The GATE LODGES of MUNSTER:

a gazetteer

The GATE LODGES of MUNSTER:
a gazetteer

J.A.K. Dean

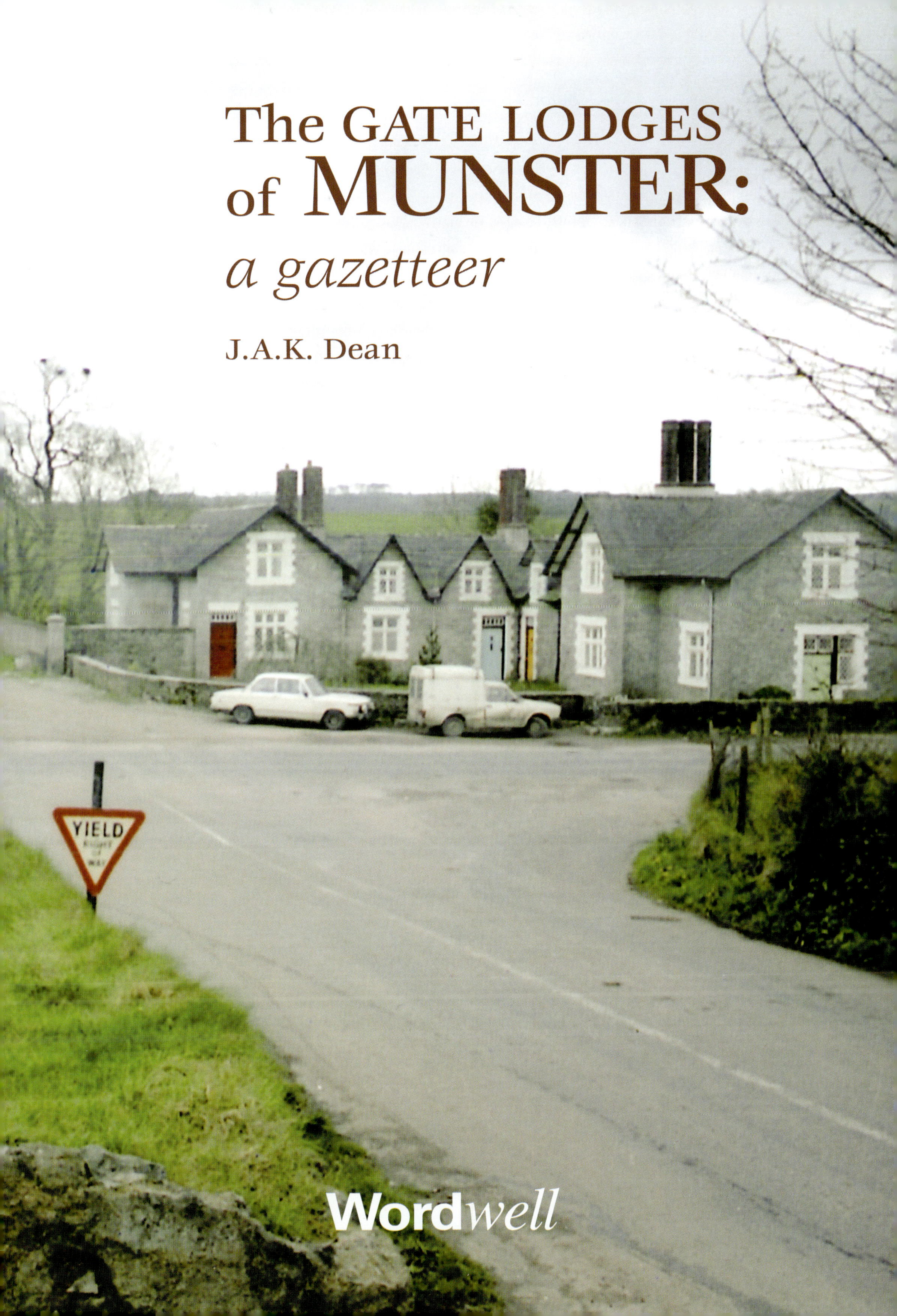

Wordwell

In fond memory of Nigel Temple

First published 2018
Word*well*
Unit 9, 78 Furze Road,
Sandyford Industrial Estate, Dublin 18, D18 C6V6
Tel: +353-1-2933568
Email: office@wordwellbooks.com
Web: www.wordwellbooks.com

ISBN: 978-0-9933518-5-3

British Library Cataloguing-in-Publication Data.
A catalogue record for this book is available from the British Library.

Front cover illustration: Old Glandore gate, Ardfert Abbey, Co. Kerry (courtesy of Tommy O'Connor).
Back cover illustration: Flesk Castle, Co. Kerry.

Front flap illustration: C.F. Anderson's design for Portlaw lodge, Gurteen Le Poer, Co.Waterford (courtesy of Count Anthony de la Poer).
Back flap illustrations from top: Deenagh Lodge, Killarney House, Co. Kerry; front gate, Hollybrook, Co. Cork (courtesy of Otho & Myra Perrott); and main gate, Walshpark, Co. Tipperary (courtesy of Otho & Myra Perrott).

Title-page illustration: Principal entrance concourse, Coolmore, Co. Cork (courtesy of Jim Shaw).

The publisher gratefully acknowledges financial assistance from the School of Irish Studies Foundation, the Irish Georgian Society and the Esmé Mitchell Trust.

Typeset in Ireland by Wordwell Ltd.
Copy-editor: Emer Condit.
Cover design: Ger Garland.

Printed by Gráficas Castuera, Pamplona.

CONTENTS

FOREWORD

This is the third of four volumes recording the gate lodges of the four provinces of Ireland, the first of which, published in 1994, covered Ulster, while the second appeared in 2016 and dealt with Leinster. The third and present volume deals with the province of Munster and follows the same excellent format as its two predecessors.

In the course of his work over the years the author has travelled the length and breadth of Ireland, in addition to scrutinising the various editions of Ordnance Survey maps, photographing and undertaking measured surveys of surviving examples, and tracking down old photographs and drawings of those which have disappeared. He also undertook research in many institutions and private collections in both Ireland and the United Kingdom.

Many readers will have favourites; mine include the extraordinary gate pillars at Castle Freke, Co. Cork, completely constructed of local shale, including their crowning oversized ball finials—a remarkable survivor. The splendid series of lodges and gates dating from the early nineteenth century at Fota Island, Co. Cork, are another personal favourite. The Templenoe gatehouse at Dromore Castle, Co. Kerry, should be singled out because of the survival of the original architect's model.

While a huge number of lodges have been lost over the years—many since the publication of the first volume—the news is not all bad, as many have been restored by private individuals, the state and the Irish Landmark Trust; good examples in this volume include those at Annesgrove and Donerail Court, both in County Cork. The theft of urns, ball finials and even gates has sadly become a new problem for owners, as demonstrated by the theft of the unique busts of Cromwell and King William III from the front of the gate lodge at Milltown Castle, Co. Cork.

Finally, mention should also be made of the magnificent new lodge and gates recently erected at Martinstown, Co. Limerick, based on a design by Robert Adam for the north lodge at Kedleston, Derbyshire, described by the author as 'an admirable addition to the landscape and a triumphant reawakening of the Irish tradition of gate-lodge-building'. Long may it continue!

David J. Griffin

ACKNOWLEDGEMENTS

Like its companion volumes in this series on the gate lodges of the provinces of Ireland, this book might not have come to fruition were it not for the generous financial contributions of an award from the School of Irish Studies Foundation and grants from the Irish Georgian Society and the Esmé Mitchell Trust that have given me much incentive and sustenance since 1997 and for which I am truly grateful. Disappointingly, overtures from Dúchas and approaches to the Heritage Council were not so fruitful.

I am indebted to many academic institutions and places of public record: first and foremost to the staff of the Irish Architectural Archive, in particular Aisling Dunne, for patiently identifying images from a vast source, and Ann Martha Rowan and David Griffin, for readily imparting their encyclopaedic knowledge of Irish architecture. Their assistance in attributions was invaluable, as was that of Kevin Mulligan, who gave so freely of his expertise, although they must be absolved from some of my ascriptions.

For their assistance in research and facilities rendered, I am grateful to the staff of the Linenhall Library, the National Archives and the National Library of Ireland, and more specifically to Lynne Dean of Stranmillis University College Library, Jean Turner and Ken Bergin of the Special Collections Library, University of Limerick, Alan Phelan of the Erasmus Smith Trust, Brian Hodkinson of Limerick City Museum, Neil Bingham of the RIBA Drawings Collection and Justin Hobson of Country Life Picture Library.

The Valuation Office is a rich source for dating building development and I am grateful to the staff for their forbearance down the years. Without that essential tool that is the Ordnance Survey of Ireland and the 6in. maps in their various editions this work would not have been possible in any detail, so to the map librarians of Trinity College Dublin, Paul Ferguson, and Queen's University Belfast, Maura Pringle, my special thanks for permitting such easy access.

My gratitude is due to library staff in the province for their help, namely Peter Beirne (Clare), Tommy O'Connor and Eamon Browne (Kerry), and Tony Storan and Margaret Franklin (Limerick).

Conal Crossan and Stephen Fallon were especially helpful in fieldwork, while Sister Mary C. Merriman and Joan Moore were generous in providing photographs.

Particularly considerate was Count Anthony de la Poer, who made available for publication from his family archive drawings by C.F. Anderson of the Gurteen le Poer gate lodges.

Latterly Julian Humphreys contributed immensely in revealing his pioneering university thesis on the grand Irish estate entrance (particularly valuable through its research dating from as early as 1978), a subject no doubt prompted by the superb example at his own gate. I remember, too, Dr Nigel Temple making available to me his unique collection of architectural pattern-books.

Ann Marie Hajba's book on the houses of north Cork and the NIAH website were most enlightening, revealing some lodges that I might otherwise have overlooked.

To the following I am obliged for encouragement, assistance, information and illustrations, which where reproduced are acknowledged individually:

> Dr Paul Bradley, Alastair Coey, Sir Howard Colvin, Burton and Linda Dean, Felicity Duggan, Helen Duggan, Desmond Fitzgerald, Knight of Glin, Simon Graham, Vera Hardy, Michael Healy, Kieran Heffernan, Patrick Holohan, Frank Keohane, Billy McGivern, J.P. McManus, Michael Mansbridge, Seán Minshull, Gerry Murray, Eileen O'Callaghan, Freddie O'Dwyer, Michael O'Dwyer, David O'Keeffe, Helena O'Higgins, John D. O'Reilly, Joe O'Shaughnessy, Tanya Paine, Otho and Myra Perrott, Nuala Quirk, Jim Shaw, Raymond Stanley, Theresa Swan, Alison Trigg, Kathleen Villiers-Tuthill, Dr David Walker, Dr Hugh W.L. Weir, Ken Wigham and Tamsin Young.

To this majority of generous individuals who responded to my queries or volunteered information, my sincere thanks. From a minority I have not yet given up hope of a response.

Sadly, given the gestation period of this work, many of the above have passed away, and to them I dedicate this book.

I would like to thank Nick Maxwell for initially taking on this project and the staff of Wordwell for guiding it through the later stages.

Yet again, a person to whom I owe so much is Michelle McGaughey, who single-handedly transformed transient handwritten notes for three provinces into immaculate word-processed texts.

Finally, to my wife Lynne, who has lived with this obsession for 30 years and accompanied me on many a diversion, my thanks for her forbearance.

INTRODUCTION

A university project in 1964 that required the submission of a thesis on 'The gate lodge and estate entrance gates of Northern Ireland' kindled an interest that resulted in the publication in 1994 of *The gate lodges of Ulster*, which assembled those in the nine counties of that province in the form of a gazetteer.

What this study revealed in those intervening 30 years was a continuous and inexorable loss of this unique little building type and an urgent need to complete and put on record such a survey of it for the whole country. Any satisfaction felt in the completion of what was literally a long journey a further nineteen years on was tempered by the realisation of the litany of destruction of the gate lodge throughout the rest of Ireland. Thus this province-by-province study represents the culmination of some 50 years of research, recording those sad losses but also celebrating the survivors.

These books seek to increase awareness of the importance of the gate lodge as part of our architectural heritage by emphasising its uniqueness, which in print to date has mysteriously received minimal notice in contrast with the exposure given its big house, and to balance that disparity. What the porter's lodge lacks in scale and interior decoration in comparison, it more than makes up for in its extraordinary range of architectural styles, a variety in design that cloaks what is in many cases essentially little more than a rectangular box, elevated as the cream of cottages.

Beyond that basic little unadorned traditional standard cottage lodge which initially predominated in the countryside and suburbs, there emerged in equal numbers those in varied and sophisticated dress which highlight the ingenuity of their designers, augmented by the Victorians, who introduced all manner of variants based on ancient Classical and English medieval precedents, instantly recognisable as a building of individual distinction. 'Its qualities could only be achieved because it gave its designer that essential freedom which the building type possesses: isolation from other structures, indifference to the convenience of its inhabitants, and ample funding' (Mowl 1984).

The lodge became a symbol of the power, status, taste and wealth of the Irish landowner, which he strove to display at his gates to impress passers-by and neighbours—with the result sometimes revealing the vainglorious, examples of which will become apparent. Here in Munster, in addition to familiar styles, there emerged, as in the rest of the country, all manner of curiosities, such as the wonderful Gothic extravaganza at the entrance to Creagh Castle (Cork), the unique Hindu–Gothic apparition at Dromana (Waterford), the lost 'Copper Lodge' prelude to Milford (Waterford) and the dotty New Zealand Maori archway and lodge to Springfield Castle (Limerick), along with much else to admire and amuse.

So, too, there appeared regional trends, such as the chaste series of neo-Classical pilastered lodges in the Cork city suburbs, a group of Tudor Gothic structures with perpendicular traceried windows in County Cork, C.F. Anderson's innovative set of six lodges distributed about the province with their unique '*ex antis*' columns and, rather less attractive, those most strange lodges peculiar to County Limerick that were built against elevations of great stone roadside screen walls.

While these conspicuous examples do not set the Irish gate lodge apart from its counterpart in mainland Great Britain, what makes it unique to this island is its abundance, proliferating as it does here far in excess of those anywhere else on the planet.

This phenomenon may be explained by a number of factors: just as Irish big houses are considerably less grand than their British equivalents, their holdings are smaller in size—but more numerous, a circumstance not unrelated to our intricate spider's-web road network. There was, too, the call here for greater vigilance by the gates, given the history of cyclic disturbance, and not least there was also the emergence of a tradition of lodge-building.

From the halcyon years of lodge-building in Munster of the later Georgian to early Victorian period their construction gradually tailed off, surviving the Famine years, but by the turn of the twentieth century the appearance of a new porter's lodge would be a rarity indeed; 65% of those recorded in the province were in place by 1840, 30% were added during the reign of Queen Victoria, and the remainder were erected prior to World War I.

Statistically, gatekeepers' lodges identified in Munster amount to 2,775, unevenly distributed about the province depending on topography; the 197 lodges in County Kerry, for instance, appear as one every 23.8km^2, compared to the 1,275 in County Cork, occurring as one per 5.8km^2, this ratio of course influenced by their frequency in the suburbs of Cork city. An average of one lodge per 9km^2 in the province compares with double that density in Leinster (1:4.6) but more than those for Ulster (1:13.9) and Connacht (1:16.8). This converts to a national average of one lodge every 8.2km^2, contrasting with the combined average of one per 15.1km^2 in England and Wales. Whereas that latter estimate from Timothy Mowl and Brian Earnshaw's pioneering *Trumpet at a distant gate* reveals an almost equal number of lodges there, 10,000 as in Ireland, the respective land areas explain the differential in density.

Telling as these statistics are, they are as little against those that reveal losses of the lodge in Ireland, which was the main motivation for preparing these books. Much has been written and made of the loss of the big house, the destruction of which was felt nowhere more than in Munster; through neglect or wilful burnings it is estimated that at least 150 large houses succumbed—about 65 of them in County Cork, that hotbed of discontent and antagonism towards the landlord. But this almost pales into insignificance alongside the destruction of their porters' lodges: of the 2,775 recorded, 1,449 (52.2%) have gone. These losses range from 56.2% in County Limerick to 'as few as' 40.4% in County Waterford, which, being the smallest of the Munster counties, exhibits such a rich selection of lodges and, like its big estate houses, the greatest survival rates, perhaps related to the taste and quality of its landowners with a greater respect for their architectural heritage. Figures otherwise reflect the national average.

On closer analysis, taking County Cork as a representative sample, it is significant that of the 975 lodges identified from the 1841–2 Ordnance Survey only 313, or a mere 32%, remain, surely a reflection of their inferior construction and Spartan accommodation. Thereafter, those built in the Victorian period show a greater survival rate, their numbers boosted considerably no doubt by those relatively sophisticated lodges appearing in the expanding Cork city suburbs, which incidentally are proving considerably less vulnerable than their counterparts in more land-hungry Dublin.

Sadly, architectural distinction was no guarantee of a lodge's survival, as evidenced by the criminal demolition of those splendid neo-Classical examples to Gurteen-le-Poer (Waterford) and Ballynagarde (Limerick), a fate that seems also to await the equally fine lodge at Ballywilliam in the same county.

Unknown lodge, courtesy Limerick City Museum

Often the greatest losses can only be recalled by old photographs or through surviving architects' drawings, such as the entrance and lodge to Newtownanner (Tipperary), with its beautiful glazing pattern and vast trabeated gatescreen, Henry Hill's delightful Picturesque cottage proposal for Kilnap (Cork) and that lost neo-Classical lodge by C.F. Anderson opposite the gates to Gurteen-le-Poer (Waterford). While the author was at pains to locate images of lost lodges, with some success, one photograph [below left] held by Limerick City Museum has defied identification. Any information on its location would be welcome.

This spectacular demise of the gate lodge was of course not unrelated to the destiny of its landed estate, the loss of a big house often condemning its lodge. Commencing with the Great Famine, the landed classes suffered an unrelenting succession of adverse circumstances. While the building of gate lodges continued alongside that of demesne walls through the Famine period as a relief measure, the aristocracy and gentry were hit by the land wars, the Land Acts, the Great War, the War of Independence, the Civil War, the burnings and the formation of the Irish Free State, after which increased taxation and economic recession were the final nails driven into their coffin, bringing the world of the landed estates tumbling down, never to return. Properties were decimated and broken up for redevelopment; their lodges, severed from the protective umbrella of their big house, became vulnerable to road-widening or realignment, their entrance gatescreens at the mercy of modern farm machinery. They were further threatened by the greed of the developer, by ineffective protection despite an official listings process, by the vandal and not least by the misguided perception that they did not lend themselves to rehabilitation and extension.

It is a fallacy to think that the gatekeeper's lodge is too small in scale to be successfully and sensitively extended to meet acceptable modern living standards, as can be seen in many excellent improvements and additions, mainly confined to the northern province. Many of the most acceptable solutions are those that contrast with the original, often in an ultra-modern style that is subservient to it, provided that there is a clearly defined division between old and new. So often, though, the mistake is made whereby the addition is in like style and detail, which sees the visual loss of the original structure. Later 1½-storey Victorian Picturesque lodges, with their more complex outlines, greater scale and informal footprints, can be more conducive to extending in like manner. While a fundamental Georgian hip-roofed, limewashed, harled, single-storey cottage lodge with its low ceilings and confined spaces is less adaptable, it can be, and has been, retained and maintained as a quaint novelty or folly by the gates to be admired and enjoyed, and put to use for storage or as ancillary to the main house.

Whilst these gazetteers also include reference to the many fine porters' lodges to institutions such as convents, hospitals, cemeteries, schools, workhouses, lunatic asylums and gaols, they are seen as companions to Mark Bence-Jones's *A guide to Irish country houses*, that remarkable compendium which made the task of uncovering lodges and their background considerably easier. As preludes to his big houses they are considerably more numerous but, given their location, relatively more accessible.

Estate maps being a rarity, the first meaningful point of reference in their location was from the first Ordnance Survey maps for the province of 1839–42 and subsequent editions from around the turn of the twentieth century. For the dating of lost lodges these sources are crucial, as are their mention for intermediate years in the Griffith Valuation of the mid-nineteenth century and subsequent valuation books. Unfortunately, identification of gate porters in Munster from these books is minimal, unlike their counterparts in and around Dublin city. Entries for an estate are confined to identifying the occupant, his immediate lessor, 'House, Offices, Gate Lodge and Land'. Thus the books are rather more useful in revealing the landowner responsible for adding a gate lodge to his property, although there are many more potential sources for this detective work. Principal in this are the Taylor and Skinner road maps of 1777 and 1783; editions of William Wilson's *Post chaise companion* from the turn of the nineteenth century; the Ambrose Leet postal directory of 1814; Samuel Lewis's essential *Topographical dictionary of Ireland* (1837), with its lengthy list of subscribers; and the Griffith Valuation and succeeding valuation books, coupled with Isaac Slater's directories of 1846, 1856 and 1870 and the 1876 *Land owners in Ireland*. All of these can assist in establishing a change of ownership, which may indicate the date of the addition of a lodge to a property by a new owner. In this respect genealogical records can be revealing, given that many a porter's lodge dates from overall improvements to an estate which can often be connected with the succession of an heir, a coming of age or a marriage. Crucial in this are Burke's *Landed gentry*, his *Peerage and baronetage* and his *Irish family records*.

Accessible as gate lodges may be, as Robert Graham discovered in his tour of Ireland of 1835, one can still meet with a mixed reception at the gates. I well remember a particularly formidable, officious and bristling County Tipperary gatekeeper demanding to know upon whose authority photographs could be taken. More intimidating was the loud, vocal and zealous guardian of an overgrown ruin in County Waterford, delivering unseen from behind a hedge all manner of threats of violence unless I returned immediately whence I had come, and forbidding even 'the taking of notes'. Overwhelmingly, however, there was a warm welcome from the few still in occupation of Munster gate lodges, and an often-justified pride shown in the improvements and additions carried out.

Sadly, now lost will be the delights of travelling the highways, and particularly the byways, of the country with that sense of expectation of uncovering another little gem around the next corner, albeit forsaken and overgrown. As the late lamented Knight of Glin asked in conclusion to his introduction to *The vanishing country houses of Ireland*, 'Should we not remember and preserve some of this important aspect of our national heritage?'—a sentiment which should just as well apply to the gate lodge.

POSTSCRIPT

Inevitably since the lodge surveys were completed at the turn of this century, much has changed in the interim period of research and writing prior to publication; indeed, sadly, a few recent visits to Munster revealed their losses to have been relentless, and such is also the picture in the other provinces. Rather than dwelling on this, however, it would be better to admire, laud and encourage the likes of those inspired restoration works to the gate lodges at Ballycolliton (Tipperary) and Worldsend (Limerick).

IMAGE REPOSITORY

The publisher has set up an area on the Wordwellbooks website to facilitate those who want to see larger, more detailed versions of the images used in the gazetteer of this book. It is not intended as a replacement or an alternative to the book and only the images will be available there. They appear exactly as the author has supplied them.

To view any of the images in the book, you will need the reference number that appears with the entry.

To proceed

First log into http://wordwellbooks.com/gatelodges/ by typing this into the address line of your web browser.

How to find an image

You will need the gate lodge reference number and county name. For example, the gate lodge at Beech Park, Co. Clare, is referenced as No. 23 in the Clare gazetteer. To view it via this page, you should type **Clare-23** [CountyHyphen-Number] in the finder window on the page and the image will appear. *Typing **Beech Park** will not find the image.*

Where there is more than one entry per site in the book, for instance **37. Cahercon** (Co. Clare), the first image that appears in that listing can be found by entering **Clare-37a**, the second by entering **Clare-37b** and so on.

A HISTORY OF THE GATE LODGE IN MUNSTER

The gate lodge in Munster, for reasons of facility and clarity, will initially be considered to have developed in three basic forms: the pierced gatehouse tower, the single sentry-box and twin pavilions.

THE PIERCED GATEHOUSE TOWER

Aside from early tenuous precursors such as the Roman *atriensis*, the most relevant and immediate source for the gate lodge can be identified as the medieval gatehouse, which itself evolved when defensive earth banks were replaced by tall curtain walls and was created as a heavily guarded structure at the point of access to the bailey and keep within. Topped by machicolated battlements, it was to become an essential model for Victorian reproductions based on the likes of the great gatehouses to Dungarvan Castle (Waterford) and Limerick Castle (Limerick). With their circular flanking towers, they were to influence such examples as the mid-Victorian entrance to Lohort Castle (Cork). Countless other derivatives enliven the province in an infinite variety of outlines.

THE SINGLE SENTRY-BOX

By far the simplest and most instantly recognisable manifestation of the porter's lodge in the countryside is, next to its gates, that two-roomed, three-bay, single-storey home probably derived from the similarly unmistakable three-cell, four-bay vernacular Irish cottage but given a degree of architectural sophistication in an invariably more self-conscious symmetrical main front, with its central doorway more often than not below a hipped roof. This was to appear in numerous guises in the particular architectural style popular at the time of its creation, often presenting an appropriate prelude to that of its big house beyond. In this form, or plainly astylar, they were built over two centuries at the entrances to properties of the aristocracy, gentry or prosperous farmers, and this quintessential little building was to become the most familiar, accessible and admired in the Irish countryside.

TWIN PAVILIONS

It is thanks to the English traveller Thomas Dineley and sketches from his journal of 1680 that we have the earliest images on record of precedents for that most prestigious of estate entrances—twin lodges. Both views date from his time in County Clare. The now long-forgotten Ballyclogh Castle [**Fig. 1**] is shown as a tower-house approached before an enclosure between a

Fig. 1

Fig. 2

pair of matching round towers with what were presumably later conical roofs rising to ball terminals and window openings, modifications to what were previously defensive flankers, indicative of the arrival of a period of relative tranquillity. Likewise, at Mount Ievers [**Fig. 2**] was a pair of twin cubic pavilions marking the forecourt entrance to its tower-house and Jacobean extension. Distinctly decorative, with their pyramidal roofs covered in scalloped slates rising to hip-knobs, their individual chimney-stacks suggest permanent habitation. Between them, and linked by curtain walls, on an axis with the front door of the later house are

Fig. 3

entrance doors with decorative strap hinges hung on lofty carriage pillars crowned by ball finials.

From such a format was born an entrance type whose symmetry was popular with the Georgians, initially 'day and night' accommodation, an unsocial arrangement remedied about the turn of the nineteenth century when individual family units began to flank the gates, which eventually saw as many as one in ten of that configuration in Munster. These twin pavilions began to preface an avenue of an altogether lengthier, more circuitous and Romantic nature than the early formal short axial approach.

Contemporary with the Dineley sketches is an anonymous print also displaying just such an early axial approach to Ballintober House (Cork) [**Fig. 3**], it being framed by an impressive pair of Classical pillars, rusticated with decorative urns atop corniced cappings, typical of the early eighteenth century and before. Such monumental early pillars are characteristic of the period and of a type in which County Cork is rich. These pillars survive at Ballintober and at another estate of the Meade family at Ballymartle (Cork), as well as at Mitchellsfort (Cork). Significantly, none of these are known to have been originally manned, although in subsequent years they were complemented by lodges, the only survivor being a Georgian Gothic cottage of around 1780 at Ballymartle, a charming mismatch now attending its decimated gatescreen.

THE WALLED ESTATE

In common with their English counterparts, there is little evidence of porters' lodges to Irish estates before *c.* 1740, about which time landowners in the country were sufficiently confident in their personal safety to extend enclosure to their property about the greater estate rather than an immediate park or forecourt. Thus security became served by distant boundary walls, some extending for miles around thousands of acres, and none more so than at Curraghmore (Waterford), seat of the marquises of Waterford, which in 1876 comprised 39,883 acres, 'very much a little world on its own, sealed off from outsiders by its woods and hills, and by the ten mile ring of its demesne walls'. So arose the problem of securing such far-flung hidden boundaries and of monitoring their distant access gates, which in the case of Curraghmore called for twelve entrances, all requiring permanent attendance.

THE FIRST MANNED GATES

Thus was born both a new building type in the gate lodge and a new vocation in that of the gate porter, a function that was to endure for up to 200 years.

As early as 1740, proprietors would have been inviting architects to submit designs for lodges to impress at their remote gates, but whereas the honey-pot of Dublin city and its hinterland attracted the likes of Gandon, Cooley, Wyatt and Chambers, no practitioners of such eminence have been identified as being active in Cork, Limerick or Waterford, nor indeed have any local architects been uncovered as being responsible. These eighteenth-century lodges would have been the result of the efforts of amateurs or jobbing builders, such is their modesty. It was not until the opening of the next century that architects on the domestic Munster scene rose from anonymity. Being of little pretension or durability, very few early lodges survive in any case, although a singular little building on the Adare Manor estate (Limerick, *c.* 1770) stands out with its 'Batty Langley' ogee arch in cut-stone facings, now roofless and lacking its avenue; there apparently was a like lodge to Tervoe in the same county. Earlier still and owing its survival to being an integral part of another ancillary building is a two-storey gatehouse to Sir Walter Raleigh's Myrtle Grove (Cork, *c.* 1700), distinctive for its oriel window overlooking plain carriage doors alongside. This earliest known surviving gatekeeper's accommodation in the province owes its existence to a later proprietor. On the evidence of this, Dineley's Mount Ievers sketch and another example at Coolville (Tipperary), it seems that wooden carriage doors may have been common, probably to give privacy where an entrance was within sight of its big house. The Irish climate ensures that no originals survive, which may account, too, for the rarity of contemporary iron gates. Of these early examples, familiar for their ornate curvilinear Baroque wrought ironwork and perhaps with an overthrow for added impact, few survive, there being a pair at Garrettstown (Cork), whereas those at Fairfield, Kinsale (Cork), were acquired from Hollymount (Mayo).

Vulnerable, too, are stone finials as prey for thieves, and those crowning Georgian gate pillars made rich pickings, as did those vases atop the Ballintober piers, much coveted as garden ornaments. Nevertheless, they still abound in their rightful places: at Castleview, Tallow (Cork), Tinhalla (Tipperary) and Adare Manor (Limerick) finely chiselled urns remain, whilst those at Hermitage

(Limerick) are conspicuously draped. Those at Mount Desert (Cork) are accompanied on outer pillars by the popular and hospitable pineapples, of which there are other good cut-stone examples at Currah Chase (Limerick), Summerhill (Tipperary), no fewer than four to the Churchtown (Kerry) gatescreen and at Garrettstown (Cork), where a secondary gate displays rusticated ball finials raised on pedestals. The latter are commonplace, though the most remarkable of which, for being assembled in a ragstone rather than being monolithic, are at Castle Freke (Cork).

From the turn of the nineteenth century finials to entrance pillars tended towards the more personal in exhibiting the likes of family crests, revealing a whole menagerie of beasts, from eagles at Miltown (Cork) and Barry family wolves at the Fota (Cork) entrance to stags of the Powers at Faithlegg (Waterford) and Mount Richard (Tipperary) and O'Shee swans atop the gate pillars of Gardenmorris (Waterford). Not so individualised are the fine pair of sphinxes addressing one another across the entrance to Castle Hyde (Cork).

Otherwise the majority of the late Georgian estate entrances were less monumental than their predecessors, compensating with crisply chiselled examples of the stonemason's craft, Classical pillars exhibiting friezes embellished with the likes of the sunflower motifs and fluting to Racecourse Hall (Tipperary), shafts being mainly sculpted with V-jointed rustication. Wrought ironwork to gates and railings were understated but arranged as extensive tripartite gatescreens as at Richmond (Tipperary). Considerably less prolific than elsewhere in Ireland are carriage gates flanked by tall quadrant walls pierced by postilion openings.

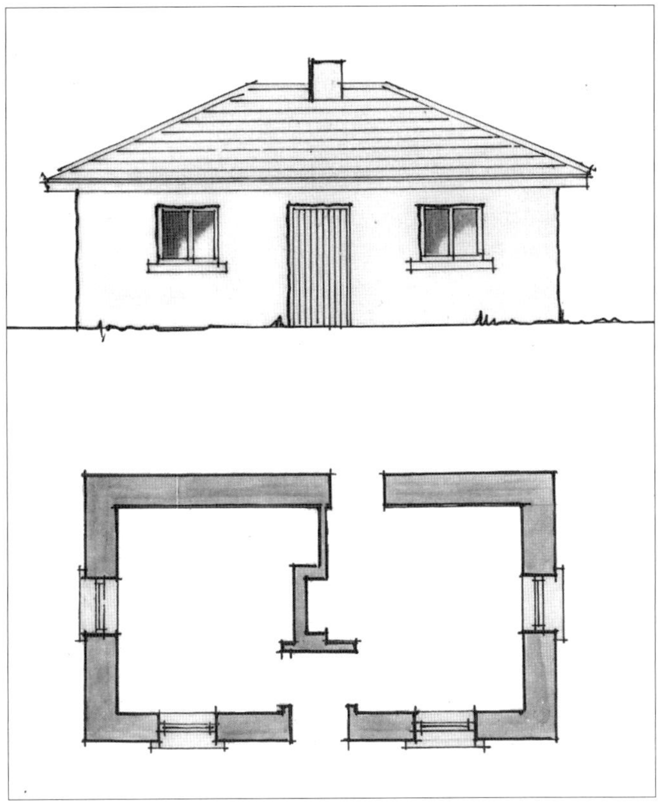

Fig. 4

THE STANDARD LODGE

By the turn of the nineteenth century these grand entrances by Munster roadsides were attended by an instantly recognisable new breed of building monitoring access to distant mansions, villas and farmhouses, mainly in the form of a simple single-storey limewashed and harled lodge on a rectangular plan with a symmetrical three-bay front below a shallow-pitched hipped roof with central chimney-stack [**Fig. 4**]. Referred to as 'standard' in the gazetteer, this simplest of plan forms comprised two rooms, one a bedroom and the other a living area, accessed via a tiny integral entrance hall, all generally devoid of any interior architectural detailing. This layout, which lacked any attached sanitary facility, lasted as typical for a century throughout the country, varying only in dimensions, and included those lodges built as accommodation for sextons of Anglican churches and gate porters to their glebe houses as part of that great building programme funded by substantial sums voted from 1801 to 1833 through the Board of First Fruits to the Established Church. These notably set a bad example as regards consideration for their employees, being particularly Spartan in their dimensions. Many were extremely cramped in accommodation compared to the three-roomed vernacular cottage, where, too, there was access to loft space afforded by a steeply pitched roof. This problem was not addressed until later in the century, when some socially minded proprietors created attic rooms by raising the eaves line higher than the ground-floor ceiling, so maintaining the accepted outline of a standard gatekeeper's lodge.

Of this quintessential and enduring 'standard' structure the earliest surviving can be found in County Tipperary at Grene Park (*c.* 1800) and Neddans (*c.* 1810), which differ little from others built later in the century at Ballyhaukish (Limerick, *c.* 1845) and Liskeveen (Tipperary, *c.* 1860), where its exaggerated soffits oversail enough to form a pretty verandah.

THE VERNACULAR COTTAGE LODGE

Of gate lodges based on a traditional steeply pitched thatched cottage there were few; no self-respecting landowner wished to have an impression of a peasant hovel by his gates. There is, though, a conspicuous surviving exception in the sweet little structure at Coolville (Tipperary, *c.* 1800), still retaining its thatch in immaculate condition. There appears also to have been a four-bay linear thatched cottage by the gates to Strancally Castle (Waterford, *c.* 1800), now lost but captured in an old photograph.

THE ECCENTRICS

This basic standard form was practical, however, compared to the lengths to which landowners were prepared to go to attract the attention and admiration of passers-by and neighbours. The first edition of the Ordnance Survey maps reveals proprietors seeking and experimenting with alternative forms by their gates. Unfortunately for the gatekeeper, these rarely considered his convenience, which was sacrificed in the interests of consequence. Nevertheless, owing to their quirkiness these attracted all manner of affectionate appellations, few of which, sadly, guaranteed their survival.

Unsocial or not, the most endearing of these forms was the circular or drum lodge often known as the 'inkpot', which could appear in an oval variant, their roofs thatched and rising to a central chimney-stack, or slate-covered, which demanded much of the roofer. Most of these delights would have contrived two rooms and perhaps a minuscule hallway. Such inconvenience could be found in the sweet little example at Coolyhane (Cork, *c.* 1810), which had gone by the turn of the twentieth century, and that rare survivor at Dick's Grove (Kerry, *c.* 1800), since much altered and extended but occupied. Later in the nineteenth century that plan form was raised a storey to realise a rather more commodious tower, seen in those castellated examples at Dripsey Castle (Cork, *c.* 1820) and Waterloo (Cork, *c.* 1815). At Rochestown Wood (Cork, *c.* 1875) is the shell of a once-spacious circular gatehouse, whilst flanking the gates to Laurentinum (Cork, pre-1835) was a 'salt and pepper' pair.

Although circular buildings were far from unheard of domestically, functioning well at large scale, their practicality reduced with their circumference. John Plaw, though, in his *Ferme ornée* (1795) convincingly opined that they 'can be viewed from every point', but to later extol them in *Sketches for country houses, villas and rural dwellings* (1800) as having the virtue of 'the figure and form being calculated to give the least resistance to the wind' was surely stretching it a bit. His further suggestion that the drum lodge could be placed on wheels that it 'might be moved at pleasure' was an interesting concept that not surprisingly failed to find favour.

This little building form was solely for the amusement of the great landowners and survived as eye-catchers or distant temples put to use in their day as places for occasional carousing or picnicking.

Hardly more convenient in layout was that with a hexagonal footprint, one of which monitored its gates from across the road at Peake (Cork, pre-1841), and the surviving beautifully restored and maintained lodge by the entrance to Shandrum Rectory (Cork, *c.* 1845), now Gortskagh. But by far the most numerous and enduring of these novelties, up to a dozen remaining, is the octagonal or 'tea caddy' lodge, the oldest being the charming Georgian Gothic example at Cloyne Palace (Cork, *c.* 1790), still kempt and obviously much loved, through to that at Rivoli (Clare, 1868). As with drum lodges, octagons came in two-storey form, as in eccentric traceried Gothic at Woodhill (Cork, *c.* 1845) and P.C. Hardwick's wonderful 'Lantern Lodge' and archway at Adare Manor (Limerick, *c.* 1860). The abandoned Flesk Castle lodge (Kerry, *c.* 1835) is likewise derelict, opposite where its entrance was, two storeys over a basement in a castellated Tudor manner to give a flavour of its big house for the visitor.

No less impressive though simply raised off a square plan is the cubic lodge with its pyramidal roof culminating in a crowning chimney-stack, a notable early version of which is the tiny cottage at Shepperton Park (Cork, *c.* 1800), with another at Heathfield (Limerick, *c.* 1825).

To date, much in the way of innovation had been achieved by variety of form but little by architectural detailing, most having remained astylar.

THE PRE-TEMPLE LODGE

The same jobbing builder may have been responsible for three significantly similar lodges at Castle View, Glanmire (Cork, *c.* 1790), Clonshire (Limerick, *c.* 1790) and Clonacody (Tipperary, *c.* 1790), all of basic rectangular plan but turned about 90° for a short elevation to become the show front, each comprised of a central opening flanked by round-headed niches, in a tentative but effective rustic Palladian style with vernacular limewashed finish below a hipped roof. All appear to have been vainly awaiting the finishing touch of the addition of a tetrastyle portico. These three modest cottages with just that hint of sophistication could be grouped with what is perhaps the most remarkable entrance lodge in Munster at Miltown Castle (Cork, *c.* 1755), of like format but with the leading façade skew-tabled, its central window in a limestone ashlar surround flanked by round-arched niches of sufficient depth to accommodate a pair of busts—of 'King Billy' and Oliver Cromwell no less, provocatively proclaiming the political proclivities of the proprietor. After surviving for centuries, they only recently fell victim to thieves. Assuming the lodge to be contemporary with its towering gate pillars, with splendid eagles atop, it may be particularly precocious and a rare early instance of architectural involvement in an Irish gate lodge.

A ROOM WITH A VIEW

Generally the simple rectangular three-bay standard lodge predominated, occasionally given a bow for effect and to assist in observing the gate, as side elevations at Seamount (Clare, *c.* 1840) and Monaincha (Tipperary, *c.* 1830), a central hall projection to be seen at Upton (Cork, *c.* 1835) or as leading fronts, in duplicate on the twin pair at Ballyseedy Castle (Kerry, *c.* 1780). Alternatively, the projection would be semi-octagonal or canted, as is the main front to the lodge at Kilbrack (Cork, *c.* 1820), advancing practically beyond its gatescreen to monitor callers.

THE BASEMENT LODGE

That lodge to Upton displays another innovation, being what appears to the visitor to be a standard type but in fact raised off a basement floor, only revealed as two-storey to the rear. It seems that some proprietors were anxious to provide their gatekeepers with generous accommodation but remained conscious of what had become the acquired perception of a gate lodge. Such basement lodges are also to be seen at Woodhouse (Waterford, *c.* 1830), Jamesbrook Hall (Cork, *c.* 1860) and Knocklofty (Tipperary, *c.* 1830).

THE GATEHOUSE

Other landowners preferred to flaunt publicly their consideration for their tenants, there being a number of manifestly two-storey gatehouses about the province, such as those at Ballywilliam (Limerick), Ballyedmond (Cork, *c.* 1830) and Glendooneen (Cork, *c.* 1835), a pair at Belgrove (Cork, *c.* 1800) and, unusually for the Church of Ireland, Kilbrogan Rectory (Cork, *c.* 1800).

THE GEORGIAN GOTHIC LODGE

The gate lodge until the turn of the nineteenth century had been a modest and unassuming affair, depending for any impact upon the variety of alternative shapes already noticed. But the period 1780–1820 saw the emergence of a passion for the Gothic style, a revival that the aristocracy and gentry embraced in transforming their homes and that was likewise applied to the humble lodge. It was more eagerly received in Munster than in the other provinces and many charming examples survive. This Georgian Gothic, as it became known, is instantly recognisable in the pointed arch or lancet window invariably containing the familiar Y-traceried sash window. Mostly this was simply applied as fenestration to the basic standard lodge, as at Rock Grove (Cork, *c.* 1800), Ballyre (Cork, *c.* 1830), with its exaggerated oversailing hipped roof, and the endearing little cottage at Odellville (Limerick, *c.* 1780). At Cloyne Palace (Cork, *c.* 1790) and Woodhill (Cork, *c.* 1845) such windows light octagonal lodges, while those at Cashel Palace (Tipperary, *c.* 1784) and Torc Cottage (Kerry, *c.* 1815) are built to more articulate plans. At Hawthorn Cottage (Cork, *c.* 1800), Beechmount (Limerick, *c.* 1800) and Kilbrack (Cork, *c.* 1820) the entrances are monitored from their pointed windows in practical canted fronts, and at New Hall (Clare, *c.* 1805) the Classical gatescreen is flanked by Gothic lodges in duplicate. More flamboyant are the ogee arches that decorate the eccentric and early Maryborough lodge (Cork, *c.* 1760). Another delightful pair of Gothic lodges by an unidentified architect were proposed for the entrance to Dromoland Castle (Clare, *c.* 1810) but were eventually discarded, probably in favour of the surviving Doric temple lodge. All of these display considerable design restraint if compared with the hugely flamboyant Gothic extravaganza that is the entrance to Creagh Castle (Cork, 1823), where both lodge and extensive gatescreen in beautifully chiselled limestone exhibit their creators' ease with the extensive Gothic vocabulary. The architects are likely to have been the brothers James and George Richard Pain, displaying the benefits of their training in the office of John Nash. This enthusiasm for the style was short-lived and it would be another 50 years before it reappeared.

THE REGENCY LODGE

Life in Ireland after the Act of Union in 1800 for a period of 30 years spanning the Regency and the reign of William IV brought intense building activity on the domestic front and a disposition towards the arch as applied to elevations in the form of recesses to emphasise openings. Popular in early nineteenth-century villas and translating to gate lodges of the period, it appears as arcading on buildings of that scale and can be seen at Cappagh (Waterford, *c.* 1845) and Knocklofty (Tipperary, *c.* 1830), while like treated lodged pairs mark the gates to Limerick Artillery Barracks (Limerick, 1807), Carrignavar (Cork, 1807) and Belgrove (Cork, *c.* 1800), where the arches rise two storeys. As a rule, the porter's lodge presented its three-bay best face to the public—to road or avenue—out of courtesy or to reflect a proprietor's polish. But in life there will always be contrary folk and just such must have created those lodges at Prospect (Limerick, *c.* 1850) and Craigbrien (Clare, *c.* 1840), both of which turn their backs to the visitor, their show fronts to be appreciated from within. At New Hall (Clare, *c.* 1805) the offence is compounded by the pair presenting their blind elevations to the approach, while both road and avenue fronts to the lodge at Riverview, Skibbereen (Cork, *c.* 1820), are windowless. Apart from being unwelcoming, the gatekeeper would have difficulty in fulfilling his function.

THE FRONTISPIECE LODGE

Overwhelmingly, however, the gate lodge faced the visitor, and in the immediate pre-Victorian period there was movement to relieve the monotony of the three-bay symmetrical façade by enhancing it with the application of a central projection or breakfront to emphasise, and crucially enlarge, the internal hallway. Invariably this would be expressed as gabled or with a Classical pediment, perhaps further enriched with column supports, either engaged or free-standing, to exhibit a porch or sophisticated portico—that most desirable of appendages to any building. This was realised in the two fine lodges to Longueville (Cork, *c.* 1815 and *c.* 1845), with their Roman Doric tetrastyle porticoes, which range in date by about 30 years but both by as-yet-unidentified architects.

THE GATE LODGE TO DESIGN

The more restrained Classical lodges are those to lunatic asylums, found as a standard pattern throughout the country, generally to a design by William Murray still to be seen at Clonmel (Tipperary, *c.* 1835) and Waterford (Waterford, *c.* 1835), both dependent for effect upon a pedimented frontispiece and segmentally arched windows. Private clients had no such financial restraints and employed the likes of *in antis* columns to frame the front doors to their lodges at Tinarana (Clare, *c.* 1836), probably by James Pain, at Modreeny (Tipperary, *c.* 1835), a sombre version by the Ballinasloe architect James Kempster at Sopwell Hall (Tipperary, *c.* 1860), the regrettably lost pedimented lodge to Ballynagarde (Limerick, *c.* 1840) with its paired columns '*ex antis*' and Corker family crest in its tympanum, and that sweet little lodge opposite the gates to Altamira (Cork, *c.* 1825), now sadly lying ruinous. At Marlfield (Tipperary, 1833) the *in antis* theme appears in duplicate to the pair of lodges by William Tinsley depending heavily on Sir John Soane.

Such Classical architectural trappings applied to the porter's lodge began to identify the input of professionals, with expertise clearly influenced by the Grand Tour. Until the turn of the nineteenth century architects, whether from home or abroad, had remained anonymous in Munster domestic architecture, but just as in the proverbial long wait for a bus to arrive only for a number to appear at once, so too was the case with architects in the province. These early nineteenth-century practitioners emerged as dynasties, fathers and sons, brothers and cousins.

William Murray, cousin of Francis Johnston, has already been noticed, but the first architectural family to arrive in the province was the Leeds-born Abraham Hargrave the Elder and his sons, one of the same name and John. There were the Pain brothers, initially sent here from London as representatives of John Nash, of whom the long-lived James settled in Limerick while the younger, George Richard, of prodigious talent evident in Cork city and beyond, was short-lived. He was an exact contemporary of that other precocious genius William Vitruvius Morrison, likewise cut down in his prime after being in practice with his father Richard Morrison, who was by far the most productive practitioner of his time in Munster and further afield. He, along with local man Thomas Deane and his son Thomas Newenham Deane, was to be knighted, and all three dominated the local architectural scene for the opening 40 years of the century. Joining these practitioners in vying with one another in creating ever more distinctive and varied versions of this new building type were J.B. Keane, erstwhile assistant in the Morrison office, a local talent in Henry Hill, the Tipperary-born William Tinsley and the gifted Charles Frederick Anderson, both of whom apparently experienced disaffection in the Famine years and emigrated to the United States.

Fig. 5

THE TEMPLE LODGE

The late eighteenth century had already seen the hint of a new gate lodge variant in that which had as its show front a short elevation of the simple rectangular format, as in those be-niched cottages at Clonshire, Clonacody and Castle View already noticed and which are but one step away from morphing into that most prestigious of structures, the Classical temple. It was Sir Richard Morrison who developed and popularised the type, which was to be offered in countless examples by him throughout the land, notably at Castlecoole (Fermanagh), Killruddery (Wicklow) and Baronscourt (Tyrone), all owing their existence to eminent English architect Sir John Soane and a plate from his 1793 *Sketches in architecture* [**Fig. 5**], which Morrison adapted for use in Munster at the gates to Bearforest Lower (Cork, *c.* 1807), now horribly disfigured, probably the pair at Ballyedmond (Cork, *c.* 1820), closest to the original concept, and Fota (Cork, *c.* 1820), where the leading front has its segmentally arched tripartite window recessed behind a screen with two columns *in antis*, a formula which Morrison was also to employ at Ballyfin (Leix). There are similar lodges at Mount Richard (Tipperary, *c.* 1825) and Rock Grove (Cork, *c.* 1825) but both probably by Morrison's erstwhile assistant J.B. Keane.

While this orientation of lodge, whereby the standard plan was turned about 90° for a short front to address the visitor, is a temple in spirit and would have lent itself to the flourish of a portico, it did not find as much favour in the province as in Leinster. In any case, it was not as a precedent a wholly appropriate model, the Greek temple being without chimney or windows. Nevertheless, there are three outstanding examples in Munster. The O'Brien family turned to the fashionable

English architect Thomas Hopper to design them a pure little Doric temple lodge at their main gate of Dromoland Castle (Clare, 1812), at which time it would have been an apt introduction to their venerable old Classical house rather than to the subsequent great Tudor Castellated replacement pile by the Pain brothers, to which it is now prelude. The neighbouring Gores of Derrymore (Clare, *c.* 1840) were clearly impressed and erected a near replica at their estate, which now lies abandoned. Meanwhile, James Pain was to prove eclectic in his interpretation of the tetrastyle Doric temple lodge at Doneraile Court (Cork, *c.* 1840). Impressive and dignified as it is in isolation, it forms but part of a conspicuous greater ensemble, the rest being that most prestigious of entrances, the triumphal archway.

THE TRIUMPHAL ARCHWAY

Munster can claim several of these grand and ultimate proclamations of a proprietor's self-esteem. The magnificent triple gateway to Doneraile Court (Cork, *c.* 1820) precedes its lodge in date by a few years sufficient to also reveal the involvement of the younger Pain brother, George Richard. The great pair of detached Ionic columns on pedestals is repeated in his almost identical entrance to Lota Beg (Cork, *c.* 1820). Elsewhere there are others, less articulate and two-dimensional, largely tripartite, round-arched and defined by Doric pilasters, the most sophisticated being at Ballygiblin (Cork, *c.* 1819) and a series of almost identical neighbouring County Tipperary archways of disparate dates at Johnstown, Ashley Park and Kilteelagh. These are all attended by detached lodges, but at Bantry (Cork, *c.* 1845), probably by C.F. Anderson, the porter's accommodation is integral with the archway, to each side and over the carriage opening, all crowned with a balustraded parapet. Likewise, at Trabolgan (Cork, *c.* 1825) the gatekeeper is confined to that most extraordinary monumental rusticated gateway, which is, for whatever reason, an almost exact copy of the stark original to the Hotel Thessulon, Paris (*c.* 1787), by the eminent French architect Claude-Nicholas Ledoux. Strangely, in Munster one had to wait until the 21st century for the type whereby the central archway is clearly defined but flanked by supportive twin lodges, as at Martinstown (Limerick, 2009). Again this is a copy, immaculate and beautifully crafted, of Robert Adam's Roman Doric North Lodge to Kedleston Hall (Derbyshire, 1762). Thankfully the triumphal archway in Munster was of such scale as to survive the advent of modern farm machinery, though at Limerick Lunatic Asylum (Limerick, 1826) both the archway and its pair of Regency lodges, blind to the road, a design from the office of Francis Johnston and William Murray, are lost without trace.

THE NEO-CLASSICAL LODGE

An old photograph shows that the grand triple archway to the People's Park (Limerick, *c.* 1875) was attended by an appropriate neo-Classical lodge and is evidence of the enduring popularity of the style, despite the revolution that was the medieval revival threatening to overwhelm it during the Victorian period. Later still was another lost lodge of the type, which from its elevated site monitored the gates to Gawsworth (Cork, *c.* 1880) opposite. The neo-Classical lodge proved particularly popular with the rising mercantile class in the 1840s, and the Cork city suburbs saw the appearance of a series of standard single-storey hip-roofed lodges with pedimented hall projections and stuccoed walls with Doric corner pilasters. They graced the length of Glanmire Road Middle and beyond in examples at Clifton (*c.* 1854), Mount Donegan (*c.* 1845), Hyde Park House (*c.* 1840), Shanakiel (*c.* 1845), Factoryville (*c.* 1855), Parkgarriff (*c.* 1845) and the Bishop's Palace (*c.* 1840), all probably by the same unidentified architect.

A particular series of lodges in County Waterford further explore a theme of square Doric pilasters; at Salterbridge (Waterford, *c.* 1849) is a splendidly restored example, eclectic in its Tudor chimney-stack, Classical pilasters and roof parapet all behind a Gothic gatescreen. Considerably more innovative are the lodges at Headborough (Waterford, *c.* 1835) and Tourtane (Waterford, *c.* 1840), both asymmetrical in their recessed porches and clearly by the same hand, possibly architect John Robertson, with his connections to the Devonshire estates of Chatsworth (Derbyshire) and Lismore Castle (Waterford). These are lodges that began to show a spirit of experimentation emerging in a growing mood of unease at the constraints of the Georgian era, which can likewise be detected at Kilrush (Clare, *c.* 1845) and Cahercon (Clare, *c.* 1835) with another strain of the neo-Classical style in two striking and inventive lodges. Here the roof is supported by columns to each leading corner marking a pair of deep recesses, thus creating a central show front, which in the case of Cahercon is blind but for a niche to display statuary. To Kilrush is a gatescreen that surely identifies its architect as J.B. Keane, being identical to that at Mount Richard (Tipperary, *c.* 1825). The form of giant 'pylon' carriage pillars and secondary cast-iron posts carrying the gates clearly identifies Keane's source as being J.B. Papworth's 1818 *Rural residences* [**Fig. 6**]. This most influential of pattern-book designs was slavishly reproduced by such as Keane and by Richard Morrison at Fota (Cork, *c.* 1820), varying only in the substitution as finials of Barry wolves at the latter and Power stags' heads at Mount Richard for Papworth's tripod urns. Tipperary-born architect William Tinsley may have been responsible for other interpretations in the gatescreens to Melview (Tipperary, *c.* 1825) and Caher Abbey (Tipperary, *c.* 1835).

Another group of considerably more imaginative

Fig. 6

neo-Classical lodges, unique to the province, reveal an architect of rare talent and versatility in Charles Frederick Anderson. What distinguishes them is the device of creating a recess in external corners to house Doric columns—'*ex antis*', so to speak—to carry pedimented gables. The type can be found distributed about Munster in splendid examples at Kilfrush (Limerick, *c.* 1837), Mooresfort (Tipperary, *c.* 1835), Ballywilliam (Limerick, *c.* 1835), Lauriston (Cork, *c.* 1845) and in duplicate at Gurteen-le-Poer (Waterford, 1843), for which the architect's delightful set of drawings survive.

THE TRABEATED GATESCREEN

Anderson complemented some of these lodges with an equally distinctive entrance screen design containing pairs of 'trabeated' postilion archways of a type that can also be seen at Lota Beg (Cork, *c.* 1840) and Newtownanner (Tipperary, *c.* 1845), which may make the lost lodge there attributable to him. This is a format probably introduced by John Hargrave at Castle Hyde (Cork, *c.* 1830) and is likely to have originated in a plate from William Pain's *The practical house carpenter* (1799). Essentially an exercise in duality, this is a gateway that depends for effect in focusing not on the main carriage opening but rather on the flanking postern gates, where they are arched in their own right yet also function as carriage pillars. Such was the popularity of this trabeated gate with the Munster landowner that it is considerably more common here than in the rest of the country. At Richmond, Glanmire (Cork, *c.* 1790), was the most monumental of examples, but for refined elegance there is none better than that at Crookstown (Cork, *c.* 1815) by the ablest of unidentified practitioners, the Doric pilasters in pristine condition, contrasting with its sad little tumbledown lodge.

SYMMETRY

Given the Georgian dilemma of how to achieve symmetry by the gates, the solution of splitting the gate porter's quarters into a duality of 'day and night' accommodation provided an ideal visual presence but was hardly convenient. Later this arrangement was superseded, finances permitting, by placing twin family units flanking the entrance, with lodged pairs eventually making up as many as one in twenty of gateways in Munster. Most of the early examples of twin lodges in the province apparent on the first Ordnance Survey maps are lost, but there are a few notable exceptions from the late eighteenth century, particularly that elegant pair at Kilbrittain Castle (Cork, *c.* 1780), each of 1½ storeys, their standard three-bay façades facing one another across the front of their now-lost gatescreen, the leading fronts relieved by round-arched niches below plaques and pedimented gables, all in fine ashlar masonry. In the same county, and equally dilapidated, are the most extensive of imposing estate entrances at Richmond (*c.* 1790) and at Castle View, Tallow (*c.* 1800), the latter pair of lodges extending forward of their gates to form a vast semicircular forecourt. Likewise abandoned and again in

County Cork are the charming and socially generous two-storey Regency twins flanking an entrance to Belgrove (*c.* 1810). On a much smaller scale are those at Ballyseedy Castle (Kerry, *c.* 1790), with their bowed single-storey fronts also thrusting forward of the gates. The Georgian Gothic taste is represented in the pair of family units at New Hall (Clare, *c.* 1805), whilst Ballynatray (Waterford, *c.* 1845) boasts two twin-lodged entrances in severe astylar manner. At Marlfield (Tipperary, 1833) is a particularly self-conscious neo-Classical pair, adapted from Sir John Soane's 1793 *Sketches in architecture* by William Tinsley from single-roomed cubes into more convenient family units. This arrangement was to combine with the castellated Tudor Gothic style in those remarkable twins linked by a delicious ogee-arched gateway at Ballysaggartmore (Waterford, *c.* 1829) for the Kiely family, designed by their talented gardener, John Smith. More immediate are Vincent Kelly's International Style bungalows impressively flanking the entrance to Nenagh Hospital (Tipperary, *c.* 1935).

By far the most common solution to that quest for balance at the gates was to site the porter's lodge across the public road on an axis with its entrance. Despite being an association inconvenient for the gatekeeper in his exposure and attendance upon the gates, it was an arrangement that amounted to as many as one in ten in the province.

What would appear to be an admirable answer to the issue of symmetry at the entrance by locating the lodge centrally between a pair of gates is only to be found at Clonea Castle (Waterford, *c.* 1830), Mayfield (Waterford, *c.* 1855) and John Hargrave's effective landmark entrance to Fota (Cork, *c.* 1830), his 1½-storey lodge with a prominent canted front. There are instances also whereby it was sought to hide the lodge altogether from the approach by integrating it into an entrance quadrant wall, as at Harrietville (Cork, *c.* 1820), Leebrook (Kerry, *c.* 1810) and Ballyard (Kerry, *c.* 1830), with little more showing than a roof above the coping or a window inserted to survey the forecourt. But generally the lodge was located deferentially behind and to one side of its gates, at least affording the porter a degree of privacy and protection in carrying out his duties.

THE MEDIEVAL REVIVAL

This search for symmetry, however, was to become of little moment; as predicted by those ground-breaking eccentric County Waterford neo-Classical lodges, a whole new aesthetic came to challenge the old order in that of the Picturesque movement or Medieval Revival. This was particularly evident in domestic architecture, where country houses were erected or made over and extended with irregular massing to achieve romantic outlines, a dream which encompassed their settings and estate buildings and found particular expression in dramatic effects at the entrance gates. Born of visions of Claude and Poussin, prompted by the writings of Payne Knight and Uvedale Price, and further influenced by such as John Nash and an increasing issue of architectural pattern-books, there began to appear all manner of interesting asymmetrical arrangements of forms and variety of texture manifest in Munster, as elsewhere in Ireland, as a Medieval Revival.

All of this required of the architect an ability to adapt to a whole new vocabulary of form and detail, something with which local men Thomas Deane, Henry Hill and C.F. Anderson had no problem, whereas the brothers Pain already had a head start, having had the perfect grounding in being versed in the new order as assistants to that pioneer of the Picturesque, John Nash.

THE PATTERN-BOOK

For the others there was the assistance and reference of the pattern-book. Already noticed have been the works of William Pain, John Soane and J.B. Papworth, influential in their versions of Classical cottages and gatescreens, but it was a whole new generation of books which was to be the greatest aid, to landowners and their designers alike, in understanding all things medieval. Leading the way were Peter Frederick Robinson with six volumes, of particular relevance being his *Designs for lodges and park entrances* of 1833, and Thomas Frederick Hunt's 1825 *Half-a-dozen hints*, each of which contributed cottage lodges to the Killarney (Kerry) estate. Designs in the form of plans, elevations and perspectives were available in a variety of ornamental English cottages, Romantic castellated gatehouses, Italianate cottages, Swiss chalets and *cottages ornés*. This wide range of compositions was to become the basis for new mansions, villas and gate lodges throughout the province. Few architects' offices or country house libraries were without an architectural pattern-book on their shelves, and the Victorian age was to see little let-up in their publication, fulfilling as they did with their seductive illustrations a demand for this newfangled Picturesque. Whilst the Robinson and Hunt books ran to numerous editions, no pattern-book was more widely referred to than John Claudius Loudon's voluminous 1833 *Encyclopaedia of cottage, farm and villa architecture*, which was a compendium of selected designs from many contributors, some architects of eminence, others not. Two such are readily identifiable at Kilrush (Clare, *c.* 1850), the original by Humphrey Repton, and Dunboy Castle (Cork, *c.* 1835), based on a design by Thomas Allason, an example of which is also to be found at Red Hall (Antrim).

BUILDING COSTS

Many of these books helpfully appended estimates of construction costs for lodges, which varied 'depending upon embellishment'; Francis Goodwin in his *Rural architecture* of 1850 offered prices for a Grecian-style lodge relative to finish as: 'Brick and Stucco £380; Brick and Stone Dressing £420; Stone £560'. Closer to home, these prices can be compared with rates quoted by Sir Richard Morrison in the range of £150 to £350, to which could be added his professional fees of 5% of building costs, with travelling expenses charged at one shilling per mile on top of that.

BUILDING MATERIALS

That £150 would presumably have built the inferior class of lodge of basic vernacular construction—the standard three-bay single-storey cottage with a harled fabric of local rubble stone below a slated hipped roof. Of mud construction there was but one example discovered, at Meldrum (Tipperary, *c.* 1780), revealed by its state of ruin. It would in any case be considered an unsuitable material for a building of such status, too redolent of a peasant cabin. Brick as a material was not readily available and would be limited to dressings for openings or as an eaves levelling course. An early exception to this is the remarkable lodge at Carnelly (Clare, *c.* 1800/*c.* 1845), which was built in two stages, the original forming an adjunct to its successor, the result of the Stamer and Burton families' sensitivities in complementing their brick-faced house. Brick did, however, become more commonplace late in the century, particularly around the greater Cork city area, prompted by that late Victorian enthusiasm for things polychromatic. That variegation was also achieved with effect by the likes of architect William Atkins, who combined the already much used grey limestone with a stratum of the red sandstone that underlies parts of counties Cork and Kerry and can be appreciated in his lodges at Cork District Lunatic Asylum (Cork, *c.* 1861) and Oak Park (Kerry, *c.* 1860). There are welcome manifestations of strata of pleasant honey-coloured sandstone in the lodges at St Patrick's Cemetery, Clonmel (Tipperary, 1886), the Lodge (Clare, 1863) and Raheen Manor (Clare, *c.* 1911), where its quarry-faced finish is subtly set off by grey limestone dressings. But generally it was that limestone that predominated as a building material throughout Munster in whatever grade of lodge, be it as a rubble core for basic harling, a more upmarket stucco finish with quoins or label mouldings in cut stone, or in an ultimate sophisticated ashlar facing, all reflecting the underlying geology of the province.

THE PICTURESQUE MOVEMENT

In common with their counterparts in the rest of the country, the Munster landowner and his architect embraced the Picturesque movement. They may or may not have been conscious of the social benefits that its adoption would bestow on their tenants, the desired effect requiring an irregularity in plan and elevation achieved by means of the application of a verandah here or an oriel window there, but crucially the addition and convenience of sanitation. Further features were introduced to enliven the skyline in eaves broken by conspicuous chimney-stacks and gablets to light attic bedrooms in steeply pitched roofs, no longer approached by a ladder but rather by a relatively easygoing staircase. These cottages can be categorised in three groups in the chronological order in which they made their appearance in the province, distinguished one from another by their roof configuration: *Cottage Orné*, English Picturesque Cottage and Tudor Manor House Cottage.

THE *COTTAGE ORNÉ*

Owing more in its origin to the English cottage than to the Irish peasant cabin is this endearing rustic 'biscuit tin' genre, notable for its thatched roof, mostly hipped and taken down to undulating eaves carried on tree-trunk supports creating verandahs. Its early appearance in Munster is probably due to an introduction here by James and George Richard Pain, fresh from their apprenticeship in the office of John Nash, and the Reptons and the influence of the likes of their Blaise Hamlet (Gloucestershire). To them can be attributed the ruined structure at the gates to Mount Shannon (Limerick, *c.* 1825) and the immaculate cottage outside the main entrance to Adare Manor (Limerick, *c.* 1828). By an unidentified designer is that at Rosanna (Cork, *c.* 1825), while the exquisite 'Deenagh Lodge' on the Killarney (Kerry, 1834) estate survives almost undiluted from T.F. Hunt's *Half-a-dozen hints* (1825), with its tall, octagonal, Tudor-style chimney-pots atop its delicious undulating thatched hipped roof, the verandah marked by tree trunks supporting the eaves. The 2nd earl of Kenmare must have had a selection of pattern-books, for 'Reen Cottage' (Kerry, 1839) on the estate is another delightful composition, taken from P.F. Robinson's *Designs for lodges and park entrances* (1833), combining attributes of both the English Picturesque Cottage and the Tudor Manor House Cottage, where decorative bargeboards and skew-table gables mix.

These two variants are distinguishable by the contrasting treatment of their gables. The English Cottage is defined by its roof extending beyond the gable walls to terminate in ornately carved bargeboards, whereas the roof of the Tudor Manor style abuts its gable walls, which finish as cut-stone skew-tables invariably rising from moulded kneeler blocks that serve to stop the fascia boards. The requisite raising of eaves heights and steepness of gables for this new fashion afforded the opportunity to display motifs such as mock arrowloops, quatrefoils and shields with family crests, monograms and date-stones, serving also to relieve areas of blank wall. Likewise common to both is medieval detailing in variety with flat, Tudor or pointed arches to openings often transomed and mullioned, with decorative squared or latticed glazing patterns in cast iron to simulate the leaded lights of the Tudor period, all below label- or hood-dropping mouldings.

CAST IRON

It was indeed serendipitous that the advent of cast-iron manufacture should coincide with this newfound enthusiasm for things medieval, for it was a material infinitely more affordable than that which it purported to be. In addition, the discovery of this process revolutionised the ironwork of gatescreens, which became infinitely chunkier, and assisted in the mass production and repetition of countless Gothic motifs, replacing the rather more subtle and restrained late Georgian wrought ironwork.

THE ENGLISH PICTURESQUE COTTAGE

While not all practitioners were at ease with this new vocabulary—and there are many examples which testify to this, the perpetrators of which remain anonymous—this is far from the case with an outstanding and innovative English Picturesque Cottage at Bellmount (Cork, 1831), built on three floors to take advantage of its site, sloping from the avenue to a babbling brook behind, but which sadly lies abandoned and derelict. Identifiable as the architect for another admirable, but lost, lodge at Kilnap House and Mill (Cork, *c.* 1835) is the Cork-born Henry Hill; if built as proposed, this was a truly delightful cottage with exaggerated bargeboards and a thick thatch, very much in the Robinson pattern-book manner. Hill may also have been responsible for the surviving lodge at Newborough (Cork, *c.* 1835), with its distinctive cluster of Tudor-style octagonal chimney-pots. Outside Bandon is another notable example in the lodge at Clancool (Cork, *c.* 1840), though lacking its entrance and avenue and much altered for the worse. Likewise worthy of note is the pretty, rambling little lodge at Dromquinna (Kerry, *c.* 1874) by the Belfast-born architect Thomas Drew, which has a relative in the lodge at faraway Tubber-na-Carrig (Down), doubtless also by him.

The impact made on Munster architecture by the Pain brothers cannot be overemphasised, initially in variety and quality and latterly, after the death of the younger, in quantity. They again displayed their comfort with the Tudor Revival style in the fine Picturesque lodge at Ciamantha (Tipperary, *c.* 1840) and the extraordinary gathering of cottages at the gates to Coolmore (Cork, *c.* 1837), a veritable village of eight estate workers' cottages, any one of which could have housed the gatekeeper. Their provenance is clear from an array of striking brick chimney-stacks, some formed in spirals of dogtooth specials identical to those of 'Dial Cottage' in Blaise Hamlet (Gloucestershire).

The English bargeboarded cottage remained popular into the mid-nineteenth century, being purveyed by a Munster-born professional in William Atkins, who designed the very fine and commodious lodge at Muckross (Kerry, 1861) to impress Queen Victoria on her visit there, and probably those at Castle Freke (Cork, *c.* 1855).

THE TUDOR GOTHIC LODGE

At this time there emerged a series of singular Tudor Gothic lodges set apart and distinguished by their distinctive glazing pattern of Perpendicular Gothic wooden tracery. Dating from the 1840s and all in County Cork, at Killinardrish, Raleigh, Leamlara (demolished) and the castellated gatehouse of Drishane Castle, they may be attributed to architect Thomas Deane through there being identical windows in the big houses of Dromore Castle (Kerry) and Horsehead (Cork) known to be by him. There is little to compare with this fourteenth-century revival anywhere else in the country.

THE TUDOR MANOR LODGE

William Atkins was again to display his abilities with the outstanding skew-tabled Tudor Manor lodge to complement his vast pile that is Cork District Lunatic Asylum (Cork, *c.* 1861). It will be seen that he was to prove just as adept in the Italianate and Romantic Castellated styles. Sir Thomas Newenham Deane likewise exhibited talent in his output of Tudor Revival lodges, all commodious essays in grey limestone for his Tipperary gentry clientele. In Picturesque English Cottage mode is a fine example at Killoshehane (Tipperary, *c.* 1867) with intricately carved bargeboards and a pretty porch, while in Tudor Manor style is that at Walsh Park (Tipperary, *c.* 1865), with two each for the Carden estates of Barnane (Tipperary, 1863) and Templemore Abbey (Tipperary, *c.* 1865). While the skew-tabled variant did not find favour amongst the gentry and aristocracy until mid-century, such was not the case with the ultimate of fanciful structures emanating from the Middle Ages.

THE ROMANTIC CASTELLATED LODGE

While there is nothing in Munster to compare in scale with those vast castellated entrance complexes in the other three provinces at Markree Castle (Sligo), Duckett's Grove (Carlow) and Shane's Castle (Antrim), they remain unsurpassed in their sheer number and variety of compositions in the province. The Munster landowner was a romantic, and he and his architect graced the countryside with all manner of fairytale castle gates with fantastic outlines. Richard Morrison led the way with his design for Thomastown Castle (Tipperary, *c.* 1815), a wholly appropriate introduction to the Mathews' fantasy mansion, the lofty pierced medieval gatehouse of irregular outline with its external staircase tower related to similar entrances from the Morrison office at Glenarm Castle (Antrim) and Borris (Carlow). While the genre is noted for this eccentricity of outline, most early examples tended towards the symmetry of old in the likes of William Robertson's gatehouse at Cork Gaol (Cork, 1824) and the twin-lodged gateway to Burton Park (Cork, *c.* 1830), which mysteriously had a twin at Clonskeagh Castle (Dublin South). With little pretence towards defence, in perfect symmetry is that extraordinary castellated pair of Gothic lodges in the outer gate to Ballysaggartmore (Waterford, *c.* 1829), which display all manner of features associated with the type in their crenellations, mock machicolations, cross arrowloops and other Tudor Gothic motifs besides.

Showing scant regard for authenticity and consciously asymmetrical is the striking decorative complex that is the castellated Gothic essay at Ardfert Abbey (Kerry, *c.* 1870), which remains proud and maintained despite surviving its big house and avenue; dominating the village, it is quite possibly another example of the versatility of architect William Atkins.

At Lohort Castle (Cork, *c.* 1876) is a perfectly symmetrical composition of a pair of round towers flanking a Tudor gateway, an example of a genuine Irish tower-house approached via a Victorian fake. There is, too, a most impressive, severe and forbidding prelude by the Pain brothers to Elm Park (Limerick, *c.* 1840), with only slit windows providing light for the unfortunate gatekeeper, though the carriage archway, now redundant as such, provides for a bright modern living area. The huge and peculiar gateway to Macroom Castle (Cork, *c.* 1825) with its great telescopic towers dominates the town square, its accommodation alongside maintaining a degree of symmetry.

But generally in a 60-year period such symmetry was anathema to the spirit of the Picturesque movement, which depended for effect upon irregularity in its drama of outline. This predominated mainly in the form of a miniature keep or tower-house as gatehouse in combination with a carriage arch, a typical ensemble often dominated by an octagonal or round spiral stair-cum-flagstaff tower which would climb beyond to give onto a roof or imaginary ramparts.

The most satisfying examples of such are those by that short-lived genius Benjamin Woodward in his creations for Dromore Castle (Kerry, 1850) and Annesgrove (Cork, 1853), almost identical but for an oriel window overlooking the approach to the latter which shows the architect to have spared some consideration of illumination for the occupants. But for authenticity one need look no further than two superb and evocative gatehouses at Castle Oliver (Limerick, *c.* 1848) by the York-based architect George Fowler Jones, where little more than arrowslits provide light, and that, combined with their prominent stair turrets, one in the form of a bartizan, makes for the most convincing of such entrances in Munster, if anything enhanced by their dereliction; they remain defiant.

The Pain brothers continued to delight in creating an impressive round tower gatehouse in Nash manner at Castlegarde (Limerick, *c.* 1823) and perhaps in those charming rustic crenellated pasteboard Gothic entrances to Glin Castle (Limerick, 1815–36). While all of these romantic structures may have raised the prestige of their inhabitants over that of the neighbours, they did little for their comfort, the accommodation often having been contrived to achieve the desired external effect, rooms being ill-lit and misshapen and connected via pokey staircases; such is the sturdiness of their construction, however, that they survive in numbers.

Wholly independent of their gates are free-standing eye-catcher battlemented towers in the Gothic drum lodge standing distant from its entrance at Waterloo (Cork, *c.* 1815) and the three-storey Tudor octagon opposite the gates to Flesk Castle (Kerry, *c.* 1835). Such was the passion for castellations that a landowner of modest means would simply apply a crenellated parapet to the hall projection of a standard lodge and label-mould a few openings, as at Castle Widenham (Cork, *c.* 1830), probably another James Pain design, or, failing that, crenellate his gate pillars or the quadrant walls, like those at Leebrook (Kerry, *c.* 1850).

THE HYBRID LODGE

Often the Picturesque is manifest in the simplest of references and none the worse for that, as can be appreciated in that endearing little structure at the entrance to Glengarriff Castle (Cork, *c.* 1825), where a rustic standard lodge in exposed ragstone is embellished with basic label mouldings to pretty windows and the oversailing roof crowned with diagonally set Tudor chimney-stacks. Many of these standard lodges were to emerge as a sort of mongrel, a cross between the Classical style of old and the newfangled Tudor whereby detailing from both was mixed. Whether born of indecision, naivety or wilfulness on the part of the proprietor or his builder matters little, as it conceived a building of considerable charm in its own right. This melding of the Roman palazzo and the English Tudor manor house saw toothed quoins and modillion-bracketed eaves alongside latticed glazed casements below label mouldings or bizarre pediments decorated with fancy bargeboards, as at Cregg (Tipperary, *c.* 1825) and the pleasant lodge at Garrykennedy (Tipperary, *c.* 1860), compounded by columns *in antis*, whilst at Laurentinum (Cork, *c.* 1835) Tudor label-moulded windows are framed by Classical pilasters.

THE ITALIANATE LODGE

Popular as the Tudor Picturesque proved, enduring until the end of the century, old habits die hard and the Classical tradition was never forsaken, continuing to find favour alongside in an Italianate or sort of Romanesque whereby round- or semicircular-arched openings became the norm, enhanced with moulded surrounds or prominent voussoirs and keystones, corners emphasised by toothed quoins and eaves oversailing enough to accommodate and feature decorative modillion brackets, these details often repeated in the chimney-stacks, all commonly characterised by lined stucco walls.

Increasingly forthright in detail the Italianate lodge

appeared, to complement new villas of merchants in the vicinity of the growing conurbations about Cork city, Limerick, Tralee, Clonmel and Waterford. Leading the way, monitoring that most exclusive of public promenades is the splendid lodge on the Mardyke Walk (Cork, *c.* 1845), with its arcaded front of semicircular-arched openings in like recesses. In contrast, at Convamore (Cork, *c.* 1855) is an austere version identifiable as being by James Pain from the gatescreen with his half-barrel pedimented pillars, which became a trademark of his at Grange (Limerick, *c.* 1850), Killishen (Clare, *c.* 1845) and Derry Castle (Tipperary, *c.* 1850).

William Atkins displayed his eclecticism twenty years apart in pink sandstone at a restrained Aghadoe (Kerry, *c.* 1835), a quirky little lodge at South Hill (Kerry, *c.* 1855) and perhaps that sophisticated example outside the gates to Carrig (Cork, *c.* 1860) in Cobh. To the Limerick-born William Fogerty can be attributed lodges at Beech Park (Clare, *c.* 1860) with its Palladian window, Edenvale (Clare, *c.* 1866) with its Soaneian tripartite window and, undoubtedly by him, Waterpark (Clare, *c.* 1870). He displayed his versatility in a Picturesque bargeboard variant of the latter for the Lodge (Clare, *c.* 1863) and probably Mulkear (Limerick, *c.* 1875), with its prominent bracketed frieze.

Concurrent with the Picturesque lodge there developed in the Victorian period the L-plan, a layout which benefited the gatekeeper considerably, necessitating as it did the addition of a third room, the internal corner thus formed creating greater scope for the designer. At Solsborough (Tipperary, 1863) Denis Hanly, builder-cum-architect of Nenagh, formed a pretty arcaded verandah to the front door, just as he had done at Glasshouse (Offaly). So, too, John Skipton Mulvany of Dublin had designed two lodges for Minella (Waterford, *c.* 1862), one of which, on an L-plan, features an arrowhead window with his particular brand of arched heads below brutally bracketed eaves and verges, replicating a design he had created for Mountanville (Dublin South).

Samuel Ussher Roberts seems to have inherited the patronage of the wealthy Malcomson family at the end of Mulvany's career, apparent in the eye-catching gate lodge at Woodlock (Waterford, *c.* 1865), raised off a T-plan formed by the living room being flanked by deep arched recesses below a lofty parapeted roof. Its equally striking and imaginative gatescreen, with massive sculptural staged pillars and voluptuous scrolled iron gates, is exactly as Roberts provided for Tulira Castle (Galway). By contrast, on a standard plan, but no less prominent for that, is the lodge at Leemount (Cork, *c.* 1870) by an unidentified architect, conspicuous for all the trappings of the Italianate being applied in a thoroughly decadent little number with iron cresting to its ridges, moulded dressings and spring-course, a corbelled chimney-stack atop and an equally ornate complementary gatescreen. The style persisted as a sort of neo-Romanesque or *Rundbogenstil* in an abundance of round-arched openings, often in groups of two or three. The impressive gatehouse at Norwood (Cork, *c.* 1861) with its leading hip-gabled front displays just such a bipartite attic window amongst moulded bands, architraves and sill corbels. The latter are exhibited as beautifully sculpted acanthus leaves to the shelves of niches on the two extravagant late lodges at Lissard (Cork, 1896), set off by deeply V-jointed rustication.

While all these examples in the province are derived from the Roman palazzo, precious little is representative of the Tuscan farmhouse or *villa rustica* other than perhaps a solitary instance in one of the lodges at Glenstal Castle (Limerick, *c.* 1875), that great neo-Norman pile commenced 40 years earlier. The impression is prompted by its 'belvedere' tower, which dominates an otherwise single-storey ensemble of disparate forms, united solely by a corbelled eaves course.

THE CURIOSITIES

At the main gate of Glenstal Castle (Limerick, *c.* 1874) is a singular little structure, whose designer was clearly at pains to provide a foretaste of what lay beyond the gates, with its sawtooth-arched entrance porch in Norman manner and quirky corner windows with colonette supports, the whole exuding an ecclesiastical feel. An oddity it may be but it palls, as does all else in the province, against the Cappoquin entrance to Dromana (Waterford, *c.* 1835). There in an idyllic setting, as prelude to a relatively plain mansion of the Villiers-Stuart family, is a Hindu-Gothic temple as gate lodge, day-and-night accommodation with delicious ogee-arched windows, straddled by a central onion dome with minarets alongside and approached by an elegant bridge over the River Finnisk. Designed by Martin Day, who must have based his design on that of Joseph Good for the North or William IV gate of 1832 to Brighton Pavilion (Sussex), it served as a reminder for Henry Villiers-Stuart and his young bride Pauline Otto of their honeymoon in that English seaside resort. As a wag once quipped, the Taj Mahal had come to Brighton and pupped—so perhaps had the Pavilion visited Dromana and done likewise! Unique to Ireland, it, Sezincote House (Gloucestershire) and Brighton Pavilion represent the only examples of the style in the British Isles. Where Connacht can boast its Swiss Chalet and Leinster its French Renaissance Château, neither can compete with the whimsy of this Dromana gate.

While it is possible to categorise the New Zealand Maori style, there for whatever reason, at Springfield Castle (Limerick, *c.* 1845), not so the now-lost 'Copper Lodge' which used to mark the gate to Milfort (Waterford, *c.* 1864), a thoroughly whimsical 1½-storey drum lodge, the 'copper' probably confined to its ogee-domed roof, else being cast iron from the Turner Works in Dublin which formed an embracing verandah and an opulent lanterned gatescreen.

UNFULFILLED DREAMS

While some such bizarre apparitions were realised, many more practical proposals were never implemented and remained on the architect's drawing-board—or, in the case of Thomas Cundy the Elder, in his notebook. He must have felt particularly hard done by, as he prepared sketches for at least seven entrances, ranging from pretty verandahed cottages through twin lodges to triumphal archways, for the Coolmore (Cork, *c.* 1815) estate of W.H.W. Newenham, only for them to be forgotten apparently in favour, twenty years later, of the extraordinary and unlikely 'village' of cottages built about the main gate by the Pain brothers. The pretty pair of Georgian Gothic cottages intended to grace the gates to Dromoland Castle (Clare, *c.* 1810) also failed to see the light of day, their unknown author disappointed. Martin Day's triumphal arch design for Dromana (Waterford, 1836) may, however, have been superseded by his Hindu-Gothic caprice. Other English architects were to have their proposals rejected, although in each case they were otherwise well rewarded with large commissions from their Irish clients. E.W. Godwin's apt miniature redoubt for the entrance to Dromore Castle (Limerick, *c.* 1870) was turned down, while at Killarney (Kerry, *c.* 1877) George Devey's sweet little Arts and Crafts cottage was not executed.

COMPATABILITY

Architectural writers of the early nineteenth century, when the building of gate lodges was proliferating, were much exercised in debate over its suitability as prelude to its big house—whether or not it should reflect the architecture within. Most were agreed that it should, and generally Munster landowners complied with this precept. Typical were the forthright observations of the architect Robert Lugar, expressed in his *Architectural sketches for cottages, rural dwellings, and villas* (1805):

> 'Lodges should be in due character with the house, and mark its style distinctly. A more flagrant error can scarcely be committed, than to give the lodge a character opposite to that of the house. If the house be Gothic, make the lodge Gothic also; and if Grecian, then let the lodge be Grecian; but mixing one style with the other, as is frequently seen, makes us think but little of the mind that thus invades every idea of common sense; and I am persuaded a man of taste, on viewing this gross violation and incongruity of design, would feel something less than respect for the sense of the possessor. To a mansion I would have a handsome arched entrance, perhaps with columns, and two lodges, in accordance with the character of the house (it is not requisite that the same order should be adopted), the gates of iron, and the plantation near of fancy trees, interspersed with oaks, &c. As an entrance to a villa, one neat lodge, of stone, white brick, or stucco, may be sufficient; the piers of the same materials as the lodge, and the gates of iron.'

Where there are exceptions in the province there may be good reason for conflict in styles, namely where a lodge is not contemporary with the main house. At Dromoland Castle (Clare), for instance, the chaste little Doric temple by the gates was designed by Thomas Hopper in 1812, when the O'Briens' residence was a homely old Classical house rather than the great castellated pile that the Pain brothers devised to replace it. By the same token, it seems that the fantastic Tudor Gothic lodges at Ballysaggartmore (Waterford) were intended for a replacement house for the Kielys' plain early house, before the money ran out. But whereas the Pains again provided a wholly appropriate Classical triumphal archway and lodge to the venerable old house in that manner that is Doneraile Court (Cork), at neighbouring Creagh Castle they may also have been responsible for the extravagant Gothic lodge and gatescreen serving as introduction to a near-contemporary gracious Classical house of the Brazier-Creagh family.

Generally a lodge would be in accord with its big house if the two were of an age, but if it was a later addition, say at the opening of a new access, it would follow the fashion of its time, regardless of what was within.

MULTIPLE LODGES

By the 1870s any self-respecting proprietor of a holding of upwards of 100 acres required a lodged gate with a trustworthy person in attendance. On larger estates with distant entrances out of sight there would be little limit to their number. Generously belodged were the demesnes of Currah Chase (Limerick), Killarney (Kerry) and Trabolgan (Cork), each with seven porters distributed about their boundaries. At Adare Manor (Limerick), where the estate is divided by a public road, there were eleven gates to be supervised, while the vast acreage of Curraghmore (Waterford) employed twelve gatekeepers, in part necessitated by internal fenced enclosures such as the deer-park. This does not include the eight semi-detached estate workers' cottages by the 'Sallyhene Gate', one of which no doubt housed the porter. Likewise ensuring maximum supervision is the gathering of eight terraced houses by the main Coolmore (Cork) entrance.

THE GATE PORTER

The gatekeeper became one of the most important members of staff of a country house estate, the public face of the family within, being entrusted with the authority to monitor visitors. As the first line of defence, beyond close communication with his employer, the porter decided to whom the gate would be opened or closed. Its being shut and locked was crucial in retaining livestock or deterring extraneous elements, particularly those vagrants and vagabonds who were a constant nuisance roaming the roads of rural Munster. The estate entrance was also a place for deliveries of provisions and attendance upon the post-chaise, and at the largest of properties the principal gate would have been a centre of considerable activity.

Such duties could only be entrusted to the likes of a respected retired butler, and the extent of his vigilance was dependent upon the state of the country at that time or the attitude of the particular proprietor, which was reflected in the reception that a visitor or tourist could expect at the gate. Accounts of early travellers in Munster are revealing of respective proprietors' inherent hospitality or desire for privacy. In 1788 Revd Daniel Augustus Beaufort, on one of his regular absences from his parish, was told by the gatekeeper to Dromoland House (Clare) that 'every gent' was welcome to drive through Sir Lucius O'Brien's grounds. Henry D. Inglis in 1834 found that there was free admission for all town inhabitants to Lord Kingston's park of Mitchelstown Castle (Cork), and a year later the Scottish tourist Robert Graham was able to 'enter one gate and out the other' at Fota (Cork), Tervoe (Limerick) and Kilbree (Cork), whereas he was refused this convenience by Mr Oliver at Inchera (Cork). At Doneraile Court (Cork) he had to skirt the demesne wall, as the main gate was locked and there was no attendant lodge—a deficiency that was to be remedied about five years later. Likewise, in 1835 John Barrow on tour experienced difficulty in gaining entry to Curraghmore (Waterford), being 'uncivilly refused' initially by an officious porter before eventually finding 'civility' within.

DIVERSIFICATION

Later in the century the gate lodge was losing its function as a place of security, particularly in the vicinity of Cork city or the town of Limerick, where it was complementing many of the new villas of the *nouveaux riches* and emerging as little more than a status symbol, but still making that all-important architectural statement. Lodges increasingly became home to a gardener or a coachman, the opening or closing of the gates being left to a dutiful wife.

There had already been instances of this diminution in the essential function of the gate lodge earlier in the century, where by necessity they were pressed into service in an alternative or even dual role. Frequently they were built, or adapted for use, as schoolhouses, as at Lloydsborough (Tipperary, pre-1840), New Lawn (Clare, pre-1840), 'Fortane School' at Rochelle (Cork, *c.* 1880) and Dromagh Castle (Cork, pre-1841), which later in the nineteenth century served as a post office, as did that at Glencairn Abbey (Waterford, 1902), presumably all after the establishment of the Penny Post in 1840. The lodge at Treanlewis (Limerick, pre-1840) in mid-century was for a while an auxiliary workhouse, while that at Arbour Hill (Tipperary, pre-1839) served as a dispensary. At a gate to Dromoland Castle (Clare, 1887) was built a commodious lodge primarily to house the gamekeeper, the porter's role presumably being filled by his wife.

The Land Wars of the 1880s, however, saw a call for a return to their original function of defence by the gates. Disturbances in rural areas and threats to landowners saw the need for 'Constabulary Barracks', particularly in County Tipperary, where lodges at Dovea (*c.* 1850), Spring (*c.* 1850) and Suir Castle (pre-1841) were converted for that purpose, and similarly at Conigar (Limerick, pre-1841).

THE VICTORIAN GATESCREEN

As the century progressed and tastes in architecture increasingly diversified, so too had the Victorian gatescreen equally become the focus of an architect's inventive mind, realising all manner and variety in attracting attention. Far removed from the tried and tested, the square Georgian pillar was transformed into something altogether more imaginative, sculptural and varied.

There was no better exponent than William Atkins, as exemplified by a range of conspicuous carriage pillars designed to complement his gate lodges. In County Kerry at Ballard (*c.* 1855) and Oakpark (*c.* 1860) they are heightened by chamfered shafts elegantly broached below cappings with coved friezes, the latter decorated with acanthus leaves, whilst at South Hill (*c.* 1855) the chamfered shafts terminate in Classical cappings of four semicircular pediments.

Wearing his Tudor Gothic hat, he created at Muckross (Kerry, 1861), in expectation of Queen Victoria's visit, weighty pillars defined by layered cappings and buttresses to leading faces and other chiselled features besides, a recipe he surely also presented at the entrance to Castle Freke (Cork, *c.* 1855), here with 'lucarnes', and at least influenced those of the Sisters of Mercy Convent (Kerry, 1894) in Tralee. In the same innovative and forthright vein are Sir Thomas Drew's playful pillars at Dromquinna (Kerry, *c.* 1874), with their pepperpot tops.

Equally forthright and unrestrained was complementary chunky ironwork to gates and railed quadrants displaying a range of motifs.

THE HIGH VICTORIAN LODGE

The later nineteenth century was not noted for architectural reticence, and in a period known as High Victorian the gate lodge was no exception. Domestic architecture was to come in previously explored styles to be augmented by others, presented separately but quite commonly as a mix of two or even more. In some cases this was born of ignorance but mostly it was by design, a case of an architect vying with others in search of the unique. In achieving this, their quest would be emphasised by a new enthusiasm for greater colour contrasts to elevations as polychrome in a variety of materials.

But it was the Tudor Revival that dominated into the mid-Victorian period, appearing in all manner of imaginative interpretations. From quiet beginnings, in a sort of transition, were essays by T.N. Deane in his institutional lodges at Killarney Lunatic Asylum (Kerry, 1873) and Queen's College (Cork, 1864). As simple 1½-storey rectangular boxes, they depend for effect upon an apparently haphazard but well-considered fenestration, the latter having a strategically placed gablet and porch, clearly descended from the lodges of his erstwhile partner Benjamin Woodward at Clontra (Dublin South) and St Austin's (Carlow).

Less restrained was William Atkins's lodge at Cork District Lunatic Asylum (Cork, *c.* 1861), of like form but conspicuous for his choice of contrasting masonry. It was surely he too who selected the Glanmire red sandstone with grey limestone dressings for that outstanding little lodge at St Vincent's Orphanage (Cork, *c.* 1860). In these materials Atkins showed himself to be an able exponent of Ruskinian Gothic in his Venetian version at Oakpark (Kerry, *c.* 1860) with its ogee-arched openings, but for quirkiness there is little to surpass William Henry Lynn's interpretation of the style at the entrance to the now-lost mansion at Caher Park (Tipperary, *c.* 1863), its subtle grey variegated stone lifted by a thoroughly eccentric articulation of forms that includes an arrowhead bay window, which is a feature common to his brick versions of this lodge at Mount Temple (Dublin North) and Ashurst (Dublin South). This is a device also employed in J.J. O'Callaghan's outstanding lodge at the Holy Ghost Hospital (Waterford, *c.* 1880), with its conspicuous relieving arch in soaring gables defined by pretty perforated bargeboards, a leftover from the Picturesque English cottage, which continued to find favour with designers until the end of the century to ever more robust and commodious structures. At the gates to Blarney Castle (Cork, *c.* 1875) John Lanyon, for whatever reason, forsook the Scots Baronial style of the big house in favour of the Picturesque cottage, with its porch-cum-verandah a fine example of the carpenter's craft in its turned posts and eaves balustrade, a design copied at the entrance to Farran Lodge (Cork, 1909). At Blarney Castle and the exceptional lodge at St Patrick's Cemetery, Clonmel (Tipperary, 1886), with its fancy bargeboards, octagonal

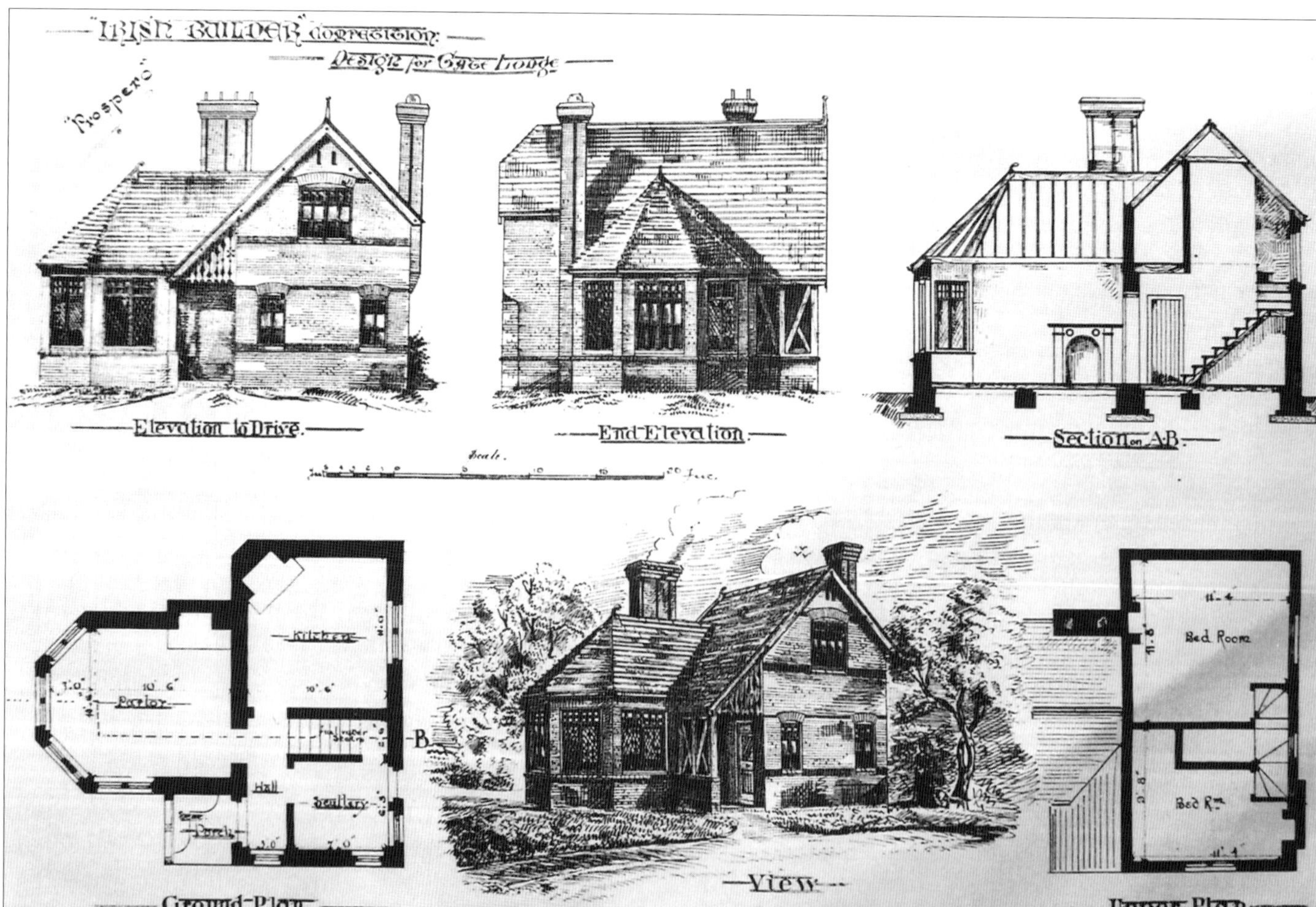

Fig. 7

Tudor chimney-stacks and mullioned and transomed windows, are grotesque earthenware dragon hip-knobs, an increasingly popular feature. On the massive gatehouse to Coolkelure (Cork, 1879), with its great watch-tower, are similar sculpted beasts, while the porch has an apex in the form of a miniature king-post truss. The latter became a common characteristic of gables at the close of the century, there being hammerbeam devices to the apexes of cottages at Curraghmore (Waterford, *c.* 1890), while the five late Victorian lodges at Dromoland Castle (Clare, *c.* 1887) feature a carved pointed arch infill with pretty perforations for relief.

Carved ornate bargeboards were not a lost art, for there are spectacular fretted examples at Mocollop Castle (Waterford, 1882) and Park View or Ardnacarrig (Cork, *c.* 1890), that most decorative of lodges of the High Victorian age, with its plethora of architectural motifs in a rare red brick and earthenware scalloped tiles to roof and as attic gable hanging, framing a striking jettied oriel with Elizabethan scrolled strapwork over a Palladian window, a feature also to be found in the saucy bungalow at Gortmore (Waterford, 1898), here flanked by porch and verandah recesses, with roughcast walls as a sort of Queen Anne Revival concoction, a harbinger of the Arts and Crafts movement.

THE ROMANESQUE LODGE

Nor was the Italianate lost, for it endured into this period in a form of Pisan Romanesque architecture conspicuous for its round-arched openings arranged as bi- or tripartite windows linked by a spring-course, as in the gatehouses to Norwood (Cork, *c.* 1861) probably by Alexander Deane the younger, and South Abbey (Cork, *c.* 1880). There is also a charming single-storey example at Clifton or Ardfoile (Cork, *c.* 1865), its hooded Venetian arches with dividing colonettes.

ARCHITECTURAL COMPETITION

If by now there had been any doubt that the gate lodge had been accepted as a distinct building type in its own right, this will have been allayed by the student competition instigated by the English architect William Isaac Chambers in the *Irish Builder* magazine, the results of which were published on 15 June 1882. Those awarded second and third prizes [**Figs 7 and 8**] both had Munster connections: respectively Daniel Edward Synan

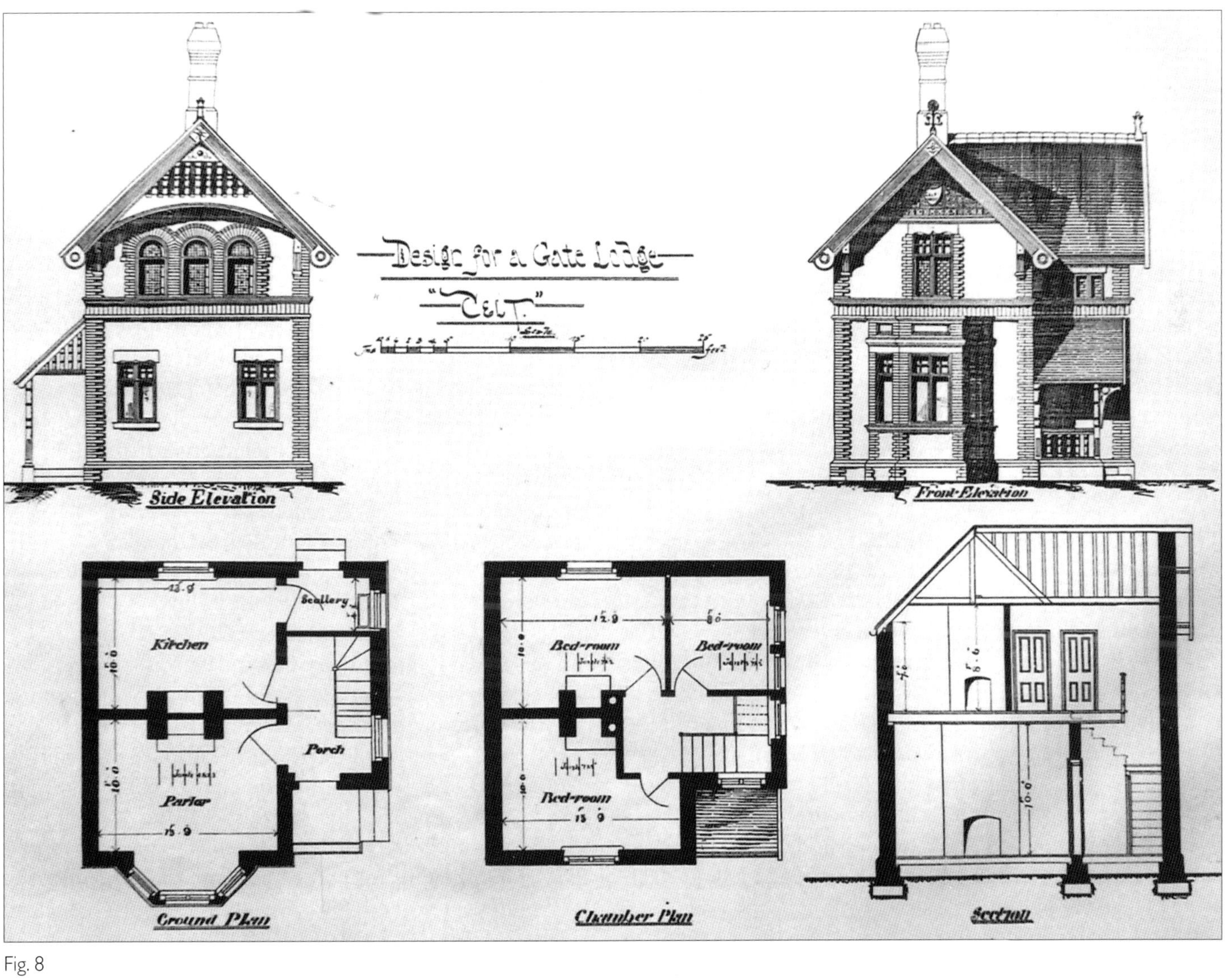

Fig. 8

of Cork, who was then seventeen years old, and Thomas K. Hogan subsequently of Cahir, neither of whom seems to have gone on to set the world alight. All three placed entries showed a scant student respect for economy in their typically robust, decorative and commodious late Victorian designs, evidence of the coming trend for a greater mix of surface finishes.

THE RAINBOW LODGE

The final decades of the century saw the advent of brick as a more common facing material in Munster, often presented as polychrome in a variety of calcium silicate cream or Staffordshire Blue relieving a local red brick as string-courses or lintels, mostly fashionable in the vicinity of Cork city, the better examples of which are at Woodville (Cork, *c.* 1880), Westboro (Cork, *c.* 1880), Glanmire Rectory (Cork, *c.* 1890), the Good Shepherd Convent (Cork, *c.* 1890), Bruree (Limerick, *c.* 1890), Shamrockville (Limerick, 1907) and that at Liss Ard (Cork, 1896), seemingly lacking its railway platform.

THE ELIZABETHAN REVIVAL LODGE

Likewise, the turn of the twentieth century saw a tendency towards roughcast and pebble-dash wall finishes, often presented in association with what was to become almost a prerequisite—Elizabethan black and white or half-timbered work, an effect often applied to gable apexes or attic storeys. Christened 'Stockbrokers' Tudor', it became populist in Edwardian times and remains beloved of developers to this day in all manner of questionable interpretations, some quite convincing. It appears tentatively in the decorative lodge at Adare Manor (Limerick, 1898) and the 1½-storey ornamental cottage at Glenbarraghane (Cork, 1895), there combining with earthenware tile hanging, incongruous in its Georgian Castletownshend setting. There is no such restraint in its application in the single-storey lodge at Milford (Limerick, *c.* 1900), while in that at Greenmount (Waterford, *c.* 1905) on the Devonshire estate no wall remains free of the effect in a striking example.

THE ARTS AND CRAFTS LODGE

The transition between the High Victorian period of architecture and that of the so-called Arts and Crafts movement in Ireland was far from clear-cut before it emerged in any purity, there persisting that fusion, or confusion, of styles in architects' quest for originality. To add further to the difficulty in distinguishing one from the other in style and date was the continuing twenty-year time-lag in the latest architectural fashion crossing the Irish Sea. This was further compounded by those two London-born practitioners J.P. Seddon and George Devey, each precocious in his own right in precipitating the Arts and Crafts style in Munster.

On the domestic architectural scene in the province, amongst the aristocracy and gentry there seems to have been little confidence at this time in home-grown architects, most placing their faith in English-based practitioners. At Rossdohan (Kerry, *c.* 1875), in the idyllic setting of the Kenmare River, on a causeway approach to the house is the first Arts and Crafts cottage in Munster. To designs by John Pollard Seddon, it is conspicuous for its boulder-faced walls, exposed chimney-breast and hipped gables. Contemporary was a building spree on the Killarney or Kenmare estate, which saw the construction of George Devey's ill-fated neo-Tudor mansion as part of a commission that included designs for some of his spontaneous cottages, one of which anticipated the Arts and Crafts movement. This 'Lackabane Lodge' at Killarney House (Kerry, *c.* 1877) might best be described as having descended from a Tyrolean chalet, with its first-floor balconies and immaculately turned balustrades, defined too by its clay tile hanging, a material much *de rigueur* for the period and particular to the imaginative late *cottage orné* at the gate to Ballybrado Farm (Tipperary, *c.* 1880) by the far-flung architectural partnership of Robert Watt of Belfast and James Otway of Waterford, the lodge with its romantic verandahs and dormers presumably by one and its Classical gatescreen by the other. By the Edwardian period came the characterful little brick lodge by G.R. Ryan of Waterford at Shamrockville (Limerick, 1907) and Clifford W. Smith of Limerick's highly imaginative lodge at Raheen Manor (Clare, *c.* 1911), a chunky affair in quarry-faced sandstone with chamfered battered corners and nicely contrasting cut-limestone colonettes *in antis* to its recessed entrance porch.

The Dublin-born Frederick William Higginbotham displayed his eclecticism in two lodges, one a smart neo-Tudor Revival cottage (Tipperary, 1914) that once gave introduction to John Nash's vast Shanbally Castle, the other an innovative Picturesque lodge with recessed corner porch for Mountain Lodge (Tipperary, 1908). Further remarkable and diverse examples of the Arts and Crafts movement, again emanating from London drawing-boards, are to be seen in the delightful compositions at the Beamish and Crawford Brewery (Cork, 1902) in an Elizabethan Revival manner with half-timbered gables and fine dated cartouche by the Houston brothers, Alfred Charles and John Lloyd; at Hollybrook (Cork, *c.* 1905) is a jewel of the province's architecture in an original and apt preparation for its contemporary big house, with its Diocletian window, Classical portico and quirky chimney dormers with requisite plain red clay tiles, as devised by R.S. 'Robin' Balfour; at Dooneen Cottage (Kerry, 1909) is the most authentic and unprepossessing of all in a Lutyens-cum-Voysey-inspired composition, with its simple white roughcast battered walls and steeply hipped roof of red clay tiles, by the little-known architect John Wornell.

THE LAST LODGES

This eccentric phase of domestic building proved to be a brave final fling of the Irish landowners. The accumulating circumstances that had beset them since the Famine eventually conspired to break them, the Great War, taxation and recession combined proving to be the last straw.

It was left to the new government's funded institutions to keep alive the tradition of lodge-building. At Queen's College (Cork, 1929) it was probably O'Flynn and O'Connor who added their version of Ruskinian Gothic, dictated to some extent by the use of salvaged materials from its predecessor. But it was mainly due to local authority health boards' foresight that the International Style is manifest through the gifted Vincent Kelly, 'the doyen of Irish Hospital architects in the 1930s'. He returned from a Grand Tour of the Continent a devotee of the Finnish architect Alvar Aalto, an influence seen in his hospitals and their lodges at Listowel (Kerry, *c.* 1930), Cashel (Tipperary, *c.* 1940) and Nenagh (Tipperary, *c.* 1935), where the entry is via a pair of his lodges, all flat-roofed with curved smooth-rendered walls uncluttered by detail.

That the tradition of lodge-building is not dead we can thank the late Ambrose Congreve for the three unassuming neo-Georgian examples at Mount Congreve (Waterford, 1950). It is some comfort that there remains some scope for accumulating personal wealth sufficient for a private landowner to indulge himself and even revive the 'big house' building tradition, as at Martinstown (Limerick, 2009) with, on public view, its beautifully crafted Adam Revival 'Kedleston Lodge'.

GUIDE TO THE GAZETTEER

Entries are numbered and listed county by county for ease of reference. Each entry heading gives the *NAME* of the property with its *LOCATION*. This heading (or subheading, where there is more than one lodge) is followed by the *DATE* of the building's construction, its *ARCHITECT* and, should there be little or nothing evident on site, its *CONDITION*. Proposals which remain unexecuted are also indicated. An *ILLUSTRATION* generally precedes the *DESCRIPTION*, and *REFERENCES* complete the entry.

NAME
Title of house, demesne or institution with which a lodge is associated, the name given being that when it was first known to have been 'lodged'; any previous and subsequent titles of a property are cross-referenced.

LOCATION
The nearest town or village.

DATE
Where a date-stone or documentary evidence is lacking, the date of construction is deduced from visual assessment. If a lodge has been demolished, is ruinous or so altered as to be unrecognisable, a date is given as 'pre-' that of the earliest Ordnance Survey map on which it appears. Occasionally, where a gate lodge is referred to in a valuation book offering a more accurate date of erection, this is noted. (For dates of the Ordnance Survey maps and Griffith valuations see the bibliography.)

ARCHITECT
In the absence of a documentary source, attributions are made on stylistic grounds or on the evidence of associated building activities. Such ascriptions are made with varying degrees of certainty, ranging from 'perhaps', through 'possibly' to 'probably'. 'Architect not known' indicates a design sufficiently sophisticated as to suggest the hand of a professional architect or talented amateur but with no positive attribution possible.

CONDITION
This is recorded solely where a lodge within the time-span of the survey (which took place between 1996 and 2006) was discovered to have been demolished. Inevitably more demolitions have occurred since.

ILLUSTRATIONS
Photographs and drawings are by the author unless otherwise credited. Note of the original architect, artist or photographer is followed (in parenthesis) by the owner or holder of such material. Most architecturally significant lodges are illustrated. Some of lesser merit have also been included, as they have been demolished and their record is considered of importance.

DESCRIPTION
Reference to a lodge being 'standard' indicates that its ground-floor main elevation is three-bay symmetrical, the front door flanked by windows. In addition to a physical description of the structure, an attempt has been made to relate it to other building phases on the estate, to the big house and to the family, proprietor or patron responsible. Over 4,000 sites have been visited in the course of this study and some have, of necessity, not been surveyed for some time; changes have thus occurred in the interim, especially in urban areas. Where known, the identities of gate porters have been recorded.

ABBREVIATIONS

BPB	Burke's *Peerage and baronetage* (various editions; London, 1861, 1873, 1903, 1925, 1929).
DB	*The Dublin Builder.*
DEP	Burke's *Dormant and extinct peerages* (various editions; London, 1844, 1883).
IAA	Irish Architectural Archive.
IADS	*Irish Architectural and Decorative Studies: Journal of the Irish Georgian Society.*
IAR	*Irish Arts Review.*
IB	*The Irish Builder.*
IFR	Burke's *Irish family records* (London, 1976).
IGS	Irish Georgian Society.
JCHAS	*Journal of the Cork Historical and Archaeological Society.*
LG	Burke's *The landed gentry of Great Britain* (various editions; London, 1853, 1863, 1875, 1882, 1886, 1894, 1912, 1952).
LGI	Burke's *The landed gentry of Ireland* (various editions; London, 1886, 1904, 1912, 1958).
LOI	*Land owners in Ireland 1876* (reprint; Genealogical Publishing Co., Baltimore, 1988).
NAOPW	National Archives: Office of Public Works Collection.
NGI	National Gallery of Ireland.
NIAH	National Inventory of Architectural Heritage (available at http://www.buildingsofireland.ie/).
NLI	National Library of Ireland: Drawings Collection.
OS	Ordnance Survey.
PGI	*Parliamentary Gazetteer of Ireland 1844–1845* (3 vols) (Dublin, London and Edinburgh, 1846).
RIBA	Royal Institute of British Architects: Drawings Collection.
TCD	Trinity College Dublin.
Thom's	*Thom's Irish Almanac and Official Directory* (various editions; Dublin, 1844–1910).

COUNTY CLARE

1. ADELPHI, Corrofin; *c.* 1860.
The lodge post-dates the charming villa considerably, perhaps having been built after 1854 when William Fitzgerald (1789–1872) succeeded to the estate on the death of his unmarried brother. It is a rubble-built single-storey structure difficult to date owing to its having been adapted to serve as a garage, losing a bow front in the process.
LGI (1904).

ANNALY LODGE (see THE LODGE)

2. ANNEGROVE, Clonlara; pre-1910; *demolished.*
A property in 1855 of James Joynt, the porter's lodge to which was added after 1840.
Griffith 1853–63.

3. ARAN VIEW, Milltown Malbay; *c.* 1845.
On an elevated and exposed site is this single-storey standard gatekeeper's lodge on a square plan with rendered walls, its pyramidal roof with clipped eaves rising to a central chimney-stack; derelict. Not existing on the 1840 OS map, it was recorded in the 1855 valuation on the property of John Carroll.
Griffith 1853–63.

4. ASHLINE PARK, Ennis (2).
Like their pleasant late eighteenth-century big house, both lodges have been demolished, having previously also served a Beechpark House (not to be confused with Beech Park [*q.v.*] further north again) and survived a public road realignment. Each was in place by 1840 to the seat in 1837 of Robert Mahon (1793–1858) of that family in neighbouring Cahircalla [*q.v.*].
Lewis 1837; *LGI* (1904); Weir 1986.

5. AUGHAVOHER, Lisdoonvarna; pre-1840; *demolished.*
A summer seat in 1837 of Francis Gore of Derrymore [*q.v.*], the gate lodge to which had gone by 1916.
Lewis 1837; Weir 1986.

6. AYLE, Tulla; *c.* 1830.
To the modest, and now lost, farmhouse occupied in 1814 by Thomas B. Woods and subsequently in 1837 by James Macnamara

was this relatively innovative lodged entrance. Sited forward of its gatescreen, the single-storey cottage, raised in a coursed rubble, has a bowed end which matches the convex quadrant across the approach, where the outer pillar is repeated as a pilaster on the lodge's road elevation. Between is a triple gateway contained by four further square stone pillars, each with a banded frieze and domed capping. The porter had the convenience of alternative door access to both the front and the rear of the gates; derelict.
Leet 1814; Lewis 1837.

7. BALLINTLEA LODGE, Sixmilebridge; *c.* 1845.
A plain single-storey standard porter's lodge with harled rubble walls and steeply gabled roof. Derelict, it is accompanied by a gatescreen of monolithic square stone carriage pillars flanked by rustic ogee quadrant walls, probably built for John Peter Kelly (1775–1871), whose father had come into the property through marriage to a daughter of the Roche family, the previous proprietors.
LGI (1904).

8. BALLYALLABAN, Ballyvaughan; pre-1840; *demolished.*
An antique seat associated through time with the O'Brien family, the lodge to which had been removed by 1916.
Griffith 1853–63; Weir 1986.

9. BALLYALLA [1], Ennis; pre-1840; *demolished.*
In Cloonteen townland was a sizeable house, removed by 1920, to be outlived by its porter's lodge, an estate in 1855 of John Enright which was subsequently renamed 'Templemaley'.
Griffith 1853–63.

10. BALLYALLA [2] or BALLYALLIA, Ennis; pre-1840/*c.* 1850.

The estate of the Stackpoole family, the original gatekeeper's lodge to which commanded an entrance off an old county road which was later absorbed into the property; a new lodge was built in its present setting next to the realigned road by Andrew Stackpoole, who had succeeded to the place on the death of his father in 1812.

This is a smart single-storey building built off a butterfly plan in smooth modern rendered finish, its gabled wings featuring Classical carved paired modillion brackets to verges and eaves, and paired round-headed casement windows with Tudor label mouldings over. Across the angle is a gabled breakfront containing an elliptically arched fanlight to a panelled door flanked by round-headed niches. Occupied and extended, its chunky chimney-stack bearing the satellite dish. Modest punched ashlar carriage pillars minus their gates but flanked by twentieth-century chunky timber postern gates; beyond, shallow concave quadrants form an extensive segmental turning area, mirrored across the road to create a greater circular forecourt.
LGI (1904).

11. BALLYCASEYMORE, Bunratty; pre-1839; *demolished.*
A property in 1814 of John Canny, prior to which it was the residence of Sir John Riggs-Miller. The long tree-lined avenue lies lodgeless.
Leet 1814; Weir 1986.

BALLYCLOGH CASTLE (see A HISTORY OF THE GATE LODGE IN MUNSTER)

12. BALLYCONNOE, Lisdoonvarna; pre-1840; *demolished.*
A property in the mid-nineteenth century of the Creagh family, the original house on which was already in ruins in 1840. At some time alternatively known as 'Prospect Lodge'.
Griffith 1853–63.

13. BALLYCUGGARRAN, Killaloe; pre-1910; *demolished.*
A lodge built after 1840 to a holding in 1855 and 1876 of Marcus Patterson.
Griffith 1853–63; *LOI.*

14. BALLYCUNNEEN, Hurler's Cross; pre-1840; *demolished.*
A late Georgian villa associated for much of the nineteenth century with the O'Halloran family.

BALLYHICKEY (see HAZELWOOD)

15. BALLYKEEL, Kilfenora; *c.* 1820.
Opposite the gates is a two-storey three-bay gabled house with stuccoed ground floor and banded roughcast upper storey; the relatively generous accommodation is probably explained by its other function in 1840 as a constabulary barracks, thus created as security for the Lysaght family. There is a

good late Georgian gatescreen of four stone pillars and flanking postilion openings, one now blind.

Leet 1814.

16. BALLYLEAAN LODGE, Killadysert; pre-1840/*c.* 1880.

The lost house of the Coppinger family is survived by its gate lodge, which is a substantial 1½-storey three-bay gabled affair with roughcast walls enhanced with toothed brick dressings and quoins. This was built as a replacement for a predecessor of his ancestors opposite the gates by John Charles Coppinger O'Connell Bianconi, so called through the estate passing down female lines.

Weir 1986.

17. BALLYLINE, Crusheen; pre-1910; *demolished.*

A property at some time also known as 'Millbrooke', which was damaged by fire and rebuilt to designs of William Fogerty in 1865 for Augustine Butler, a commission which may also have included the provision of the porter's lodge.

DB (15 December 1865).

18. BALLYNAHINCH, Tulla; *c.* 1840.

A lodge that probably assumed its present shape through evolution during the proprietorship of Capt. Charles George Martin O'Callaghan (1821–95), who succeeded to the estate in 1829 as a minor. Single-storey on a T-plan with a hipped roof, the main wing projects to the avenue to terminate in a canted end below an equivalent roof. In a good punched ashlar, it now lies derelict with a corrugated iron lean-to roof imposed. Perhaps improved and altered around 1874, when architect E.H. Carson was designing 'farm offices'.

LGI (1904); *IB* (15 February 1874).

19. BALLYQUIN, O'Briensbridge; pre-1840; *demolished.*

A seat of the Arthur family since the seventeenth century, subsequently renamed 'Glenomera' around 1810.

20. BALLYVALLEY, Killaloe; *c.* 1810.

A property that passed around 1810 from the Carr family to Revd Standish Grady Parker (d. 1848) of Castle Lough, Co. Tipperary, but apparently occupied by his uncle, William Parker. The lodge probably dates from that transition, originating as a single-storey standard Georgian Gothic cottage with harled walls below a hipped roof, the central of its three lancet-headed openings having since been altered from doorway to window; much modernised and extended in like manner. Alongside is a very fine and probably older gatescreen in Classical style from the Carr era, comprised of four tall ashlar pillars with plain friezes and extending moulded corniced cappings, all crowned by splendid rusticated ball finials. Angled wing walls in nicely contrasting whitened rendering contain stone-dressed and keystoned postern openings (that to the right-hand side is blind).

Wilson 1803; Leet 1814; *LGI* (1904).

21. BALLYVAUGHAN UNION WORKHOUSE, Ballyvaughan; *c.* 1852; *demolished.*

Both the main building, which first opened for admissions in 1852, and its gatekeeper's lodge have gone.

O'Connor 1995.

22. BALLYVOE, Ennis; pre-1840/pre-1910; *demolished.*

The original lodge of the Keanes has gone, as has its later replacement on a slightly different site, the latter built subsequently for the Gibson family.

Weir 1986.

23. BEECH PARK, Ennis; *c.* 1860; architect possibly William Fogerty.

The Keane family moved here from Ballyvoe [*q.v.*] in the early nineteenth century, but the single-storey standard gate lodge was a later addition to the property by Marcus Keane (1815–83), who inherited it on the death of his father in 1839. A positively outstanding little lodge in a robust neo-Palladian style, located outside its gates (now missing, like the big house), it is in a sad state of dereliction but not beyond saving. The oversailing hipped roof has carved modillion brackets to the soffit carried about the verge of the projecting hall with its round-headed, moulded-surround fanlit doorway. To each side are narrow semicircular-arched windows with plain banded surrounds in rendered walls broken by a bold stone string-course which embraces the building to meet the charming Venetian window to the road elevation. An inspirational design by an as-

yet-unidentified architect who must also have been responsible for the lodge to nearby Edenvale [*q.v.*].

Leet 1814; *LGI* (1904); Weir 1986.

BEECHPARK (see ASHLINE PARK)

24. BELLE ISLE, Castleconnell; *c.* 1810.

A single-storey standard hip-roofed lodge with oversailing eaves, latterly extended by a bay and having its doorway blocked up. Presumably built for James Young, who is recorded here in 1814. Gateway removed.

Leet 1814.

25. BELMONT, Milltown Malbay; *c.* 1825.

The most basic yet quintessential of Irish gate lodges. Although single-storey standard, nothing is quite symmetrical, its one-over-one sash windows on each side of a sheeted door in limewashed rubble walls below a steeply pitched hipped, almost pyramidal, roof with clipped eaves, very large slates rising to a crude chimney-stack off-centre of its minimal ridge; derelict. Adjacent is the most modest of gatescreens to match with a blocked-up postilion gateway and a gateless carriage opening. A property in 1814 of William Butler.

Leet 1814.

26. BELVOIR, Kilkishen (2).

The sorry remains of a fascinating demesne with its ruined early nineteenth-century Tudor Gothic house, chapel and folly building. Sadly now lacking its pre-1840 entrances with their paired lodges, neither of which survived to 1922; indeed, a replacement opposite the northern gate is also no more. A property after 1814 of David J. Wilson, who succeeded his father John Wilson here, eventually passing through marriage to the Lynch family.

Bence-Jones 1988; Weir 1986.

27. BIRCHFIELD, Ennistimon (2).

Cornelius O'Brien MP (1772–*c.* 1860) was a devotee of the Picturesque, in particular the Tudor Castellated style, evident in his lookout tower at the Cliffs of Moher and the octagonal corner turrets, crenellated parapets and label mouldings on his mansion. Thomas Lacy, on tour in 1861, informs us: 'The celebrated Thomas Steele, Esq., who was a friend of the late proprietor, and an engineer and architect of no mean pretentions, drew the plan of this building'. Sadly, not only has his creation not endured down the centuries but neither have the estate's pre-1840 gate lodges, that at the main gate now superseded by a twentieth-century replacement, displaying wavy bargeboards to its breakfront porch and similar fascias to its canted end. The immaculate uncoursed stone facings and trefoil-perforated crestings perhaps reflect its predecessor. Alongside is a good early nineteenth-century straight gatescreen of four square pillars and flanking walls containing postilion openings. The rear lodge lies ruinous.

Lewis 1837; Lacy 1863; Weir 1986.

28. BLACKWATER, Ardnacrusha; *c.* 1845.

A property in 1855 comprising Blackwater flour mill, miller's house, offices and land of 139 acres, then, eighteen years earlier and as late as 1870 of Samuel Caswell. His lodge, a standard single-storey, hip-roofed, harled cottage at Barry's Cross, opposite its gates, now serves as a shop.

Lewis 1837; Griffith 1853–63; Slater 1870; Flynn 2013.

BUNAVORY (see CRAGG)

29. BUNCRAGGY, Clarecastle (2).

In 1838 Fraser described 'the old and neglected but beautifully situated seat of the noble family of Burton'. Another property of the marquises of Conyngham of Slane Castle, its neglect was due in part to absenteeism and its being let to others. It was nevertheless occupied by colonel of the Clare militia Sir Francis Nathaniel Pierpont Burton (1766–1832), whose twin brother had inherited the marquisate in 1787 and who may have been responsible for adding at least the existing main entrance to the estate.

North gate; *c.* 1800.

In its original state this was a perfectly delightful little single-storey standard rustic Irish porter's lodge with just that touch of sophistication in its 'Wyatt' or tripartite multi-paned windows, in limewashed harled walls, on each side of a simple boarded doorway below a hipped roof with basic

chimney-stack central to its ridge. That Wyatt influence is explained by the famous architect James Wyatt working around 1785 for Sir Francis's father at Slane Castle, Co. Meath. The little lodge has recently been saved from dereliction and likely extinction in rehabilitation—but at a cost. Alongside is a fine late Georgian gatescreen consisting of four square ashlar pillars, awaiting reinstatement of their moulded cappings, containing straight railed screens with postern gates matching the carriage gates with their spear tops and husk motifs. There is similar ironwork at Carrigoran [*q.v.*] and an identical gatescreen at Doonass [*q.v.*].

South gate; pre-1840; *demolished.*

The lodge to the secondary entrance lay opposite its gates.

Leet 1814; Fraser 1838; *BPB* (1929); Colvin 2008.

30. BUNNAHOW, Crusheen (2).

There survives a single-storey gabled structure, now in use as a farm building, near a pair of sophisticated late Georgian square ashlar pillars with moulded cappings. Probably built by either William Butler (d. 1823) or his son of the same name (1784–1871). Likewise dating from before 1840, the lodge opposite the main gate had gone by 1916, as has its big house.

LGI (1904); Weir 1986.

31. BUNRATTY EAST, Bunratty; *c.* 1830.

Located forward of its gates is this single-storey standard lodge with roughcast and a hipped and gabled roof containing loft accommodation. The fine gatescreen has moulded cappings and flame finials to its stone pillars. Presumably built for Thomas Studdert (1779–1870), who in 1825 had succeeded his father of the same name, who was building the house around 1807.

Dutton 1808; *LGI* (1904).

32. BUNRATTY WEST, Bunratty; pre-1840; *demolished.*

A 'post office' located by the entrance to a property in 1837 of the Palliser family, then in 1855 of Richard Dawson, as shown on the 1840 and 1922 OS maps may have had the dual function of porter's lodge.

Lewis 1837; Griffith 1853–63.

33. BURTON HILL, Cratloe; *c.* 1825.

A property, at some time also known as 'Killeely', doubtless founded by the Burton family, which by 1846 had as proprietor Edward Hodges Goggin. The entrance screen has good fancy cast-iron gates and carriage pillars with vases atop, whilst forward of them is an earlier single-storey standard gatekeeper's cottage, rendered with banded surrounds to modern windows below a steeply hipped roof; occupied and much extended.

Slater 1846.

34. BUSHY PARK, Ennis; pre-1840; *demolished.*

An estate since the late eighteenth century of the Macnamara family of Ennistimon [*q.v.*]. By 1921 the porter's lodge had been demolished and the avenue rerouted westwards to a new entrance.

Taylor and Skinner 1778; 1783; Weir 1986.

35. CAHER, Caher; *c.* 1870.

An unprepossessing, big and derelict two-storey, four-bay, gabled mid-Victorian gatehouse, once commanding the gatescreen of four rusticated pillars with four-faced pedimented cappings, flanked by good shallow concave railed quadrants. Situated at the entrance to a demesne in the mid-nineteenth century of William O'Hara.

Griffith 1853–63; *LUI*.

36. CAHERBANE, Newmarket-on-Fergus; pre-1840; *demolished.*

Only some original outbuildings survive on the estate of the Creagh family, both their big house and its gate lodge having gone. Recalling the latter, by the old entrance, is a modern interpretation of a porter's lodge. In red rustic brick, this bungalow has a red-tiled hipped roof from which projects a gabled central hall.

37. CAHERCON or CAHIRACON, Killadysert; *c.* 1835; architect possibly J.B. Keane.

The most innovative and noteworthy country house entrance complex in the province is this extraordinary Classical composition, frustratingly by an architect not yet identified. Although having suffered some indignities down the years, it thankfully survives largely as it appears in early twentieth-century photographs.

Clearly by a designer of some invention, and tentatively attributed to J.B. Keane on the strength of his lodge at Kilrush [*q.v.*], the single-storey lodge is essentially square in plan with a shallow pyramidal roof rising to the central stone chimney-stack, its capping with mutule brackets, a feature repeated about the eaves, which project beyond the sculpted frieze. Faced in limestone ashlar, the main avenue front is of five bays, those to the external corners in the form of open porches over which the frieze passes to be carried on single fluted Doric columns. The elevation is dominated by a unique central pedimented frontispiece that breaks the eaves and contains a round-

IAA

Country Life

headed niche to display a beautiful Greek goddess statue. Flanking this aedicule is a pair of bipartite casements with, perversely, pretty Gothic traceried lights and subtle keystones over—a window repeated about the structure.

The gatescreen is equally creative, with the aedicule feature repeated as carriage pillars-cum-semicircular-arched and pedimented postilion openings, each framed by engaged Doric columns. Beyond are heavily decorative railings on dwarf walls extending initially as straight screens to secondary iron pillars, past which they continue as convex quadrants before terminating in plain stone pillars, but not before being interrupted on each side by a squat Doric column on a recessed-panel plinth, apparently serving no purpose unless originally bearing more statuary. Sadly, the 'sentry-box' postilion arches have been desecrated—adapted and reduced in ludicrous fashion to permit modern traffic passage. So too have the windows been spoiled by the removal of the glazing pattern, while the delightful heathen goddess has been replaced by a less scantily clad Madonna, signifying that this is now the entrance to a religious establishment. The great mansion was in 1837 home to Bindon Scott and his son John, who were responsible for commissioning this memorable overture, which James Fraser was moved to mention in 1838: 'The entrance gate is a remarkable feature'.

Lewis 1837; Fraser 1838; Weir 1986.

38. CAHERCALLA, Ennis; pre-1840; *demolished.*

A house which probably owes its appearance to Capt. Charles Mahon (1789–1874), who was resident here in 1837, having acquired it between 1814 and 1824 from David E. England. The lodge may have been contemporary with those early nineteenth-century improvements.

Leet 1814; Pigot 1824; Lewis 1837; *LGI* (1904).

39. CAMBRAI, Killaloe; *c.* 1890.

A turn-of-the-century development of house, outbuildings and gate lodge for Henry Lefroy (1860–1935), named to recall his French ancestry. This is a sturdy single-storey structure with high eaves to its steeply pitched hipped roof, rising to its late Victorian brick chimney-stack. Faced in stucco-effect rendering, it would be standard format but for the bay window projecting to the avenue, with mock half-timbered work to its gable and a bipartite sash window. Occupied, with what looks like an older cottage at right angles to it.

IFR; Weir 1986.

40. CAPPAGH, Ennis; *c.* 1845; *demolished.*

Surviving are the remains of good mid-Georgian entrance pillars with moulded plinths and cut-stone scrolls, presumably from the time here of the Kirwan family. A single-storey three-bay brick-built porter's lodge was added across the road sometime between the 1840 OS and the valuation of 1855, when Cappagh was the seat of John Curtin.

Griffith 1853–63; Weir 1986.

41. CAPPAGH LODGE, Kilrush; pre-1840; *demolished.*

The early gatekeeper's lodge, perhaps from the residency of one John Trousdell, recorded here in 1814, or his successor Randal Borough, seems to have had a late Victorian replacement thanks to the arrival of the South Clare Railway. Neither survives.

Leet 1814; Lewis 1837.

42. CAPPATEEMORE, Ardnacrusha; pre-1840; *demolished.*

Opposite the entrance was a two-bay two-storey porter's lodge, removed in the late twentieth century. An early seat of the Bindon family, by the mid-nineteenth century it had been acquired by Christopher Delmege.

Griffith 1853–63; Weir 1986.

43. CARNELLY, Clarecastle; pre-1840/*c.* 1845.

A very grand mid-eighteenth-century Palladian-style house, built for George Stamer probably to designs of his brother-in-law, architect Francis Bindon, in pretty pink brick; it passed out of that family's hands and around 1865 became a property through marriage of Francis Nicholas Valentine Burton (1842–83) of Carrigaholt Castle [*q.v.*].

A lodge built appropriately in brick, albeit orange, in Flemish bond with raised

toothed quoins in the same material, the window soldier arches and elliptical porch head masterfully spanned with gauged voussoirs. Single-storey standard in faintly Italianate form, the tall eaves and verge to hipped roof and its gabled entrance projection having angled brackets, an unusual feature also to be seen on a Hazelwood [*q.v.*] lodge. The modern plastic windows probably reflect squared bipartite casement predecessors; this lodge, presumably built during the tenancy of John O'Brien (1840–9), apparently fronts an earlier brick-built cottage—probably for the last male Stamer to live here, George William Stamer (d. 1819)—to form a double pile, partly screened by a giant Irish yew from its elegant gatescreen, at the head of a long straight avenue on an axis with the front door of the house. Four Classical pillars, the same as those at Hazelwood, define a straight triple gateway, the carriage opening flanked by postern gates framed by matching spear-topped railings on dwarf walls.

Slater 1870; *LGI* (1904); Weir 1986; www.landedestatesnuigalway.ie.

44. CARRICKPATRICK, Milltown Malbay; pre-1840; *demolished.*

A seat in 1814 of Robert Crow, which by 1855 was the residence of George Lysaght.

Leet 1814; Griffith 1853–63.

45. CARRIGAHOLT CASTLE, Carrigaholt; pre-1910; *demolished.*

The porter's lodge probably formed part of the redevelopment of the estate in the mid-nineteenth century by Henry Stuart Burton (1808–67), who built the present house to replace the old MacMahon castle.

Mason 1814–19, vol. 2; Lacy 1863; *LGI* (1904).

46. CARRIGORAN, Newmarket-on-Fergus (2).

A fine estate and late eighteenth-century mansion of a branch of the Fitzgerald clan, the two gatekeepers' lodges to which are later replacements for those apparent from the OS map of 1839.

Kilnasoolagh gate; pre-1839/*c.* 1850; architect probably James Pain.

On the northern avenue is a replacement lodge and contemporary gatescreen in which can be detected the hand of Limerick architect James Pain, for there is an identical entrance to Convamore, Co. Cork [*q.v.*], where he is known to have worked, and like screens at Kilkishen [*q.v.*], Grange, Co. Limerick [*q.v.*], and Derry Castle, Co. Tipperary [*q.v.*]. Here is a triple gateway of six limestone ashlar pillars with raised and fielded panels and familiar half-barrel-capped/semicircular-pedimented cappings, containing decorative cast-iron gates and matching railings. Behind is a distinctive single-storey standard lodge in crisp modern rendering, recent extensions not compromising its original form. The main gables and that of the projecting hall display exaggerated extending verges with paired carved brackets continued from the oversailing eaves which return to create open pediment features—Classical were it not for the quirky intrusion of perforated Picturesque bargeboards. To the front door is a rectangular fanlight and elsewhere two-over-two sash windows. The chimney-stack rose off the original back wall, a feature of many of Pain's lodges. Presumably built for Sir Edward Fitzgerald, who succeeded to the property as 3rd baronet on the death of his father in 1847.

Carrigoran gate; pre-1839/*c.* 1890.

William Walter Augustine Fitzgerald inherited Carrigoran in 1877 and built this generous gatehouse to supersede a predecessor at this southern approach. A typically uncompromising late Victorian affair, faced in stone with raised toothed brick dressings to latticed casement windows. Two-storey, three-bay and gabled with a similarly treated porch; from the avenue end projects a single-storey rectangular bay window below a tripartite attic casement with a strangely remote Tudor label moulding. The gateway looks to be about 50 years older, with very fine ashlar pillars having fluted friezes and moulded cornices, those flanking the carriage opening now sporting modern ball lanterns. Spear-topped railings also display husk motifs, the whole nicely framed by whitened roughcast concave quadrant walls beyond but probably lacking two pillars and a pair of postilion gates.

The property now houses a nursing home.

BPB (1903); *LGI* (1904); Bence-Jones 1988.

CARROWBANE (see CAHERBANE)

47. CARROWDOTIA, Kilrush; *c.* 1835.

A plain and derelict single-storey standard cottage, rendered, with a chimney-stack to each gable. A property in the early nineteenth century of the Daxon family.

Leet 1814; Lewis 1837.

CARROWGAR LODGE (see MOY)

48. CASTLE CRINE, Sixmilebridge; *c.* 1845.

The lovely old Georgian Gothic 'castle' of the Butler family was regrettably demolished in the 1950s but magically survives in microcosm at the gate in the shape of an early Victorian gatekeeper's lodge reflecting its erstwhile big house in detail, with its Y-traceried lancet windows and crenellated parapets. Saved from ruin by the foresight of its owners and restorers, it is dominated by a single-bay, two-storey 'keep' with two-bay single-storey wing alongside containing the entrance porch—a charming little Picturesque composition. Unfortunately, restoration has stopped short of the return of its weatherproofing limewashed harling, leaving exposed its fabric of rubble stone and brick dressings. Equally disturbing is its main feature, the remarkable round corbelled bartizan to the main parapet, now looking particularly precarious without its attendant castellations. Originally built for Henry Butler at the entrance to a once-proud demesne with magnificent gardens, wooded parkland and an artificial lake, its original gates reconstructed at the 'Wells' church.

Weir 1986.

49. CLAREABBEY RECTORY, Clarecastle; *c.* 1822.

Built during the long perpetual curacy from 1815 until his death of Revd William Young (1789/90–1847) is a plain, rendered, single-storey hip-roofed structure, its main three-bay front addressing the park, the entrance doorway to the left-hand side blocked up, the short single-bay avenue elevation comprised of a window of squared casements. Doubtless contemporary with the building of the glebe house in 1822, which from the mid-nineteenth century became a private house of the Pilkington family subsequently renamed 'Glenard'.

Lewis 1837; Weir 1986; Leslie and Crooks 2010.

50. CLAREVILLE, Ennis; pre-1840; *demolished.*
By 1921 the residence, in 1855 of James F. Macnamara, and its porter's lodge had both been removed.
Griffith 1853–63.

51. CLARISFORD, Killaloe; *c.* 1825.
A noble house built as the episcopal palace for Revd Robert Fowler (1724–1801), bishop of Killaloe and Clonfert, in 1774 to designs of Thomas Cooley. Its porter's lodge and entrance are altogether more modest, probably dating from the time (1823–8) of the Rt Revd Alexander Arbuthnot (1768–1828). Single-storey standard and hip-roofed, the left-hand window of its elongated three-bay front extends beyond the gatescreen; toothed dressings; much improved and occupied. The modest carriage pillars are of rubble stone with a segmentally arched postilion opening in the right-hand boundary wall. The property passed out of church hands in 1977.
Weir 1986; IAA; Leslie and Crooks 2010.

52. CLONBOY, O'Briensbridge; pre-1840/*c.* 1870.
Surviving its big house, demolished in the 1940s, is this single-storey standard lodge with steeply hipped roof and rendered walls, its main front prolonged to the right-hand side with a flat-roofed bay window to the road elevation. Modernisation makes dating difficult but its brick chimney-stack suggests a mid-Victorian rework or rebuild, probably after Robert Lidwill Brown inherited the estate on the death of his father in 1870.
LGI (1904); Weir 1986.

53. CLONDERLAW, Labasheeda; *c.* 1830.
Forward of the entrance with its crude chunky pillars with 'bap' finials is a standard single-storey porter's lodge with oversailing eaves to its hipped roof; occupied. Probably built for George Studdert (d. 1857), who had succeeded to the place by 1814.
Leet 1814; *LGI* (1904).

54. CLONMONEY, Bunratty; *c.* 1830.
A single-storey standard three-bay gabled cottage subsequently enlarged by a bay to the right-hand side, roughcast and latterly modernised with a projecting lower entrance hall; occupied. A property in 1837 of Dennis Canny, probably leasing from the Westropp family.
Lewis 1837; Weir 1986.

55. CLONRUSH RECTORY, Whitegate; *c.* 1815; *demolished.*
A lodge possibly contemporary with the building of the glebe house around 1814 for the incumbent, Revd James Martin (d. 1824), perhaps also to designs of James Sheane, architect of the rectory.
Weir 1986; Leslie and Crooks 2010.

56. CLOONEENAGH, Cooraclare; pre-1840; *demolished.*
A gentry farmhouse in 1855 of John O'Kelly, at the base of the long straight avenue to which was a porter's lodge.
Griffith 1853–63.

57. CLOONEY, Fair Green (2).
The ancestral home of the Bindon family, of whom the painter and architect Francis Bindon was one and may have designed the early house, the later lodge to which survives.

North entrance; *c.* 1815.
A single-storey standard cottage with wide window openings in pastel pink-washed harled walls and with a chimney-stack to each gable; derelict. Alongside are the remains of a fine mid-Georgian gatescreen of ashlar pillars with moulded plinths and corniced cappings.

By 1853 the estate had been run down by the spendthrift Burton Bindon, on whose behalf it was sold through the incumbered estates court, he having emigrated to Australia. Six years later the property was purchased by his daughter and her husband Joseph Hall, who restored the demesne, refaced the old house in the Italianate manner and added a new lodged entrance to designs of the Dublin architect E.H. Carson.

South entrance; 1863; architect E.H. Carson.

In a rather more subdued Italianate style than the house but displaying equally crisply chiselled punched limestone in its toothed quoins and plain surrounds to windows and segmentally headed doorscreen which continue to plinth level, all in otherwise stucco-effect rendered walls. Single-storey standard, its hipped roof rises from a cut-stone eaves band to the chimney-stack with plinth and corniced capping. Now derelict and blocked up, its doorway having been side and fanlit.

The mansion has lain a forlorn burnt-out shell since 1924.
DB (15 February 1863); Bence-Jones 1988; Lyons 1993.

58. CLOONMORE, Tulla; *c.* 1845.
Next to a minimal gate sweep is this dinky standard lodge with wide modernised windows in roughcast walls below a steeply hipped roof with paired carved modillion brackets to soffits. Like its modest gentry farmhouse, now restored and inhabited. The property in 1855 of James Molony, surgeon and physician in Tulla.
Griffith 1853–63; Slater 1856.

COOLREADY (see ST CATHERINE'S)

59. COOLREAGH, Bodyke; 1914.
Surviving from the time here of Ralph Westropp (1800–83) is a pretty mid-nineteenth-century gatescreen of cast iron with a curly-wurly anthemion motif repeated in its gate pillars and railings. Elevated from this is the 1½-storey porter's lodge, with tall eaves and mildly skew-tabled gable over a three-bay front with two-over-two sash windows and door to the right-hand side in roughly harled walls; derelict, with the datestone in a gable marking the status of the proprietor, Capt. George O'Callaghan-Westropp (b. 1864), as justice of the peace and high sherriff for County Clare. He had been left the property to comply with the will of his maternal uncle, Ralph Westropp, whose surname he accordingly assumed.
Lewis 1837; *LGI* (1904); Weir 1986.

CORNFIELD (see FORT FERGUS)

60. THE COTTAGE, Parteen; pre-1840.
By the roadside lies the blocked-up four-bay elevation of a gatekeeper's lodge to a property in 1846 and 1870 of Donough McCreagh or McCraight.
Slater 1846; 1870.

61. CRAGBRIEN, Ennis (2).
An estate since 1712 of the Stacpoole family to which there were two lodged gates.

South entrance; *c.* 1810.
Next to a modest gatescreen lies the front elevation of a single-storey standard rubble-built cottage, presumably created for George Hogan Stacpoole (1745–1812), barrister, whose fifth son succeeded to Cragbrien.

North entrance; *c.* 1840.

The Very Revd William Henry Stacpoole (1787–1847) would have been responsible for this once-pretty porter's lodge, which rather impolitely turns its back to the road and faces the park with its standard three-bay front. Single-storey with a hipped roof and the stump of an octagonal brick chimney-stack in Tudor Picturesque manner, as are the bipartite cast-iron latticed casement windows set in stucco-effect walls with planted rendered toothed quoins. Now in a sad abandoned state, a large opening gouged out where its left-hand window once was.
IFR; Weir 1986.

62. CRAGG, Tulla; pre-1840; *demolished.*
A long-time seat of the Molony family, the lodge to which lay opposite its gates and seems also to have commanded the entrance to neighbouring Bunavory. It had been removed by 1922.

63. CRANAGHER, Fair Green; *c.* 1830.
Lying derelict opposite the gates is a single-storey hip-roofed gatekeeper's lodge, asymmetrical with an off-centre chimney-stack and the doorway of its three-bay front to the left-hand side of square casement windows in rendered walls. Built for 'the Vampire' Bindon Blood (1775–1855), who had succeeded to the estate as a minor in 1784.

LGI (1904); Weir 1986.

64. CRATLOE WOODS, Cratloe; pre-1840/*c.* 1845; architect possibly James Pain.

The antique seat of the Stafford O'Brien family, of whom Augustus Stafford O'Brien Stafford (d. 1857) extended and altered the property with the introduction of Tudor Revival elements, reflected in its pretty Picturesque porter's lodge, all attributable to the Limerick-based architect James Pain. Replacing an earlier lodge at the other side of the gateway is this single-storey cottage raised off a T-plan with steeply pitched gables, probably originating with ornamental bargeboards, but retaining its coupled brick chimney-stack and pretty cast-iron latticed casement windows in striking maroon-washed rendered walls. From the leading avenue gable extends a little gabled hall; occupied and well tended.

Bence-Jones 1988.

CULLAUN CASTLE (see LOUGH O'CONNELL)

65. DANGAN, Tulla; pre-1910; *demolished.*
A lodge built after 1840 on a property since the seventeenth century of the Creagh family; lost, like its big house.

66. DEER PARK, Bunratty (2).
Neither lodge survives; that opposite the west gate seems to have been one of a pair of semi-detached cottages. A seat in 1814 of Simon O'Donnell, who was succeeded here before 1837 by Edward Maunsell, probably the Revd Edward Eyre Maunsell of Fort Eyre, Co. Galway, who in 1818 married Elizabeth Studdert of Bunratty.

Leet 1814; Lewis 1837; *LGI* (1904).

67. DERRYMORE, O'Callaghan's Mills (3).
The fine ashlar mansion with *porte-cochère* of the Gore family having been demolished, little remains now of any architectural sophistication on their estate other than the chaste little temple lodge at the south entrance.

Main gate; *c.* 1840; architect perhaps J.B. Keane (*above*).
Bearing such a close resemblance to the principal lodge of 1812 to Dromoland Castle [*q.v.*], this must have been built with it in mind, possibly adapted by J.B. Keane. Constructed in rubble facings, the main body of the structure is faced with a cut-limestone tetrastyle pedimented portico of Doric columns with corresponding pilasters behind, which define the bays of one-over-one sash windows flanking the central doorway of its short avenue front. This lodge differs from Hopper's at Dromoland only in having column bases and substituting frameless windows for architraved blind recesses to the main façade. Tragically, his little gem lies abandoned and derelict, its entrance screen destroyed.

Secondary gate; pre-1840; *demolished.*

Inner gate; pre-1840; *demolished.*
This entrance would have been rendered redundant when public roads were absorbed into the demesne as avenues around 1840, a process which has since been reversed.

LGI (1904); Weir 1986.

68. DERRYOWEN COTTAGE, Tubber; pre-1840; *demolished.*
A property in the early nineteenth century and the centuries before of many a Christopher Lopdell.

Leet 1814; Lewis 1837; *LGI* (1904).

69. DESMOND VILLA, Kilkee; *c.* 1845.
The seat in 1846 of Capt. G.H. Fitzgerald, whose house has gone and the place overrun by modern housing development, to be remarkably survived by its dapper little gate lodge. Single-storey standard with stone facings below a hipped roof.

Slater 1846.

70. DOOLIN CASTLE, Lisdoonvarna; *c.* 1820.
A not-quite-symmetrical single-storey standard cottage with whitewashed rendered walls and a chimney-stack to each gable. Now offering bicycle hire. An estate of the Macnamaras of Ennistimon [*q.v.*], of whom William Nugent Macnamara (1775–1856) would have added the lodge, which now survives their house, burnt in the Troubles.

LGI (1904); Weir 1986.

71. DOON, Broadford; *c.* 1820.
Opposite a now-avenueless entrance is a totally dilapidated single-storey three-bay harled lodge, one end hipped, the other gabled to accommodate a loft room, probably a later addition. It marginally outlives its big house, in the late eighteenth century of the Massy family though thereafter let by them to Richard Hart, followed by the Butler family.

Taylor and Skinner 1778; 1783; Leet 1814; Weir 1986.

72. DOONASS, Castleconnell; *c.* 1800; *demolished.*

Hugh Dillon Massy (d. 1807) was created 1st baronet in 1781, which he marked by building a new house with a fine square of offices and probably the gate lodge, of which, though lying in ruins, enough survives to reveal it as having been a single-storey hip-roofed structure with evidence of Georgian Gothic lancet openings. The excellent straight entrance screen of later date is comprised of six Classical ashlar pillars containing a triple gateway, the postilion gates in railed screens with spear and husk motifs, the whole by the same hand as the identical entrance to Buncraggy [*q.v.*]. The big house likewise lies a shell. By 2017 lodge removed and screen badly damaged.

Beaufort, 1764–1808; Wilson 1803; *BPB* (1861).

73. DREWSBOROUGH, Scarriff; pre-1920; *demolished.*
A lodge probably added to the estate, originally of the Drew family, around 1855, when it was purchased by Michael Skehan.

Griffith 1853–63; Weir 1986.

74. DROMOLAND CASTLE, Newmarket-on-Fergus (8).
Clare's architectural jewel is this magnificent estate and mansion of the O'Brien family, now hopefully saved for posterity in its new and fitting role of luxury hotel. Mainly the creation of Sir Edward O'Brien, 4th baronet (1773–1837), who had succeeded to the property in 1795, he displayed great caution before deciding to replace the old Classical mansion in a completely newfangled style rather than extend it in like manner. He sought alternative designs from home and abroad over a period of about seven years, receiving plans from the eminent English practitioner Thomas Hopper and the home-grown Sir Richard and William Vitruvius Morrison before choosing the design of the brothers Pain, James and George Richard, erstwhile assistants of that master of the Picturesque Castellated style John Nash, in whose manner they created the grand rambling fantasy castle and ancillary buildings. Work commenced in 1819 and took nineteen years to complete.

That there was at least one gate lodge to the estate in Sir Edward's father's time is clear from an entry in the diary of Revd Daniel Augustus Beaufort, who visited in 1788: 'the seat of Sir Lucius O'Brien ... At the gate of Dromoland, we applied for leave to drive thro' the grounds, which the Porter told us every gent was welcome to do—so we went on by a pretty lake ... the antique mansion ... a large old house, not regular and only part of a vast design intended to connect with a castle, since pulled down'. That Sir Edward was rather more decisive in commissioning a new gate lodge for the main gate is clear from the splendid little neo-Classical temple, which is all that the unfortunate Hopper has to show for all his work, in a style that was wholly appropriate as an introduction to the old house. It did, though, rather pre-empt what the Pains may have offered a decade later as a suitable prelude to their grand design. Perhaps Hopper was thankful for small mercies, for there was another proposal for the front entrance in another, unidentified, hand that was discarded.

Unexecuted design [1]; *c.* 1810; architect not known (*top*).
This is a charming, if naive, drawing, unsigned and undated, for a pair of lodges to flank the gateway, a 'Plan of Portors Lodges, for the New Entrance to Drummoland, The Seat of Sir E. O'Brien Bt.', which shows twin cottages, their generosity of accommodation perhaps too extravagant for the client. Each was intended to be a single-storey standard three-bay below a shallow hipped roof; the central bay extends as a pedimented portico with four cluster-columns, behind which a pointed-arched front door with diamond panels is flanked by lattice-glazed lancet lights. On each side flat-arched squared windows set in like recesses are embraced by Tudor label mouldings, a feature curiously repeated on a wide chimney-stack which would have contained a flue from a fireplace in each of the four main rooms. From each 17ft by 10ft living room to the park front is 'a Wyat window looking towards the approach to the house'.

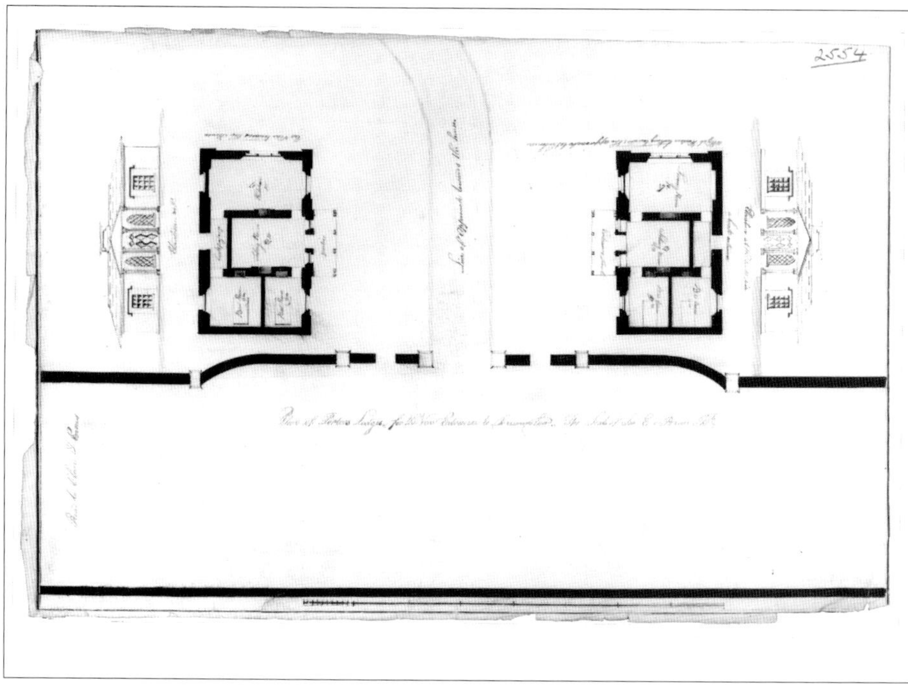

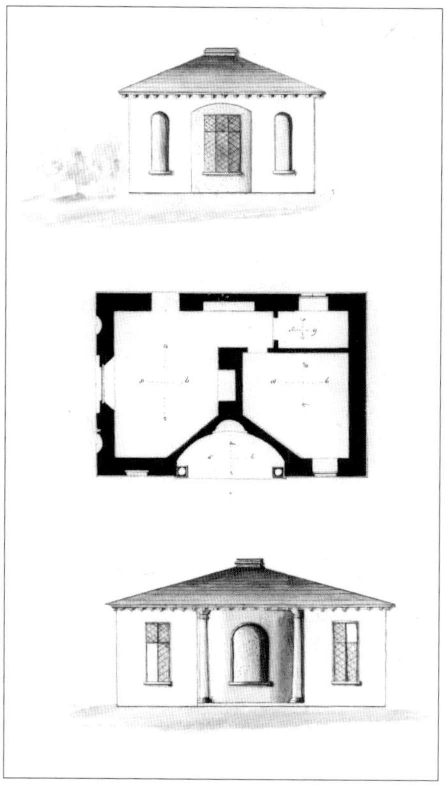

Unexecuted design [2]; *c.* 1810; architect not known (*left*).
Perhaps intended as an alternative Classical proposal for the above, and likewise anonymous, was this other apparently unrealised design of considerable character. Single-storey and hip-roofed with corbelled eaves, it displays two principal fronts, each three-bay, the short one having the living room window in a segmentally arched recess flanked by a pair of narrow round-headed niches, the long one with a window to each side of a central segmental-arched recess flanked by a pair of Tuscan columns *in antis* framing another larger niche within, probably intended as a sheltered seat; the only doorway is relegated to the rear.

Main entrance; 1812; architect Thomas Hopper.

An extraordinarily well-documented building, the fourteen surviving drawings

74. Thomas Hopper's design for the main lodge to Dromoland Castle. (All drawings for Dromoland, National Library of Ireland)

demonstrate the meticulousness of its architect, or perhaps his client, and that it was built precisely as intended. In the form of a chaste Greek temple, were it not for Egyptian overtones in its tapering moulded and shouldered openings. All in an immaculate ashlar construction, the short avenue front is three-bay, its glazed and panelled doorway flanked by blind windows, all behind a pedimented tetrastyle portico of unfluted Greek Doric columns with corresponding pilasters to all corners. Originally simply two-roomed, lit by squared casement windows, it has latterly been extended to an L-plan, with the addition to the rear in like manner. The lodge at Derrymore [*q.v.*] is a close copy.

Surprisingly for an estate of this size, it remained served by a single lodged gate until late in the nineteenth century, when the 6th baronet and 14th Lord Inchiquin, Edward Donough O'Brien (1839–1900), added a further six lodges about the perimeter, all to generous proportions.

South entrance; 1887; architect not known.
Faced in rubble stone, this is a relatively simple 1½-storey gabled affair with pretty perforated foiled bargeboards, newly slated, occupied and well maintained.

South-west entrance; 1887; architect not known.
A large 1½-storey gabled structure of an L-plan, with a single-storey hip-roofed hall in the internal corner. Finished in roughcast with brick dressings, arches and quoins. Occupied.

North-west entrance; pre-1922; *demolished.*

North-east entrance; 1887; architect not known.
A strangely dilapidated, deserted but still attractive ornamental 1½-storey lodge with decorative carved fascias and bargeboards to a steeply pitched roof of red earthenware roof tiles with scalloped bands, rising to a perforated crested ridge broken by a red-brick chimney-stack with sawtooth corbelled

capping. Rectangular in plan, with an asymmetrically projecting hall that has a brick oculus feature above the front door, its narrow sidelights all dressed in brick with gauged soldier arches in coursed rubble walls; rectangular-paned bipartite casement windows elsewhere similarly highlighted.

East entrance; 1887; architect not known.

A very fine and commodious single-storey late Victorian lodge built off an irregular plan in random coursed rubble facings with smooth stone quoins and red-brick dressings to a variety of single, bi- and tripartite squared sash windows. Highly decorative fascias and bargeboards with ornamental quatrefoil toes and fancy brackets as support to extended wall-plates and ridges. To an internal angle is a pretty High Victorian Gothic porch with carved posts, brackets and bargeboards pierced with an attractive foliated trefoil motif. All admirably rehabilitated with an attic conversion and roof windows in a newly slated roof with scalloped courses for relief and a red crested ridge.

South-east entrance; 1887; architect not known.

Another spacious lodge, explained by its main role as accommodation for the estate gamekeeper. As with the other porters' lodges, it is in a late Victorian Picturesque-cum-Arts and Crafts transitional style; 1½-storey on an L-plan, it exhibits ornamental carved foiled fascias and bargeboards with hip-knobs to its very steep gables, scalloped slate bands and perforated crestings with a lofty red-brick-banded and corbelled chimney-stack. Faced with random coursed rubble and dressed with smooth stone quoins and toothed brick dressings to rectangular-paned casement windows. To the leading gable is a single-storey glazed rectangular bay window, while to the internal corner is a carved wooden porch below a lean-to roof. To the rear are associated single-storey outbuildings in like style. Occupied.

Beaufort 1764–1808; Heaney 1999; *BPB* (1929); Lee 2006; NLI drawings (AD 2554, 2568, 2576–89).

75. DROMORE, Ruan; pre-1840; *demolished.*
The old avenue to the family home of the Crowes has become a public road, with the loss of the porter's lodge, suffering the same fate as the big house.

Weir 1986.

76. EDENVALE, Ennis; pre-1840/*c.* 1866; architect possibly William Fogerty.

A superb little lodge in the Italianate style by an able but unidentified practitioner, probably the same as was responsible for that to neighbouring Beech Park [*q.v.*]. Single-storey standard and hip-roofed, its wide soffit is relieved by bold carved modillion brackets that continue about the verge of an open-

pedimented porch breakfront with a round-headed archway having moulded surround and a keystone, which also features on the low, segmentally arched windows to each side and the wide tripartite casements on opposing end elevations. All in smooth rendering and raised on a plinth, as is the prominent chimney-stack with its wide corniced capping in mid-Victorian Classical manner.

Well tended, on display behind a railed enclosure, it replaced a semicircular cluster of three estate cottages opposite the gates, probably for Richard Stacpoole (1828–91), who inherited the estate in 1866 on the death of his father. Now a nursing home.

LGI (1904).

77. ELM HILL, Clonlara; pre-1840; *demolished.*
Sometime seat of the Bouchier family, by 1837 it was home to a Mrs Davis, and eighteen years later the residence of Joseph Wallplate.

Lewis 1837; Griffith 1853–63; Weir 1986.

78. ENNIS DISTRICT LUNATIC ASYLUM, Ennis; *c.* 1870; architects probably Fogerty and Adair.

An impressive institutional building designed by W. Fogerty and A.C. Adair, built between 1863 and 1868, now Our Lady's Hospital. The conspicuous porter's lodge, probably by the same practice, sits solid and immovable as a large, square, single-storey Italianate affair with a pyramidal roof now minus a chimney-stack. Constructed in rubble stone with channelled dressings, its two-bay front to the avenue comprising a semi-octagonal bay window with, as elsewhere, segmentally arched openings and two-over-two sash windows. Alongside was the recessed and open porch (now enclosed), which also opened as two bays on the three-bay front, the third bay being a window with moulded surround, keystone and corbelled sill in a recess to plinth level, repeated on the opposing front. What remains of the gatescreen shows it to have been equally formidable, with its sturdy channel-rusticated pillars and friezes with oversailing cappings in durable granite; quarry-faced uncoursed stone quadrants survive beyond.

Williams 1994; O'Dwyer 1997a.

79. ENNISTIMON, Ennistimon; *c.* 1845; *demolished.*
A porter's lodge datable through not appearing on the first OS map but valued by 1855 as the property of Capt. Francis Macnamara (d. 1873), who had just acquired it from the Finucane family.

PGI; Griffith 1853–63.

80. ERRINA, Clonlara; *c.* 1840.
A tiny, overgrown, ruinous, single-storey hip-roofed gatekeeper's lodge with its main single window bay to the avenue. A property associated in 1837 with James Lysaght, followed nine years later by James Kelly MP.

Lewis 1837; Slater 1846.

81. ERRINA HOUSE, Clonlara; *c.* 1835.

The remains of a charming little Tudor Revival lodge built to the seat in 1837 of George Vincent. Single-storey below a shallow hipped roof with diagonally set chimney-stack and extensive oversailing soffit to limewashed harled walls, with irregular fenestration having a degree of sophistication in its label mouldings to the main wide window and Tudor-arched doorway complete with spandrels. Subsequently horribly abused, the main window being gouged out as a doorway for farm use.

Lewis 1837.

82. FAIRY HILL, Parteen; pre-1840; *demolished.*
One Jasper White is recorded here until his death in 1808; it subsequently became the residence in 1837 of E. Burnard Esq. and by 1855 of John McDonnell.

Lewis 1837; Griffith 1853–63; *LGI* (1904).

83. FENLOE, Newmarket-on-Fergus (2).
Two lodges built after 1840, probably both by Hugh Palliser Hickman (1805–83), who succeeded to the estate in 1824.

East entrance; pre-1922; *demolished.*

West entrance; *c.* 1850.
Now a four-bay gabled affair, immaculate but altered in modernisation, a sophisticated moulded lugged door-case surviving the improvements.

LGI (1904); Weir 1986.

84. FINAVARRA, Finavarra (2).
The condition of its gate lodges graphically reflects the state of decay of this once-proud estate of the Skerrett family, now virtually treeless and the big house in ruins.

South gate; *c.* 1810.

Built for Major William Skerrett (d. 1818) and now almost ruinous is this single-storey Georgian Gothic lodge, its harled rubble walls contrasting satisfyingly with the rusticated cut-limestone dressings to the flat-arched doorway and little lancet windows. Gradually being shrouded in the ivy that has already engulfed the chimney-stack, which rises where there was once a hipped roof with cut-stone eaves band. Alongside is a pair of V-jointed rusticated squat carriage pillars now framing a modern galvanised farm gate.

North gate; *c.* 1860.
William Joseph Skerrett (1819–74) succeeded to the property at birth but six months after the death of his father, and added this secondary lodge about 40 years later. Plain single-storey standard and hip-roofed, its walls smooth-rendered, the central projecting flat-roofed hall flanked by boarded-up windows. Nearby is an earlier gatescreen of cast-iron perforated pillars with anthemion motifs and knobbed cappings carrying railed gates with palmette finials. The site is being overrun by liberated garden shrubs.

LGI (1904); Weir 1986.

85. FIRGROVE, Bunratty (2).
John McMahon, who is recorded as proprietor here in 1838, would have known the early, westerly lodged gate, in place before 1839. The additional secondary entrance was created probably after the long-lived John Peter Kelly (1775–1871) had taken up residence. Of the original estate buildings only the farmyard and offices survive, with one of the entrance screens, a triple gateway with six cut-stone pillars, having found a new home at Drumline House, Newmarket-on-Fergus.

Fraser 1838; *LGI* (1904); Weir 1986.

86. FORTANEBEG, Tulla; pre-1840; *demolished.*
Both the big house of the Westropp family and its porter's lodge opposite the entrance are things of the past.

87. FORT FERGUS, Killadysert; pre-1840/*c.* 1870.
A rather gauche single-storey lodge built off an L-plan, finished in smooth rendering in contrast with conspicuous toothed stone

quoins, dressings and voussoirs. Below the gables with their carved ornamental bargeboards are relieving round-headed niches with moulded surrounds. In the internal angle are nice double-leafed glazed panel doors with a Tudor-arched head, in keeping with the coupled chamfered brick chimney-stacks at the meeting of ridges; sympathetic additions to the rear. This is a replacement for an earlier porter's lodge on the site, for Major William Hawkins Ball, who may also have been responsible for the earlier gatescreen, perhaps dating from around 1855, when he purchased the estate through the incumbered estates court. This is a triple gateway with good sturdy cast ironwork having an anthemion motif at the carriage gates meeting rails. The Classical pillars with plain friezes are framed by extensive shallow concave quadrant walls in uncoursed random cut stone.

Major Ball had been preceded here by Daniel O'Grady in 1837 and by a Mr Evans in 1814, prior to which it was the seat of the Ross Lewin family, from whom it had passed to John Stacpoole by 1800.

An entrance that also served Cornfield House, which, unlike Fort Fergus, survives.

Leet 1814; Lewis 1837; Bence-Jones 1988; Weir 1986.

GLENARD (see CLAREABBEY RECTORY)

GLENOMERA (see BALLYQUIN)

88. GLENWOOD, Sixmilebridge (2).
Neither the house nor its two mid-Victorian lodges survive, but the entrance on the old western approach is worthy of notice. Perhaps a portent of the turreted Gothic house once within is this boulder-built rustic gatescreen, one of the flanking walls containing a low grottoesque pointed-arched postern gate—all a suitable medium for sapling roots and ivy. Pretty but more delicate carriage gates repeat the Gothic theme with their arcaded rails, quatrefoil motifs and scroll-topped meeting rails. All perhaps a vision of John Gabbett, who was resident in 1852.

Griffith 1953–63; Weir 1986.

89. GRANAGHAN CASTLE, Newmarket-on-Fergus; pre-1840; *demolished.*
Another property in the nineteenth century of the Molony family, whose main seat was Kilnacrandy [*q.v.*], which was let to the Hewitts. Their lodge, at the base of the tree-lined lakeside northern approach, like its big house has gone.

Griffith 1853–63; Weir 1986.

90. HAZELWOOD, Quin (3).

Otherwise known as Ballyhickey after its townland, this now-lost house was the seat of the Singleton family, only one of whose lodges, all built after 1840, survives.

On the southern avenue is a single-storey hip-roofed lodge in limewashed harled walls of two different periods. Initially it would seem to have been built off an L-plan with bipartite, rectangular-paned casement windows of around 1845. About 25 years later a two-bay wing was added with plain one-over-one sash windows when an angled eaves bracket feature, just as at Carnelly [*q.v.*], was applied about the whole, the leading gabled avenue projection being a gambrel with a decorative roundel in the apex. Similarly, the early Victorian slender ashlar gate pillars with chunky contemporary ironwork appear to have been complemented with mid-Victorian quarry-faced random stone ogee quadrants. All would seem to have been the work of John Singleton, whose main seat was at Quinville Abbey [*q.v.*] nearby, and his younger brother, Hugh Brady Singleton.

LGI (1904).

91. HERMITAGE, Ennis; pre-1840; *demolished.*
Another estate of Robert Keane (1774–1839) of nearby Beech Park [*q.v.*], the miniature three-bay lodge to which must have been erected in his lifetime but was removed in the late twentieth century.

Leet 1814; *LGI* (1904).

92. HURDLESTON, Broadford; pre-1840; *demolished.*
A shooting lodge designed by William Fogerty of Limerick for William Bentley, the gate lodge to which served an earlier house on the site, that family being recorded here in the eighteenth century.

LOI; Williams 1994; Weir 1986.

93. IBRICKANE LODGE, Milltown Malbay; pre-1920.
Surviving is a rather nasty single-storey standard flat-roofed affair with round-headed windows, perhaps from the late nineteenth century. The avenue leads to a modest single-storey farmhouse, originally associated with the O'Gormans and subsequently in the nineteenth century of the Studdert family.

LGI (1904); Weir 1986.

94. ISLANDMAGRATH, Clarecastle; pre-1840.
The remains of a single-storey gabled lodge, ruinous and overgrown, to a property in 1855 of Edward Maunsell.

Griffith 1853–63.

95. KILGORY, Tulla (2).
Neither the house nor its two pre-1840 gate lodges survive. That to the northern approach was opposite the entrance, at the head of a long, straight, tree-lined avenue. The property passed to the O'Connells from the O'Callaghan family on the death of Edmond O'Callaghan in a duel in 1791.

LGI (1904); Weir 1986.

96. KILKISHEN, Kilkishen (2).
The fine estate of the Studdert family, who came by it through the marriage in the early eighteenth century of Thomas Studdert of Bunratty Castle to Madame Cusack. It was his grandson of the same name (*c.* 1790–1873) who carried out improvements to the property, replacing the main entrance and lodge.

Kilkishen gate; pre-1840/*c.* 1845; architect probably James Pain.

The gatescreen is attributable to James Pain of Limerick, being identical to those at Convamore, Co. Cork [*q.v.*], Grange, Co. Limerick [*q.v.*], Derry Castle, Co. Tipperary [*q.v.*], and Carrigoran [*q.v.*]. Six cut-limestone pillars with moulded recessed panels and distinctive semicircular cappings with anthemion motifs to their tympana contain extensive limestone ashlar quadrant walls flanking a triple gateway with chunky ironwork to matching railings and gates. The gate lodge, presumably also by the architect, is identifiable through the chimney-stack rising off the rear wall. Now tragically a shell choked in ivy, it is still recognisable as having been a distinctive composition in limestone ashlar. Single-storey and built off an irregular plan, from which a hall projects to the road with narrow sidelights and a canted bay window extends towards the avenue. The quality of its detail and durability of material would justify its rehabilitation as a more edifying introduction to the fine late eighteenth-century house beyond.

Kilmurry gate; pre-1840; *demolished.*
Surviving at this secondary entrance is a screen of ogee quadrants framing four cylindrical stone pillars with fluted friezes; late Georgian.

LGI (1904); Weir 1986.

KILLEELY (see BURTON HILL)

97. KILLOFIN, Labasheeda; *c.* 1850; *demolished.*
A single-storey three-bay gate lodge apparently contemporary with a villa built by Charles Keane, who was already proprietor here in 1837.

Lewis 1837; Weir 1986.

98. KILMORAUN, Clarecastle; pre-1840; *demolished.*
The gate lodge stood until 1986 opposite the gates to a property that belonged from as early as the seventeenth century to the Daxon family, from whom it was on long-term lease to the Davorans in the early nineteenth century.

Leet 1814; Griffith 1853–63; Weir 1986.

99. KILNACRANDY, Quin; pre-1922; *demolished.*
A lodge built after 1840 to a property in 1855 of Croasdaile Molony, whose family was also associated with nearby Granaghan Castle [*q.v.*].

Griffith 1853–63.

100. KILRUSH, Kilrush (3).
In its heyday a magnificent seaside estate of the Vandeleur family, devastated by the loss to an accidental fire in 1897 of its noble mansion and subsequent abandonment. Largely built in 1808, perhaps along with two early porters' lodges that have similarly succumbed, one being replaced remarkably promptly.

South gate; pre-1841; *demolished.*

100. Kilrush. North gate.

Originally opposite its entrance, a lodge probably of some presence, given the quality of the remaining gatescreen, which is a handsome tripartite gateway, its bow-topped postern gates having matching iron railings with spear tops, husk motifs and rope-wreath ornamentation, all framed by four cut-stone pillars with plain recesses but now missing the carriage gates.

North gate; pre-1841/*c.* 1845; architect probably J.B. Keane.
A striking lodge that had an equally substantial predecessor, possibly lost through the same circumstance that took the big house. Single-storey and hip-roofed with paired carved soffit brackets, built mainly in a coursed rubble essentially off a square plan were it not for recesses to the avenue front, the eaves of each corner carried on octagonal columns with corresponding Doric pilasters and round-headed niches within. One access is the entrance porch to the consequently created central hall with tripartite window in dressed limestone, further emphasised by a gablet over. A semi-octagonal bay window,

with equivalent roof and under-panels of big quarry-faced blocks, oddly views the park rather than the entrance. The gatescreen is yet another in the country based on a design from J.B. Papworth's pattern-book *Rural residences* (1818), here adapted to form an extensive entrance of six mammoth stone pillars, each articulated with Egyptian pylon-

fashion tapering frontispieces with moulded recessed panels. Chunky ogee iron railings on dwarf-walled quadrants of a pattern repeated in the postern gates and those of the carriage opening, with fleur-de-lis finials and meeting rails crowned by a feature displaying symbols of the three kingdoms—shamrock, rose and thistle. That the architect was J.B. Keane there is little doubt, for precisely this design of gatescreen was presented by him to the O'Loughlin family for their lodgeless Drumconora House in the county, along with a neo-Classical porch proposal for that place which, too, was realised here on the face of the otherwise plain big house. There is a lodge of similar footprint at Caheracon [*q.v.*].

Town gate; *c.* 1850.

Col. Crofton Moore Vandeleur (1808–81), who succeeded to the property in 1828, added not only the replacement north gate but also this new and more convenient lodged approach from Kilrush. Based on a design of 1801 by Humphrey Repton for Blaise Castle in Somerset, which he illustrated in his *Landscape gardening* (1803) and which was popularised by J.C. Loudon's edited reprint (1840). In a Tudor Gothic castellated style, it presents itself as a single-bay gatehouse, of two storeys divided by a stone string-course, the lower floor with a pointed-arched window, the upper having a wide tripartite multi-paned sash light with label moulding crowned by machicolation, probably missing an original castellated parapet. Attached alongside is an elliptically arched carriage gateway, lacking its wooden doors, balanced by a square turret, all crenellated, in a pleasant rubble stone finish, as, no doubt, was the derelict gatehouse now cloaked in a drab grey rendering. Approached across a bridged river.

Papworth 1818; Loudon and Repton 1840; *LGI* (1904); NIAH; drawing in Clare County Library.

101. KILTANON, Tulla (2).

In 1845 'the seat of James Moloney ... the demesne is a feature of great beauty amidst a bleak and neglected country'. Now the fine old house lies in ruins since its burning in the 1930s, and only a gate lodge survives as relief in the landscape.

South gate; pre-1840/*c.* 1845.

Presumably built by the aforementioned James Molony (1785–1874), the last in a succession of the family of that name, replacing a predecessor on the site. On the main approach, this is a plain 1½-storey standard affair with rendered walls, mildly skew-tabled main gables and a lower projecting gabled hall. Much modernised and occupied. The gates are more notable in the decorative cast-iron pillars with anthemion features and spear-topped railed screens terminating in outer square stone dome-capped pillars.

North gate; pre-1840; *demolished.*

A third porter's lodge is noticed under Nutgrove Cottage [*q.v.*], an associated Molony holding on the estate.

LGI (1904); Weir 1986.

102. KINCORA LODGE, Killaloe; *c.* 1845.

Attorney Thomas O'Brien is recorded here in 1846, although nine years later he had been succeeded by Captain Frederick Lowe RN; one of these two was responsible for adding the gatekeeper's lodge at the entrance to the tree-lined avenue from the south-east. Single-storey with rendered walls on an L-plan, with carved modillion brackets to the soffit of its hipped roof, the leading wing being canted with an equivalent roof but spoiled by a later glazed porch and modern windows.

Slater 1846; Griffith 1853–63.

103. KNAPPOGUE CASTLE, Quin (2).

The present fascinating mansion evolved down the years from its origin as a genuine defensive late fifteenth-century tower-house of the Macnamaras, who remained in possession for 200 years before it became home to the Scott family of Cahercon [*q.v.*], by whom it was disposed of through the incumbered estates court in 1855. The new owner took possession of a property already boasting two lodged gates. This was Theobald Fitzwalter Butler (1806–81), the 14th Baron Dunboyne, who had succeeded to the title and possessions sufficient to finance a second home beyond his Kildare estates and to carry out improvements and extensions here to nineteenth-century standards, and to upgrade the entrances accordingly. His architect was James Pain of Limerick, at the time a 76-year-old practitioner well versed in the appropriate Tudor Gothic Castellated Picturesque fashion.

'East Gate'; pre-1840/*c.* 1858; architect James Pain.

So called and thus inscribed on the entrance screen, behind which Pain inherited an early hip-roofed single-storey lodge that he extended rather awkwardly with the addition of a further room, independently hip-roofed in its own right, giving both outsized curved eaves brackets, concealed behind a tall curtain wall with crenellated parapet. This he incorporated in an informal gatescreen with a cut-stone carriage archway with a pointed head, flanked by a pair of lofty square castellated turrets, beyond which is a lower and longer curtain wall containing a similarly arched postilion opening with dressed stone surround in roughcast finish, likewise crenellated.

'West Gate'; pre-1840/1858; architect James Pain (*below*).

Another disappointing composition where the new lodge has not been integrated, the early lodge being replaced and its successor left divorced from the entrance screen. The latter, in a high-quality punched ashlar, is

103. Knappogue Castle 'West Gate'.

comprised of matching crenellated curtain walls with square turreted stops, but any symmetry is lost in the peculiar arrangement of the central gateway, which is dominated by a grand round machicolated and castellated tower that is in fact the postern gateway, with pointed arched doorways, a structure which also served as a carriage gate pillar, the other a simple square one of normal proportions. Behind is a single-storey standard hip-roofed porter's lodge, with roughcast walls distinguished by large toothed cut-stone quoins and dressings to openings. On the keystone to the central doorway is inscribed 'A.D. 1858'. Latterly extended by two bays to the right-hand side.

BPB (1929); Weir 1986; Lyons 1993; Lee 2006.

KNOCKANIRA (see MULVIHILL)

104. LAKYLE, Broadford; *c.* 1850.
A very derelict, ivy-shrouded, single-storey stone-built cottage with a chimney-stack to each end and a shed added to the left-hand gable. A property in 1855 of Daniel Lenihan, the big house now demolished.

Griffith 1853–63; Weir 1986.

105. LANDSCAPE, Castleconnell; *c.* 1830.

A seat in 1837 of P.W. Creagh Esq., occasionally let down the century to others before being developed in the early twentieth century into a large, rambling Elizabethan Revival mansion. But the early Creagh porter's lodge survives in its original state as a characterful little structure, single-storey with high eaves to accommodate a loft room, having a typical Regency soffit with paired carved brackets under a steeply hipped roof. The principal short single-bay front contains a tripartite casement window with banded surround, while the two bipartite windows to the road are similarly treated in startling whitened roughcast walls. Occupied and immaculately maintained.

Lewis 1837; Weir 1986.

106. LARCH HILL, Ennis; pre-1840; *demolished.*
A lost house, the residence in 1846, and probably nine years earlier, of land agent Pierce Carnick.

Lewis 1837; Slater 1846.

107. LATOON, Clarecastle (2).
Both lodges to a property in 1855 of John Lynch were built after 1840.

East gate; *c.* 1860.
A standard three-bay single-storey cottage with chimney-stacks to each of the gables of its steeply pitched roof. Built in a coursed rough stone. A sturdy survivor but derelict.

North gate; pre-1922; *demolished.*
The lodge was situated opposite its entrance on a road formed after 1840.

Griffith 1853–63.

108. LEADMORE, Kilrush; pre-1840; *demolished.*
A property associated in the nineteenth century with the Brew family.

Weir 1986.

109. LEITRIM, Kilmihill; *c.* 1845.
Opposite the gates is a basic standard single-storey gabled lodge constructed in stone with basic skew-tables to a now-corrugated iron roof. A modest estate in 1855 of William Crowley.

Griffith 1853–63.

LISMEHANE (see MARY FORT)

110. LISMOYLE, Newmarket-on-Fergus; *c.* 1810.
A standard single-storey cottage with tiny windows in harled walls with a brick eaves band to its hipped roof. Derelict and suffering the indignity of having an opening gouged out of its front for garage use. A property early in the nineteenth century of the O'Donoghue family.

Weir 1986.

111. THE LODGE, Broadford; 1863; architect William Fogerty.
'A shooting lodge is in course of erection, on the estate lately purchased by Colonel Henry White at Broadford, Co. Clare. An entrance and keeper's lodge are also in progress on the same estate. The buildings are in the Gothic style, of the local sandstone, with cut limestone dressings, and ornamental bargeboards. Mr W. Fogerty, of Limerick, is the architect.' A graphic description from the *Dublin Builder* magazine of what materialised and what survives intact of this fine development in a gate lodge which is the perfect introduction to its big house in style, in materials, with its uncoursed rubble finish, and in detail, with its scalloped slate roof bands, perforated wavy bargeboards and exaggerated hip-knob and semi-octagonal bay window with equivalent roof to one gable. Single-storey standard and symmetrical but for its bay window and sole chimney-stack to the opposing gable; bipartite casement windows in chamfered surrounds flank the entrance breakfront with its fanlit Tudor Gothic arched opening containing a sheeted door with ornamental strap hinges. At a distance is a gatescreen in like manner with chamfered pillars and steep tiered cappings. Built for the young Lt.-Col. Charles William White (1838–90), fifth son of the 1st Baron Annaly of Luttrellstown Castle, Co. Dublin, after which title this property is also known. Fogerty designed a lodge of identical proportions for Waterpark [*q.v.*] but in an Italianate cloak.

DB (1 March 1863); *BPB* (1929).

112. LOUGH O'CONNELL, Kilkishen; pre-1840/*c.* 1855.

In a delightful woodland setting are the sad, dilapidated remains of a once-pretty single-storey Picturesque English Country Cottage lodge, raised off an L-plan with steeply

111. The Lodge, Broadford.

pitched gables, with a lower-gabled hall tucked into the internal angle and a semi-octagonal bay window to one wing. Now minus its roof over limewashed harled walls, it was a replacement for an earlier, equally ill-fated lodge, though not past salvation. Nearby is a ruined gatescreen of shallow ogee quadrant walls flanking toppled monolithic stone drum pillars. All seemingly an appropriate prelude to the ruinous house within, initially built for the Steele family, which passed through marriage of a niece to the Studderts, of whom Robert Wogan Studdert (1816–97) probably erected the replacement lodge after the death of his father in 1851. A property subsequently renamed 'Cullane Castle'.

LGI (1904); Weir 1986.

113. MARY FORT, Tulla (2).

The very fine demesne of the O'Callaghan family, latterly renamed 'Lismehane' and now a commercial concern.

Main gate; *c.* 1825.

An entrance created by George O'Callaghan (1788–1849), who succeeded his father to the property in 1818. This is an example of a pleasant Regency gate lodge suffering at the hands of the 'improver'. Single-storey standard below an oversailing hipped roof, it has a distinguishing feature in its three-bay elevation being expressed as a breakfront to the avenue façade. This, however, has been stripped of its original protective harled finish to reveal its limestone rubble fabric, with the consequent loss of impact of the fine cut-stone keystoned door surround. To compound matters, modernisation has seen the intrusion of inappropriate casement windows in the wide openings. The extent of roof overhang at each corner suggests that there may originally have been ornamental post support. The impressive entrance screen was once a triple gateway framed with fluted friezes and moulded corniced cappings with iron gates and matching railings, as so often seen in the county with their spear tops and husk drapes. Beyond are shallow concave quadrant walls in exposed rubble, probably once also more effectively in a limewashed harled finish.

Secondary gate; *c.* 1870.

Separated from its estate by a new public road is this single-storey four-bay pebble-dashed cottage with a dormer window, forward and alongside big vermiculated pillars and quadrants. Presumably an improvement by Capt. John O'Callaghan (1830–1912), who inherited the property on his father's death.

LGI (1904).

114. MERVILLE, Milltown Malbay; pre-1840; *demolished.*

Both house and porter's lodge have gone; a holding in 1837 of John Carroll.

Lewis 1837.

MILLBROOK (see BALLYLINE)

115. MILLBROOK, Killaloe; pre-1840; *demolished.*

A milling business and proprietor's house in 1837 of James Watson.

Lewis 1837.

116. MILTOWN, Milltown Malbay; pre-1840/pre-1920; *demolished.*

A grand marine residence of the Morony family, now run as a school. The original lodge to the south-west was opposite its gates, subsequently superseded by one within the curtilage of the property. Another lodged gate to the south-east appears to have been shared by Wellington House [*q.v.*].

117. MOANMORE COTTAGE, Kilrush; pre-1840; *demolished.*

The modest homestead in 1855 of Francis Cox, but not too modest to have had a lodged gate.

Griffith 1853–63.

118. MORELANDS, Limerick; pre-1840; *demolished.*

The seat in 1814 of Abraham Abell, which by 1855 was occupied by Daniel Cullen.

Leet 1814; Griffith 1853–63.

119. MOUNT ALLON, Broadford; *c.* 1845; *demolished.*

The house, now ruined, was approached past a plain single-storey three-bay gate lodge. The proprietor in 1855 was parish priest Revd Patrick Quaid (1801–68).

Griffith 1853–63; Weir 1986.

120. MOUNT BAYLEE, Kilkishen; pre-1840; *demolished.*

An estate in 1837 of H. Baylee Esq.

Lewis 1837.

121. MOUNT CATHERINE, Clonlara; pre-1910.

Opposite the gates is probably what began as a late Victorian lodge, perhaps once standard with a hipped roof, much extended subsequently to the right-hand side by a bay and to the left-hand side to form an L-plan; roughcast and occupied. A property of the Lloyd family.

Weir 1986.

122. MOUNT IEVERS, Sixmilebridge (3).

One of the finest early Georgian mansions in the country seems not to have had an entrance worthy of it since the removal of the highly significant and distinguished late seventeenth-century pair of twin cubic single-storey pavilions to the immediate walled forecourt of the earlier house, with lofty chimney-stacks and pyramidal roofs rising to ornamental finials and between which on an axis with the front door was a pair of tall pillars with ball finials framing carriage doors with prominent strap hinges. A precursor of things to come.

South gate; *c.* 1820.

At the village entrance is a basic standard cottage in harled rubble below a shallow-pitched gabled roof with clipped eaves. The roadside elevation is three-bay with a segmentally arched doorway, alongside the gate sweep of shallow concave quadrant walls between outer pillars with ball-less pedestals and inner ones with gadroons on beds of rope mouldings as cappings. Built in the time of Eyre Ievers (1797–1860).

North gate; pre-1923; *demolished.*

A short-lived lodge erected after 1840.

LGI (1904); Bence-Jones 1988; Humphreys 1979.

123. MOUNT PLEASANT, Kilrush; pre-1840; *demolished.*

A now-lodgeless property with its house roofless, once home to the Cox family.

124. MOUNT PROSPECT, Killaloe; *c.* 1845.

A lodge to a property previously known as 'Aylevawn Cottage', the residence in 1855 of Major Alfred Scott. Apparently once single-storey standard and hip-roofed, half-removed, only that portion forward of its gates remaining, they being notable for two octagonal limestone carriage pillars.

Griffith 1853–63.

125. MOUNT PROSPECT, Milltown Malbay; pre-1840; *demolished.*

A lodge opposite its gates to a marine villa in 1855 of George Lysaght; gone by 1920.

Griffith 1853–63.

126. MOUNT SHANNON, Mountshannon; *c.* 1845.

A house, lodge and gates erected around 1840 for the Tandy family. The distinguished entrance is comprised of a triple gateway of fine ironwork with palmette finials and acroteria to the carriage piers but particularly notable for the containing outer punched-ashlar convex quadrants and four innovative cut-stone pillars, the chamfers to which are stopped by pendants supporting unusual corner projections to the cappings. All encrusted delightfully in the lichen of centuries. Not so the distant lodge, with its modern sanitising rendering with sharp arises and inappropriate modern windows. A single-storey standard cottage with elliptically arched fanlit doorway below an oversailing hipped roof and extended to the right-hand side. The once-splendid house lies as a romantic ruin.

Weir 1986.

127. MOY, Lahinch; *c.* 1840.
Opposite the entrance is a derelict single-storey standard gabled cottage added for Sir William Fitzgerald (d. 1847), whose main seat was Carrigoran [*q.v.*] and who had succeeded to the estates on the death of his brother in 1834.

BPB (1929); Weir 1986.

128. MOYNOE, Scarriff; pre-1840; *demolished.*
The residence in 1814 and 1845 of Sir John Reade, the probable builder of the lodge.

Leet 1814; *PGI.*

129. MOYRIESK, Fair Green (2).
The present house is but a portion of the once-magnificent mid-eighteenth-century Classical mansion of the Macnamaras and subsequently the Vesey-Fitzgerald family, of which neither of its pre-1840 gate lodges survives.

130. MULVIHILL, Ennis; pre-1840; *demolished.*
David Mulvihill is recorded as resident in 1814, his family living on here until the mid-nineteenth century, when the place became known as 'Knockanira', its lodge set well back from the road.

Leet 1814.

131. NEWGROVE, Tulla (3).
Another sad example of a once-proud demesne fallen to ruin, its big house demolished, ornamental lake dried up and porters' lodges removed, all that remains being the walled garden and the main entrance gateway. A seat of the Browne family.

East gate; pre-1840/pre-1922; *demolished.*
Both the early lodge opposite the gates and its successor within the boundary have gone.

Middle gate; pre-1922; *demolished.*

West gate; pre-1840; *demolished.*
An extraordinary survivor is this peculiar gatescreen of seemingly different ages. Angled straight walls of uncoursed random quarry-faced masonry of mid-Victorian origin terminate in sophisticated ashlar aedicules as pavilions with moulded plinths and round-headed niches, both ivy-capped. In the centre is the triple gateway, framed by a pair of square stone pillars with plain friezes and moulded corniced cappings, repeated on the four inner cylindrical pillars which contain latticed ironwork to the outer screens and the lower postern gates which have sunburst motifs over, all in contrast with the relatively traditional railed carriage gates.

Weir 1986.

132. NEW HALL, Clarecastle (2).
Charles MacDonnell purchased Killone Abbey in 1764, elegantly refaced it in brick as it today endures, and renamed it. It would seem to have been his grandson, John MacDonnell (1789–1850), who added lodges at its distant gates, succeeding to the estate on the death of his father in 1803.

Lough Killone gate; *c.* 1805.

On the distant entrance from the south to a beautiful lakeside backdrop is this forlorn shell of a Georgian Gothic gatekeeper's lodge, displaying in its dereliction rubble construction with brick-dressed openings to its pointed-arched three-bay symmetrical front; standard with a chimney-stack to one gable and a little loft window to the other. By 2017 totally obscured by ivy.

Main gate; *c.* 1805.

If this fine twin pair of single-storey lodges is anything to go by, Charles MacDonnell may not have been of a particularly hospitable disposition; they display blind façades to the visitor, whilst their showpiece fronts were reserved for his viewing across the park. Each is a perfect mirror image of the other; below hipped roofs they exhibit irregular three-bay elevations of lancet-headed openings of two tiny Y-traceried windows alongside similarly arched sheeted doors in stone toothed dressed surrounds, their voussoirs meeting in keystones, all in harled rubble walls. They face each other with cut-stone round-arched niches across the front of a triple gateway of Classical ashlar pillars, with dentil-coursed cappings, on which are hung spear-topped contemporary railed gates. All now shamefully neglected.

LGI (1904); Bence-Jones 1988.

133. NEW LAWN, O'Callaghan's Mills; pre-1840; *demolished.*
Not quite opposite the gates was the porter's lodge, later converted into 'Fortanne School', to a property in 1837 of Captain H. Westropp.

Lewis 1837.

134. NEWTOWN, Clonlara; pre-1840; *demolished.*
Not quite on an axis with the entrance opposite was the lodge to a seat in 1814 and 1837 of Andrew Walsh.

Leet 1814; Lewis 1837.

132. New Hall, Clarecastle. Main gate.

IAA

NUTGROVE COTTAGE (see KILTANON)

135. O'BRIENSBRIDGE RECTORY, O'Briensbridge; pre-1840; *demolished.*

In 1837 the glebe house had been recently built on six acres of land presented by Thomas Westropp of nearby Ross House [*q.v.*], its gate lodge presumably contemporary and both built by Revd Richard Coplen Langford (1790–1855), incumbent from 1832 to *c.* 1839.

Lewis 1837; Leslie and Crooks 2010.

136. PARADISE HILL, Killadysert; pre-1840/*c.* 1870; architect J. McCurdy.

An aptly named property, in 1685 granted to Richard Henn, whose family must have found it inconvenient; for five generations thereafter they were absentees, letting the estate on the banks of the Shannon estuary to a succession of tenants, one of whom in 1855 was Augustus Arthur from Ballyquin [*q.v.*], who had as his gatekeeper Michael Galvin. The Henn family returned to the place in the person of barrister Thomas Rice Henn (1814–1901), revitalising it with the help of Dublin architect John McCurdy, who replaced the old house with one in the French Château style, and the gate lodge more in the English Cottage Picturesque manner. Unlike the house, it survives much as built but for the modern alien casement windows and the loss of bay windows to leading gables, one rectangular lean-to, the other canted. Built on

Benedictine nuns of Kylemore Abbey

what is essentially an L-plan, single-storey over a basement and raised in stucco-effect finish, its steep gables are decorated with bold carved perforated bargeboards that rise to ornamental cast-iron hip-knobs on the ridges of a slated roof with scalloped courses. A breakfront hipped gable to the rear retains its lean-to glazed bay window, while in the internal corner is a minuscule double-gabled glazed hall with a band of blank shields, a Tudor motif repeated on the main gables. Now distinctly run-down and missing its original pretty wooden gatescreen of picket fence and Tudor Gothic carriage posts.

Griffith 1853–63; *LGI* (1904); Weir 1986; Williams 1994.

PARTEENALAX (see THE COTTAGE)

PROSPECT (see THORNBERRY)

PROSPECT LODGE (see BALLYCONNOE)

137. QUILTY, Quilty; *c.* 1850.

Here are the ruins of a single-storey standard, hip-roofed, stone-built, harled cottage of indeterminate date, erected after 1840 but recorded to the property in 1855 of Thomas Crowe which was renamed 'Salus' by the turn of the twentieth century.

Griffith 1853–63; Weir 1986.

138. QUINSBOROUGH, Parteen; pre-1840/*c.* 1845; architect perhaps J. Pain.

A quite grand country house, as befits its connections with two of Ireland's noble titled families. Built in 1767 for George Quin (1729–91), a younger son of the earl of Dunraven of Adare Manor, Co. Limerick [*q.v.*], it passed through his daughter and heir by her marriage to the Taylours, marquises of Headfort, Co. Meath, to her son, Lord George Quin (1792–1888), who assumed that surname in 1813. The replacement porter's lodge is sufficiently original and

sophisticated to be attributable to an architect of some standing—James Pain had his office in nearby Limerick and had already worked for the Dunraven family. Single-storey and basically square in plan, it has segmentally bowed corners containing similarly arched casement windows in rendered walls which are further articulated by wide pilasters with plain recesses, cleverly mirroring the entrance pillars. Projecting towards the avenue is a sturdy portico with square Doric outer pillars and a pair of octagonal columns *in antis* carrying a shallow pediment that extends from an otherwise hipped roof, the frieze of which continues about the lodge as an eaves band. A later addition in like manner projects toward the road. What was a triple gateway has now lost its original carriage pillars and retains only the postern gates, framed by rendered concave quadrant walls. If not built for Lord George Quin then it was erected for Martin Honan, who had taken up residence here by 1846.

Slater 1846; *BPB* (1929).

139. QUINVILLE ABBEY, Quin; *c.* 1780.

In 1827 John Singleton (1793–1877) commenced the transformation of his father's old house into a modern Tudor-Gothic symmetrical manor house, probably to designs of the Pain brothers. Edward D'Alton Singleton on his death in 1814 also passed on to his son a fine entrance lodge, which serves to this day, surviving thanks to its unusually generous accommodation and recent sensitive rehabilitation and extension. Single-storey standard of rare length, it is also notable for its hipped gables, large slates and a wide, low, pointed-arched doorway in striking white harled walls. In contrast to this Gothic detail is the Classical gatescreen, with square stone carriage pillars having miniature moulded corniced cappings, a postilion opening with small recessed-panel pillar and basic ogee quadrant walls beyond.

LGI (1904); Weir 1986.

Benedictine nuns of Kylemore Abbey

136. Paradise Hill, Killadysert.

140. RAHEEN MANOR, Tuamgraney (2).
While the big house has gone, it is surprisingly survived by both of its contrasting gatekeepers' lodges, each reflecting a different era of the estate's ownership.

Tuamgraney gate; *c.* 1830.

An original single-storey lodge describing an octagon on plan, faced in punched random coursed masonry, with an octahedral roof that rises to a two-flue, four-cluster chimney-stack. As built, the octagonal plan comprised a wide canted porch with a gabled pediment feature supported on a pair of octagonal posts, behind which is a symmetrical three-bay façade. This has since been enclosed with innovative sloped glazing in the manner of an airfield control tower. Lovingly maintained.

In 1837 this was a seat of Revd Thomas B. Brady, whose family had been here since the previous century but whose interest ceased when it was sold through the incumbered estates court around 1854 to William John Harrison Moreland, whose contribution to the property may have been the exceptional identical gatescreens to both entrances. These are comprised of triple gateways with four ashlar pillars which are Classical in form, with moulded plinths, corniced cappings and gate stops with beautifully carved acanthus leaf-scrolled tops but inscribed with Gothic moulded recesses to shafts with traceried tops of cusped foils and, in the friezes, quatrefoil motifs.

By 1911 Raheen had been purchased by the traveller, poet and writer Sidney Royse Lysaght (1856–1941), who gave the house a make-over in Arts and Crafts style that year to designs of William Clifford Smith, doubtless responsible for the delightful gate lodge.

East gate; *c.* 1911; architect W.C. Smith.

Smith was clearly influenced by the Tuamgraney lodge, for he incorporated many of its features, such as an open pillared entrance porch, bevelled corners and a cluster of four octagonal chimney-flues. Single-storey standard in random quarry-faced masonry with ashlar dressings below a hipped roof. In innovative Arts and Crafts manner, the entrance porch is screened by a triple opening with miniature Tuscan columns *in antis* on dwarf walls, with square external corners broaching to permit canted triple sash corner windows over. The damaged gatescreen is flanked by contrasting crenellated concave rubble quadrants from the Lysaght era.

Even lacking its big house, the estate remains an architectural surprise and delight.

Lewis 1837; Griffith 1853–63; *IFR*; Weir 1986; IAA.

141. RATHLAHEEN, Newmarket-on-Fergus; pre-1839; *demolished.*
An estate since 1660 of the Vandeleur family of Kilrush [*q.v.*] on which only some outbuildings survive.

LGI (1904).

142. RATHLUBY, Kilkishen; *c.* 1850.
A basic single-storey standard lodge faced in stone with red-brick soldier arches below a shallow-pitched gabled roof with minimal skew-tables. A holding in 1855 of Henry Bridgeman.

Griffith 1853–63.

143. RIVOLI, Ennistimon; 1868.

A wholly charming and compact porter's lodge; single-storey octagonal with octahedral roof rising from its carved bracketed eaves to the single-flue banded octagonal chimney-stack. Plain rendered walls have round-headed openings alternating between one-over-one sash windows and blind recesses, except that facing the avenue, from which projects a gabled entrance porch with semicircular-arched doorway and carved bargeboards with hip-knob over. Abandoned and allegedly haunted! The contemporary shallow concave quadrants and chunky pillars are in a quarry-faced masonry. Along with the house, a development for wealthy Ennistimon solicitor James Shannon, far from the Piedmont town.

Weir 1986.

144. ROCKFOREST, Tubber (2).
Both lodges opposite their gates, neither of which remain, were in place by 1840, probably built by Bindon 'the Vampire' Blood (1775–1855), who had another property, Cranagher House [*q.v.*].

LGI (1904); Weir 1986.

145. ROSE HILL, Clonlara; *c.* 1835.
A single-storey standard, harled, hip-roofed cottage; derelict and surrounded by a farmyard. A property in 1837 of P. O'Callaghan Esq.

Lewis 1837.

146. ROSMANAGHER COTTAGE, Sixmilebridge; pre-1923.
All that survives opposite the entrance is a ruin of the gate lodge to a now-lost house, in 1855 of Robert Ker D'Esterre, who by 1870 had been succeeded here by Henry V. D'Esterre.

Griffith 1853–63; Slater 1870.

147. ROSS, O'Briensbridge (2).
An estate of a succession of occupants, from the late eighteenth century of Thomas Pearce, followed in 1814 by John Blake and in 1837 by Thomas Westropp. Neither entrance is in pristine condition.

Principal gate; pre-1840.
A single-storey structure opposite a handsome gatescreen of V-jointed rusticated stone pillars with exaggerated cornices to cappings.

Secondary gate; *c.* 1825.

On the north-western approach alongside its gateway is a pleasant but modest single-storey hip-roofed structure, with doorway and window as its main two-bay road front in whitewashed harled walls off an almost square plan. Derelict.

Taylor and Skinner 1788; 1783; Wilson 1803; Leet 1814; Lewis 1837; Weir 1986.

148. ROSSLEVIN, Ennis; pre-1922; *demolished.*
The residence in 1855 of Revd James W. Rynd, which he thereafter rented out.
Griffith 1853–63.

149. ROXTON, Corrofin; *c.* 1910; *demolished.*
A once-fine seat of the Blood family, reduced in the twentieth century to the present ruinous state. Curiously, its gate lodge was first valued as late as 1913, when the property passed from James Darling Wilson to his widow Mary.
Weir 1986.

150. ST CATHERINE'S, Bodyke; pre-1920.
A lodge built after 1840 probably for Ralph Westropp, who had inherited the property by marrying Catherine O'Callaghan in 1852. It now lies ruinous at the base of the western avenue to a house previously known as 'Coolready'.
LGI (1904).

SALUS (see QUILTY)

151. SANDYMOUNT, Milltown Malbay; pre-1840; *demolished.*
A property in 1814 of John Kerin. Neither the house nor its gate lodge, situated opposite the entrance, survives, the latter a shell by 1920.
Leet 1814.

152. SEAMOUNT, Liscannor; *c.* 1840.

A delightful single-storey standard lodge opposite the gates, symmetrical but for a big semicircular bow bulging from the right-hand end, paying little heed to the entrance. Its semi-conical roof extends from an otherwise hipped roof, from which projects a gabled breakfront hall, the doorway Tudor label-moulded, as are the flanking bipartite sash windows in harled walls. The gatescreen is comprised of railed quadrants on dwarf walls with slender monolithic pillars. The gatekeeper in 1855 was Bridget McGwann, employed by Cornelius O'Brien of nearby Birchfield [*q.v.*].
Griffith 1853–63.

153. SMITHSTOWN, Sixmilebridge; pre-1840; *demolished.*
A property which had a succession of occupants in the early nineteenth century: a Mr Watt in 1802, Anthony Sheehan twelve years later, followed by John Macnamara, any one of whom could have built the lodge, which had been removed by 1951.
Weir 1986.

154. SPRINGHILL, Ardnacrusha; pre-1840; *demolished.*
House and lodge have gone, both dating from the early nineteenth century and belonging to a property of the McAdam family.
Leet 1814; Lewis 1837.

155. STAMER PARK, Ennis; pre-1840; *demolished.*
Originally a seat of the Stamer family, it was occupied by the Finucanes in the first half of the nineteenth century.
Weir 1986.

156. STREAM MOUNT, Parteen; pre-1840; *demolished.*
An 82-acre estate in 1852 of Martin Honan Burke, whose house now lies in ruins.
Griffith 1853–63; Weir 1986.

157. SUMMERHILL, Clonlara; pre-1840; *demolished.*
Neither the main house nor its gate lodge, sited not quite opposite the entrance, survives, although the latter, a good mid-Victorian straight railed gatescreen, remains, along with some outbuildings and the back return of a residence in the early nineteenth century of Revd Charles Massy (1767/8–1817), followed by his only son, Hugh Dillon Massy, who lived on here until 1842, when he succeeded to a baronetcy on the death of his uncle and left for his new inheritance, Doonass House [*q.v.*]. The gatescreen may date from the advent of the Vincent family.
Leet 1814; *BPB* (1861); Weir 1986; Leslie and Crooks 2010.

158. SUN VILLE, Kilkishen; *c.* 1830.
Lying derelict on an elevated site is a tiny standard rubble-built lodge, gabled with basic skew-tables to a corrugated iron roof. A property in 1814 of John O'Halloran, who by 1837 had been succeeded here by T. Studdert Esq.
Leet 1814; Lewis 1837.

TEMPLEMALEY (see BALLYALLA [1])

159. THORNBERRY, Lahasheeda; pre-1840/*c.* 1850.
On an elevated mound overlooking an insignificant entrance is this dinky single-storey standard rendered porter's lodge with a chimney-stack to each gable and minimal skew-tables. This would seem to be the replacement for a predecessor on a slightly different site, built for William Henry Studdert (d. 1867), who is recorded here in 1837, the fifth son of George Studdert of neighbouring Clonderlaw [*q.v.*].
Lewis 1837; *LGI* (1904).

160. TINARANA, Tuamgraney; *c.* 1836; architect not known.
The year 1836 was a momentous one for Simon George Purdon (1797–1862), for on 1

February he inherited Tinarana on the death of his father and on 11 August he married Louisa Elizabeth Eleanor, daughter of the 1st Lord Ponsonby of Imokilly. This very fine Classical lodge may be one of the improvements carried out to the estate to impress his bride and in-laws. Single-storey standard below a shallow hipped roof from which projects, not quite centrally, a pedimented breakfront containing a double-leafed panelled doorway with rectangular fanlight flanked by a pair of Tuscan columns *in antis*. In the tympanum is the Purdon crest—a Dexter arm embowered, holding a broken staff—over which, incongruously, is a hip-knob, perhaps part of later modernisation which included a late Victorian chimney-stack replacement. In roughcast walls are casement windows with stone plinth and smooth eaves band carried about the frontispiece. Nearby, the impressive gatescreen appears to be of two periods. Octagonal stone carriage pillars are flanked by short, railed concave quadrants stopped by tall square pillars with moulded recessed shafts and over-panels of foliated and floral carving. Alongside are postilion gates with architraves and segmental arches. All immaculately maintained. A little building of some sophistication, perhaps owing to the hand of architect James Pain.
LGI (1904).

161. TINTRIM, Whitegate (3).
An estate, previously in County Galway, of John Anthony Burke until his death in 1863 at the age of 101. His two lost gatekeepers' lodges, located well within the property, were erected before 1838. Despite appearances, the pleasant surviving lodge may be as recent as 1900, judging by one remaining multi-paned Arts and Crafts window. Single-storey standard, square in plan, with a pyramidal roof rising to a central chimney-stack, its walls harled and cream-washed below oversailing eaves, the projecting hall similarly roofed. Occupied and overlooking a gatescreen with cylindrical gate pillars.

Weir 1986.

162. TOONAGH, Ennis (2).
The late eighteenth-century residence of the O'Brien family has been survived by its gatekeepers' lodges.

North entrance; pre-1840/*c.* 1855.
Opposite the gates is a replacement lodge on the site of its predecessor, apparently built for Poor Law inspector Henry William Lucas, who was leasing the house from Cornelius O'Brien. It is a 1½-storey rendered gabled structure with Irish pilaster quoins and a projecting central single-storey gabled hall with a round-headed fanlit doorway, flanked by mini-buttresses. All framed by ornamental cast iron railings, which were probably mirrored across the road but swept away by widening.

South entrance; *c.* 1875.
By 1870 Toonagh was the residence of William Henry McGrath, who probably added the secondary lodge; to the left-hand side of its gates is a large two-storey, three-bay, plain, gabled late Victorian house.

Griffith 1853–63; Slater 1870.

163. TROMEROE, Quilty; pre-1840; *demolished.*
Both porters' lodges opposite the entrance and its big house, in 1814 home to Charles Mahon, have gone.

Leet 1814; Weir 1986.

164. TROUGH CASTLE, Blackwater; *c.* 1850.
According to Lenihan in 1866, this was 'the castellated residence of General Sir Charles Routledge O'Donnell [1796–1870], colonel of the 18th Hussars', although the *Irish Builder* magazine six years later records that architect William Sidney Cox designed a castellated mansion here for Lt.-Col. John Wyse O'Donnell. In any case, this was a delightful toy castle, now in ruins, survived by a rather less Romantic estate entrance. The standard single-storey lodge lies deserted and blocked up, its gabled roof now with a corrugated-iron finish behind a parapeted front elevation with a crudely banded door-case and rendered pilaster quoins. Flanked by stone concave quadrant walls, which reflect the gatescreen across the road.

Lenihan 1967; *IB* (1 June 1872).

165. TROUGH COTTAGE, Blackwater; pre-1840; *demolished.*
A typical late Georgian single-storey-over-basement villa, in 1852 the residence of William Walsh, whose porter's lodge had been removed by 1938.

Griffith 1853–63.

166. VIOLET HILL, Broadford (2).
A seat in 1809 of Exham Vincent, succeeded by James Going, who was resident here in 1837, either of whom may have built the early porter's lodge.

North gate; pre-1840; *demolished.*
The lodge opposite the entrance had gone by 1922.

South gate; *c.* 1870.
A now much improved single-storey lodge with a pyramidal roof and a gabled entrance breakfront, rendered and only datable from the quarry-faced masonry of its entrance pillars. Perhaps built for the lessee William Blennerhassett.

Weir 1986.

167. WATERPARK, Clonlara; *c.* 1870; architect William Fogerty.

The previous house of the Bindon family was purchased by John Lecky Phelps (1815–81) and in 1869 was transformed into a much larger Italianate residence by the eclectic Limerick architect William Fogerty, whose commission also included a design for the complementary gatekeeper's lodge. Sadly, the big house has already been demolished and its lodge is in an advanced state of decay, although not beyond rehabilitation. A once-jaunty single-storey standard composition in the Italianate manner, with exposed rafter toes and bold brackets to main verges and that of the gabled breakfront, which displays a panelled front door with a moulded-surround round-headed fanlight with impost course. To each side simple casement windows have moulded surrounds, while the road elevation has a semicircular-arched window and the opposing front, enjoying views of the park, has a semi-octagonal bay window with equivalent roof. The conspicuous chimney-stack with corbel course and curved capping is reflected in the four stone entrance pillars with their chamfered shafts, which contain very fine arcaded cast ironwork of gates and matching concave railed screens on dwarf walls, all of which is strikingly well maintained in contrast to the dereliction of its fine lodge, of which there is a Picturesque version by Fogerty at the Lodge [*q.v.*], Broadford.

Lewis 1837; *IB* (1 May 1869); *LGI* (1904); Weir 1986.

168. WELLINGTON COTTAGE, Milltown Malbay; pre-1840; *demolished.*
A marine villa in 1855 of Edward Morony, the lodge to which, opposite the entrance, seems to have been shared by Milltown House [*q.v.*].

Griffith 1853–63.

169. WESTPARK, Milltown Malbay (2).
Neither the house nor its two pre-1840 porters' lodges survive to a property in 1855 of John N. Russell, leasing from Burdett Morony, who was then letting one of the lodges to Henry Morony.

Griffith 1853–63.

170. WILLOWBANK, Ennis; pre-1840; *demolished.*
An estate in 1814 and 1824 of Edward B. Armstrong, and in 1837 of Edmund J. Armstrong.

Leet 1814; Pigot 1824; Lewis 1837.

171. WOODPARK, Bunratty; *c.* 1830.
A single-storey shallow-gabled cottage, derelict and put to farm use. Its now-lost big house was residence in 1837 to M. Dalton Esq.

Lewis 1837.

172. WOODPARK, Mountshannon (2).
Two gatekeepers' lodges built for Philip Reade (1793–1883), who succeeded to his father's estates in 1801 as a minor.

South gate; pre-1920.
A lodge built after 1840 that has either been replaced by or transformed into a twentieth-century bungalow.

North gate; *c.* 1855.

A 1½-storey lodge in the English Picturesque Cottage manner, built off an L-plan, with chunky carved wooden perforated foiled bargeboards and earthenware fleur-de-lis cresting to ridges. Done over in a crisp modern rendering, the leading gable containing a canted glazed bay window with equivalent roof below a little loft light, all on an elevated site.

Griffith 1853–63; *LGI* (1904)

COUNTY CORK

Entries in close proximity to Cork city are distinguished by [N] or [S] depending upon their location north or south of the River Lee.

1. ABBEYSTREWERY CHURCH OF IRELAND CHURCH, Skibbereen; *c.* 1890.

Of main interest at the entrance to the parish church off Bridge Street is the conspicuous Gothic gate. In random uncoursed masonry, its pointed archway is dressed in hewn stone contained by a skew-capped and kneelered gable with finial atop, the apex to which bears the inscription: 'Erected by His Parishioners & Friends to the Memory of the Revd. Canon James Goodman M.A. 20 Years Rector of this Parish of Abbeystewery 12 Years Professor of Irish in Trinity College Dublin. Died 18th January 1896 Aged 67 Years.' Railed quadrants and matching postilion gates. Considerably less pretentious is a drably rendered two-storey hip-roofed house with gabled breakfront to the avenue, appended to the gable end of the adjacent terrace. The entrance archway may be by W.H. Hill & Son, they having expertly extended the old church of 1827 in 1890.

Lewis 1837; Williams 1994.

2. ADELAIDE PLACE, Cork [N]; *c.* 1835.
A modest single-storey hip-roofed structure, its main entrance front single-bay and with two windows to the avenue elevation. At the gate to an exclusive late Georgian terrace development associated with the Beale family, of whom Joshua's gatekeeper in 1852 was Pat Kearney.

Griffith 1853–63.

3. ADMIRALTY, Cobh; *c.* 1886.
At the entrance to a great Italianate pile built for the British navy is a set of stone gate pillars with vermiculated rustication contemporary with the big house, as is the

lodge. An example of a late Victorian mix of the Picturesque and Italianate styles, single-storey on an irregular plan, with end gables hipped but that to the avenue projection fully gabled and with ornamental carved perforated geometrical bargeboards, below which is a rectangular glazed bay window with its own roof. Alongside this, in an internal angle, the panelled front door shelters below a canopy created as a catslide to the main roof, supported on a solitary wooden bracket. Rendered, with applied toothed quoins and dressings to narrow round-arched windows; ridge of serrated earthenware cresting interrupted by corbelled rendered chimney-stacks with octagonal pots. Subsequently home in the twentieth century to the Sisters of Mercy, now St Benedict's Priory.

4. AFGHAN, Cork [N]; *c.* 1845; *demolished.*
A house, gate lodge, offices and garden recorded in 1852 on Glanmire Road Middle, its proprietor being James Kane, bookseller and stationer in the city. Neither apparent on site nor on the 1841 OS map.

Griffith 1853–63.

5. AGHADA, Rostellan; *c.* 1830.
A plain hip-roofed single-storey porter's lodge with a two-bay front to the approach. Improved and occupied. A seat in 1837 of J.J. Roche, the house having been built for the Roche family around the turn of the nineteenth century to designs of the elder Abraham Hargrave.

Lewis 1837; Bence-Jones 1988.

6. AGHADA RECTORY, Aghada; *c.* 1860.
Although the glebe house originated in 1814, the gatekeeper's lodge was not added until the incumbency of Revd William Robinson or his successor and nephew Revd Thomas Townsend. It is an unremarkable 1½-storey gabled affair with clipped verges and roughcast finish, its three-bay front having a minimal flat-roofed hall projecting from the left-hand side. Occupied.

Lewis 1837; Slater 1856; 1870; *IFR.*

7. AGHADOE, Killeagh (3).
Here are the pitiful remains of an ancient estate of the de Capell Brooke family, its big house a shell and all lodges in place by 1842 having been demolished in the twentieth century.

Lewis 1837; Bence-Jones 1988.

8. AGHAMARTA CASTLE, Crosshaven; pre-1842; *demolished.*
A seat in 1837 of Carew O'Grady, of that Limerick family, the gate lodge to which may have been doomed through being in the path of the Great Southern Railway.

Lewis 1837.

9. AGHAVINE, Ballymadog; pre-1841; *demolished.*
A property in 1853 of Michael Neville.

Griffith 1853–63.

10. AGHAVRIN, Coachford; pre-1841; *demolished.*
An estate in 1814 of William Crooke, 23 years later succeeded here by Thomas E. Crooke. Subsequently renamed 'Olans', its gate lodge had been removed by 1938.

Leet 1814; Lewis 1837.

11. AGHERN, Aghern; pre-1841/*c.* 1887.

With the remnants of an old Desmond castle attached, the house was probably initiated by the Gifford family; a porter's lodge was added across the road from the gates. In 1805 the property was acquired by Spotswood Bowles (1784–1864) of the Mount Prospect, Curraglass [*q.v.*], family, whose great-nephew of the same name (b. 1854), after inheriting in 1886, created the surviving entrance and replacement gate lodge at the foot of a beech-lined avenue.

Two brash and monumental cut-stone chamfered carriage pillars display raised vermiculated panels and deeply friezed cappings with apologetic ball finials. To one side is a free-standing pedestrian archway with ornamental bargeboarded gables, balanced to the other side by a single-storey standard lodge in rubble facing with punched ashlar quoins and polychromatic stone voussoirs to flat-arched openings, the gable one of which, with its tripartite sash window, escaped modernisation. Blind to the road, its carved soffit brackets project from a singular ornamental frieze with continuous bracket trim. The steeply pitched pyramidal roof rises to a replacement for its chimney-stack—an apt stable-like louvred ventilator, the prelude to what is now Aghern House Stud.

LGI (1904); Pike and Hodges 1911; Hajba 2002.

12. AGHINAGH RECTORY, Macroom; *c.* 1835; architect possibly J. Pain.

A quintessential Anglican glebe house built in 1814, to which a gate lodge was not added until later. It is a typically formal single-storey standard affair, with the charming additions of label mouldings and diagonally set brick chimney-stacks in the newfangled Tudor style. In whitewashed harled walls are pretty bipartite pointed-arched casement windows below the oversailing eaves of the shallow-pitched roof, which is peculiarly hipped to the road but gabled to the park. Occupied and immaculately maintained. Quite conceivably a design of James Pain, who was architect to the Board of First Fruits in Munster at that time, working on behalf of Revd S. Gerrard Fairthough, rector.

Lewis 1837; IAA.

AGRICULTURAL INSTITUTE (see MUNSTER MODEL FARM)

13. AHANESK, Ballynacorra (2).
William Oliver Jackson (1806–81) seems to have acquired Ahanesk Lodge as younger son of W.H.R. Jackson of Castleview, Glanmire [*q.v.*], around the time of his father's death in 1851, improving the property with the addition of two gatekeepers' lodges.

East gate; pre-1934; *demolished.*

West gate; *c.* 1850.
Outside its gates is a plain single-storey standard cottage with a pyramidal roof and diagonally set chimney-stack. Derelict.

Griffith 1853–63; *LG* (1894).

14. AHERLA, Farran; *c.* 1810.
Here are the sad remains of a single-storey hip-roofed lodge in harled rubble finish, with a single-bay elevation to the avenue comprised of an opening in a pointed-arched recess. A property in the early nineteenth century of the Barter family.

15. ALDWORTH, Mallow; pre-1841.
The ruins of a standard single-storey hip-roofed cottage of indeterminate age lie at the gates to a large late eighteenth-century house occupied by a succession of owners and tenants between the mid-eighteenth and nineteenth centuries—identified as the Bolster, Foott, Lombard and Hunt families.

Hajba 2002.

18. Altamira, Liscarroll.

Humphreys

16. ALDWORTH LODGE, Mallow; pre-1841; *demolished.*
A seat associated from the late eighteenth century with the Bolster family.

17. ALLOWDALE, Banteer; pre-1841; *demolished.*
An estate of the Webb family, whose big house is a ruin and its gate lodge opposite the gates removed.

18. ALTAMIRA, Liscarroll; *c.* 1825; architect not known.
In 1822 the Whiteboys attacked and burnt the mansion of William Purcell (d. 1837). His response was to restore it and, one can suppose, he took the opportunity to improve security with the addition of a gate lodge to the demesne. While his house remained plain, all architectural daring was invested in this fine little building opposite its entrance. Single-storey standard in an ashlar finish, with wide bipartite casement windows below rectangular recessed panels as relief under tall clipped eaves of a shallow pyramidal roof rising to the central chimney-stack. Central is a sophisticated Classical porch with a pair of Doric columns *in antis* in support of a pediment, the tympanum of which contains the finely chiselled Purcell bearings of four boars' heads and the family motto: AUT VINCAM AUT PERIBO ('Either conquer or suffer'). Sadly, this important structure lies neglected and in an advanced state of dereliction, though not beyond saving.

LGI (1904); Hajba 2002.

19. ALTAMOUNT, Millstreet; pre-1842; *demolished.*
A residence in the early nineteenth century of Revd John Charles Mongan.

20. ALTAVILLA, Douglas; pre-1841; *demolished.*
Listed as the residence in 1837 of J. Woodrooffe MD, practising from South Mall in Cork city, it was by 1870 renamed 'Norwood'.

Lewis 1837; Slater 1870.

21. ANNAKISHA, Doneraile (2).
Both lodges, in place by 1841, one opposite its gates, had been demolished by 1937. A seat of the Nagle family, the house has likewise perished.

22. ANNEBROOK, Cobh; pre-1841; *demolished.*
The seat in 1814 and 1837 of Patrick Ronayne.

Leet 1814; Lewis 1837.

23. ANNE MOUNT, Carrigtohill; pre-1841; *demolished.*
A late eighteenth-century house built by Sir Riggs Falkiner (d. 1797), presumably named after his second wife, was dramatically developed into an Italianate pile around 1883 by John Murphy. In the intervening years it was home to Revd Charles M. Coghlan and Nicholas Marshall Cummins. The house was destroyed by fire in 1948, its lodge lost not long later.

Townsend 1815; Griffith 1853–63; Pike and Hodges 1911; *BPB* (1929); Bence-Jones 1988.

24. ANNESGROVE, Castletownroche (3).
On his father's death in 1849, Richard Grove-Annesley (1815–92) inherited the demesne,

24. Annesgrove, Castletownroche.

previously known as Ballyhemmick, complete with three lodged entrance gates, at least one of which he promptly replaced to a notable design by the celebrated and short-lived Benjamin Woodward.

North gate; 1853; architect Benjamin Woodward.

A Romantic Castellated composition in uncoursed rubble stone, essentially a one-up/one-down miniature square keep, its upper room reached via a spiral stair contained in an octagonal turret, counterbalanced by a prominent chimney-stack which rises to break the crenellated parapet. The façades are enlivened by a

pointed-arched doorway, single, bi- and tripartite Tudor Gothic windows with immaculately carved foiled heads containing leaded lights and, to the leading front, a finely chiselled plaque containing the family's quartered shield. Alongside is the great pointed carriage archway with hood moulding and foliated dripstones, capped by castellated ramparts whimsically accessible from the bedroom. Wooden carriage gates have a delightful carved Gothic poppy motif to the meeting rail. All admirably restored as holiday accommodation by the Irish Landmark Trust. There is an earlier version of this design by Deane and Woodward at Dromore Castle, Co. Kerry [*q.v.*].

Middle gate; *c.* 1815.

Dating from the time of Lt.-Gen. Arthur Grove-Annesley (1774–1849) is this plain single-storey roughcast cottage, two-bay by two below a hipped roof with oversailing eaves and later unsightly flat-roofed additions. Occupied.

South gate; pre-1841/*c.* 1850; architects possibly Deane and Woodward.

A sturdy, square, pretty single-storey lodge with oversailing eaves to its pyramidal roof

rising to the central chimney-stack. Two-bay by one with bipartite label-moulded windows, there is much delightful Gothic detailing in the highly decorative frieze and exquisite ornament to the reveals and doors of the entrance vestibule. It is rare for a porter's lodge to exhibit such internal attention to detail, perhaps further evidence of the work of Benjamin Woodward. A replacement for an earlier lodge on the site. Entrance screen of ogee quadrants with charming and unique draped upper rail to its iron screen.

BPB (1929); Bence-Jones 1988; Humphreys 1979; Williams 1994; O'Dwyer 1997b.

25. ANNGROVE, Carrigtohill; *c.* 1825.

A long, low, rendered single-storey cottage, its five bays comprised of one tripartite and three bipartite casement windows below a roof with hipped gables surmounted by three chimney-stacks, not quite symmetrically positioned. Occupied. Opposite the entrance to a seat in 1814 and 1853 of Francis Wise.

Leet 1814; Griffith 1853–63.

26. ARAGLIN LODGE; pre-1841.

Charles Frederick Anderson designed a pretty fishing lodge here in the 1830s for Edward King, Viscount Kingsborough (1795–1837), who was not to live long to enjoy it and, predeceasing his father by two years, failed to succeed him as earl of Kingston at Mitchellstown Castle [*q.v.*]. There is nothing of Anderson at the gate, its lodge being a derelict and modest gabled cottage with a corrugated-iron roof.

Power 2000; *IAR* (2002).

27. ARBUTUS LODGE, Cork [N]; pre-1841; *demolished.*
A villa in 1852 of Randall Howe, the lodge to which had gone by 1902.

Griffith 1853–63.

ARDCAEIN (see ST ANNE'S HILL)

ARDCAIRN (see ROSE HILL, Ballintemple)

28. ARDFALLEN, Douglas; *c.* 1860.
A small single-storey standard lodge with a pyramidal roof over rendered walls with plain opening surrounds and Irish pilaster quoins. Occupied. Part of the redevelopment of 'Ballinlough Cottage' when the place was acquired in 1859 by William Hoare before it quickly passed to the Lunhams.

ARDFOILE (see CLIFTON)

29. ARDMANAGH, Skull; pre-1842; *demolished.*
A seat in 1814 of Richard N. Somerville, which by 1837 was occupied by Major John Wynne.

Leet 1814; Lewis 1837.

30. ARDMANNING, Cork [S]; pre-1841; *demolished.*
A property in 1837 of W.D. White.

Lewis 1837.

ARDNACARRIG (see PARK VIEW)

31. ARDNAGASHEL, Glengarriff; pre-1842; *demolished.*

Surviving is a large carriage archway with a pointed head and castellated parapet in a pleasant slate stone. Perhaps of *c.* 1810 and, if so, it and its lodge may have been built for Arthur Hutchins (1770–1838), who succeeded his father in 1787. The gate porter in 1852 was Cornelius Lyons.

Griffith 1853–63; Everett 2001.

32. ARDNAGEEHA, Rathmore; *c.* 1840.
A tiny single-storey standard lodge with a hipped roof above rendered rubble walls with square windows. Derelict and overgrown. Presumably contemporary with the big house, built in 1837 by Daniel McCartie (1785–1849).

Hajba 2002.

ARDNALEE (see CARROLINA)

ARDNALEE (see PROSPECT HILL, Ballincollig)

33. ARDNAVILLING, Cloyne; *c.* 1860.

A lofty 1½-storey gabled gatehouse in a harled finish contrasting boldly with toothed dressings and quoins and lintels expressed. The irregular three-bay front is comprised of a two-bay gabled breakfront containing the doorway to the left-hand side, now missing its gabled canopy, below paired attic windows, repeated on the side gable. Mildly ornamental perforated foiled bargeboards and distinctive latticed windows almost

achieve a Picturesque effect. Nearby are magnificent cast-iron concave Gothic arcaded railed quadrants contained by four chamfered stone pillars with layered cappings. All apparently, with the big house, part of a development around 1860 for John Litton.

Williams 1994.

34. ARDOGEENA, Durrus; pre-1842; *demolished.*
An estate in 1837 of Richard Tomson Evanson.

Lewis 1837.

35. ARDRUM, Blarney (5).
The fate of this once-grand estate was sealed in 1846 by the marriage of its owner, Sir George Conway Colthurst, 5th baronet (1824–78), to the heiress of the Jefferyes estate, when it was abandoned in favour of her inheritance of Blarney Castle [*q.v.*]. His large Georgian mansion was eventually demolished, and of its set of porters' lodges, in place by 1841, already in 1852 only three

were identified by the valuation, manned by Thomas Russell, David Burns and Catherine Walsh. Today only that at the Cloghroe gate on the old north-western approach survives, remarkably occupied and in good heart.

Generous in size, single-storey standard but not quite symmetrical below a steep hipped roof, its roughcast walls contain segmentally arched windows on each side of a wide doorway, all openings having smooth banded surrounds but with inappropriate replacement inserts. Dating from around 1820 during the time of the 4th baronet, Sir Nicholas Conway Colthurst (1789–1829).

Griffith 1853–63; *BPB* (1929); Bence-Jones 1988.

36. ARLISTOWN, Ballymartle; pre-1934; *demolished.*
A lost lodge, built after 1841 for the Lane family.

ASHBOURNE (see TOUREEN LODGE)

37. ASHFIELD, Fermoy; pre-1841; *demolished.*
John William Anderson of the Fermoy House [*q.v.*] family married in 1823, perhaps the date of building the house and its gatekeeper's lodge.

Pigot 1824; Hajba 2002.

38. ASHGROVE, Cork [S]; pre-1842; *demolished.*
A seat in the late eighteenth century of the Williams family which by the mid-nineteenth century was home to Michael Bucke. Its lodge had been removed by 1934.

Taylor and Skinner 1778; 1783; Griffith 1853–63; *LGI* (1904).

39. ASHGROVE, Great Island (3).
A country property well furnished with estate buildings, at the heart of which is the big plain house of *c.* 1800 built for Councillor Richard Frankland to designs of Abraham Hargrave, once served by three lodged entrances.

North gate; *c.* 1810.
On the main approach, the very fine late Georgian tripartite gateway, comprising four ashlar pillars with scroll-topped gate stops and moulded cornices, is accompanied by a fascinating variety of structures. Within, where the porter's lodge should be, is the Georgian Gothic 'coach-house' with an antique miniature keep alongside. Without is the single-storey lodge, much altered and added to down the years to not quite obscure its original rustic Gothic cloak with what

remains of lancet glazing in whitewashed roughcast walls below a hipped roof with simple clipped eaves. Occupied.

South gate; pre-1841; *demolished.*

East gate; *c.* 1820.

Now a commodious residence in a pleasant exposed rubble finish is what was surely a pair of semi-detached cottages, 1½-storey below a hipped roof. The road front displays a two-bay pedimented breakfront, the tympanum of which contains an attic window; flanking are what would originally have been separate doorways. To the meeting of ridges is a plain two-flue brick chimney-stack—all quaint were it not for the plastic windows.

Townsend 1815; Bence-Jones 1988.

40. ASHGROVE, Macroom; pre-1842; *demolished.*

The residence in 1814 and 1852 of Richard Ashe lay in ruins and lodgeless by 1939.

Leet 1814; Griffith 1853–63.

ASHTON COURT (see BELLEVUE, Youghal)

41. ASHTON GROVE, Glanmire; pre-1841; *demolished.*

A property in 1853 of Thomas J. Cleary, owner of the nearby corn mill.

Griffith 1853–63.

42. ASHTON, Cork [S]; pre-1841; *demolished.*

The seat in 1814 and 1837 of John Cotter.

Leet 1814; Lewis 1837.

43. ASHTON LAWN, Ballintemple; *c.* 1880.

In a mellow orange brick with black relieving bands and a stone plinth is this single-storey lodge with asymmetrical front façade; gabled, with corbelled brick eaves brackets and earthenware ridges with occasional sawtooth cresting. Occupied. A property that originally comprised two pairs of semi-detached villas.

44. ASSOLAS, Kanturk; *c.* 1840.

A delightful group of buildings created by a succession of families, none of whom felt the need for a presence at the gates until the arrival in 1831 of Sir William Wrixon-Becher, 1st baronet (1780–1850), of Ballygiblin [*q.v.*]. Like the big house, his lodge is luxuriantly creeper-clad, disguising the coursed rubble stone facings of a 1½-storey three-bay structure with gablets and a chimney-stack to each of its main gables. Occupied, with its avenue removed.

Hajba 2002.

45. ATKINVILLE, Donnybrook; pre-1842/*c.* 1845.

The early lodge to a seat of the Atkin family, located distant from its entrance, was replaced by a successor next to the gate. The new owner was Thomas Clarke, whose impressive gatescreen has the new name of the place, 'Summerlea', inscribed over each lintel of a pair of postern arches in cut stone which acted as supports to the carriage gates, all framed by plain ogee quadrant walls. The scene is now run-down, with the shifting of one archway to permit passage of modern farm machinery, and overseen by the sadly dilapidated lodge. Plain single-storey standard in a whitewashed harled finish with a chimney-stack to its road gable. A pair of square casement windows flank a doorway with restricted headroom.

Lewis 1837; Griffith 1853–63.

46. AUDLEY, Cork [N]; *c.* 1860; *demolished.*

A property in an 1863 valuation shown to have been greatly improved by Charles Cotton to include the addition of a gate lodge. It was a modest single-storey standard, rendered, gabled cottage. On its footprint is a convincing 1½-storey standard Gothic 21st-century replacement with pointed-arched openings. The eminent Cork architect William Henry Hill made this his home from around 1880 until his death in 1911.

AVONCORE (see MILLVIEW)

AVONDHU (see BALLYELLIS)

47. AVONMORE, Fermoy; *c.* 1875.

A mid-Victorian development of villa and porter's lodge for Roderick O'Flanagan, the latter being a single-storey standard affair with a steeply hipped roof with decorative earthenware cresting, hip-knobs and carved soffit brackets. Square windows with Tudor label mouldings in rendered walls flank a doorway with round-arched fanlight below a gabled canopy carried on flimsy replacement wooden brackets, part of modernisation which saw the loss of its chimney-stack. Crude entrance pillars with roughcast to shaft panels and the tympana of pedimented cappings.

Hajba 2002.

48. BALLEA CASTLE, Carrigaline; pre-1842; *demolished.*

A charming converted seventeenth-century tower-house of the Hodder family with a modern bungalow at its gate.

49. BALLINABOY, Ballinhassig; *c.* 1835.

A standard single-storey hip-roofed cottage, with carved soffit brackets above bipartite one-over-one sash windows in roughcast walls on each side of a hideous projecting flat-roofed hall. Occupied. Miniature ogee quadrant walls and pillars with moulded panels. All to a house in 1837 of John Molony described then as 'a handsome modern mansion'.

Lewis 1837.

50. BALLINAMOTE, Cork [N]; pre-1841; *demolished.*

Latterly renamed 'Tracton Park', this was a seat in 1837 of J. Chatterton.

Lewis 1837.

51. BALLINCOLLIG ARTILLERY BARRACKS, Ballincollig; *c.* 1820.

The Ballincollig Gunpowder Mills, established in 1794, were purchased in 1805 by the Board of Ordnance and the barracks built as protection against the Napoleonic threat. By 1837 Samuel Lewis found that the barracks formed 'an extensive quadrangular pile of buildings, having in the eastern range the officers' apartments, and on the western side an hospital and a neat church, built in 1814. The buildings contain accommodation for 18 officers and 242 non-commissioned officers and privates, and are adapted to receive eight field batteries.' Strangely, of the three entrances to the site both 'West Gate' and 'Main Gate', with its pair of large limestone carriage pillars, remained lodgeless, while the sole permanent presence on the road boundary was at 'East Gate', so called. This survives in the shape of a single-storey standard lodge below a pyramidal roof, lying derelict and blocked up behind an extensive gatescreen of six pillars containing a pair of carriage openings and two segmentally arched postilion gates, the whole flanked by wide concave quadrant walls pierced with defensive gun-slits.

Lewis 1837; Heritage Centre pamphlet.

BALLINCOLLIG ORDNANCE SUPERINTENDENT'S HOUSE (see ORIEL)

52. BALLINCURRIG COTTAGE, Douglas; pre-1841; *demolished.*

A seat in 1837 of William C. Logan.

Lewis 1837.

53. BALLINCURRIG, Douglas; *c.* 1900.

An estate of the Coppinger family, at the gate to which is a plain two-storey brick gabled gatehouse.

54. BALLINDEASIG, Nohaval; pre-1841; *demolished.*

A seat in the nineteenth century of the Kenefic family.

55. BALLINDERRIG, Little Island; *c.* 1835.

A modest single-storey standard three-bay roughly harled cottage with a chimney-stack to each gable. Derelict. A 133-acre holding in 1852 of Jane Cantillon.

Griffith 1853–63.

56. BALLINDEENISK, Watergrasshill; 1912.
Until the mid-nineteenth century the property was served by a modest farmhouse occupied by Catherine Keefe, which was then transformed by the Fell family, who erected the new house as part of an enclosed yard complex. The property was further expanded at the turn of the twentieth century by Robert Gibbons Fell, who added the lodge whose first occupant was Thomas Hoolihan. It is an ample single-storey gabled structure, with a five-bay symmetrical front of two-over-two sash windows flanking the projecting side-entry gabled hall. Of rubble construction, rendered to sides and rear, its red earthenware tiled ridge broken by a single off-centre red-brick chimney-stack with sawtoothed corbelling.
Griffith 1853–63.

57. BALLINDINIS, Castlemartyr; pre-1842; *demolished.*
A property of sufficient status to warrant a pair of lodges at its gate, which on the 1935 OS map are shown reduced to shells. Home to the Garde family, Thomas in 1814 and Charles by 1824.
Leet 1814; Pigot 1824.

58. BALLINDINISK, Belgooly; pre-1841/*c.* 1860.
Until 1853 there was here a modest house and gate lodge of Benjamin Jeffers on a farm of 256 acres. By 1856 it had been acquired by John Thomas Cramer (1820–73) of Rathmore [*q.v.*], who transformed the property, building a new house, to be known as 'Cramer's Court', and rerouting its approach to the south, at the entrance to which he added a replacement porter's lodge. This has been latterly extensively reworked to appear as a twentieth-century 1½-storey bungalow, but retains some original detailing in Tudor-style label mouldings to windows and its single-storey gabled hall projection.
LGI (1904).

BALLINGLANNA (see GLENVILLE)

59. BALLINKEEN, Millstreet; pre-1936; *demolished.*
Both the house and its lodge, built after 1841, on an estate of the Williams family have been removed.

60. BALLINPHELLIS, Inishannon; pre-1841; *demolished.*
A property in 1837 of W. Barter Esq., the porter's lodge to which had gone by 1940.
Lewis 1837.

61. BALLINTEMPLE BRICKWORKS, Ballintemple; pre-1841; *demolished.*
A concern in the mid-nineteenth century of Jeremiah Foley, brick and tile dealer in the city.
Slater 1846; Griffith 1853–63.

62. BALLINTERRY, Rathcormack; pre-1841; *demolished.*
An estate that incorporated an early castle and house of *c.* 1710, which passed from the earls of Barrymore to the Ross family and from 1821 to 1862 was home to Archdeacon 'Black Billy' Ryder.
Bence-Jones 1988.

63. BALLINTOBER, Ballinhassig (2).

The once-proud and antique demesne of the Meade family, to which in 1841 both lodges were in place, one opposite the entrance to the home farm, while at the main gate remains a magnificent pair of lofty carriage pillars in V-jointed rusticated masonry with scroll-topped gate stops, plain friezes and oversailing moulded-corniced cappings which used to carry fluted urns, as depicted in an old print of 1650 at the head of an approach axial with the house, whence they have been repositioned. At the western entrance there survives an equally monumental pair of carriage pillars with pilastered faces, the likes of which are also to be seen at the approach to Mitchellsfort [*q.v.*] and another Meade property of Ballymartle [*q.v.*] nearby. Neither lodge nor house has proved as durable.
ffolliott 1958; 1970; Bence-Jones 1988.

64. BALLINTUBBRID, Midleton; *c.* 1845.
Sited forward of its gates is this much-altered and extended single-storey hip-roofed gatekeeper's lodge in a rendered finish, with a shallow canted bay below an eaves line decorated with continuous scalloped fascia board. Although not shown on the 1841 OS map, Griffith in 1853 values a house, offices, gate lodge and 180 acres of Edward Heard (1791–1861), who succeeded to the estate on the death of his father in 1821.
Griffith 1853–63; *LGI* (1904).

65. BALLINTUBBRID LODGE, Midleton; *c.* 1845; *demolished.*
A lodge built between 1841 and 1853 for Henry Overend.
Griffith 1853–63.

66. BALLINURE, Blackrock; pre-1841; *demolished.*
A seat in 1837 of W. Crofts, subsequently of the Perrier family.
Lewis 1837.

67. BALLINWILLIN COTTAGE, Mitchelstown; *c.* 1840.
In exposed coursed rubble masonry with brick dressings to openings is what appears to be a standard single-storey lodge below a shallow hipped roof but in fact is a gatehouse disguised, with a basement storey. Re-roofed but unoccupied. In 1837 'the property of the Earl of Kingston, and occasionally the residence of his lordship's agent', then Denis O'Brien. A property said to have been built *c.* 1777 for the agriculturalist Arthur Young and latterly called 'Ballywillin House'.
Lewis 1837; Hajba 2002.

68. BALLINVONARE, Doneraile; *c.* 1825.
Opposite the gates, its harled walls in a pretty sepia wash, is a terrace of gabled estate workers' cottages, presumably built by the then proprietor of the estate, John Harold-Barry.
LGI (1904).

69. BALLYADAM, Midleton; *c.* 1850.
A standard gabled lodge in chiselled random masonry below scalloped fascias and bargeboards to a roof crowned with a brick chimney-stack. Derelict. A house in 1853 of Henry Barry (d. 1868), eleventh son of William Barry of Rockville.
LGI (1904).

70. BALLYANNAN, Midleton; pre-1841; *demolished.*
In 1750 Smith recorded a deer-park of Viscount Midleton, which in the early nineteenth century was occupied by the Adams family before Fraser in 1838 found that 'the fragments of some ruined gate piers and a few scathed Beech trees point out where, not very many years ago, stood Ballyanan'. By 1853 Viscount Midleton's gate lodge lay empty.
Smith 1893; Leet 1814; Lewis 1837; Fraser 1838; Griffith 1853–63.

71. BALLYBANE, Shanagarry; *c.* 1810.
Alongside and forward of its entrance is a simple standard single-storey gabled gatekeeper's lodge, harled and whitewashed. Extended by a bay to the right-hand side and 'improved' with replacement concrete roof tiles and plastic windows. Occupied. A seat in the early nineteenth century of the Gaggin family.
Pigot 1824; Lewis 1837.

72. BALLYBRACK, Douglas; pre-1902; *demolished.*
A lodge built after 1841 on a property that passed from the Heards to the Lane family around that time.

73. BALLYBRICKEN, Ringaskiddy; pre-1841; *demolished.*

A once-proud estate of the Conner family, with its fine eighteenth-century house now overrun by a huge industrial complex but in 1835 'a pretty situation and much wooded'. The gate lodge in 1853 was home to William Bolster, porter to Daniel Conner.

Heaney 1999; Griffith 1853–63.

74. BALLYBUTLER, Churchtown; pre-1841; *demolished.*
A property in the early nineteenth century of the Leahy family alternatively known as 'Butlerstown'.

75. BALLYCLOGH RECTORY, Ballyclogh; pre-1841; *demolished.*
A glebe house built in 1824 by Revd John Chester, its lodge possibly contemporary. Now a private house.

Lewis 1837; Hajba 2002.

76. BALLYCLOGH, Glanworth (2).
The property of the Barry family has been devastated, with the loss of its 'handsome mansion in the Elizabethan style' and the demolition of both of its lodges, which dated from before 1841.

Lewis 1837; Bence-Jones 1988.

BALLYCLOUGH (see BALLYGLASS)

77. BALLYCRENANE, Mogeely; *c.* 1855.
A plain 1½-storey lodge, gabled with high eaves and the remains of continuous bracket bargeboards and fascias over roughcast walls with smooth banded surrounds to openings. Derelict. Two older, low, V-jointed rusticated entrance pillars nearby. An old seat of the Tyntes, from whom it passed to the Wallis family before the porter's lodge was added by James Ellis.

Smith 1893; Griffith 1853–63.

78. BALLYDELOHER RECTORY, Riverstown; 1891.
A plain roughcast hip-roofed lodge with high eaves over the two-window-bay avenue front and a lower hip-roofed hall projection from the short road elevation. Occupied. Added during the incumbency of Revd Charles Westropp Roberts.

BALLYDERRIF (see GARRANE MILL)

79. BALLYEDEKIN, Castlemartyr; pre-1842; *demolished.*
The residence in 1824 and 1837 of Capt. John Leech.

Leet 1814; Lewis 1837.

80. BALLYEDMOND, Midleton (6).
The former splendid property of the Courtenay family, now missing its fine mansion but remarkably retaining most of its gatekeepers' lodges, all of which were built within a twenty-year period of improvements by George Courtenay (1795–1837) and his father Robert, whom he predeceased.

'Ballyrichard' gate; *c.* 1840.
A standard single-storey lodge with very lofty eaves to the hipped roof, oversailing a later flat-roofed hall projection. Occupied and located at the south-western extreme of the old estate.

Curragh South gate; *c.* 1830.

Likewise remote from the demesne proper is this fine gatehouse, in pristine condition. Two-storey standard in crisp re-rendering below a dominant shallow hipped roof with exaggerated oversailing eaves, the soffit of which displays carved modillion brackets. The symmetrical three-bay main front has at first-floor level three rectangular blind recesses as relief, but appearing as upper-storey windows above two-over-two sashes on other elevations.

Curragh North gate; pre-1841/*c.* 1845.
By the entrance to 'Pheasants Wood' on the roadside is this single-storey standard cottage with segmentally arched openings in rubble-faced walls below a steeply hipped roof with a delicate scalloped fascia. Derelict. A replacement for a longer structure on the site.

'Water Lodges' gate; *c.* 1825.

So called for their proximity to the Owenacurra River behind, on the western approach to the ancillary outbuildings is this twin pair of single-storey hip-roofed lodges, their three-window-bay façades with cast-iron latticed casements fronting the road in roughcast finish. Linked by the plainest of gatescreens, behind which shallow-pitched gabled hallways confront each other across the access, with scalloped bargeboards projecting from below main fascia boards with finely carved sawtooth pattern. The first OS map identifies only the left-hand cottage functioning as a porter's lodge.

Ballyedmond Bridge gate; *c.* 1820/*c.* 1870; architect possibly Sir Richard Morrison.
At the main entrance to the house, conspicuously sited on a right-angled bend on the road from Midleton, is a remarkable pair of lodges distantly terminating an earlier gatescreen. A tripartite gateway comprised of an inner pair of cylindrical pillars is flanked by larger square ones with recessed panels in cut stone, the whole framed by stucco-effect convex quadrant walls stopped by further

drum pillars. This is all of a familiar pattern much purveyed by architect Richard Morrison. It is doubtless significant that in 1814 brother and sister George and Eliza Mary Courteney married sister and brother Caroline Augusta and John Smith-Barry, for the latter of whom the architect was working at Fota [*q.v.*]. The extraordinary, and later, gate lodges replaced an earlier pair but still show the posthumous influence of Morrison, who had pedalled just such a pattern and built throughout the country a design which he in turn had borrowed from Sir John Soane's *Sketches in architecture* (1793) [**Fig. 5**, p. 6]. Thrusting forward of the gatescreen, these lofty lodges display in their short fronts a wide, once-tripartite window in heavily reticulated surrounds continuing as a segmental head which breaks a heavy stone string-course, relief below the high eaves of its hipped roof. Beyond, the sweep continues further in short concave wing walls stopped by tall square Classical pillars, likewise decorated with the same reticulated masonry. Admirably restored were it not for the inappropriate replacement windows and artificial 'slates'.

East gate; pre-1841; *demolished.*
Soane 1793; *LGI* (1904); *IFR*; Bence-Jones 1988.

81. BALLYELLIS, Mallow (2).
An estate of the Hare family, Viscounts Ennismore and earls of Listowel, who in the nineteenth century leased it first to Arthur Gethin Creagh, from whom it passed, through an earlier marriage, around 1840 to Kilner Brazier (d. 1874), who was responsible for the later gate lodge.
East gate; pre-1841; *demolished.*
A lodge located within the property, superseded by that on the town approach.
West gate; *c.* 1845.

An impressive Classical tripartite gateway composed of pillars with moulded recesses and corniced cappings on which are hung good cast-iron gates with palmette finials and floral motifs, the whole framed by concave quadrant walls, all very formal and in contrast to the delightful porter's lodge. Single-storey standard and gabled with plain rendered walls, it is a typical Irish hybrid with its traditional pilaster quoins nicely highlighted, Classical margined sash windows and exceptionally pretty Picturesque perforated bargeboards to main gables, extending as fascia boards along the main front before rising up the central gablet to emphasise a double-leaved entrance doorway below. Well tended and extended sensitively to the rear. The big house was demolished in 1977, by then having been renamed 'Coláiste De La Salle' and latterly 'Avondhu'.
Lewis 1837; Fraser 1838; O'Flanagan 1975; *LGI* (1904).

82. BALLYGAGGIN, Cork [S]; pre-1841; *demolished.*
A property in 1852 of Edmond Murphy, the gate lodge of which appears later to have been shared at a communal gate to the Munster Model Farm [*q.v.*].
Griffith 1853–63.

85. Ballygiblin, Cecilstown.

83. BALLYGARRETT, Mallow; pre-1841; *demolished.*
A residence in the late eighteenth–early nineteenth century of the Kell family. Both their house and its lodge have gone, the latter removed by 1935.
Hajba 2002.

84. BALLYGARVAN, Carrigaline; pre-1842; *demolished.*
The estate in 1837 of Joseph Coghlan.
Lewis 1837.

85. BALLYGIBLIN, Cecilstown; *c.* 1840.
William Wrixon-Becher (1780–1850) was created a baronet in 1831 and engaged William Vitruvius Morrison to design him a new residence appropriate to his new standing, a mansion in the Tudor Revival style favoured by the young architect.
By the gate is a relatively plain, gabled 1½-storey cottage with a single-storey half-hip-roofed hallway, all so altered as to preclude any attribution to Morrison. Occupied. Nearby is an impressive ashlar entrance archway, its carriage opening round-arched below an entablature carried on Doric pilasters. To each side are like-headed postern gates with moulded architraves in contrasting rubble wing walls. Conceivably built by Wrixon-Becher in 1819 to welcome home his new bride, the actress Elizabeth O'Neill.
Pike and Hodges 1911; *BPB* (1929); McParland *et al.* 1989.

86. BALLYGLASS, Ballyduff; pre-1841; *demolished.*
Also known as Ballyclough, in 1837 a property of Edward Creed, its gate lodge situated opposite the gate of its north-western approach.
Lewis 1837.

87. BALLYGRADY, Ballygrady; pre-1841; *demolished.*
In 1837 this was 'the neat cottage residence of J. Purcell, Esq.', which three years later was leased to Daniel Watson; the first OS map shows it in 1841 to have been renamed 'Fortwilliam'. By 1903 its gate lodge had been removed.
Lewis 1837; Hajba 2002.

88. BALLYHUBBO, Charleville; *c.* 1880.
An estate in the early nineteenth century of the Roches, later passing to the Daly family, of whom John R. Daly probably added the porter's lodge. Mysteriously, Michael Fitzgerald of neighbouring Fortlands House [*q.v.*] in 1907 engaged Limerick architect Brian E.F. Sheehy to invite tenders for alterations and additions to Ballyhubbo, which may account for the early twentieth-century windows in the lodge, with their upper small-paned, bottom-hung lights. Otherwise single-storey and hip-roofed on an L-plan, a like-roofed hallway projecting from the end elevation, its walls are finished in stucco effect and the ridges highlighted with red earthenware canted tiles with trefoil perforations, stopped by scrolled hip-knobs.
IB (20 April 1907); Hajba 2002.

89. BALLYMACMOY, Killavullen; pre-1841; *demolished.*
Surviving at the entrance is a very fine late Georgian gatescreen comprised of six ashlar pillars with plain friezes and cornices, descending in height from the carriage opening, the postilion gates flanked by concave quadrant walls. Presumably its lost lodge was contemporary and of an age with the big house, built for James Hennessy, of brandy fame, in 1818, the year of his marriage.
O'Flanagan 1975; Hajba 2002.

90. BALLYMAGOOLY, Mallow; *c.* 1810.
Outlasting the house is what was a three-bay single-storey hip-roofed cottage with clipped eaves. Now extended in like manner by a right-hand bay to form a main front of four bipartite casement windows. Derelict. Previously named 'The Garrison', recalling its use in the Williamite Wars, it was subsequently renamed 'Chesterfield' after Richard Chester, before being acquired by the

Courtenay family of Ballyedmond [*q.v.*] through marriage to a daughter of John Nash, the lodge probably being added when the Courtenays took possession.

O'Flanagan 1975; Hajba 2002.

91. BALLYMALOE, Cloyne (2).
A delightful property, home down the centuries to a succession of diverse families before Clement John Forster was recorded here in 1824 and 1838, to be succeeded by John Litchfield, whose family settled here for the remainder of the century and beyond.

North gate; *c.* 1825.
A single-storey porter's lodge built off a square plan with rendered walls below a pyramidal roof. Single-bay to the road and having a pair of bipartite casement windows with segmental heads as the park elevation; it lies unoccupied.

South gate; pre-1841; *demolished.*

Pigot 1824; Fraser 1838; Slater 1846; Bence-Jones 1988.

92. BALLYMARTLE, Ballymartle; *c.* 1800.

ffolliott

A dear little single-storey Georgian Gothic lodge, commanding the area before its gatescreen with a three-bay short front of pointed-arched openings, the simple sheeted door flanked by tiny lancet windows with a naive glazing pattern, in rendered walls below a steeply hipped roof that originally had a finish of small slates. Presumably built for Revd Richard Meade (1763–1814), either when he married in 1802 or on his succession two years earlier to the estate on the death of his uncle, Revd John Meade (1720–1800), rector of Ballymartle. The noble Classical entrance gates look to be mid-Georgian, with the lofty carriage pillars (one now missing) in ashlar with moulded plinths, corniced cappings and distinctive central frontispieces of Doric pilasters, just as at Mitchellsfort [*q.v.*] and the western entrance to Ballintober [*q.v.*]. Completing the tripartite gateway, the postern openings are flanked by secondary pillars with ball finials, the left-hand one of which is linked to the lodge by a concave quadrant wall. There is a very similar lodge to nearby Glinny House [*q.v.*]. The big house lies ruinous.

ffolliott 1958; 1971b.

93. BALLYMONEY RECTORY, Ballineen (2).
A glebe with a rectory built in 1789, by 1837 'in the centre of some extensive improvements' and having one of its two porters' lodges, in place by 1841, both opposite their gates. It now lies in ruins, survived by a tiny single-storey hip-roofed structure with a short, symmetrical three-bay elevation to its avenue, dating from around 1810. The later secondary lodge has been demolished.

Lewis 1837.

94. BALLYMORE COTTAGE LOWER, Cobh; pre-1841; *demolished.*
A property in 1837 of W. Joseph Coppinger.

Lewis 1837.

95. BALLYMORE COTTAGE UPPER, Cobh; *c.* 1840.
A nicely restored and tended single-storey gabled lodge, originally three-bay, subsequently extended by a bay to the left-hand side and with a projecting gabled hall added to the other end. Later black-and-white mock Tudor work to one gable, with a margined window below. Occupied. A seat in 1837 of R.B. Shaw of Monkstown Castle [*q.v.*].

Lewis 1837.

96. BALLYMORE, Cobh; pre-1841; *demolished.*
An estate in 1837 of Joseph H. Bennett, later of Bennett's Court [*q.v.*] nearby, when Ballymore was leased to the Hare family.

Lewis 1837.

97. BALLYMOUNTAIN, Ovens; pre-1842; *demolished.*
A lodge that had been removed by 1943 from a holding in 1837 of William Penrose.

Lewis 1837.

98. BALLYMURPHY LODGE, Aghern; pre-1841; *demolished.*
A property long associated in the nineteenth century with the Creed family, whose house lies in ruins.

Hajba 2002.

BALLYNABOOLA (see GLANMORE)

99. BALLYNACARRIGA, Kilworth (2).
Neither of the pre-1841 porters' lodges survives to this seat of the Pyne family. At the eastern gate remains an entrance screen of quarry-faced rusticated pillars and ogee railed quadrants, probably a replacement built for the Corbans, who purchased the place in the late 1850s. Opposite is a two-storey house of *c.* 1860.

Bence-Jones 1988.

100. BALLYNACORRA, Ballynacorra; pre-1841; *demolished.*
A residence in the first half of the nineteenth century of John Garde.

Leet 1814; Pigot 1824.

101. BALLYNAGAUL, Glanmire; pre-1841; *demolished.*
Subsequently renamed 'Glenmore', a property in 1853 of Daniel Foley, the lodge to which had gone by 1936.

Griffith 1853–63.

102. BALLYNAHOW, Kilworth; pre-1935; *demolished.*
A gatekeeper's lodge built after 1841 at the base of a straight beech-lined avenue, probably by William Campbell, the resident in 1853.

Griffith 1853–63; Hajba 2002.

103. BALLYNAMONA, Shanballymore; pre-1841; *demolished.*
The site of a castle in 1837 'the ancient family residence of Garret Nagle, Esq., about to be rebuilt'. This Garrett Nagle (1776–1853), who in 1790 succeeded to the estate on the death of his father of the same name, may also have commissioned a complementary porter's lodge, perhaps even to designs of Patrick Nagle, an architect (and brother?) of Cork, noted in an 1846 directory. It had been removed by 1937.

Lewis 1837; Slater 1846; *LGI* (1904).

104. BALLYNOE, Cobh; pre-1841; *demolished.*
Latterly renamed 'The Hermitage', it was home in 1837, and as late as 1876, to an Abraham Hargrave, doubtless of that family of architects.

Lewis 1837; *LOI.*

105. BALLYNONA, Dungourney (2).
An estate in the early nineteenth century of Richard Harding Wigmore, whose successor in 1853, Henry Wigmore, had John Mullins as one of his gatekeepers. Both lodges, dating from before 1842, have been demolished. Nearby is an extraordinary three-storey Gothic folly building, often mistaken for a gate lodge.

Leet 1814; Pigot 1824; Griffith 1853–63.

106. BALLYORBAN EAST, Monkstown; *c.* 1860.
At the gates to a holding in 1852 of Joseph England is a plain, gabled 1½-storey cottage.

Griffith 1853–63.

107. BALLYPHILIP, Glanmire; pre-1841/pre-1936; *demolished.*
An estate in 1837 of Samuel Adams Austen, whose family was leasing it to John Forrest by 1852, when the valuation described his gatehouse as dilapidated and unoccupied. This is shown on the first OS map as being circular in plan, subsequently replaced by a successor, likewise demolished.

Lewis 1837; Griffith 1853–63.

108. BALLYRE, Killeagh; *c.* 1830.

Sited forward of its entrance behind one of a modest pair of rubble quadrant walls is this dear little single-storey standard *cottage orné*, apparently Georgian Gothic with its pointed-arched openings, but the latticed lights probably dating it later to the advent of cast iron and thus more likely to have been built for Crofton Uniacke (1791–1864), who succeeded his father of the same name in 1831. At the gates to a fine gentry house built by the latter, it lies derelict, its double-leafed doorway flanked by a pair of lancets in limewashed harled walls below an outrageous oversail of the steeply pitched hipped roof, thatched but now disguised by a layer of corrugated iron. A sleeping beauty, its awakening defied by the attentions of passing vandals.

IFR.

109. BALLYROBERT CASTLE, Aghern; *c.* 1826.

The original castle of the Barrys and its estate were acquired in 1826 by Michael Mackay, who built a new house nearby and presumably this modest complementary porter's lodge. Single-storey standard below a hipped roof, its narrow windows in a harled front elevation forming part of a concave entrance quadrant. Derelict.

Hajba 2002.

110. BALLYVA, Clonakilty; pre-1842; *demolished.*

A seat in 1837 of Michael Galway.

Lewis 1837.

111. BALLYVALOON, Blarney; pre-1938; *demolished.*

A lodge built after 1841 on a property in 1851 of Arthur Williamson.

Griffith 1853–63.

BALLYVISTEALE (see BROOKLODGE)

112. BALLYVODOCK, Midleton; pre-1841; *demolished.*

An estate in 1824 and 1837 of Henry Wigmore, later to be found at Ballymona [*q.v.*], the lodge to which had been removed by 1934.

Pigot 1824; Lewis 1837.

113. BALLYVOLANE, Aghern; pre-1841; *demolished.*

An ancient seat of the Coppingers of Barry's Court [*q.v.*], subsequently acquired by the Pyne family.

Hajba 2002.

114. BALLYWILLIAM, Kinsale; pre-1841; *demolished.*

A seat in the early nineteenth century of Benjamin Barter, subsequently let to Henry Cole Bowen of Bowen's Court [*q.v.*].

Lewis 1837; Griffith 1853–63.

BALLYWILLIN (see BALLINVILLIN COTTAGE)

115. BALTIMORE, Baltimore; pre-1842; *demolished.*

The residence in the first half of the nineteenth century of the Freke family.

Leet 1814; Slater 1856.

116. BANTRY, Bantry (4).

Commanding one of the most idyllic of views over Bantry Bay is this mansion, mostly the creation of Richard White (1800–68), 2nd earl of Bantry, who began contemplating its transformation many years before the death of his father in 1851 when on his frequent shopping sprees to the Continent as Viscount Berehaven. Richard inherited two porters' lodges on the coast road, both of which he superseded, one having become redundant when he replaced the old, more remote stable courtyard by new buildings forming the grand forecourt to the extended house; both his new gatekeepers' lodges reflect subtle architectural reference to its giant pilasters. He is thought to have had advice in his building ventures from C.F. Anderson, whose influence is possibly seen at each entrance.

Town gate; *c.* 1845; architect possibly C.F. Anderson (*above*).

Recently admirably restored is this fine ashlar gatehouse in the form of a triumphal archway into which is integrated, above and on each side of the segmentally arched carriage gateway, porter's accommodation. Three-bay and two-storey, each bay is defined by a basic pilaster, or pier, rising through a plain frieze to carry ball finials crowning a balustrade—much as the big house. To each side of the big wooden carriage gateway are panelled doorways, with six-over-six sash windows to the upper floor. The whole is framed by cruder concave rubble quadrant walls terminating in big square ashlar pillars.

Secondary gate; *c.* 1845; architect possibly C.F. Anderson.

From the road this appears the most unprepossessing of entrances, a narrow sheeted wooden gateway flanked by a pair of plain cut-stone carriage pillars interrupting the tall rubble estate wall, pierced to the left-hand side by two windows to the porter's lodge behind. Once in, the visitor discovers secreted a relatively sophisticated single-storey standard cottage below an oversailing hipped roof, the eaves of which are supported on four cast-iron pillars. Behind this is a series of recess-panelled Corinthian pilasters framing the doorway and the bipartite margined glazed sash windows, their sills almost taken to ground level in rendered walls. In 2000 abandoned and dilapidated.

LGI (1904); *Country Life* (20 July and 3 August 1989); IAA; Howley 1993.

117. BANTRY RECTORY, Bantry; pre-1842.

A much-altered structure, transformed into a modern bungalow of four bays below a steeply hipped roof with a projecting glazed gabled porch and replacement windows.

118. BARNABROW, Cloyne; *c.* 1800.

Across the road is a charming single-storey standard Georgian Gothic cottage, with pointed-arched openings and Y-traceried glazing in rendered walls with toothed quoins below a steeply hipped roof. Occupied and contrarily located well off-centre of its entrance opposite, which is comprised of rubble pillars with lancet niches framed with ogee-walled quadrants. Probably built for Timothy Lane, who is recorded as proprietor in 1814.

Leet 1814.

119. BARRY'S COURT, Carrigtohill (2).
An ancient seat of the Barry family, who forsook it in the eighteenth century to make way for the Coppingers, from whom it passed through marriage in 1867 to a nephew, Morgan John O'Connell (1811–75).

South gate; pre-1841; *demolished.*

North gate; pre-1841/*c.* 1870.
A picturesque replacement lodge, presumably for O'Connell, with the fancy bargeboards, beloved of that age, to main gables and gablets. A three-bay 1½-storey rendered structure, symmetrically flanked by single-bay single-storey wings, its segmentally arched brick heads left exposed. Occupied, much extended and modernised, and bypassed by road realignment. In 1853 William Coppinger had Edmund Cotter as one of his gatekeepers.

Griffith 1853–63; *LGI* (1904); Bence-Jones 1988.

120. BARRY'S LODGE, Carrigtohill; pre-1841; *demolished.*
A seat in 1824 and 1837 of David Barry.

Pigot 1824; Lewis 1837.

BATHVIEW (see LAUREL HILL)

121. BAURLEIGH, Kilbrittain; *c.* 1810.
Forward of its gates and forming a stop to the left-hand concave quadrant wall is this plain single-storey standard roughcast gabled lodge with tiny windows. Derelict. In 1837 W. Moore Esq. was resident in 'Borleigh'.

Lewis 1837.

122. BEACH, Bantry; *c.* 1855.
A solid, no-nonsense entrance ensemble, gatescreen and lodge in a neat random rubble, the latter single-storey standard with square-paned tripartite casement windows on each side of a tall, double-leafed, round-arched doorway. Commendably rehabilitated, though missing a chimney-stack from its hipped roof in the process. Architect C.F. Anderson built a house here in the 1840s for J. O'Connell, presumably the Jeremiah O'Connell recorded in the valuation of ten years later. The lodge is unlikely to have formed part of his commission, he having been forced by the Famine to emigrate to the USA in 1849.

Griffith 1853–63; IAA.

123. BEAMISH AND CRAWFORD BREWERY, Cork [S]; 1902; architects Houston and Houston.

A startling addition to the Cork city streetscape was this Edwardian gatehouse designed by the brothers Alfred Charles and

John Lloyd Houston of London in an Elizabethan Revival style. Gabled and 1½-storey, it rises off an L-plan, its lower storey to the road stone-faced but brick beyond, supporting a striking attic floor in half-timber effect. Its leading gable apex contains the date of construction in a cartouche on a bed of shamrocks, over a tripartite small-paned casement window which is bracketed past the ground-floor canted bay windows. A roof catslides over the internal angle to create a hallway, while the outline is further enlivened by a half-hipped gable and a pair of towering diagonally set brick chimney-stacks.

IB (10 April 1902); Williams 1994; RIBA 1993.

124. BEARFOREST LOWER, Mallow (2).
Architect Richard Morrison in 1807 furnished his client Robert Delacour with designs for one of his Soane-inspired Classical villas, a commission which included at least one of the porters' lodges.

Principal gate; *c.* 1807; architect Richard Morrison.

Despite being ravaged at the hands of the twentieth-century 'improver', there is just sufficient surviving in its form to recall one of Morrison's temple lodges, probably much as that to Fota [*q.v.*]. On an impressive elevated site was a single-storey hip-roofed structure; its short show front probably comprised a tripartite window recessed behind a pair of columns *in antis*—doubtless Doric to reflect those to the house. The very high oversailing eaves would have accommodated a small gabled entrance hall on a side elevation with a balancing projection on the opposing front, thus forming a cruciform plan favoured by the architect and like the villa design influenced by an illustration in John Soane's *Sketches in architecture* (1793). The fine tripartite gateway is surprisingly conventional for Morrison, with its six Classical square pillars, of V-jointed rustication and moulded corniced cappings, all contained by wide rubble-built concave quadrant walls.

Secondary gate; pre-1841; *demolished.*
Perhaps another design by Morrison for Robert Delacour, upon whose death in 1846 the demesne was lost to the family.

Soane 1793; *LGI* (1958); McParland *et al.* 1989.

125. BEARFOREST UPPER, Mallow; *c.* 1820.
Both the first OS map of 1841 and the 1935 edition suggest that there was a pair of lodges incorporated in this very extensive gatescreen, but today only a single two-storey two-bay house remains to the right-hand side, roughly harled below a hipped roof, and derelict. Two adjacent access gates are flanked by wide ogee quadrants. A property in the early nineteenth century of the Seward family.

Pigot 1824; Hajba 2002.

126. BEAUMONT, Ballintemple (2).
This once-rural and proud mansion of the Beamish family on the outskirts of Cork city is no more, having been overrun by twentieth-century suburban development. Both of its pre-1841 lodges have suffered the same fate of demolition.

BEECHFIELD (see PENCIL HILL)

127. BEECH HILL, Cork [N] (2).
A property in 1837 of Michael Salmon which he later let to Col. Marcus Beresford, when there was one lodged gate adjacent to the house.

East entrance; *c.* 1840.

A single-storey standard hip-roofed lodge with plain quoin bands and Tudor label mouldings to windows. Nearby is a later gatescreen of around 1870, consisting of four pillars with moulded round-headed recessed panels and four-pedimented cappings, probably added by Maurice Murray, whose family annexed land to the west and added a lengthy new approach to the park.

West entrance; *c.* 1870; *demolished.*
This secondary lodge was probably built when the site was split up to accommodate what was to become St Raphael's Asylum [*q.v.*] next door.

Lewis 1837; Griffith 1853–63; Slater 1870; *Thom's.*

128. BEECHMOUNT, Carrigrohane; *c.* 1845.
The seat in 1853 of Revd John Cahill. Forward of its gatescreen on the road's edge is a single-storey gabled rubble-built cottage, a two-window bay to the carriageway and a

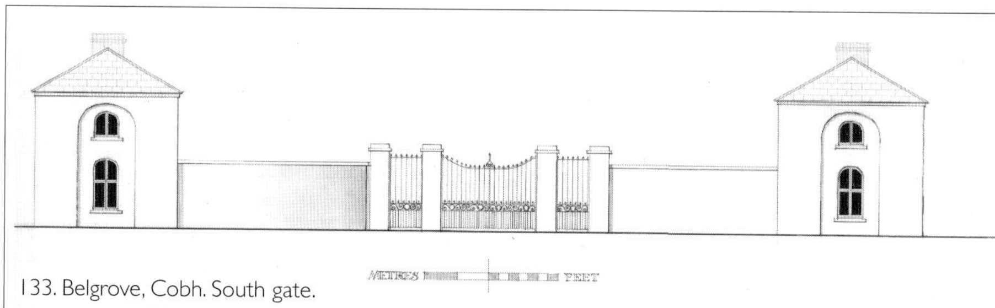

133. Belgrove, Cobh. South gate.

tall lancet light monitoring the approach below ornamental bargeboards carried beyond as fascia boards. Behind is a later two-storey gabled extension in like materials, linked by a diminutive gabled hallway with spiky hip-knob.

Griffith 1853–63.

129. BEECHMOUNT, Coachford; pre-1842; *demolished.*
The residence in 1837 and 1852 of Thomas Godfrey MD.

Lewis 1837; Griffith 1853–63.

130. BEECHMOUNT, Inishannon; pre-1841.
Said to have been built for the Payne family, who also had Upton [*q.v.*], across the road, it was occupied in 1814 by a Mrs Minton and in 1837 by John Hornibrook. Beautifully restored, which cannot be said for its unfortunate lodge, which may have originated as a single-storey standard gabled affair but has latterly suffered all manner of hideous twentieth-century accretions. Derelict.

Leet 1814; Lewis 1837.

131. BEECHMOUNT, Mallow; pre-1841; *demolished.*
A property in 1824 of Major William Russell, after whom by 1837 it had become home to Revd Sackville R. Hamilton, the local Church of Ireland rector, leasing from Thomas Lysaght, whose family later occupied it.

Pigot 1824; Lewis 1837; Griffith 1853–63.

132. BELFORT, Charleville; pre-1841; *demolished.*
A seat in the early nineteenth century of the Reeves family that from *c.* 1840 onwards was the residence of the Clancys. Its lodge had been removed by 1935.

Lewis 1837; Slater 1846.

133. BELGROVE, Cobh (3).
The old estate of John Harper, which passed through the marriage in 1749 of his daughter and co-heir Jane to William Bagwell of the Marlfield, Co. Tipperary [*q.v.*], family. The Bagwells lived here occasionally until the 1830s, from which time it was leased to a Mr and Mrs Townsend but around 1837 more permanently to Revd George Gumbleton, who effected several improvements.

Waterside gate; pre-1841; *demolished.*

South gate; *c.* 1810.
From the Bagwell era are the sleeping remnants of a once-important rustic Regency gatescreen consisting of a pair of one-up/one-down cubic gatehouses, their front doors facing one another distantly across the entrance forecourt, linked by convex walled quadrants to a modest tripartite gateway. Each structure is in harled rubble, their single-bay leading fronts of round-headed window openings set in like arched recesses below shallow-pyramidal roofs. Derelict and overgrown.

North gate; *c.* 1830.

Alongside the gate is a pair of commodious and identical five-bay symmetrical part-single-storey, part-1½-storey semi-detached gabled estate workers' cottages in a limewashed harled finish. Each has a projecting central hallway below a catslide roof with a pretty quadripartite Tudor Gothic window flanked by bipartite and single ones, taller and with the remains of Y-tracery. Abandoned.

Smith 1893; Townsend 1815; Heaney 1999; Lewis 1837; Griffith 1853–63; *LGI* (1904).

134. BELLAIRE, Cork [S]; pre-1841; *demolished.*
A seat in the early nineteenth century of the Perrier family.

Lewis 1837; Griffith 1853–63.

135. BELLEVIEW, Bandon; pre-1841; *demolished.*
A property in 1851 of James Wrinn that by 1870 had become the parochial house.

Griffith 1853–63; Slater 1870.

136. BELLEVILLE, Cork [N]; pre-1841; *demolished.*
The residence in 1837 of Daniel Murphy, whose gate lodge had gone by 1902.

Lewis 1837.

BELLEVILLE (see CLIFTON LODGE)

137. BELLE VUE, Cobh; pre-1841; *demolished.*
The residence in 1837 of Dr Crotty, RC bishop of Cloyne, part of the grounds to which around 1850 were sold off, the avenue discontinued and a replacement lodge built on the site to serve the new house, 'Charleston' [*q.v.*], to the south-east.

Lewis 1837.

138. BELLE-VUE, Cork [N]; pre-1852; *demolished.*
A lodge identified by the Griffith valuation, not apparent on any map or on site. A property in 1837 on Tivoli Road of John William Topp, secretary and treasurer of the Cork Dispensary, who by 1852 was leasing it to Denis Brennan.

Lewis 1837; Slater 1846; Griffith 1853–63.

139. BELLEVUE, Fermoy; *c.* 1830.
Fronting the road is a derelict standard gabled plain cottage, harled and with a projecting hall with a very shallow-pitched gabled roof. An estate once of the Glissan family called 'Mount Glissan', it had been sold by 1814 to Thomas Dennehy.

Leet 1814.

140. BELLEVUE, Mallow; pre-1935; *demolished.*
A property in the mid-nineteenth century of Mrs Jane Frances Hartland.

Slater 1846; Griffith 1853–63.

141. BELLEVUE, Monkstown; pre-1934; *demolished.*
A seat in 1837 and 1856 of Capt. Nicholas S. Parker which by 1870 had been acquired by James Ignatius Murphy, co-founder of a local brewery and probable builder of the entrance lodge, from which time only half of a red-brick gatescreen of *c.* 1880 survives.

Lewis 1837; Slater 1846; 1856; 1870; *LGI* (1904).

142. BELLEVUE, Youghal; pre-1842; *demolished.*
A property that had a succession of owners in the nineteenth century before the house was replaced in 1898 by the present Arts and Crafts pile that is 'Ashton Court'.

Pike and Hodges 1911.

143. BELLMOUNT, Crookstown; 1837; architect not known.
A once-exquisite and quite unique Picturesque Gothic lodge, now tragically reduced to a crumbling shell; together with the bridge over which it is approached, its babbling brook and the gentleman's villa awaiting on the hill beyond, it forms part of an idyllic and romantic scene. Apparently 1½-storey to the avenue, it in fact has a basement

143. Bellmount, Crookstown.

storey at stream level, having originated as a square plan rising to a skew-table gable to each front with spiky stone hip-knobs, one inscribed with the date of construction. Single-bay to the road, there is a rectangular oriel window at intermediate level with big diamond panes. Another oriel on sturdy brackets ornaments the avenue elevation, but this with pointed lights, above the symmetrical three-bay entrance. To the park façade are the remains of a more elaborate Tudor Gothic casement with cusped head. All in a plain rendered finish with what looks like a later 1½-storey gabled addition to the rear, it contrasts with associated rubble-built retaining outworks which extend along the river to incorporate the pretty bridge. A remarkable structure, erected for the wealthy owner of the nearby Bellmount flour mills, Thomas Herrick, preceding his later villa on the hill. A fairytale scene surely worthy of restoration.

Lewis 1837.

144. BELLVIEW COTTAGE, Cork [N]; pre-1841; *demolished.*
A property in the mid-nineteenth century of Mary Callaghan, latterly renamed 'Carrig'. Its description in the 1852 valuation as 'Gate House' and its appearance on the first OS map suggest that its accommodation spanned an entrance archway.

Griffith 1853–63.

145. BELMONT, Douglas (2).
All that survives of the pre-1841 porters' lodges and entrances is a screen to the western gate consisting of six dainty cylindrical stone posts with shallow concave quadrants. A small estate that saw a rapid succession of occupiers in the nineteenth century.

146. BELVIEW, Douglas; pre-1842; *demolished.*
A seat in 1837 of Edward Lucette, succeeded by Richard B. Porter, the gatekeeper's lodge to which had gone by 1934.

Lewis 1837; Griffith 1853–63.

147. BENNETT'S COURT, Cobh (2).
Home to the Bennetts of Ballymore, neither of whose pre-1841 gate lodges survives.

Side gate; pre-1841; *demolished.*

Shore gate; pre-1841/pre-1934; *demolished.*
The previous porter's lodge was replaced at the other side of the entrance after 1841, it too having been removed although its gatescreen remains. Of *c.* 1845, the wide, shallow-walled concave quadrants flank a pair of postilion openings, each in the form of a round-arched opening with keystone and framed by Irish pilaster rustication. Frustratingly, Bence-Jones in 1988 describes an 'Impressive gate lodge with portico', apparently lost without record. Presumably built for Joseph Henry Bennett (d. 1861), who was in residence in 1853 and earlier to be found at Ballymore [*q.v.*].

Griffith 1853–63; *LG* (1886); Bence-Jones 1988.

148. BENNETT'S GROVE, Clonakilty; pre-1841; *demolished.*
An estate in 1814 of Francis Bennett, by whom it was being leased in 1837 to Herbert Gillman. The gate lodge had gone by 1902.

Leet 1814; Lewis 1837.

149. BESBOROUGH, Blackrock; pre-1841; *demolished.*
The lodge is survived by a gatescreen of *c.* 1830 comprised of four stone drum pillars, each with a peculiar gadrooned finial of Portland stone, all linked by carriage gates and concave railed quadrants of matching spear-topped rails. A property in 1783 of the

Allen family, in 1814 of J. Spence and from 1837 of Ebenezer Pike (1806–83).

Taylor and Skinner 1778; 1783; Leet 1814; Lewis 1837; *LGI* (1904).

BETSBOROUGH (see FERN HILL, Dromahane)

150. BETTY VILLE, Kanturk; pre-1841; *demolished.*
The estate in the early 1800s of Charles Bastable, who was succeeded here by John Therry between 1824 and 1837.

Leet 1814; Pigot 1824; Lewis 1837.

151. BILBERRY, Midleton; pre-1936; *demolished.*
A lodge built after 1841 opposite the entrance to a seat in the nineteenth century of the Cardo family.

152. BIRCHHILL COTTAGE, Blarney (2).
Both pre-1841 lodges to a property in the mid-nineteenth century of John Travers have been demolished.

Griffith 1853–63.

153. BISHOPSTOWN, Cork [S]; pre-1841; *demolished.*
A seat in 1852 of John Lewis.

Griffith 1853–63.

154. BLACKROCK CASTLE, Blackrock; 1828; architects G.R. and J. Pain.

Best seen from the opposite shore of Lough Mahon, at the entrance to which it is like a sentinel, the most illustrated of Cork sights. A most picturesque of structures, erected in

1828 by Cork Corporation after a fire, off the foundations of a tower built in 1604 by Lord Deputy Mountjoy. Designed by George Richard and James Pain as a fairytale castle and occasional residence during his year of office for the lord mayor in a manner in which the brothers were well versed, having been assistants of the great John Nash.

Across the entrance courtyard is the carriage archway with Tudor head flanked by a pair of slender square turrets relieved by mock arrowloops, all crenellated, as is the porter's lodge to which it is linked by a postilion archway. In like limestone ashlar, it provides simple rectangular single-storey accommodation, with a chamfered, mullioned bipartite window to the visitor. An inscribed stone plaque gives the date of commencement as 1828 and the precise date of completion of Saturday 3 March 1829, in addition to a list of office-bearers for both years.

Lewis 1837; *PGI.*

155. BLARNEY CASTLE, Blarney (3).
The Jefferyes family built their ill-fated eighteenth-century mansion next to the legendary keep of the McCarthys of Muskerry, and before its burning in 1820 they formed the curiosity of 'Rock Close', a landscaped garden to which was dedicated its own gate lodge, since lost. In 1846 Sir George Conway Colthurst (1824–78) of Ardrum [*q.v.*] married Louisa Jane Jefferyes, heiress of the Blarney estate, and around 1874 they set about reviving the neglected property as their new home. On an alternative site, their architect John Lanyon designed them a Scots Baronial pile, much as his Belfast Castle masterpiece, and complemented it with at least one gatekeeper's lodge.

Principal gate; *c.* 1875; architect John Lanyon (*below*).
Substantial in its own right but more Picturesque English cottage than Scots Baronial in style is this 1½-storey gabled gatehouse raised off an L-plan in cut-stone random facings. Each wing has chamfered mullioned windows with relieving arches, tripartite to the lower floor and bipartite to attic rooms. In the internal corner, the main roof catslides over to form a lofty verandahed entrance porch with striking carved wooden balustraded frieze. The roof retains its enhancing canted slate bands, serrated earthenware crestings, wonderful winged-beast finials and ornamental foil and wave bargeboards, but a late nineteenth-century photograph shows the lodge to have latterly lost its finely fretted apex features and the great corbelling to its brick chimney-stack.

Secondary gate; *c.* 1875; architect possibly John Lanyon.
A single-storey solid standard composition in coursed exposed rubble, with brick relief in its two chimney-stacks and segmentally headed opening arches, toothed dressings and quoins, the central doorway flanked by a pair of sidelights.

Lawrence photograph (2970R); *BPB* (1929); Bence-Jones 1988; Williams 1994.

156. BLARNEY WOOLLEN MILLS, Blarney; pre-1841; *demolished.*
A thriving mid-nineteenth-century concern of Martin Mahony, who in 1837 employed 120 persons in spinning and dyeing woollen yarns and had in 1852 Pierce Carroll across the road from the entrance as gatekeeper.

Lewis 1837; Griffith 1853–63.

157. BLOOMFIELD, Douglas; pre-1841; *demolished.*
A property in 1814 of William Cuthbert that was occupied 23 years later by W.J. Sheehy.

Leet 1814; Lewis 1837.

158. BLOSSOM GROVE, Glanmire; *c.* 1820.
Alongside the gatescreen with plain pillars and fronting the road is a standard three-bay lodge below a steeply hipped roof with a pronounced bellcast extending sufficient to cover a minimal entrance breakfront, now a window. The whole complex now finished in white pebble-dash, the modern plastic windows contained in plain smooth surrounds. Occupied. A property in 1852 of William Casey.

Griffith 1853–63.

National Library of Ireland

159. BON SECOURS CONVENT, Cork [S]; *c.* 1890.
At the Western Road, on what was then perceived as a more salubrious approach leading to an avenue bridged over the River Lee, is this commodious, nondescript, rendered two-storey gatehouse, long and three-bay. Alongside are two tall cast-iron late Victorian carriage posts with recessed panels, roundels and ball finials. Inscribed in a side wall: 'Bon Secours Convent'. The convent building was initially completed by 1881.

160. BOWEN'S COURT, Kildorrery (5).
Elizabeth Bowen, the twentieth-century novelist, in her autobiography bemoans how she had to sell her beloved mid-eighteenth-century Bowen's Court in 1959 and the subsequent breach of trust which saw its demolition, and she wistfully describes the approaches to it from the various gates. All three entrances were lodged in 1841, the year that her grandfather, Robert Cole Bowen (1830–88), inherited the estate. After attaining his majority he carried out improvements to the property, which included replacement of two of those porters' lodges.

Lower gate; pre-1841/1873.
Replacing a predecessor further up the avenue from Farahy is this single-storey standard lodge with steeply hipped roof from which projects a gabled entrance breakfront with basic wavy bargeboards, the apex of which contains a stone inscribed 'R.C.B. 1873'. In a plain rendered finish, removed from the breakfront to reveal the brick-dressed rubble construction, part of an ill-advised modernisation that included the indignity of new plastic windows and doorway. The straight cast-iron gatescreen has contemporary loop-topped rails and ball-finialled posts and gives access to St Coleman's Church of Ireland church and its graveyard, in which are the remains of Elizabeth Bowen and her husband.

Middle gate; pre-1841/1885.
Likewise superseding an earlier porter's lodge within the property is a gabled 1½-storey six-bay symmetrical structure, its two central bays in a breakfront, roughcast in an otherwise rubble-faced finish, in the apex of which is the inscription 'R.C.B. 1885' below a shallow-pitched gable extending from the main steeply gabled roof with crude wave and foil bargeboards. Possibly having originated as a pair of semi-detached estate workers' cottages.

Upper gate; *c.* 1835.
Opposite the gates at the western avenue is this single-storey five-bay symmetrical gabled lodge, its six-over-six sash windows in harled rubble walls, the central bay in a shallow gabled entrance breakfront. Derelict and overgrown. Across the road is a very fine tripartite gateway framed by cut-stone walled quadrants contained by four square ashlar pillars, straight railed screens with four inner cast-iron posts.

LGI (1904); Bence-Jones 1988.

161. BOYLEGROVE, Inchigeelagh; pre-1842; *demolished.*
Home to the Boyle family, whose lodge had gone by 1904.

162. BRADE, Leap; pre-1842; *demolished.*
The big, plain, mid-eighteenth-century gentry house of the Jervois family was occupied by Revd E.P. Thompson by 1837, reputedly having been squandered by them.
Lewis 1837; Bence-Jones 1988.

163. BRIDE PARK, Tallow; pre-1841; *demolished.*
A house that, from its building by Revd Stephen Rolleston around 1775 until 1844, went through a succession of various owners before becoming a settled family home of the Powers.
Hajba 2002.

164. BRIDE VIEW, Ovens; *c.* 1845.
Also known by its townland name of 'Knockanemore', it was a property in 1852 of Samuel Hawkes, presumably the builder of this pleasant single-storey standard hip-roofed gatekeeper's lodge with a rubble stone finish and cusped, foiled bargeboards to its projecting gabled hallway. Occupied.
Griffith 1853–63.

165. BRIDESTOWN TOWERS, Glenville; pre-1935; *demolished.*
Until the mid-nineteenth century a seat of the Morgan family, the gate lodge to which, built after 1841, had been reduced to a shell opposite its gates by 1935.
Bence-Jones 1988.

166. BRIDGEFIELD, Castlemartyr; pre-1842.
By the Womanagh River lies the rubble shell of a lodge to a property in 1853 of Henry Connell.
Griffith 1853–63.

167. BRIDGEMOUNT, Macroom; pre-1842; *demolished.*
A seat of the Townshend family, whose porter's lodge, located well within the property, had been removed by 1940.

168. BRINNY RECTORY, Brinny; 1900.
A plain single-storey standard lodge with a pyramidal roof and one-over-one sashes in roughcast walls. Built for Revd R.F. Clarke opposite the entrance to a rectory of *c.* 1840. Derelict.
IB (1 June 1900).

169. BRITFIELDSTOWN, Nohaval (3).
An estate for a century of the Roberts family before they sold it in 1853.
East entrance; pre-1841; *demolished.*
North entrance; pre-1841; *demolished.*
West entrance; *c.* 1830.
A charming survivor is this single-storey porter's lodge built off a square plan in rubble stone facings, with a pyramidal roof rising steeply to a tiny brick chimney-stack. A two-window bay to the approach, its openings with elliptical arches. In use. Probably built by Sir Thomas Howland Roberts (1804–64), who succeeded as 3rd baronet and to the property on the death of his father in 1828. The house has gone the way of two of its lodges.
BPB (1929); Glin *et al.* 1988.

170. BROADALE, Donnybrook; pre-1842; *demolished.*
A modest holding in 1852 of Patrick Desmond, now obliterated by a modern housing estate.
Griffith 1853–63.

171. BROOKDALE, Dungourney (2).
A seat in 1837 of the Ormsby family, who by 1853 were leasing it to James Bull, one of whose gatekeepers was then Ellen Guiry. Both lodges, built before 1842, have been demolished.
Lewis 1837; Griffith 1853–63.

172. BROOKFIELD, Cork [S]; *c.* 1870.
A 1½-storey gabled structure with an irregular three-bay front to the road, its segmentally arched openings in a cream brick to reflect that of the big house. A development before 1874 of house and porter's lodge for Thomas and Francis M. Jennings.

173. BROOK LODGE, Fermoy; *c.* 1865.
A compact single-storey standard hip-roofed lodge with two-over-two sash windows on each side of a panelled door in a lugged surround. Derelict but surviving its big house, the residence before his death in 1857 of John Dennehy, who was succeeded here by his son, Major-Gen. Sir Thomas Dennehy (b. 1829).
LGI (1904).

174. BROOK LODGE, Glanmire; pre-1842; *demolished.*
A seat of the Martin family, whose lodge had gone by 1936.

175. BROOKLODGE HOUSE, Glanmire (2).
Neither of the lodges, one opposite its gates and each in place by 1841, survives. A property in the early nineteenth century of the Phair family which also went by the name of its townland, 'Ballyvisteale'.

176. BROOKPARK, Dunmanway; pre-1841; *demolished.*
In 1852 a 53-acre property of John Hamilton but recorded 38 years earlier as home to R. Cox Bowden.
Leet 1814; Griffith 1853–63.

BROOKSIDE (see THE RETREAT, Mallow)

177. BROOK VIEW, Glanmire; *c.* 1820.
A single-storey standard three-bay cottage with limewashed rendered walls below a hipped roof with clipped eaves. Occupied. A house with twelve acres in 1852 of Francis Mason.
Griffith 1853–63.

178. BROOK VILLE, Glanmire (2).
One of the lodges remains to what in the early nineteenth century was a seat of Cornelius O'Callaghan (b. 1788).
Principal entrance; *c.* 1810.

Apparently this expansive and once-impressive gatescreen was to have incorporated a pair of twin lodges, each of standard single-storey type, their symmetrical three-bay fronts to form part of it. In fact, only the right-hand one materialised, its counterpart merely forming a façade, once harled, with blind segmentally arched 'windows' on each side of a postern opening with elliptical head. These flank a good pair of late Georgian cut-stone carriage pillars with moulded corniced cappings, which are repeated to terminate the framing shallow concave quadrant walls beyond. The whole now lies run-down, with the lodge derelict. It seems to have had a later Victorian make-over, having a chimney-stack to each gable and a smooth rendered finish to contrast with the otherwise rubble walls.
Secondary entrance; pre-1841; *demolished.*
The first OS map shows a lodge to one side of the south-western access to Brook Ville, immediately opposite the gate to Brooklodge House [*q.v.*].
LGI (1958).

179. BROOMFIELD, Midleton; pre-1841.
A seat in 1837 of Daniel Humphreys, the lodge to which is now a gabled ruin engulfed in Russian vine.
Lewis 1837.

180. BROOMHILL COTTAGE, Mitchelstown; pre-1841/*c.* 1845.
Replacing a predecessor by the road is this standard single-storey hip-roofed cottage with a gabled porch. Much modernised, with plastic window intrusions and extended to the left-hand side with a return to form an L-plan. A property in 1852 of James Gearn.
Griffith 1853–63.

181. BROOMHILL, Coachford; pre-1938; *demolished.*
Previously called 'Ellen Ville', an estate in 1852 of William Tait to which the gate lodge was added after 1842.
Griffith 1853–63.

182. BROOMLEY, Tracton; pre-1842; *demolished.*
A seat in 1837 of George Daunt that lay in ruins by 1834.
Lewis 1837.

183. BROTHERS FORT, Inishannon; pre-1841/pre-1890; *demolished.*
A residence in 1837 and 1852 of William Whiting, to which both the early lodge and its larger successor on the site had gone by 1903.
Lewis 1837; Griffith 1853–63.

184. BURGES, Killeagh; pre-1842; *demolished.*
By 1935 the gatekeeper's lodge, to an estate in 1837 of William Hall, had been removed.
Lewis 1837.

185. BURREN, Timoleague; *c.* 1875.
A single-storey hip-roofed four-bay structure, with brick as segmentally arched openings and toothed dressings and quoins in an otherwise roughcast finish. Occupied and opposite its entrance to a property in 1876 of James Sealy.
LOI.

186. BURTON PARK, Churchtown; *c.* 1830; architect not known.
An ancient seat of the Percevals, earls of Egmont, which was acquired around the turn of the nineteenth century by Revd Matthew Purcell (d. 1845), rector of Churchtown and Dungourney, who improved the approach with this impressive entrance. In a Tudor Gothic castellated style, it consists of a pair of twin single-storey, single-bay, plain-parapeted boxes linked by a lofty carriage archway with Irish crenellated parapet. The whole composition, including its convex quadrant wing walls, is in a drab grey rendering relieved by Tudor archways to openings (those to the accommodation now blind, with 'Burton' and 'Park' plaques over), toothed stone quoins, dressings and voussoirs, mock cross-arrowloops to spandrels and, high on the parapet, the Purcell bearings on an embossed plaque displaying their saltire between four boars' heads and crest over in a hand couped above the wrist erect holding a sword—just as can

be seen on the lodge to their nearby property of Altamira [*q.v.*]. A mystery is why there was an identical entrance to Clonskeagh Castle on the outskirts of Dublin.
LGI (1904); Bence-Jones 1988; Dean 2016.

187. BUSHY PARK, Glenville (2).
Richard Gifford Campion was the proprietor in 1837. Both lodges, curiously attendant upon the same gate in 1841, had been demolished by 1935.
Lewis 1837.

188. BUTLERSTOWN, Courtmacsherry; pre-1842; *demolished.*
The lodge to a property in 1837 of Jonas Travers was located opposite his gates.
Lewis 1837.

189. BUTLERSTOWN, Glanmire (3).
An estate in the first half of the nineteenth century of the Martin family, who were responsible for the two earlier lodges.

South gate; pre-1841.
A ruinous single-storey standard structure below a pyramidal roof, its three-bay symmetrical front addressing the park and a two-window bay to the avenue, on the opposing end to which is attached incongruously an extension with a chimney-stack to each gable.

Middle gate; *c.* 1830.
Opposite the entrance are single-storey gabled estate workers' cottages with basic broad label mouldings to openings, one of which is identified on the first OS map as a gate lodge.

North gate; 1907.
A charming little building in the same format as an eighteenth-century porter's lodge. Single-storey standard and gabled, its roof catslides to form a central entrance canopy carried on a pair of carved bracketed posts. In a roughcast finish, the wide window openings have Tudor-style label mouldings curved centrally to convey confusing information. The lodge is first valued in 1907, when Henry Joyce was proprietor, but must have been given a facelift a decade later, as suggested by the date displayed and a monogram of his successor, a Colonel Pickford—stamping his personality on it.
NIAH.

190. BYBLOX, Doneraile; *c.* 1800.
Long associated with the family of Robert Fennell Crone since he built his stately gentry house in 1793, it is outlived by the ruins of its porter's lodge, still identifiable as having been a single-storey rubble-built structure, its three-bay principal front with doorway to the left-hand side. In rather a better state is its Georgian gatescreen, comprised of four square Classical pillars, the outer pair with urn finials, containing ogee quadrant walls, a carriage gateway and two postern openings.
Irish Ancestor (1971).

186. Burton Park, Churchtown

191. CAHERAGH RECTORY, Drimoleague; *c.* 1845.

Doing an impression of a Georgian Gothic lodge is this rubble-built gabled single-storey lodge with harled finish, displaying a lancet window to the short road front and a pair of flat-arched casements to the avenue, all containing cast-iron latticed glazing inserts. Derelict.

192. CAHERDUGGAN, Ballincurrig (2).
The sedate late Georgian villa built by Cornelius O'Callaghan (1756–1831), who came into the property through his marriage

in 1781 to Mary Davies, daughter of the previous owner, and who may also have added the two lost porters' lodges to his estate, both built by 1842. It now has been allowed to deteriorate almost beyond recall.

Pike and Hodges 1911; *LGI* (1958).

193. CAHERMONE, Midleton; *c.* 1840.
Although a seat of the Brodricks, Lords Midleton, the 4th and 5th earls being absentees, it was occupied for much of the first half of the nineteenth century by the earl's agent, Thomas Poole (1773–1854), who lived here in preference to his own estate of Mayfield [*q.v.*]. In his time was built a two-storey three-bay gabled gatehouse, much transformed in modernisation, its rubble stone fabric exposed with brick dressings to new windows. Nearby, the gatescreen of tall pillars and concave quadrants is liberally relieved by round-headed niches.

BPB (1929); ffolliott 1958.

194. CAHERMORE, Rosscarbery (2).
The residence in 1837 of Thomas Hungerford (1789–1861), which he had inherited in the year of his birth upon his father's death.

South entrance; pre-1842; *demolished.*

North entrance; pre-1842.
The shell of a single-storey rubble-built cottage, its gabled avenue front containing a single window.

LGI (1904).

195. CAIRN, Fermoy; pre-1841; *demolished.*
The Revd Richard Dane Freeman is recorded here in 1844.

Hajba 2002.

196. CAMEATRINGANE, Castletownbere; pre-1842; *demolished.*
A seat in the early 1800s of the O'Sullivan family.

197. CAREW'S WOOD, Castlemartyr; *c.* 1820.
A nicely restored single-storey standard lodge in exposed uncoursed rubble below a hipped roof. Built for Henry Boyle, 3rd Lord Shannon (1771–1842), who had succeeded to the title and estates in 1807 and whose mother lived on here before her death in 1827.

BPB (1929).

198. CAREYSTOWN, Whitegate; pre-1935; *demolished.*
A gatekeeper's lodge built after 1841 to a holding in the mid-nineteenth century of William Murray Hickson.

199. CAREY'S VILLE, Fermoy; *c.* 1830.
A plain single-storey standard lodge with harled walls and a chimney-stack to one of its gables. Derelict and sited opposite the gates to an estate in 1837 of Edward Kiely Carey, who would seem to have succeeded Peter Carey around 1824.

Pigot 1824; Lewis 1837.

CARRIG (see BELLVIEW COTTAGE)

200. CARRIG, Cobh; *c.* 1860; architect perhaps William Atkins.

Located forward of its gates is this excellent little lodge in a rather more jaunty Italianate style than its austere contemporary big house, visible at the head of a short avenue. Single-storey on an L-plan, in a smooth rendered finish with bracketed shallow-pitched oversailing bargeboards. The leading gable to the footway is two-bay of one-over-one sash windows in recesses to ground level, rising to round arches with banded surrounds from a spring-course with a blind *oeil-de-boeuf* over. Dominating the roof is a decorative chimney-stack with 'barrel' flue covers, while the site constraints dictate the positioning of an entrance porch to one end, with its gabled roof supported on a pair of chunky square Doric piers. In contrast are the two elegant drum carriage pillars with incised Greek key-patterned friezes. A development in the suburbs of the town for John C. Atkins, which hints further at an attribution to Cork architect William Atkins.

Slater 1870.

201. CARRIG PARK, Mallow; *c.* 1790.

David Franks succeeded to the estate on the death of his father in 1780 and may have been responsible for this singular Georgian Gothic lodge, now an ivy-covered shell next to a lost entrance and avenue. Rubble-built in the shape of a handball court, its monopitched roof rising to a standard three-bay symmetrical road front comprised of pointed-arched openings. There is a porter's lodge of like form to Woodview, Kilworth [*q.v.*]. To complete the scene, the big house has lain in ruins since the 1920s.

LGI (1904).

202. CARRIGABRICK, Fermoy; *c.* 1830.
Probably originating as a single-storey standard gabled lodge, subsequently extended by a bay, it has two-over-two sash windows in roughcast walls. Occupied and immaculate. A holding in 1852 of Nicholas William Roche.

Griffith 1853–63.

203. CARRIGACUNNA CASTLE, Killavullen (2).
Next to the old keep of the Nagle family is the villa built around the turn of the nineteenth century by Henry Baldwin Foott (d. 1878), who revitalised the estate and added two porters' lodges.

East entrance; *c.* 1845.
A plain single-storey lodge in rubble facings, with modern enlarged windows and a chimney-stack to each of its shallow gable ends. Occupied and extended.

West entrance; pre-1841/*c.* 1870.
Now a symmetrical five-bay single-storey hip-roofed affair, with mid-Victorian rock-faced pilaster quoins to main block and the hip-roofed hall projection. Presumably once a three-bay standard cottage contemporary with the good surviving late Georgian gatescreen comprised of shallow concave rubble quadrants and a triple gateway contained by V-jointed rusticated square Classical pillars.

Townsend 1815; O'Flanagan 1975; *LGI* (1904).

204. CARRIGANARRA COTTAGE, Ballincollig; pre-1841; *demolished.*
A small estate in 1852 of Benjamin Hutchings.

Griffith 1853–63.

205. CARRIGANARRA, Ballincollig; *c.* 1840.
A modest single-storey gabled roughcast structure, the original front door to the avenue now a window, to be superseded by a flat-roofed hall extending to the road. Occupied. A property in 1852 of Daniel Reardon.

Griffith 1853–63.

206. CARRIGDUVE, Ballintemple; pre-1841; *demolished.*
A property in 1837 of George Sherlock, who had purchased it from the previous occupant, the architect Sir Thomas Deane.

Lewis 1837.

207. CARRIGDUVE HOUSE, Ballintemple; pre-1841; *demolished.*
A villa leased from the 1830s by Sir Thomas Deane to his partner and brother-in-law Richard Notter, one of whom may have designed not only the house but also its porter's lodge.

Lewis 1837; O'Dwyer 1997b.

208. CARRIGEEN HALL, Tallow (3).
The sad remains of a once-proud and important estate of the Peard family, their imposing mansion and all of its gatekeepers' lodges having been demolished. What survives of the central and principal entrance

gates reveals the probable involvement of architect Richard Morrison, working for Henry Peard, who had inherited the property on the death of his father in 1799. Of a familiar pattern that he perpetuated throughout the land, the tripartite gateway has a pair of drums as carriage pillars flanked by larger square ashlar pillars, with recessed panels, containing walled quadrants. A bungalow now occupies that lodge site.

LG (1863).

209. CARRIGMAHON, Monkstown; *c.* 1810.
A seat in the nineteenth century of The O'Grady of Kilballyowen, Co. Limerick [*q.v.*], its lodge a modest affair. Single-storey standard roughcast with a central breakfront and hipped gables, it has been much extended.

CARRIGMORE (see MOUNT DONEGAN)

210. CARRIGMORE, Cork [N]; pre-1841; *demolished.*
A property in the suburb of Sunday's Well, in 1852 the residence of Richard Newman, a butter merchant in the city, its ground subsequently absorbed into the District Lunatic Asylum [*q.v.*] site.

Slater 1846; Griffith 1853–63.

211. CARRIGMORE, Enniskean (2).
Previously the site of Connerville House of the Conner family, from whom it was purchased in 1837 by William Lysaght, probably having with it the lodge at the eastern gate. James Lysaght built the present replacement house in 1842 before the estate was acquired as an incumbered estate in 1853 by the 3rd earl of Norbury, who let it to James L. Holmes.

East gate; pre-1841; *demolished.*
This broad, straight avenue ran from the house about 600 yards between two very lofty walls, overgrown with ivy, at the extremity of which was a high and massive iron gate. During the 1798 Rebellion the whole length of the avenue was commanded by cannon managed by French artillerymen. The then proprietor, Roger O'Connor (a Conner), was hoping, by leaving the gates open, to lure and entrap the Redcoats. The contemporary account fails to mention the presence of a gatekeeper or his lodge. The ploy failed.

West gate; *c.* 1845; *demolished.*
Surviving road-widening is a fine neo-Classical gatescreen comprised of four chunky pillars with tapering recessed panels and ring-and-palmette-motif cast ironwork.

Burke 1854–5; Pike and Hodges 1911; Lyons 1993.

212. CARRIGNAVAR, Carrignavar (3).
In 1837 Samuel Lewis found 'the seat of Justin McCarty, Esq. ... an old mansion pleasantly situated above a romantic glen, and surrounded by a very extensive demesne'. This Justin McCarty (1786–1864) had inherited an old tower-house, at the entrance to at least two approaches to which he added porters' lodges. His grandson, Lt.-Col. Frederick Fitzgerald McCartie (b. 1851), who succeeded him in 1900, further enhanced the place by greatly extending and remodelling the old residence to designs by James F. McMullen in 1903.

South entrance; pre-1841; *demolished.*

East entrance; pre-1841; *demolished.*
The date-stone '1813' incorporated in the new gatescreen hints at the date of construction of the lost lodge opposite the entrance.

North entrance; 1807/1909.

A pair of tiny Classical single-storey rectangular lodges; although twins in appearance, they were not so in conception. The 1841 OS map indicates only the right-hand lodge, the '1807' date-stone upon which confirms its date of erection. Its companion displays the date '1909', which suggests that James McMullen was given the task of creating a greater impression upon the passer-by. They still succeed in doing that without having any practical function, being maintained blocked-up in a smooth rendering, distantly fronting the road, with their single-bay 'window' elevations having segmental heads and raised toothed dressings in like arched recesses on plinths with toothed quoins. The old door openings face each other across a wide forecourt enclosed by ogee-walled quadrants that meet the two surviving pillars of an original triple gateway, still exhibiting their ball finials.

Lewis 1837; *IB* (17 December 1903); *LGI* (1904); Williams 1994.

213. CARRIGOON [1], Mallow; pre-1841.
A once-fine demesne, in 1851 held by Timothy Collins, since devastated by a commercial quarry concern. Strangely located in Lacknamona townland next to its similarly, and more correctly, named neighbour.

Griffith 1853–63.

214. CARRIGOON [2], Mallow; *c.* 1750/*c.* 1860.

Reputed to have been a gate lodge is this substantial seven-bay vernacular cottage, more likely to have been a farmhouse in its own right, later assuming the new role to a grander replacement dwelling (since demolished) associated with the Nash and Curtin families. Up a long lane is the gabled structure with skew-tables to what was a thatched roof, now replaced by corrugated iron, its walls quaintly limewashed, with little two-over-two sash windows. To reflect its new function, it was given new mid-nineteenth-century ornate scalloped fascia boards and a decorative carved gabled canopy to the front door. Derelict but in use as a farm building.

Leet 1814; Hajba 2002.

215. CARRIGRENANE, Glanmire; *c.* 1810.
Backing onto the shore of Lough Mahon with a blind elevation are the ruins of a single-storey Georgian Gothic lodge with a hipped roof and lancet windows in brick-dressed, harled rubble walls. A seat in 1837 of John M. Ashlin, the year of the birth here of his architect son, George.

Lewis 1837; Bence-Jones 1988.

216. CARRIGRHU, Cobh; *c.* 1870; *demolished.*
Savage French (1840–1922), an eldest son, married in 1869 and, whilst his father was until 1878 in residence in the neighbouring family home of Cuskinny [*q.v.*], had this new house ready for occupation that year for his bride; the gate lodge is presumably contemporary.

LGI (1958).

217. CARRIGROHANE CASTLE, Ballincollig; *c.* 1850/*c.* 1880.
A plain, rendered four-bay structure, probably later extended from an original three-bay front, when it may also have gained its decorative plastered opening surrounds and the sawtooth-corbelled brick chimney-stack to its steeply hipped roof. Probably built for local mill-owner Augustus Robert McSweeney, who incorporated the antique castle of the Barrett family into his new house around 1846.

Bence-Jones 1988; O'Dwyer 1997b.

CARROKEAL (see CASTLE VIEW, Mallow)

218. CARROLINA, Cork [N] (2).
Both lodges, to a property latterly renamed 'Ardnalee', built before 1841 have been demolished. Presumably originally named after the Carroll family, who were here in 1837.

Lewis 1837.

219. CASHEL, Rosscarbery; pre-1842; *demolished.*
A lodge opposite the gates to an estate in 1837 of William Wolfe had gone by 1903.

Lewis 1837.

220. CASINO, Castlemartyr; pre-1842; *demolished.*

A property in the town, home in 1814 to a Mrs Hyde, followed by Thomas Bell.

Leet 1814; Slater 1846.

221. CASTLE BERNARD, Bandon (6).
Formerly called 'Castle Mahon', this stronghold of the O'Mahonys was acquired in the early seventeenth century by the Bernard family, whose Classical house, built in 1806, was burnt down in the Troubles of 1921. The estate, much divided east–west by the Bandon River and by a public road, was thus in need of surveillance at distant gates. Three lodges were in place by 1841 to the demesne proper, while a further two were added thereafter to the deer-park by James Bernard, 2nd earl of Bandon (1785–1856), who had succeeded to the estates and title on the death of his father in 1830.

Bernard's Bridge gate; pre-1841; *demolished.*
The outer entrance on the eastern approach from the town in Gully townland, located near the bridge over the Bridewell River of 1823, the lodge to which in 1852 was occupied by Catherine Antice.

Inner gate; pre-1841; *demolished.*
Situated within the demesne only yards from the above on the same approach.

Principal gate; pre-1841/*c.* 1855.

The only porter's lodge on the estate to have survived almost intact, if not without escaping the attention of the moderniser. Replacing a predecessor across the avenue, it presents in stark white rendering a striking finish to the road, its double gable with beautiful and elaborately carved scrolled bargeboards that rise to relatively plain hip-knobs from decorative turned pendants, which also stop the alternating wave and foiled fascia boards. Contemporary are the pretty wooden-latticed casement windows, slits to the loft and Picturesque canopies to the ground floor. The avenue front is late twentieth-century, with a gabled porch alongside a feature rubble chimney-breast.

Killmountain gate; pre-1841; *demolished.*
The westernmost of the lodges to the deer-park is survived by four buttressed entrance pillars.

Shinagh gate; *c.* 1845; *demolished.*
On a northern access to the deer-park was a lodge manned in 1852 by porter J. Forde.

South deer-park gate; *c.* 1845.
Here are the sad remains of a once-fine Tudor Gothic lodge, its main skew-table gabled one-bay front containing a pointed-arched cut-stone attic window with Y-tracery in a harled rubble wall above a projecting single-storey canted entrance hall. Ruinous and overgrown.

Lewis 1837; Griffith 1853–63; *BPB* (1929); Bence-Jones 1988; Lawrence photograph (5732R).

222. CASTLECOOKE, Kilworth; pre-1841/1899.

Supplanting an earlier lodge on the site is this substantial two-storey gabled gatehouse on an estate long associated with the Cooke family. Perhaps originating as a semi-detached pair, it has lost much character in recent alterations, with the insertion of bland plastic windows, new synthetic roof 'slates' and the loss of its skew-tables, from which prominent kneelers survive rather aimlessly. The whole structure is clad in quarry-faced uncoursed random stone, with shouldered openings and peculiar triangular lintels decorated with petalled paterae and ring motifs. To the leading apex is installed a shield inscribed with the date and the monogram of Colonel William Cooke-Collis (1847–1933), who inherited the property from his father in 1882. He is likewise remembered in a stone to one quadrant wall, but dated '1896' and with the additional monogram 'W.J.', presumably of the mason. The big house was burnt by the IRA in 1921.

IFR; Hajba 2002.

223. CASTLECOR, Kilbrin; pre-1841; *demolished.*
Of the porter's lodge, only a two-window-bay elevation of rubble survives in the right-hand entrance quadrant wall, perhaps dating from the time here of Edward Deane Freeman (1760–1826), whose family was in possession of Castlecor for two centuries until it was sold as an incumbered estate in 1852 to William Norton Barry.

LGI (1904); Lyons 1993.

224. CASTLE EYRE, Union Hall; *c.* 1820.
Addressing the road was a single-storey hip-roofed structure, three-bay with doorway to the right-hand side, subsequently extended by a bay to the opposing end, its two-over-two sash windows in whitewashed rendered walls. Occupied. A property in 1814 of Col. W.S. Limerick, by 1902 it had been renamed 'Listarkin'.

Leet 1814.

225. CASTLE FREKE, Rosscarbery (3).
The beautiful marine seat, previously Rathbarry Castle, of the Barry family, from whom it was purchased by the Frekes, devolving by marriage into the Evans-Freke family, Barons Carbery. Its big house developed over the late eighteenth and early nineteenth centuries, as funds dictated, to various designs of Richard Morrison and the Pain brothers, mainly for the 6th baron, John Evans-Freke (1765–1845), who had succeeded his cousin in 1807. From the era of the cousins, one of its two porters' lodges, at the south and west gates, survives, although it would seem to have been George Patrick Percy Evans-Freke (1810–89), who became the 7th baron on the death of his uncle, who further enhanced the property with two new gatehouses, one to the eastern approach.

South entrance; *c.* 1800.

Overlooking Rosscarbery Bay is this complex of structures of various ages, the most notable being the gate pillars, probably of early eighteenth-century origin, constructed of local shale to form a pair of cylinders crowned by outsized ball finials on pedestals remarkably of like composition. Upon these are hung twentieth-century iron gates, whilst a wing wall with postern opening links them

to the slate-hung seaward-facing gable of an otherwise harled humble single-storey cottage, extending a hipped roof to the park with a single wide tripartite window and four-over-four square-paned sashes. Projecting from a now-blind avenue elevation is a Picturesque gabled hallway with ornamental carved bargeboards and little buttressed cheeks, clearly one of the 7th baron's improvements of *c.* 1850. Abutting the rear wall is a most odd single-roomed addition with a canted end but gabled to the road with a rubble stack aloft. Charming and occupied.

East entrance; *c.* 1855; architect probably William Atkins.

An impressive and generously scaled lodge with outbuildings and an extensive gatescreen; 1½-storey, built off an L-plan in random rubble construction, with dressed stone to its label-moulded attic windows, the single-storey canted avenue gable window and the rectangular road bay with its tripartite pointed-arched head now unfortunately missing its chamfered mullions. Continuing the Tudor Gothic Picturesque English Cottage theme are the trefoil incised foiled bargeboards to main gables and that of the dormer window. A lean-to verandah porch in the internal angle with its carved post supports and lofty stone chimney-stacks enhance the Romantic effect. The great semicircular forecourt, with its railed concave quadrant dwarf walls and railings with repeating quatrefoil, has distinctive chunky cut-stone pillars with buttresses and Tudor Gothic lucarnes to layered cappings, so reminiscent of those to Muckross House, Co. Kerry [*q.v.*], by architect William Atkins.

West entrance; pre-1842/*c.* 1855; architect possibly William Atkins.

Another capacious 1½-storey Picturesque rubble-faced lodge, built off a T-plan without any stone detailing but having a canted single-storey bay window in a round-arched recess on the avenue gable, fancy foiled and pierced bargeboards to main gables and that of a gablet. In an internal angle is a single-

storey lean-to hall and to the roof a hefty buttressed and corbelled chimney-stack. Replacing a predecessor on the site.

Brewer 1825; Pike and Hodges 1911; *BPB* (1929); ffolliott 1970; Bence-Jones 1988; IAA.

226. CASTLE HARRISON, Charleville (2).

Both gatekeepers' lodges—that within shown on the 1841 OS map—have been demolished. There is a fine big plain early eighteenth-century gentry house of the Harrison family, of whom Standish Henry Harrison (d. 1865) added the later lodge on the southern approach around 1845.

Griffith 1853–63; *LGI* (1904).

227. CASTLEHAVEN RECTORY, Castletownsend; *c.* 1820.

A single-storey stone cottage below a hipped roof with projecting soffit. Whitewashed and much extended into a double-pile structure. Occupied. Probably contemporary with the glebe house.

228. CASTLE HYDE, Fermoy (2).

The noble pavilioned mansion of the Hyde family, magnificently sited on the north bank of the River Blackwater, assumed its present appearance around 1801 through designs of Abraham Hargrave the Elder for John Hyde II (d. 1832), who may also have been responsible for the elegant main entrance gates. Both porters' lodges would seem to have been added by his son, John Hyde III (1803–85), who will also be remembered for subsequently selling the property in 1851 as an incumbered estate.

Eastern entrance; *c.* 1835.

A charming and decorative 1½-storey hip-roofed cottage built in exposed rubble facings; standard and unusually commodious. Prettily glazed tripartite windows, centrally six-over-four sashes flanked by latticed sidelights, grace both ground and first floors, where they break the eaves as hip-roofed gablets, including that to the central bow, which rises to full height and contains a panelled doorway with rectangular fanlight. Lovingly maintained in a bonny garden.

Western entrance; *c.* 1830.

A bulky single-storey standard lodge in roughcast, with small, square, latticed cast-iron casement windows flanking a porch to the front door, its gable projecting from the high-eaved hipped roof—altogether deferential in elegance to the splendid gatescreen. Apparently based on a plate in William Pain's *The practical house carpenter* of 1799, it is constructed in ashlar and comprises two trefoil-arched postilion gates, each flanked by a pair of massive square Classical piers with moulded plinths and friezes of triglyphs and metopes with bucrania. The entablatures are topped by inadequate dainty Coade stone sphinxes, which face each other across the carriage opening. There is a more faithful reproduction of it at Rockingham (Roscommon).

Pain 1799; O'Flanagan 1975; *LGI* (1904); Bence-Jones 1988; Lyons 1993; Kelly 1990.

229. CASTLE JANE COTTAGE, Glanmire; pre-1841; *demolished.*

A property in 1837 of Robert Martin that contained a cloth mill had by 1902 simply become 'The Cottage'.

Lewis 1837.

CASTLE JANE (see POULACURRY)

230. CASTLE JANE HOUSE, Glanmire; pre-1841; *demolished.*

The seat in 1837 of Richard Martin.

Lewis 1837.

231. CASTLE JANE VILLA, Glanmire; *c.* 1840; architect not known.

Outside its entrance gates is this most delightful and unusual of ornate Tudor Gothic lodges in pristine condition. Single-storey and gabled in a smooth whitened rendering, its symmetrical three-bay front has charming rectangular-paned sash windows

in trefoil-arched cases within Tudor-headed openings, flanking a frontispiece of a flat-roofed canted bay window similarly glazed with pointed-arched casings, below a gablet decorated like the main gables, with cusped and foiled carved bargeboards connected by scalloped frilled fascia boards. To the leading gable apex is a Tudor-arched niche below a spiky hip-knob. Now called 'Glenkeen', it was the seat in 1852 of Robert Martin, who had probably moved from nearby Castle Jane Cottage [*q.v.*] in the townland.

Griffith 1853–63.

232. CASTLE KEVIN, Doneraile; pre-1841; *demolished.*

Formerly a seat of the Roches, it was transformed by Edward Badham-Thornhill in the 1830s into a romantic castle, the entrance screen to which was an apt prelude, with its crenellated concave quadrant walls framing two late Georgian square ashlar pillars, now spoiled by a crude modern overthrow. Its gate lodge opposite has gone.

Lewis 1837; Bence-Jones 1988.

233. CASTLE LANDS, Carrigrohane (2).

A property of 48 acres of Richard Martin in 1852, when its main approach was from the south.

Early entrance; pre-1841; *demolished.*

The second OS map shows a lodge, its short front with hall projecting to the avenue.

By 1890 the place had been redeveloped, the house enlarged and renamed 'Rockrohan', with another lodge added.

Later entrance; *c.* 1860.

On the northern avenue is this excellent 1½-storey standard gabled lodge in a rendered finish, with shallow gables decorated with carved scrolled bargeboards. The pretty Picturesque theme is emphasised by cast-iron latticed bipartite windows below label mouldings. The main front is dominated by a wide gablet, below the attic window of which projects a single-storey gabled hall. By the road is a good contemporary gatescreen of wide concave railed quadrants with palmette and anthemion motifs, which extend to carriage gates hung on pillars that

have round-headed niches below hood mouldings with little pendant dripstones. A property by 1857 of Philip W. Bass, who remained here until the end of the century.

Griffith 1853–63; *LOI.*

234. CASTLE MAHON, Blackrock; pre-1902.

A nondescript single-storey, gabled and much-'improved' structure to an estate in the nineteenth century of the Chatterton family, of whom General Sir Charles Chatterton (1796–1872), 3rd (and last) baronet, may have been its builder, having succeeded to the place in 1855 on the death of his brother.

IFR.

235. CASTLE MARTYR, Castlemartyr (3).

The erstwhile mansion of the Boyles, earls of Shannon, by whom it was created over 200 years to form, along with its 'Charming garden retreat', 'fine timber and artificial waters', a place of fascination for visitors. One of these was that peripatetic cleric Revd Daniel Augustus Beaufort, who came here on 16 September 1788 and recorded in his diary: 'Lord Shannon's gateway—lately built in very bad stile, in imit of Gothick—The house is very large but not at all handsome'. The amateur architect accompanied this description with a sketch of the former, which shows a castellated structure formed of a pair of identical two-storey single-bay turrets, with pointed windows and seemingly machicolated parapets, flanking a lower, similarly topped central portion with a single pointed window. To one side was tacked a flat-roofed entrance hall. This has surely not survived and the 1842 OS map gives no clue as to its location, but there is a hint as to the date of a similar curiosity at the present main gate.

Early town entrance; *c.* 1780.

This perhaps remains as further testimony to the taste in architecture of Richard Boyle (1727–1807), who had become the 2nd Lord Shannon on his father's death in 1764. Here, effectively sited at the head of the main street, are what appear to be a twin pair of lofty two-storey roughcast gatehouses, each comprised of single-bay square turrets with pointed windows rising to corbelled crenellated parapets, containing blind central bays. A slightly closer inspection, however, reveals them to be little more than sham toy-castle façades, as flimsy as stage sets with mock windows. Those to the right-hand structure would have lit a gate lodge abutting the rear, which survives as a blocked-up overgrown shell. Did it have a companion across the avenue? Certainly not since the OS surveyors were here in 1842.

What is clear is that the 4th Lord Shannon, Richard Boyle (1809–68), considered this inferior accommodation and replaced or supplemented it with a new porter's lodge nearer the main street.

Late town entrance; *c.* 1855; *demolished.*

Michael O'Dwyer

A relatively substantial, faintly Tudor Picturesque-style single-storey lodge, its steeply pitched hipped roof with tall eaves projected to form a verandah carried on square wooden posts, thinly bracketed. Built off an L-plan, the roughcast walls contained transomed and mullioned casement windows with squared glazing. In the internal angle was a later flat-roofed draught porch with finely carved crenallated parapet. Demolished in 1982, to be survived by its predecessor.

Barn Wood entrance; *c.* 1870.

Henry Bentinck Boyle (1833–90) succeeded as the 5th earl of Shannon in 1868 and built his quirky little lodge at the distant gate to the western approach. Single-storey and gabled in attractive rubble finish with toothed brick dressing and quoins, its irregular three-bay front elevation is notable for the doorway and slit window occupying a corner recess as entrance porch, the eaves over, with sawtooth fascia in 'railway' manner, carried on a pair of post supports.

Beaufort 1764–1808; De Latocnaye 1984; Barrow 1836; *BPB* (1929); Bence-Jones 1988.

236. CASTLE MARY, Cloyne (3).
Revd Robert Longfield (d. 1843) inherited the estate, once of his cousins, the earls of Longueville, on the death of his father in 1819, thereafter leaving the property to his son with two lodged gates, one at least of his creation.

Inner gate; pre-1841; *demolished.*

South gate; *c.* 1820.

A generous 1½-storey standard late Georgian lodge in a limewashed harled finish below a hipped-gabled roof, its openings having Tudor label mouldings—early evidence of the coming of the Picturesque to Ireland. Occupied. Nearby, the impressive gatescreen is comprised in the main of twin segmental arches, one containing a postilion doorway, the other a balancing blind recess, both flanked by a pair of tall, square, rubble stone piers on each side of the wide carriage opening.

North gate; *c.* 1880.

Mountifort John Courtenay Longfield (1858–1929) succeeded to the place as a minor of six years of age, and on the evidence of the fancy earthenware crestings to this lodge built it not long after his coming of age. The fleur-de-lis pattern adorns the ridges of a gabled 1½-storey structure erected off an irregular T-plan in a coursed random stone, with basic Tudor-style label mouldings to openings conspicuously lacking dripstones. In the leading internal angle is tucked a little gabled hall breakfront, the whole on a nicely manicured elevated site.

LGI (1904); *IFR.*

237. CASTLE PARK, Kanturk (2).
A compact estate whose earliest known occupant was John Howard in the 1750s. Also known as 'Paal', it was in 1814 recorded as 'Paul' of Maurice O'Donnell, who may have been the builder of the original elongated gatekeepers' lodges. Around 1895 Kingsmill G. Priestley acquired the property and carried out improvements, which included replacement of both lodges.

East entrance; pre-1841/*c.* 1897.

Single-storey standard but raised off an

ample square plan. Below an oversailing pyramidal roof, rising to a square-set chimney-stack, is a three-bay front, its openings having dainty label moulding. The central doorway under a pretty chinoiserie rectangular fanlight contains a very fine five-panel door, perhaps salvaged from its predecessor. All in a crisp rendered finish. The good Classical late Victorian gatescreen has contemporary decorative ironwork.

West entrance; pre-1841/*c.* 1897.

On an elevated site, much as the above, with the same squared glazing to transomed and mullioned casement windows but with a diagonally set chimney-stack for variety. Run-down entrance and avenue.

Leet 1814; Hajba 2002.

238. CASTLETOWNSHEND, Castletownshend (3).
The romantic seat of the Townshend family in its idyllic setting is now lodgeless, those to the demesne proper and that opposite the 'Home Farm' gate, all built before 1842, demolished.

CASTLE VIEW (see CLASHDUFF)

239. CASTLE VIEW, Blarney; *c.* 1810.

IAA

Sited outside its basic gatescreen, monitoring the approach, is this charming limewashed harled cottage with steeply hipped roof, the high eaves to which allow attic space. The principal front doubtless originated as being two-bay, now having lost much character through the loss of its six-over-six Georgian sashes and the intrusion of a new doorway to one side. A property recorded in 1814 as the residence of Henry St Leger.

Leet 1814; IAA photograph (S/694/4).

240. CASTLE VIEW, Buttevant; pre-1841; *demolished.*
A seat in 1801 and 1837 of Barry Gregg, whose gate lodge had gone by 1937.

Lewis 1837; Hajba 2002.

241. CASTLE VIEW, Glanmire; *c.* 1790.
An estate inherited on the death of his father

in 1797 by Warren Hastings Rowland Jackson (d. 1851), which he thereafter graced with this little porter's lodge, which seems also to have served neighbouring Ditchley. Single-storey below a shallow, almost pyramidal, hipped roof with oversailing eaves. There is a degree of rustic Palladianism in its principal front of a pair of round-arched niches flanking the doorway (now a nasty modern window) in a rendered finish framed by a granite plinth and V-jointed toothed quoins. There are almost identical lodges at Clonacody, Co. Tipperary [*q.v.*], and Clonshire, Co. Limerick [*q.v.*], probably originating from a pattern-book rather than by a common hand.

LG (1894).

242. CASTLE VIEW, Macroom; pre-1841; *demolished.*
A holding in 1814 of Thomas Brown which by 1837 had passed to Patrick Ronayne.

Leet 1814; Lewis 1837.

243. CASTLE VIEW, Mallow; pre-1841.
A single-storey standard affair below a hipped roof in roughcast finish, its back return forming an L-plan. All much altered, with a lean-to extension to the avenue. Occupied. A property which went under the name of 'Mount Watts' after the Watts family, which by 1814 was occupied by a Major Rogers but ten years later was a seat of the Williamsons of nearby Dromore, Old [*q.v.*]. It was latterly called 'Carrokeal'.

Leet 1814; Pigot 1824; Hajba 2002.

244. CASTLE VIEW, Tallow (2).
Here are the pathetic remnants of a once-proud property, the fine mansion house having been built in 1791 by Robert Warren Gumbleton of the Castle Richard, Co. Waterford [*q.v.*], family. Also known as 'Glanatore', it had a suitably imposing main entrance screen.

South gate; *c.* 1800; architect not known.

Just discernible in the undergrowth are a pair of sophisticated little Classical two-roomed pavilions, their principal fronts to the highway's edge, each in the form of a doorway in a coved recess (in the manner of Richard Morrison villas) with segmental arch and narrow string-course in harled rubble walls below a pedimented gable defined by cut stone. These guard a vast semicircular forecourt with concave-walled quadrants before a grand triple ashlar gateway comprised of a pair of H-structures, each in the form of a postern gateway flanked by tall pillars, crowned by the remains of vases with

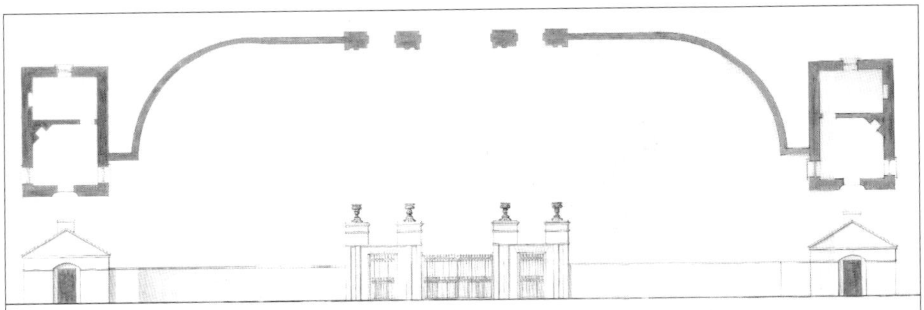

244. Castle View, Tallow. South gate.

gadrooned pedestals (part reconstructed in the accompanying drawing). Upon these are hung delicate and delightful Gothic wrought-iron gates, now giving access to a field.

North gate; *c.* 1845.

At the secondary approach, to the farmyard, is this single-storey standard gabled cottage with pointed-arched openings, built in an earlier style for Richard Gumbleton (d. 1849). Derelict.

LGI (1904); O'Flanagan 1975; Bence-Jones 1988.

245. CASTLE WARREN, Ringaskiddy; pre-1841; *demolished.*

'A spacious mansion erected in 1796', in 1837 the seat of Robert Warren junior, whose porter's lodge faced its entrance gates.

Lewis 1837.

246. CASTLE WHITE, Ballincollig (2).

An estate of the White family, in 1837 of George Martin White. Both the early lodge built before 1842 and its replacement, necessitated by the arrival of the railway, have been demolished.

Lewis 1837.

247. CASTLE WIDENHAM, Castletownroche (2).

The old castle of the Viscounts Roche was granted to the Widenham family, who extended it, although it assumed its present extensive pseudo-Tudor Gothic appearance at the hands of Henry Mitchell Smyth (d. 1850) in the 1830s, when the last of the male Widenhams, his father-in-law Charles, was still in residence. Opposite the main entrance to the estate is the perfect prelude.

South gate; *c.* 1830; architects perhaps G.R. and James Pain.

In an excellent limestone ashlar with beautifully crafted detailing is this characterful little lodge. Single-storey standard with an oversailing pyramidal roof broken by the castellated parapet of the central entrance breakfront, the diagonal buttresses of which frame a triple hood moulding which embraces the Tudor-arched doorway and its lancet sidelights. To each side are bipartite windows with chamfered mullions and reveals, below delicate label mouldings, perhaps lacking their original cast-iron glazing pattern. Delightfully nestling in its tended shrubberied setting.

North gate; pre-1841.

A large single-storey hip-roofed structure of little pretension.

Heaney 1999; O'Flanagan 1975; *LGI* (1904); Bence-Jones 1988.

248. CHARLEMONT, Douglas; pre-1841; *demolished.*

The seat in 1837 of Charles Evanson, whose porter's lodge was opposite his gates.

Lewis 1837.

249. CHARLEMONT TERRACE, Cork [N]; pre-1841/*c.* 1855.

A range of sixteen three-storey homes extending from the earlier block of Waterloo Terrace [*q.v.*], the old detached gate lodge to which was superseded by this unique replacement tacked on to the gable end of the new terrace. Two-storey and single-bay, the same tall windows as beyond in like understated Classical proportions, its rendered façade checked and relieved by a moulded eaves frieze and a deep course at first-floor level continued from the terrace. Extended to the rear in basic fashion, curved to the line of the public footpath. Capless remains of a pair of Classical gate pillars with moulded recessed panels.

250. CHARLESTON, Cobh; *c.* 1850.

About 1850 a portion of the land previously associated with 'Bellevue' [*q.v.*] was hived off, its gate lodge replaced and a new avenue constructed from the same entrance to serve Charleston, whose first owner was Thomas Hoskin Tarrant. This is a pretty 1½-storey gabled standard English Picturesque Tudor-

style cottage, faced in a hewn uncoursed sandstone with label mouldings to openings, high eaves, continuous bracketed carved bargeboards and a pair of octagonal chimney-pots. The triple gateway is Classical, with inner pillars corniced and having pedestals now lacking finials. The outer pillars have gadrooned cappings framed by palmette-topped railed screens.

Griffith 1853–63.

CHARLEVILLE PARK (see SANDERS PARK)

251. CHERRYHILL, Newtownshandrum; *c.* 1845.

The lodge built for George Harding is a single-storey standard cottage with a steeply hipped roof and wide rectangular windows on each side of the doorway with flat-arched fanlight in rough harled walls.

Lewis 1837; Griffith 1853–63.

CHESTERFIELD (see BALLYMAGOOLY)

252. CHIPLEE, Ballintemple; pre-1841.

A single-storey two-window-bay elevation is all that survives as an extension of the right-hand ogee entrance quadrant. There is one postilion opening and '1761' on one gate pillar. A property in 1814 of R. Harvey, by 1837 it had passed to Paul Maylor.

Leet 1814; Lewis 1837.

253. CHRISTCHURCH, Cobh; *c.* 1866; architect probably Henry Hill.

At the entrance to Cobh Church of Ireland church and its 'parsonage' is this ivy-clad, dramatically extended single-storey gabled lodge in red-brick facings nicely contrasting with toothed stone quoins and dressings to chamfered bi- and tripartite windows with lead-effect glazing, no doubt reflecting lost latticed cast-iron originals. To the steep gables are High Victorian Gothic bargeboards pierced, with trefoil toes to echo the church's transept tracery across the laneway. Occupied. Henry Hill designed the church in 1863–4 and the glebe house shortly after.

254. CHURCH HILL, Ballineen; pre-1841/*c.* 1870.

The Desertserges parish rectory, in 1837 occupied by Revd Mountifort Longfield, to which the surviving lodge is a replacement. It is a single-storey square two by two-bay structure, with distinctive toothed stone quoins and dressings in otherwise roughcast walls below a pyramidal roof, a brick stack rising off the rear wall.

Lewis 1837.

255. CHURCHTOWN, Churchtown; pre-1841; *demolished.*
An estate in the early nineteenth century of the Crofts family, in which they sold their interest around 1840; thereafter the 143 acres became one of many properties willed to his family law agent Sir Edward Tierney by the dissolute 5th earl of Egmont.
Griffith 1853–63; Hajba 2002.

256. CITTADELLA LUNATIC ASYLUM, Cork [S]; pre-1841; *demolished.*

In 1837 Samuel Lewis records: 'Private lunatic asylum ... belonging to Joshua Bull, Esq., was established by the late Dr Hallaran, in 1798, and has secluded pleasure grounds for the use of patients'. The gate lodge seems also to have served neighbouring 'Springville' [*q.v.*].
Lewis 1837.

257. CLANCOOL, Bandon; *c.* 1845; architect not known.

A perfect example of the Tudor Picturesque Revival was this English cottage lacking some of its original fancy bargeboards and glazing pattern, now in a setting of twentieth-century suburbia. Off a requisite informal plan, its main body is 1½-storey, with an arrowhead bay window below a label-moulded attic window to the road. From opposing sides extend single-storey extensions, one an entrance porch with Tudor archway in a breakfront, the other a room retaining its continuous bracket bargeboards with quatrefoil toes, and a rectangular bay supported by diagonal buttresses. In a drab roughcast finish; remaining is a fine trio of octagonal chimney-pots to cap the effect. Built for Thomas Wall Hewitt (1776–1857), who must have been *au fait* with the latest architectural pattern-books of Hunt and Robinson.
LGI (1904).

CLANLOUGHLIN (see LEE BANK)

258. CLANRICARDE, Ballintemple; *c.* 1875.
A development of a clear site which included a single-storey standard lodge below a bellcast hipped roof and a big red-brick chimney-stack. Now plain, modernised and put to office use. The Italianate main house was 'still unfinished' at the time of the 1866/7 valuation and was apparently completed for Henry Hope several years later.

259. CLARAGH, Millstreet; pre-1936; *demolished.*
A lodge built after 1841 for one of the Pomeroy family.

260. CLARAVIEW, Millstreet; pre-1841; *demolished.*
An eleven-acre property acquired around 1845 as a presbytery to the neighbouring Roman Catholic church.
Griffith 1853–63.

261. CLARAVILLE, Mallow; *c.* 1860; *demolished.*
A villa built after 1841 by Rogers Johnson, which he named after his wife. A bungalow now identifies the site of the lost gate lodge, which was probably contemporary with the house. By 1876 Joseph Bullen had renamed the place 'Hermitage'. Original carriage pillars survive, with recessed moulded panels and dainty ball finials.
LOI; Hajba 2002.

CLAREMONT (see MYRTLEVILLE)

CLARENS (see KNOCKREA [1])

262. CLASHDUFF, Cork [S]; pre-1841; *demolished.*
A seat in the early nineteenth century of the French family.

263. CLASHDUFF, Midleton (2).
Both lodges built before 1841 to an estate in 1837 of Peter Warner have been demolished. Later renamed 'Castle View'.
Lewis 1837.

264. CLASSES, Ballincollig; pre-1841; *demolished.*
A property in 1837 of H. Minhear Esq., the lodge to which fifteen years later was manned by Samuel Kean, gate porter to William O'Callaghan. It had gone by 1939.
Lewis 1837; Griffith 1853–63.

265. CLEVE HILL, Ballintemple; pre-1841; *demolished.*
The suburban house in 1837 of Samuel Perrott.
Lewis 1837.

266. CLIFFORD, Kilavullen; *c.* 1810.
In 1815 this was 'a new seat ... of Richard Martin', whose lodge lies very derelict, having been a standard single-storey harled and gabled structure with the later addition of a bay to the right-hand side. Nearby is a fine pair of tall mid-Georgian gate pillars, with plinths, friezes, cornices and scroll-topped gate stops, now minus their pineapple finials.
Townsend 1815.

CLIFTON (see WATERVIEW)

267. CLIFTON, Ballintemple; pre-1841/*c.* 1865; architect not known.

A seat in the first half of the nineteenth century of John Moore Travers (1768–1853), a barrister in the city of Cork, whose porter's lodge was located to the left-hand side of the present gateway. After his death the place was acquired by Thomas Masters Usborne, who replaced Travers's lodge with this showy survivor to the other side of the gate. Dating from around 1865 and by an unidentified architect, its single-storey singular double-gabled principal front is exposed to the road, one set back to accommodate the overlapping catslide-roofed hallway and each containing a large Italianate bipartite window with round-headed archway below dripstoned hood moulding with Venetian tracery supported on a stone Tuscan columnette, a pattern nicely repeated in the panelling of the semicircular-arched doorway in chamfered surround. Beautifully maintained in smooth rendering with paired side windows and decorative verge brackets. Some tall entrance pillars survive in stone, chamfered with heavily corbelled mid-Victorian cappings. A property subsequently renamed 'Ardfoile', home now to Our Lady of Apostles Convent.

Leet 1814; *Thom's*; *LGI* (1904).

268. CLIFTON, Cork [N] (2).

The house, when it was home to Nicholas Murphy (1783–1852), was served by an early nineteenth-century lodge off Leycester's Lane to the rear which had been removed by 1902 and superseded around 1854 after John Nicholas Murphy (1815–89) succeeded his father, perhaps to mark his year of mayoralty of the city, or his wedding the following year to a Leahy of Shanakiel [*q.v.*], where there is a lodge with like characteristics. A splendid little Classical lodge of a type in which the Cork suburbs abound. By an unidentified architect, it is simply single-storey standard but abounding in Doric pilasters to decorate its rendered walls, bound by a plain frieze to a shallow oversailing hipped main roof and that of the hall projection. Strikingly occupying an elevated site with a tripartite chimney-stack but suffering the indignity of modern casement windows. An entrance all the better suited to the proprietor's standing, conspicuous to the Glanmire Road, with its contemporary gatescreen of gate pillars with their round-arched moulded recessed panels. Now the entrance to a convent. There are similar lodges at Factoryville, Mount Donegan and the Episcopal Palace.

Bence-Jones 1988; *IFR*.

269. CLIFTON LODGE, Ballintemple; pre-1853; *demolished.*
A modest property in 1853 of Henry Woods, valued then with a gate lodge but not evident on any OS map.

Griffith 1853–63.

270. CLOGHEEN, Buttevant; *c.* 1830.
An unprepossessing porter's lodge, single-storey rendered and gabled with clipped verges, probably latterly extended from a three-bay standard structure to the left-hand side, when it may also have gained its back return. Erected for Lt.-Col. Arundel Hill (d. 1839) after he had built the replacement house, itself demolished in the early 1990s.

Pigot 1824; Lewis 1837; Hajba 2002.

271. CLOGHER, Shanballymore; *c.* 1825.
An estate of the Nagles, at whose main seat of Ballynamona [*q.v.*] they resided, leaving Clogher on long lease to the Lowe family, of whom George Bond Lowe (1784–1839) was an improver. He gave the house a new entrance front and built the out-offices which the lodge precedes. Single-storey standard, hip-roofed and built in random rubble facings, its central doorway now sealed and the entrance relocated to one end, but its cast-iron latticed casement windows surviving. Like the big house, it lies derelict.

Hajba 2002.

272. CLOGHROE, Blarney (2).
A Georgian house occupied between 1814 and 1837 by Joseph Capell Fitzgerald, his lodge a charming prelude.

Main entrance; *c.* 1825.

A cottage with limewashed harled walls. Single-storey standard with a shallow pyramidal roof rising to a diagonally set chimney-stack, its high oversailing eaves sheltering a breakfront hall with a nasty door, flanked by pretty, wide tripartite casement windows with shouldered heads. Nearby are the remains of a suitably rustic triple gateway with basic pillars and convex quadrant walls. By 1852 the estate was let to Thomas Keogh, whose gatekeeper was James Walsh. Occupied.

Secondary entrance; pre-1841; *demolished.*
On the northern approach is a pair of replacement twentieth-century semi-detached dwellings.

Leet 1814; Lewis 1837; Griffith 1853–63.

273. CLONDROHID RECTORY, Macroom; *c.* 1820.
A plain single-storey gabled cottage on an L-plan, its two-bay rendered window elevation to the road with modern inserts. Superintending the gates to the graveyard and to the glebe house of 1813, with which it may be contemporary.

Lewis 1837.

274. CLONDULANE, Fermoy; *c.* 1860.
Derelict and shrouded in rampant *Lonicera* hedging is a single-storey hip-roofed structure of Italianate appearance with rusticated quoins, its main front of two windows with banded surrounds and lugged lintels to their segmental heads, but otherwise harled. Opposite the gates to a house in the mid-nineteenth century of Robert Briscoe, who worked the adjacent extensive flour mills.

Lewis 1837; Griffith 1853–63; Slater 1856; 1870.

275. CLONEEN, Carrigtohill; pre-1841; *demolished.*
A property in 1853 of Robert Lunham, the gate lodge to which may have been integral with an entrance archway, the whole having gone by 1936.

Griffith 1853–63.

276. CLONMOYLE, Coachford; *c.* 1845; *demolished.*
A lost lodge, built sometime between the first OS map of 1841 and its recording in the 1852 valuation of a property of a Jonathan Bruce (1819–88), probably of Milltown Castle [*q.v.*], leasing from Charles Colthurst.

Griffith 1853–63; *LGI* (1904).

277. CLONMULT, Clonmult; pre-1936; *demolished.*
A lodge built after 1841 to an estate in 1853 of Pierce Power.

Griffith 1853–63.

278. CLONTAFF, Union Hall; pre-1842; *demolished.*
The residence in 1814 of William Horan; by 1837 it had been acquired by Richard Townsend, which name is recorded here as late as 1876.

Leet 1814; Lewis 1837; *LOI*.

279. CLONTYMON LODGE, Cork [S]; pre-1841; *demolished.*
A seat in the Knockrea suburb occupied in 1853 by Revd William Shaw.

Griffith 1953–63.

280. THE CLOSE, Castletownroche; *c.* 1870.
Maurice Hickey rented the property in 1868 and proceeded to rebuild the house, landscape the grounds and doubtless add this porter's lodge as part of the improvements. A single-storey standard structure with a pair of chimney-stacks and high eaves to its hipped roof over wide windows and a minuscule fanlight to the front door. Occupied and improved.

Hajba 2002.

281. CLOVER HILL, Blackrock; pre-1841; *demolished.*
The proprietor in 1837 was Charles Connell, whose lodge has been replaced by a bungalow on the site.

Lewis 1837.

282. CLOYNE CATHEDRAL, Cloyne; *c.* 1810.
A 1½-storey sexton-cum-gatekeeper's lodge, located remote from its entrance in a bland modern rendering, its age betrayed by the hipped gables. Occupied.

283. CLOYNE PALACE, Cloyne; *c.* 1790.
A rare and cherished survival is this superb example of a 'tea caddy' lodge (*above*)—a single-storey Georgian Gothic structure on an octagonal plan with Y-traceried sash windows in pointed-arched openings in roughcast walls. Overhead is an octahedral roof with exposed rafter toes, rising to the little octagonal chimney-stack. Probably built during the episcopacy of Richard Woodward (1726–94), bishop of Cloyne (1781–94). The palace became a private house in 1836, when the diocese was united with that of Cork.

Lewis 1837; ffolliott 1971b.

284. CLOYNE PRESBYTERY, Cloyne; pre-1853; *demolished.*
A good Classical Regency villa survives the gatehouse recorded in the 1853 valuation; not identified on the 1841 OS map.

Griffith 1853–63.

285. CLYDA, Mallow; pre-1841.
A property held in the early nineteenth century by the Haines family but sublet to a succession of tenants, in 1814 to Joseph Barry, later to Thomas Townsend and by 1837 to Revd Michael Henry Becher. The single-storey steeply hip-roofed lodge is barely detectable through a variety of subsequent additions and alterations.

Leet 1814; Lewis 1837; *LGI* (1904); Hajba 2002.

286. COACHFORD RECTORY, Coachford; *c.* 1815.

Probably contemporary with the building of its glebe house in 1812 is this single-storey late Georgian roughcast lodge with a shallow hipped roof over an irregular three-bay main front which catslides over the left-hand hall projection. A plain structure, featureless but for a tiny Y-traceried lancet window, which reveals its age, in the road elevation. Occupied.

Lewis 1837.

287. COBH CEMETERY, Cobh; *c.* 1850.

Near the ruins of Clonmell church is the standard 1½-storey gabled lodge in a pleasant random rubble facing with high eaves to accommodate a gabled canopy or porch (now lost). Decorated with carved 'fang' bargeboards and fascias and crowned by a pair of square chimney-stacks on a common base. In use.

288. COBH FORT, Cobh (2).
A steeply sloping seven-acre military ordnance ground, in an enclosure bounded on the shore by mid-eighteenth-century star works and above by tall, late eighteenth-century rubble walls, which contained a hospital, barracks, coastguard accommodation and two lodges monitoring the entrance. While that at the lower gate, dating from before 1841, has been replaced by a modern bungalow, the upper lodge represents the sole original structure to remain on the site, albeit of later date.

Of about 1880, it curiously turns its back on the entrance to enjoy a splendid sea view. It is a lofty and sturdy 1½-storey affair in a plain rendering, relieved to some extent by a string-course at first-floor level which runs through the single-storey breakfront doorway, now obliterated by a lean-to hallway. Six-over-six sashes below a steeply pitched roof with a stack to each gable.

289. CODRUM, Macroom; pre-1842; *demolished.*
The estate in the first half of the nineteenth century of the Warren family, descended from that of Warren'scourt [*q.v.*] and Crookstown [*q.v.*], of whom John Warren was succeeded here around 1830 by his son, John Massey Hutchison Warren. Their porter's lodge had been removed by 1939.

Leet 1814; Lewis 1837; *BPB* (1929).

290. CODRUM WEST, Macroom; *c.* 1810.

Centrally sited between the gateways to parallel driveways is this single-storey Georgian Gothic hip-roofed lodge with pointed-arched windows, two-window bay to the road, four to each side, probably extended by two bays with commendably matching openings but with subsequent lead-effect glazing inserts. Immaculately maintained in a crisp modern rendering with later carved fascia boards and corner pendants in the Picturesque tradition, with a gablet over the doorway. Some original wrought-iron gates survive, hung on plain rebuilt rubble pillars. A seat in the early nineteenth century of the Ashe family.

Lewis 1837.

291. COMBERMERE COTTAGE, Carrigtohill; *c.* 1820.
The pretty cottage-style gentry residence in 1837 of James Keane, to which its contemporary porter's lodge has been retained as a curiosity by the gate. Single-storey standard, hip-roofed, tiny and twee.

Lewis 1837.

CONNERVILLE (see CARRIGMORE, Enniskean)

292. CONVAMORE, Ballyhooly (2).
A restrained Classical mansion was added to an existing house in the 1830s for William Hare (1751–1837), 1st earl of Listowel, to designs of the Cork-based brothers George Richard and James Pain. By 1838, like the client, the younger architect had died, but James, on the evidence of one of the replacement lodges, had been retained years later to work for another William Hare (1801–56), the 2nd earl or his like-named and long-lived eldest son, William Hare (1833–1924), the 3rd Lord Listowel.

Country gate; pre-1841/*c.* 1855; architect James Pain.

Superseding an older lodge on the site is this single-storey standard capacious structure built off a cruciform plan. Gabled with a central back return and a projecting hall, which contains a lugged moulded architrave to the doorway below a sculpted stone shield with a coronet in the apex. Flanking are wide window openings (now with modern inserts) treated as entablatured breakfronts or aedicules in cut stone in an otherwise drab rendered finish. As with other Pain lodges, the chimney-stack rises off the rear wall. It is a building that, with its gatescreen, has marked similarities to those at Derry Castle, Co. Tipperary [*q.v.*]. The six-pillared entrance is comprised of outer ogee-walled quadrants and straight inner cast-iron railings with matching carriage gates. This distinctive ashlar pillar design with raised panels and semicircular-pedimented, half-barrel capping is also to be seen at Grange, Co. Limerick [*q.v.*], and in County Clare at Carrigoran [*q.v.*] and Kilkishen [*q.v.*].

Village gate; pre-1841/*c.* 1900.

A 1½-storey replacement lodge with hipped gables and a gabled breakfront in an Arts and Crafts style.

The mansion was burnt down in 1921.

BPB (1929); Bence-Jones 1988.

293. COOLCOUR, Macroom; *c.* 1830.

An exercise in duality is this single-storey lodge, two single-bay hip-roofed wings of which extend to each side of an entrance

recess. In a roughcast finish, what were six-over-six sash windows are set in rectangular recesses, while two chimney-stacks are positioned to further the balanced effect. Presumably built for William G. Browne, who succeeded to the property in the 1830s.

Brewer 1825; Lewis 1837.

294. COOLE ABBEY, Fermoy (2).

An antique estate with an impressive mid-eighteenth-century house of the Peard family, neither of the lodges to which now enhances the approaches.

North gate; pre-1841.

A standard single-storey gabled affair so altered as to defy accurate dating.

South gate; pre-1841; *demolished.*

Surviving is a good Georgian gatescreen, its shallow concave quadrant walls relieved by cut-stone pilasters, contained by six graceful pillars with moulded cornices and plinths and scroll-topped gate stops. Probably an improvement for Henry Peard (d. 1797) or his son Richard Peard (d. 1839).

LG (1863).

295. COOLINEY, Charleville; *c.* 1840.

Opposite the gates is the derelict and modest single-storey standard cottage with steeply skew-tabled gables, the effect not improved by a replacement concrete tiled roof finish and a cement rendering to walls. The proprietor in 1837 and 1851 was Robert Weldon.

Lewis 1837; Griffith 1853–63.

296. COOLKELURE, Dunmanway; 1879; architect Henry Hill.

An extraordinarily brash mid-Victorian gatehouse erected to two storeys on a

cruciform plan with forthright detailing and materials, quite symmetrical but for a hefty chimney-stack which breaks the fleur-de-lis earthenware cresting. The apexes of the steeply pitched bellcast gables are ornamented with carved trussed woodwork, while below is random coursed ashlar with contrasting quoins, a conspicuous string-course, cross arrowloops and a variety of bi- and tripartite mullioned sash windows, some with semicircular heads. To the front is an open porch with Gothic arch and round heads to the side, and a room over. At opposing ends are single-storey bay windows, one rectangular and the other

semi-octagonal. To the rear is a remarkable three-stage square stair tower with single and bipartite slit windows, culminating in a pyramidal roof with exposed rafter toes and a cast-iron finial. The whole is further adorned within and without by a variety of sculpted grotesque mythical beasts, including the Shuldham griffin, a date-stone and a monogram of the client, Edmund Anderson Shuldham (1826–1904), commissioner of this whimsy.

LGI (1912); Williams 1994.

297. COOLKIRKY, Ballymartle; pre-1841; *demolished.*
A property in 1837 of Thomas Herrick, the lodge to which had been removed by 1934 but is survived by its gatescreen with four stone pillars having recessed panels and corniced cappings, framed by shallow concave quadrants; cast-iron gates with roundel and palmette motifs.

Lewis 1837.

298. COOLMAIN CASTLE, Kilbrittain; pre-1842; *demolished.*
A delightful rambling eclectic house created by the Stawell family and from the mid-nineteenth century by the Bernards of Castle Bernard [*q.v.*]. Eustace Stawell was the last of his family recorded here in 1837. The lodge opposite his gates had gone by 1902.

Lewis 1837; *LGI* (1904); *BPB* (1929).

299. COOLMORE, Carrigaline (2).
William Worth Newenham (1761–1814) inherited the estate as a minor on the death of his father in 1766 and commenced improvements to the property with the building of his new residence in 1788. By 1815 the thoughts of his son, William Henry Worth Newenham (1785–1842), upon his succession had turned to transforming the approaches, and to this end he had engaged the unfortunate English practitioner Thomas Cundy the elder—unfortunate in that the architect, through the evidence of his charming sketch-book, produced at least seven designs for his client for lodges in the whole range of architectural styles then in vogue, from pretty verandahed and trellised standard cottage to Italianate, Tudor Gothic, a pair of chaste pedimented Regency lodges linked by a Classical archway and great Triumphal gateways, one triple and lodgeless, the other with integral twin 'day and night' accommodation. Not one of these materialised on site, and twenty years later, a decade after Cundy's passing, Newenham was still agonising over new avenues, as revealed in the journal of the Scottish tourist Robert Graham on 11 July 1835:

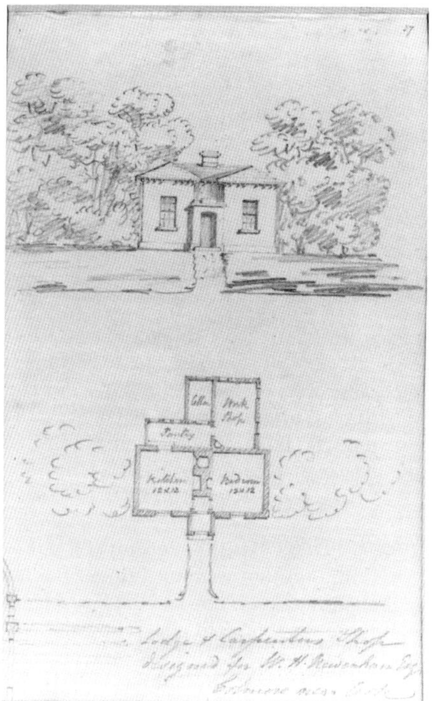

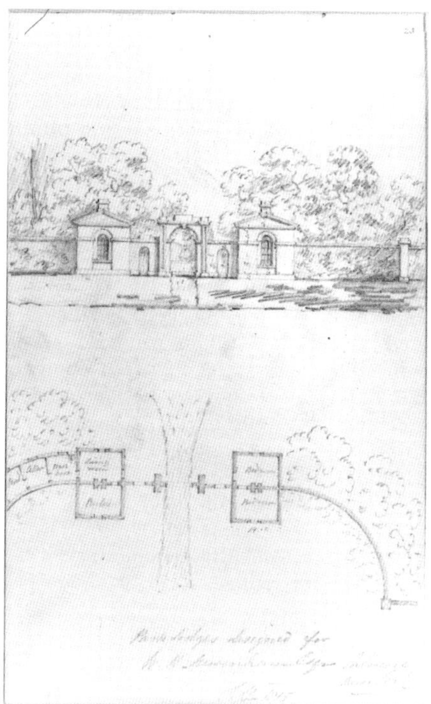

British Architectural Library, RIBA, London

> 'Mr Newenham is much puzzled at present about the entrance to his house. There is a magnificent avenue of elm trees, which runs almost from the park wall to the door of the house. Whether to bring the approach along that line, or by a more circuitous one, which shows more of the grounds, and the other great wood of the place to much more advantage, is the question. The man who is always on the spot ought to determine this question; but, at present, I think I would complete the present approach thro' the interior of the grounds for common purposes. I would have the other, too, as a dress approach, or to retire by, or use as a riding when the fancy struck the visitors at the place.'

In fact, the grand straight avenue to the house survives to this day and by 1838 the problem of policing its gate had eventually been resolved, for a drawing of what exists has survived, signed by James and George Richard Pain, showing a thoroughly practical solution which also answered a need for improved accommodation for Newenham's estate workers.

Principal entrance; *c.* 1837; architects James and G.R. Pain.
Here the Cork-based architects have innovatively gathered for maximum impact

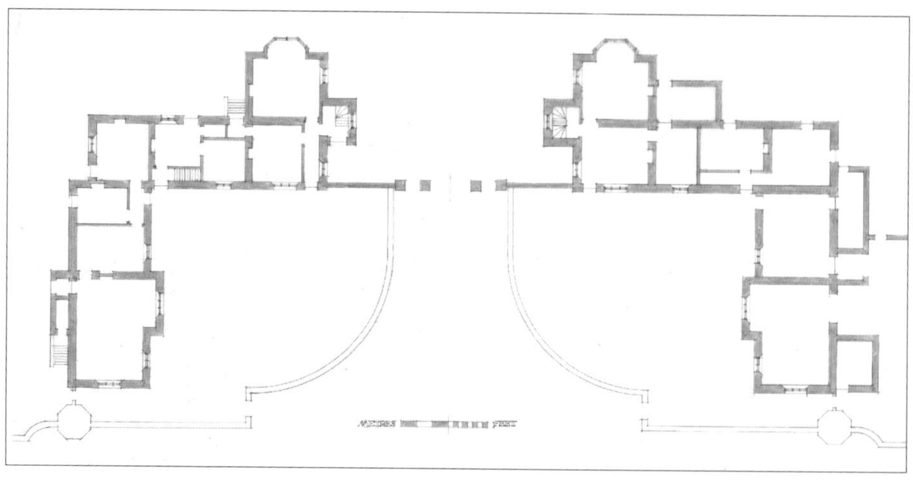

eight English Picturesque cottages as a veritable village, arranged in two mirror-image irregular ranges, creating a grand forecourt to the gates. All 1½-storey in a rubble stone with brick toothed quoins and dressings to simply sheeted door openings with pretty arcaded mouth-organ fanlights and to transomed and mullioned lattice-glazed casement windows. The roofscape is enlivened by a variety of gables and attic gablet windows, the whole crowned by a selection of tall circular, octagonal and diagonally set square brick chimney-stacks arranged singly, in pairs or in threes, all in the spirit of the architects' erstwhile master John Nash, seen at the likes of Blaise Hamlet (Gloucestershire). Either, or both, of the cottages which flank the modest tripartite pillared gateway may have housed the gate porter. All in occupation and in surprisingly good condition, with the insertion of modern windows being the main blemish on this pictorial scene. The illustration is a redrawing of the Pains' original plan.

Secondary entrance; pre-1841/*c.* 1850; architect possibly James Pain.

On the Carrigaline driveway is this Tudor Revival lodge, 1½-storey with parapeted eaves, kneelers and skew-table gables. Not quite three-bay symmetrical, its central projection with chamfered label-moulded windows flanked by a window bay and the hood-moulded pointed-arched porch doorway, over which is a Newenham quartered shield. Occupied and well maintained in a smooth modern rendered finish. A replacement doubtless built for Revd Edward Henry Newenham (1817–92) when he succeeded his uncle to the estate in 1849.

Heaney 1999; *LGI* (1904); Bence-Jones 1988; IAA; RIBA Drawings Collection (Cundy Sketch-book, pp 23, 37, 96–9).

300. COOLROE, Ballincollig; pre-1841; *demolished.*
An old seat in the eighteenth century of the Wetheral family, the lodge to which has been replaced by a twentieth-century bungalow.

Smith 1893; Taylor and Skinner 1778; 1783.

301. COOLYHANE, Macroom; *c.* 1810; *demolished.*

IAA

The most delightful of single-storey drum lodges with round-headed openings in limewashed harled walls below a thatched conical roof, probably contemporary with the big house, in 1837 'the seat of Richard Ashe Esq. . . . recently erected'.

Lewis 1837; IAA photograph (39/35).

302. COOMLOGANE, Millstreet (2).
The big house built next to the town by Denis McCarthy O'Leary was demolished in 1955, to be survived by one of its two lodges, both added by John McCarthy O'Leary (1814–96), who succeeded his father in 1829.

North gate; pre-1936; *demolished.*

South gate; *c.* 1845.
A standard single-storey hip-roofed lodge with an eaves frieze band and 'Irish pilasters' defining the bays. Occupied and 'improved' with new plastic windows and the addition of a gabled glazed hall with corrugated-iron roof.

LGI (1904); Hajba 2002.

303. COOPERVILLE, Macroom; pre-1842; *demolished.*
A property in 1837 of W. Warsop Cooper, the lodge to which was a ruin by 1938.

Lewis 1837.

304. CORBALLY, Glanmire; pre-1841; *demolished.*
The lodge is survived by a good rustic gatescreen of limewashed harled pillars and walls, that to the left-hand side containing a round-arched niche, perhaps all built for William John Sheehy (d. 1868), who succeeded his father to the estate in 1806.

IFR.

305. CORBALLY, Kanturk; pre-1841; *demolished.*
A seat in 1824 of Patrick and Timothy Shine, the porter's lodge to which, not quite opposite its gates, had been removed by 1937.

Pigot 1824.

306. CORK CITY GAOL, Cork [N]; 1824; architect William Robertson.

Surviving from the original massive complex is this imposing entrance barbican in a locally quarried sandstone as coursed facings. A symmetrical five-bay Tudor Castellated composition, approached via double steps to the central doorway in an elliptically arched recess flanked by three-storey canted bays rising to Irish crenellated parapets. Flanking two-storey wings contain label-moulded dressed and mullioned bipartite windows and terminate in mock machicolated and castellated parapets. Designed by William Robertson of Kilkenny in 1818, with Thomas Deane acting as contractor.

Windele 1849; O'Dwyer 1997b.

307. CORK CITY GASWORKS, Cork [S]; *c.* 1830.

All that remains of an extensive establishment is this pleasant legacy, a single-storey Classical porter's lodge faced in squared limestone masonry, its principal two-bay front of round-arched openings with spoked glazing, below a basic pedimented gable. Railed gatescreen with pediment-capped limestone pillars.

NIAH.

308. CORK DISTRICT LUNATIC ASYLUM, Cork [N] (2).
A vast institutional pile built between 1847 and 1852 to Tudor Gothic designs of William Atkins was extended by him in 1861 to create 'an interminable façade and panoply of

spires spectacularly sited to dominate the valley to the Lee'. To this he provided a wholly appropriate introductory gatekeeper's lodge at the main gate.

Principal entrance; *c.* 1861; architect William Atkins.

In like High Victorian Gothic and the same polychromatic limestone-dressed sandstone facings of its brooding backdrop is this 1½-storey composition on a simple rectangular plan but rendered informal with irregular fenestration, a projecting porch from the right-hand side and a sole gablet breaking the high front eaves. The steep gables terminate in skew-tables off kneelers, a diagonal buttress to a leading corner, while the ridge is broken by a sturdy battered chimney-stack. Openings are enhanced by a variety of square and pointed arches arranged as single and bipartite lancets with finely chiselled chamfered reveals and random toothed dressings to match the quoins. There is a very similar lodge to St Vincent's Orphanage [*q.v.*].

Secondary entrance; *c.* 1860.

Occupying the site of a previous lodge that served the Carrigmore [*q.v.*] estate, absorbed to accommodate the huge complex, is this plain 1½-storey standard lodge, in roughcast finish and with ornamental bargeboards to gables. Derelict.

Williams 1994; O'Dwyer 1997a.

309. CORK FEVER HOSPITAL, Cork [S]; *c.* 1865; architect possibly W.D. Smith; *demolished.*

Built as an adjunct of the Union Workhouse of 25 years earlier, to designs of William D'Esterre Smith, its porter's lodge probably forming part of his commission from Cork Union Board of Guardians.

IAA.

310. CORKBEG, Whitegate; pre-1841; *demolished.*

The island demesne of the Uniacke Penrose-Fitzgeralds, the causeway approach to which was guarded on the main road by the porter's lodge—like its big early nineteenth-century house, lost to make way for an oil refinery.

Bence-Jones 1988.

311. CORRAN, Inishannon; pre-1841; *demolished.*

A seat in the nineteenth century of the Hornibrooke family, the gatekeeper's lodge to which was located remote from the public road.

312. CORTIGAN, Mallow; pre-1841; *demolished.*

Another property of the Jephson family, secondary to that of their main seat of Mallow Castle [*q.v.*] on the opposite bank of the Blackwater. Probably occupied as a dower house or by an agent.

313. COSHEEN, Castletownsend; pre-1841; *demolished.*

Alternatively known as 'Point' when Richard Boyle Townsend was given by Lewis as occupant in 1837, although his dates are given as 1756–1826 or 1827, depending on the source. Its lodge was sited distant from the county road.

Lewis 1837; *LGI* (1904); *IFR*.

314. COTTAGE, Coachford; pre-1841; *demolished.*

Almost uniquely for the Ordnance Survey, the 1841–2 map describes the lodge opposite its gates as 'Old Gate Lodge'. Its antiquity then must have militated against it, for it had gone by 1938. A property in 1814 and 1837 of John Pyre.

Leet 1814; Lewis 1837.

315. COTTAGE, Doneraile; *c.* 1835.

A standard single-storey lodge with two-over-two sash windows in harled walls and loft space permitted by its gabled roof, a brick chimney-stack to the left-hand side. It survived the big house, first recorded in 1807 as the residence of John Norcott MD, who died in 1843.

Hajba 2002.

316. COURT MACSHERRY, Courtmacsherry (2).

'The marine villa of the Earl of Shannon', whose main seat was Castle Martyr [*q.v.*], it became in the mid-nineteenth century home to Ladies Jane and Elizabeth Boyle, spinster daughters of the 3rd earl, apparently shared by the Leslie family, John Leslie being recorded here in 1837. There are two pretty porters' lodges.

Coastal gate; *c.* 1835.

A striking 1½-storey *cottage orné* with a hefty banded chimney-stack to the ridge of a slated hipped roof, steeply pitched to prompt visions of a lost thatch. The eaves to avenue and road fronts are broken by gablets, each containing a lattice-glazed lancet attic casement window. The three-bay symmetrical entrance front has a basic gabled porch flanked by wide windows with tripartite pointed-arched insets, with another on the road elevation, the whole finished in a whitened crisp rendering. All lovingly tended.

Inland gate; *c.* 1845.

A dapper single-storey standard lodge, its walls in stucco effect with wide windows containing tripartite inset casements with round heads, a pattern neatly repeated in the panelled door. Below the high oversailing soffits of the shallow hipped roof is a plain frieze, a feature also to be seen under the chimney capping.

Lewis 1837; *PGI*; Griffith 1853–63; *BPB* (1929).

317. COVENTRY, Cork [S]; pre-1842; *demolished.*

A roadside property of the Sarsfields of Doughcloyne House [*q.v.*], much tenanted down the years, in 1814 by the Revd Beaufort, but vacant by 1852. Its gatekeeper's lodge had been removed by the turn of the twentieth century.

Leet 1814; Griffith 1853–63.

CRAMER'S COURT (see BALLINDINISK)

318. CREAGH CASTLE, Doneraile (2).

Windele in 1841 was moved to record that 'The Gateway is the handsomest thing of the kind I have seen in the country, being entirely Gothic, formed of panelled piers, surmounted by ogee crocheted pinnacles with finials, etc., the arches depressed, the workmanship is excellent'. Nor has it been exceeded since as the most extravagant and lavishly detailed Tudor Gothic entrance in Ireland, the avenue of which leads to an impressive medieval tower-house and a most restrained Classical house, erected only twelve years earlier. Did William Johnson Brasier-Creagh (1782–1827) and his brother George Washington Brasier-Creagh (1797–1876) intend to embellish their father's house sufficiently to justify its dramatic prelude? An architect is not recorded, but the Pain brothers, George Richard and James, would seem to have been the sole locally based practitioners with the ability. The form of the gatescreen is also redolent of that at Castle Leslie, Co. Monaghan, designed around 1812 by John Nash when the Pains were assistants in his London office.

Principal gate; *c.* 1827; architects probably G.R. and J. Pain.

An immaculately tooled limestone ashlar tripartite gateway, the central carriage opening spanned by a Tudor arch below Gothic arcading and a crenellated coping, all contained by octagonal turrets with recessed panels rising to crocketed finials. To each side the like-arched postilion openings are label-moulded with spandrels of quatrefoils

and mouchettes, stopped by buttressed piers crowned by poppy-topped finials. Beyond, extensive concave quadrant walls terminate in square pillars embellished with recessed pointed tracery to shafts and octagonal columns to each corner, from which spring crown spires rising to support spirelets. The gate ironwork is suitably chunky, with complementary Tudor Gothic detailing. Datestone. Within is an exquisite single-storey standard lodge with its main façade in corresponding style, having just a hint of Hindu Gothic with its octagonal piers to main corners and those of the tall entrance frontispiece rising to spirelets in the manner of minarets and containing castellated parapets. The double-leafed doorway is set below a hood-moulded Tudor arch and an arcaded apron course above. To each side are little rectangular breakfront bays with bipartite four-over-four sash windows below their own hood mouldings and crenellated parapets. While the architect has not been identified, the remarkable quality of the stonework can be attributed to masons called Regan of Doneraile, and the stonecutters identified as two men named Flynn from Dromore Cross.

Secondary gate; *c.* 1820.

Alongside a plain gateway is an equally ordinary and derelict pair of 1½-storey three-bay symmetrical semi-detached cottages.

LGI (1904); Pike and Hodges 1911; de Breffny and ffolliott 1975; Dean 1994.

319. CREAGH, Skibbereen; *c.* 1820.

A property listed in 1814 as the residence of Alexander O'Driscoll and subsequently acquired by William Wrixon-Becher (1780–1850) of Ballygiblin [*q.v.*], who was created a baronet in 1831. Now the setting for outstanding gardens, its lodge is a much-modernised two-storey, three-bay gatehouse. Adjacent is a new gatesweep with cat and dog finials.

Leet 1814; *BPB* (1929).

320. CREAGH RECTORY AND CHURCH, Skibbereen (2).

Both the porter's lodge built by 1842 and that added by 1902 have been demolished, to be survived by a pleasant group of glebe house of *c.* 1820, church of about 1810, the remains of its predecessor and the graveyard.

Lewis 1837.

321. CREGANE, Liscarroll; *c.* 1840.

In exposed limestone is the standard gatekeeper's lodge, with tall eaves to accommodate loft rooms lit by skylights in its oversailing hipped roof; mouth-organ fanlight to front door. Derelict. There is an almost identical lodge to Knockhouse Farm [*q.v.*] nearby, likewise a property in the vast estates of the earls of Egmont. Cregane in 1844 was occupied by the Hutchins family.

Hajba 2002.

322. CREGG CASTLE, Fermoy; pre-1841; *demolished.*

A lofty Georgian mansion, like the neighbouring Castle Hyde [*q.v.*] of the Hydes, but for much of the early nineteenth century home to Colonel William Stewart through his marriage to a Hyde.

Leet 1814; Fraser 1838; Hajba 2002.

323. CREGGANE, Rosscarbery; *c.* 1835.

The seat in 1814 of Richard Dunscombe, although the gatekeeper's lodge is likely to have been added by his successor, Robert Starkey, who was resident by 1837. The first OS map reveals the single-storey lodge to have survived in outline much as then, with its back return and entrance porch to the right-hand side of the avenue front, both gabled, while a canted end addresses the road below an equivalent roof. Exceedingly solid, being faced in a rubble stone also used to create soldier-arched openings, its windows being casement replacements in Edwardian style with fixed multi-squared uppers. The ridge is broken by a hefty brick-built chimney comprised of a conjoined pair of diagonally set stacks on a rectangular base. Admirably restored.

Leet 1814; Lewis 1837.

324. CROBEG, Doneraile; *c.* 1805.

A thoroughly delightful little single-storey hip-roofed lodge with limewashed harled

walls. The short main avenue front displays a charming pointed-arched doorway with tiny integral sidelights, while that to the road is a two-windowed elevation. Sadly derelict, overgrown and returning to nature. Built for barrister George Stawell (1770–1825), who acquired the property in 1803 but whose pleasant home was demolished in the 1980s.

LGI (1912); Hajba 2002.

325. CROOKSTOWN, Crookstown; *c.* 1825.

Probably pre-dating its porter's lodge is this chaste and striking Classical gateway, its carriage opening flanked by twin ashlar trabeated postilion archways, each round-headed with archivolt and keystone and framed by pairs of Doric pilasters carrying an entablature. Contrasting pleasingly are whitewashed rubble quadrant walls. Probably built in the time here of Revd Robert Warren (d. 1830), who had succeeded to the estate on the death in 1811 of his father, Sir Robert Warren of nearby Warren'scourt [*q.v.*]. Relatively unsophisticated and hopelessly dilapidated is the single-storey standard lodge built in rubble off a square plan, its shallow pyramidal roof rising to a tiny central chimney-stack. Its sole architectural feature is a cut-stone string-course which steps over doorway and bipartite casement windows as label mouldings. Might building of the gateway have stretched funds when it came to providing a complementary lodge?

BPB (1929).

326. CROSSHAVEN, Crosshaven; *c.* 1835.

In contrast to the big, sombre Classical house is this Georgian Gothic-style lodge, built off a square plan with a pyramidal roof terminating in a little chimney-stack. Exposed rubble walls contain pointed-arched openings with neatly toothed brick dressings. Occupied and well maintained, but its original windows lost to bland modern latticed lead-effect replacements. Probably built by Thomas Hayes II (1813–1900), who had inherited the property as a minor on the death of his father in 1817.

IFR.

327. CRUISKEEN LODGE, Cork [S]; pre-1842; *demolished.*

A secluded property, both house and its lodge sited distant from the road; home in 1852 to Jeremiah Carroll.

Griffith 1853–63.

328. CULLIG TOWNLAND, Churchtown; pre-1841.

To an anonymous house, in 1851 of the Coghlan family, is a plain four-bay single-storey gabled cottage of doubtful age. Occupied.

Griffith 1853–63.

329. CURRA, Ballinclashet; pre-1841; *demolished.*

A property in the mid-nineteenth century of Samuel Buck, the lodge to which had been removed by 1934.

Griffith 1853–63.

330. CURRAGHBOWER, Lombardstown; pre-1936; *demolished.*

A holding of the Bolster family, of whom George Bolster, after succeeding to it in 1842, built the adjacent flour mill and perhaps added the porter's lodge, retaining an interest in the place until 1900.

Hajba 2002.

331. CURRAGLASS, Tallow; pre-1841; *demolished.*

Another seat of the Gumbleton family of nearby Castle View [*q.v.*] and Fort William [*q.v.*] and Castle Richard [*q.v.*] in County Waterford, improvements to which were carried out in the early nineteenth century by Henry C. Gumbelton (d. 1834). The lodge had been removed by 1935.

Townsend 1815; Pigot 1824; *BPB* (1929).

CURRAVARAHANE (see THE FARM)

332. CURRYCLOGH, Bandon; pre-1841; *demolished.*

Gone by 1942 was the porter's lodge to a property in 1851 of Denis O'Donoghue.

Griffith 1853–63.

333. CURRYMOUNT, Churchtown; *c.* 1840; architect not known.

A house, built around 1780 by one John Gregg, which gradually assumed its present mid-Victorian appearance through improvement and additions of the O'Leary family and Alexander McCarthy. David O'Leary is recorded as occupant in 1840 and would seem to have built this precocious and commodious gatehouse in the newfangled Tudor Picturesque manner. Two-storey standard and perfectly symmetrical, with fine foiled bargeboards to the main gables and that of the entrance breakfront, contrasting with the pleasant cut stone of the principal front. Openings are conspicuously highlighted by painted toothed brick dressings and heavy label mouldings framing the sheeted front door with rectangular fanlight and original windows remarkably retaining their innovative multi-squared cast-iron centre pivot openers. Occupied, well maintained and reassuringly durable in its own mature planted setting.

Hajba 2002; NIAH.

334. CUSKINNY, Cobh; *c.* 1835; architect possibly James Pain.

Architect James Pain was engaged to prepare a scheme to reface the old plain family mansion in the new Tudor Revival manner, a proposal that never materialised, probably owing to the death of his patron, Savage French, in 1834. There survives just a hint of that commission in the gate lodge with its Tudor label mouldings to openings, perhaps carried out for Sampson Towgood Wynne French (1807–78), who succeeded his father to the estate. Now an otherwise modest single-storey standard structure with a shallow gabled roof, having lost much in modernisation with its rendered walls, replacement windows, a one-bay extension

to the left-hand side and a gawky recent chimney-stack probably having replaced a feature Picturesque original. Rather less attractive is a pair of big brutal Classical carriage pillars with squat ball finials.

LGI (1904); Pike and Hodges 1911; IAA.

335. DANESFORT, Mallow; pre-1841; *demolished.*
An early nineteenth-century house, built by James Butler Stopford to replace a cottage on the site, which by 1837 was home to his brother-in-law, Capt. Edmund Lombard (d. 1848). Like its porter's lodge, it has been demolished.

Lewis 1837; Hajba 2002.

336. DARLING HILL, Monkstown; pre-1841; *demolished.*
A property in 1837 of W.R. Daltera Esq., whose gatekeeper's lodge had gone by 1934.

Lewis 1837.

337. DAVIS' CASTLE, Grenagh; pre-1841; *demolished.*
A lodge removed by 1938 to a seat in 1851 of Henry Hassett.

Griffith 1853–63.

338. DEANESFORT, Inishannon; pre-1842/*c.* 1870.
A standard 1½-storey lodge with toothed stone dressings and quoins in pebble-dashed walls, its single-storey gabled hall projection with foiled bargeboards below eaves broken by two front gablets in a steeply gabled roof having an ornamental earthenware canted cresting with trefoil perforations and fleur-de-lis hip-knobs. A replacement for an earlier porter's lodge on the site. A property in 1851 of Revd Somers Payne, who also had nearby Upton [*q.v.*].

Griffith 1853–63.

DEANROCK (see SUMMERSTOWN [2])

339. DEELISH, Macroom; pre-1842; *demolished.*
An estate in the nineteenth century of the Harnett family. Their lodge, distant from its gate, had gone by 1938.

340. DEELISH, Skibbereen; pre-1842; *demolished.*
By the River Ilen, the lodge opposite the entrance to a seat in 1850 of Henry Marmion had been removed by 1944.

Griffith 1853–63.

341. DERREEN, Coachford (2).
Both gatekeepers' lodges built before 1842 to an estate in 1837 of William Crooke have been demolished.

Lewis 1837.

342. DERRY COTTAGE, Coachford; pre-1841; *demolished.*
Part of the neighbouring estate of Derry [*q.v.*] associated with the Gibbs family, from whom it was rented by Revd William Meade in 1837 and by Thomas Barrett in 1852. The lodge had gone by 1938.

Lewis 1837; Griffith 1853–63.

343. DERRY, Coachford (2).
The family seat in 1814 of Daniel Gibbs and 23 years later of John Bennett Gibbs.

West gate; *c.* 1840.
Not quite opposite its gates is a five-bay symmetrical roughcast gabled cottage, occupied and much modernised.

North gate; pre-1841; *demolished.*
What was probably the principal entrance distant from the Kanturk road, the lodge at which had been removed by 1938.

Leet 1814; Lewis 1837.

344. DERRY, Rosscarbery; *c.* 1840.

A house built for himself around the turn of the nineteenth century by Revd Horatio Townsend (1750–1837), rector of Clonakilty and Carrigaline, historian and author of *A general and statistical survey of the county of Cork* (1815). The splendid 1½-storey Tudor Picturesque English Cottage-style porter's lodge by the entrance may, however, have been added after his father's death by Revd Chambre Corker Townsend (d. 1852). Built off a spacious cruciform plan, it elevates loftily to steeply pitched gables relieved by blind oculi and decorated with eccentrically carved bargeboards, the ridges meeting at a trio of diagonally set flues. This medieval theme extends to label mouldings with dainty pendant dripstones, in what were harled walls, above bipartite six-over-four sash windows, the upper of which had pretty ornate glazing. The triangular-arched doorway is now framed in rubble stone, the fabric having been exposed in what deserves to be a faithful restoration project. Otherwise-plain entrance pillars have cappings mimicking the lodge roof.

Townsend 1815; *IFR*.

345. DESERT COTTAGE, Ballineen; pre-1841; *demolished.*
A property in 1853 of Mrs Susan McDonnell which by 1903 was 'Knockmacool' and lodgeless.

Griffith 1853–63.

DESERTSERGES RECTORY (see CHURCH HILL)

346. DIAMOND HILL, Ballintemple; pre-1902; *demolished.*
A house, and its attendant lodge, erected after 1841, its proprietor in 1870 Mr Attill Wellwood.

Slater 1870.

DISTILLERY COTTAGE (see MIDLETON DISTILLERY)

DITCHLEY (see CASTLE VIEW, Glanmire)

347. DONERAILE COURT, Doneraile (2).
The noble house and estate of the St Leger family since 1630, both of its entrance lodges dating from the early nineteenth century, that at the main gate announced by a magnificent triumphant archway.

Principal entrance; *c.* 1840; architects probably J. and G.R. Pain.

In deeply rusticated V-jointed ashlar is this Classical triumphal triple gate of *c.* 1820, its round-headed arches with moulded archivolts below entablatures, that of the tall carriage opening crowned by a die, broken by a keystone and flanked by a giant pair of detached Ionic columns on pedestals, the whole central to a vast segmental forecourt with walled quadrants. Robert Graham, visiting in July 1835, found the equally sturdy iron gates impenetrable: 'here I met the first disappointment of the day. I expected to get in at an approach to Lord Doneraile's park where I first touched it and to have driven through the grounds and then proceeded to Mallow; but the gate was locked and no lodge at hand. So I was obliged to skirt the outside of the park wall.' An

attendant lodge was built about fifteen years later for Hayes St Leger (1786–1854), who had succeeded as 3rd Viscount Doneraile in 1819. It is an important single-storey temple structure in ashlar, the three gables of its T-plan pedimented, that of the downstroke with a tetrastyle portico of chunky Doric columns forward of the symmetrical three-bay entrance front; there are architraved openings of six-over-six sash windows on each side of the panelled doorway. Surely a complex by the brothers Pain, James and George Richard, the latter having designed an almost identical archway at Lota Beg [*q.v.*] and being recorded in the Doneraile Papers as having carried out an inspection here of earlier 'Proposals and estimates of masonry for sweep wall and lodges in Doneraile Court'. The masons responsible are identified as Phil Mohily, Thomas Fitzgerald, E. Stack and John McCarthy.

Secondary entrance; *c.* 1825; architects probably J. and G.R. Pain.

Altogether more prosaic on the southern approach is this single-storey roughcast cottage with high eaves and paired chimney-stack to the hipped roof. To the long avenue front is a pair of square bipartite latticed cast-iron casement windows, the lodge entered from the road elevation. This hint of Tudor Picturesque contrasts with a fine Classical triple gateway, its ashlar pillars with scroll-topped gate stops and ball finials.

Heaney 1999; Pike and Hodges 1911; *BPB* (1929); Malins and Glin 1976; NLI (Doneraile Papers: MS 34,106).

348. DONICKMORE, Clonmult; pre-1853; *demolished.*

A lodge identified to a property in the 1853 valuation of John Ronayne, obvious neither on the OS maps nor on site.

Griffith 1853–63.

349. DONNYBROOK, Doneraile; *c.* 1870.

A single-storey standard lodge notable for its front façade of red brick in Flemish bond, containing rectangular three-over-three sash windows and doorway in smooth dressings below singular ribbed label mouldings, all framed by a recess created by advancing piers and the oversailing eaves of a pyramidal roof no longer rising to a central stack—replaced by that on a side wall. Derelict and succumbing to vegetation. Built for Arundel Hill, the surviving V-jointed rusticated stone pillars with dainty moulded cappings look to be late eighteenth-century.

Hajba 2002.

350. DONNYBROOK, Donnybrook; *c.* 1845; *demolished.*

A lodge built sometime between the Ordnance Survey of 1842 and the valuation ten years later on the estate of Thomas Jones.

Griffith 1853–63.

351. DONNYBROOK ROPE FACTORY, Donnybrook; pre-1852; *demolished.*

Not identifiable on the OS maps was the gate lodge to an establishment with house, offices and four acres in 1853 of Bartholomew Gibbings (b. 1786) of Gibbings Grove [*q.v.*].

Griffith 1853–63; *LGI* (1904).

352. DOON, Kinsale; pre-1841; *demolished.*

The residence in 1852 of Revd John R. Webb, the gate lodge to which had gone by 1939.

Griffith 1853–63.

353. DOUGHCLOYNE [1], Cork [S]; pre-1842/*c.* 1870.

On the death in 1868 of Philip Sarsfield it was his nephew, Dominick Ronayne Sarsfield (1828–92), who probably built this distinctive gatehouse as a replacement lodge. Whereas its predecessor was located distant from the public road, this 1½-storey structure has a short gabled façade comprised of a two-bay ground floor fronting the footway, the

sheeted doorway with faintly pointed head flanked by a tiny sash window, one-over-one like the big centrally positioned bipartite attic window over. This is all arranged in striking, loosely patterned, polychrome squared masonry finish. Occupied.

LGI (1904).

354. DOUGHCLOYNE [2], Cork [S]; *c.* 1825.

A very modest single-storey standard gabled cottage to a property in 1814 of a Mr Haynes which by 1837 was home to James Simpson Esq. Thereafter it became home to Philip Sarsfield (d. 1868), son of Dominick Ronayne Sarsfield of neighbouring Doughcloyne [1] [*q.v.*], but after whose death it went into decline.

Leet 1814; Lewis 1837; Griffith 1853–63; *LGI* (1904).

355. DOUGLAS FARM, Douglas; pre-1841; *demolished.*

A seat of Frederick Olden in 1852, by which time the place had been upgraded to 'Douglas Hall'.

Griffith 1853–63.

356. DOUGLAS, Douglas; pre-1841; *demolished.*

An estate in 1814 of William Lumley but the residence 23 years later of T. Fitzgerald Esq.

Leet 1814; Lewis 1837.

357. DOUGLAS, Kilworth; pre-1841; *demolished.*

A late Georgian house of the earls of Mountcashel, subsidiary to their main seat of Moore Park [*q.v.*], probably built as their dower house but occupied in 1837 by Henry

Decie and later by the dowager Lady Mountcashel.

Lewis 1837; Griffith 1853–63.

358. DOWNDANIEL, Inishannon; *c.* 1835.
A singular 2½-storey gabled structure in stucco-effect finish with one surviving label moulding. Derelict, next to two entrance accesses with drum pillars that led to the house in the early nineteenth century of Chambre Coker, upon whose death around 1830 it passed to Revd R.L. Conner.

Leet 1814; Pigot 1824; Lewis 1837.

359. DRIPSEY CASTLE, Coachford; *c.* 1820/*c.* 1860.

At the entrance to the old fifteenth-century McCarthy moated castle and a Georgian house of the Colthurst family is this fascinating group of structures—to one side a three-storey rubble-built round tower with mock arrowloops and corbelled, Irish-crenellated parapet, probably built as little more than an eye-catching folly, seemingly succeeding a pair of plain square Georgian carriage pillars with moulded cappings. Within is a simple single-storey gabled cottage, likewise rubble-built, its three-bay avenue front with doorway to the left-hand side, all modernised in mid-century with the addition of banded opening surrounds to new one-over-one sash windows and very pretty bargeboards carved into cusped foils and pierced with quatrefoils. Both structures probably originated in the time of Major John Bowen Colthurst (1779–1848), who inherited the property on his father's death in 1815. It is likely to have been his grandson, Joseph Colthurst (1812–82), who initiated the improvements after his succession to the estate in 1865.

IFR; Killanin and Duignan 1962.

360. DRIPSEY LODGE AND PAPER MILLS, Dripsey (2).
The prosperous scene in 1837 of 'the Dripsey paper-mills, belonging to Messrs Magnay and Co., and situated in a deep and well-wooded glen; the buildings are of handsome appearance, and the works afford employment to a number of persons, varying from 70 to 100, in the manufacture of large quantities of paper for the English market'. Although water was the lifeblood of this establishment, it became its downfall, with flooding from the creation of the reservoir that severed the avenues from their house but spared both entrances.

West gate; pre-1842; *demolished.*

East gate; pre-1842.
The large, plain, two-storey gatehouse remains, without a feature to date it.

Lewis 1837.

361. DRISHANE CASTLE, Millstreet (4).

NLI

NLI

Next to a fifteenth-century keep of the McCarthys the Wallis family built themselves a big Georgian house, which successive Victorian generations were to transform into a rambling Tudor Castellated mansion, a process commenced by Henry Wallis (d. 1862) who preceded the first phase at the main gate with a dress rehearsal for what was to be visited upon the house and which was to prove a wholly appropriate prelude.

South entrance; *c.* 1835; architect possibly Sir Thomas Deane.
A Picturesque composition, irregular in outline and dominated by a two-storey octagonal structure with pasteboard machicolation below a crenellated parapet, the windows to which an old photograph shows containing wooden traceried Tudor Gothic glazing reminiscent of the work of Sir Thomas Deane, and probably label-moulded, like the big house. To the rear rises an attached circular stair tower, preceded by an entrance porch with pointed-arched openings—all castellated, as are the lofty square carriage pillars and extensive rubble curtain walls beyond. Now lying boarded up and abandoned but maintained in startling white livery as some sort of statement—a sad reminder of halcyon days.

Town entrance; pre-1842; *demolished.*
A lodge opposite its gates, removed in the mid-twentieth century.

Lackabane Wood entrance; pre-1842.
A plain and derelict single-storey, four-bay, hip-roofed, limewashed harled cottage with two-over-two sash windows.

Wallis's Bridge entrance; 1870; architect not known; *demolished.*
Henry Aubrey Beaumont Wallis (1861–1926) inherited the estate on his father's death in 1868, and his first contribution to its development was this romantic and forbidding three-bay two-storey gatehouse in a bold quarry-faced sandstone finish, with porter's accommodation extending above the wide, pointed-arched carriage access, lit by round-headed slit windows with Y-tracery. A crowning crenellated parapet with mock machicolation extends between a tall octagonal spiral stair turret and a balancing square corbelled bartizan atop a two-stage diagonal buttress. Once situated in the corner of a vast concourse with boundary wall punctuated by squat round turrets, the gatehouse is ludicrously survived solely by its lonesome stair tower. The date-stone conveys the time of its construction, when the Owennagloor River was bridged to replace 'stepping stones'.

Latterly home to the Convent of the Holy Infant Jesus.

Lawrence photographs (10324R; 10328R; 10329R); *IFR*; Bence-Jones 1988.

362. DRISHANE, Castletownsend (2).
A graceful villa built overlooking Castlehaven Bay around 1790 by Thomas Townsend Somerville (d. 1811), whose son, Thomas Somerville (1797–1882), complemented the pretty demesne with a couple of porters' lodges.

Front gate; *c.* 1830.

A two-storey shallow-gabled gatehouse on a T-plan, much altered and sanitised in modernisation with a bland, crisp grey rendering, but retaining some delightful square-paned bipartite casements with Gothic cinquefoiled heads to the ground-floor openings. Built tight to the rear of the left-hand rubble quadrant entrance wall; the right-hand wall contains a curved bench over which is a plaque commemorating Vice-Admiral Boyle Townshend Somerville (1863–1936) and another nicely sculpted with the family crest and motto: 'Fear God in Life'.

Rear gate; *c.* 1830.

A fine rustic Italianate cottage, single-storey with shallow oversailing gables off an L-plan, the wing to the road displaying a lattice-glazed, mullioned and transomed casement window with a small blind *oeil-de-boeuf* over for relief in a limewashed harled finish. Mysteriously lying neglected and derelict in an area of much-sought-after holiday accommodation.

LGI (1904); Pike and Hodges 1911.

363. DROMACULLEN, Coachford; pre-1842; *demolished.*
A property in 1852 of John Connell, leased from the Woodley family.

Griffith 1853–63.

364. DROMADDA, Castlemartyr (2).
A seat in the early nineteenth century of Warham Durdin (1769–1822), after whose death it was acquired by George Courtenay (1795–1837). One of these two may have added the dignity of a pair of lodges to the main entrance and a single lodge to the secondary gate further west, with its entrance encroaching on the highway. None survive.

Leet 1814; Pigot 1824; *LGI* (1904); *IFR.*

365. DROMAGH CASTLE, Banteer (2).
Originally a property of the O'Kiefs, by 1814 it was the seat of Nicholas Philpot Leader (1773–1836), upon whose death it passed to his eldest son (1810–80) of the same name. The only remaining evidence of their presence here is a fine castellated stable yard and one Classical gateway, the house having been destroyed by the IRA in 1921.

North entrance; pre-1841; *demolished.*

Surviving the lodge opposite is an extensive and ornate gatescreen comprised of a triple access, the ironwork of its gates and secondary pillars, with their anthemion motifs in hooped tops, repeated in the railed quadrants, the whole contained by stone pillars with cappings relieved by recessed 'lunettes'.

South entrance; pre-1841; *demolished.*

Another structure across from its gates, the primary function of which in the nineteenth century was as a 'schoolhouse'; by the following century it served as a post office.

Leet 1814; *PGI*; *LGI* (1904); Williams 1994.

366. DOMANEEN, Mallow; pre-1841; *demolished.*
The residence in the 1840s of the Bolster family.

O'Flanagan 1975.

367. DROMAVANE, Murragh; pre-1841; *demolished.*
A property in 1852 of Thomas Munn.

Griffith 1853–63.

368. DROMBEG, Rosscarbery (2).
In 1814 the seat of John Baldwin; by 1837 he had been succeeded here by Revd Jonas Travers Jones, who may have added the gatekeepers' lodges on acquiring the place.

Glandore gate; *c.* 1820.

A tiny, modest, single-storey hip-roofed cottage, with a hefty chimney-stack to the road elevation and a two-bay avenue front of casement windows in a crisp modern rendering.

Rosscarbery gate; *c.* 1820.

On an elevated site opposite the gates, what was a relatively sophisticated lodge, now having lost some character in modernisation. Single-storey standard below a tall-eaved hipped roof from which projects a pedimented hallway, its large fanlit doorway, like the quoins in toothed rusticated stone dressings, flanked by tiny replacement casement windows.

Leet 1814; Lewis 1837.

369. DROMBROW, Bantry; *c.* 1855.
Probably by the same jobbing builder as the lodge to nearby Beach [*q.v.*] is this single-storey standard lodge below an oversailing hipped roof, constructed in a rubble finish with brick surround to the round-arched doorway. Having been here since the 1790s, the White family parted with it in 1853 to a retired army major, Arthur Bury Wilkinson (*c.* 1805–73), who presumably commissioned the building of the porter's lodge and further enhanced the estate, subsequently noted for its water lilies and rhododendrons.

Everett 2001.

370. DROMCARRA, Inchigeelagh; pre-1842; *demolished.*
The seat in 1837 of Joseph M. Barter.

Lewis 1837.

371. DROMDEER, Doneraile; pre-1841; *demolished.*
The Norcott family were in residence between the late eighteenth century and 1844, when it was leased to Charles Campion. Their house was demolished in the 1990s, its porter's lodge having preceded it by 1937.

Hajba 2002.

372. DROMDIHY, Killeagh; pre-1934; *demolished.*
Sadly little remains of the fine development of 1833 by Roger Green Davis, who built the handsome winged Classical house, now in ruins, and a lodge, added after 1841 opposite its gates.

Lewis 1837.

373. DROMORE, Mallow (2).
Both lodges, built before 1841, have been replaced by twentieth-century dwellings, that to the north-west survived by an original gatescreen and limestone pillars with recessed panels and two-tiered pyramidal cappings. The old seat of the Newman family, now 'Nazareth House'.

DROMORE, OLD **(see OLD DROMORE)**

374. DROMRAHAN, Killnavullen; *c.* 1845.
Like the house and its ancillary buildings, the 1½-storey gabled gatekeeper's lodge is faced in a distinctive red sandstone, with a miniature like-roofed hall projection from the avenue front. Occupied and modernised. A development for Thomas Franks (1805–75) of the Rockforest [*q.v.*] family.

LGI (1904); Hajba 2002.

DRUMCORA **(see CARRIGDUVE)**

375. DUARRIGLE CASTLE, Millstreet; *c.* 1892/*c.* 1944.
Originally an O'Keeffe estate with a subsequent chequered history, the big house having been rebuilt by the Justice family in

1806 in Romantic Castellated style before falling on hard times, suffering in the Famine, being sold as an incumbered estate in 1851 and thereafter passing through a succession of occupants. In all this time it remained lodgeless, but this was remedied by the Crofts family in 1892. Its valuation of 10/- reveals a certain modesty and by 1922 it was 'down'. Despite appearances, what survives is a 1940s rebuild, a commodious two-storey structure with apparently random fenestration to the avenue with squared glazing, some transomed and mullioned. To the park is a single-storey one-bay addition with pasteboard castellated parapet, while the road front is single-bay below a hipped end, all in a smooth rendered finish which contrasts with the harled rubble on adjoining curtain walls, which flank a round-headed crenellated carriage archway. A convincing and appropriate castellated Georgian style mix, ironically now the prelude to a sad overgrown ruin.

Hajba 2002.

376. DUNBOY CASTLE, Castletownbere (2).
A beautiful and romantic estate, the scene of much tragedy, the great house having been burned down by the IRA in 1921. It had been abandoned unfinished after Henry Lavallin Puxley's wife died in childbirth, which followed his elder brother's short drunken tenure of the place and the death in their 30s of his grandfather and grand-uncle. It was these brothers, John Lavallin Puxley (1800–37) and Henry Puxley (1797–1828), who oversaw the early transformation of a Georgian house into a neo-Gothic castellated fairytale mansion, with an appropriate prelude at the gates in like manner.

Main entrance; *c.* 1835; architect Thomas Allason.

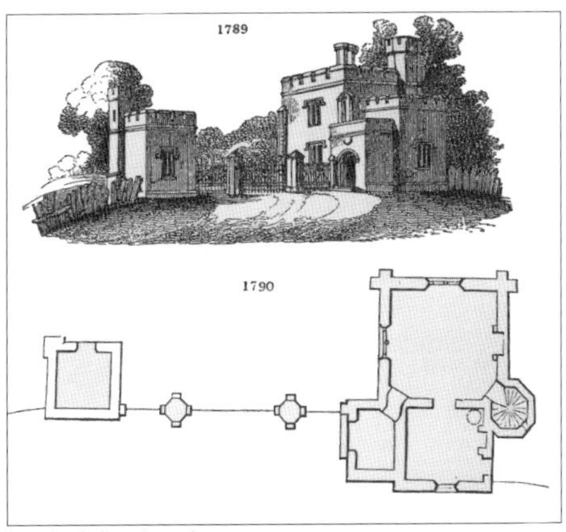

Loudon's *Encyclopaedia*

Whether the relatively obscure architect Thomas Allason (1790–1852) was directly commissioned for the work here is not known. If not, this splendid architectural group was taken from a design published in J.C. Loudon's popular *Encyclopaedia of cottage, farm and villa architecture* (1833), from which it varies only in being considerably loftier than illustrated and its stair tower being telescopic and circular rather than octagonal. The gatekeeper's accommodation is an expert irregular arrangement of interrelated boxes, with crenellated parapets, comprising, according to Loudon, 'a sitting-room and scullery on the ground floor, and three bedrooms over'. While the porch has a pointed-arched opening, the fenestration in harled rubble walls is otherwise a variety of label-moulded single and bipartite windows with pointed mullioned and transomed tracery. A relatively flimsy iron gatescreen (probably missing a pair of stone carriage pillars) links to a miniature keep in its own right, intended by Allason as a coal store. An impressive composition allowed to go to ruin, a process hopefully to be reversed to an introduction befitting the recently restored mansion now at the heart of a luxury hotel complex. There is a later interpretation of Allason's design at Red Hall, Co. Antrim.

Rear entrance; pre-1842; *demolished.*

Loudon 2000; *LGI* (1904); Bence-Jones 1988; Dean 1994; Everett 2001; Colvin 2008.

377. DUNDANION CASTLE, Blackrock; *c.* 1832; architect probably Sir Thomas Deane; *demolished.*
The tourist John Barrow in 1835 records that 'The modern castle takes the name from that of the ruins of an old one still existing in the grounds . . . is one of those numerous villas which have sprung up within the last few years. The present house of Dundanion has been recently built by Sir Thomas Deane, and is tastefully fitted up.' The Cork architect had moved from adjacent Carrigduve [*q.v.*] and doubtless planned his own porter's lodge, which the 1841 OS map shows to have been cruciform in plan.

Barrow 1836; O'Dwyer 1997b.

378. DUNDERROW COTTAGE, Dunderrow; pre-1841; *demolished.*
The occupant in 1837 was Revd R. Halburd, leasing from the Kearney family; the gate lodge had gone by 1939.

Lewis 1837.

379. DUNDERROW RECTORY, Dunderrow; pre-1939; *demolished.*
The glebe house was erected in 1921, although its porter's lodge was an addition later in the century, located across from its entrance gates.

Lewis 1837.

380. DUNDULLERICK EAST, Ballincurrig; pre-1841; *demolished.*
Like its neighbouring sister seat of Dundullerick West [*q.v.*], a property of the Barry family to which James Barry (1782–

1846) succeeded on the death of his father in 1824. His porter's lodge lay opposite its gates, separated by an extensive entrance sweep.

IFR.

381. DUNDULLERICK WEST, Ballincurrig (2).

Both lodges, one opposite the entrance and built before 1841, have been demolished. The estate of Edmond Barry (1794–1862), which he inherited on his father David's death in 1820.

IFR.

382. DUNGOURNEY RECTORY, Dungourney; pre-1853; *demolished.*

A porter's lodge recorded in the Griffith valuation in the incumbency of Revd William Wilson, identifiable neither on an OS map nor on site. Now a private house.

Griffith 1853–63.

383. DUNKEREEN COTTAGE, Inishannon; *c.* 1810.

A standard single-storey gabled cottage with a projecting eaves band above harled rubble walls. Latterly extended by a bay to the left-hand side. Derelict. A seat of the Hornibrook family.

384. DUNKETTLE, Glanmire (4).

Of the four lodges existing in 1841 only one survives, two on the southern boundary having been demolished by 1902 and that to the west removed since, to be survived by a good gatescreen. Remaining on the northern approach is this quintessential Irish gate lodge. Single-storey standard with wide bipartite casement windows on each side of a twin-leafed panelled door, in limewashed harled walls below bracketed oversailing eaves to its shallow pyramidal roof, which rises to a tiny, diagonally set chimney-stack. It lies pitifully derelict beyond a tripartite gateway of four good ashlar Classical pillars with contemporary iron gates, all framed by rubble-walled quadrants. A main entrance complex of *c.* 1825 from the time of Jonas Morris, who inherited the estate in 1822 on the death of his father, who had built the handsome Palladian-style house.

LG (1882); Bence-Jones 1988.

385. DUNMANWAY COTTAGE, Dunmanway; pre-1842/*c.* 1883.

Lost is the lodge of the Cox family to their early Victorian villa, to be replaced by this perky two-storey gatehouse with a perfectly symmetrical front façade. Its central doorway is dominated by an ornate canopy with pretty fretted cusped foil bargeboards and quatrefoil toes, so steeply pitched as to reach the eaves of the hipped roof flanked by the bedroom windows. All finished in a smooth rendering relieved by ceramic tiles as a first-floor string-course and a feature over the front door. Inappropriate modern casement windows. Enclosed by a well-manicured hedge and iron gate, probably salvaged from the previous entrance. Of more sturdy cast iron are the concave railed quadrants and two remaining postilion gates of a once-tripartite gateway, to be survived by five of six original Classical pillars with moulded plinths and recessed panel shafts. Dating from the ownership of John Atkins, when in 1883 its valuation was doubled to £2.

386. DUNMORE, Douglas; 1897.

The so-called 'Dunmahon Lodge' is a single-storey standard hip-roofed porter's lodge, with dentil course to its chimney-stack and 'Irish' pilaster quoins, and a projecting entrance hall with hipped roof. Like the main house, a development for Richard A. Atkins. Occupied.

DUNSLAND (see FACTORY HILL)

387. DURRUS RECTORY, Durrus; pre-1842; *demolished.*

The delightful glebe house was built in 1831 by the rector, Revd Edward Jones Alcock, who doubtless complemented it with a contemporary gate lodge.

388. EAST GROVE, Great Island; *c.* 1820.

A charming Picturesque rustic Italianate villa built for the Bagwells of Marlfield, Co. Tipperary [*q.v.*]. Approached via a remote and impressive entrance forecourt enclosed by crenellated rubble walls broken by a round-headed carriage archway and the leading short front of a Gothic porter's lodge, its single bay monitoring the approach with a pointed-arched sash window in a like recess below a bracketed oversailing gable. Rendered and lacking its Y-traceried glazing, a strangely discordant prelude to what is within.

Heaney 1999.

388. East Grove, Great Island.

389. EAST HILL, Cobh; pre-1841.

Perched precariously on the hillside is this much reworked and extended lodge, apparently having had a shallow hipped roof. Occupied. A property in 1837 of Capt. Thomas Stubbs.

Lewis 1837.

390. EASTLY COTTAGE, Mallow; pre-1841; *demolished.*

In 1824 and 1852 noted as the residence of Miss Mary Anne Lombard.

Pigot 1824; Griffith 1853–63; Hajba 2002.

391. EAST VIEW, Cork [N]; *c.* 1835.

The seat in 1837 of 'J. Leicester Esq., a very pretty villa in the cottage style commanding a splendid view down the river towards Passage'. This Joseph Leycester also added this splendid porter's lodge, which has since suffered from subsequent alterations and extensions in replacement windows and an unpleasant glazed hall. Apparently conceived as a single-storey pyramidal-roofed structure built off a square plan, the exaggerated oversailing eaves extending to cover a rectangular glazed bay window to the avenue front, which was framed by recessed-panel corner pilasters with rosette motifs. Extended initially in sensitive fashion by a matching bay to the right-hand side below an elongated roofline and rendered finish to correspond. The entrance pillars with incised panels and moulded scroll-topped gate stops look to date from around 1865 in the time of

William Leycester. A property also noted for its 'shrubberies and plantations, which form a most interesting botanical study'; latterly known as 'Ennismore'.

Lewis 1837; Windele 1849; Slater 1856; 1870.

392. EDEN HALL, Mallow; pre-1936; *demolished.*
Until around 1855 a seat of Joseph Carpenter, thereafter home to Thomas Carmichael, the lodge dating from after 1841.

Griffith 1853–63; Slater 1856.

393. EGLANTINE COTTAGE, Mallow; pre-1841.
A single-storey hip-roofed, stone-faced structure, much altered and extended with a loft conversion. The entrance screen has basic ogee quadrants and a pair of sphinxes, one decapitated. A small demesne in 1851 of James Welply.

Griffith 1853–63.

394. EGLANTINE, Cork [N]; pre-1841; *demolished.*
The property in 1852 of Reuben Deaves, merchant in the city.

Griffith 1853–63.

395. EGMONT, Churchtown; pre-1841; *demolished.*
One of the many properties of the earls of Egmont in the vicinity, this leased out to David Quinlan (d. 1835) and subsequently to John Hawke Bolster. Its lodge lay deep within on the eastern approach.

Hajba 2002.

396. EGMONT VILLA, Kanturk; *c.* 1830; *demolished.*
A fine Regency villa built on the site of an old McCarthy stronghold by Neptune Blood, the lodge to which may have been contemporary.

Lewis 1837.

397. ELM GROVE, Cork [N]; 1878.
The pitiful remains of a stuccoed overgrown shell of a lodge and its blocked-up entrance screen, at the access to an older house, added to the property that Edward Flynn had then acquired.

398. ELM PARK, Farran; *c.* 1830.
Initially a single-storey standard gabled lodge in rendered finish with a like-roofed central hall projection, alongside which the right-hand bay was subsequently extended. The estate in 1837 of Valentine Barry, which later passed to the Orpen family.

Lewis 1837.

399. ELM VALE, Doneraile; pre-1841; *demolished.*
A late Victorian house, built for Charles W. Wyatt. Its predecessor belonged a century earlier to the Foott family; it was subsequently let in 1801 to Henry Lysaght and in the mid-1800s to the Duggans.

Lewis 1837; Hajba 2002.

400. ENDSLEIGH, Douglas; pre-1841/pre-1902/*c.* 2000.
A property in the mid-nineteenth century of Alleyn C. McCarthy, the surviving porter's lodge to which bears little resemblance in outline to the cruciform plan shown on the first OS map nor to the simple rectangle apparent on the 1902 edition, which was probably incorporated into the present exercise in duality. Linked by a flat-roofed hallway, two single-bay gables have modern continuous bracket bargeboards that ornament a single-storey blandly rendered structure with plastic windows.

Griffith 1853–63.

ENNISMORE (see EAST VIEW)

401. EPISCOPAL PALACE, Cork [S]; *c.* 1840; architect possibly J. Pain.

While the palace dates from the late eighteenth century, its gatekeeper's lodge was added 50 years later, in the episcopacy of the Right Revd Samuel Kyle DD, bishop of Cork, Ross and Cloyne. It is in a very fine neo-Classical form in which the city abounds, particularly north of the river. Single-storey standard but raised from a cruciform plan off a pronounced plinth, with Doric pilastered external corners and a plain frieze below a shallow hipped roof. Rear return and central front hallway projections are gabled, the latter with a good moulded-panel front door. From the avenue elevation extends a semi-octagonal bay window under an equivalent roof, its windows margined sashes in smooth rendered walls. The bay monitors a contemporary entrance screen comprised of a pair of tall carriage pillars with acanthus leaf-decorated friezes and chunky cast-iron gates with matching short, railed concave quadrants. There are lodges akin to this at Clifton, Hyde Park House, Factoryville, Mount Donegan and Shanakiel, all attributable to one or both of the Pain brothers, of whom James was working on St Mary's Cathedral nearby in 1843.

Slater 1846; Bence-Jones 1988.

EVERSLEIGH (see JANEVILLE)

402. FACTORY HILL, Glanmire; *c.* 1840.
The neo-Classical entrance screen is a tripartite gateway of minimal concave railed quadrants framing a central pair of carriage pillars of the tapering pylon type pioneered by J.B. Papworth, each crowned by antifixes containing sculpted anthemion motifs nicely corresponding to the hoop-topped gates with repeating husk features. The gatekeeper's accommodation is substantial in a two-storey gatehouse with a pyramidal roof rising to a central stack. The central entrance breakfront

has a blind recess over the doorway and below a gablet with trefoil-pierced bargeboards. The lovely first-floor bipartite casement windows with latticed glazing serve to distract from the appalling modern ground-floor replacements. A small estate in 1837 and 1846 of William Litchfield, later renamed 'Dunsland' to contain a new neo-Elizabethan mansion of the Pike family.

Lewis 1837; Slater 1846; Pike and Hodges 1911.

403. FACTORY HILL HOUSE, Glanmire; pre-1841; *demolished.*
A small Palladian-style house of the Hoare family, subsequently home to Thomas Martin, the gate lodge to which had gone by 1902.

Bence-Jones 1988.

404. FACTORYVILLE, Douglas (2).
The residence in 1814 of P. Besnard Esq. and subsequently in 1837 of the splendidly named Julius Caesar Besnard, proprietor of the neighbouring Douglas Rope Manufactory. The original pre-1842 lodged gate was moved westwards around 1855 to the present congested road junction. This is a stylish

single-storey standard neo-Classical lodge, with an oversailing shallow hipped roof over an embracing plain frieze carried on Doric pilaster quoins resting on a plinth, all in a drab grey rendered finish, with narrow one-over-one sash windows flanking the central hall projection, likewise hip-roofed; occupied. The excellent gatescreen emphasises how the lodge could benefit from a paint scheme to subtly emphasise its fine detail; it perhaps dates from the time here of James Wheeler Pollock in 1870, by which time the place had been renamed 'Mount Grange'. Each carriage pillar has a plain recessed panel to the shaft but a decorative recessed fan motif to its frieze. There are very similar, if earlier, lodges in the city suburbs at Clifton, Hyde Park House, Mount Donegan and Shanakiel and at the Episcopal Palace, attributable to James Pain.

Leet 1814; Lewis 1837; Slater 1846; *Thom's*.

405. THE FARM, Bandon (2).
In 1841 a property, alternatively known as 'Curravarahane', of the Hon. Lt.-Col. William Smyth Bernard (1792–1863), youngest son of the 1st Lord Bandon of Castle Bernard [*q.v.*] nearby, upon which by 1837 he had built 'a handsome house in the Elizabethan style' and was later to endow with a couple of lodged gates.

East entrance; *c.* 1855.
A plain 1½-storey gabled gatehouse with very high eaves to its symmetrical three-bay front. Occupied.

West entrance; *c.* 1845.
What may have been a standard single-storey

structure with a symmetrical front of three pointed-arched openings has latterly been raised a storey to an ungainly gabled affair with peculiar skew-tables rising to stone arrowhead finials, but all in pleasant rubble facings. These alterations see the front door becoming a window with squared sashes below lofty eaves. Much extended.

Lewis 1837; *BPB* (1929).

406. FARRAN LODGE, Farran (2).
A fine Italianate house of around 1880 designed by Robert Walker of Cork for William Clarke (1803–84), with whom his son, Thomas Clarke (1834–1911), kept faith when a replacement gate lodge was commissioned decades later.

East entrance; pre-1842/1909; architects Robert Walker and Son.

Superseding an earlier lodge of the Penrose family, on the same site as its predecessor across from the gates, is this substantial Arts and Crafts creation. The excellent original triple gateway of *c.* 1810 survives in its tall square ashlar pillars, which have moulded cappings and fine urn finials with fluted bands. Contemporary spear-topped iron gates and matching railings complete the required Georgian symmetry, whereas across the road the Edwardian designers felt no such constraint: 1½-storey gabled, built off an L-plan in pebble-dashed finish, its leading gable presents a 'half-timbered' apex. The ridge is dominated by a pair of large corbelled brick chimney-stacks, while the roof catslides over the internal angle to form a 'colonial' verandah-cum-entrance porch, its eaves with a balustraded frieze carried on elegant carved posts. The architects must have been familiar with John Lanyon's lodge at Blarney Castle [*q.v.*].

West entrance; pre-1938; *demolished.*
A lodge built after 1842, perhaps part of the commission which led to a 'Contract for erection of an Entrance Gate Lodge & 4 cottages on the lands of Farran, Co. Cork, for William Clarke at an estimated cost of £1,100. Plans and specifications by Robert Walker & Son'.

Lewis 1837; *IB* (20 March 1909); *IFR*.

407. FARRANFADDA TOWNLAND, Ballylickey; pre-1852; *demolished.*
A property of Robert White of Glengarriff Cottage [*q.v.*], leased to Timothy Lumsden in 1852, the valuation then identifying a gate lodge, nothing of which is apparent in the townland, on site or on the OS maps.

Griffith 1853–63.

408. FELTRIM, Cork [S]; pre-1841/*c.* 1870.

Long a seat of the Fagan family, whose previous porter's lodge, if contemporary with the surviving gatescreen, was of around 1810. The fine Classical pillars in limestone ashlar display wide moulded cappings, recessed panel shafts and scroll-topped gate stops. The attendant replacement lodge is a typical mid-Victorian Italianate/Tudor Picturesque hybrid; single-storey below a hipped roof, the large gabled entrance hall projection has perforated foiled bargeboards and a spiky hip-knob over a label-moulded window with pendant dripstones, while the low side-entry doorway has a semicircular head. The smooth rendered walls are bound by a continuous sill band and a conspicuous bracketed frieze, a feature repeated below the chimney-stack capping. Probably built by Charles Addis Fagan (1829–1903) on his succession to the property.

LGI (1904).

409. FERMOY COLLEGE, Fermoy; *c.* 1840.
A single-storey standard gabled cottage with perforated wave and foil bargeboards and roughcast walls. Nasty monopitch return. Derelict. What in 1824 was 'an excellent seminary for boarders' and was in 1837 'conducted by Dr Fahie, for the preparation of young gentlemen for the university, was originally built by the late Mr Anderson for a military college', he being John Anderson of nearby Fermoy House [*q.v.*].

Pigot 1824; Lewis 1837.

410. FERMOY COUNTY HOSPITAL, Fermoy; pre-1935; *demolished.*
According to the 1852 valuation a lodge had not yet been built.

Griffith 1853–63.

411. FERMOY, Fermoy; pre-1841; *demolished.*
Surviving the sad loss of both mansion and its gatekeeper's lodge is a handsome gatescreen in the form of a wide railed segment with a series of twelve square pillars, rusticated, plinthed and corniced. The late Georgian house was built by John Anderson, a native of Dumfries who settled here 'with a small fortune' as an army contractor, becoming a pioneer in public transport and the carriage of mail in Ireland, and laying out the town of Fermoy before going bankrupt in 1816.

Curwen 1818; O'Flanagan 1975; Bence-Jones 1988.

412. FERN HILL, Clonakilty; pre-1841; *demolished.*
An estate in 1837 of W.F. Atkin, whose gate lodge lay opposite its gates.
Lewis 1837.

413. FERN HILL, Mallow; pre-1841; *demolished.*
A seat of a branch of the Townsend family, who lived here intermittently over the centuries; previously known as 'Betsborough', it was let to an abundance of lessees and was the birthplace of Thomas Russell (1767–1803), United Irishman and librarian of the Linenhall Library, Belfast. Capt. H. Porter was resident from 1799 to 1817, followed by Matthew Seward. The house was in ruins by 1936, to be briefly outlasted by its lodge.
Hajba 2002.

414. FERNEY, Blackrock; pre-1841; *demolished.*
The suburban seat in 1814 of a Mrs Coote, who by 1837 had been succeeded by J.H. Manley Esq.
Leet 1814; Lewis 1837.

415. FERNHURST, Cork [S]; 1885.
A plain late nineteenth-century 1½-storey gabled roughcast lodge added to his property by Thomas Donovan, who was then also extending the house.

416. FIRGROVE, Inishannon; *c.* 1890.

A standard single-storey hip-roofed lodge built forward of its entrance gates on an awkward sloping site in attractive stone facings. Three-bay to the visitor, leaded casement windows flank its central glazed lobby contained below the oversailing soffit, as are two tall canted bay windows facing the park. The triple gateway was probably taken from an early, eastern avenue and re-erected here when the main approach was altered. Odd gadrooned 'jelly-mould' finials crown the carriage pillars, with their moulded cappings and scroll-topped stops. Work probably dating from the residency of Thomas S. Quinn.
LOI.

417. FIRHILL, Monkstown; *c.* 1860; *demolished.*
A seaside villa and lodge built for Sir John Arnott (1814–98), founder of the department chain and mayor of Cork (1859–61), whose main seat was at Woodlands, Cork [N] [*q.v.*]. The house was subsequently renamed 'St Aubyn's'.
BPB (1929).

418. FIRVILLE, Macroom; pre-1841/*c.* 1900.

To replace a lodge probably contemporary with 'the recently erected mansion of Philip Harding Esq.' in 1837 is this extraordinary successor—an amply proportioned 1½-storey gabled affair clad in shiplap boarding below a corrugated iron roof. To the avenue the attic storey oversails a ground-floor room to form flanking recesses, the eaves carried on bracketed posts. The road-front eaves are broken by a central flat-roofed 'gablet' loft room, while from the rear there appears some solidity in the corbelled brick chimney-stack.
Lewis 1837.

419. FIR VILLE, Mallow; *c.* 1820.
To complement 'the seat of R. Atkins, Esq., a square house in a pretty lawn' in 1844, is the modest single-storey standard, rendered, hip-roofed lodge with wide windows below a later decorative carved fascia board of double-pointed foil pattern.
O'Flanagan 1975.

420. FLAXFORT, Glanmire; *c.* 1810.
A long, single-storey cottage in limewashed rubble construction, three-bay with its blocked-up doorway to the right-hand side and a brick chimney-stack to each gable. Derelict. Another seat of the Martin family of Glanmire.

421. FLINTFIELD, Millstreet; pre-1841; *demolished.*
A lodge, replaced by the twentieth-century bungalow on the site, at the entrance to a property in the eighteenth century of the Chinnery family, who subsequently let the place to a series of tenants—Barry Cotter being in residence in 1802 and 1814, followed by Dr Denis O'Connell in 1837. A gate porter, William Sweeney, also farmed the land hereabouts in the later nineteenth century, his descendants now occupying the bungalow.
Hajba 2002.

422. FLORAVILLE, Cork [S]; pre-1841; *demolished.*
A seat in the late eighteenth century of John Swete, subsequently tenanted.

423. FLOWER LODGE, Ballintemple; pre-1841; *demolished.*
The suburban property in 1837 of R. MacMullen Esq.
Lewis 1837.

424. FORTLANDS, Charleville; *c.* 1810.
A nice little single-storey standard late

Georgian Gothic porter's cottage, unusually of brick-faced construction given a painted finish, its front of three pointed-arched openings with unfortunate modern windows. Subsequently enlarged from a rectangular to a square plan, giving it a pyramidal roof rising to a diminutive brick chimney-stack. The Batwell family is recorded here in 1802 in the person of Lullum Batwell, who was here twelve years later. Admirably tended.
Leet 1814; Hajba 2002.

425. FORT LISLE, Cobh; pre-1841; *demolished.*
A seat of the Stubbs family, both their residence and its gatekeeper's lodge having gone by 1934.

426. FORT RICHARD, Nohaval; pre-1841; *demolished.*
An estate inherited as 'Killowen' by Richard Galwey (1757–1826) through his marriage to a St Leger girl around 1787 and promptly renamed. His eldest son John succeeded him, living here until his death in 1860.
IFR.

FORTWILLIAM (see BALLYGRADY)

427. FORTWILLIAM, Milford; *c.* 1840; *demolished.*
A very early Victorian cottage-style house with fancy bargeboards built by William Barry; its contemporary gatekeeper's lodge lay across the road from the estate entrance.
Hajba 2002.

428. FORT WILLIAM, Cork [N]; pre-1841; *demolished.*
A demesne with a late Georgian house built by William Massy Baker (d. 1829), of the Lismacue, Co. Tipperary, family, succeeded here by his son Godfrey Thomas Baker.
Leet 1814; *LGI* (1904).

429. FOTA, Carrigtohill (5).
One of the great demesnes of Ireland in its spectacular island setting owes almost all architecturally to John Smith-Barry (1793–1837). Succeeding to Fota in 1801 at the age of eight, after his coming of age he acquired a reputation for lavish living, a suitable venue for which he created with the assistance of the leading architectural practice in the country. Sir Richard Morrison and his son William Vitruvius completely transformed and enlarged the old house and designed an appropriate grand entrance to the estate.

Main gate; *c.* 1820; architects Sir R. and W.V. Morrison.

A splendid composition adapted from a design by John Soane in his *Sketches in architecture* (1793) [Fig. 5, p. 6], its short principal front here given a Greek Doric pair of fluted columns *in antis*, setting the scene for those to the portico on the big house. These are set forward of the tripartite window within a *pronaos*, any loss of daylight being compensated for by the lofty eaves line of a shallow hipped roof. Single-storey but on a grand scale in beautifully chiselled limestone ashlar, with laurel wreath motifs to the frieze below a bold bracketed soffit. From opposing side elevations are balancing gabled projections housing closet and entrance hall, flanked by six-over-six sash windows in lugged surrounds. All to a plan much favoured about the country, in the county at Bearforest Lower, and beyond at Killruddery, Co. Wicklow, Castlecoole, Co. Fermanagh, and Ballyfin, Co. Laois, where it is repeated elevationally. At the latter, as here, the Morrisons faithfully reproduced a gatescreen from J.B. Papworth's *Rural residences* (1818) [Fig. 6, p. 8], copied right down to the iron secondary piers. The noble triple gateway is dominated by mammoth carriage pillars as tapering 'pylons', personalised with recessed panels containing the family motto, *Boutez En Avant*, embossed therein, and crowned by proud Smith-Barry wolves over ribboned laurel wreaths. Secondary cappings feature scrolls and floral motifs, the whole framed by extensive quadrants, their walls in a

contrasting whitened render finish. Both lodge and gates recently admirably saved from dereliction.

On 17 July 1835 the Scottish visitor Robert Graham recorded his visit: 'drove along Mr Smith Barry's wall till I came to his magnificent new entrance, where he has lately made a very handsome new gate and lodge. This improvement, including the approach, is said to have cost him £4,000. There is thriving fine plantation on each side of the approach ... I came out by another gate, more modest than the first one, close by the bridge which connects Footay island with the great or Cove island.'

Belvelly Bridge gate; *c.* 1830; architect John Hargrave.

Perrott

Modest by Fota standards but still an impressive introduction, to a design clearly showing Morrison influence in the basic cruciform plan of the lofty lodge but here with a canted leading front and equivalent roof (now lacking its octagonal chimney-stack), in a rubble finish, the ground-floor windows reflected above the cut-stone string-course in 'blind' attic windows. Much extended to the rear, the porter's accommodation with its little gabled wings is central to another extensive gatescreen, here flanked by a pair of triple entrances contained by a series of cylindrical ashlar pillars. Presumably Hargrave succeeded the Morrisons here, having also designed a castellated folly tower on the estate. There is an almost identical lodge by him at Clifton Lodge, Co. Meath.

As today, James Fraser in 1838 found that 'The entrance gates at either end of the island are remarkably spacious, unique, and distinct in their character, from each other', and that 'Strangers are admitted to see this place by writing their names in a book kept at the entrance lodge'. Two other gatekeepers' lodges on the perimeter of the estate did not warrant mention by those early tourists.

Slatty Bridge gate; *c.* 1830.

At the entrance to the circuitous northern 'Cork Drive' approach to the house is this attractive single-storey cottage below a hipped roof with conspicuous bracketed soffit over pleasant rubble stone walls, the principal front of which to the road contains three latticed glazed casement windows; the entrance is at the rear.

Secondary gate; *c.* 1820.

On a short southern approach is this very plain single-storey standard hip-roofed cottage.

Fota Castle gate; *c.* 1830; architect John Hargrave; *demolished.*

On the westernmost tip of the island were the

eye-catcher tower and its gate lodge, plans for which were provided by architect John Hargrave, the former in ruins, the latter lost.

Soane 1793; Papworth 1818; Heaney 1999; Fraser 1838; uncatalogued Henry Hill notebooks, Cork City Museum; *Country Life* (11 and 18 September 1986); McParland *et al.* 1989.

430. FOUNTAINSTOWN, Crosshaven; pre-1842; *demolished.*
An estate of the Hodder family, whose lodge, located remote from the road, had gone by 1935.

431. FRANKFIELD, Frankfield; pre-1841; *demolished.*
Prior to its sale as an incumbered estate in 1855, a seat of the Lane family, whose representative in 1837 was Samuel Lane.

Lewis 1837; Lyons 1993.

432. FRANKFORT, Cork [N]; 1881; *demolished.*
One of a series of villas built along Glanmire Road Middle in the early 1870s, this being first occupied by Francis Cade, who later added a porter's lodge to the property at the junction with Tivoli Road.

433. FRANKFORT, Curraglass; pre-1841; *demolished.*
Home to the Woodley family that lies in ruin, its lodge in the same state by 1936.

434. FRIENDLY COVE, Durrus; pre-1842; *demolished.*
Nathaniel Evanson was in residence in 1814, succeeded by Richard Tomson Evanson by 1837, their lodge gone by 1902.

Leet 1814; Lewis 1837.

435. GALWEY'S DYKE, Cork [S]; pre-1841; *demolished.*
A small park sandwiched between the Mardyke Walk and its lodged access from Western Road, a property until the mid-nineteenth century of the Galwey family.

436. GARDEVILLE, Murragh; *c.* 1845; *demolished.*
A property of Revd W. Hall in 1837, lodgeless then and in 1844 before one was recorded in the 1852 valuation, when Gardeville was the residence of Sarah Hosford.

Lewis 1837; Griffith 1853–63.

437. GARRANCLOYNE, Carrigtohill; *c.* 1840.
The most unpretentious of single-storey standard lodges in a cement-rendered finish, with just the suggestion of skew-tables to its gables. Derelict. A holding in 1853 of Hughes Martin.

Griffith 1853–63.

438. GARRANE HOUSE AND MILLS, Mitchelstown; *c.* 1835.
'On the river Funcheon, is an extensive bleach-green, with flax and tucking mills, and machinery for carding and spinning wool, to which a power-loom for the manufacture of blankets has been lately added by the proprietors, Messrs J. & F. Atkins.' This addition, recorded in 1837, could conceivably have formed part of improvements to the establishment which included the building of the porter's lodge. It remains as a standard single-storey structure over a part-basement in exposed coursed masonry with shallow segmental brick arches and dressings below a hipped roof. Reroofed but sealed up. Sometime later renamed 'Ballydrerriff'.

Lewis 1837.

439. GARRANE, Cork [S]; pre-1841; *demolished.*
A property in 1852 of Francis Hemmis.

Griffith 1853–63.

440. GARRETTSTOWN, Ballinspittle (4).
Here are the remains of a grand design, perhaps incomplete, for a central Palladian mansion with a great forecourt flanked by wings connected to pavilions, which survive as comfortable villas in their own right—the dream of James Kearney, allegedly prosperous through his smuggling activities. All around are noble gateways and the remains of some of their lodges, likewise having suffered the ravages of time.

East gate; pre-1842; *demolished.*

The principal entrance, suitably extensive, at the centre of which is a towering pair of cylindrical carriage pillars of about 1750, constructed in a slate rubble with dressed cappings which formed the base to large pedestalled ball finials, much akin to those at Castle Freke [*q.v.*]. Here are the remnants of contemporary mid-Georgian iron gates and alongside a dressed postern opening with hood-moulded pointed arch and containing a fine studded wooden door.

West gate; *c.* 1800.
Opposite a wide gateless sweep with concave quadrants is a long, low, 1½-storey gabled vernacular cottage with two-over-two sash windows in limewashed harled rubble walls.

North-west gate; pre-1842.
Across the road from the entrance; a ruin.

North-east gate; pre-1842.
All that survives of this porter's lodge is a sealed-up lancet opening to the right-hand side of the gateway.

Smith 1893; *LG* (1863); Bence-Jones 1988.

THE GARRISON (see BALLYMAGOOLY)

441. GARRY CLOYNE, Blarney; *c.* 1835.
V-jointed rusticated carriage pillars retain one harled ogee quadrant wall, opposite which is the single-storey porter's lodge with a canted front probably built for John Travers (d. 1854), proprietor in 1837 of the property which comprised the castle of the Clancarthys and his house, 'spacious and well-built on rising ground looking over a fine lawn of more than 100 acres, surrounded by fine plantations'.

Lewis 1837.

442. GARRYHANKARD, Inishannon; pre-1842; *demolished.*
A property, perhaps a dower house to northern neighbour Upton [*q.v.*], which was in decline by 1851 and had been removed by 1900.

443. GARRYHANKARDMORE, Inishannon; pre-1842; *demolished.*
A seat in the early nineteenth century of the Wiseman family, from whom by 1837 it had become home to T. Biggs Esq., its lodge having gone by 1942.

Leet 1814; Pigot 1824; Lewis 1837.

444. GAWSWORTH, Carrigrohane; *c.* 1880; architect not known; *demolished.*

Gerry Murray

A property in 1852 of Russell Fitton (*c.* 1805–64), named after the family's ancestral home of Gawsworth Hall in Cheshire, which subsequently passed into the hands of Robert Pratt (1835–1910) through his marriage to Sarah Fitton. It was he who improved the place by the creation of a new entrance in the form of a fine cast-iron screen, the central pillars of which sport elegant urns and the outer elephants' heads as the family crest. Across the road on an elevated site was an impressive sophisticated neo-Classical gatekeeper's lodge, the loss of which is a scandal. Single-storey standard on a cruciform plan, probably stuccoed, it displayed Doric pilasters to each of its external corners below an embracing entablature, each of its gables, including its central entrance porch, pedimented. The chimney-stack with moulded capping rose off the rear wall at the back return junction.

Griffith 1853–63; *LGI* (1904); Fairbairn 1986.

445. GIBBINGS GROVE, Charleville (2).
The ancient seat of the Gibbings family, previously called 'Tourmore', to which Bartholomew Gibbings added at least one of its gatekeepers' lodges.

East entrance; pre-1841; *demolished.*

West entrance; 1829.
Behind an extensive entrance sweep of shallow walled quadrants with crenellated copings and one dwarf round-arched

postilion gateway is the most perfectly dotty of lodges. A fundamental single-storey hip-roofed cottage has its short avenue front faced in an eccentric façade with an 1829 inscription, although it probably exhibits some contributions from later proprietors. Doubtless influenced by the porter's lodge at nearby Milltown Castle [*q.v.*] (which had a Gibbings connection), its modern roughcast walls have a smooth banded surround framing a parlour window flanked by a pair of niches, all segmentally arched. Overhead, the crazy gable is dressed in punched limestone displaying a central roundel below a hood-moulded four-centred Tudor arched feature, the skew-table gable crowned by a distinctly ecclesiastical Tudor-Gothic finial to which has been added a weather-vane. Across the road is a corresponding walled screen, central in which is a pillared stile access to estate land beyond.

LGI (1904).

446. GILL ABBEY, Cork [S]; *c.* 1835; *demolished.*

The park was absorbed in the 1860s into a larger site for the Queen's University College [*q.v.*], its big house removed and the little lodge apparently given a second floor in a mock Elizabethan transformation in 1865. 'Before' and 'after' drawings preserve for posterity a record of the perfectly presentable single-storey two-roomed hip-roofed lodge with a central gabled hall projecting, having side entry and bipartite casement windows set in rectangular recesses to ground level. The double-flue chimney-stack rose off the rear wall. The last occupant of the house was Revd Charles Leslie, who had refused to vacate it and enable transfer of the grounds for college use, but this was resolved by his unexpected death in 1846.

Murphy 1995; NAOPW drawings (5HC/4/892-1).

447. GLANANORE, Castletownroche (2).

West entrance; pre-1841.

The original gate serving the estate of the Purcell family, of whom Revd James George Purcell (d. 1843) was the last, the porter's lodge sited opposite now in ruins, with only rusticated pilaster quoins remaining of the front elevation.

East entrance; *c.* 1840.

The next occupant was another cleric, Revd Thomas Hoare (1779–1835), whose widow lived on here until her passing in 1865. This lodge was probably erected single-storey on a square plan, its irregular three-bay front with doorway to the left-hand side in a harled finish below a pyramidal oversailing roof with cast-iron post supports, these fluted with acanthus leaf capitals and more ornamental ironwork applied to the fascia boards. Derelict. Shallow concave harled quadrant walls form the entrance screen, with plain stone pillars and one postilion gate.

Griffith 1853–63; *LGI* (1904); *BPB* (1929); Hajba 2002.

GLANATORE (see CASTLE VIEW, Tallow)

448. GLANAVIRANE, Ballinspittle (2).

The seat in 1837 of J. Howe Esq., in whose family it remained for the rest of the century.

North gate; *c.* 1820.

A tiny, square, gabled standard cottage with bipartite casement windows in limewashed harled walls. Early twentieth-century roof replacement.

South gate; *c.* 1830.

On the principal approach is this standard single-storey, clipped-eaves, hip-roofed lodge retaining square-paned casement windows in crisp modern rendered walls, reroofed with synthetic slates and leaded hips. Pretty ironwork forms a triple gateway with four square pillars, each with moulded plinths and cappings and unusual fluted shafts; in contrast, pleasant rubble quadrant walls.

Lewis 1837.

449. GLANDALANE, Fermoy; *c.* 1820.

An entrance to the predecessor of the present Edwardian turreted pile, another property in the first half of the nineteenth century of Robert Briscoe of neighbouring Clondulane [*q.v.*] and his adjacent flour mills. The entrance lodge is a single-storey hip-roofed harled cottage with a hint of pretension in its leading short front, comprised of a bipartite cast-iron latticed main window set in a recess formed by extending piers. To the park is a pair of single like-glazed casements. Derelict and no longer monitoring the contemporary double gateway of square ashlar pillars with moulded corniced cappings and very fine sculpted pine cone finials atop.

Griffith 1853–63.

450. GLANDORE, Glandore (2).

James Redmond Barry came here in 1824 as a young man and remained for 50 years, leaving a reputation for being an improving and philanthropic landlord and a gate lodge apparently from each extreme of his tenure.

North entrance; pre-1842; *demolished.*

On the early avenue survives a peculiar rubble-built structure, tall and containing a lancet opening, perhaps the remains of eccentric gatekeeper's accommodation.

South entrance; *c.* 1865.

Barry created this lengthy new approach from the south-east which crossed a public road and built this spacious sentinel on an elevated site by the gate. Two-storey and gabled on an L-plan, it retains perforated wave and foil bargeboards with quatrefoil pierced toes and hip-knobs. From the leading gable extends a canted single-storey bay window overlooking the gateway; all in a modern roughcast finish, the whole effect spoiled by the loss of original detailing and the insertion of hideous twentieth-century metal window replacements. Flat-roofed additions. Deeply V-jointed rusticated stone carriage pillars.

Lewis 1837; *Thom's*.

451. GLANMIRE, Glanmire; pre-1841; *demolished.*
A seat in 1837 of Edward Morrough (b. 1785), whose widow lived on here until her death in 1869.

Lewis 1837; *LGI* (1904).

452. GLANMIRE RECTORY, Glanmire; *c.* 1890.

On Kilroan Glebe a nice essay in polychrome brickwork—orange in Flemish bond relieved by cream brick as sill and head courses and to cambered arches. Three-bay with doorway to the right-hand side below a pretty gabled canopy on curved carved brackets. High oversailing eaves to its hipped roof accommodate attic rooms. Sensitively extended in like manner. The gatescreen, in more variegated brick, has an Edward VII postbox built into an outer pillar.

453. GLANMORE, Charleville; *c.* 1865.
Previously called 'Ballynaboola' after its townland, it was owned by the Tynte family, who sold it in 1816 to Michael Russell. It was his grandson (b. 1845) of the same name who added the gate lodge opposite its gates after his father's death in 1859. A plain and rather gawky single-storey standard affair, with tall eaves to its steeply pitched hipped roof giving loft space. In a recent sand/cement finish, the fanlit door is set in a breakfront flanked by one-over-one sash windows. Occupied. Across the road is a pretty gatescreen of ogee railed quadrants with fleur-de-lis finials repeated on the triple gateway.

LGI (1904); Hajba 2002.

GLASSON'S AVENUE (see MOUNT ALTO)

THE GLEN (see KILLURAGH)

454. GLEN PARK, Kanturk; pre-1841; *demolished.*
The old house of the O'Brien family lies ruinous, its gatekeeper's lodge opposite the entrance having gone by 1937.

GLENAVON (see MILLBANK)

455. GLENBARRAGHANE, Castletownsend; 1895; architect not known.

Previously 'Laputa' and lodgeless until the advent of the Coghills in Sir John Joscelyn Coghill, 4th baronet (1826–1905), and his eldest son Sir Egerton Bushe Coghill, 5th baronet (1853–1921), both of whom married Somerville girls of neighbouring Drishane [*q.v.*] and opened up a new access to the house from the west, building an impressive Arts and Crafts porter's lodge at the gate. Addressing the approach to the Georgian village is this incongruous 1½-storey commodious mock-Elizabethan composition, its gable elevation unspoilt, with a half-timbered apex over a quadripartite square-paned window framed in a red terracotta tile-hung attic storey separated by a bellcast and coving from the pleasant rubble stone ground floor. The standard three-bay avenue front is disfigured by a dominant later two-storey grey roughcast protrusion consisting of a room above a crudely pillared porch.

BPB (1925).

456. GLENBURNE, Glanmire (2).
Both pre-1841 lodges to an early nineteenth-century 'Cottage Gothic' by architect Henry Hill, the residence in 1837 of A. Lewis Esq., have been demolished.

Lewis 1837; Bence-Jones 1988; IAA.

GLENCAIRN (see ROSEVIEW)

457. GLENDOONEEN, Ballymartle; *c.* 1835.
Like its big late Georgian house, the porter's lodge is hip-roofed and two-storey but doubtless originated in the time here of Revd J. Stoyte as a single-storey standard cottage. It still retains delightful Tudor-style label-moulded bipartite lattice-glazed casement windows in modern roughcast, over which has subsequently been added a second storey

with four-over-four bipartite sashes. Immaculate. The gatescreen contains a tripartite gateway with hoop-topped rails and octagonal iron posts with crenellated tops.

Lewis 1837.

458. GLENGARRA, Killeagh; *c.* 1800.
Here are the sad remains of a Georgian Gothic lodge engulfed in *Rhododendron ponticum*. Single-storey standard with a hipped roof over Y-traceried pointed-arched windows in harled rubble walls. Built for James Uniacke.

459. GLENGARRIFF CASTLE, Glengarriff (2).
The romantic estate with its now-derelict rambling Castellated Gothic house was created by the younger brother of the 1st earl of Bantry, Colonel Simon White (d. 1838), sometime around his marriage in 1801 to the heiress Sarah Newenham of Maryborough [*q.v.*]. He further adorned the property with other fanciful structures but neither of his gate lodges retains a flavour of these times.

North gate; pre-1842.
A tripartite gateway which does reflect past Gothic delights in its cut-stone pillars with layered cappings and shafts having ogee-arched recesses and quatrefoil motifs. Opposite and distant is a plain, single-bay, hip-roofed rendered gatehouse so modernised as to defy accurate dating.

South gate; pre-1842; *demolished.*

LGI (1904); Everett 2001.

460. GLENGARRIFF COTTAGE, Glengarriff; pre-1842; *demolished.*
Both the house by the shore, in 1846 home to Robert Hedges White (b. 1810), and its lodge had gone by 1890.

Slater 1846.

461. GLENGARRIFF LODGE, Glengarriff (2).
The charming romantic *cottage orné* retreat created around 1815 from conversion of a plain predecessor by Richard White (1767–1851), the future 1st earl of Bantry. Over a mile distant to the east, he complemented this with a porter's lodge at the entrance to the meandering approach through wood and deer-park and across two rivers and three townlands.

Drumaclarig South gate; *c.* 1825.
A delightful single-storey standard lodge, its Georgian Gothic detailing giving just a flavour of what to expect beyond. Built in a pleasant grey rubble, not quite symmetrical, with its pedimented porch projecting slightly off-centre to accommodate the chimney-stack to the ridge of an oversailing hipped roof.

The windows are bipartite with Y-traceried glazing below Tudor-style label mouldings, while within the segmentally arched entrance is revealed a beautiful Georgian Gothic door-case with Classical pilasters, pointed-arch panelling and a Y-traceried semicircular fanlight. Sadly, the chimney has lost its original trio of diagonally set brick stacks in insensitive alterations which also saw the disappearance of pretty cusped carved bargeboards and barley-twist hip-knobs to the porch. The gatekeeper in 1853 was John Ironmonger.

Drumaclarig North gate; *c.* 1852.

A lodge probably added, opposite the entrance, by the 2nd earl of Bantry (1800–68) after succeeding his brother to the title, its first porter being Daniel Turner. A single-storey rendered affair, modest but much modernised, with an additional bay and a projecting gabled glazed hallway.

Griffith 1853–63; Lawrence photograph (1991); *LGI* (1904); Everett 2001.

GLENKEEN (see CASTLE JANE VILLA)

GLENMERVYN (see JANEMOUNT)

GLENMORE (see BALLYNAGAUL)

462. GLENSESKIN, Douglas; 1906; architect not known.

A very pleasing and competent Arts and Crafts composition which appears as a single-storey standard lodge, or double-fronted bungalow, with horizontal emphasis in its red-brick plinth to sill level and, to the underside of the exaggerated oversailing bracketed roof soffit, half-timbered strapwork containing metal bipartite casement windows on each side of a herringbone-sheeted front door flanked by a pair of carved angle brackets to a little pedimented canopy that breaks the eaves of the shallow-pitched pyramidal roof, which terminates in a central chimney-stack. To the road elevation a bay window extends to the fascia board. A house and gate lodge first valued in 1906, of W.B. Barrington.

463. GLENVIEW, Fermoy; pre-1841.

Here are the remains of a single-storey standard lodge evident only in a three-bay front elevation to a property, in 1851 of Elizabeth Buchanan, leased by George Bevan Lukey, probably that in 1837 known as 'Lukeyville'.

Lewis 1837; Griffith 1853–63.

464. GLENVIEW, Midleton; pre-1841; *demolished.*

A typical late Georgian villa of 1780, home in 1814 to George Courtenay, probably the same of Dromadda [*q.v.*].

Leet 1814; *LGI* (1904).

465. GLENVIEW, Skibbereen; pre-1842; *demolished.*

An estate of the Levis family, whose lodge lay opposite their gates.

466. GLENVILLE, Glanmire; pre-1841; *demolished.*

The seat in 1814 of J. Newsom Esq., succeeded by 1837 by Edward Newsom, latterly renamed 'Ballinglanna' after its townland.

Leet 1814; Lewis 1837.

GLENVILLE (see THE MANOR, Glenville)

467. GLENWOOD, Kilworth (2).

A development of around 1840—house and lodges built for Major Peter Teulon after he moved from Ennismore Cottage, Cobh, where he was recorded in 1837.

West gate; *c.* 1840.

A single-storey standard lodge with tall eaves to its hipped roof and Tudor-style label mouldings to openings in modern rendered walls. Occupied. Innovative cut-stone carriage pillars chamfer and taper from square plinths to octagonal cappings. Contemporary ironwork to gates decorated with palmette finials and husk features below.

East gate; *c.* 1840.

Almost identical to its counterpart but with

a more pronounced roof oversail, the lodge is at right angles to the road, commanding a forecourt to a triple gateway giving avenue access oblique to the carriageway. Good tapering pillars with nice ogee 'cushion' cappings.

Lewis 1837; Slater 1846.

468. GLINNY, Ballymartle; *c.* 1800.

An endearing little Georgian Gothic cottage, possibly by the same jobbing builder of the lodge to nearby Ballymartle [*q.v.*]. Single-storey standard, with pointed heads to doorway and flanking high-silled windows below a hipped roof. Its character survives extension and modernisation despite a recast roof of synthetic slate and replacement windows in crisp rendering. An estate in 1837 of G.N. Dunne Esq.

Lewis 1837.

469. GLYNTOWN COTTAGE, Glanmire; pre-1841.

A seat of the Hill family, now destroyed by a motorway cutting. The lodge lies in ruins, only a now-blind front elevation upright, with quadrant entrance walls nearby.

470. GLYNTOWN, Glanmire; *c.* 1825.

In 1815 'a very handsome seat, built by the late Samuel McCall', since demolished, to be survived by the gate lodge built by his son, James McCall. Outside the demesne curtilage is the very basic single-storey hip-roofed harled cottage which commanded the forecourt with its best front—a naive attempt at sophistication in a short, three-bay symmetrical façade of V-jointed rusticated ashlar with wide windows below an embracing cut-stone pediment; derelict and blocked-up. The gatescreen is equally condemned; all that remain of the original are a massive pair of squat indestructible stone pillars with raised and fielded panels and cappings. These are just as those to Oldtown [*q.v.*] nearby, where they frame a tripartite iron gateway, missing here. The big house has suffered the ultimate fate.

Townsend 1815; *LG* (1853).

471. GOOD SHEPHERD CONVENT, Cork [N]; *c.* 1885; architect probably George Ashlin.

George Coppinger Ashlin's great Gothic Revival convent, Magdalen asylum and industrial school in raw variegated materials on the hill is neatly preceded by this 1½-storey gabled lodge in like manner and polychromatic finish of red brick, with cream highlights in its toothed quoins and string-courses, further embellished in stone as skew-tables and kneelers and forming spring blocks and keystones to segmental pointed-arched window openings which also contain some smart corbel detailing to the reveals. To the ridge is a dainty, diagonally set chimney-stack with sawtooth course. The grand chamfered Classical cut-stone pillared carriage gateway is awkwardly linked to the projecting hallway by a concave quadrant of variegated brick containing a postern opening. All presumably allied to some stage of the architect's commission.

Williams 1994; IAA.

472. GOOLDSHILL, Mallow; pre-1935; *demolished.*
A property of the Goold family to which the porter's lodge was added after 1841, since removed to make way for industrial development.

473. GORTAGLANNA, Kilbrittain; *c.* 1810.
A plain 1½-storey gabled gatekeeper's lodge, sensitively maintained and occupied, with a two-window-bay elevation to the road. For long a seat of the Scott family.

474. GORTAGOULANE, Cork [S]; pre-1841/1869; *demolished.*
A holding in 1852 of Edward Mulcahy, the lodge to which seems to have been replaced by a later owner, Thomas Sealy.

Griffith 1853–63.

475. GORTNAHORNA, Kilbrittain (3).
Not one of the lodges that existed in 1841 has survived, that to the middle gate having gone by 1890. At the northern entrance remains a good straight screen of six pillars and a tripartite gateway. An antique estate of the Sealy family, its big house having succumbed to 'the troubles'.

GORTSKAGH (see SHANDRUM RECTORY)

476. GRAIG, Shanballymore; pre-1841; *demolished.*
The residence, otherwise 'Graigue', in the early nineteenth century of James Hill, the porter's lodge to which had gone by 1903.

Leet 1814; Lewis 1837; Hajba 2002.

477. GRANGE, Ballincollig; *c.* 1850.
A plain single-storey gabled structure with a three-window principal front in a rendered finish. Occupied and modernised. Recorded as the property in 1814 and 1853 of John Hawkes.

Leet 1814; Griffith 1853–63.

478. GRANGE ERIN, Douglas; pre-1842; *demolished.*
The seat in 1837 of W.E. Penrose Esq.

Lewis 1837.

479. GREENFIELD, Ballincollig; pre-1841; *demolished.*
An estate of the Carleton family going back to the mid-nineteenth century, both gatekeeper's lodge and big house having been removed by 1939.

480. GREENFIELD, Clonakilty; pre-1842; *demolished.*
The residence in 1837 of Henry Galway, otherwise Gallwey (*c.* 1794–1850).

Lewis 1837; *IFR.*

481. GREENFIELD, Kanturk; *c.* 1830.
For a century the property of the Allen family, whose interests in it terminated with the death of Philip Allen in 1832; its typical Irish traditional porter's lodge dates from around that time. Single-storey standard with an off-centre chimney-stack to the ridge of a steeply pitched oversailing hipped roof. Modern casement windows in rendered walls. Occupied. Complementary plain gatescreen with convex-walled quadrants.

Hajba 2002.

482. GREEN LODGE, Coachford; pre-1842; *demolished.*
The property in 1837 of R. Coppinger Esq., the gate lodge to which had gone by 1938.

Lewis 1837.

483. GREEN PARK, Youghal; pre-1842; *demolished.*
A house in 1837 of Capt. H. Parker RN, whose lodge had been removed by 1935, its site occupied by terraced housing at the entrance to what is now a hotel.

Lewis 1837.

484. GREENVILLE, Carrigtohill; *c.* 1830.
A long, low, much-improved, roughcast single-storey gabled cottage with a projecting entrance hall, still in occupation. A small estate in 1837 of Richard Barry, one of fourteen siblings, one of whose younger brothers, Garrett, succeeded him here.

Lewis 1837; *IFR.*

485. GREENVILLE, Crookstown; pre-1841; *demolished.*
A Classical villa designed by architect Henry Hill for Benjamin Swete, who is recorded here in 1837. The gate lodge may have formed part of that commission.

Lewis 1837; IAA.

486. THE GROVE, Cobh; 1864.
Like neighbouring Norwood [*q.v.*], a development for builder Alexander Deane, comprising a regulation rendered mid-Victorian suburban villa and contemporary Italianate gate lodge, which predicts the big house in its own semi-octagonal bay window below an equivalent roof to the gable end overseeing the gates. Single-storey with a three-window elevation to the park and gabled hall extending to the road on the opposing front, its gables displaying prominent moulded verge brackets; the ridge is broken by a pair of chimney-stacks with bold bands and plinths. Derelict and boarded-up.

487. GROVE HILL, Passage West; pre-1841; *demolished.*
In 1837 the residence of John C. Irvine.

Lewis 1837.

488. GURRANE COTTAGE, Kilworth; pre-1890; *demolished.*
A property of builder-cum-architect Alexander Deane (*c.* 1790–1869), who reworked an earlier house for himself and complemented it with a gate lodge on the site of an older structure.

Hajba 2002; IAA.

489. GURRANE, Kilworth; *c.* 1865.
An unassuming house designed and built for his son Charles by Alexander Deane, reflected by its equally unpretentious gate lodge, which is a grey roughcast single-storey standard affair, sometime later extended to the left-hand side by a bay, two chimney-stacks defining the original gables. Occupied. Rather more sophisticated chamfered moulded pillars with good palmette terminals to the cast-iron gates of its entrance.

Bence-Jones 1988; Hajba 2002.

490. GURTEEN, Bandon; *c.* 1855.
The sadly neglected remains of a pretentious 1½-storey gabled porter's lodge. With a gable to the avenue front, just discernible through rampant greenery is some of its rich cut-stone detailing in the form of corbelled 'shelf' sills, toothed dressings and moulded shoulders to window heads. Built for Thomas Barter.

Griffith 1853–63.

491. GURTEENARD, Kanturk (2).
The elegant late eighteenth-century house has been served by two lodges from successive centuries.

Early lodge; *c.* 1830.
Not quite opposite the gates is this plain single-storey standard cottage with a facing of pleasant honey-coloured rubble, with a brick chimney-stack to each of its gables. Latterly adorned with canopies to openings and shutters. Probably built in the time here of the Begley family.

Late lodge; *c.* 1940.
A charming minuscule structure set well back from the entrance in a wooded setting, masquerading as something older, with its single-storey standard format and projecting central gabled hall. Reflecting the big house

with its six-over-six sash windows in cut-stone masonry below a slightly bellcast hipped roof with small slates and a chimney-stack to each end. It first appears in the valuation books as a 'workman's house' in 1962 when Liam Hutch was proprietor, although probably built for the previous owner, Mathew Bourke, who had acquired the property from the Bastable family.

492. GURTEENROE COTTAGE, Macroom; pre-1842; *demolished.*
A seat in 1814 of John Pyne, which by 1852 had passed to James Welply.

Leet 1814; Griffith 1853–63.

493. HADWELL LODGE, Whitegate; *c.* 1800.
The residence in 1814 of Revd Dr Robert Austen, in 1824 also recorded at Midleton Rectory [*q.v.*]. Here are the ruins of his Georgian Gothic porter's lodge, with the remains of lancet openings in rubble walls.

Leet 1814; Pigot 1824.

494. HANOVER HALL, Macroom; pre-1842; *demolished.*
The old bridged avenue access is disused and its lodge, in ruins in 1938, removed. A property in 1814 of John Harding, and 23 years later of J. Bowen Esq.

Leet 1814; Lewis 1837.

495. HARDINGVILLE, Dromcolliher; pre-1841; *demolished.*
Surviving is a gatescreen comprised of four 'Irish pilastered' pillars and harled ogee quadrants with a single postilion opening. At the entrance to a late eighteenth-century house of the Harding family.

496. HARRIETVILLE, Mallow; *c.* 1820.
A single-storey whitewashed gabled cottage, one short front of which, with later foiled bargeboards, curves to form one of the concave quadrant entrance walls. Occupied. Revd John Lombard (*c.* 1758–1847), rector of Kilshannig from 1800, is recorded as living here in 1814 and until his death. Previously a property of Major Henry Croker of neighbouring Quartertown [*q.v.*], who named it after his wife Harriet Dillon, whom he married in 1793.

Leet 1814; *IFR*; Hajba 2002.

497. HAWTHORN COTTAGE, Mallow; *c.* 1800.

Just apparent through the undergrowth are the dilapidated remains of a single-storey Georgian Gothic porter's lodge with a canted leading front containing pointed-arched Y-traceried windows. Early in the nineteenth century a residence of William Lombard, whose widow Ellen is recorded as still living here in 1853.

Griffith 1853–63; Hajba 2002.

498. HAWTHORN HILL, Inishannon; pre-1842; *demolished.*
A property in 1814 of David Hanes (Haynes?) that by 1837 was the residence of J. Godwin Esq., the gate lodge to which had gone by 1890.

Leet 1814; Lewis 1837.

499. HAWTHORN VILLA, Bandon; *c.* 1870.
A two-storey gabled gatehouse with symmetrical three-bay front, much modernised with cement rendering, plastic windows and synthetic slates. Occupied. The residence in the mid-Victorian years of Christopher Dowden, maltster in the town.

Slater 1856.

500. HAYFIELD, Coachford; pre-1841/*c.* 1900.
A smart, modernised 1½-storey gate lodge built on the site of its predecessor, probably from compensation for the railway line that severs the avenue to the rear. Rendered and three-bay symmetrical with two gablets over, breaking the eaves of an oversailing hipped roof with trefoil-perforated earthenware ridge cresting. From the rear rises a typical late Victorian corbelled red-brick chimney-stack. Like the first lodge, flanked by gatescreens, two pillars of which are topped by cast-iron urns. An estate in 1852 of Henry Lindsay, from whom it passed to Richard Barter MD, in whose hands it became neglected before being acquired and improved *c.* 1900 by John Kelleher.

Griffith 1853–63.

501. HAZLEWOOD, Doneraile; 1819.

The Lysaght family acquired the estate in 1819 through the marriage of the daughter of William Atkins to William Lysaght (1800–38), who then redeveloped the place with a new house, entrance screen and porter's lodge. Although the latter is a pleasant and extensive low, cruciform, hip-roofed, wisteria-clad roughcast cottage, it bears little relationship to the original. The early OS maps show a rectangular plan with a short front addressing the avenue. The relatively unaltered contemporary entrance screen is a tripartite gateway, its round-arched pedestrian openings flanking V-jointed rusticated ashlar carriage pillars with moulded corniced cappings, one crowned by a pedestalled obelisk, the other by an oriental lion. Beyond, this impressive introduction is completed by walled concave quadrants and lower rusticated pillars.

IFR.

502. HEATHBURN HALL, Carrigaline (3).
An estate in the early nineteenth century of George Daunt, whose original porter's lodge survives on what was then the sole approach.

East gate; *c.* 1820.

A lovely late Georgian Gothic single-storey standard cottage on a square plan, its steeply hipped roof rising to a single-flue chimney-stack. In harled rubble walls are narrow pointed-arched openings, the windows in a highly decorative cast-iron latticed and Y-traceried pattern also to be found in the gatekeeper's lodge to Woodlands, Inishannon [*q.v.*]. Occupied and beautifully maintained. Alongside is the entrance screen of four plain pillars with cast-iron ball finials.

In 1882 the property was purchased by Lt.-Col. Frederick George Shaw, who further embellished it by extending the house and creating two additional lodged entrances.

Middle gate; *c.* 1885.
A commodious two-storey standard hip-roofed gatehouse, a veritable villa in its own right with some quirky detailing. To the eaves is an embracing scalloped fascia board broken by catslide roofs to first-floor oriel windows; that to the road is arrowhead-shaped, while to the avenue a canted variant projects centrally, carried on a bracket with

the monogram 'S'. The ground floor is surrounded by a 'colonial' corrugated-iron-roofed verandah carried on paired posts, behind which the round-arched spoked fanlit front door is flanked by tripartite casement windows with corbelled sills.

West gate; *c.* 1905.

A striking little building, not of its time, looking to be of mid-Victorian origin. Single-storey standard, faced in a mellow brick finish in English garden wall bond, its semicircular-arched fanlit doorway flanked by six-over-six sash windows, while from the road front extends a canted bay window with its own roof below a perforated fish-scale fascia board to the eaves of the steeply hipped main roof. Abandoned. By the gate is a contemporary 'E VII R' postbox.

Pike and Hodges 1911.

503. HEATHERSIDE HOSPITAL, Buttevant; *c.* 1910.

On the slopes of the Ballyhoura Mountains is this large institution, founded in 1909 as a tuberculosis sanatorium, the entrance to which is marked by this strangely flimsy 'seaside' chalet bungalow behind a suburban hedge. The core of the 1½-storey lodge has a rectangular plan with timber-clad walls below an oversailing steeply hipped roof of corrugated-iron finish with little gabled dormer windows to opposing pitches, solidity only apparent in its masonry chimney-stacks and later additions.

504. HEATHFIELD, Ballymartle; pre-1842; *demolished.*
By 1942 the gate lodge, to an estate in 1837 of Henry Bastable, had gone.

Lewis 1837.

505. HEATHFIELD TOWERS, Youghal; *c.* 1865.
Nothing but a shell is left of the extraordinary remains of a fantasy castle and outbuildings, the conceit of the Revd Pierce William Drew (b. 1799), long the rector of Youghal. He lived across the road at Brook Lodge before acquiring old Heathfield House around 1860, demolishing it and redeveloping the site in stages, eventually adding the porter's lodge. Unlike the big house this is relatively conventional, sited outside its gates and now no longer presiding, in its dereliction, over an unkempt forecourt. Single-storey, hip-roofed and constructed with solid rubble facings, the principal short front having a single window with basic label moulding; shrouded in undergrowth, two solid chimney-stacks dominate the ridge. Alongside is a pair of chunky ornate gate pillars with recessed panels and exaggerated corbelled cappings in typical mid-Victorian fashion, giving onto a redundant approach—all a fair reflection of the dereliction beyond.

LGI (1904).

506. HERMITAGE, Glanmire; pre-1841/*c.* 1870.
On the site of a predecessor is this mid-Victorian single-storey standard roughcast lodge, with a central modern glazed hall tucked in below the extending soffit of the tall eaves to a roof with a chimney-stack to each gable. At the gates to a late Georgian house probably built by Richard Rowland, occupied in 1853 by Eliza Martin.

Leet 1814; Griffith 1853–63.

HERMITAGE (see CLARAVILLE)

THE HERMITAGE (see BALLYNOE)

507. HETTY VILLE, Belgooly; pre-1841; *demolished.*
A property in 1814 of John P. Heard.

Leet 1814.

508. HIGHLAND COTTAGE, Ballintemple; pre-1841; *demolished.*
A suburban seat in 1852 of Thomas Fitton, which by 1890 had become 'Lisnacairn'.

Griffith 1853–63.

509. HIGHLAND COTTAGE, Monkstown; pre-1841; *demolished.*
An estate in 1852 of Mrs Sarah Phillips.

Griffith 1853–63.

510. THE HIGHLANDS, Glanmire; pre-1890; *demolished.*
A property massively developed between 1841 and 1890, when a gate lodge was added, probably for Patrick Gleeson, who leased the place during the second half of the nineteenth century from the Welland family.

Griffith 1853–63.

511. HIGH PARK, Castle Lyons; pre-1841; *demolished.*
The seat in the early nineteenth century of Revd John Ware Edgar, both his house and its porter's lodge removed in the twentieth century.

Pigot 1824; Lewis 1837.

512. THE HILL, Douglas; pre-1842; *demolished.*
The lodge has been replaced by a modern bungalow, to be survived by its gatescreen of punched rusticated ashlar with postilion openings. The residence in 1837 of Alexander O'Driscoll, who had perhaps come from Creagh House [*q.v.*], Skibbereen.

Lewis 1837.

513. HILL LODGE, Cobh; pre-1841; *demolished.*
A seat of a branch of the Scott family, by the twentieth century known as 'Belmont'.

514. HILLSGROVE, Skibbereen; pre-1842; *demolished.*
A property acquired around 1855 from George Pinchin by Paul Limerick, the original straight approach to which was replaced by a more circuitous and mysterious avenue, its new access by a pre-existing structure which seems to have then been put to use as a porter's lodge.

Griffith 1853–63.

515. HODDERSFIELD, Crosshaven (2).
William Hodder married thrice but died without leaving male issue in 1787, leaving his estates to his nephew, William Henry Moore-Hodder I, an improver who by 1815 had 'lately converted a very old fashioned house and demesne into a fine country seat'. This was to designs of the elder Abraham Hargrave, who may also have furnished plans for the gazebo in the demesne and perhaps the two gatekeepers' lodges. Both the mansion and the original lodges have been demolished.

Inland entrance; pre-1841; *demolished.*

Coastal entrance; pre-1842/*c.* 1870.
Succeeding to the property on the death of his father in 1859, William Henry Moore-Hodder III (b. 1846) built this replacement lodge. To its main front two finialled gablet windows break the eaves of a roof with chimney-stacks to each gable. All in mellow brick facings, one-over-one sash windows with segmental heads flank a little gabled glazed entrance hallway. Occupied.

Townsend 1815; *LGI* (1904).

516. HOLLYBROOK, Skibbereen (2).
An old house built by John Becher in 1751 remained lodgeless until his grandson, Richard Henry Hedges Becher, remedied that 100 years later on the main eastern approach. The family neglected the place and leased it for half a century before its acquisition by Lt.-Col. Anthony Hickman Morgan, who

transformed the place, replacing the Becher house with a grand new Arts and Crafts mansion and two complementary gatekeepers' lodges.

Front gate; *c.* 1850/*c.* 1903; architect Robert Shekleton Balfour.

Whilst the Scottish architect's design for the big house is relatively conservative, this lodge (*above*), although also in a Queen Anne Revival manner, is quite outstanding and innovative. It is all the more ingenious if it is a reworking of its mid-nineteenth-century predecessor. Now 1½-storey on an elongated octagonal plan, the attic accommodation occupies a steeply pitched hipped roof finished in striking red earthenware plain tiles, its bedrooms lit by eccentric minuscule flat-roofed dormers contained at each end by towering chimney-stacks. To the contrasting roughcast ground floor are tripartite multi-paned casement windows below segmental heads flanking a front door that lies recessed behind a wide tetrastyle Doric portico with a mutuled entablature, the pediment to which is tile-hung and delightfully frames a keystoned Diocletian window.

Rear gate; *c.* 1903; architect probably R.S. Balfour.

Contemporary with its counterpart but less imaginative is this big two-storey hip-roofed gatehouse, again with red earthenware tiles to steep pitches and bellcast eaves over segmentally headed rectangular-paned casement windows in Voysey-like roughcast walls. The single-storey hall projection sports another Diocletian window.

Bence-Jones 1988; *IFR*; Lyons 1993; Shaffrey and Shaffrey 1985; Williams 1994.

517. HOLLYHILL, Kinsale; *c.* 1840.

A plain single-storey lodge faced in rubble with an ungainly outsized projecting gabled hall, the main roof tall-eaved and steeply hipped. Derelict, next to a run-down avenue, described in 1750 as being 'above an English mile long', to a house of Francis Roche. Subsequently in 1852 the residence of Simon Bohane.

Smith 1893; Griffith 1853–63.

518. HOLLYHILL HOUSE, Kinsale; pre-1841; *demolished.*

In the nineteenth century linked to its neighbour and sister house of Hollyhill [*q.v.*] by a long straight avenue with a porter's lodge on the boundary, both since removed. In the first half of that century it was home to the Newman family but by 1852 was the residence of Mary Anne Collis.

Leet 1814; Griffith 1853–63.

HOLLYMOUNT (see MOUNT DESERT FARM)

519. HOME FOR INCURABLES, Cork [N]; *c.* 1885; architect Henry Hill and Son.

Off Military Road, the great institution in polychromatic brickwork and stone dressings is approached via a characterful little gatekeeper's lodge in red brick, 1½-storey off a simple rectangular plan, its elevations enlivened by a delightful single-storey wooden glazed bay window below a bellcast roof; the main hipped roof eaves are broken by hip-gabled gablets containing paired four-over-four sash windows with segmental pointed arches. Doubtless contemporary with the completion in 1881 of the Home, now a hotel.

IAA.

HONAN (see SUMMERHILL, Cork [N])

520. HOP ISLAND, Rochestown (3).

Approached via a causeway, until the turn of the nineteenth century this was 'Red Island', successively home to a Mr Lane (1783) and Revd Mr Saunders (1804) before the Edwards family took it for the rest of the century. The inner, pre-1841 lodge, like its successors, has been demolished. An old boat-house took on the role of porter's accommodation for a period before yet another was built on the mainland, occasioned by the arrival of the Cork Blackrock and Passage Railway.

Taylor and Skinner 1778; 1783; Wilson 1803; Leet 1814; *LOI.*

521. HORSEHEAD, Passage West; pre-1841; architects possibly Thomas and Kearns Deane; *demolished.*

Described by Samuel Lewis in 1837 as 'of Samuel Lane, Esq., an elegant mansion in the Tudor style of architecture, situated amidst beautiful scenery', it was in fact built in 1836 to designs of Thomas and Kearns Deane, whose commission doubtless included the contemporary gate lodge.

Lewis 1837; Lyons 1993; Williams 1994.

522. HUNTING HILL, Castletownroche; pre-1841; *demolished.*

A lodge no longer marks the entrance to the long, straight, beech-lined avenue from the north to a thatched cottage residence in 1814 of William Dwyer. This lodge may have been contemporary with the addition of a new slated Regency villa by Thomas Dwyer.

Leet 1814; Hajba 2002.

523. HYDE PARK, Cork [N]; *c.* 1835.

A property presumably founded by the Hydes of Castle Hyde [*q.v.*], it was leased to Jeremiah Murphy (b. 1779) and his son Jeremiah Stack Murphy, the latter presumably having added the gate lodge, which is a single-storey stuccoed hip-roofed affair with a breakfronted doorway. Much improved and extended into a double-pile structure. Wide entrance with concave quadrants.

Lewis 1837; *IFR.*

524. HYDE PARK HOUSE, Cork [N]; *c.* 1840; architect not known.

Another one of that fine genre of neo-Classical Doric lodges which grace the entrances to gentry and merchant villas in the northern suburbs of the city. This one, built for James Morrogh (*c.* 1794–1868), is likewise rendered single-storey on a cruciform plan with plinth, pilastered external corners and a plain frieze to its shallow hipped roof. Modern windows do little for the effect. Impressive stone carriage

pillars with pedimented cappings: keystoned, round-topped, moulded recessed panels and moulded plinths, framed by convex dwarf quadrant walls below opulent cast-iron railings, which all looks later than the lodge—perhaps the result of subsequent road-widening. Similar lodges are at Clifton, Mount Donegan, Factoryville, Shanakiel and the Episcopal Palace. A property latterly renamed 'St Mary's'.

Lewis 1837; *LGI* (1904).

ILECASH (see ROCKVILLE, Fermoy)

525. ILEN LODGE, Drimoleague; pre-1842; *demolished.*
A small estate in 1853 of Revd Richard L. Connor.

Griffith 1853–63.

IMMACULATA MOUNT AVERNIA (see WOODFORT)

526. INCHERA, Glanmire (2).
An early nineteenth-century house built by Charles Silver Oliver of the Castle Oliver, Co. Limerick [q.v.], family, who was succeeded on his death in 1817 by his eldest son, Silver Charles Oliver (d. 1878) of the 10th Hussars, who was certainly responsible for adding the front lodge, manning it with a porter who was not to be impressed by casual visitors.

North gate; *c.* 1830.
On 17 July 1835 the Scottish tourist Robert Graham recorded: 'On coming to the gate of Mr Oliver's demesne, who has made a mound and private bridge leading to his house ... I applied for permission to drive through his grounds ... The gatekeeper would not allow the car to enter.' What he failed to describe was this single-storey standard hip-roofed, rendered hybrid lodge, with Classical pilasters defining corners and framing wide windows with basic Tudor-style label mouldings. A Picturesque diagonally set chimney-stack pierces the roof where the ridge used to be, but now removed thanks to extensive additions and alterations which see an inappropriate new concrete-tiled finish allied to equally unpleasant modern window replacements. Some good contemporary ironwork survives to gates and railings.

South gate; pre-1841; *demolished.*

Heaney 1999; Bence-Jones 1988; *IFR.*

527. INCHICLOGH, Bantry (2).
The White family took possession of the property in the 1790s and it was Richard White, nephew of the 1st earl of Bantry, who from 1827 supervised extensive improvements to Inchiclogh, which may have involved the creation of the two porters' lodges before 1842. Both, along with the big house, have perished, lost like their fine demesne.

Everett 2001.

528. INISHCARRA RECTORY, Inishcarra; pre-1841; *demolished.*
A glebe house with conflicting dates for its construction of 1794 and 1816. The porter's lodge, intriguingly, is shown on the first OS map as being circular—a 'drum lodge' opposite the gates probably contemporary with one of those years and maybe inspired by the early incumbent the Revd Hon. George De la Poer Beresford (1765–1841), grandson of the 1st earl of Tyrone, later to become bishop of Kilmore and Ardagh. The lodge had been removed by 1890. The rectory on the banks of the River Lee is now a private house.

Townsend 1815; Lewis 1837; *BPB* (1929).

529. IVY HILL, Douglas; pre-1841; *demolished.*
The residence in 1853 of the Very Revd Horace Townsend Newman, dean of Cork (d. 1864).

Griffith 1853–63; *LGI* (1904).

530. JAMESBROOK HALL, Cloyne (2).
The grand house since the eighteenth century of the Adams family, the entrances to which remained lodgeless until after the succession as a minor in 1817 of Richard Wallis Goold-Adams (1802–73), and even then, it seems, following his 1852 marriage.

Coastal entrance; pre-1890; *demolished.*
Built after 1841 on a site by Cork Harbour close to a previous unidentified structure.

Inland entrance; *c.* 1860.
A rustic whitewashed rubble-built tripartite gateway with plain screen walls and wooden gates, giving way to what appears to the visitor to be a single-storey standard lodge but is revealed to the rear as a two-storey gatehouse. A pleasant structure of rubble construction with brick as quoins and dressings and with segmental arches to six-over-six sash windows, its gables with pretty carved bargeboards. Well maintained and extended sensitively and imaginatively to one side.

LGI (1904); NIAH.

531. JANEMOUNT, Glanmire; *c.* 1830; *demolished.*
What has now been transformed into the Arts and Crafts mansion known as 'Glenmervyn' was a pretty early Victorian Tudor Picturesque villa, which explains the conspicuous fantasy entrance. Now lacking its tiny lodge is a Tudor carriage archway with castellated parapet running between a pair of crenellated octagonal turrets flanked by screen walls. Constructed in rubble stone, now startlingly picked out in white livery, a creation for William Hickie (1768–1847) of Killelton, Co. Kerry [*q.v.*].

LGI (1904); Pike and Hodges 1911.

531. Janemount, Glanmire.

532. JANEVILLE, Ballintemple; pre-1841; *demolished.*
A little suburban park in 1852 of Joseph Woodley Lindsay, his villa and its gatekeeper's lodge swept away to make way for modern housing development.

Griffith 1853–63.

533. JANEVILLE, Bandon; *c.* 1830.
Squeezed in behind a crude crenellated concave quadrant wall of a gatescreen with arched postilion openings is a plain single-storey hip-roofed lodge, any features obscured by a flat-roofed hall projection. Home in 1851 of Revd Henry Gillman, leasing from the Cornwall family of neighbouring Park View [*q.v.*], the property latterly renamed 'Eversleigh'.

Griffith 1853–63.

534. JANEVILLE, Cork [S]; pre-1841; *demolished.*
The mortuary chapel of St Joseph's Cemetery [*q.v.*] now occupies the site of the old porter's lodge to a property in 1852 of Timothy Dongan.

Griffith 1853–63.

535. JANEVILLE, Kilworth; 1867.
Like the plain mid-Victorian house built by Edward Peter O'Gorman, there is an equally unassuming and contemporary gabled gate lodge with like-roofed projecting hall flanked by flat-roofed extensions in the internal angles. Occupied.

LOI.

536. JOHN'S GROVE, Shanballymore; *c.* 1800.

In an enchanting sylvan setting is this delightful rubble-built cottage, now divested of its harled finish. Single-storey standard, facing the road alongside the modest gates and framed by walled quadrants, its tiny windows flank a sheeted door below the high eaves which, along with the hipped gables, permit modest attic space, the chimney-stack off-centre to accommodate it. Derelict. An estate in 1797 of Edmund Glover, who by 1814 had been succeeded here by John Glover.

Leet 1814; Hajba 2002.

537. JOHNSTOWN, Carrigtohill; pre-1841; *demolished.*
Down the years a much-leased property, in the late eighteenth century a seat of the Sarsfield family and subsequently home in 1853 to John Courtenay of Ballyedmond [*q.v.*].

Taylor and Skinner 1778; 1783; Wilson 1803; Griffith 1853–63.

538. JOHNSTOWN, Douglas; *c.* 1820.
A plain rendered gabled single-storey cottage, two-window-bay front to the road, subsequently lengthened by a further two bays. Occupied. A 65-acre holding in 1853 of Daniel Caddigan.

Griffith 1853–63.

539. KEALE, Millstreet; pre-1842; *demolished.*
A house built in 1834 by John Leader (1796–1839) to replace a predecessor, an improvement which may have included the addition of the porter's lodge.

LGI (1904); Hajba 2002.

540. KEIL BUI, Cloyne; pre-1841; *demolished.*
Lewis Gibson is recorded as resident here in 1814 and 1837.

Leet 1814; Lewis 1837.

541. KENT RAILWAY STATION, Cork [N]; 1893; architect not known.

The terminus to the Great Southern and Western Railway was rebuilt from 1891 onwards in a striking Ruabon red brick from Denbighshire and a new access created off Lower Glanmire Road, incorporating a porter's lodge in like material. Little more than a sentry-box but boasting a chimney-stack for its occupant, it is central to an extensive railed gatescreen with hefty pillars in a contrasting stone which also forms plinth and sill courses to the lofty lodge, notable for its leading canted front with narrow one-over-one sash windows.

IAA.

542. KILBARRY, Clondulane; pre-1841; *demolished.*
A stone on the outbuildings bears the date '1808' and the monogram of Robert Wigmore, whereas 'the splendidly situate and hospitable mansion of Henry Wigmore' is a replacement house of 1842 described by O'Flanagan two years later. The lodge on the northern approach had been removed by 1890.

Leet 1814; O'Flanagan 1975; Hajba 2002.

543. KILBARRY, Cork [N]; pre-1841; *demolished.*
A Barry property in 1852 leased to George Wise.

Griffith 1853–63.

544. KILBARRY, Macroom; pre-1842; *demolished.*
A 116-acre estate, in 1837 of James Barry.

Lewis 1837.

545. KILBERRIHERT, Macroom; pre-1842.
Alongside the gates of a property in 1837 of R.B. Crooke Esq. is a ruined three-bay standard cottage.

Lewis 1837.

546. KILBOLANE CASTLE, Milford; *c.* 1800.

A venerable house built around 1695 by John Bowen and improved a century later by the Bruces of Miltown Castle [*q.v.*], who refaced it and probably built the Gothic porter's lodge opposite its gates. It remains a shell, its wide, rubble-built, three-bay, almost symmetrical façade displaying rare ogee-arched openings, all maintained as a curiosity minus its hipped roof and sealed up. Across the road the gatescreen appropriately has ogee-walled quadrants, contained by four plain square limestone ashlar pillars.

Bence-Jones 1988; Hajba 2002.

547. KILBOY, Cloyne; pre-1841; *demolished.*
The demesne's proprietor in 1824 and 1870 is noted as Francis Rowland.

Pigot 1824; Slater 1870.

548. KILBRACK COTTAGE, Doneraile; pre-1841; *demolished.*
Another old seat of the Creagh family of Creagh Castle [*q.v.*] and Laurentium [*q.v.*]. Michael Creagh (1771–1845) lived here before moving to the latter upon his father's death in 1833, when the place was let to the local parish priest.

LGI (1904).

549. KILBRACK, Doneraile; *c.* 1820.

An estate of a junior branch of the Stawells of Kilbrittain Castle [*q.v.*] which was home to William Stawell (d. 1830) and his nephew, the local rector, Revd Francis Stawell (1784–1866). Their entrance is a good tripartite gateway of square limestone ashlar pillars with moulded plinths and corniced cappings—Classical and grey in comparison with its Georgian Gothic-style lodge, admirably rehabilitated in a pastel pink livery alongside. Single-storey, it projects beyond the connecting screen wall in a canted front with pointed-arched Y-traceried sash windows to the road, below a semi-octahedral roof. Within, a two-bay entrance elevation commands the gates, a hefty chimney-stack rising off the opposing wall and toothed quoins to all corners.

LGI (1912).

550. KILBREE, Cloyne (2).
Both gatekeepers' lodges to a property in 1837 of Samuel Wallis Adams Esq. have been demolished. In place by 1842, the Scottish tourist Robert Graham failed to notice them in his account of a visit on 18 July 1835: 'called at Mr Adam's of Kilbrea from whose lady we got a key which enabled us to drive in at what they call the Cloyne gate, and out at the gate leading to the town or village, which is inconsiderable'.

Heaney 1999; Lewis 1837.

551. KILBRITTAIN CASTLE, Kilbrittain; *c.* 1780; architect not known.

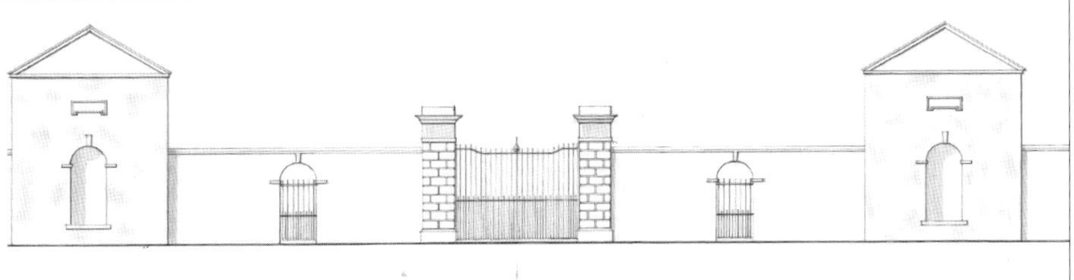

551. Kilbrittain Castle, Kilbrittain.

Here are the vestiges of an important Palladian-style entrance comprised of a pair of 1½-storey lodges once linked by a 40ft-wide gatescreen; they represent the earliest surviving twin non-defensive examples in the county. The visitor is met by a pair of short and lofty blind harled rubble façades, each relieved by a round-arched niche with spring and keystones, with an uninformative cut-stone plaque between it and the pedimented gable. They face each other with their high eaves over three-bay openings, all treated as per the niches, whilst the park gables display upper-storey windows and chimney-stacks. Not beyond restoration to its pomp, the entrance formed the perfect frame on an axis to the mansion on the hill beyond, which now appears as an irregular mid-Victorian creation as transformed from a more appropriate Classical house built by Jonas Stawell (1700–67) about 1740 on the site of an older sixteenth-century McCarthy tower-house. The illustration is conjectural in respect of the gatescreen.

Smith 1893; *LGI* (1912); Bence-Jones 1988.

552. KILBROGAN RECTORY, Bandon; *c.* 1800.

For an Anglican rectory porter's lodge this is an unusually commodious structure, a two-storey hip-roofed gatehouse in a cream-washed harled finish, its short single-bay elevation to the roadside with pointed-arched ground-floor window below a square one to the upper storey. Alongside is an equally rustic gatescreen of four bold plain pillars which contain short concave quadrant walls, each with a now-blind postilion opening, all in a finish co-ordinating with the house, which faces the avenue with irregular fenestration and a single-storey projecting hip-roofed hallway. Derelict, but maintained up to a point in a dense tree canopy. Probably built for Revd John Kenny DD (d. 1814), rector in 1796.

553. KILBURN or KILBYRNE, Doneraile; *c.* 1835.

A lost house, itself built in 1828 by James Grove White (1791–1866) to replace a predecessor burnt down five years earlier by the Whiteboys. The lodge at the entrance to the northern approach is an uninspired affair. Single-storey with a roughcast three-bay front elevation, the doorway to the right-hand side below an oversailing hipped roof. Occupied. There are nice Gothic hooped tops to the gate and their concave quadrants.

LGI (1904); Pike and Hodges 1911.

554. KILCASCAN CASTLE, Ballineen (2).

In 1837 'the seat of W.J. O'Neill Daunt Esq., a handsome castellated mansion embosomed in young and thriving plantations'. The Romantic Regency seat was created around 1830 by Daunt (1807–94) after he had inherited the place upon his father's death in a duel in 1826.

West entrance; pre-1841; *demolished.*

A lodge that had been removed by 1890.

East entrance; pre-1841.

Across the road from its gates but strangely removed is the ruin of a rubble-built gatekeeper's lodge.

Lewis 1837; *LGI* (1904).

555. KILCOLMAN, Ballineen; pre-1841; *demolished.*

An estate in 1837 of Adderley Beamish Esq. (d. 1866), who later took the additional surname of Bernard. His house has likewise gone, having been burnt in 1921.

Lewis 1837; *LGI* (1904); Bence-Jones 1988.

556. KILCOLMAN PARK, Ballineen; *c.* 1840.

An attractive 1½-storey three-bay gabled cottage, its ground floor in a boldly pointed rubble finish with a gabled front door canopy and two pretty attic gablets over. A seat in 1837 of W. Lamb Esq.

Lewis 1837.

KILCRENAGH (see WOODSIDE)

557. KILCRONE, Cloyne; *c.* 1800.

An entrance that reflects different eras of development on the estate. The gatescreen of around 1870 has pillars of deeply punched rusticated masonry and contemporary decorative palmette-finialled railings and carriage gates, a replacement by Clement F. Lawless when he came by the property and made alterations to the old eighteenth-century house, previously of the Hanning family. Across the road is their traditional Irish Georgian Gothic cottage lodge. Single-storey standard in a harled finish, its low

flat-arched doorway flanked by a pair of lancet windows below a clipped-eaves steeply pitched hipped roof, the ridge of which is broken by a conspicuously off-centre brick chimney-stack. Derelict. Possibly built for John Hanning, who was in residence in 1814.

Leet 1814; Slater 1870; Bence-Jones 1988; IAA photograph (S/675/6).

558. KILCRUMPER CEMETERY, Kilworth; *c.* 1850.

A very plain, derelict, single-storey roughcast lodge, its three-bay front with doorway to the right-hand side and gables having cursory skew-tables. Next to the ruins of old Kilcrumper church. Probably built in the incumbency of the Revd Francis Brady.

Griffith 1853–63.

559. KILCRUMPER RECTORY, Kilworth; pre-1841; *demolished.*

A large glebe house, otherwise known as Kilmore Rectory, built in 1820 by the wealthy bachelor incumbent, Revd Thomas Newenham (1797–1849), who was to succeed to Coolmore [*q.v.*] in 1842. The porter's lodge was probably contemporary with the rectory.

Lewis 1837; *IFR.*

560. KILDINAN, Glenville (2).

Edward Roche (1771–1855) succeeded his father Edmund here on his death in 1823. Both their gate lodges built before 1841, one well within the demesne at an inner boundary, have been demolished.

BPB (1929).

561. KILFINNAN CASTLE, Glandore; pre-1842; *demolished.*

A property in 1837 of J. Ranclaud Esq., leasing from the Hussey de Burghs of Donore, Co. Kildare, an old house given mock castellations.

Lewis 1837.

562. KILGARRIFF, Clonakilty; *c.* 1815.

A single-storey hip-roofed lodge on an L-plan with two-bay elevations to road and avenue, in a limewashed harled finish. Derelict. A seat in 1837 of Capt. Alfred Davies.

Lewis 1837.

563. KILHESSEN LODGE, Bandon; pre-1841; *demolished.*

A 95-acre holding in 1852 of James Jellett.

Griffith 1853–63.

564. KILLAHORA, Carrigtohill; *c.* 1820.

A derelict, plain, single-storey standard gabled gatekeeper's lodge to a property in 1837 of John Martin Esq.

Lewis 1837.

565. KILLANEER, Enniskean; pre-1841; *demolished.*
The seat at the turn of the nineteenth century of John Beamish, the lodge to which was situated distant from the county road.
LGI (1904).

566. KILLANY, Kinsale; pre-1841; *demolished.*
Resident on the estate in 1837 was T. Markham Esq.
Lewis 1837.

KILLEAGH (see WESTPARK)

567. KILLEE, Mitchelstown; *c.* 1845.

The Palladian house of the Montgomerys, belatedly complemented by this singularly retarded little lodge by the gate, appearing to date from the turn of the nineteenth century. Single-storey in a limewashed harled finish, its hipped roof has clipped eaves to three sides extending to oversail the two-bay avenue front of doorway and a wide window, which may have had a verandahed post support as its sole decorative feature. Built for Revd William Quin Montgomery (d. 1869). Derelict.
LGI (1904).

568. KILLEENA, Skibbereen; pre-1842; *demolished.*
A seat in 1837 of Revd John Wright, whose gate lodge had gone by 1902, by which date the house was in ruins.
Lewis 1837.

KILLETRA (see MOUNT RUBY)

569. KILLINARDRISH, Coachford; pre-1841/*c.* 1845; architects possibly Sir Thomas and Kearns Deane.

A distinctive little Tudor Gothic lodge which had a predecessor on the site opposite the gates. Originating as a single-storey extended octagon on plan, with an equivalent roof and an entrance offshoot, it displays single and tripartite label-moulded openings in smooth rendered walls containing Perpendicular Gothic traceried windows. The delightful Tudor-arched double-leafed panelled door is flanked by a pair of sidelights, while the Gothic theme extends to a pair of diagonally set chimney-stacks with pointed-arched recessed panels. There is some loss of the previous glazing pattern in an otherwise admirable restoration, which includes a gabled extension in similar style. A property in 1837 of R.B. Crooke Esq., which by 1852 was the residence of Robert I.O. Donohoe. There is an identical glazing pattern in the county at Kilcascan Castle [*q.v.*] and the lodges at Leamlara [*q.v.*], Raleigh [*q.v.*] and Drishane Castle [*q.v.*].
Lewis 1837; Griffith 1853–63.

570. KILLORA LODGE, Carrigtohill; *c.* 1835.
A single-storey hip-roofed lodge with oversailing soffits on an L-plan, its smooth rendered walls framed by crude pilasters, the leading window set in a rectangular recess to ground level. In the internal angle is a later flat-roofed hallway. Derelict. Dating from the time here of Revd Robert Bury (d. 1853).
Lewis 1837; Griffith 1853–63; *LGI* (1904).

571. KILLOWEN COTTAGE, Newmarket; pre-1841; *demolished.*
A holding of the Creagh family, let in the early nineteenth century to the Stannards, the lodge to which had gone by 1936.
Leet 1814; Pigot 1824.

572. KILLURAGH, Castletownroche; pre-1841; *demolished.*
The house built by E. Badham Thornhill around 1790 was by 1837 the residence of Cornelius Linahan. Later named 'The Glen', it was destroyed by fire in the 1950s, its lodge having gone by 1935.
Lewis 1837; Hajba 2002.

573. KILMAHON RECTORY, Shanagarry; pre-1842; *demolished.*
A gate lodge perhaps contemporary with the glebe house, variously recorded as dating from 1794 or 1805. By 1919 the former was vacant and a decade later was described in the valuation notes as 'now uninhabitable'.
Townsend 1815; Lewis 1837.

574. KILMALODA, Timoleague; pre-1841; *demolished.*
The estate of a branch of the Beamish family, the porter's lodge to which served the old house replaced in 1872 for Sampson Beamish. The lodge had gone by 1902.

575. KILMALODA RECTORY, Timoleague; pre-1841; *demolished.*
A glebe house built in 1790 or 1813, so contradictorily noted, the lodge possibly of an age with it.
Townsend 1815; Lewis 1837.

576. KILMARNOCK LODGE, Monkstown; *c.* 1845; *demolished.*
A lodge that probably dated from the house's being greatly enlarged by Henry Westropp O'Donovan (1812–70), resident here in 1853.
Griffith 1853–63.

577. KILMEEN RECTORY, Ballingurteen; *c.* 1820.
'... [T]here are large plantations around the glebe-house the residence of the Rev. E.H. Kenny. The glebe-house was erected by the last incumbent, with the aid of £100 from the late Board of First Fruits, in 1791.' The lodge looks to be of slightly later date and was probably added by Revd Kenny. Standard 1½-storey with tiny one-over-one sash windows to a road elevation in sepia-washed harling. Gabled, with a chimney-stack to each; a skylight and cast-iron latticed casement light the attic floor. Derelict.
Lewis 1837.

578. KILMORE, Inishannon; *c.* 1800.
A single-storey standard cottage with high pointed-arched openings in harled rubble walls below tall eaves to the steeply pitched roof, with a chimney-stack to each gable. Derelict. An estate in 1814 of William Popham.
Leet 1814.

579. KILMURRY, Kilworth; pre-1841/*c.* 1855.

Thomas St John Grant (1822–68) inherited the estate as a minor, with its modest house and porter's lodge by the roadside, upon his father's death in 1832. It was not until twenty years later that he embarked on a major redevelopment of the property, perhaps not unrelated to his marriage in 1849 to Eliza Anna Louisa Hoare of Glanamore [*q.v.*]. The works comprised a splendid new neo-Classical mansion, outbuildings with an '1856' date-stone, and a replacement gate lodge and entrance appropriate to the place. Regrettably this now lies abandoned and ivy-infested, a fitting prelude to the desolation beyond. Single-storey and gabled on an L-plan, its stucco finish containing on the avenue elevation a single wide window opening below a crudely corbelled mantle canopy. The roof is skew-tabled, with a fine pair of cut-stone plinthed chimney-stacks to ridges. The once-impressive gatescreen is comprised of a triple gateway with Classical stone pillars, each chamfered, having recessed panels and four pediment-faced cappings. The extensive concave railed quadrants display rosette and palmette motifs to match the gates.
LGI (1904); Hajba 2002.

580. KILNAP GLEN HOUSE AND FLOUR MILL, Cork [N]; pre-1841; *demolished.*
An establishment of the Shaw family, flour factors, millers and corn and flour merchants, in 1852 of William Shaw. There survives a drawing for a 'Sketch of a Lodge for William Shaw Esq.', dated October 1835, which depicts a delectable English Tudor Picturesque cottage with thatched roof. In the P.F. Robinson manner and thus not quite symmetrical, it is 1½-storey and three-bay

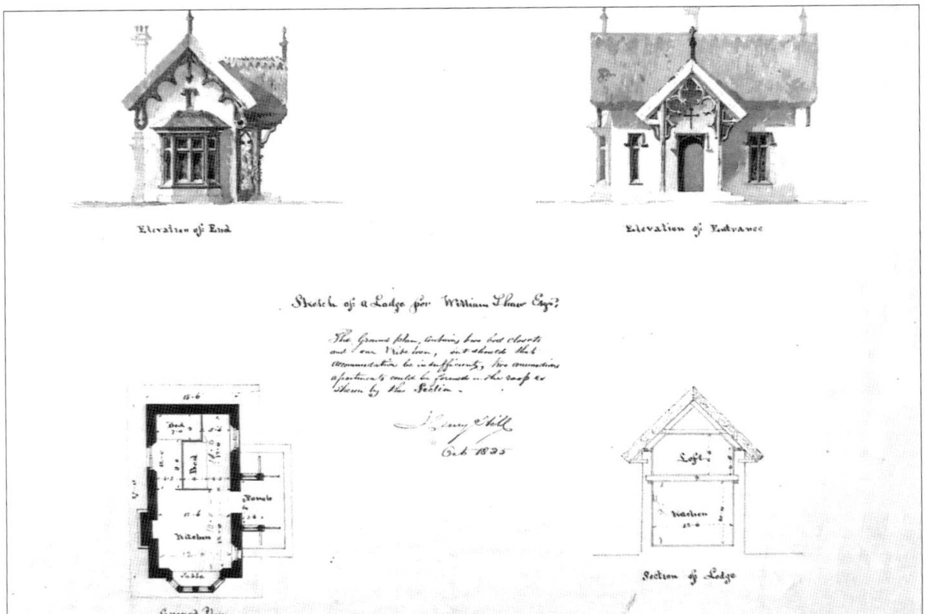

580. Kilnap Glen House and Flour Mill, Cork [N] (IAA).

with thatched roof and highly decorative exaggerated carved cusped bargeboards with mouchette toes to main gables and that of the rustic canopied porch. To one end is a glazed canted bay window, transomed and mullioned, as are the other single and bipartite casements below label mouldings. The OS maps suggest that this was in fact built in handed form by the gate. The accompanying illustration is a copy of an original drawing by Henry Hill in the collection of the Allen family of Ballymaloe House [*q.v.*].

Griffith 1853–63; IAA (photograph S/2307/18 & S/2308/1,2).

581. KILNAP, Cork [N]; pre-1841; *demolished.*
The residence in 1852 of Honoria Cooke.

Griffith 1853–63.

582. KILORGA, Castlemartyr; *c.* 1790.
An antique single-storey standard gabled cottage with tiny windows, now sporting green shutters on a background of burgundy painted rubble. Modernisation extends to new concrete roof tiles. Maintained derelict. Gateless. A seat in 1814 of Mr Michael McCarthy.

Leet 1814.

583. KILPATRICK, Bandon; *c.* 1910.

Other than the modern plastic windows in a drab cement rendering, this is a pleasant 1½-storey gabled gatehouse of generous proportions, with the doorway to the right-hand side of a three-bay main front, directly over which are three pretty gablets with, like the main gables, carved ornamental bargeboards and earthenware hip-knobs stopping trefoil-perforated crestings. To a gable one-over-one late Victorian sash windows remain. A property which lay unoccupied in 1852, the immediate lessor being William Whiting of nearby Brothersfort [*q.v.*], the lodge being added somewhat later by the subsequent proprietor, John Good, who had acquired the estate around 1890. His gatekeeper in 1912 was John Connor.

584. KILRUSH, Ballineen; pre-1841.
All that remains of the gatekeeper's lodge to a seat in 1837 of Captain Andrew Poole is an ivy-covered rubble-built gabled ruin.

Lewis 1837; *LGI* (1904).

585. KILSHANNIG, Rathcormack; pre-1841; *demolished.*
Described in 1844 as 'one of the princely seats of Edmund Roche, Esq.', the magnificent Palladian mansion had been built in 1765–6 for Abraham Devonsher to designs by Davis Duckart, but nothing of its entrance remains, the lodges having gone by 1935. The first OS map indicates that this was an extensive gatescreen framed by a pair of lodges, an appropriate reflection of the pavilioned splendour within.

O'Flanagan 1975; Bence-Jones 1988.

586. KINOITH, Shanagarry; *c.* 1919.
From 1860 a lodgeless property developed by Joshua Strangman, a situation not remedied until the early twentieth century with the building of a most convincing imitation of a porter's lodge from 80 years earlier. Single-storey standard on a square plan with a pyramidal roof rising to a central chimney-stack. Smooth-rendered on a plinth, its one-over-one bipartite sash windows have basic Tudor-style label mouldings. The earlier entrance has nice, simple, pointed 'hooped' railings and gates. Built for Wilson Strangman.

587. KNIGHT'S LODGE, Charleville; pre-1841/*c.* 1920.

A house built in 1795 by Robert Featherstone was entered past a little square lodge to the right-hand side of the gatescreen. By 1890 this had gone, not to be replaced until years later at the other side of the approach. This is a peculiar hybrid lodge, its two-over-two sash windows below Tudor style label mouldings contrasting with an Italianate porch with square Doric pillars and, within, a round-headed fanlight to the glazed double-leafed doorway, which leads into a gabled room that projects from the single-storey hip-roofed main body of the grey rendered structure; earthenware cresting and ball-topped hip-knob to the ridges. Built around 1920 for Mr Owen Binchy on an irregular plan in a mid-Victorian manner.

Hajba 2002.

588. KNOCKANE, Castlemartyr; pre-1842; *demolished.*
The seat in the early nineteenth century of the Garde family, whose lodge was in ruins by 1935.

Leet 1814; Lewis 1837.

KNOCKANEMORE (see BRIDE VIEW)

589. KNOCKANROE, Carrignavar; pre-1841/pre-1890; *demolished.*
An estate in the mid-nineteenth century of Robert A. Rogers. Both the early lodge and its successor at the other side of the entrance have gone.

Griffith 1853–63.

590. KNOCKDUFF, Kinsale (2).
A property occupied by a succession of various residents down the years, from Lt.-Gen. Sir T. Browne in 1837, in whose time both entrances were already lodged, to John F. Lee and in 1870 Thomas Hornibrook.

South gate; *c.* 1835/*c.* 1890.
The first OS map shows a rectangular plan with central front projection, which by the end of the century had increased to a cruciform imprint with the addition of a back return, as it appears today but much latterly extended from the park gable and thoroughly restored. Single-storey gabled with modern continuous bracket bargeboards, its attractive

rubble walls with pointed-arched openings dressed in brick having Georgian Gothic-style Y-traceried modern windows. The central doorway is flanked by supporting lancet lights in an admirable rehabilitation awaiting a softening planted setting.

North gate; pre-1841/*c.* 1890.
A 1½-storey standard lodge with rubble stone facings, with toothed brick quoins and dressings to segmentally arched openings. A gabled replacement for a predecessor.

Lewis 1837.

591. KNOCKEVEN, Cobh; 1867.
An extensive single-storey symmetrical lodge, its hipped roof with carved soffit brackets continued over a central breakfront with decorative pilasters framing two windows. Flanking, in rendered walls, are paired windows, the ridge crowned by two balancing chimney-stacks, like the main structure, on plinths. The large villa was built in 1863 for Simon Hardy at a cost of £2,000.

592. KNOCKGLASS, Castlemartyr; pre-1842; *demolished.*
An estate in the early nineteenth century of the Hennis family.

593. KNOCKHOUSE FARM, Churchtown; *c.* 1845.

A very sturdy and well-built single-storey standard lodge in attractive stone facings, its rectangular fanlit front door flanked by six-over-six sash windows, all below a high-eaved oversailing hipped roof with a banded chimney-stack. Almost identical to the lodge at nearby Cregan [*q.v.*], which likewise was a property that passed upon the death in 1841 of the 5th Lord Egmont to his agent and solicitor Sir Edward Tierney. The lodge lies abandoned and dilapidated, ripe for restoration.

Griffith 1853–63.

KNOCKMACOOL (see DESERT COTTAGE)

594. KNOCKMORE, Carrigaline; *c.* 1850.
The first OS map of 1842 and the valuation of eight years later show that a stable block preceded the building of house and lodge, then recorded as a 184-acre property of John Martin. This porter's lodge is a plain standard gabled cottage, still in occupation.

Griffith 1853–63.

595. KNOCKMOURNE RECTORY, Curraglass; pre-1841; *demolished.*
A glebe house built in 1827 by Revd Thomas Spread Campion for £1,223; this sum doubtless covered the erection of a round 'inkpot' caretaker's lodge, which sadly had been removed by 1890.

596. KNOCKNAGAPPUL, Ballinadee; *c.* 1835.
Originally a standard single-storey lodge, subsequently raised an extra storey. Gabled, with roughcast upper floor above smooth-rendered walls containing a double-leafed door flanked by later two-over-one sash windows. A property in 1851 of Francis Croker.

Griffith 1853–63.

597. KNOCKNAHORGAN MILL, Sallybrook; pre-1841; *demolished.*
'The woollen manufacture was established here in 1822, by Messrs Lyons and Hanly, whose factory, in a secluded part of the vale of Glanmire, contains 30 looms, and affords employment to 200 persons.' A century after Samuel Lewis recorded this in 1837, it had become 'Silverspring Starch Works'. A lodge presumably contemporary with its foundation. See also Silverspring Woollen Mills.

Lewis 1837.

598. KNOCKREA [1], Cork [S]; *c.* 1855; architect not known.

An excellent little neo-Classical single-storey standard lodge, rendered with recessed panel pilasters to external corners below a shallow oversailing hipped roof with carved soffit brackets, which extends over a projecting hall flanked by rectangular-paned casement windows. To the Blackrock Road are later carriage pillars in stone on a plinth with quarry-faced masonry, recessed moulded panelled shafts and, below the triangular capping with floral motifs, an egg-and-dart corbel and friezes inscribed 'Knockrea'. To one side is a bricked-up postilion opening with chamfered surround in punched limestone and a segmental head. A property previously called 'Clarens', to which the lodge was added by Robert Raves.

Griffith 1953–63.

599. KNOCKREA [2], Cork [S]; *c.* 1855.
A big, plain, two-storey gabled gatehouse to a property on the Douglas Road in 1853 of William Harvey; previously called 'Summerville'.

Griffith 1853–63.

600. KNOCKREA TOWNLAND, Cork [S]; pre-1841; *demolished.*
Located next to the rear of Feltrim [*q.v.*], in 1853 surgeon and physician Christopher Bull enjoyed a little pleasure park of an acre, recorded in the valuation with garden house, gate lodge and garden.

Slater 1846; Griffith 1853–63.

601. KNOCKROBIN, Kinsale; *c.* 1830.
A standard single-storey roughcast gatekeeper's lodge with a chimney-stack to each gable. Modernised and occupied. A seat in 1837 of Captain Edward Bolton, to which survives a gatescreen with concave quadrant walls with sealed-up postilion opening and balancing round-headed niche.

Lewis 1837.

602. LACKENDUFF, Clonakilty; pre-1841.
An estate in 1837 of J. Lucas Esq., at the gates to which lies a ruined gabled cottage.

Lewis 1837.

603. LAKELANDS, Blackrock; pre-1841; *demolished.*
The site of an important collection of exotic plants built up in the late nineteenth century by brewer, philanthropist and gardener William Crawford, whose ancestor of the same name is recorded as living here in 1814 and 1837.

Leet 1814; Lewis 1837.

604. LAKE LODGE, Glanmire; pre-1841; *demolished.*
The residence in 1837 of John Martin.
Lewis 1837.

605. LAKEMOUNT, Murragh; pre-1841; *demolished.*
A house in 1852 of John James Baylie MD.
Griffith 1853–63.

606. LAKE VIEW, Blackrock; pre-1841; *demolished.*
The suburban seat in 1837 of William Prettie Harris.
Griffith 1853–63.

607. LAKEVILLE, Ballintemple; pre-1841; *demolished.*
A Georgian house in sixteen acres, latterly renamed 'Ravens Court', in 1853 the residence of James Morgan.
Griffith 1853–63.

608. LAPLAND, Douglas; pre-1842; *demolished.*
A 56-acre holding in 1852 of William Carr, whose gate lodge was removed around 1900.
Griffith 1853–63.

LAPP'S ASYLUM (see WHITE CASTLE)

609. LARAGH, Bandon; *c.* 1835.
Robert Graham called here on 30 July 1835 to find 'An excellent house, with suitable offices, thrashing mill by water etc., have been erected ... The whole of this land which has only been three years in the possession of Mr Swanston, has already adopted much the appearance of a Berwickshire or East Lothian farm.' John Swanston may by then have appended the gate lodge as part of his development of the property. It is a 1½-storey harled cottage with a high-eaved hipped roof which catslides over two bays of its three-bay symmetrical main front, having the support of three rustic poles. Occupied, with a pair of dormer windows added.
Heaney 1999.

610. LARCH HILL, Coachford; pre-1890; *demolished.*
A property in 1852 of Patrick Hassett, who probably created the approach from the west after 1841 which connected with the public road next to an existing cottage, which seems then to have assumed the role of gatekeeper's lodge.
Griffith 1853–63.

611. LAUREL HILL, Fermoy (4).
In 1833 'The handsome house built by the parish priest, called Laurel Hill, is destined by that reverend gentleman as the future convent for the Sisters of Mercy, and is to be occupied by the nuns of that benevolent order'. By 1841 it already boasted two porters' lodges and by 1853 the site was being engulfed by institutional building, subsequently extended in 1869 and much thereafter. Two further gate lodges were added to the rear on a new, tortuous pedestrian approach from Princes Street to what had become the Loreto convent. Only one lodge survives. At the head of a steep, circuitous, overgrown track lies this little dilapidated lodge. Three-bay, single-storey, gabled, with plain bargeboards, its walls rendered with segmentally arched openings, the doorway to the left-hand side. The chimney-stack suggests a date of construction of *c.* 1870.

612. LAUREL HILL, Monkstown; pre-1841; *demolished.*
A small estate in 1852 of Ralph Uvedale, the gate lodge to which was in ruins by 1890.
Griffith 1853–63.

613. THE LAURELS, Fermoy; 1892.
A property now known as 'Linden' is approached via a single-storey standard gabled lodge forward of its gatescreen. All in a drab grey rendering, with six-over-six sash windows below a plain frieze and Doric pilasters framing the doorway. Extended by a bay to the rear of the left-hand entrance quadrant wall. Within is the contemporary, and likewise grey, mid-Victorian villa built for William Fagan St Leger (1853–1916), who in 1886 had married and acquired this site; the following year he had 'a new house in progress', which by 1891 was considered by the valuer to be 'built in superior manner' and accompanied by a gate lodge.
BPB (1929).

614. LAURENTINUM, Doneraile (3).
Michael Creagh (1771–1845) succeeded to the old Georgian family house within a demesne descending to the Aubeg River on the death of his father, Arthur Gethin Creagh, in 1833, inheriting two lodged gates, one of which he promptly updated.

Outer gate; pre-1835/*c.* 1835.

Here was a pair of lodges flanking the old entrance screen by the roadside, reputedly circular in plan. Their replacement within and set back from the avenue is a single-storey standard lodge, its three bays framed by basic limestone pilasters contrasting with harled panels containing doorway and square windows below delicate Tudor-style label mouldings. Over is a shallow pyramidal roof rising to a diminutive chimney-stack. Deserted. Good sturdy cast-iron contemporary carriage gates are flanked by concave quadrant walls between four plain cut-stone pillars.

Inner gate; *c.* 1800.
Alongside the remains of the old gatescreen is a derelict, plain, single-storey standard cottage, harled, with a chimney-stack to one shallow gable.
LGI (1904).

615. LAURISTON, Cork [S]; *c.* 1845; *demolished.*
A house and lodge built soon after 1841, valued in 1852 as a property of William Lumley Perrier.
Griffith 1853–63.

616. LAURISTON, Glanmire; *c.* 1845; architect probably C.F. Anderson.

IAA

A lodge and gatescreen almost identical to those at Gurteen Le Poer, Co. Waterford [*q.v.*], by architect Charles Frederick Anderson. This is a superb and imaginative asymmetrical single-storey neo-Classical design, with a bold entablatured parapet which continues to form pediments to leading gables. Two opposing fronts have Doric columns '*ex antis*' framing architraved windows and corbelled sills in rendered walls, while from the principal front off-centre extends a portico with square Doric pillars *in antis*. Beautifully presented but the whole effect hideously compromised by a modern glazed draught lobby across the entrance. This is approached through an equally impressive gatescreen comprised of a pair of Classical postilion arches doubling as carriage pillars, with entablatures and incised panelled shafts (just as at nearby Lota Park), all framed by shallow concave quadrant walls. Built for Nicholas David Murphy, attorney in the city.
Slater 1846; *IFR*; IAA photograph (S/694/9).

LAVANAGH (see TEMPLEVILLE)

617. LEADINTON, Ballincurrig (3).
Otherwise known as 'Reddington', this once-proud demesne of the Atkins family is now lacking its big house and porters' lodges at the bases of the grand avenues.

618. LEAMCON, Skull; pre-1842; *demolished.*
A property in 1814 and 1837 of R.E. Hull Esq. In 1853 it was occupied by William Hull, whose gatekeeper was Denis Dawley.
Leet 1814; Lewis 1837; Griffith 1853–63.

619. LEAMLARA, Carrigtohill; *c.* 1835; architects possibly Sir Thomas and Kearns Deane; *demolished.*

Pike and Hodges

The delightful old mansion of seventeenth-century origin and its demesne have been swept away, along with the wonderful little porter's lodge opposite the entrance. Garrett Standish Barry (d. 1864) succeeded to the estate on his father's death in 1821 and this was to be his major architectural legacy. Single-storey and raised off a T-plan, from the main gabled body of which the living room extended to the road below a hipped roof crazily oversailing but sufficient to cover a charming canted oriel window from which the gatekeeper could view the gatescreen through sumptuous Perpendicular Gothic traceried glazing, exactly as that in the lodges to Killinardrish [*q.v.*], Raleigh [*q.v.*] and Drishane Castle [*q.v.*], and as the Deane brothers introduced to Dromore Castle, Co. Kerry [*q.v.*], and possibly Kilcascan Castle [*q.v.*]. Topping the ridge was a lofty pair of Tudor-style stone chimney-pots, octagonal like the dome-capped stone gate pillars across the road, with their ornate chunky contemporary iron gates.

LGI (1904); Pike and Hodges 1911; Bence-Jones 1988.

620. LEEBANK, Carrigrohane (2).
A seat on the river's edge in 1837 of Thomas Parker, whose lodge was then on an approach from the south. Around 1845 the public road was realigned, thus isolating it from the property, and a replacement lodge was erected by a new avenue created for Noble D. Parker MD further to the east. Both lodges have been demolished, the place by 1890 having been renamed 'The Lodge'.

Lewis 1837; Griffith 1853–63.

621. LEE BANK, Cork [N]; pre-1841; *demolished.*
A property subsequently known as 'Clanloughlin' was the residence in 1837 of Robert Hatton.

Lewis 1837.

LEE CARROW (see MARYVILLE COTTAGE)

622. LEE COTTAGE, Cork [S]; *c.* 1845; *demolished.*
A porter's lodge erected on Gaol Walk after 1841 for Henry Osborne Seward, whose property has been overrun by the University College.

Griffith 1853–63.

LEEMOUNT (see WOODHILL)

623. LEEMOUNT, Ballincollig (2).
A seat of the Fuller-Harnett family, from whom it was acquired in the early nineteenth century by Capt. Thomas Otho Travers (*c.* 1785–1844), when the house designed for him by John Hargrave was approached from two lodged gates.

North entrance; *c.* 1820; *demolished.*
A tiny, nondescript, limewashed gabled cottage with a two-window elevation to the road.

Principal entrance; pre-1841/*c.* 1870; architect not known.

Henry Lindsay Young became the new proprietor about 1869, replacing the previous lodge and gates with this assured access on the city approach, a single-storey standard lodge with lavish Italianate detailing. Rendered smooth and immaculate with pronounced V-jointed toothed quoins and moulded-surround, segmentally arched windows on each side of a hip-roofed entrance breakfront with round-headed doorway, its moulded surround rising from a spring-course. The steeply pitched hipped roof rises to a ridge embellished with conspicuous ironwork cresting broken by the central chimney-stack with plinth and corbelled capping. The triple gateway consists of chamfered ashlar pillars, with corbels to layered pyramidal cappings, on which are hung opulent mid-Victorian iron gates.

Lewis 1837; *Thom's*; *LGI* (1904); *IFR.*

624. LEE MOUNT, Passage West; pre-1841; *demolished.*
A residence in 1850 of John Smithwick.

Griffith 1853–63.

625. LEEVIEW COTTAGE, Cork [N]; pre-1841; *demolished.*
The lodge to a property in 1852 of William Harrington, 'druggist' in the city, had been removed by 1902. A long rectangular structure, its site and that of Bellville next door have been absorbed into a hotel complex.

Slater 1846; Griffith 1853–63.

626. LEHENAGH, Cork [S]; pre-1842; *demolished.*
A seat in 1814 of the Newenham family which by 1837 had passed to Charles Mathew (*c.* 1793–1871), a younger son of the Thomastown, Co. Tipperary [*q.v.*], family.

Leet 1814; Lewis 1837.

627. LEHENAGHMORE, Cork [S]; pre-1842; *demolished.*
T. Curtis Esq. was proprietor here in 1837, his porter's lodge located opposite the gates.

Lewis 1837.

628. LEIGHMONEY, Kinsale; pre-1841; *demolished.*
A residence in 1851 of John C. Kearney.

Griffith 1853–63.

LINDEN (see THE LAURELS)

629. LINDVILLE, Ballintemple (2).
Originally a property of John Lindsay, after whose death in 1828 it was acquired by Thomas C. Osborne, who utilised and expanded it as a private lunatic asylum. Both its gatekeepers' lodges, built before 1841, have been demolished.

Lewis 1837; *LGI* (1904).

630. LIRIAS, Farran (2).
Both pre-1842 lodges have been demolished, that to the north having gone by 1890. An estate in the early nineteenth century of the Ellard family, from whom it was let in 1853 to Benjamin Barter.

Lewis 1837; Griffith 1853–63.

631. LISHEENS, Ballincollig; pre-1841; *demolished.*
A 108-acre holding in 1837 of Richard Donovan, whose lodge by 1939 was a ruin.

Lewis 1837.

632. LISLEAGH, Ballyclogh; *c.* 1845.

A modest though solidly constructed single-storey standard lodge, with a steeply hipped roof topped by a disturbingly puny off-centre brick chimney-stack. Faced in a good coursed limestone rubble taken to punched ashlar quoins, its small-paned windows flank the rectangular fanlit doorway. Derelict. Contemporary is the gatescreen comprised of four cut-stone pillars with moulded plinths, plain friezes and corniced cappings, which contain ogee rubble quadrants and ornate cast-iron gates with fleur-de-lis finials and floral motifs. Built by William Culmore.

Griffith 1853–63; Hajba 2002.

633. LISLEE RECTORY, Courtmacsherry; *c.* 1815.
'The glebe-house was built in 1813 by a gift of £100 and a loan of £750 from the Board of First Fruits', a figure which may not have sufficed to cover the cost of what appears to be a contemporary porter's lodge. It lies a shell, missing its hipped roof, having been of harled rubble, the main front three-bay with a pair of wide window openings and doorway to the left-hand side.

Lewis 1837.

LISNACAIRN (see HIGHLAND COTTAGE)

634. LISNAGAR, Rathcormack (3).
A house much altered since its foundation in 1730 by Col. Redmond Barry. It now appears as an English Tudor manor house, created around 1824 by William Tonson, 2nd Lord Riversdale (1775–1848). Sadly, nothing survives at the various entrances to reflect the style within.

Village gate; pre-1841/*c.* 1870.
Successive OS maps reveal a gate lodge much altered down the years. Single-storey standard roughcast, with a chimney-stack to each gable and a gabled canopy on carved brackets over the front door. Occupied and modernised.

Middle gate; pre-1841; *demolished.*

South gate; pre-1841; *demolished.*
A gatekeeper's lodge opposite its entrance that had been removed before 1890.

The valuation identifies the three gatekeepers in 1853 as Margaret Scannell, Mary Collins and Pat Callaghan.

Pigot 1824; Griffith 1853–63; Bence-Jones 1988.

LISNALEE (see PROSPECT, Ballintemple)

635. LISQUINLAN, Castlemartyr (2).
An old seat of the Uniacke family, represented at the turn of the nineteenth century by Robert Uniacke (1751–1814), after the death of whose son of the same name without issue in 1832 it passed to his granddaughter, Louisa Pettitot, and her husband, James Penrose of Woodhill [*q.v.*], and hence descended to their son, Robert Uniacke-Penrose-Fitzgerald (1800–57).

Main entrance; *c.* 1820.
On the northern approach is this single-storey standard harled cottage with clipped eaves to its hipped roof. Derelict.

Rear entrance; pre-1842; *demolished.*

IFR.

636. LISSA, Doneraile; pre-1841; *demolished.*
An estate with naval connections, having passed in 1801 to Vice-Admiral Henry Evans from the Nash family, into which he had married. Around 1824 the new-built house was acquired from the Norcotts by Captain Charles Corker RN (d. 1877), who changed its name to 'Corker Lodge'. Its porter's lodge lay opposite the entrance.

Lewis 1837; *LGI* (1904); Hajba 2002.

637. LISS ARD, Skibbereen (4).
Henry Winthrop O'Donovan (1812–90) succeeded his brother in 1870 as The O'Donovan and commenced a rebuilding programme on the estate, to be carried on by his son, Morgan William O'Donovan II (1861–1940). Apart from a large new neo-Classical house near its predecessor, the demesne was to be entered via four conspicuous lodged entrances, the later two of which form a pertinent prelude to the mansion.

Tower gate; *c.* 1870.

On the southern approach, by Abisdealy Lough, in a drab grey rendered finish is this striking two-storey castellated gatehouse in Romantic Medieval manner. Quite symmetrical, its three-bay façade punctuated by a variety of segmentally arched openings, the wide carriage archway flanked by blind recesses, the bays defined by staged buttresses. The first-floor porter's accommodation is lit by central bipartite two-over-two sashes and flanking lights, all crowned by crenellated parapets stopped at each corner by little round pepperpot bartizans.

Carrigfadda gate; 1880; architect not known.

An exercise in polychrome brickwork is this commodious 1½-storey gabled lodge on the northern avenue, its fronts dispersed with a series of round-arched openings, windows paired and dressed in alternating cream and orange brick in Flemish Garden wall bond, the three-bay avenue front not quite symmetrical, with a fanlit doorway below a bold double sawtooth string-course defining the first floor. Scalloped slate bands relieve the roof, on the ridge of which the chimney-stack is central. Railway architecture rather at odds with that of the big house.

Skibbereen gate; 1896; architect not known.

Single-storey below an oversailing hipped roof, in an otherwise bold V-jointed channelled rendered finish to its three-bay elevations is a liberal parade of round-headed niches, all framed in smooth-rendered recesses with moulded surrounds terminating in pretty acanthus leaf

carvings and shelves supported on guttaed console brackets. The niche to the avenue façade is flanked by a pair of two-over-two sash windows with moulded surrounds below segmental heads; niches to the road front flanking a double-leafed panelled doorway below a segmental arch with keystone and prominent voussoirs. The gatescreen has six pillars in matching rustication with moulded cappings containing railed dwarf quadrant walls and tripartite gateway.

Castletownsend gate; 1896; architect not known.

Differing from the Skibbereen gate only in boasting loftier gate pillars.

IFR.

638. LISSELAN, Clonakilty; *c.* 1890; architect probably Sir T.N. Deane.

In 1843 William Bence-Jones (1812–82) inherited a modest home and property on a potentially idyllic site on the banks of the Argideen River. A decade later he was transforming the place in landscaping about his new turreted French château home to plans of Lewis Vulliamy. Further furnishing of the demesne with workers' cottages came after the architect's death in 1871, and included a striking gate lodge probably to designs of Sir Thomas Newenham Deane. Remotely located opposite its entrance is this 1½-storey Arts and Crafts cottage on a basic L-plan but innovatively elevated in a roughcast finish with a varied roofscape. Projecting to the road in a canted front, its face tapers at attic level as a gablet in the steep semi-octahedral roof. The other wing stops in a hipped gable, the roof catsliding over the internal angle, via a miniature arrowhead dormer window, to form the entrance porch. From the opposing elevation rises a lofty chimney-stack.

LGI (1904); Bence-Jones 1988.

LISTARKIN (see CASTLE EYRE)

639. LITTLE ISLAND, Glanmire (2).

Referred to as 'Wallingstown' after the townland in 1837, when it was the residence of Phineas Bury, one in a succession of the family of that name to live here. Both its lodges, in place by 1841, have been demolished, and the big house is in ruins.

Lewis 1837; *LGI* (1904).

640. LOCHCARRIG, Ballynacorra; pre-1841; *demolished.*

A seat in 1837 of Henry Garde, who was letting it to William Humphreys by 1853.

Lewis 1837; Griffith 1853–63.

THE LODGE (see LEEBANK)

641. LOHORT CASTLE, Cecilstown (3).

The twelfth-century tower-house of the McCarthys, remarkably still in partial occupation, has been in the possession of the Perceval family down the years. Sited in an octagonal ornamental demesne, it has been subjected to various alterations over time, the major of which, carried out around 1826, in 1835 impressed the Scottish visitor Robert Graham, who remarked on the improvements effected by Charles George Perceval I (1756–1840), 2nd Baron Arden: 'It is delightful to see the state of his ground, farmhouses and cottages ... He does this at immense sacrifice ... He builds, or contributes to build, farm houses, and the cottages are all new, neat and in good order. Many of the farm houses stand in a kind of lawn, with large transplanted single trees, intended in the long run, to give them a parkish-like appearance.' From this period may date the early porters' lodges.

Outer gate; pre-1841; *demolished.*

A lost lodge by the village that presided over the entrance to a long, straight, southbound avenue, which turned westwards at right angles by the secondary lodge.

Intermediate gate; *c.* 1820.

Returning to nature are the sad remains of a single-storey standard Georgian lodge with shallow hipped roof and harled rubble walls, its front elevation relieved by a gabled breakfront.

Inner gate; *c.* 1876; architect not known.

In 1874 Charles George Perceval II (1845–97) succeeded his uncle as 7th earl of Egmont and two years later began further alterations, giving the tower-house roof a romantic outline and creating a grand gatehouse to the forecourt in a sort of medieval manner. To the visitor it presents a large, hood-moulded, two-centred carriage archway integral to a perfectly symmetrical façade, being flanked by two-storey bows with transomed and mullioned windows, the whole bound by a

IAA

mock machicolated and castellated parapet, central to which is a carved plaque containing the Perceval coat of arms. There is much else to admire in a beautifully sculpted frieze of shamrocks on what at first sight would appear to be a pair of lodges but was in fact created as accommodation supplementary to the tower-house. Viewed from within, the rear elevation is relieved by a dramatic pair of lofty crenellated circular spiral-stair turrets. It has lain a shell since 1921, having been torched along with the castle by the IRA. An architect for the works has yet to be identified.

About that time a new northern approach was formed, to which remains an impressive tripartite gateway of four muscular chamfered pillars with heavily sculpted cappings, accompanied by elegant contemporary iron gates. Strangely, there was never a lodge here, as if the money finally ran out.

Heaney 1999; Pike and Hodges 1911; *BPB* (1929); Bence-Jones 1988; IAA photograph (S/858/2).

642. LONGUEVILLE, Mallow (5).
The antique seat of the Longfield family, their graceful Classical Georgian block being reflected in two of its lodged entrances.

Inner gate; *c.* 1815.
Single-storey standard and hip-roofed, but notable for its splendid sophisticated tetrastyle Roman Doric pedimented portico in stark white paint contrasting with the drab grey rendering of the walls, let down further by nasty modern plastic windows which flank a good glazed-panel double-leafed doorway. Occupied. Probably built for Lt.-Col. John Longfield (1767–1842), who had succeeded to the property on his father's death in 1815.

South gate; pre-1841; *demolished.*
A lodge no longer presiding over the entrance from the Mallow–Killarney road, which bridged the parallel canal.

Kilgobban outer gate; pre-1841; *demolished.*

Kilgobban inner gate; *c.* 1845.
A relatively undistinguished single-storey, elongated, gabled roughcast cottage, three-bay to the avenue with a central gabled porch projection, its ridge below the line of the tall main eaves. To the leading gable are carved wooden bargeboards over a single window with a basic label moulding.

Side gate; *c.* 1845.

A new approach created for Richard Longfield (1802–89), graced by another fine neo-Classical gatekeeper's lodge and a complementary triple gateway in a wide ogee railed screen with ashlar pillars, those to the carriage opening crowned by lanterns. Grander in scale than the inner lodge, having lofty oversailing bracketed eaves to a shallow hipped roof, its tetrastyle pedimented portico less correct, with slender Doric columns paired to frame the fanlit double-leafed panelled front door. To each side the tall nine-over-six sash windows are effectively displayed by brick dressings in rubble walls with cut-stone toothed quoins beyond; to the ridge is a hefty ashlar chimney-stack typical of the early Victorian period.

LGI (1904); Bence-Jones 1988.

LORETO CONVENT, Fermoy (see LAUREL HILL)

643. LOTA, Glanmire; pre-1772; *demolished.*
A watercolour from around 1772 painted by William Osborne Hamilton shows the pavilioned Palladian-style mansion built on the north bank of the Lee estuary for Robert Rogers about seven years before to designs of Davis Ducart. In the foreground by the coast road is a single-storey standard gabled lodge forward of its triple gateway, the carriage opening of which is flanked by trabeated postilion archways. By 1857 the scene in an illustration accompanying the sale of this by now incumbered estate had changed little, but the lodge by then was behind a convex quadrant wall. By *c.* 1890 it was shown as square on plan, having increased from a shallow rectangle on the 1841 OS map, all prior to its twentieth-century removal.

Bence-Jones 1988; Crookshank and Glin 2002; Lyons 1993.

644. LOTA BEG, Glanmire; pre-1841/*c.* 1845; architects James and G.R. Pain.

Windele in 1849 records 'until lately, the seat of D. O'Callaghan, Esq., M.P. ... The house is a plain square building without wings. The gateway is a beautiful piece of architecture, and will not fail to catch the attention.' Since attracting the affectionate appellation of 'O'Callaghan's Gate', it is indeed still so positioned as to catch the eye on leaving Cork City for Glanmire. This impressive Classical Triumphal carriage archway, its round-headed opening with moulded archivolts and keystone, is surmounted by an entablature supported on a pair of detached Ionic columns on pedestals, just as the Pain brothers also designed for Doneraile Court [*q.v.*], except here the ashlar work is unrusticated and the central die is the base for a fine canine sculpture. This is said to be the 'dashound' commemorated by its grateful owner, the rich butter merchant Daniel O'Callaghan MP, which saved him from drowning in the estuary nearby. Flanking the grand gateway and separated from it by short railings are secondary pillars containing screen walls, each with an opening for dwarf postilions, the copings with highly ornamental lantern ironwork. Apparently dating from *c.* 1820, when O'Callaghan came by the demesne, he later replaced the old lodge he had acquired with the surviving structure around 25 years later. Single-storey on a square plan below high eaves to the pyramidal roof which rises to a central chimney-stack, its avenue elevation unusually blind, save for the central pedimented entrance porch, the ashlar walls relieved by quoins in contrasting stone. The 1841 OS map indicates its predecessor to have been a large lodge with a circular plan, by then probably already antique and dilapidated, perhaps dating from the time of the Galwey family, who settled here in 1673, building the first house on the site, which subsequently passed around the turn of the nineteenth century to Sir Richard Kellett (1764–1853), who had married a Galwey in 1788.

Windele 1849; *BPB* (1929); *IFR*.

645. LOTA LODGE, Glanmire; pre-1841; *demolished.*

The delightful canopied and bowed Regency villa of the Smith-Barry family of Fota [*q.v.*], its lodge probably having been contemporary.

646. LOTA MORE, Glanmire; pre-1841/pre-1890; *demolished.*

A noble mid-eighteenth-century house early associated with the Rogers family of neighbouring Lota [*q.v.*], subsequently given wings probably by subsequent lessees, the Harrisons, who occasionally sublet the demesne to a succession of occupants before it was acquired around 1856 by Sir William Hackett as an incumbered estate. A lithograph that accompanied that sale reveals the triple entrance gateway and its porter's lodge with a porthole window to the attic on the coast road gable and a smoking chimney-stack to the other. This was latterly replaced by a successor on the other side of the entrance, likewise lost.

Smith 1893; Pigot 1824; Griffith 1853–63; Lyons 1993.

647. LOTA PARK, Glanmire; pre-1841; architect possibly C.F. Anderson; *demolished.*

Lyons

The pleasant 1801 villa built by John Power, which had a succession of owners before being purchased about 1835 by Jeremiah James Murphy (1795–1851), the likely creator of the gatekeeper's lodge and gatescreen. The lithograph view that accompanied the incumbered estate auction of 1857, when it was bought by Col. N. Ludlow Beamish, shows the lodge as a single-storey hip-roofed structure with a luxuriant wooded backdrop. Its gates survive in the form of a pair of elegant Classical miniature trabeated postilion arches with moulded plinths, incised panel shafts and died entablatures, flanking the carriage opening. Its being identical to the entrance to Lauriston suggests the hand of architect Charles Frederick Anderson.

Lewis 1837; *IFR*; Bence-Jones 1988; Lyons 1993.

648. LOTAVILLE, Glanmire (2).
Front entrance; *c.* 1810.

Probably contemporary with the original house are these vestiges of a Georgian Gothic cottage of brick and rubble construction, all that is left of which is an elevation to the road; single-storey and two-bay, of blocked-up pointed-arched hood-moulded openings, a window and doorway.

Rear entrance; *c.* 1825.

A diminutive single-storey standard lodge with openings framed by rendered pilasters and plinth, the windows modern squared casements below a hipped roof that rises almost pyramidally to a tiny chimney-stack. Elementary gate pillars with basic ball finials.

Griffith 1853–63; Lyons 1993.

649. LOUGH EIRC, Glanmire; pre-1841; *demolished.*

Alternatively 'Lough Eric' or latterly 'Lochlair', another property offered for sale in 1857 by William Kissane Rogers as an incumbered estate, initially acquired by Benjamin Wood with a sitting tenant in Jane Morris. The lithograph view accompanying that sale reveals a simple single-storey pyramidal-roofed cottage with a central chimney-stack and door and window to the road, bound by the perimeter wall alongside a single gateway.

Griffith 1853–63; Lyons 1993.

650. LOUGH HYNE COTTAGE, Baltimore; *c.* 1830.

Idyllically situated is the villa in 1837 of D. McCarthy Esq., a late nineteenth-century photograph of which also shows its porter's lodge as a single-storey structure with steeply pitched hipped roof and a central semi-octagonal entrance projection to the avenue front. This has since been raised a storey into a rather ungainly house with nasty stone facings.

Humphreys

Lewis 1837; Lawrence photographs (4915R & 4919R).

651. LOUGHLEA, Buttevant; *c.* 1860.

Set well back from its entrance is a ruinous single-storey gate lodge with a rubble-built chimney-stack to each gable. Probably erected for Robert Deane Freeman, who improved the property in the mid-nineteenth century.

Hajba 2002.

652. LOUGH VIEW, Cork [N]; pre-1841; *demolished.*

A property in 1852 of Joseph Hayes on the Youghal Old Road, once rural, now suburban—both house and lodge gone.

Griffith 1853–63.

653. MACROOM CASTLE, Macroom; *c.* 1825.

While the castle eventually met its final end at the hands of the IRA in 1922, what was a fifteenth-century stronghold of the McCarthys, rehabilitated in the early nineteenth century by Robert Hedges Eyre, is survived by a most extraordinary gatescreen from that latter period. A remarkable example of castellated Romanticism dominates the town square like a giant stage set in a series of circular tiered towers arranged symmetrically, the two tallest flanking the Tudor-arched carriage gateway below a panel of slate hanging, the whole rising to crenellated parapets with mock machicolations in a rubble-faced construction punctuated by a variety of flat- and pointed-arched openings. Extending at one side, a two-storey gatehouse in like material and style monitors the forecourt with its two impressive guardian cannons. A striking piece of streetscape, now a tourist attraction and office.

Pigot 1824; Fraser 1838; Bence-Jones 1988; Lawrence photograph (176 I).

654. MAGLIN, Ballincollig; *c.* 1840.
Forward of its gates is a well-maintained, roughly harled, standard gate lodge, the eaves of its hipped roof high to accommodate a little gabled hall with arrowhead-arched openings; modern windows. The proprietor in 1852 was James Barry, with 95 acres.

Griffith 1853–63.

655. MALLOW CASTLE, Mallow (2).
An old sixteenth-century castle of the Desmond family, acquired in the following century by the Jephsons, whose descendant, Sir Charles Denham Orlando Jephson-Norreys (1799–1888), inherited the estate around 1820, in 1838 being created the 1st (and last) baronet and assuming the additional surname. He set about transforming what Revd D.A. Beaufort described in 1788 as a house 'low and mean' into an early Victorian 'Tudorbethan' mansion with the assistance of the English architect Edward Blore, who may also have advised on upgrading the main gate lodge.

Town gate; pre-1841/*c.* 1845.

The first OS map indicates a porter's lodge with a basic rectangular plan, presenting a short front to the forecourt. This may well form the nucleus of the present gatehouse, a re-formation into this irregular structure, partly single-storey, partly two-storey, partly gabled and partly hip-roofed, all in a pleasant rubble construction with a canopy across both the front door and the rectangular bay window alongside; modern metal windows. The gatescreen is older, having high rubble walls contrasting with Classical ashlar pillars terminating in corniced cappings and outsized ball finials on pedestals.

Country gate; *c.* 1845.
A single-storey standard lodge, its brick-dressed rubble fabric exposed, with a projecting rendered porch, wave and 'fang' bargeboards contrasting with the plain main gables. A lancet doorway is flanked by modern windows; alterations include a single-bay extension to the right-hand side and the application of peculiar plastic discs to gables. Occupied.

Beaufort 1764–1808; O'Flanagan 1975; Bence-Jones 1988; www.parliament.uk.

656. MALLOW CEMETERY, Mallow; *c.* 1865; architect not known.
A very smart gate lodge to St Gobnait's Roman Catholic cemetery, in a good squared random rubble facing taken to courses. Standard 1½-storey with foiled bargeboards to its steeply pitched gables and to the single-storey projecting hallway with its Tudor-arched doorway and little sidelights.

656. Mallow Cemetery, Mallow

Otherwise the wooden mullioned and transomed windows are conspicuous for their tiny squared glazing pattern. The fleur-de-lis-crested ridge is broken by a bulky banded stone chimney-stack. The equally fine triple gateway has chunky cast ironwork with palmette, anthemion and rose motifs framed by quarry-faced stone pillars and concave rubble quadrants.

657. MANCHE, Ballineen; *c.* 1870.
Overlooking the Bandon River is the faintly Italianate house built in 1824 for Daniel Conner, to replace the old home of 'Connerville', to designs of G.R. Pain. The demesne remained lodgeless until Mr Conner was succeeded by his son of the same name (1798–1880) on his death in 1848. Through the undergrowth can be detected the sorry remains of a single-storey porter's lodge with a steeply hipped roof and an irregular three-bay front, a central slit window being flanked by one considerably wider and an ornamental gabled entrance porch to the right-hand side. The latter has continuous bracket carved bargeboards rising from pendants to a central decorative hip-knob, all supported on a pair of chamfered wooden posts. Dominating the ridge is a central chimney-stack in smooth red brick.

Dublin Penny Journal (19 December 1835); *LGI* (1904).

658. THE MANOR, Dunmanway; pre-1842/*c.* 1900.
A villa built in 1819 by the Cox family, the gate lodge by the road's verge probably contemporary with it, though what remains today dates from later, either a replacement or a transformation of the original for John Thomas Rashleigh Lucas (b. 1863), who inherited the place in 1896 on the death of his father Jasper, who had purchased it from the Coxes. It appears as a bland, grey-rendered, three-bay two-storey house with label mouldings, modernised and occupied.

LGI (1904); Pike and Hodges 1911.

659. THE MANOR, Glenville (2).
An old estate of the Coppinger family, originally called 'Mount Pleasant' and later 'Glenville Park', which was purchased around 1780 by Dr Edward Hudson, who built a new house near its predecessor. A century later the property had passed by marriage to Sir Edward Hudson Hudson-Kinahan (1828–92), who, to reflect his elevation as 1st baronet in 1887, commissioned architect Sandham Symes to greatly enlarge the house. Neither gate lodge appears to date from this phase of improvements; both were in any case in an advanced state of dereliction in 2000.

South gate; pre-1841.
An impressive entrance sweep with six cylindrical pillars, its gate lodge across the road but strangely removed from them. On an elevated site, approached up a flight of steps, are the laurel-smothered ruins of a harled single-storey structure with a chimney-stack to each gable.

North gate; pre-1890.
Built after 1841 was this three-bay single-storey cottage, now a shell opposite the gates.

Lately the home of the architectural historian Mark Bence-Jones.

BPB (1929); Bence-Jones 1988.

660. MANSFIELD, Passage West; *c.* 1845; *demolished.*
A gatekeeper's lodge added after 1841 to a property in 1850 of Henry O'Hara.

Griffith 1853–63.

661. MARBLE HILL, Ballintemple; pre-1841; *demolished.*
In 1852 Michael Cagney was gatekeeper to Samuel Keays, salmon merchant in the city. Today house and lodge have given way to housing development.

Griffith 1853–63.

662. MARDYKE WALK, Cork [S]; *c.* 1845; architect not known.
An excellent single-storey, neo-Classical, flat-cum-hipped-roof lodge in smooth rendering on a square plan, with two main three-bay fronts in a series of round-headed openings of spoke-glazed sash windows having moulded surrounds and under-panels set in like-arched recesses. The entrance in a breakback has a pilastered door-case, its panelled double-leafed door continuing the semicircular-arched theme. A photograph

662. Mardyke Walk, Cork [S].

NLI

from the turn of the twentieth century shows it in its heyday standing guard over the gated entrance to the walk, a triple iron gateway with overthrow to the carriage opening, created to control access by vehicular traffic and monitored by the constable, who would emerge from his lodge to open them at dawn and close them at sunset. They were manufactured by ironmonger Thomas Barnes of Hanover Street in the city.

Lawrence photograph (515 C).

663. MARSHTOWN, Ballyduff (2).
Otherwise 'Marston', in 1844 'the residence of R. Gumbleton, Esq., is built in the ornate cottage style, which harmonises well with the surrounding scenery'. This was probably the same Richard Gumbleton (*c.* 1788–1849) of nearby Castle View [*q.v.*], whose old house survives still, having served as a porter's lodge to the grander and ill-fated later residence built for himself by Basil Orpen years later but burnt down in 1921.

North entrance; *c.* 1800.

A long, low, single-storey gabled affair with irregular fenestration of four Georgian Gothic lancet windows (one blind) to the road but on the opposing elevation to the park square-headed openings, including the doorway in a vernacular breakfront. The ridge is broken by a pair of sturdy stone chimney-stacks, while the walls are now rather bland in a modern rendered finish. The 1841 OS map suggests that the road front has lost a breakfront in modernisation.

South entrance; *c.* 1860; *demolished.*
Said to have been in a retro-Gothic style, the lodge doubtless formed part of Orpen's development of the estate.

O'Flanagan 1975; Hajba 2002.

664. MARYBOROUGH, Douglas (2).
A big mid-eighteenth-century mansion of the Newenham family, relatively plain, any architectural novelty having been lavished on its fanciful gate lodge by the main gate.

South entrance; *c.* 1760.

de Breffny and ffolliott

Forward of the lost gatescreen, its standard three-bay façade to the back of the footpath, this extraordinary lodge has survived relatively unscathed despite the efforts of recent 'improvers', having lost its central chimney-stack and wonderful rustic crow-stepped gables and had its front door converted to a window. Single-storey in a harled finish, it displays a variety of eccentric Gothic detailing: the opening with framing surrounds; the ogee-arched doorway crowned by a fleur-de-lis motif; the flanking Y-traceried pointed-arched windows with 'quiffs' ascending to chinoiserie pagoda terminals; and spear-topped Gothic lunette features on the main gables and that of the entrance breakfront.

North entrance; *c.* 1845; *demolished.*
A lodge built at the rear gate by Edward Eyre Newenham.

Griffith 1853–63; Bence-Jones 1988; de Breffney and ffolliott 1975.

665. MARYLAND, Aghada; *c.* 1840.
A tiny, derelict, single-storey lodge on a square plan, with pyramidal roof and central chimney-stack, a two-window-bay elevation to the avenue. A seat in 1837 and 1856 of Joseph Haynes.

Lewis 1837; Slater 1856.

666. MARYSBOROUGH, Glanmire; pre-1841; *demolished.*
The estate until 1843 of the Wallis family, their final representative here being James Wallis, whose lodge had gone by 1890.

Bence-Jones 1988.

667. MARYVILLE COTTAGE, Passage West; *c.* 1825.
A derelict single-storey standard porter's lodge with an oversailing hipped roof, its eaves high to accommodate the semicircular-arched spoked fanlight to the front door in harled walls. A property in the early nineteenth century of the Abbott family which became 'Lee Carrow' later in the century.

668. MARYVILLE, Ballineen; pre-1841; *demolished.*
A lost lodge opposite the gates to a seat of the Hosford family.

669. MARYVILLE, Ballintemple; pre-1841; *demolished.*
The seat in 1837 of John Lindsay.

Lewis 1837.

670. MARYVILLE, Kilworth (2).
A house built *c.* 1830 for Laurence Corban, proprietor of the neighbouring flour mill, which he founded on the Funshion River in 1818. Both lodges, that to the rear opposite the gates, were in place by 1841 and, like the mill, are things of the past.

Bence-Jones 1988; Hajba 2002.

671. MARYVILLE, Youghal; pre-1842; *demolished.*
An estate in 1824 and 1837 of Thomas Taylor, the lodge to which had gone by 1936.

Pigot 1824; Lewis 1837.

672. MAWMORE, Bandon; pre-1841; *demolished.*
The residence in 1837 of Capt. Samuel Beamish-Bernard (*c.* 1783–1853).

Lewis 1837; *LGI* (1904).

673. MAYFIELD, Bandon; *c.* 1870.
Standing well back and opposite the entrance is a simple two-storey, three-bay symmetrical gabled gatehouse, over-modernised in a smooth rendered finish with plastic windows. Of indeterminate age, perhaps dating from the addition of a porch to the house in 1872—if so, carried out for Hewitt Poole (1812–1903), who had inherited the property on the death of his father in 1854.

LGI (1904); ffolliott 1958.

674. MAYFIELD, Cork [N]; pre-1841; *demolished.*
A house and lodge probably built about 1815, the date of the wedding of proprietor James John Cummins (1795–1862) to Lucia Swete of Floraville [*q.v.*], he having been the fourth son of Nicholas Cummins of Tivoli [*q.v.*] and Woodville [*q.v.*].

IFR.

675. MEESHAL, Coachford; pre-1841; *demolished.*
Samuel Lewis in 1837 gives a clue as to the provenance and date of the porter's lodge:

'Myshell of Dr Barter, whose demesne of 200 acres, formerly an improfitable waste, has, since 1826, been reclaimed and brought into a state of high cultivation'. At the gate is a replacement in the gate lodge style.

Lewis 1837.

MENLOE (see WEBB VILLE)

676. MERTON, Cobh; *c.* 1835.

A fine Regency maritime villa, in 1837 home to R. Morrison Esq., whose gate lodge survives as a rather gauche affair, not least because of nasty modern windows in its wide openings. A standard 1½-storey gabled lodge in a smooth rendered finish, the three-bay front gathered below linked label mouldings. The tall eaves display carved joist ends, while the early foiled bargeboards are abbreviated by peculiar later two-storey projections to each gable. Occupied.

Lewis 1837.

677. MIDDLETON PARK, Cobh; *c.* 1867.

A lodge built to give added status to a development of exclusive semi-detached villas created in the 1860s on land belonging to the Rushbrooke family. A lovingly maintained single-storey gabled cottage with triangular-arched chamfered openings with hood mouldings, a pair to one end, its front elevation probably once standard three-bay, with a central doorway now converted to a window in a modernisation which also saw the left-hand opening being disfigured as a flat-arched picture window, in rendered walls. The original mid-Victorian chimney-stack survives atop a synthetic slated roof. John Leonard was gatekeeper in 1901.

678. MIDLETON ENDOWED SCHOOL, Midleton; *c.* 1810.

The college was founded in 1696 by Lady Elizabeth Villiers, afterwards countess of Orkney, and by 1837 was 'a seminary of very high character'; only nine years later, however, Slater's *Directory* reported that 'the establishment has since fallen into decay', before the 1870 edition reassured readers that 'it now appears to be reviving'. Today it

flourishes, as does the little gatekeeper's lodge by the gates, which consist of two lofty ball-finialled ashlar carriage pillars in V-jointed rustication, reflected in the toothed stone quoins of the short single-bay leading front of the lodge alongside. Its bipartite casement window has a later chamfered surround in the roughcast wall. Single-storey, it presents a standard three-bay elevation within, below a very shallow hipped roof. Occupied.

Lewis 1837; Slater 1846; 1870; Killanin and Duignan 1962.

679. MIDLETON DISTILLERY, Midleton; *c.* 1825.

Originally the site for a woollen enterprise and subsequently a military barracks before being sold in 1824 by Lord Midleton to the Murphy brothers, who established the famous distillery here which by 1837 was 'producing 400,000 gallons of whiskey annually, and affording employment to 180 persons'. To lend *gravitas* to the concern they erected a sober entrance archway, the segmental carriage opening surmounted by a

pediment with an '1825' date-stone in its tympanum. In ashlar, it is supported by plain, low postern gateways (one blind). This was complemented by a single-storey hip-roofed porter's lodge, contemporary with it but sometime later extended towards the approach to create a verandahed porch, the irregular three-bay façade within comprised of blocking stone-dressed openings with keystones in whitened contrasting rendering. Currently the information office of what is now a museum and heritage centre.

Lewis 1837; Townsend 1997.

680. MIDLETON LODGE, Midleton; pre-1841; *demolished.*

A property of the Coppinger family but leased in the first half of the nineteenth century to a succession of tenants: Warham Durdin, Marcus Lynch, Revd William Wray Maunsell, bishop of Limerick, and Joseph Barry MD.

Mason 1814–19; Pigot 1824; Lewis 1837; *LGI* (1904).

681. MIDLETON RECTORY, Midleton; pre-1841; *demolished.*

A porter's lodge that may have been contemporary with the glebe house of 1794.

Townsend 1815.

MIDSUMMER LODGE (see TOWERVILLE)

682. MILLBANK, Fermoy; *c.* 1840.

Later to be renamed 'Glenavon', the gatekeeper's lodge was probably added by David Reid (1761–1845) not long before his death. A single-storey hip-roofed structure, with a principal short front containing the doorway below a canopy framed by quoins in rendered walls; two-window bay avenue elevation. Occupied.

Hajba 2002.

683. MILLBRO, Carrigrohane; *c.* 1830.

Here is the pathetic shell of a single-storey standard lodge, minus its hipped roof, still showing the vestiges of a hybrid of the period, with rudimentary Classical pilasters defining the bays which contain simple Tudor-style label mouldings over wide openings, all in a harled finish. The all-cast-iron entrance screen is comprised of a triple gateway with pineapple-topped posts, spear finials and highly decorative carriage gate meeting rail terminal. The seat in 1852 of Martin Hayes.

Griffith 1853–63.

684. MILLBROOK COTTAGE, Mallow; *c.* 1845.

A small, single-storey standard roughcast gate lodge with six-over-three sashes, foiled 'stalagtite'-carved bargeboards and a tiny back return, at the entrance to the mill-owner's house of the adjacent Mallow Flourmills, the proprietors of which in 1846 were William and Kingsmill Brady.

Slater 1846.

685. MILLBROOK, Bandon; *c.* 1845.

A very smart and well-maintained lodge, built for the proprietor, John Hurley, through the proceeds of his adjacent brewery. Single-storey standard in a whitened smooth rendering, its new plastic windows recalling the margined glazing of its predecessors, singly on each side of the hall projection, with its slit lights and hipped roof, and a tripartite window to the park. The main shallow hipped roof rises to a wide central chimney-stack, its moulded panelling reflecting those on the four fine Classical entrance pillars with their plain friezes and multi-moulded cappings.

Slater 1846.

686. MILLEEN, Rosscarbery; pre-1842; *demolished.*
The property in 1837 of Revd William Jennings.

Lewis 1837.

687. MILLFIELD HOUSE AND MILLS, Cork [N]; pre-1841; *demolished.*
The house of the proprietor, corn mills, offices, kiln and gate lodge on five acres, in 1846 of Thomas Dawson.

Slater 1846; Griffith 1853–63.

688. MILLFORT, Mallow; pre-1841; *demolished.*
A house built in the early eighteenth century by George Foott which by 1839, in the time of his great-grandson (d. 1844) of the same name, had gone to ruin. Both it and its gate lodge had been removed by 1890.

LGI (1904); Hajba 2002.

689. MILLSTREET UNION WORKHOUSE, Millstreet; *c.* 1852; architect probably George Wilkinson; *demolished.*
Presumably a lodge contemporary with the main building, inevitably to a design by George Wilkinson, which was open for admissions in 1852.

O'Connor 1995; IAA.

690. MILL VIEW, Kanturk; *c.* 1810.

A seat in 1814 of the O'Callaghan family, which ten years later had been acquired by the Lloyds. The lodge survives as a single-storey hip-roofed structure, two-window-bay to front and back, the former elevation with later glazed canted bay windows taken to the eaves of an oversailing soffit. Partly pebble-dashed and partly limewashed harling, what was once the short show front to the avenue is now horribly disfigured by a hideous flat-roofed hall projection. Derelict.

Leet 1814; Pigot 1824.

691. MILLVIEW HOUSE AND DISTILLERY, Midleton; pre-1841; *demolished.*
All is now swept away from this site where in the early nineteenth century was a thriving distillery of Daniel Donovan by the Owennacurra River but by 1853, 'In consequence, however, of the happy progress of temperance', it had been transformed into flour mills of Margaret O'Donoghue, house and mills being later renamed 'Avoncore'.

Pigot 1824; Slater 1846; Griffith 1853–63.

692. MILTON, Bandon; *c.* 1800.

A late Georgian house, in the mid-nineteenth century a residence of the Swete family. Presumably the single-storey three-bay traditional cottage gate lodge is contemporary—a delight, maintained in limewashed rubble construction with the most basic of skew-tables rising up each gable to a chimney-stack. The 1842 OS map shows the lodge to have been flanked by entrance gates, since departed.

Griffith 1853–63.

693. MILTOWN CASTLE, Charleville; *c.* 1725; architect not known.

A quite unique gate lodge and noble gateway, both from the eighteenth century but probably a generation apart in date, preceding the present modest house of *c.* 1781 to which they trumpet access. The tall, elegant Classical ashlar carriage pillars with scroll-topped gate stops and wide moulded cornices carry majestic eagles clasping ball

finials. Beyond are extensive, shallow, ogee-walled quadrants in an effectively contrasting whitened rendering with crenellated copings, terminating in squat pillars with more ball finials. This gatescreen of around 1725, which gave onto a previous castellated house, was perhaps erected by Thomas Evans to mark his wedding in 1722. His death in 1753 coincided with the marriage of his daughter Mary that year to George Bruce, who may have added this extraordinary lodge on thus coming by the estate. The basic single-storey cottage presents its striking short front to the avenue as an unusual and sophisticated ashlar façade with an arcade of three keystoned, round-headed arches with surrounds, that to the central window moulded, flanked by a pair of brick-lined niches containing busts, one of Oliver Cromwell and the other of King William III—highly provocative and remarkable survivals for 250 years until they recently fell prey to thieves. Above is a lofty blank gable trimmed by skew-tables, rising to a platform for a sculpted lion couchant.

LGI (1904); *BPB* (1929); Bence-Jones 1988; Hajba 2002.

694. MINEHILL, Millstreet (2).
The seat in 1814 of Denis McCarthy was home to John Cooke Wallis a decade later, when he probably added at least one of the gatekeepers' lodges. By 1852 he had forsaken the place, leasing it to the Burton family.

South gate; pre-1841; *demolished.*

North gate; *c.* 1820.
A standard single-storey hip-roofed gate lodge with plastic replacement windows.

Leet 1814; Pigot 1824; Griffith 1853–63.

695. MIRAMAR, Cobh; pre-1897; *demolished.*
Built after 1877, a short-lived lodge to a mid-Victorian house probably built by barrister Francis Woodley (1817–82), which later became home to his widow's second husband, the Cork East Riding surveyor Samuel Alexander Kirkby.

IFR; IAA; O'Donoghue 2007.

696. MISHELLS, Bandon; pre-1841; *demolished.*
An estate in 1814 and 1837 of William Conner that by 1851 had been acquired by Thomas Gash, a descendant of whose here was the magnificently named Masculine Gash.

Leet 1814; Lewis 1837; Griffith 1853–63; *LOI.*

697. MITCHELLSFORT, Watergrasshill (2).

South entrance; pre-1841.
Opposite its gates is the forlorn, ivy-shrouded shell of a single-storey three-bay lodge.

North entrance; pre-1841; *demolished.*
Across the road from the vacant gate lodge site is a majestic pair of cut-stone pillars in V-jointed rustication with Doric pilaster frontispieces, scroll-topped gate stops and exaggerated moulded cappings. Now flanking a public road access, perhaps the

survivors of a quartet at the head of the old principal avenue. There are similar pairs at the western gate to Ballintober [*q.v.*] and at Ballymartle [*q.v.*], probably also mid-eighteenth-century and thus the introduction to an earlier house of the Mitchells, the late Georgian replacement for which itself lies a ruin.

Bence-Jones 1988; *Irish Ancestor* **2** (1985).

698. MITCHELSTOWN CASTLE, Mitchelstown (4).
'... [T]he splendid seat of the Earl of Kingston, is a noble and sumptuous structure of hewn stone, in the castellated style, erected after a design by Mr Pain, of Cork, at an expense of more than £100,000 ... it is in contemplation to erect an entrance lodge, on the model of Blackrock castle, near Cork.' Sadly, this grand plan remained only in contemplation and certainly never materialised, probably owing to lack of funds after 'Big George' King, 3rd Lord Kingston (1771–1839), had completed the huge gaunt Tudor Castellated pile in 1825 to designs of James and George Richard Pain. This had been erected to replace the 'large and magnificent building' finished as recently as 1776 for his father, whom he succeeded in 1799. The Pain brothers' doubtless grand and appropriate herald to the excesses within would nevertheless have conflicted aesthetically with the approach through the elegant Georgian Kingston Square.

Town gate; pre-1841; *demolished.*
What did transpire at the foot of a 'short and pleasant avenue' seems from the first OS map to have been a relatively modest lodge located at what Graham in 1835 stated to be 'the sole public entrance to the park' and which Inglis advised a year earlier gave 'Free admission to Lord Kingston's park, is a great advantage, possessed by all the inhabitants'. This generosity was in evidence in 1844, when the profligate 4th earl as 'the hospitable lord of the castle always receives strangers with a hearty welcome'. The gate lodge was

sited forward of an extensive segmental entrance screen from which survives a solitary pair of cut-limestone octagonal turrets with crenellated cappings. These may well be credited to William Downes Webber, who managed the estate and had married the widow of the 5th Lord Kingston in 1873, writing: 'An early improvement affected by me was the erection of the front gate and piers of the Demesne. The gateway designed by Payne had never been built by Ld. K, so the old and dilapidated piers and gate remained, which I replaced with a design more suitable to the castle.'

White gate; pre-1841.
Far to the west off the Buttevant road is a 1½-storey gabled and much-modernised structure in cement rendering and applied quoins, all probably a recent replacement for an earlier lodge.

Limerick gate; *c.* 1820.
A single-storey hip-roofed affair with tall eaves, barely recognisable as such, with later extensions, including a disastrous flat-roofed addition across its front elevation.

Killaclug gate; *c.* 1875.
On the northern approach is this five-bay single-storey cottage with an asymmetrical façade of brick segmental-arched openings with toothed dressings in rubble stone walls. Hip-roofed to the visitor and latterly extended from the opposing gable. Modern windows. Probably another initiative of William Downes Webber, who undertook several 'desirable improvements' for which he obtained loans of £3,000 from the Board of Works, several labourers' houses being built within and outside the demesne.

Big George's castle failed to survive a century, being burnt down in 1922 by the IRA before subsequently being demolished.

Inglis 1835; Heaney 1999; Lewis 1837; O'Flanagan 1975; *Country Life* (18 April 1963); *IAR* (2002); Power 2000.

699. MITCHELSTOWN RECTORY, Mitchelstown; *c.* 1809.
A single-storey hip-roofed lodge, extended

and developed into a twentieth-century bungalow. Seemingly contemporary with the glebe house erected in 1809 by Revd Dr Austin thanks to a gift of £100 and a loan of £1,000.

Lewis 1837; Pike and Hodges 1911.

700. MOATVILLE, Charleville; pre-1841; *demolished.*
A secondary seat in the early nineteenth century of John Boles Reeves of Belfort [*q.v.*] that by 1837 was on long lease to the Ryan family.

Lewis 1837; Hajba 2002.

701. MODELIGO HOUSE, Ballyduff (2).
Not to be confused with the neighbouring house of the same name, it was built around 1836 by Daniel O'Neill, who probably then complemented it with a porter's lodge.

East entrance; pre-1841.
A standard single-storey hip-roofed structure in sandstone rubble construction. Now ruinous, it may well be a replacement for an O'Neill predecessor for Henry Braddell (1827–1913), who took up residence on expiry of the former's lease in 1848. He considerably extended the house in 1877, perhaps then adding the secondary lodged gate.

West entrance; pre-1890; *demolished.*

Hajba 2002.

702. MOGEELY, Curraglass; pre-1841; *demolished.*
Next to the ruined stronghold of the earls of Desmond is the house built by Charles Henry Walsh, who probably also erected a contemporary gate lodge in the early 1830s.

Lewis 1837; Hajba 2002.

703. MONABEG, Fermoy; pre-1841; *demolished.*
In 1844 'the pretty seat of John Allen' had its lodged gate off Thomas Street.

O'Flanagan 1975.

704. MONARD, Blarney; pre-1841; *demolished.*
A property in 1852 of Joseph Nash.

Griffith 1853–63.

705. MONARD AND COOLOWEN IRONWORKS, Blarney; *c.* 1825.
In 1837 Abraham Beale was the 'proprietor of the Monard ironworks, an extensive manufactory for spades and shovels, to which is attached a dyewood mill'. By 1850 Beale was dead, and it was probably his successors, Robert and John Leslie, who raised an existing standard three-bay lodge by half a storey to accommodate a gabled attic with a chimney-stack to one end. Now roughcast, a string-course defines the early eaves line, while the previous tiny squared window glazing has been lost and a flat-roofed porch added.

Lewis 1837; Griffith 1853–63.

706. MONFIELDSTOWN, Rochestown; pre-1841; *demolished.*
The property in 1837 of Thomas Cuthbert Kearney of the Garrettstown [*q.v.*] family, whose big house and gate lodge have been removed to make way for suburban housing.

Lewis 1837.

707. MONKSTOWN CASTLE, Monkstown (2).
The multi-gabled fortified house built in 1636 by Anastasia Archdekin, both lost lodges to which may date from two centuries later, the estate by the turn of the nineteenth century having been acquired by Bernard Shaw, grandfather of the dramatist George Bernard Shaw. The distant northern lodge was around 1845 purloined as the location for a new lodge and entrance to Parkgarriff [*q.v.*].

Bence-Jones 1988.

708. MONROE, Carrigaline (3).
A seat of N.G. Seymour in 1837, when but one lodge was in place.

Middle gate; pre-1841; *demolished.*
In ruins by 1890, when this entrance had been discontinued in favour of a new approach further east; it was subsequently reinstated but without a lodge.

East gate; *c.* 1845.
An access created after 1841, possibly by Ralph Westropp (1813–96), and latterly closed, to be survived by its porter's lodge. A charming cottage of vernacular appearance—two-storey and single-bay, with irregular fenestration comprised of the front door and lone window over in a rubble finish, a chimney-stack to one of its gables.

West gate; pre-1890; *demolished.*
Opposite its gates, a short-lived gatekeeper's lodge erected after 1841.

The house was subsequently renamed 'Ravenswood'.

Lewis 1837; Griffith 1853–63; *IFR*.

709. MONTPELLIER, Donnybrook; pre-1842; *demolished.*
An estate in 1837 of Revd Morgan O'Donovan (1760–1839), rector of Dundurrow and from 1829 The O'Donovan.

Lewis 1837; *LGI* (1904).

710. MOORE PARK, Kilworth (3).
The family seat of the Moore family, earls of Mountcashell, whose house Brewer in 1825 found 'commodious rather than elegant, in an architectural point of view'. Burnt down in 1908, it was survived by its porters' lodges.

Deer-park entrance; pre-1841; *demolished.*
Located south-east of the house by the River Funshion, opposite its gates and at an oblique angle, was an exceptionally long rectangular building.

Kilworth entrance; *c.* 1835.
A single-storey standard, hip-roofed, mildly Tudor Gothic lodge, with a plain frieze and toothed quoins framing flat-headed windows in Tudor-arched recesses on each side of a flat-roofed hall projection with pointed-arched doorway, all in a crisp modern rendered finish. Occupied and commanding a wide entrance screen of concave-walled quadrants with two postilion openings, at the head of the northern avenue. Presumably

created for Stephen Moore, 3rd earl of Mountcashell (1792–1883), who succeeded his father in 1822.

Downing Bridge entrance; pre-1841; *demolished.*

Brewer 1825; *BPB* (1925).

711. MOUNT ALTO, Cobh (2).
Gate lodges to each end of Glasson's Avenue, off which in 1897 was the sole dwelling, a mid-Victorian Gothic Revival house said to have been built by a Mr Ensor, salvage merchant.

South entrance; pre-1897; *demolished.*
A lodge built after 1841 opposite the access.

North entrance; *c.* 1860.
A standard single-storey hip-roofed cottage, recently rehabilitated, gaining a hip-roofed canopy to its front door but losing a chimney-stack.

712. MOUNT BEAMISH, Ballineen; pre-1841; *demolished.*
A house in 1815 'much improved and enlarged by its present possessor, the Rev. Samuel Beamish' (1753–1834), its lodge perhaps dating from that phase of improvements or built by his son, John Samuel Beamish (*c.* 1776–1858).

Townsend 1815; *LGI* (1904).

713. MOUNT BERNARD, Bandon; pre-1841.
A bland 1½-storey standard gabled structure of indeterminate age, to a property in 1851 of William Smyth Bernard (1792–1863), fourth son of the 1st earl of Bandon of Castle Bernard [*q.v.*].

Griffith 1853–63; *BPB* (1929).

714. MOUNT CONWAY, Douglas; pre-1842; *demolished.*
A property in 1837 of H. Sharpe Esq., presumably leasing from the Conway family.

Lewis 1837.

715. MOUNT CROZIER, Cobh; pre-1841; *demolished.*
An old house of the Crozier family which by the early nineteenth century was on lease to a succession of occupants, in 1824 to the Rt Revd Dr Coppinger.

Pigot 1824.

716. MOUNT DESERT FARM, Cork [N]; pre-1841/*c.* 1880.
The seat in 1837 of T.J. Wise, whose early lodge was replaced by the surviving one, probably by his descendant Edward Wise. It is a single-storey hip-roofed affair in orange brick and of little architectural merit. A property by 1890 renamed 'Hollymount'.

Lewis 1837; *LOI.*

717. MOUNT DESERT, Cork [N] (4).
The demesne since 1703 of the Dunscombe family, who since its purchase extended the old house into an extensive mansion. By 1841 the property boasted three lodged entrances, the principal of which was superseded by the present main gate after the succession of Nicholas Dunscombe (1807–76) in 1835.

North gate; pre-1841; *demolished.*

Inner gate; pre-1841; *demolished.*
At a crossing of busy estate roads was a lodge that served a number of gates.

Early gate; pre-1841; *demolished.*
The old main entrance, which was superseded when the approach was routed further west.

Principal gate; *c.* 1865.

de Breffny and ffolliott

An exuberant Classical tripartite gateway of V-jointed rusticated ashlar pillars surmounted by pineapple and vase finials, the postern gate openings and carriage gates crowned by elaborate scrolled wrought ironwork containing the Dunscombe arms and rising to pike-head finials, the gates equally decorative but the whole recently drastically truncated. Across the road, backing onto the River Lee, is Nicholas Dunscombe's replacement main lodge—a highly articulate single-storey hip-roofed composition of three-bay standard appearance with apparently later wings, like the house, but the whole in fact of an age. The front door, in a gabled breakfront with frieze and pilastered Doric sides, has been reduced to a window in modern alteration and extension. All in a smooth rendered finish, it is effectively dominated by a central triple-flue chimney-stack.

LGI (1904); Pike and Hodges 1911; Bence-Jones 1988; de Breffny and ffolliott 1975; IAA photo (S/701/11).

718. MOUNT DONEGAN, Cork [N]; *c.* 1845; architect not known.
A very fine little neo-Classical porter's lodge, clearly by the same hand as those to Clifton [*q.v.*] and Hyde Park House [*q.v.*] in the vicinity. A single-storey gabled structure on a cruciform plan with pilasters as quoins on a smooth rendered finish, but the whole disastrously impaired by a nasty prefabricated flat-roofed extension across its front. There survives a good pair of complementary carriage pillars with recessed moulded panels of keystoned round arches, differing only from those at Hyde Park House in having flat, rather than pedimented, cappings. All for Daniel Donegan, wax and tallow chandler, after whose passing the place was occupied by Nicholas Murphy, who renamed it 'Carrigmore'.

Griffith 1853–63.

719. MOUNT EMLA, Douglas; pre-1842; *demolished.*
A holding in 1837 of John Barnes.

Lewis 1837.

720. MOUNTFORD LODGE, Fermoy; pre-1841.
Only two walls stand of a rubble structure, a short front of which addressed the avenue to a property in 1837 of brothers Capt. Peter Collis (1793–1871) and Revd George Gun Collis.

Lewis 1837; *LGI* (1904).

MOUNT GLISSAN (see BELLEVUE, Fermoy)

MOUNT GRANGE (see FACTORYVILLE)

721. MOUNT LEADER, Millstreet (2).
Here are the vestiges of a once-fine demesne of the Leader family, their big house an overgrown ruin, with the remnants of an ornamental lake and a tree- and rhododendron-lined avenue from a now-lost main lodged gateway.

Town entrance; pre-1842; *demolished.*

Country entrance; pre-1842/*c.* 1870.
The first OS map indicates a standard lodge, rectangular on plan, its central hall projecting to the avenue. What survives bears no relation to this imprint, being an irregular planned replacement of before 1890, presumably built for Capt. Henry Eustace Leader (1833–76), who succeeded to the estate on the death of his father and his marriage in 1868. In a crisp, white, modern smooth-rendered finish is this single-storey structure with oversailing hipped roof,

notable for a quirky five-sided room extending from the left-hand side next to a gableted doorway and its delicate Y-traceried Gothic sash windows below arrowhead arches. It stands guard over a dilapidated gatescreen of wide cut-stone concave quadrants on the southern approach.

IFR; Hajba 2002.

722. MOUNT MARY, Ballinhassig; pre-1842; *demolished.*
Remote from its gateway was this lodge to a property in 1837 of William Fortune, which by 1850 had been acquired by Daniel Lombard.

Lewis 1837; Griffith 1853–63.

723. MOUNT MASSY, Macroom; *c.* 1800.

Although the 'handsome seat' of the Hutchinson Massy family is in ruins, it is survived by its substantial Georgian Gothic gatekeeper's lodge. Beyond a plain gatescreen is the single-storey standard structure in a pleasant rubble finish, displaying asymmetrical fenestration of pointed-arched openings below an oversailing pyramidal roof rising to a central chimney-stack. In 1852 the property was leased to Revd Somers Payne, whose gatekeeper was Jeremiah Leary.

Griffith 1853–63.

724. MOUNTPATRICK COTTAGE, Glanmire; *c.* 1825; architect possibly G.R. Pain.

Raised on a sturdy platform is a diminutive and attractive hip-roofed single-storey lodge in a smooth rendering, its bays, two-windowed to the avenue and a doorway to one end, defined by pilasters with moulded recesses, all openings with hood-moulded pointed Gothic heads. A property occasionally known as 'Tower Hill' through the presence in the grounds of Mathew's Tower, erected in honour of Father Theobald Mathew by William O'Connell to a design by George Richard Pain, who may just have been responsible for the porter's lodge. In a wall by the entrance is a stone plaque with the inscription 'Enterance (*sic*) to Mount Patrick'.

Bence-Jones 1988.

725. MOUNT PLEASANT, Bandon; pre-1841; *demolished.*
In 1815 the seat 'of Henry Baldwin ... The house which seems rather more than necessarily large, has as yet but a naked appearance from want of timber.' Whilst a Henry Baldwin was still in residence in 1851, doubtless having remedied the tree deficiency, his porter's lodge is no more, having been replaced by a modern house.

Townsend 1815; Griffith 1853–63.

726. MOUNT PROSPECT, Bandon; pre-1841; *demolished.*
The big house in 1824 was home to Mrs Beamish and thirteen years later to Mrs Bradshaw. A structure opposite its gates had gone by 1890.

Pigot 1824; Lewis 1837.

727. MOUNT PROSPECT, Curraglass; pre-1841; *demolished.*
A home between 1746 and 1879 to three generations of George Bowles.

LGI (1904).

728. MOUNT PROSPECT, Passage West; pre-1890; *demolished.*
A post-1841 mid-Victorian development, which included a porter's lodge, for William Browne, of which only his villa survives.

Griffith 1853–63.

729. MOUNT RIVERS, Carrigaline; pre-1842; *demolished.*
An estate in 1837 of Michael Roberts.

Lewis 1837.

730. MOUNT RIVERS, Fermoy; pre-1841; *demolished.*
The seat in the early nineteenth century of Matthias Hedley and his son Mathias Christopher Hedley, whose gatekeeper's lodge was removed around 1980.

Leet 1814; Slater 1846; Hajba 2002.

731. MOUNT RUBY, Mallow; pre-1841; *demolished.*
Initially the ancestral seat of Thomas Ruby, it passed by marriage to the Flynn family, who leased it to a succession of occupants, to some of whom it became 'Killetra' after its townland. The gate lodge had gone by 1890.

Hajba 2002.

732. MUCKRIDGE, Youghal; pre-1842; *demolished.*
The seat in 1814 and 1824 of Richard Fitzgerald and in 1837 of William Fitzgerald, whose 'tasteful and hospitable mansion' was reached via a long avenue and between a pair of lodges at its head, both gone by 1890.

Leet 1814; Pigot 1824.

733. MUCKRUSS, Clonakilty; *c.* 1840.
In 1837 this was home to Mrs Henry Beamish, whose husband was of the Kilmalode [*q.v.*] branch of that family. Outside the entrance and rather remote from it is a singular gate lodge in the form of a seven-bay structure in harled rubble, its symmetrical front of a central round-headed fanlit doorway flanked by six narrow windows. The roof with high oversailing eaves accommodates loft rooms between two stone chimney-stacks. Derelict and succumbing to undergrowth.

Lewis 1837; *LGI* (1904).

734. MUNSTER MODEL FARM, Cork [S]; *c.* 1855; architect probably Frederick Darley.

An agricultural school in the form of a formal Elizabethan mansion, a standard design to be found throughout the country to plans of Frederick Darley for the Board of Works, here dating from 1853. Its fine gate lodge lacks the curvilinear gables of the main block but rather has Tudor Revival kneelered skew-table gables, probably also by Darley but in more relaxed mode, it being on an irregular L-plan. Single-storey, its pleasant uncoursed cut-stone facings punctuated by transomed and mullioned single, bipartite and tripartite casements, the main gables relieved by mock arrowloops, while that of the hall, which advances from the internal angle, displays a blank shield. To the roof is a chimney-stack with a row of cut-stone triple octagonal flues. Modern gatescreen.

Williams 1994; IAA.

735. MURRAGH RECTORY, Murragh; *c.* 1810.
In 1815 Townsend recorded 'a new and very elegant glebe-house, latterly erected by the Rev. Ambrose Hickey'. It was in fact built five years earlier, and Lewis in 1837 found it to be 'handsome and commodious'. Its porter's lodge is probably contemporary and an unusually commodious gatehouse: two-storey with a chimney-stack to each gable; two-bay upper storey over a not-quite-symmetrical three-bay ground floor with little central single-storey gabled hall, all in whitened rendering. Nice rustic rubble gateway.

Townsend 1815; Lewis 1837.

736. MYLANE HALL, Ovens; pre-1841; *demolished.*
A property in 1852 of Jeremiah Horgan, whose gate lodge had been removed by 1890.

Griffith 1853–63.

737. MYROSS WOOD, Leap (2).
The porters' lodges built before 1842 have been demolished; both were probably added by John Sealy Townsend (d. 1852).

LGI (1904).

738. MYRTLE GROVE, Youghal; *c.* 1700.

The remarkable and unique survival that was Sir Walter Raleigh's Tudor manor house of 1586, subsequently acquired by Richard Boyle, 1st earl of Cork, and then inhabited by a variety of owners and tenants down the centuries but little altered. Perhaps not quite as antique is the gatehouse integrated with the two-storey outbuilding, its clipped gable end, alongside impenetrable wooden entrance doors and basic square pillars, displaying a grand first-floor glazed canted oriel window with multi-paned casements below a lead ogee roof, strategically placed to overlook the forecourt. Whereas crudely roughcast, the side elevations reveal their rubble construction and gablets breaking the eaves lines.

Lewis 1837; Bence-Jones 1988.

739. MYRTLE HILL, Cork [N]; (2).

Lovers' Walk gate; *c.* 1830.
In nice exposed rubble stone is this otherwise unremarkable single-storey lodge with an oversailing hipped roof, lying abandoned.

Lower Glanmire Road gate; *c.* 1860; *demolished.*
A lodge appended to the end of Myrtlehill Terrace at the foot of a tortuous route to the big house above. There are the remains of a straight, railed mid-Victorian gatescreen with recessed panel pillars.

A property in 1852 of Revd Rowland Gray, and by 1863 of James Harding.

Griffith 1853–63; *Thom's*.

740. MYRTLEVILLE, Crosshaven; *c.* 1810.
Outside its gates, a two-window bay elevation monitoring the forecourt, is a much-modernised single-storey lodge, square on plan, with its pyramidal roof crowned by a central chimney-stack. Occupied. A property in 1837 of a Dr Shea.

Lewis 1837.

741. MYRTLEVILLE, Douglas; pre-1841; *demolished.*
A seat in the early nineteenth century of the Cummins family, subsequently renamed 'Claremont'.

IFR; Lyons 1993.

742. NADRID, Coachford; pre-1842; *demolished.*
Here are the remnants of a rather grand entrance, its porter's lodge survived by a carriage opening flanked by pairs of tall rubble-built pillars, each containing a screen wall with round-arched postilion gateway. Erected either by Joseph Woodley (*c.* 1771–*c.* 1809), his successor to the estate, James Edward Galwey (1781–1827), his son James Galwey (1808–47) or even Henry Davies O'Callaghan (1790–1858), who was in residence by 1837.

LGI (1958); *IFR.*

NASHVILLE (see ROSNALEE)

NAZARETH (see DROMORE)

743. NETTLEVILLE, Coachford; *c.* 1820.
A single-storey standard gatekeeper's lodge with oversailing hipped roof and original six-over-six sash windows on each side of a later projecting gabled hall with round-arched doorway and modern crazy-paved facings. Occupied. Doubtless built for Capt. Robert Nettles (d. 1831), whose mansion, in contrast, lies a pitiful shell.

LGI (1904).

744. NEWBERRY, Mallow (2).
A venerable old seat of the Newman family, the main entrance to which was from the north, an avenue that led to St Senach's Church.

Old gate; pre-1841; *demolished.*
Probably superseded in favour of the present approach around 1845, when the gate pillars were probably those re-erected at the new gate.

New gate; *c.* 1845.
Almost completely obscured by saplings are the remains of a single-storey standard hip-roofed harled lodge of Georgian Gothic appearance with a lovely pointed-arched doorway. Opposite is the more obvious and familiar gatescreen, earlier than the lodge and conspicuous for its perverse arrangement of pillars. To the extremes a lofty and noble Classical ashlar pair with exaggerated moulded cappings and Newman eagles aloft and scroll-topped gate stops, which suggests that they were removed here from the earlier entrance. This sophistication gives way to basic rustic rubble screen walls topped by lower ashlar pillars, likewise having gate

stops and moulded cappings but crowned by delightful and hospitable pineapple finials. While lodge and inner gatescreen probably date from the time here of Adam Newman, the grand pillars may be the creation of his grandfather Richard in the early eighteenth century. Their house is no more.

LGI (1904); ffolliott 1970.

745. NEWBOROUGH, Ballinclashet; *c.* 1835; architect probably Henry Hill.

An exquisite example of a Picturesque English Country cottage, popularised through the pioneering work of the English architects John Nash and P.F. Robinson, here probably interpreted by the Cork practitioner Henry Hill, who is recorded as designing a house near Kinsale for Achilles Daunt. George Achilles Daunt dwelt here in 1837 in his 'retired and pleasant residence'. The 1½-storey lodge, gabled on an irregular plan, is faced in pleasant rubble stone and is dominated by a massive external chimney-breast terminating in a pair of Tudor Revival octagonal brick stacks. From the road projects a single-storey rectangular bay window with some latticed glazing below its own hipped roof rising to a slit attic window. The avenue elevation has a catslide breakfront, from which projects further a gabled hall with Tudor-arched doorway under the sole surviving foiled bargeboards. A partly creeper-clad delight, proudly maintained. Peculiar hexagonal-patterned replacement roof finish.

Lewis 1837; IAA.

746. NEW COURT, Skibbereen; pre-1842; *demolished.*
In 1815 Revd Townsend considered that, in the vicinity, 'of the new houses, the most deserving of mention seem to be Newcourt of Becher Fleming', who was still in residence in 1838.

Townsend 1815; Fraser 1838; ffolliott 1958.

747. NEWENHAM TERRACE, Cork [S]; *c.* 1860; *demolished.*
Named after the developer and landlord Revd Edward Henry Newenham of Coolmore [*q.v.*], a row of eight houses dating from the mid-nineteenth century, which originally had the prestige afforded by its own lodged entrance.

748. NEWMARKET, Newmarket (3).
Now home to St Joseph's Convent, this was 'the seat of the old and respectable family of Aldworth, who have a large and handsome mansion house', built in the early eighteenth century on land granted in 1621 to Sir Richard Aldworth. Of the three gate lodges in evidence in 1842 both to the rear approaches have been demolished, while to the front avenue there are tantalising hints of the old lodge in openings with pointed and ogee arches incorporated into the present structure. The ogival theme, suggestive of the mid-eighteenth century, is repeated in the entrance quadrants, perhaps created in the time here of Richard Aldworth (1694–1776) at the foot of 'an avenue of ash ... said to have been planted in the reign of Queen Elizabeth'.

O'Flanagan 1975; *PGI*; *LGI* (1904); Pike and Hodges 1911.

749. NEWTOWN, Bantry; pre-1842.
Of the gate lodge, a chimney-stack protrudes through the ivy that is choking a single-storey ruin with the suggestion of a hipped roof. A property in 1824 and 1837 of Michael Murphy, whose family had leased it from the earls of Kenmare since 1754, the arrangement between the families ending acrimoniously in 1844.

Pigot 1824; Lewis 1837; Everett 2001.

750. NEWTOWN, Mallow; pre-1841; *demolished.*
An estate in the early nineteenth century of Edward Gardener, the gate lodge to which was at the head of a long straight avenue from the north.

Hajba 2002.

751. NORTHESK, Glanmire; *c.* 1835.

A single-storey standard hip-roofed gate lodge with oversailing eaves, displaying a typical stylistic blend of its time, the bipartite casement windows below Tudor label mouldings in bays defined by deeply incised rustic Classical pilasters. The whole in limewashed harled walls having a frieze decorated by a pattern of perforations and sawtooth band, a feature repeated in the pillars to the gate sweep, appropriately in the form of circular turrets in limewashed finish, heralding the big house within. It is an early Georgian house romanticised with crenellations and round tower additions by James Carnegie, which he reflected in his lodge and gatescreen.

Lewis 1837; Bence-Jones 1988.

752. NORTH PRESENTATION CONVENT, Cork [N]; *c.* 1810.

'The North Presentation convent was founded in Chapel-street in 1799, and removed to the present house in Clarence-street in 1808 ... the average attendance of children at the school is 600, one third of whom are clothed annually by a subscription of the citizens: the buildings with chapel form a handsome pile.' The children thus described in 1837 may well have seen the lodge as single-storey off what is now Gerald Griffin Street. Today it appears as an unpretentious two-storey gabled gatehouse, its two-window-bay elevation to the footpath, squared Georgian-style lights to the ground floor but two-over-two Victorian sashes over, below a bracketed eaves frieze. Alongside are tall angled walls, one containing a pedestrian doorway, flanking a carriage archway.

Lewis 1837.

753. NORWOOD, Cobh; *c.* 1861; architect perhaps Alexander Deane.

A fine mid-Victorian villa, complete with verandah and belvedere tower on an irregular plan, its Italianate style aptly announced at the gate by a striking gate lodge, likewise informal in layout and matching in style. In a smooth rendering, its 1½-storey gable addresses the avenue, a pair of one-over-one sash attic windows with round heads united by a spring-course, below which is a rectangular bay containing a Palladian window with its own hipped roof. The road elevation is blind but for a gablet window, while to the park extends a single-storey wing, again with a pair of semicircular-arched windows, here with two-over-two sashes, alongside which the doorway projects below a catslide roof. Concave railed quadrants frame matching iron gates on suitably Italianate stone pillars with recessed

panels, carved cappings and rusticated plinths. By 1876 the property had been bequeathed by Joseph and Caroline O'Meara to the Sisters of Mercy as an orphanage, but it was originally built as a private residence in about 1858 by the builder and developer Alexander Deane, its lodge probably dating from a few years later, when the valuation increased by £5. The first proprietor was Nicholas Murphy (*c.* 1823–1900) of the distilling family.

IFR.

NORWOOD (see ALTAVILLA, Douglas)

754. OAKGROVE, Coachford; pre-1841.

The estate in 1837 of John Bowen (1798–1870), which he inherited on the death of his father in 1824. His gate lodge has been replaced or drastically worked over, the big house likewise rebuilt after a fire *c.* 1820.

Lewis 1837; *LGI* (1904); Bence-Jones 1988.

755. OAKLANDS, Bandon; 1866.

A plain 1½-storey gate lodge, its steeply pitched roof over a three-window-bay principal front. Occupied. A property developed on a virgin site by Richard Wheeler Dogherty.

756. OAK MOUNT, Ballingurteen; pre-1841; *demolished.*

James Gillman is recorded as resident here in 1814 and 1853; the porter's lodge had been removed by 1900.

Leet 1814; Griffith 1853–63.

757. OATLANDS, Ballinclashet; *c.* 1820.

Doubtless contemporary with the building of the house, in 1837 described as 'of Capt. Knolles, a handsome modern mansion', the lodge is a basic single-storey hip-roofed affair with clipped eaves and harled rubble walls, the single-bay front to the avenue, doorway and a two-window-bay elevation to the rear. This proprietor was in fact Thomas Walton Knowles.

Lewis 1837.

758. O'DONOVAN'S COVE, Durrus; pre-1841; *demolished.*

The evocatively named property in 1824 of Richard O'Donovan, by 1837 succeeded here by Timothy O'Donovan.

Pigot 1824; Lewis 1837.

OLANS (see AGHAVRIN)

759. OLD COURT, Doneraile (2).

An estate from early times of the Watkins family, from whom it was leased around the turn of the nineteenth century to Jonas Stawell, who built a new house, but the place remained lodgeless until after it was acquired in 1853 as an incumbered estate by James Morrogh (1810–84), of the Glanmire House [*q.v.*] family, who remedied that with the erection of two contrasting gatekeepers' lodges.

Principal gate; *c.* 1855.

Sadly neglected and overgrown but still

759. Old Court, Doneraile.

retaining some of its rich detailing is a single-storey standard gabled cottage, its stuccoed walls embellished with toothed stone quoins and dressings to the doorway, which also exhibits a little applied pediment over. Below the high eaves with their exposed rafter toes are lattice-glazed bipartite casement windows with moulded sills and surrounds and unusually crowned by little entablatures with rosette brackets above that again. Next to it is a splendid tripartite Classical gateway of four grand V-jointed rusticated stone pillars on generous plinths, with finely chiselled moulded cappings supporting rather less sophisticated pedestal-less ball finials.

Secondary gate; *c.* 1855.

On an elevated site is this rather more vernacular lodge, having only dereliction in common with its near neighbour. Single-storey standard with small openings in harled walls, lacking both its hipped-gable roof and its avenue.

Leet 1814; *LGI* (1904); Lyons 1993; Hajba 2002.

760. OLD COURT, Rochestown (2).

A seat formerly of the Norris family, subsequently occupied by the Goolds, in 1815 of Sir Francis Goold, of which it was then said that it 'owes all its beauty to the present possessor, who built a handsome house, and adorned the grounds'. It was also he who presumably added the early gate lodge before his death in 1818.

Main entrance; *c.* 1815.

On the northern approach is what is shown on the early OS maps to have been a singular lodge with an elongated hexagonal plan, doubtless with an equivalent hexahedral roof, since squared off to the rear and thus presenting an 'arrowhead' front to the avenue. Single-storey and much 'improved' in a grey rendered finish with modern windows. The big squat ashlar secondary pillars with their boldly moulded cappings and raised and fielded panels are identical to those at Glyntown [*q.v.*]. These flank a triple gateway of elaborate ironwork, the main carriage posts decorated with miniature urns supporting scrolled lantern frames having pendant anthemion motifs. All regrettably run-down, in a sylvan setting probably reminiscent of the next phase in the estate's history.

On the death of Sir Francis Goold the place was inherited by his nephew, the 2nd baronet, Sir George Goold (1778–1870), of whom it was said on its sale as an incumbered estate in 1852: 'During the two-and-thirty years that Sir George Goold has been in possession of this property, he has been nearly twenty-six an absentee! ... of course every acre of Oldtown shows neglect.' The purchaser and new owner was Alexander Glasgow, who before his passing in 1874 effected a renaissance of the estate, erecting a new porter's lodge at the western gate.

Monfieldstown entrance; *c.* 1855.

The ruin of a harled, rubble-built, single-storey rectangular lodge, its main front having had a left-hand breakfront, by what is now a public woodland walk.

Townsend 1815; *LG* (1863); *BPB* (1929); Lyons 1993.

761. OLD DROMORE, Ballynamona; 1860.

An old landed estate with a long and confused history of building on the site, initially from the days of the Newman family and then the Deanes, earls of Muskerry. What is clear is that its entrances remained lodgeless until after the arrival of the Williamson family, who purchased it in 1803, the Revd Benjamin Williamson creating a long new avenue to the south and placing a lodge opposite its entrance in 1860. And a relatively undistinguished affair it is, with basic wide label mouldings to the openings of a 1½-storey gabled roughcast structure with a later gabled porch. Modernised and occupied.

Bence-Jones 1988; Hajba 2002.

762. OLD GRANGE, Douglas; pre-1890; *demolished.*

A property in 1852 of Hatton A. Condron, its lodge built after 1842.

Griffith 1853–63.

763. OLDTOWN, Coachford; pre-1842; *demolished.*

The residence in 1837 of Simon Crook(e), the gate lodge to which was removed early in the twentieth century.

Lewis 1837.

764. OLDTOWN, Shanballymore; pre-1841; *demolished.*

A house associated in the eighteenth century with the Creagh family was replaced around 1816 by Henry Evans RN, who by the time of his death in 1842 had risen to the rank of vice-admiral. The gate lodge, which may have been contemporary with the house, had gone by 1935.

LGI (1904); Hajba 2002.

765. OLD WOOD, Douglas; pre-1841; *demolished.*

The residence in 1852 of Revd Robert Holboyd, previously curate of Dunderrow parish.

Lewis 1837; Griffith 1853–63.

766. ORIEL, Ballincollig (3).

The superintendent's house of the Ballincollig Ordnance [*q.v.*], which Lewis puts into context: 'This place is chiefly distinguished as a military depôt, and for its extensive gunpowder mills, formerly carried out under the superintendence of

Government, but, after having been for some years discontinued, recently purchased by the present proprietors, and now in full operation ... In appropriate situations, and adjoining these establishments, are the residences of the different persons superintending the works'—in 1837 the new owner being Thomas Tobin, who was still in possession fifteen years later. In 1841 the house was accessed via a looped driveway, each of its gateways guarded by a gate lodge. By about 1850 both had been demolished in favour of the surviving replacement at the eastern entrance, marked by a contemporary gatescreen of railed concave quadrants and four stone pillars of V-jointed rustication and four-faced pedimented cappings—Classical, in contrast to the generously proportioned English Picturesque 1½-storey lodge sited across the entrance from its predecessor. Much modernised for the worse, with a bland, smooth-rendered finish and the loss of its chimney-stack and some of its pretty Tudor Revival lattice-glazed casements, it nevertheless retains ornate perforated trefoil and wave bargeboards to its road gable and that of an avenue gablet which breaks the eaves of a very steeply pitched roof, with its bands of decorative serrated tiles.

Lewis 1837; Slater 1846.

767. OVERTON, Bandon; pre-1842; *demolished.*

Beside Overton Cotton mill, in 1837 the house was the residence of a Colonel Clerke.

Lewis 1837.

768. OYSTERHAVEN, Kinsale; pre-1841; *demolished.*

According to Revd Horatio Townsend, in 1815 this was a seat of the Hodder family but by 1851 was occupied by Charles Daly.

Townsend 1815; Griffith 1853–63.

769. PALLASTOWN, Belgooly; *c.* 1830; architect not known.

Otherwise 'Palacetown', this was an estate of a branch of the Townsend family; although it was mainly their spinster or widowed womenfolk who were in residence, Samuel Philip Townsend (*c.* 1777–1864) added a sweet little porter's lodge. Single-storey

769. Pallastown, Belgooly

standard, essentially square on plan, its shallow hipped roof with oversailing eaves and bold carved soffit brackets rising to a tall, perky chimney-stack, banded with conspicuous base and capping. The main avenue front is notable for its round-headed openings, the windows in the form of Venetian arches, the doorway panelled, all picked out by dark surrounds in whitewashed rendered walls. To the park is a hipped-roofed extension in like manner. Entrance gate swept away.

Lewis 1837; *IFR*.

770. PARK FARM, Sallybrook; pre-1890; *demolished.*
A 179-acre farm in the mid-nineteenth century of Henry Morrogh, its lodge built after the 1852 valuation.

Griffith 1853–63.

771. PARK, Doneraile; *c.* 1810.
A single-storey standard gabled gate lodge with two-over-two sash windows in harled walls. Derelict. A property previously known as 'Ballingrane', its lodge probably built after passing from the Hennessy family to Arthur Norcott.

Wilson 1803; Pigot 1824; Hajba 2002.

772. PARK, Killeagh; *c.* 1860.
A most odd little porter's lodge, being single-storey in the form of a double pile to the avenue, each of its clipped gables being unequal and its fenestration of a pair of bipartite one-over-one sash windows flanking the front door being likewise asymmetrical, reflecting its evolution. All in a whitewashed rendered finish, the taller ridge displaying a less-than-elegant crenellated earthenware cresting. Occupied, modernised and extended, the right-hand gable being that originally built for Charles William Talbot-Ponsonby (1843–1927), a naval lieutenant who came to live here in the 1860s after his family had leased the property to the Hudsons for many years previously, perhaps on the occasion of his wedding in 1868. The following year he commissioned H. and A. Hill, architects of Cork, to alter and enlarge the old house.

LGI (1904); *IB* (1 December 1869).

773. PARK, Kilworth; pre-1841; *demolished.*
The birthplace of David Richard Pigot (1797–1873), lord chief baron of Ireland, in whose long absence on official duties it was leased to the family of his wife, the Payes.

Hajba 2002.

774. PARKGARRIFF, Monkstown; *c.* 1845.

A property in 1850 of David Cagney, the probable builder of this genteel little single-storey lodge in a smooth rendered finish on a cruciform plan. Rendered Classical by dainty Doric corner pilasters that rise off a plinth to a plain frieze to the eaves, which continue about the shallow gables, combining with the bargeboards of which to resemble pediments. Modern windows mar the effect. This was built on a site previously occupied by the northern lodge gate to Monkstown Castle [*q.v.*] and a new approach created therefrom.

Griffith 1853–63.

775. PARK VIEW, Bandon (2).
By the north bank of the Bandon River, this small estate on the outskirts of the town was sustained in the nineteenth century by proceeds from alcoholic drink, initially from the brewery of Henry Cornwall, from whose time the early gate lodge dates, and subsequently from around 1885 from the Bandon Distillery of Allman and Co.; the later lodge was built for the director of that concern, James Clugston Allman II (1822–1911).

North gate; *c.* 1830.
Now derelict is this single-storey hip-roofed structure with bipartite sash windows, latterly extended to a double pile.

South gate; *c.* 1890; architects possibly W.H. Hill and Sons.

A sumptuous 1½-cum-single-storey concoction raised in Flemish bond orange brickwork off an irregular plan, a combination of the Tudor Revival English Cottage Picturesque style with its rich and intricately pierced bargeboards and hip-knobs, and a touch of the Queen Anne Revival Arts and Crafts manner in its rectangular attic oriel window with mullions and transoms and Jacobean strapwork over, incorporating the 'A' monogram. This is set in a background of serrated earthenware tile-hanging with a bellcast sufficient to cover a canted bay window below, flanked by carved wooden bracket supports to the jettying. To the internal angle the main roof catslides steeply down to create an entrance porch with turned posts and round-arched access. To the other gable is another little canted bay window with an equivalent lead roof. The main roof rises with scalloped slate bands to a crested ridge dominated by a hefty corbelled chimney-stack, now blandly rendered. Squat chamfered brick carriage pillars with lanterns over and contemporary late Victorian railed quadrants on dwarf walls, but modern entrance gates.

Lewis 1837; Slater 1870; *Thom's*; Townsend 1997.

PARSONAGE (see CHRISTCHURCH RECTORY, Cobh)

776. PEAKE, Coachford; pre-1841; *demolished.*
Opposite the gates to a seat in 1814 of Henry Lindsay was a lodge, hexagonal on plan, removed in the early twentieth century.

Leet 1814.

777. PEMBROKE, Passage West; pre-1841; *demolished.*
Surviving the lost lodge and the big house are its four good stone gate pillars with recessed 'pylon' panels. An estate in the early nineteenth century of Thomas Parsons Boland.

Leet 1814; Lewis 1837.

778. PENCIL HILL, Doneraile (2).

Outer gate; *c.* 1820.

A tiny single-storey limewashed and harled cottage with clipped eaves and hipped roof, its two-bay main front comprised of the doorway and a low, wide window. Derelict.

Inner gate; *c.* 1825.

A delightful single-storey porter's lodge, its leading short front bowed with a bipartite window of four-over-two sash windows. Derelict.

A seat in the early nineteenth century of Harmer Spratt, the place being renamed 'Montevideo' by 1837 before reverting to 'Pencil Hill', and then assuming the name 'Beechfield' in the twentieth century.

Leet 1814; Lewis 1837; Hajba 2002.

779. PETERBOROUGH, Cork [S]; pre-1841/*c.* 1860.

A much-modernised 1½-storey gabled affair with a pair of gablets, alongside the gates, probably a replacement for a predecessor to a property in 1814 of Charles Perry. By 1852 it was the residence of Cornelius Coghlin.

Leet 1814; Griffith 1853–63.

POINT (see COSHEEN)

780. POPE'S HILL, Cork [N]; pre-1841; *demolished.*

Both the big house and its extensive gatekeeper's lodge on Pope's Road have succumbed to modern housing development. A property in the early nineteenth century of the Clarke family.

781. POULACURRY CLOTH MILL, Glanmire; pre-1841; *demolished.*

On the Glashaboy River, a big concern in 1837 of William Thorley, then employing up to 100 people, the gate lodge to which, distant to the north, was a shell by 1890.

Lewis 1837.

782. POULACURRY, Glanmire; *c.* 1830.

The seat in 1814 of Hugh Lawton, his lodge a single-storey plain gabled affair with a blind elevation to the road and a two-bay return to the avenue, having two-over-two sashes in roughcast walls. Occupied. Basic entrance pillars with ball finials. Latterly renamed 'Castle Jane'.

Leet 1814.

783. PRESENTATION CONVENT, Youghal; *c.* 1890.

The so-called 'South Abbey Lodge' is a striking 1½-storey late Victorian structure, its main hip-gabled short front addressing the road in a smooth rendered finish with generous Italianate detailing. Moulded string-courses define the first-floor level and the spring of heavily moulded round-headed arches to openings—the bipartite attic window with one-over-one sashes divided by a Doric 'pillarette' above the two-bay ground floor of window and fanlit doorway. There is a good pair of cut-stone carriage pillars with octagonal cappings, the shafts with chamfers tapering to square bases. Contemporary spiky ironwork.

784. THE PRIORY, Cobh; *c.* 1845.

Like the pretty marine villa within, the single-storey gate lodge is a Tudor Revival-cum-Italianate hybrid, with a diagonally placed chimney-stack to a shallow-pitched roof and tripartite wooden lattice-glazed window in an exposed coursed rubble finish, all so typical of the early Victorian period. A property in 1853 of Revd Francis Newport.

Griffith 1853–63.

785. PRIORY, Newmarket; pre-1890; *demolished.*

Not quite opposite the gates, a lodge built after 1841 to an estate in the mid-Victorian period of Edward Stannard, the house having been built in 1779 by John Philpot Curran, later of Priory, Co. Dublin.

Leet 1814; Griffith 1853–63; Hajba 2002.

786. PROHUST, Dromina; pre-1841; *demolished.*

A late Georgian villa built by Jonathan Bruce with which its porter's lodge may have been contemporary. Surviving at the entrance are peculiar square pineapple finials.

Lewis 1837; Hajba 2002.

787. PROSPECT, Ballintemple; *c.* 1840.

A little Classical lodge presumably built for Carden Terry, resident here in 1837. Single-storey in a smooth rendering, its corners defined by basic pilasters with plain panels, its main front single bay of a bipartite window with margined glazing, set in a recess below a shallow-pitched hipped roof with exaggerated oversailing eaves further emphasised by long, carved soffit brackets. V-jointed rusticated concave entrance quadrants frame cast-iron posts and gates with delicate anthemion motifs, by 'Nash of Cork'—William Nash, wrought-iron manufacturers, Faulkiner's Lane, Cork. The property was later renamed 'Lisnalee' by a subsequent owner.

Lewis 1837; Slater 1846.

788. PROSPECT, Glandore; pre-1842; *demolished.*

The seat in 1837 of John Morris Jr, latterly renamed 'Shorecliffe'.

Lewis 1837.

789. PROSPECT, Glanmire; *c.* 1830.

A plain single-storey gabled roughcast cottage, its irregular three-bay front having a later glazed porch to the doorway. A property in 1853 of Charles McCarthy.

Griffith 1853–63.

790. PROSPECT, Youghal; pre-1842; *demolished.*

Both the house, in the early nineteenth century of William Hudson, and its lodge had been removed by the end of that century.

Slater 1846.

791. PROSPECT HILL, Carrigrohane; *c.* 1832/*c.* 1870.

There was a porter's lodge at the entrance to the house built in 1832 by Anthony Morgan,

but the present building on the site has the form of a later Victorian replacement, probably erected when the new owner, John Stephen Collins (1834–1906), came by the property and styled it 'Ardnalee'. This single-storey standard gabled structure, with a wing in like manner to one side, presents itself in a pleasant rubble with brick dressings—all very attractive but never as intended, having had its original Classical rendered cloak and detailing removed. Of this livery but a single-panel double-leafed door survives as a clue in a breakfront hall with projecting bargeboards over. Otherwise immaculately preserved, with modern rectangular-paned wooden casement windows. Nearby is the once-complementary fine Classical tripartite gateway of six stone pillars with moulded cappings and plinths, the carriage pair of more substance with recessed panels, slightly tapering to mildly pedimented tops with dainty iron lanterns. These frame short ogee quadrants of plain spear-topped railings, contrasting with more elaborate gates.

Lewis 1837; *LGI* (1912); Bence-Jones 1988.

792. PROSPECT HILL, Dunmanway; pre-1842; *demolished.*

The seat in the nineteenth century of the Bryan family.

793. PROSPECT VILLA, Ringaskiddy (2).

A lost demesne of the Burke family, 'the elegant residence of Lieut.-Col. Thomas Burke' in 1837, when there was a single lodged entrance.

West gate; pre-1841; *demolished.*

East gate; *c.* 1855.

The later main entrance, probably added by the same proprietor, sadly now reflects the dereliction within. Across a narrow carriage opening a pair of twin single-storey two-roomed lodges confront one another with their canted fronts, each with openings below bold, joined label mouldings, the parapets over defined by string-courses and moulded coping stones. Strangely, this

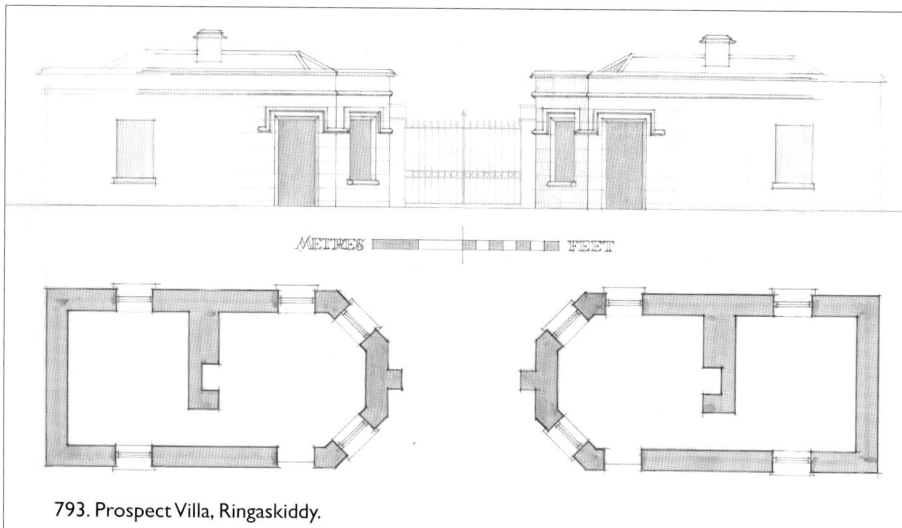

793. Prospect Villa, Ringaskiddy.

decorative ashlar facing reduces to but a rubble finish to the rear of each structure. A once-distinctive prelude, now lying as ivy-covered, sapling-infested shells, their forecourt a dump.

Lewis 1837; Griffith 1853–63.

794. QUARTERTOWN, Mallow; pre-1840; *demolished.*

Major Henry Croker (1758–1836), of the Ballynagarde, Co. Limerick [*q.v.*], family, came by Quartertown demesne through his marriage to heiress Harriet Dillon in 1793. This late Georgian house and its gatekeeper's lodge opposite the gates have gone, to be survived by the latter as a pair of good tall limestone ashlar carriage pillars with moulded corniced cappings and scroll-topped stops, perhaps contemporary with an earlier house on the site.

IFR; Hajba 2002.

795. QUEEN'S COLLEGE CORK, Cork [S] (4).

In 1845 the Colleges (Ireland) Act was placed on the statute book to provide for the further education of Roman Catholics, and the centres of Belfast, Galway and Cork were chosen for new universities. In 1846 architect Sir Thomas Deane was appointed to prepare plans for the latter, having already recommended the old Gill Abbey estate [*q.v.*] as its site; work commenced the following year and was completed by 1849. The old gate and its lodge to Gill Abbey were adopted as the early college entrance but, like the later additional ones, were to experience some degree of upheaval.

Gaol gate; *c.* 1835/1866; architect J.H. Mellon; *demolished.*

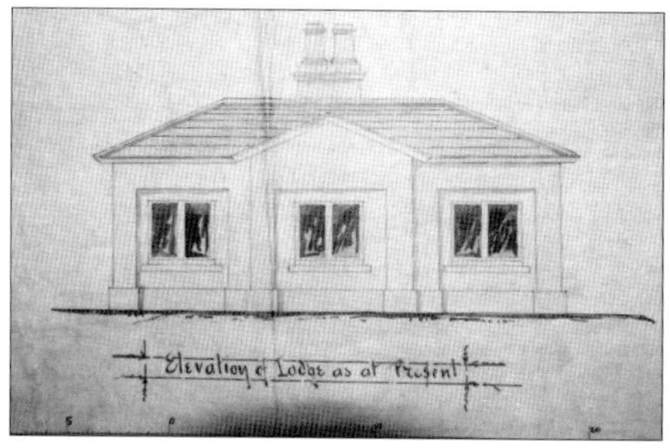

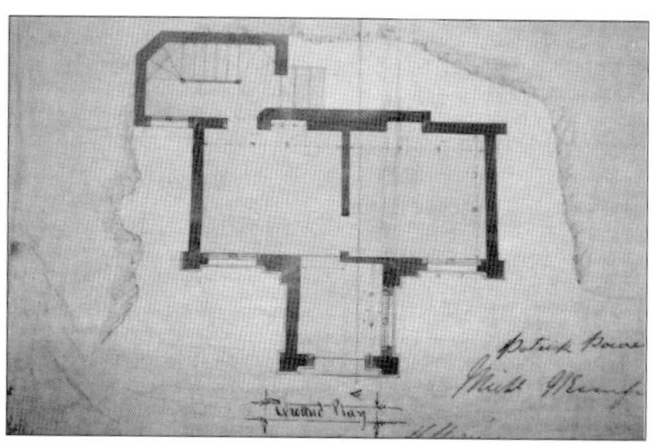

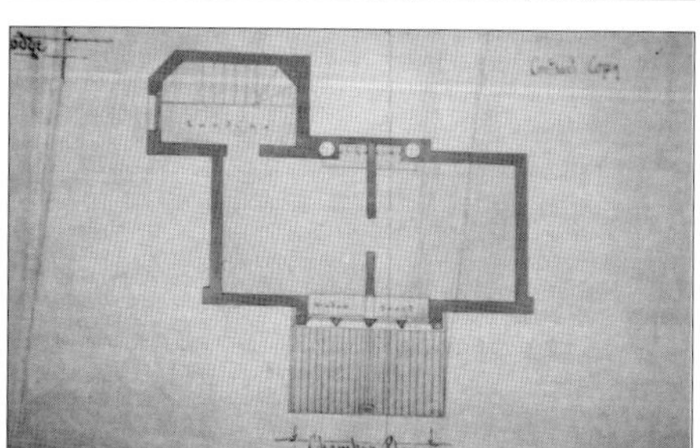

795. Queen's College Cork.
Above—plans and elevations of present and proposed gate, 1865. End elevations and sections showing proposed additions to old gate lodge, 1866. (OPW 5HC/4.892: National Archives.)

What the college authorities inherited was a smart little single-storey, hip-roofed, three-bay, mildly Classical gate lodge, as can be seen from 'existing' and 'proposed' drawings prepared by architect J.H. Mellon, whom they had commissioned to enhance its accommodation and transform it dramatically into a 1½-storey hip-gabled affair with a jettied half-timbered upper floor in Elizabethan style, with a multi-paned gablet window lighting the attic bedrooms. The original projecting hall was likewise given a Tudor make-over. There was clearly little resolve to promote this western gate as an entrance, it being in a less than salubrious location by the jail, and in any case it was too remote from the city, so perhaps mercifully this lodge had a limited life, being removed in the twentieth century. It is survived by the splendid decorative iron gates designed by E.T. Owen in 1870 and manufactured by the Perrott foundry, rehung here in 1929 after removal of the first Western Road entrance and displayed in the very arches which contained them as the ground floor of the doomed gatehouse, salvaged and reassembled in an uncoursed random ashlar with dressed segmental pointed carriage and pedestrian arches below a stepped coping, the apex of which contains the college's arms and the motto *Where Finbarr Taught Let Munster Learn.*

College Road gate; 1864; architect T.N. Deane.

A commodious lodge in Ruskinian Gothic manner, very much akin to the lodges of Deane's erstwhile colleague Benjamin Woodward at St Austin's, Co. Carlow, and Clontra, Co. Dublin, though here a gabled version with skew-tables and kneelers, one rising to a battered chimney-stack. It is raised off a rectangular plan in uncoursed rubble limestone facings, its fenestration of label-moulded single and tripartite Tudor arches irregularly distributed, the 'lych-gate' gabled wooden porch placed below a bipartite gablet which breaks the eaves with its bold stone gutter brackets, just as at St Austin's. The accompanying gatescreen is in the form of a

double gateway, the little postern opening pointed alongside the four-centred arched carriage gate, over which the stepped coping contains, in uncoursed cut stone, a datestone '1849', it having been re-erected here after previously gracing the quadrangle to the main complex. This approach was nevertheless considered 'a back road, through an impoverished district ... very inconvenient and dirty, especially in winter', and it was always the college's ambition to have the main and prestigious access from the Western Road. This they eventually realised after the clearance of some intrusive and unsightly hovels.

Old Western Road gate; 1879; architect Enoch Trevor Owen; *demolished.*

The most spectacular and handsome of the entrance lodges was once sited preceding a bridge spanning the River Lee's South Channel, leading to a serpentine avenue approach to the college. While the bridge was swept away by a 1916 flood, the gatehouse was sadly replaced in 1929. It was a lofty gabled Medieval Revival/Arts and Crafts affair, its 1½-storey porter's accommodation lit by a variety of single, bipartite and tripartite mullioned, pointed-arched windows irregularly distributed in limestone masonry over the segmentally pointed-arched carriage and postern openings. All was not totally lost, for the archways were incorporated in the Gaol gatescreen and the windows can be recognised in the new lodge nearby.

New Western Road gate; 1929; architects probably O'Flynn and O'Connor.

This replacement porter's lodge, set well back from its gatescreen, is a sturdy 1½-storey gabled building with like entrance projection and minimal back return, an exercise for the architects in giving a new home to details salvaged from its predecessor. Recognisable as irregular fenestration is a variety of single, bipartite and tripartite square and pointed-arched openings arranged in uncoursed random cut stone. Likewise reused are the 1879 chimney-stacks and doubtless skew-tables and kneelers. Similarly, it (distantly) monitors traffic over a new bridge further east and preceded by a wide railed iron screen framed by a giant pair of ashlar round-arched pedestrian openings.

Murphy 1995; Dunne 1995; O'Dwyer 1997b; IAA; NA (OPW 5HC/4/892-1).

796. RAFFEEN, Monkstown; pre-1841; *demolished.*

A lodge, which by 1934 was a shell, to a property in 1814 of William Warren, which 23 years later was the residence of T. Dorman Esq.

Leet 1814; Lewis 1837.

797. RALEIGH, Macroom; *c.* 1845; architect possibly Sir T. Deane.

A superb little Tudor Gothic creation, two-bay by two-bay on a square plan below a pyramidal roof, its bays delineated by plain vertical panels, plinth and frieze, which frame delightful label-moulded bipartite and tripartite Perpendicular Gothic Y-traceried windows. All in a smooth rendered finish, occupied and beautifully maintained. There are identical windows to the lodges at Leamlara [*q.v.*], Drishane Castle [*q.v.*] and nearby Killinardrish [*q.v.*], which recall work by Sir Thomas Deane and his brother Kearns. A seat in 1846 of James Minhear.

Slater 1846.

798. RATHCALLAN, Castlemartyr; pre-1842; *demolished.*

A holding in 1814 of William Garde, which by 1846 had passed to the Eager family.

Leet 1814; Slater 1846.

799. RATHCOURSEY EAST, Cloyne; pre-1841; *demolished.*

A seat of the Lyons family, the gate lodge to which had been removed by 1934.

800. RATHCOURSEY WEST, Cloyne (2).

A big, unassuming Georgian house, recorded as the home between 1814 and 1876 of John Smyth.

North entrance; pre-1890; *demolished.*

A lodge built after 1841.

South entrance; *c.* 1845.

On an elevated site is this charming single-storey standard gabled cottage in a limewashed rubble finish, with eccentric fenestration of a two-over-two sash window to one side of the front door and a contrasting wider bipartite lattice-glazed casement to the other. Occupied.

Leet 1814; *LOI.*

801. RATHDUANE, Millstreet; pre-1841; *demolished.*
An estate in 1814 of Owen McCarthy, who by 1844 had been succeeded here by Jeremiah E. McCarthy.

Leet 1814; O'Flanagan 1975.

802. RATHHEALY, Fermoy; pre-1841; *demolished.*
The seat in the late eighteenth century of the Bryan family, which by 1837 was occupied by John Lucas (1816–57).

Taylor and Skinner 1778; 1783; Wilson 1803; Lewis 1837; *LGI* (1904).

803. RATH LEE, Cork [N]; pre-1841; *demolished.*
The property in the 1850s of Richard Dowden.

Griffith 1853–63.

804. RATHMAHER, Kanturk; pre-1841; *demolished.*
Neither the house, in 1837 of C. Purcell Esq., nor its lodge survives.

Lewis 1837.

805. RATHMORE, Kinsale (3).
The demesne until his death in 1817 of Marmaduke Cramer, who was succeeded by his eldest son, John Thomas Cramer (d. 1845), who in 1837 enjoyed 'a handsome mansion embosomed in flourishing plantations', approached through three lodged entrances. One of these was a prestigious pair, probably the earliest, which has not survived. The others have fared little better.

West gate; *c.* 1830.
A ruinous single-storey roughcast cottage with a main two-window-bay avenue front below the remains of carved soffit brackets of a now-missing hipped roof. Nearby are four big corniced entrance pillars and two postilion gates.

East gate; *c.* 1810.
A very derelict single-storey harled rubble structure with a hipped roof and a later tiny gabled hall projecting to the old avenue.

LGI (1904).

806. RATHPEACON HALL, Cork [N]; pre-1890; *demolished.*
A gate lodge built after 1841, probably part of improvements carried out for George D. Atkinson to the property previously called 'Rathpeacon Cottage'.

Griffith 1853–63.

807. RATHPEACON, Cork [N] (2).
The proprietor in 1852 of an establishment that included a corn mill was Richard Thomas, although he then leased the mill-owner's house to William Lefanu. The gatekeepers then were Michael Lynch and John Coleman, who manned the approach in a double line of defence.

Outer gate; *c.* 1830.
A single-storey standard lodge in limewashed rendering, with a high plinth and narrow slit windows below a pyramidal roof. Occupied.

Inner gate; pre-1841.
A rubble ruin.

Griffith 1853–63.

808. RATHROE, Millstreet (2).
Both pre-1841 lodges located opposite their entrances have been demolished, as has the big house, in 1824 and 32 years later home to Denis McCarthy.

Pigot 1824; Slater 1856.

RAVENSCOURT (see LAKEVILLE)

RAVENSWOOD (see MONROE)

809. RAVENSWOOD, Fermoy; 1902.

A commodious lodge built to complement the contemporary villa, semi-detached with 'Innisfallen', as an early Edwardian development for George Francis Hodder (1852–1908), his neighbour in Ravenswood being P.H. Dickson. Single-storey, rendered, gabled and raised off a T-plan, its long three-bay façade to the footpath shows a regular pattern of bipartite one-over-one sash windows with arrowhead arches. To the avenue the main gable contains a rectangular-glazed bay window below its own bellcast roof and surmounted by carved foil and perforated scallop bargeboards, the canopied porch which projects from the internal angle alongside similarly decorated with a carved screen support. Beyond there is a later extension to match, with a continuation of the bold corbelled eaves, while brick highlights are seen in toothed quoins, string-courses and the chimney-stack at the meeting of ridges, which repeats the corbel feature to its capping. Its first gatekeeper in 1903 was Thomas Fitzgerald.

IFR.

810. THE REANTES COTTAGE, Nohaval; *c.* 1790.
By the gate is a pair of small, single-storey, gabled, semi-detached three-bay cottages of rubble construction, now lying ruinous. A house and corn mill in 1852 the property of Luke J. Shea.

Griffith 1853–63.

811. RENNY, Ballyhooly; pre-1841; *demolished.*
Successively owned by the Spencer family followed by the Nagles, it was in 1815 home to Revd Christopher Wallis, who was succeeded here by Henry Smyth around 1826. By 1890 both the house and its lodge had gone, leaving but an outbuilding.

Townsend 1815; Lewis 1837; Hajba 2002.

THE RETREAT (see RIVERVIEW, Bandon)

812. THE RETREAT, Clonakilty; *c.* 1835.
The delightful single-storey Gothic villa rebuilt by the Gillman family from a dwelling in 1851 of Richard Beamish. The porter's lodge is single-storey, with a shallow, canted, leading three-window elevation and originally two-bay to the avenue with a round-arched doorway, the brick arches in rubble facings. Incorporating loft space, it has been nicely extended up the avenue, with trefoil-perforated earthenware crestings on synthetic slated roof.

Griffith 1853–63; Pike and Hodges 1911.

813. THE RETREAT, Mallow; *c.* 1850.
A much-modernised two-storey gatehouse with a three-bay ground floor and two-bay upper storey below a pyramidal roof. Perhaps built by the Williamson family, who acquired the property through the incumbered estate court. Subsequently renamed 'Brookside'.

Hajba 2002.

814. RICHMOND COTTAGE, Sallybrook; pre-1841.
On an elevated site is this single-storey standard hip-roofed gatekeeper's lodge—much extended, a flat-roofed brick monstrosity obscuring it. A property in 1852 of Revd John Halvey.

Griffith 1853–63.

815. RICHMOND, Cork [N]; *c.* 1900.

On St Patrick's Hill, the late Georgian villa originally known as 'Ashley' remained lodgeless until it was acquired around 1884 by Sarah M. Mayne, although the lodge was not valued until 1902. Standard 1½-storey, with chimney-stacks to gables ornamented with carved Tudor Picturesque bargeboards,

at odds with the otherwise Classical detailing. Set in stucco-effect rendering, the round-arched fanlit doorway and flanking segmentally headed sash windows have, in their banded surrounds, over-panels that cleverly disguise the first floor. To the tall eaves is a deep frieze of console brackets and, to the gables, semicircular-arched two-over-two sashed attic windows, one of which addresses the public footpath, alongside which is a more sophisticated pilastered and pedimented pedestrian doorway. Now an Ursuline convent.

816. RICHMOND, Fermoy; pre-1841/*c.* 1890.

In 1844 this was 'Richmond Lodge the tasteful residence of H. Smyth, Esq.'. From Henry Smyth it passed to Thomas Walker, and later in the century to John Furlong, who extended the old villa and gave it an Italianate cloak; he replaced the old porter's lodge with the surviving typically brash late Victorian 1½-storey affair, with its single-storey hip-roofed outshot with blind arcading forming an L-plan. All in a smooth rendering and with red-brick highlights, the main front to the avenue contains in the apex a canted oriel attic window on brackets above a pair of windows with segmental brick arches and relieved by sill and head bands. Alongside, one main roof pitch catslides over the internal angle to form an entrance porch. From the early 1920s the property became home to St Mary's Presentation Convent.

O'Flanagan 1975; Slater 1870; Hajba 2002.

817. RICHMOND, Glanmire; *c.* 1790; architect not known; *demolished.*

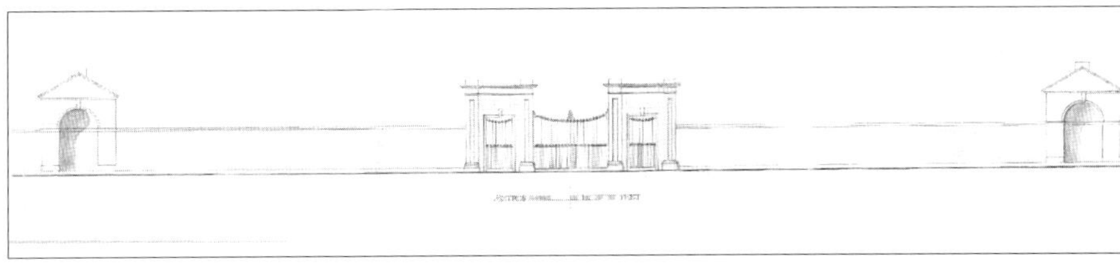

The pitiful overgrown remains of a once-noble and sophisticated gateway built for Sir Henry Mannix (1740–1822), barrister, probably to celebrate his creation as first, and last, family baronet in 1787, having succeeded to the estate on the death of his father ten years earlier. Two grand trabeated postilion archways in ashlar with moulded architraves and keystones are framed by plain pilasters supporting entablatures, beyond which tall ogee-walled quadrants terminated in a distant pair of pedimented aedicules which contained deep round-headed keystoned niches, the right-hand of which had a doorway, an entrance in the frontispiece to a porter's lodge which the first OS map suggests was not one of a pair. A central acroterion may have functioned as its chimney-stack. The Mannix mansion has been likewise reduced, its old approach abandoned. The drawing is conjectural in respect of the left-hand lodge.

Journal of the Pembrokeshire Historical Society **14** (2005); IAA photographs (S/695/4&5).

818. RICHMOND LODGE, Ballintemple; pre-1890; *demolished.*
A porter's lodge built after 1841 to a property in 1853 of William Clarke.

Griffith 1853–63.

819. RICHMOUNT, Bandon (2).
A late Georgian house presumably built by John Sealy (1769–1836), who succeeded his father Richard to the estate in 1789. It was burnt in 1922, the lodges faring little better.

Front entrance; pre-1841.
All but gone, except for a rubble stone main elevation with two sealed-up windows alongside its gates.

Rear entrance; pre-1841; *demolished.*

LGI (1904); Bence-Jones 1988.

820. RINGABELLA, Crosshaven (2).
An estate with late Georgian house of the Hodder family, with gatekeepers' lodges of contrasting quality.

Inland gate; *c.* 1825.
An unprepossessing single-storey roughcast cottage, its roof part-gabled, part-hipped, sited outside the entrance, with a three-window-bay elevation extending in a lean-to hall. Occupied.

Coastal gate; *c.* 1840; architect not known.
A lodge in fine ashlar facings with singular detailing in bold roll mouldings to plinth and eaves, and moulded surrounds to shallow triangular-arched casement windows framed by plain corner pilasters. Single-storey on a

square plan, with single-bay elevations below a pyramidal roof rising to a paltry chimney-stack. Occupied and rose-clad, by a disused avenue.

Both lodges presumably built in the time of Francis Hodder.

Bence-Jones 1988.

821. RINGACOLTIG, Cobh; *c.* 1890.
A single-storey gabled cottage, much modernised with plastic decorative bargeboards and newly louvred two-over-two sash windows in a main two-bay rendered front. First valued in 1896, with John Fitzgerald as gatekeeper to Theodore Carroll in his distant seaside villa.

822. RINGMAHON CASTLE, Blackrock; pre-1841; *demolished.*
The demesne in 1837 of James Murphy (1769–1855), founder in 1825 of the noted distillery. Surviving at the entrance are pineapple finials to the pillars.

Lewis 1837; *LGI* (1904); Bence-Jones 1988.

823. RINGMAHON COTTAGE, Blackrock; pre-1841; *demolished.*
A 27-acre holding in 1852 of Richard Tivey.

Griffith 1853–63.

824. RINGVIEW, Monkstown; *c.* 1860.
A mid-Victorian single-storey rendered gabled cottage with ornamental bargeboards and a principal two-bay front of two-over-two sash windows. Occupied. A property of the Bailey family in the mid-nineteenth century.

825. RIVERDALE, Kilbrittain; *c.* 1830.
A seat in 1837 of Thomas Bayly, whose gate lodge survives, a derelict single-storey standard structure with cast-iron squared casements in harled rubble walls below a hipped roof.

Lewis 1837.

826. RIVERSDALE, Riverstown; pre-1841; *demolished.*
In 1853 the house of John Carmichael, whose gatekeeper was then John Reardon.

Griffith 1853–63.

827. RIVERSTOWN COTTAGE, Glanmire; pre-1841.
Here are the scanty remains of a single-storey structure, a lodge in 1853 to a 52-acre farm of Denis Murphy.
Griffith 1853–63.

828. RIVERSTOWN, Glanmire; pre-1841; *demolished.*
The early eighteenth-century house of the Browne family, chiefly notable for its plasterwork by the Francini brothers and the demesne 'containing a very considerable extent of the largest and finest trees in the country'. Its lodge, opposite the gates at a public crossroads, was removed in the twentieth century.
PGI; Bence-Jones 1988.

829. RIVERVIEW, Ballincollig; *c.* 1850.
Conspicuously sited on a right-angled bend of the road and forward of its entrance is this single-storey standard rendered gabled cottage, plain and latterly extended by an extra bay. Occupied. A small eight-acre holding in the 1850s of Henry Curtis.
Griffith 1853–63.

830. RIVERVIEW, Bandon; pre-1841; *demolished.*
The residence of local barrister Thomas Kingston Sullivan in the mid-nineteenth century, by the end of which it had been renamed 'The Retreat'.
Griffith 1853–63.

831. RIVERVIEW, Skibbereen; *c.* 1820.
A single-storey rubble-faced gabled cottage, blind to both road and avenue, fenestrated to the park. Much modernised, restored and extended to four bays. Occupied. Nearby is a basic gatescreen with concave rubble quadrants and postern openings. A property in 1814 of Cornelius O'Driscoll, it was home a decade later to Arthur Atteridge, who was still in residence in 1846.
Leet 1814; Pigot 1824; Slater 1846.

832. ROCHELLE, Cork [S]; pre-1841/*c.* 1880.
Surviving from the original entrance is the gatescreen, comprised of a pair of tall plain limestone carriage pillars, with moulded plinth tops, flanked by high concave quadrant walls. What was probably a contemporary late Georgian lodge has been replaced by the present late Victorian gatehouse. Two-storey in limestone rubble with toothed red dressings and quoins below a hipped gable roof. A central single-storey entrance hall with perforated foiled bargeboards projects to the avenue. It was at some time extended to the left-hand side in its later role as a schoolhouse. A property in 1837 of R.W. Topp, it later became a seminary.
Griffith 1853–63.

833. ROCHE MOUNT, Whitegate (3).
Like the neighbouring estate of Trabolgan [*q.v.*] of the earls of Fermoy, this was a property of the Roche family, not one of the gate lodges to which, all in place by 1842, has survived, that within on the western approach having been removed by 1890. The later OS maps reveal the principal lodge to the south to have had a plan of some complexity.

834. ROCHESTOWN WOOD, Rochestown; *c.* 1875.

A mildly Tudor multi-gabled house, originally built in 1860 by Harriett St Leger Purcell, who in 1874 married George Roch of Woodbine Hill, Co. Waterford [*q.v.*], and lived on here after his death twenty years later. Although the lodge was first valued in 1918 when the property was home to Denis Hurley, who had acquired it from Sir Henry O'Shea, it probably dates from considerably earlier. This is a commodious two-storey drum lodge of rubble construction, with rendered walls lacking windows and conical roof in its present ruinous state. To the external wall is a feature chimney-breast.
LGI (1904); Pike and Hodges 1911.

835. ROCK CLIFF, Ballintemple; *c.* 1835.

Otherwise 'Rockcliffe', this was a property in 1846 of Wright Sherlock, a merchant in the city. Good chunky cast iron forms a tripartite gateway, the postilions with flat arches on each side of a pair of carriage pillars with recessed panels and moulded cornices to four-faced segmental stone cappings with sculpted fan features. The single-storey rendered lodge is three-bay with a shallow hipped roof and central projecting like-roofed side-entry hall projection, the soffits emphasised by carved paired brackets extending from an eaves band. Modern window inserts spoil the effect. Occupied.
Slater 1846.

836. ROCK COTTAGE, Passage West; *c.* 1845; *demolished.*
The seat of the Parker family, of whom Miss Catherine Anne Parker, the eighth daughter of Michael Parker, was resident, living on here until her death in 1869 at the age of 97.
Griffith 1853–63; *LGI* (1904).

837. ROCK GROVE, Coachford; *c.* 1800.

Once hip-roofed is this shell of a single-storey standard Georgian Gothic gatekeeper's lodge with pointed-arched openings in harled rubble walls. A seat of the Good family in the early nineteenth century.

838. ROCK GROVE, Glanmire; *c.* 1825; architect probably J.B. Keane.

A fine example of the alternative orientation for a simple rectangular two-roomed gate lodge, with a short elevation displayed as the show front. Evolved from Sir John Soane's design 'Intended for an Entrance to a Gentleman's Seat' and pioneered about Ireland in a host of lodges by Sir Richard Morrison, here it is developed—surely by John B. Keane, once an assistant in the Morrison office—in a neo-Classical composition identical to that at Mount Richard, Co. Tipperary [*q.v.*], and the lost example known to have been by Keane at Stradone, Co. Cavan. Single-storey on a cruciform plan below a shallow hipped roof, it presents a once-tripartite window below a segmental arch set in a deep recess framed by piers with recessed panels and embossed laurel wreath motifs, all in a smooth rendered finish. The central skew-table gabled hallway to one side is balanced by a like closet projection to the opposing façade. Occupied and well maintained. The other similar lodges were attended by complementary gatescreens, taken from a design by J.B. Papworth, in the form of giant tapering 'pylon' ashlar pillars and robust cast ironwork, but nothing such has survived here to the lodge commissioned by Simon Dring (d. 1833), who had succeeded to the estate in 1811, perhaps to mark his year as high sheriff of County Cork in 1827. James Reardon was gatekeeper in 1853.

Soane 1793; Papworth 1818; Griffith 1853–63; *LGI* (1904); Dean 1994.

839. ROCK, Inishannon (2).
An estate in 1837 of John Gillman, both of whose porter's lodges, built before 1841, have been demolished, that to the north having gone by 1890, the other lost to modern road realignment.

Lewis 1837.

840. ROCK LODGE, Carrigrohane; pre-1890.
The property in 1853 of Henry Osborne Seward, to have been found also at Lee Cottage [*q.v.*], the gate lodge to which was built after 1841 but by 1890 had been isolated by a new avenue access.

Griffith 1853–63.

841. ROCK LODGE, Monkstown (2).
A seat of John Galwey in 1837, when the house was approached by a sole lodged gate from the south-east.

Coastal entrance; pre-1841/pre-1890; *demolished.*
A gatekeeper's lodge shown on the first OS map as a simple square on plan which 50 years later is indicated with a very different elongated imprint with small projections front and back, presumably a replacement for the Perry family, who were here by 1856.

Inland entrance; pre-1890.
Although '1813' is inscribed on the right-hand entrance quadrant, the gate remained lodgeless until the mid-nineteenth century. This is a big two-storey hip-gabled gatehouse, partly pebble-dashed, with twentieth-century rendered surrounds to openings; two-bay upper storey over three-bay symmetrical ground floor with a central glazed porch and, to the road, a single-storey bay window.

Lewis 1837; Slater 1856; 1870; Griffith 1853–63.

842. ROCKENHAM, Passage West; pre-1841.
The pretty Regency seat recorded in 1837 as the residence of Noble Johnson (1798–1880), whose porter's lodge lies a harled gabled ruin on an irregular plan.

Lewis 1837; *LGI* (1904); Pike and Hodges 1911.

843. ROCKFIELD, Kanturk; *c.* 1835.
A simple 1½-storey standard gabled lodge in a roughcast finish with a gabled entrance canopy. Occupied, with its back to the avenue. Probably built for Christopher Crofts Nash (1824–73) after he succeeded to the property on the death of his father John in 1832. Also known as 'Ballyheen' after its townland.

LGI (1904).

844. ROCKFOREST, Killavullen (2).
The lovely old mid-eighteenth-century bow-fronted house of the Cotter family, now almost halved in size, one of whose lodges remains intact.

Rockforest West gate; pre-1841; *demolished.*
By 1890 the lodge was a shell.

Rockforest East gate; *c.* 1820/*c.* 1860.
A plain-walled gatesweep with recessed panelled pillars in contrast with fine acanthus leaf-cupped swagged urns. The left-hand quadrant contains the postern arch and terminates in the modest 1½-storey gabled lodge forward of the forecourt, its two-window-bay principal front in a stuccoed finish reduced to roughcast beyond. Probably built for Sir James Laurence Cotter I (1748–1829) and raised an attic storey by his grandson, Sir James Laurence Cotter III (1828–1902), who succeeded as 4th baronet on the death of his father in 1834 to 'a noble place; the house is very extensive, but much out of repair'.

O'Flanagan 1975; *BPB* (1929); Bence-Jones 1988.

845. ROCKFOREST LODGE, Killavullen; *c.* 1835.
A late Georgian villa, in 1837 of Pierce Creagh, to which is a tiny single-storey standard three-bay cottage with wide openings to accommodate bipartite windows and double-leafed door in a rendered finish below the hipped roof; three-bay end elevation. Derelict but in use. Modest tripartite gateway with short concave-walled quadrants framing pillars with V-jointed rusticated faces.

Lewis 1837.

846. ROCKFORT, Inishannon; *c.* 1840.
A small, gabled, 1½-storey mildly Picturesque cottage with a single-storey gabled hall extending from the road elevation. In pleasant exposed rubble, much modernised with new serrated bargeboards but plastic windows. Occupied. A property in 1837 of Stephen Lewis, succeeded by John T. Hornibrook.

Lewis 1837; Griffith 1853–63.

847. ROCKMILL LODGE, Rockmills; pre-1841.
A fishing and shooting lodge built in 1776 by Colonel Richard Aldworth of Newmarket Court [*q.v.*], who on his death in 1824 left the place to the next resident, his wife's nephew, Charles Deane Oliver (1771–1829), whose gate lodge lies ruinous, a semblance of its standard single-storey three-bay front elevation apparent.

LGI (1904).

ROCKROHAN (see CASTLE LANDS)

848. ROCKVALE, Castletownroche; pre-1841; *demolished.*
An estate in the eighteenth century of the Stannards, from whom it passed through an 1800 marriage to the Eustace family, who resided at their main seat of Robertstown, Co. Kildare, letting Rockvale to a succession of tenants—Francis Fosberry being recorded here in 1814, and Patrick Nagle in 1830.

Leet 1814; *LGI* (1904); Hajba 2002.

849. ROCKVALE, Mallow; pre-1841; *demolished.*
'... [T]he recently erected mansion' of Samuel George Beamish, so described in 1837, was in 1851 let by him, and by 1890 had been reduced in size, its lodge a shell.

Lewis 1837; Griffith 1853–63.

850. ROCKVILLE, Fermoy; pre-1841; *demolished.*
A villa of early nineteenth-century appearance, pleasantly situated on the River Blackwater, its design attributed to John Hargrave; it was home in 1814 to Major-General Orde, followed for many years by Revd James Mockler, rector of Castle Hyde. The property was subsequently renamed 'Ileclash'.

851. ROCKVILLE, Macroom; pre-1842; *demolished.*
A property in 1837 and after of Thomas Radley, whose porter's lodge had been removed by 1938.

Lewis 1837.

852. ROCKY ISLAND GUNPOWDER MAGAZINE, Cobh; *c.* 1810; *demolished.*
Samuel Lewis in 1837 remarks that the neighbouring land of 'Hawlbowling was

Mr and Mrs Hall

fortified and made the ordnance depôt, and the Lords of the Admiralty made it the only naval vitualling depôt in Ireland; and Rocky island was excavated and made the chief gunpowder magazine of the southern part of the kingdom'. His reference to 'excavation' probably explains the absence of a lodge on the OS maps, whereas an 1840 engraving in Mr and Mrs S.C. Hall's *Ireland, its scenery, character &c.* reveals the front elevation of a little guardhouse outside a monumental entrance archway. The latter survives in limestone ashlar as a Classical composition, its deep entablature and pair of Doric pilasters framing the round-arched gateway. The short main elevation of the lodge was two-bay of doorway and window, likewise flanked by a pair of Doric pilasters supporting a full-width pediment. It otherwise appears to have been buried in an embankment. The island now is the site of a crematorium.

Lewis 1837; Hall 1841–3.

853. ROOKHURST, Monkstown; *c.* 1890.
A late Victorian lodge in railway style, with its polychromatic battered chimney-stack, earthenware crestings and carved hip-knobs to fretted bargeboards. Single-storey in orange brick with stone string-course, its openings bipartite with central sash boxes below keystones in segmental arches. A property founded by Ralph Westropp (1774–1822), and long held thereafter by his son Hodder, which seems to have been redeveloped by John Daly, alderman and JP for Cork city (1880–84). 'Ashleam' is inscribed on a gate post.

LGI (1904); *Thom's*.

854. ROSANNA, Carrigrohane; *c.* 1825.

A charming 1½-storey *cottage orné*, its steeply pitched hipped thatch displaying a prominent modern hip-gabled dormer. Square windows arranged as three-bay by two in an exposed rubble construction with basic pilasters. On an elevated site, it overlooks a good tripartite gateway of six pillars with plain friezes and corniced cappings and containing contrasting whitened short concave-walled quadrants. A seat overlooking the River Lee, in the early nineteenth century a residence of the Webb family, in 1837 known as 'West Hill' and then of Revd John Webb LLD.

Lewis 1837.

855. ROSE COTTAGE, Lombardstown; pre-1841; *demolished.*
In 1844 'the pretty dwelling of Mr Leahy', described a century earlier under its townland name of 'Drumrastill' as 'a good house and improvement of the Wrixons'. Its gatekeeper's lodge had by 1936 been allowed to deteriorate to a shell.

Smith 1893; O'Flanagan 1975.

856. ROSE HILL, Ballintemple; pre-1841; *demolished.*
Subsequently renamed 'Ardcairn', a property in 1814 of a Dr White which by 1852 had passed to Thomas Johnston.

Leet 1814; Griffith 1853–63.

857. ROSE HILL, Ballynacorra; *c.* 1845; *demolished.*
A seat in the mid-nineteenth century of a branch of the Barry family, its gatehouse recorded in the 1853 valuation but not indicated on the 1841 OS map, presumably built when John Barry succeeded to the place after Augustus W. Barry.

Lewis 1837; Griffith 1853–63.

858. ROSE HILL, Donnybrook; pre-1842; *demolished.*
A 47-acre holding in 1852 of Henry Hall, who followed the 1837 proprietor, W. Lane Esq., here.

Lewis 1837; Griffith 1853–63.

859. ROSE LODGE, Ring; pre-1841; *demolished.*
A property in 1852 of William B. Warren.

Griffith 1853–63.

860. ROSEMOUNT, Farran; *c.* 1830.
A nondescript 1½-storey gabled affair raised off an L-plan, one wing extending in line with the estate wall and flanked by a pair of entrances, one of which is in the form of tall rubble pillars framed by convex quadrant walls containing blind round-headed recesses, perhaps originally postilion arches. A seat in 1837 of William Hawkes.

Lewis 1837.

861. ROSENEATH COTTAGE, Cobh; *c.* 1870.
Opposite its gates, sandwiched between road and railway cutting, is this plain, rendered, single-storey gabled lodge with a two-bay front, the right-hand window in a gabled breakfront facing the entrance. Possibly built during the mid-Victorian occupancy of proprietor Capt. William L. Tooker.

862. ROSEVIEW, Cork [S]; *c.* 1835.
What was a single-storey standard gabled lodge with a chimney-stack to each end was subsequently extended by a bay. Rendered, with ornamental carved bargeboards to main gables and the entrance canopy. This evidence of the Picturesque fashion favoured in the Regency period is not reflected by the gatescreen. Four V-jointed rusticated Classical corniced pillars contain concave-walled quadrants, one with a postilion opening. In 1853 the property, off old Blackrock Road, was home to Eliza O'Connor; latterly renamed 'Glencairn'.

Griffith 1853–63.

863. ROSEVILLE, Cork [N]; pre-1841; *demolished.*
A 28-acre holding on the Old Youghal Road, in 1852 of Stephen Cave.

Griffith 1853–63.

864. ROSKEEN, Banteer; pre-1841; *demolished.*
A house built in 1837 by Pierce Power, the four limestone entrance pillars to which now give onto a disused avenue. The gatekeeper's lodge must have been of some significance, given that O'Flanagan in 1844 was moved to notice 'a highly improved spot, the porter's lodge at the entrance is built of variegated freestone, and has a handsome appearance', now no more.

O'Flanagan 1975; Hajba 2002.

865. ROSNALEE, Banteer (2).
Originally a property of the Nash family, with the appropriate appellation of 'Nashville', it passed through an 1800 marriage to Nicholas Philpot Leader (d. 1836) of Mount Leader [*q.v.*], whose son William Leader (d. 1860) enlarged the house, changing its name and erecting an additional porter's lodge to the side gate. Neither it nor the original front entrance lodge (nor the big house) survived the arrival of the Irish Land Commission in the 1930s.

LGI (1904); Hajba 2002.

866. ROSSACON, Newmarket; *c.* 1825.
Opposite the entrance was a single-storey standard lodge, probably with a pyramidal roof, recently beautifully restored and sympathetically extended to a four-bay front of exposed rubble with two-over-two sash windows and half-doors. Occupied. An estate from 1772 leased to the Nash family of Rockfield [*q.v.*], who themselves sublet it in the early nineteenth century to a succession of occupants, noted as Daniel Egan (1814), Nathaniel Warner (1824), John Homan (1826) and George Kirkland Tivy (1829).

Leet 1814; Hajba 2002.

867. ROSSLINE, Newmarket (2).
One of many properties in the county willed on the death of the 5th Lord Egmont in 1841 to his legal representative Sir Edward Tierney, here let in 1852 to John Noonan with 80 acres.

Principal entrance; *c.* 1840.
A bland and derelict single-storey standard, cement-rendered, steeply gabled affair, located not quite opposite its gates.

Secondary entrance; pre-1841; *demolished.*
A lost lodge to a lengthy wooded drive from a distant southerly gate.

Griffith 1853–63; Hajba 2002.

868. ROSSMORE, Carrigtohill; pre-1841.
The ruins of a gate lodge to a seat in the early nineteenth century of Thomas Coppinger, whose gatekeeper in 1853 was Michael Toomy.

Griffith 1853–63.

869. ROSTELLAN CASTLE, Rostellan (3).
The site of yet another important lost mansion, here of the O'Brien family, marquises of Thomond, of whom the 1st and 2nd effected improvements to the mid-eighteenth-century house before apathy set in. The 3rd marquis was recorded in 1835 as having 'begun to ornament in the gothic

style, thro' the medium of the Dublin architect, Mr Morrison. But he tired of the expense and stopped short, after very little was done except to a wing, which contains the offices, and which has been finished off.' The decline was further ensured with his death in 1855, when the title became extinct and the property was auctioned as an incumbered estate, but one of the gate lodges remains.

Saleen gate; pre-1841; *demolished.*

Farsid gate; *c.* 1835.

Originally a standard 1½-storey gabled structure in pleasant exposed rubble finish with tall eaves and later banded surrounds to openings; three-bay round-headed blind arcade to the park gable. Extended by a bay in sympathy. Occupied.

East gate; pre-1841; *demolished.*

Heaney 1999; *BPB* (1929); Bence-Jones 1988; Lyons 1993.

870. ROXBOROUGH, Midleton; pre-1841; *demolished.*

A property in the early nineteenth century of the Ball family but by 1837 of a Mr McSweeny, the gatekeeper's lodge to which had gone by 1890.

Leet 1814, Lewis 1837.

871. RUSHMOUNT, Kilworth (2).

A seat in 1824 of Denis Geran, his Georgian house about a decade later being given a fashionable new Picturesque Gothic front partly reflected in work to one of the gate lodges, probably for Daniel Geran.

Principal gate; *c.* 1820.

A plain single-storey standard late Georgian lodge with a hipped roof, given an early Victorian gabled hall projection with ornamental bargeboards. Subsequently subjected to twentieth-century improvements with a roughcast finish, modern window replacements and an unsightly flat-roofed addition next to the hall. Occupied.

Secondary gate; pre-1841; *demolished.*

At the head of a short avenue nearer the house was a square porter's lodge opposite the entrance, removed by 1890.

Pigot 1824; Lewis 1837; Hajba 2002.

872. RYE COURT, Crookstown; *c.* 1830; architect not known.

A most conspicuous entrance, with a sophisticated Classical lodge presiding centrally over an extensive segmental forecourt. Single-storey with a main short ashlar front flanked by a pair of gateways, its single window having a moulded surround and like sill course between framing corner pilasters which support an entablatured pediment. Wing walls on each side extended to elaborate cast-iron carriage gates hung on sturdy and distinctive circular pillars, half of their shafts in the form of boldly fluted drums on square bases. The cappings are similarly square, crowned by four-faced round pediments containing boldly sculpted anthemion motifs. All created for John Tonson Rye by an unidentified designer who produced identical pillars for Upton House [*q.v.*]. The big house was burnt in 1921, its lodge sadly derelict and boarded-up.

LGI (1904); Bence-Jones 1988.

SACRED HEART CONVENT, Clonakilty (see SCARTAGH COTTAGE)

SACRED HEART CONVENT, Cobh (see NORWOOD)

873. ST ANNE'S HILL, Blarney.

A site which experienced the most remarkable redevelopment, from the unprepossessing early house and its 87-acre estate of Thomas Barter to the emergence in 1856 of Ireland's first hydropathic establishment, the creation of his physician grandson, Richard Barter (1802–70), which grew further after his death in the hands of his son, Richard H. Barter. This included the building of a new house on the land, 'Ardcaein', complete with its own porter's lodge. The huge institution declined in the new century before its sale in 1952 and today lies in ruins, unlike the surviving gate lodges.

Main entrance; pre-1841/*c.* 1875.

On the site of the gate lodge to the old Barter house is this attractive replacement in the form of a single-storey bungalow on an L-plan, in a roughcast finish with toothed brick quoins and dressings to openings. Perforated wavy bargeboards decorate the gables, the main roof extending in a catslide over the internal angle to form a pretty balustraded entrance verandah with post supports and fretted brackets to the eaves. Plastic door and windows. Occupied.

Ardcaein entrance; *c.* 1870.

A plain roughcast structure with a two-bay window main elevation below the lofty eaves to its gabled roof. Built within the St Anne's Hill estate to serve a new house occupied at the turn of the twentieth century by Sir Richard Barter (d. 1916), knighted for his services to agriculture.

Guy 2017; Wikipedia; IAA.

ST AUBYN'S (see FIRHILL)

874. ST COLMAN'S COLLEGE, Fermoy; *c.* 1856; architect probably J.P. Hurley.

Dominating a hill of the same name

overlooking the town is this huge Italianate institution in a sandstone/limestone mix. Extended in 1884, its gatehouse dates from the original 1856 college building and reflects it in style and materials. It is in fact one of a semi-detached pair, both forthright two-storey with a three-bay symmetrical main gabled front and with skew-tables and kneelers in limestone, which is likewise employed as bold toothed quoins and dressings to its round-headed openings in otherwise sandstone random rubble facings; keystones enhance the ground-floor arches and an oculus relieves the lofty gable. Now independent of the school complex and put to commercial use. Likely to have formed part of the commission of architect John Pine Hurley, who designed the college in 1855 for Bishop Timothy Murphy.

IAA; NIAH.

875. ST FINBARR'S CEMETERY, Cork [S]; *c.* 1880; architect not known.

To the largest graveyard in the city is this impressive and generous accommodation for a gatekeeper but in the main for his principal role of cemetery superintendent. A tall, 1½-storey, steeply multi-gabled house on an irregular plan in polychrome stone, with toothed quoins and chamfered dressings to square-headed windows below relieving arches of variegated alternate voussoirs. Two leading wings, the left-hand of which is a later addition, create a recess containing a single-storey lean-to entrance porch with shouldered arches carried by delightful foliated capitals on colonnettes. To the road is a gabled breakfront, and four lofty brick chimney-stacks augment the roof line. An extensive railed gatescreen has fine cut-stone chamfered Tudor Gothic pillars, their cappings gabled with roll-topped ridges and foiled features.

876. ST FINBARR'S SEMINARY, Cork [N]; *c.* 1890; architect probably S.F. Hynes.

Outside the gates is this neat 1½-storey standard lodge in polychromatic brickwork, with cream highlights introduced in eaves, sill and head courses and as alternate voussoirs to segmentally arched openings to two-over-two sash windows and the fanlit doorway. The theme is taken into the corbelled chimney-stacks to each gable. A not-inappropriate prelude to the Bishop's Palace and the great High Victorian Gothic Revival institutional building on the hill, built around 1885 for the Most Revd Dr Delany to designs of Samuel Francis Hynes, whose commission doubtless included the entrance lodge.

Williams 1994; IAA.

ST FRANCIS'S CONVENT (see SANS SOUCI)

ST GOBNAIT'S CEMETERY (see MALLOW CEMETERY)

877. ST JOHN THE BAPTIST RC CHURCH, Lisgoold; pre-1841; *demolished.*
Opposite its gates, a long rectangular structure which survived into the twentieth century.

878. ST JOSEPH'S CEMETERY, Cork [S]; pre-1841; *demolished.*
'The quondam botanic garden, once so popular as a place of recreation, was sold in 1826, and its new proprietor, the celebrated Father Theobald Mathew, has changed its gaieties into a mournful cemetery, after the plan of Père la Chaise at Paris—it is now very beautiful, but very sad.' It is not clear whether the old porter's lodge graced the gardens or was built for the new graveyard gate. What is evident is that the present flat-roofed affair is not worthy of notice.

Slater 1846.

ST JOSEPH'S COLLEGE (see WILTON)

ST JOSEPH'S CONVENT (see NEWMARKET)

879. ST LUKE'S HOME, Cork [N]; *c.* 1885; architect probably W.H. Hill and Son.
A 'Home for Protestant Incurables' designed by W.H. Hill and Son about 1881 in a red brick reflected in its quirky 1½-storey gate lodge, having to each front a hip-gabled gablet with a scroll-ended earthenware ridge tile, each with segmentally arched two-over-two sash attic windows in pairs, breaking the eaves of its steeply hipped roof. From the main front extends a single-storey rectangular-glazed bay window, likewise hip-roofed.

Williams 1994.

880. ST MARIE DE L'ISLE CONVENT, Cork [S]; pre-1890; *demolished.*
Architect William Atkins designed his great High Victorian Gothic complex from 1850 with its main front permitting solely pedestrian access, carriages entering via a carriage arch to the rear monitored by a porter's lodge from Convent Place.

Williams 1994.

881. ST MARY'S COLLEGIATE CHURCH, Youghal; *c.* 1850; architect possibly Edward Fitzgerald.

The largest medieval parish church still in use in Ireland, after lying roofless for 300 years, was controversially restored in 1851–8 by local architect and historian Edward Fitzgerald, who in the general reinstatement of the site may have been responsible for the splendid little Tudor Gothic lodge. Originally three-bay, having subsequently been extended by a bay to the left-hand side, and probably raised from single-storey with attic accommodation, its leading gable alongside the gatescreen is skew-tabled above a good moulded lancet light. Within, its not-quite-symmetrical front has a gabled entrance breakfront, in the apex of which is a square plaque with carved foils clasping a blank shield. Below is the shallow-pointed arched doorway, label-moulded as are the windows to each side, chamfered in pleasant uncoursed rubble. The extensive straight triple gateway is in like style; a pair of distant label-moulded shallow-pointed arched postilion openings, the copings of which are stepped over more blank shields, flank short railings on each side of the carriage pillars. Similarly in cut stone, cruciform in plan section and rising off bold moulded plinths, their recessed panels with foiled tops in gabled cappings eccentrically surmounted by square gabled finials crowned by tiny 'knobs'. The contemporary wrought ironwork displays a repeating Tudor Gothic quatrefoil motif.

Killanin and Duignan 1962.

ST MARY'S (see HYDE PARK HOUSE)

ST MARY'S PRESENTATION CONVENT, Fermoy (see RICHMOND)

ST PATRICK'S HOSPITAL (see ST VINCENT'S ORPHANAGE)

882. ST RAPHAEL'S BLIND ASYLUM, Cork [N]; *c.* 1870; *demolished.*

The sophistication of the surviving handsome Greek Revival entrance screen suggests its lodge to have been of some significance—shown with an irregular plan on the OS maps. Wide with railed quadrants, the triple gateway is contained by tall stone pillars, their shafts decorated with Soaneian incised panels below fluted friezes to pedimented cappings with plain acroteria. An institution along with the main building of the Sisters of Charity, who acquired it not long after Francis Lyons had built his residence here.

883. ST VINCENT'S CONVENT, Cork [N] (2).
An establishment of the Sisters of Mercy off Vincent's Avenue.

Outer gate; *c.* 1880.

The impressive triple gateway has a main carriage entrance flanked by massive square limestone pillars with, alongside, lofty red sandstone walls containing limestone-dressed postern openings. Behind is the less-than-impressive 1½-storey three-bay

884. St Vincent's Orphanage, Cork [N].

gabled lodge, probably having lost much character in modernisation, now rendered in stucco-effect containing plastic windows and doorway to right-hand side. To the roof are nasty flat-roofed dormers; the red-brick chimney-stacks to each gable suggest a late Victorian origin.

Inner gate; pre-1890; *demolished.*

884. ST VINCENT'S ORPHANAGE, Cork [N]; *c.* 1860; architect probably William Atkins.
More than holding its own is this fitting foretaste of the great Gothic Revival backdrop—a busy little lodge (*above*) on an elevated site, its red sandstone ashlar contrasting starkly with white toothed limestone dressings to angles and chamfered slit windows. Single-storey, presenting a canted end to the road below an equivalent roof that rises steeply to a wrought-iron finial that stops the serrated earthenware cresting of a ridge broken by a battered chimney-stack in a matching variegated stone. Otherwise there are skew-table gables, that of the hall which extends to the avenue containing a wide, hood-moulded, pointed-arched doorway. The bipartite entrance gateway is in like manner, with a little shouldered-arched postern opening alongside tall, slender, ashlar carriage pillars with multi-gabled cappings and sculpted finials atop them. The lodge is so akin to that at Cork District Lunatic Asylum [*q.v.*] as to be attributable to William Atkins. Now St Patrick's Hospital.

O'Dwyer 1997a.

885. SALLYBROOK HOUSE AND PAPER MILLS, Sallybrook; pre-1841; *demolished.*
In 1837 'the property of James Hodnet, Esq., at present employing about 30, and when in full work 70 persons'. Fifteen years later it had converted to a woollen factory of Alexander Nicholls.

Lewis 1837; Griffith 1853–63.

886. SALLYPARK, Liscarroll; *c.* 1855.
A plain 1½-storey standard gabled lodge, much modernised in roughcast with plastic windows and door, gabled entrance canopy and synthetic slates. A seat of the Lowe family, which they let for most of the early nineteenth century, the house in 1837 was in ruins but must have been later rebuilt to justify the addition of a gate lodge to the estate, probably during the occupancy of William Foote around 1850, when George Bond Lowe was the lessor.

Lewis 1837; Griffith 1853–63.

887. SANDERS PARK, Charleville; *c.* 1835.

To a distinctly Classical house of late Georgian appearance is this remarkable two-storey octagonal gatehouse with an octahedral roof, its eaves broken on the entrance face by a steeply pitched gablet with ornamental bargeboards, its toes supported on carved brackets—a feature probably added around 1865. Otherwise apparently of Regency origin, with large transomed and mullioned lattice-glazed casement windows in plain rendered walls. Presumably inspired by Christopher Sanders (1808–39), who inherited the property on the death of his father in 1819, the first of four brothers to succeed to it. A remarkable survival, it remains occupied; its old avenue has become a public road, the big house lost.

IFR.

888. SANDY HILL, Macroom (2).
A property in close proximity to the town, in 1814 occupied by Revd John Orpin, which for much of the remainder of the century was the residence of Thomas S. Coppinger, one of whose gatekeepers in 1852 was John Buckley. Both pre-1842 lodges have been demolished.

Leet 1814; Griffith 1853–63.

889. SANS SOUCI, Ballintemple; pre-1841/1883.
A seat on the Blackrock road in 1837 of R.B. Shaw Esq., presumably the same of Monkstown Castle [*q.v.*]. The surviving lodge is a replacement, built when the place became home to the Very Revd H.F. Neville. A plain red-brick gabled affair, raised off an L-plan and extended to a double pile at the rear. Occupied.

Lewis 1837.

890. SARSFIELD COURT, Sallybrook; pre-1890; *demolished.*
Named after the neighbouring ancient mansion of the Sarsfield family was this short-lived villa of Charles Putland of Bray Head, Co. Wicklow, which was swept away to make way for St Stephen's Hospital, its gate lodge first being identified by valuation notes of 1948!

891. SCARTAGH COTTAGE, Clonakilty; pre-1841/*c.* 1880.

A single-storey four-bay structure, two with gables over, now roughcast with a sidelit front door, semi-octagonal bay window to the right-hand side and a louvred lunette to one of its gables. Probably originating as a basic cottage from the early eighteenth-century sojourn here of the Galway family, but subsequently much altered and elongated to receive the Sisters of the Sacred Heart Convent, from whose time dates the elaborate ecclesiastical gatescreen of *c.* 1880: a triple gateway with a pair of very finely chiselled stone carriage pillars with roll-moulded corners and gabled cappings containing blank shields in cusped clasps and fleur-de-lis ridges. The splendid scrolled and foliated ironwork is set off by convex quadrants of uncoursed punched random masonry.

Lewis 1837.

892. SEA COURT, Courtmacsherry; pre-1842.

A decent old house of *c.* 1760 built by the Powell family, from whom it passed to the Longfields with the marriage of Henry Longfield (d. 1851) of Waterloo [*q.v.*] to Mary, only daughter and heiress of John Powell. Surviving at the entrance are basic concave rubble quadrant walls containing postilion openings, now sealed. Alongside to the road are the ruins of a one-bay front elevation of its porter's lodge.

LGI (1904); Pike and Hodges 1911.

893. SEYMOUR VILLE, Youghal; pre-1842; *demolished.*

A small estate in the mid-nineteenth century of Richard Torbuck.

Griffith 1853–63.

894. SHAMROCK LAWN, Douglas; pre-1841; *demolished.*

Recorded in 1814 as a seat of Samuel Wiley, which by 1837 and as late as 1870 was home to William P. Robinson.

Leet 1814; Lewis 1837; Slater 1870.

895. SHANAKIEL, Cork [N]; *c.* 1845.

Probably built for Robert Morrison, the occupant in 1852, is this tiny single-storey hip-roofed lodge, harled and pinkwashed with a two-window-bay main front. Occupied. Adjacent is the gatescreen of stone pillars with recessed panels and a flanking straight-arched postilion opening with balancing niche.

Griffith 1853–63.

896. SHANAKIEL HOUSE [1], Cork [N] (2).

A villa on the 18-acre seat in the early nineteenth century of Daniel Leahy, initially approached by two avenues, one of which was abandoned later in the century.

Sunday's Well Road gate; pre-1841; *demolished.*

Once the principal avenue, which by 1890 had been removed along with its porter's lodge.

Shanakiel Road gate; *c.* 1845; architect not known.

An excellent single-storey, hip-roofed, three-bay, smooth-rendered lodge with a central semi-octagonal entrance hall projection below an equivalent roof, the ridges meeting at a chimney-stack once with recessed panel faces. From the park front extends a rectangular bay, its external corners like elsewhere defined by Doric pilasters, which with the eaves frieze give a neo-Classical identity, all perhaps by the same hand as the lodges about the city to the Episcopal Palace, Mount Donegan, Clifton, Hyde Park and Factoryville, here the margined glazing to its casement windows giving a clue to its early Victorian date.

Lewis 1837; Griffith 1853–63.

897. SHANAKIEL HOUSE [2], Cork [N]; pre-1841; *demolished.*

A house by the Shanakiel Road, whose avenue and lodge had by 1890 already gone, its demise being predictable in 1852, as it was described in that valuation as being unoccupied and dilapidated, the absentee owner then being Nelson McCarthy, butter merchant in the city.

Slater 1846; Griffith 1853–63.

898. SHANBALLY, Glenville (2).

In the time here of John Welsh in 1837 there were porters' lodges to both avenues from the north, neither having survived, that to the Glenville gate having been removed before 1890.

Lewis 1837.

899. SHANDRUM RECTORY, Charleville; *c.* 1845.

All is not as it first seems in this pleasant Classical villa and its porter's lodge, both being of later origin than they appear, the latter particularly affecting to be of 50 years earlier with its pointed-arched openings. In an attractive rubble finish is this sweet miniature single-storey sentry-box on a unique hexagonal plan, its hexahedral roof rising from a cut-stone eaves band to terminate awkwardly in a square chimney-stack. Recently admirably cleared of undergrowth and restored as a curiosity by the gate to a contemporary glebe house built for the Revd William Bunbury, who was clearly charmed by the Georgian Gothic lodge to 'Fortlands' [*q.v.*], which he was renting while awaiting his rectory's completion. Late in the century following his death the place became known as 'Gortskagh House'.

Slater 1846; 1856; 1870; Griffith 1853–63.

900. SHEPPERTON PARK, Leap; *c.* 1800.

A remarkable survivor, forward of and elevated from its gates in whitewashed rubble walls, is this most basic of single-storey gatekeepers' lodges, minuscule but containing three rooms, having three single-bay elevations with bipartite

rectangular-paned casement lights, its square plan with a shallow-pitched pyramidal roof rising from an eaves course to the central chimney-stack. Presumably built for the plain old Georgian house by John Townsend (d. 1810). His namesake grandson's gatekeeper in 1853 was James Daly.

Griffith 1853–63; Pike and Hodges 1911; *IFR.*

901. SHIPPOOL, Inishannon (3).

In 1837 'a handsome residence in a richly-wooded demesne, sloping gradually to the water's edge', then of Capt. William Henry Herrick (1784–1863), who had succeeded his father to the estate as a minor in 1796 and subsequently built at least two of its porters' lodges.

Frankford Bridge gate; pre-1841; *demolished.*

A lodge at the head of an exceptionally long avenue from the north, parallel with the Bandon River and the public road.

Middle gate; *c.* 1810.

At the principal entrance is this cute little single-storey standard lodge, quirky in its lofty eaves to a roof, gabled and chimneyed to the park and hipped to a road elevation, distinguished solely by a round-arched niche with pronounced keystone and spring voussoirs in a stucco finish carried about the main avenue façade with likewise semicircular-headed fenestration, the windows with Georgian Gothic Y-traceried glazing pattern. The entrance screen is comprised of extensive concave quadrant walls, square stone pillars and carriage gates with a big ornate meeting-rail finial.

South gate; *c.* 1830.

A single-storey hip-roofed cottage with two-bay elevations of two-over-two sash windows in limewashed stucco-effect walls. Occupied. Here too is an ornamental finial to the carriage gates, and wide harled quadrant entrance walls.

Lewis 1837; *LGI* (1904).

SHORE CLIFFE (see PROSPECT, Glandore)

902. THE SHRUBBERY, Cork [S]; pre-1890; *demolished.*
A traditional Georgian-style villa built *c.* 1850 for Charles Beamish of brewers Beamish and Crawford, its lost lodge presumably contemporary. Now the site of 'Fitzgerald Park'.
Griffith 1853–63.

903. SIDNEY, Cork [N]; *c.* 1850.
To an older house of the Fitzgibbon family is an undistinguished standard single-storey lodge, gabled with like breakfront hall, in exposed red sandstone rubble with cream toothed brick dressings. Modernisation has seen the loss of its chimney-stack, the insertion of plastic windows and plain bargeboards.

904. SILVER SPRING, Cork [N]; pre-1841; *demolished.*
A seat in 1837 of Joseph King Cummins (1788–1842).
Lewis 1837; *IFR.*

905. SILVERSPRING WOOLLEN MILLS, Sallybrook; pre-1841; *demolished.*
'The woollen manufacture was established here in 1822, by Messrs Lyons and Hanly, whose factory, in a secluded part of the vale of Glanmire, contains 30 looms, and affords employment to 200 persons', according to Samuel Lewis in 1837. Its gate lodge lay distant to the south, its long avenue parallel with the river.
Lewis 1837; Griffith 1853–63.

906. SISTERS OF GOOD SUCCOUR CONVENT, Cork [S]; *c.* 1860.
A 1½-storey rendered gabled lodge with dormers. Occupied.

SISTERS OF MERCY CONVENT, Cobh (see ADMIRALTY)

907. SKULL RECTORY, Skull; pre-1842; *demolished.*
A lodge doubtless built during the incumbency here of a Traill, both the Revd Anthony (1755–1841) and his son Robert (1793–1847) being rectors here before the latter's death from Famine Fever.
LGI (1904).

908. SMITHGROVE TERRACE, Cork [N]; pre-1841; *demolished.*
A terrace of seven houses, the landlord of which in 1852 was James Smith, whose gatekeeper was then Pat Killen.
Griffith 1853–63.

909. SMITHVILLE, Castletownshend; *c.* 1840.
A seat in 1837 of Thomas Townsend, whose lodge stands as a single-storey standard cottage, hip-roofed, like its back return, with chunky chimney-stacks, suffering the indignity of a nasty lean-to hall projection and modern windows. Occupied.
Lewis 1837.

910. SNUGBOROUGH, Cork [S]; pre-1841; *demolished.*
The cosy-sounding seat in 1837 of T. Nelson Esq., probably the proprietor of the adjacent nursery garden.
Lewis 1837.

911. SNUGMORE, Kinsale; pre-1841; *demolished.*
An estate in 1814 of Achilles Daunt, which by 1837 was the residence of Charles Newenham.
Leet 1814; Lewis 1837.

912. SOUTH ABBEY, Youghal; pre-1853/*c.* 1880; architects possibly Robert Walker and Son.

The 1853 valuation reveals that there was an earlier lodge on the site, perhaps on the imprint of the present building, to an establishment described in 1837 by Samuel Lewis: 'At the south entrance of the town a handsome convent for nuns of the Presentation order has been erected, towards the expense of which £2,000 was received from Mrs Gould of Doneraile; attached to it are a small chapel and the female national schools'.

Against the backdrop of the vast sandstone and limestone Romanesque-style convent is its relatively diminutive gatehouse of nevertheless generous proportions and losing little in comparison in a contrasting painted rendered finish; 1½-storey and presenting a bold and decorative Italianate short front to the road, below its hipped gable are round-arched openings with moulded surrounds rising from spring bands, the bipartite attic window having a colonnette dividing one-over-one sashes on a corbelled sill whilst the ground floor is two-bay, including the entrance door. The chamfered corners are repeated on the ashlar gate pillars, tapering from square plinths to octagonal cappings.
Lewis 1837; Griffith 1853–63; NIAH.

913. SPAMOUNT, Millstreet; *c.* 1860.
The earlier house was previously approached from the west, its entrance immediately opposite that to Coomlogane [*q.v.*], the gate lodge to which probably monitored the two gates, both properties having been associated with the McCarthy O'Leary family. Sometime after 1841 a new house was built, with an additional long, straight, lodged avenue created from the south. This is an unpretentious single-storey gabled affair, with a two-window bay to the approach in a whitened rendered finish, a low-gabled hall extending from the avenue front. In 1852 the occupant was Denis O'Connell.
Griffith 1853–63; Hajba 2002.

914. SPIRE VIEW, Glanmire; *c.* 1830.

Alongside the modest gateway on a sloping site is this two-storey split-level structure, the survivor from a terrace of three houses. With a chimney-stack to each gable, its roughcast walls retain cast iron latticed casement windows, a survivor to the road front having a pointed head to one side of a single-storey hip-roofed modern canted extension. A property in 1852 of Edward Phair.
Griffith 1853–63.

915. SPRINGFIELD, Buttevant (2).
East gate; *c.* 1810; *demolished.*

Commandingly forward of its gatescreen and effectively forming a vista stop at a turn in the public road was this nicely proportioned 1½-storey late Georgian hip-gabled standard cottage with high eaves and two-over-two sash windows in harled walls, perfectly symmetrical but for an offset chimney-stack on a roof with skylights to the loft space. The tripartite gateway is flanked by tall rubble quadrant walls with six ashlar pillars, those to the carriage opening emphasised by ball finials. A lodge probably built for Hugh Norcott, the proprietor in 1814. There is now a replacement dwelling on the site.
West gate; *c.* 1810.
Across the county road and at an angle to it

is a single-storey standard rustic lodge with limewashed harled rubble walls below a hipped gable roof, probably once thatched but now in corrugated iron.

Leet 1814.

916. SPRINGFIELD, Killeagh; pre-1842; *demolished.*
A seat in the seventeenth and eighteenth centuries of the Bowles family.

917. SPRINGFORT HALL, Mallow (2).
Principal entrance; pre-1841; *demolished.*
The gate lodge opposite the gates was removed in 1928.
Secondary entrance; *c.* 1835.
Likewise across the road from the gates, this single-storey standard porter's lodge survives, with chimney-stacks to both gables and roughcast walls containing bipartite small-paned casement windows on each side of the sheeted door. Occupied. Probably built by James Foott, resident here in 1837, who seventeen years later sold the charming old bow-fronted villa and its land as an incumbered estate and died in Australia in 1873.

Lewis 1837; *LGI* (1904); Lyons 1993; Hajba 2002.

918. SPRINGFORT, Charleville; pre-1841; *demolished.*
A property in the late eighteenth century of the Cox family, which by 1837 they were leasing to Revd J. Bruce; its gate lodge had been removed by 1890.

Taylor and Skinner 1778; 1783; Lewis 1837; Griffith 1853–63.

919. SPRING GROVE, Kanturk; pre-1841; *demolished.*
The seat in 1814 of Arthur Bastable, which within ten years was occupied by Joseph Coppinger. Its porter's lodge had gone by 1937.

Leet 1814; Pigot 1824.

920. SPRINGMOUNT, Ballincollig; *c.* 1800.
Here are the pitiful remains of a standard single-storey, hip-roofed, rubble-built cottage, now a backdrop for hydrangea, honeysuckle, pyracantha and escallonia. A 35-acre holding in 1837 of Samuel McCarthy.

Lewis 1837.

921. SPRINGMOUNT, Glanmire; pre-1841; *demolished.*
The first OS map of 1841 shows the gatekeeper's lodge isolated from a new avenue approach from the east, and by the end of the century both it and the big house, another seat of the Glanmire Martins, had been removed.

922. SPRINGMOUNT, Mallow; *c.* 1810.
To the road's edge and forward of its gates, gutted and awaiting its fate, are the remains of a 1½-storey standard harled lodge with hipped gables, its loft room lit by a gable window. Presumably built in the time here of A. O'Connor, by 1851 the property being leased to Henry Keating by Anthony O'Connor.

Leet 1814; Griffith 1853–63.

923. SPRINGVILLE, Cork [S]; pre-1841; *demolished.*
A seat in 1852 of one Robert Dagg, the porter's lodge to which was at the end of a long alleyway from the Blackrock Road to the outbuildings at the rear.

Griffith 1853–63.

924. STAND, Fermoy; pre-1841; *demolished.*
An 85-acre farm in 1852 of Owen McCarthy, whose gatekeeper was then Timothy Keeffe. A modern bungalow stands on the gate lodge site.

Griffith 1853–63.

925. STUMP HILL, Castlemartyr; *c.* 1820.
A very basic and derelict single-storey standard harled affair, with mini-skew-table gables and a chimney-stack to each; twentieth-century stylised rendered pediment features applied over openings. The seat in 1814 and ten years later of William O'Boy.

Leet 1814; Pigot 1824.

926. SUBULTER, Kanturk; pre-1841; *demolished.*
Both the gate lodge and its big house, the home in the early nineteenth century of the Leahy family, have gone—the former, single-storey and three-bay, removed around 1970.

Hajba 2002.

927. SUMMERHILL, Cork [N]; *c.* 1820.
A plain two-storey gatehouse, with a symmetrical two-bay upper storey and three-bay ground-floor main front below a hipped roof. Round-arched postilion openings flank the carriage gates. For much of the early nineteenth century a seat of George Newenham; by the turn of the twentieth century 'Honan Home', under the care of the Sisters of Charity.

Leet 1814; Griffith 1853–63; Pike and Hodges 1911.

928. SUMMERHILL, Mallow; pre-1841; *demolished.*
A property in the late eighteenth century of the Stawell family, who by 1824 were letting it to William Lysaght, regaining occupancy before 1846 in the person of Capt. John Robert Stawell (b. 1812).

Pigot 1824; Slater 1846; *LGI* (1904); Hajba 2002.

SUMMERLEA (see ATKINVILLE)

929. SUMMERSTOWN [1], Cork [S]; *c.* 1820.
On the Glasheen Road a flat-roofed single-storey shop obscures the lower storey of what may have been quite a sophisticated building, 1½-storey roughcast and hip-gabled, with a wide pedimented road elevation containing an attic window. The proprietor in 1837 is recorded as J. Swiney Esq., followed by Revd Joseph Jervois (1778–1856).

Lewis 1837; Griffith 1853–63.

930. SUMMERSTOWN [2], Cork [S]; pre-1841; *demolished.*
Off the Togher Road, the entrance to a seat in 1852 of William Bateman, rebuilt before 1890 and more appropriately renamed 'Deanrock' after its townland but subsequently removed, like its porter's lodge.

Griffith 1853–63.

SUMMERVILLE (see KNOCKREA [2])

931. SUN LODGE, Curraglass (2).
East gate; *c.* 1830.
A single-storey standard limewashed and harled hip-roofed gatekeeper's lodge, now derelict and avenueless.
West gate; pre-1841; *demolished.*
Two structures flanked the gate on the first OS map but by 1890 had been reduced to that to the left-hand side. A house said to have been built in the 1830s by Denis Hanan.

Hajba 2002.

SUNMOUNT (see MITCHELSTOWN RECTORY)

932. SUNMOUNT, Clonakilty; *c.* 1830.
A single-storey standard shallow-hip-roofed lodge, modernised with synthetic slates, cement rendering and replacement windows. Opposite the gates to a property in 1814 of William Coates, subsequently by the 1850s home to the Alleyn family.

Leet 1814; Griffith 1853–63.

933. SUNNINGHILL, Inishannon; pre-1842.
Otherwise 'Sunny Hill', occupied in 1824 by the Stawell family, by 1837 it was a residence of the Quinns. Its lodge has been developed into a bungalow.

Pigot 1824; Lewis 1837.

934. SUNNY HILL, Mallow; *c.* 1845; *demolished.*
A lodge probably built by James Delacour (1798–1886) of the Bearforest [*q.v.*] family, who acquired the estate in 1835.

LGI (1958); Hajba 2002.

935. SUNVILLE, Carrigtohill; pre-1841.
A long, low, single-storey gabled cottage, very derelict and shrouded in Virginia creeper. A property in the mid-nineteenth century of Thomas Donovan.

Griffith 1853–63.

936. SUNVILLE, Shanagarry; *c.* 1840.
A plain single-storey rendered lodge, gabled on an L-plan, now lacking entrance gates, avenue and big house, a seat in 1846 of Major Staffard Keane (or Kane).
Slater 1846.

937. TEEVEENY, Dromina (2).
Michael Cagney acquired the estate around 1850, effecting a transformation by improving the old farmhouse, creating an impressive double courtyard of outbuildings and adding a gate lodge on the eastern approach and another opposite the entrance to the western avenue. Neither survives.
Hajba 2002.

938. TELLINGANA, Ballintemple; *c.* 1835.

A lodge much altered, extended and put to commercial use. Originally square on plan, single-storey below a very shallow pyramidal roof with tiny central chimney-stack. The main avenue front is a two-window bay, the openings round-arched with smooth surrounds in pebble-dashed panels framed by rendered 'pilasters', plinth and eaves band. The impressive gatescreen looks to be of two later dates. Chiefly of *c.* 1865 are the four square stone pillars with pedimented cappings, the carriage pair having recessed shouldered round-headed panels, much as those to Beech Hill [*q.v.*] across the river. The chamfered and shouldered-arched postilion opening probably dates from the 1880 house enlargement undertaken by Samuel H. Newson, who had been here from 1875, one of his predecessors having been Samuel Bennett in mid-century.
Griffith 1853–63; Pike and Hodges 1911.

939. TEMPLE HILL, Ballintemple; *c.* 1845; *demolished.*
A lodge erected between the dates of the first OS map of 1841 and the 1852 valuation, when John Simkin, watchmaker in the city, was in residence.
Griffith 1853–63.

940. TEMPLE LAWN, Ballintemple; *c.* 1835.

The single-storey rambling hip-roofed structure manifest today may incorporate the lodge of square plan and central hall projection to the avenue as indicated on the second OS map. Clearly much altered, lacking a chimney-stack and rendered with stylised hood mouldings applied over semicircular-arched openings, some original plain pilasters surviving below the oversailing eaves. Occupied. A property in 1852 of Patrick Michael Kelly, tanner.
Slater 1846; Griffith 1853–63.

941. TEMPLENOE, Fermoy; pre-1841; *demolished.*
The seat in 1837 of William Lane Hyde, descended from that family of Cregg Castle [*q.v.*], whose porter's lodge lay opposite its gates.
Lewis 1837.

942. TEMPLEVILLE, Ballintemple; pre-1841; *demolished.*
A property in 1837 of the Murphy family; subsequently renamed 'Lavanagh'.
Lewis 1837.

943. TERRAMOUNT, Rathcormack; pre-1841; *demolished.*
John George Nason is recorded as proprietor here in 1851, living on until 1901.
Griffith 1853–63; Hajba 2002.

944. THORNBURY, Rochestown; *c.* 1830.

A single-storey two-bay hip-roofed lodge, with basic label mouldings to wide openings with new plastic windows and a recess to the left-hand corner to form the entrance porch. Occupied. The gatescreen is comprised of roughcast ogee quadrant walls and four good castellated-capped pillars with lancet recesses—an appropriate prelude to the delightful Tudor Gothic villa, home in 1814 and 1837 to Thomas Townsend.
Leet 1814; Lewis 1837.

945. THORNHILL, Cork [S]; *c.* 1850; *demolished.*
A property in 1853 of Thomas Fitzgerald, probable builder of the gate lodge on the Boreenmanagh Road and the replacement house to the south.
Griffith 1853–63.

946. THORNHILL, Curraglass; *c.* 1820.
A single-storey roughly harled hip-roofed lodge with a short main front to the avenue. Much modernised and extended to one side. An estate in the early nineteenth century of the Nason family.
Hajba 2002.

947. TIMOLEAGUE, Timoleague; pre-1841; *demolished.*
The seat in 1837 of Col. Robert Travers (d. 1840), the gate lodge to which had been removed by 1902.
Lewis 1837; *IFR*.

948. TIMOLEAGUE RECTORY, Timoleague; pre-1841; *demolished.*
The porter's lodge, gone by 1902, may have been contemporary with its glebe house, 'a neat villa residence ... erected by aid of a gift of £100 and a loan of £900, in 1816' by the Revd Johnson.
Townsend 1815; Lewis 1837.

949. TIVOLI, Cork [N]; pre-1841; *demolished.*
An important Palladian-style mansion and its fine park adorned with fanciful temples are, along with the gatekeeper's lodge, things of the past. Created in the mid-eighteenth century by James Morrison, merchant and mayor of the city, passing by marriage to the Morgan family.
ffolliott 1958; Bence-Jones 1988.

950. TOUREEN LODGE, Carrigtohill; pre-1841/*c.* 1860.
Until his death in 1853 this was the property of Revd Robert Bury of the neighbouring Little Island [*q.v.*] family, following which it was acquired by Capt. Richard Pigott Beamish (1832–99), who renamed the place 'Ashbourne' and replaced the old porter's lodge opposite the entrance with the present structure. Single-storey on a square plan below a pyramidal roof, it displays a window and door as the main two-bay façade to the road, the openings with later banded surrounds framed by earlier pilaster features. Now a hotel.
Griffith 1853–63; *LGI* (1904).

TOWER HILL (see MOUNT PATRICK COTTAGE)

951. TOWERMORE, Fermoy (2).
A late eighteenth-century house built by a Capt. Oliver, the residence in 1837 of A. Morris Oliver. Both its lodges, in place by 1841, have been demolished.
Lewis 1837; Hajba 2002.

952. TOWERVILLE, Blackrock; *c.* 1845.
Previously 'Midsummer Lodge' and part of the Castle Mahon [*q.v.*] property, in 1837 home to Miss Jones, it was by 1852 the residence of Henry Westropp. Looking to be of earlier origin is this tiny early Victorian single-storey cottage, roughcast below a steeply hipped roof with a main two-window-bay front. Occupied.
Lewis 1837; Griffith 1853–63.

953. TRABOLGAN, Whitegate (7).
The once-proud estate of the Roche family, earls of Fermoy, is now missing most of its architectural treasures, including the mansion, and retains but two of its many porters' lodges. All seven were in position in 1842, one on the eastern avenue and three each over the length of the two northern

953. Whitegate inner entrance.

approaches, one of which had been abandoned by 1890 and its lodges demolished.

Whitegate outer entrance; pre-1842/*c.* 1860.

What remains is a commodious and well-maintained replacement for an earlier lodge on the site. Probably built by Edmund Burke Roche (1815–74) after succeeding to the property on his father's death in 1855 and his creation as 1st Baron Fermoy the following year. It is a 1½-storey gabled structure on an L-plan, with a single-storey lean-to porch in the internal angle and a later similarly roofed glazed projection to the road elevation. Smooth-rendered and having a hint of the Italianate Picturesque with a wide segmentally arched window to the avenue, sashed like the rest.

Whitegate inner entrance; *c.* 1825; architect Claude-Nicolas Ledoux.

Far along the mile-long avenue as the third and final stage of a build-up to the big house is this startling and forbidding Classical triumphal archway, its piers sufficiently massive to have contained the gatekeeper in two-storey accommodation on each side of the great carriage archway. Semicircular, it springs from a bold string-course emphasised by rusticated quoins, which continue as voussoirs to meet in a keystone that breaks the frieze of the entablature with its triglyphs, guttae and mutules. Probably built by Edward Roche (1771–1855), who succeeded in 1823, one can only speculate as to why this is an exact copy of the grand archway to Hotel Thelusson near Paris by the inventive French architect Claude-Nicolas Ledoux; perhaps he spent his honeymoon there in 1805.

BPB (1929); Bence-Jones 1988; Humphreys 1979; Wikipedia.

954. TRACTON COTTAGE, Tracton; *c.* 1820.

A single-storey roughcast gabled cottage of three bays, with a lean-to hall projection to the right-hand side. Occupied. A small five-acre demesne in 1851 of Richard Hungerford.

Griffith 1853–63.

TRACTON PARK (see BALLINAMOTE)

955. TRAFALGAR HILL, Cork [N]; pre-1841; *demolished.*

So called no earlier than 1805, a modest property listed as vacant in 1852, its lessor having been William John.

Griffith 1853–63.

956. TRAFALGAR, Cork [N]; pre-1841; *demolished.*

A property in 1837 of James and Thomas Lyons, proprietors of the Glanmire Woollen Factory.

Lewis 1837.

957. TRAMORE, Douglas (2).

The 23-acre demesne in 1837 of Thomas Somerville Reeves (1781–1863). Both the front lodge, in position by 1841, and that to the rear built thereafter have been demolished.

Lewis 1837.

958. TRANTSTOWN, Watergrasshill; pre-1841; *demolished.*

A gate lodge modestly rated in 1853 at eight shillings was then occupied by John Curtain, gate porter to John Daly, who had been preceded here as proprietor by a Mrs Pepper.

Lewis 1837; Griffith 1853–63.

959. TULLAGH CHURCH (C of I), Baltimore; *c.* 1820.

A charming whitewashed single-storey gabled cottage outside the churchyard gate, its two-bay door and window elevation fronting the road. In use and maintained. Possibly contemporary with the building of St Matthew's in 1818.

Lewis 1837.

960. TULLAGH RECTORY, Baltimore; *c.* 1820.

'The Glebe-house was built about 1818, when £100 was given and £825 lent by the late Board of First Fruits', sums which may also have gone some way towards funding its single-storey porter's lodge, which presents two windows to the road and a hipped gable to the avenue. Subsequently much extended to two sides and the roofspace converted.

Lewis 1837.

961. TULLAGREEN, Carrigtohill (2).
North gate; pre-1841; *demolished.*

961. Tullagreen, Carrigtohill, south gate.

Originally the main approach to the house, in 1824 of Robert Martin and thirteen years later of Hughes Martin.

South gate; *c.* 1870.

In 1876 another Robert Martin was in residence, probably the builder of this very pleasant Picturesque 1½-storey gabled lodge in random rubble facings, with some brick arched highlights to a rare variety of flat, segmental, semicircular and pointed heads to openings. Gables to the two-bay main front, like the main gables, rising to turned hip-knobs, which stop a ridge decorated with what remains of fleur-de-lis cresting. The rubble limestone and red sandstone mix is repeated in the simple gatescreen.

Pigot 1824; Lewis 1837; *LOI.*

962. TULLIG, Ballinhassig; *c.* 1830.

A property in 1837 and 1850 of Daniel Keller. At the entrance is a ruinous single-storey standard gabled gatekeeper's lodge in rubble construction with brick label mouldings to openings, its main front to the road, forward of the gates.

Lewis 1837; Griffith 1853–63.

963. TULLIG, Buttevant; *c.* 1840.

The seat in 1840 and 1851 of Richard Hutch, whose lodge lies abandoned and derelict as a modest solid single-storey standard structure raised in rubble facings, with minimal skew-tables and chimney-stacks to each of its gables. Tiny two-over-two sash windows flank half-doors below eaves sufficiently high to accommodate lofts.

Griffith 1853–63; Hajba 2002.

TURRET FARM (see ROCK LODGE)

964. TULLYLEASE, Dromcolliher; *c.* 1845.

In ruins is this single-storey standard lodge in good rubble facings, now minus its oversailing hipped roof over a central elliptically arched fanlit doorway. Nearby are four slender stone entrance pillars with four-sided pedimented cappings containing a triple gateway. An estate in 1837 of J.J. Sullivan, who by 1852 had been succeeded by William Sullivan.

Lewis 1837; Griffith 1853–63.

965. UMMETA, Timoleague; pre-1841; *demolished.*

In 1837 'a beautiful house on the banks of the river' of the Revd Benjamin Swete, prebendary of Kilbrittain, 23 years previously having been home to Revd A. Sealy.

Leet 1814; Lewis 1837.

966. UNDERHILL COTTAGE, Dunmanway; *c.* 1825.

Here are the pitiful remnants of a once very fine single-storey hip-roofed porter's lodge, three-bay, the central of which is a bow-fronted projecting room with a panelled double-leafed door flanked by four-over-four sash windows. Below many layers of limewash is the original stucco finish. The ridges meet at the chimney-stack, from which rises a pair of diagonally set brick flues; to one side is a rustic lean-to shed. A seat in 1837 of Benjamin Hayes Holmes, by 1853 letting it to the Hazle family.

Lewis 1837; Griffith 1853–63.

967. UNION LODGE, Carrigtohill; pre-1841; *demolished.*

A property, in 1837 of Revd W. Gifford, latterly renamed 'Carhuegarriffe'.

Lewis 1837.

UNIVERSITY COLLEGE CORK (see QUEEN'S COLLEGE)

968. UPLAND, Bandon; pre-1841; *demolished.*

An estate in the mid-nineteenth century of William Anthony Spiller.

Slater 1846; 1856.

969. UPLAND, Fermoy; pre-1841; *demolished.*

In 1837 the residence of Samuel Perrott and his son Thomas.

Lewis 1837.

970. UPPER FOREST, Coachford; pre-1842; *demolished.*

A seat in 1837 of Thomas Gollock, which fifteen years later he was leasing to John Hassett. A chalet bungalow occupies the site of its gate lodge.

Lewis 1837; Griffith 1853–63.

971. UPTON, Inishannon (2).

The residence until *c.* 1836 of Revd William Lewis Beaufort, rector of Brinny [*q.v.*], when that parish was without a glebe house. He was followed here by his fellow cleric Revd Somers Payne (1785–1857), who would seem to have been responsible for both surviving gate lodges.

North entrance; *c.* 1835; architect not known.

Alongside its gatescreen is a striking lodge, its single-storey short front displaying, in attractive rubble stone facings below a steeply hipped roof, a tripartite window comprised of a central round-headed spoked sash window flanked by similarly arched slit lights. Much improved and extended in

unobtrusive fashion; to the avenue a pair of spoked sash windows with round heads sit beside a hip-roofed projecting hall with modern double-leafed doorway below a segmental arch. The distinctive gateway has a twin at Rye Court [*q.v.*], with its drum pillars having part-fluted shafts and four-faced semicircular pedimented cappings, their tympana having exquisitely carved anthemions. Decorative cast-iron carriage gates and matching railings.

South entrance; *c.* 1835.

What first appears to the main approach as a single-storey standard hip-roofed lodge in a pleasant ragstone finish is revealed on closer inspection to be a two-storey gatehouse with an area to sides and front over which bridged steps approach the central projecting bowed hall with equivalent roof over round-arched doorway and like-headed sidelights. To each side are bipartite casement windows with lead-effect glazing reflecting their cast-iron latticed predecessors. Apart from these and the synthetic slated roof, admirably restored and maintained.

Leet 1814; Pigot 1824; Lewis 1837.

972. URSULINE CONVENT, Blackrock; pre-1841; *demolished.*

'An Ursuline convent was removed hither from Cork in 1825; it was founded in 1771, by the late Miss Honora Nagle ... and is the original of all the institutions of this class founded in Ireland. The community consists of 35 professed nuns and 6 lay sisters, and is governed by a superioress, her deputy, and a council of six. At this institution many of the daughters of the R.C. gentry are instructed.' Samuel Lewis goes on to describe the many buildings that pertained in 1837, failing to notice the porter's lodge, which no doubt was in place by *c.* 1830. Surviving is a contemporary gatescreen comprised of six square stone pillars with ball finials containing two postilion openings, scroll-topped gate stops and a cast-iron overthrow.

Lewis 1837.

URSULINE CONVENT, Cork [N] (see RICHMOND)

973. VELVETSTOWN, Doneraile; *c.* 1810.
There is little velvety about what has been visited upon this once-square hip-roofed single-storey structure, now with a hideous flat-roofed extension to the avenue and another on its road front. Now roughcast with concrete roll-tiled roof finish. Occupied. The probable builder, Thomas Lucas Crofts (1790–1851), who succeeded to the estate on the death of his father in 1811, would not be impressed.

LGI (1904).

974. VERNON MOUNT, Douglas; pre-1842; *demolished.*
When, despite its uniqueness, the late eighteenth-century villa built for sheriff, abductor and transportee Sir Henry Browne Hayes (1762–1832) remains under threat of destruction, its long avenue and porter's lodge stood little chance and have succumbed to suburban sprawl. The latter, square of plan, briefly became 'The Villa' in its own right.

ffolliott 1971a.

THE VICARAGE (see BANTRY RECTORY)

975. VICTORIA LODGE, Cork [S]; pre-1841; *demolished.*
The previous modest property was replaced by a sizeable villa around the turn of the century for John Haycroft, proprietor of a nursery garden on the site, its lodge by the roadside.

Slater 1846; Griffith 1853–63.

976. VILLA FRANCA, Cork [S]; *c.* 1860.
An unprepossessing 1½-storey gabled lodge, lying derelict. Nearby are four large entrance pillars with large corniced cappings and incised rendered shafts. A property in 1852 of James Wright, probably the builder of the first house on the site.

Griffith 1853–63.

977. VILLA NOVA, Cork [S]; *c.* 1810.
A plain single-storey, standard, roughcast, hip-roofed structure, modernised with plastic windows and a central flat-roofed hall projection. Concave entrance quadrant walls in limestone rubble containing brick-dressed pointed-arched postilion openings (now blocked up). A seat in 1837 of J. Lombard Esq.

Lewis 1837.

978. VOSTERBERG, Cork [N]; *c.* 1825.
A park that almost perpetuates the name of its Dutch creator, Daniel Vorster, which around 1750 contained 'a neat garden and improvement with canals, fountains, statues and a pretty house', to which a future owner, William Leycester (1747–1834), added the present entrance and porter's lodge. Located forward of its gates and commanding the forecourt is this dapper standard single-storey hip-roofed structure, notable for its missing chimney-stack but with a conspicuous wide pedimented entrance breakfront. Much modernised with a smooth rendering and some later applied opening surrounds to a sheeted door and latticed casement windows. The Classical tripartite gateway is comprised of four fine contemporary square ashlar pillars with moulded plinths, friezed and corniced cappings and scroll-topped gate stops, all framed by railed and walled quadrants.

Smith 1893; *LG* (1952); Bence-Jones 1988.

WALLINGSTOWN (see LITTLE ISLAND)

979. WALTON COURT, Belgooly; *c.* 1810.
With its front elevation to the road's edge is this basic single-storey standard gabled lodge in harled rubble construction with tiny four-paned casement windows. Derelict and the survivor of a pair of lodges, its companion lost like the big house, the residence in 1814 of Thomas Walton.

Leet 1814.

980. WARREN'S COURT, Crookstown; *c.* 1800.
Set 50m distant from its gates is a single-storey standard rendered lodge of square plan below a pyramidal roof. Of an age is the fine gatescreen, its carriage pillars crowned with Greek key-patterned ball finials and secondary pillars carved with chinoiserie panels and fluting; outer pillars with simple ball finials. All probably for Sir Robert Warren (1723–1811), created 1st baronet in 1784, whose 'handsome house' is no more.

Luckcombe 1780; *BPB* (1929).

981. WARREN'S COURT, Crookstown (2).
The secondary seat of the Warrens, occupied in 1837 by John Borlase Warren (1800–63), who very briefly succeeded his brother as 4th baronet at Warren's Court [*q.v.*]. Both porters' lodges built before 1841 have been demolished.

Leet 1814; *BPB* (1929).

982. WATERFALL, Ballincollig; pre-1841.
A lodge, now developed into a bungalow, probably originating from the time of Thomas Austin, recorded here in 1814 and 1837.

Leet 1814; Lewis 1837.

983. WATERLOO, Lombardstown; *c.* 1815; architect not known.
A momentous year for Henry Longfield (d. 1851) was 1815, with the death of his father, John Longfield of Longueville [*q.v.*], the birth of his first son and Wellington's famous victory demanding an obvious name for his elegant newly built Classical villa. And what more appropriate at his gate than an

introduction of military moment, an eye-catching two-storey gatehouse in the form of a tower, perfectly circular, with a conical roof concealed behind a castellated and mock machicolated parapet. The defensive pretence ceases in its big decorative hood-moulded pointed-head Gothic windows and like-arched moulded surround doorway in roughcast finish. With its later single-storey back return nicely restored, though unfortunately having lost the original latticed glazing bars in the process.

IFR; Bence-Jones 1988; Humphreys 1979.

984. WATERLOO PLACE AND TERRACE, Cork [N]; *c.* 1820; *demolished.*
A lodge leased in 1852 by Thomas Gibson from Capt. Stephen S. Mowle shortly before its replacement to make way for the Charlemont Terrace [*q.v.*] development.

Slater 1846; Griffith 1853–63.

985. WATERVIEW, Fermoy (2).
The riverside property in 1851 of Boyle Meredith. Both lodges were erected by 1841; that to the outer gate seems to have been originally a cottage subsequently employed to house a gatekeeper when the place was purchased by Revd Richard Freeman, who renamed it 'Clifton'. Both lodges have been demolished.

Griffith 1853–63; Slater 1856.

986. WATER VIEW, Passage West; pre-1841; *demolished.*
A seat in 1814 of Richard Neville Parker (1774–1832), who was succeeded here by his son of the same name.

Leet 1814; *LGI* (1904).

987. WEBB VILLE, Ballintemple; *c.* 1835.
The residence in 1837 of Revd C. Tutthill, at whose gate survives the commodious gatekeeper's lodge. Two-storey rendered with a two-over-two sash window bay to the

avenue, it presents a short canted front to the road below an equivalent roof, which is otherwise hipped. Occupied.

Lewis 1837.

988. WESTBORO, Cork [N]; *c.* 1880.

This virgin site was developed around 1870 for John W. Clery, who somewhat later added a porter's lodge to complement his new house. This is a charming single-storey standard cottage in subtle polychromatic brickwork, brown with cream highlights of the corbelled soffit and alternate voussoirs to segmentally arched windows and round-headed doorway. The bays are emphasised by plain pilasters below the oversailing hipped roof, from the ridge of which rises a slender chimney-stack having rectangular recessed panels with bold plinth and capping. Occupied.

Slater 1870.

989. WESTFIELD, Ballydehob; *c.* 1830.
In a bland cement rendering is this nondescript and derelict single-storey standard lodge with clipped eaves to its hipped roof. A property in 1853 of Revd John Coppinger, leasing from Margaret Long.

Griffith 1853–63.

990. WEST GROVE, Donnybrook; pre-1842; *demolished.*
The residence in 1837 of Mrs Susanna Baylie.

Lewis 1837.

WEST HILL (see ROSANNA)

991. WESTLANDS, Cobh; 1867; *demolished.*
A mid-Victorian development of house and adjacent workshop and docks for Joseph Wheeler. Now the Norwegian Consulate in docklands.

Slater 1870.

992. WESTPARK, Midleton; *c.* 1830.
The ruins of a once-fine porter's lodge, set well back from and opposite its gates. Hip-roofed with an oversailing soffit, single-storey and cruciform on plan with a projecting gabled hall, its openings segmentally arched of brick in stone walling. In contrast, a rather grand short front addresses the road, with a tall semicircular-arched window set off by ornamental brick pilasters and relieving arch accommodated by a gablet breaking the eaves. Also known

IAA

as 'Killeagh Farm', in 1824 the estate of William Welland.

Pigot 1824; IAA photograph (S/681/4).

993. WESTWOOD COTTAGE, Mallow; *c.* 1830.
A derelict single-storey standard hip-roofed lodge, with ornamental fascia boards over wide window openings flanking a low, sheeted doorway in roughly harled walls. Built for McCarthy Flynn, who is recorded as resident here in 1826 and 1840.

Hajba 2002.

994. WHITE CASTLE, Cork [S] (2).
A property acquired, with a single lodged access, from John O'Brien around 1855 and put to use as Lapp's Asylum, the trustees providing an additional lodge and avenue across a new bridge spanning the River Lee to Western Road.

College Road gate; pre-1841; *demolished.*
Originally the sole access to a nine-acre site in 1837 of J. Cope Esq.

Western Road gate; *c.* 1855.
What appears to have been a single-storey hip-roofed lodge with doorway to the left-hand side now extending to five-bay symmetrical in a smooth rendered finish, with modern squared plastic casements below basic hood mouldings, over which are synthetic slates and plastic gutters, fascias and soffits. Occupied and absorbed into the greater UCC complex. Good semicircular entrance with four pillars having recessed panels framing concave railings with fleur-de-lis and palmette finials.

Lewis 1837.

995. WHITEGATE, Whitegate; pre-1841; *demolished.*
A twentieth-century bungalow now occupies the gate lodge site at the entrance to the home, from her husband's death in 1832, of Mrs Gertrude Blakeney Fitzgerald, who was still in residence in 1853.

Griffith 1853–63; *IFR.*

996. WHITE HALL, Baltimore; *c.* 1825.
Opposite the gates is a very dilapidated tiny, standard, single-storey, rubble-built lodge with narrow windows below the high eaves of a steeply pitched gabled roof. Here displayed is a heraldic shield with the crest of a stag *trippant* of the Townsends, of whom Samuel Townsend (1768–1836) extended the house in 1816 as part of improvements which may have included the addition of the lodge, a process which is said to have

plunged the family into debt but they remained here until 1879.

LGI (1904); Somerville-Large 1995.

997. WHITE POINT, Cobh (2).

South entrance; *c.* 1820.
A 1½-storey gatekeeper's lodge with a little lancet light to the upper entrance gable, while seawards is a façade of two openings, one a tiny square original, the other a big new picture window. Probably built for the proprietor in 1824, Henry H. O'Brien.

North entrance; 1882; *demolished.*
A short-lived lodge built during the residency of William Raymond, leasing from the Rushbrooke family.

Pigot 1824.

998. WILLMOUNT, Cobh; *c.* 1845.
At the entrance to the seat in the mid-nineteenth century of William Deane Seymour remains a derelict single-storey standard lodge, its hipped roof with a hexagonal chimney-stack on a rectangular base.

Griffith 1853–63.

999. WILLOW BROOK, Millstreet; pre-1842; *demolished.*
Opposite the entrance was a porter's lodge, gone by 1900, to a property of the Leaders of neighbouring Mount Leader [*q.v.*] that passed to John Herbert Orpen MD (1805–62) through his marriage in 1834 to his cousin Margaret Leader.

LGI (1904); Hajba 2002.

1000. WILTON, Cork [S] (2).
Both lost lodges existed in the time of Charles H. Leslie, who is recorded here in 1814 and 1837. By 1900 the property was home to St Joseph's College.

Leet 1814; Lewis 1837.

1001. WILTON, Mallow; pre-1841; *demolished.*
An elegant late Georgian villa, in 1846 of Joseph McMullen, proprietor of the adjacent Quartertown flour mills—like the

contemporary square porter's lodge, probably built by the Molloy family.

Lewis 1837; Slater 1846; Griffith 1853–63.

1002. WINDFORD, Youghal; pre-1842; *demolished.*
A seat in 1814 of John Hudson.

Leet 1814.

1003. WINDMILL HILL, Churchtown; *c.* 1850.
A derelict 1½-storey gabled cottage in harled rubble construction to another property in 1851 of Sir Edward Tierney, beneficiary of the will of the 5th earl of Egmont.

Griffith 1853–63.

1004. WINDSOR, Carrigtohill; pre-1900; *demolished.*
Both the house and its lodge, built after 1841, have gone. A holding in 1853 of Joseph Martin.

Griffith 1853–63.

1005. WINDSOR, Douglas; pre-1841; *demolished.*
A mansion of the Bernard family, earls of Bandon, which they were leasing in 1814 to Dominick Sarsfield and by 1837 to George Cooke.

Leet 1814; Lewis 1837; Bence-Jones 1988.

1006. WOOD COTTAGE, Ballyhooly; pre-1890; *demolished.*
A porter's lodge erected after 1841 probably by George Wallace at the gates to his cosy cottage residence, which was extended around 1860.

Griffith 1853–63.

1007. WOODBROOK, Dunmanway; *c.* 1845; *demolished.*
A lodge built after the 1842 Ordnance Survey and before the valuation a decade later in the time here of Herbert Gillman, prior to which he seems to have been at Bennett's Grove [*q.v.*].

Lewis 1837; Griffith 1853–63.

1008. WOODFORT, Bandon (2).
Both lodges, in existence before 1842 within a stone's throw of one another, have been demolished; that to the north was a shell by 1900. A property in 1853 of John Ottley.

Griffith 1853–63.

1009. WOODFORT, Glanworth; pre-1841; *demolished.*
A seat throughout the nineteenth century of the Massy family, the lodge to which had deteriorated to a shell by 1935, its avenue now abandoned.

1010. WOODFORT, Mallow; pre-1841; *demolished.*
A handsome Classical mansion, much altered and let down the centuries but taken on a longer lease by the Ware family in the mid-nineteenth century. Now serving as St Patrick's Hospital.

Lewis 1837; Hajba 2002.

1011. WOODHILL, Cork [N]; pre-1841/*c.* 1845; architect not known.

Apparent from the first OS map is that this extraordinary exclamation mark by the entrance had a simple square-plan predecessor on the site and that it is a caprice of Cooper Penrose (1796–1862) upon succeeding to the demesne on the death of his father James in 1845. A two-storey gatehouse built off an octagonal plan below an octahedral roof half-concealed behind coved parapets of breakfronts to alternate faces, each of which is single-bay with large Y-traceried pointed-arched Gothic windows. The doorway, flanked by dwarf crocketed finials, has a segmental pointed fanlight below naive embossed scroll decoration. In 2000 it lay derelict, its windows sealed, the whole roughcast, awaiting restoration, forward of its earlier sober gatescreen of Classical limestone pillars.

IFR.

1012. WOODLANDS, Cork [N]; pre-1841/*c.* 1900; architect not known.

A smart single-storey Edwardian porter's lodge below a hipped roof, its rendered walls highlighted with striking polychromatic brick as vertical bands defining the two-bay roadside front and as dressings to the round-arched two-over-two sash windows. A plain eaves band with exposed rafter toes embraces the entrance elevation with its sumptuous arcaded semi-octagonal porch of semicircular arches and Roman Doric engaged columns; within, a like-arched fanlit door with slit sidelights. Banded and corbelled brick chimney-stack. Built on the site of a predecessor when the property was 'Woodland', in 1852 of William Johnston. The replacement was probably created for Capt. Loftus Percival Fitzgerald-Arnott (b. 1873) when he succeeded to the property on the death of his father, Sir John Arnott, in 1898.

Griffith 1853–63; *BPB* (1929).

1013. WOODLANDS, Dunmanway; *c.* 1850; *demolished.*
A mid-nineteenth-century development of house and lodge on twenty acres for William Wright.

Griffith 1853–63.

1014. WOODLANDS, Inishannon (2).
The seat of George Cornwall in 1837, when there was but a single lodged gate.

West entrance; *c.* 1830.
A very basic single-storey standard hip-roofed gate lodge in exposed rubble but with nasty modern windows. Occupied.

Around 1840 the demesne was acquired by Capt. William Henry Herrick RN (1784–1863) of Shippool [*q.v.*], who added another porter's lodge.

East entrance; *c.* 1845.

1015. Woodlawn, Cork [N].

A delightful little single-storey lodge—a perfect octagon with octahedral roof but tiny square chimney-stack. In a coursed facing stone containing pointed-arched Gothic openings with highly decorative cast-iron Y-traceried, 'teardrop', latticed glazing identical to those at Heathburn Hall [*q.v.*]. Well maintained in a cloak of Virginia creeper. There are complementary octagonal gate pillars.

Lewis 1837; Slater 1846; *LGI* (1904).

1015. WOODLAWN, Cork [N]; *c.* 1840.
Fronting the Sunday's Well Road footpath is an unusual single-storey three-bay lodge, a central narrow window flanked by bipartite lights, all one-over-one sashes with round head within flat-arched openings in a smooth rendering; chimney-stacks rise off each hipped end. Alongside is a tripartite gateway, its six pillars and concave quadrants conspicuous for their V-jointed channel rustication. The three-acre property in 1852 of Thomas J. Vallant.

Griffith 1853–63.

1016. WOODPARK, Lombardstown; *c.* 1850.
Here are the sad, overgrown remains of an innovatively designed single-storey lodge below a hipped roof in a harled finish, but its single-bay avenue front is of cut stone, its sophisticated door-case having unusual label-moulded detailing with corbelled 'dripstones'; the longer park and road elevations are two-bay of bipartite casements. The entrance façade is reputed to have been assembled with salvaged masonry from a dismantled church, probably for James Carmichael, proprietor in the mid-nineteenth century.

O'Flanagan 1975; Slater 1856; Hajba 2002.

1017. WOODSIDE, Carrigrohane; *c.* 1830.
A plain single-storey structure, a short gable end addressing the avenue; modern window inserts, but now derelict. Good cast-iron gate posts with 'morgenstern' finials, as there are to all rails on the ogee quadrants. A seat in the early nineteenth century of the Carleton family, by 1852 having been acquired by Horace Townsend, whose gatekeeper was then Jeremiah Corcoran. The property was later renamed 'Kilcrenagh'.

Leet 1814; Lewis 1837; Griffith 1853–63.

1018. WOODSIDE, Knockraha; 1861; *demolished.*
The house and lodge erected for Charles Cleary, the latter with a central projecting hall to the avenue and a back return, creating an L-plan. A ruin by 1934.

1019. WOODVIEW COTTAGE, Cork [N]; pre-1841; *demolished.*
A seat in 1814 of Thomas Cuthbert, which 23 years later had been acquired by Daniel Hamblin.

Leet 1814; Lewis 1837.

1020. WOODVIEW, Cloyne; *c.* 1840.
Derelict and now with its rubble fabric exposed is this 1½-storey gabled lodge with a three-window-bay elevation to the avenue, loft window to the park and a lower gabled porch with Tudor archway extending towards the road. An estate in 1824 of John Lawless and thirteen years later of Revd J.P. Lawless, rector of Inch.

Pigot 1824; Lewis 1837.

1021. WOODVIEW, Crosshaven; *c.* 1800.
The ruins of a gabled single-storey Georgian Gothic lodge, with two pointed-arched openings still discernible in harled rubble walls. Opposite the entrance to a seat in 1824 of Francis Sealy.

Pigot 1824.

1022. WOODVIEW, Glanmire; pre-1841; *demolished.*
A seat in 1837 of Jeremiah Crimmin.

Lewis 1837.

1023. WOODVIEW, Inishcarra; *c.* 1840.
A standard 1½-storey cottage with a chimney-stack to each main gable and two-over-two sash windows in limewashed harled walls on either side of a hall breakfront, its hipped roof below the main eaves. A property occupied in 1852 by Revd William Spedding.

Griffith 1853–63.

1024. WOODVIEW, Kilworth; *c.* 1820.

Set low to the road and partly hidden by the right-hand convex quadrant is an extraordinary structure like a castellated handball court, its three-bay façade to the avenue rising to a monopitched crenellated parapet. The flat-arched doorway is flanked by Gothic lancet windows in a rough harled finish. Derelict. There is a similar structure at the gate to Carrig Park [*q.v.*]. A seat of the earl of Mountcashel, occupied in 1837 by Lt. F. Prangnall RN.

Lewis 1837; Griffith 1853–63; Hajba 2002.

1025. WOODVIEW, Kinsale; pre-1841; *demolished.*
The residence in 1852 of Edward Daly, which by 1890 had been outlasted by its porter's lodge.

Griffith 1853–63.

1026. WOODVIEW, Newmarket; pre-1842; *demolished.*
Home in 1814 and 1837 to Jeremiah McCartie; it now lies in ruins.

Leet 1814; Lewis 1837.

1027. WOODVILLE, Ballyhooly; pre-1841/pre-1890; *demolished.*
The lodge lies an ivy- and elder-smothered ruin; like its big house, it seems to have been a replacement for an earlier structure on the site. An estate in 1814 of Revd William Berkley, which by 1837 was home to a 'Mrs Gibbons'—probably Anna Maria, widow of Bartholomew Gibbings of Gibbings Grove [*q.v.*], whose fourth son, Robert Edward Gibbings, succeeded her here. The 1860s redevelopment of the property was carried out by Dr William Starkey.

Leet 1814; Lewis 1837; Slater 1856; *LGI* (1904); Hajba 2002.

1028. WOODVILLE HOUSE AND CORN MILLS, Rochestown; *c.* 1880.
Now a polychromatic shell of orange and cream brickwork is this three-bay, two-storey standard gatehouse, its main ground-floor elevation with segmental arches springing from a string-course. Above are three blind recesses to correspond with the lower

openings, all in contrasting brick dressings. A big brick chimney-stack on a hefty plinth crowns the hipped roof. An establishment in 1870 of Arthur P. Harty, having earlier being a concern of the Powells.

Slater 1870.

1029. WOODVILLE, Glanmire; *c.* 1835.
By the roadside, well forward of its gates, is a rendered two-storey gabled gatehouse with fretted bargeboards, its main front having a two-bay lower storey and one over; doorway to the side elevation. Occupied. The seat of Nicholas Cummings (b. 1754) of Tivoli [*q.v.*] until his death in 1831, when it became home to his son, Nicholas Marshall Cummings (1783–1838).

IFR; Bence-Jones 1988.

1030. YOUNG GROVE, Midleton (2).
The Foulke family resided here in the first half of the nineteenth century; their lodges existed in 1841 but have both since been demolished, that to the northern gate being survived by a short avenue of antique beeches.

Leet 1814; Lewis 1837.

COUNTY KERRY

1. ABBEYLANDS, Ardfert; *c.* 1870.
A house built in 1870 for George Frederick Trench (1841–1915), agent and son-in-law of William Talbot-Crosbie of neighbouring Ardfert Abbey [*q.v.*]. Burnt in 1922, it has been reinvented as a retreat centre. At the gate is a simple rectangular, single-storey, hip-roofed rendered cottage with banded stone chimney-stack, a short two-bay elevation as principal front; alongside the doorway is a window with arrowhead arch.

BPB (1929); Bary 1994; O'Connor 1999.

2. AGHADOE, Killarney; *c.* 1835; architect probably William Atkins.

In materials and style the lodge is a suitable introduction to its house, precocious and looking more mid-Victorian. Both were designed for Charles Allanson Winn, 2nd Baron Headley, and were nearing completion in 1835 to designs by the equally precocious William Atkins (1812–87). Lewis in 1837 reveals that 'the approach is by a small but elegant bridge across a ravine, leading from the entrance gate and lodge, which are both in a corresponding style of architecture', and that the stone was taken from a quarry at Barleymount, Aglish. Sixteen years later Lacy was equally impressed: 'The entrance is commodious, the gate light and handsome, and the gate-lodge a very neat cottage with a pentagonal roof'.

An imaginative design in ashlar, it confronts the visitor, thrusting forward of its gates with a flat-roofed porch projecting from the octagonal front room. Single-storey and two-roomed with round-headed openings, it is capped by a hipped roof, atop which is a dominant chimney-stack with decorative scalloped band. Derelict and awkwardly positioned on a steeply sloping site alongside which the avenue passes over a bridge, all framed by cut-stone drum entrance pillars.

Heaney 1999; Lewis 1837; Lacy 1853; Bary 1994; Williams 1994.

AGHANA (see WOODLANDS)

3. ANN'S VILLA, Tralee; pre-1841; *demolished.*
The first OS map suggests that there was a pair of lodges at the entrance, now distinguished by a later mid-Victorian gatesweep of punched limestone pillars with 'cushion' cappings and ornamental iron railings that match the postilion gates, probably dating from the advent of Stephen Creagh Sandes (d. 1861) around 1857, or his brother Thomas, who renamed the property 'Oakvilla'. They had acquired it from its builder, Thomas Payne (b. 1795), who had called it after his beloved daughter.

McMorran and O'Keeffe 2005.

4. ARABELLA, Ballymacelligot; pre-1841; *demolished.*
The entrance site is marked by a later gatesweep of small concave quadrant walls and pillars in quarry-faced masonry of *c.* 1865, when Francis Peete was in residence. Prior to that it was a property of the Blennerhassetts, of whom Revd Arthur and his sister Arabella were two. Subsequently it passed to the Rowan family.

Taylor and Skinner 1778; 1783; Bary 1994; McMorran and O'Keeffe 2005.

5. ARDFERT ABBEY, Adfert (4).
Of this ancient demesne of the Crosbies, earls of Glandore, and its estate buildings little remains except its gate lodges, built for William Talbot Talbot-Crosbie (1817–99), all of considerably later date than the fine, but lost, late seventeenth-century house.

North entrance; *c.* 1870; architect probably William Atkins.

A replacement or reworking of a pre-1842 lodge, single-storey with a very steeply pitched roof, hipped to the rear but half-umbrello to the front over a canted avenue elevation. Much extended and inappropriately refenestrated, only the splendid cut-stone plinthed chimney-stack has escaped modernisation, saved by its inaccessibility and still betraying its likely author. Cement-rendered walls contrast with the plain rubble entrance screen.

East or deer-park entrance; 1878.
A successor to a pre-1842 lodge is this single-storey gabled affair on an irregular plan with a moulded plinth. The lofty eaves accommodate a projecting roof with a catslide on one side, and on the other, in the internal angle, a flat-roofed hallway with moulded corniced parapet and segmentally arched doorway. To each main gable is a large Venetian window with hideous modern

casement inserts, over one of which, obligingly, is a dated shield. All terribly dilapidated, with tatty cement rendering and damaged earthenware cresting. Grand ashlar Georgian gate pillars with scroll-topped stops and later gates.

Old Glandore gate; *c.* 1785; *demolished.*

The charming sketch of 1834 and an 1876 photograph reveal a single-storey two-bay Georgian Gothic cottage with Y-traceried lancet windows in rubble stone walls, gabled, with a central chimney-stack subsequently raised in search of draught, alongside a grand castellated gateway with pointed carriage arch. Built for Sir John Crosbie, 2nd earl of Glandore (1754–1815), not long after he succeeded his father to the estate in 1781. The Revd D.A. Beaufort in 1788 found it to be 'not of a piece with the rest of his old-fashioned place'. The archway was later dismantled and reassembled further south on a new approach that connected with 'several fine avenues of elm, lime and beech trees', noticed by Lewis in 1837.

New Glandore gate; 1880; architect probably William Atkins.

NLI

A surprising, splendid and extensive piece of Victoriana, totally out of keeping with this modest village setting. A plaque within the archway reveals it to be that removed from the old main entrance and rebuilt here by Patrick Dineen and his son, complete with the decorative wrought-iron gates, as the centre-piece of a new castellated complex in fine punched coursed random limestone with smooth cut-stone dressings. Dominated by Irish crenellations to the reassembled buttressed pointed archway and the little two-bay single-storey lodge alongside, with its cast-iron latticed lights to bipartite and tripartite ecclesiastically pointed windows piercing ogee quadrant walls which terminate in squat turrets; all enhanced with cross arrowloops and a Talbot-Crosbie coat of arms. A design probably to plans by architect William Atkins, who had worked for the family in 1868 on their now-lost church. An entrance now redundant since the demise of the big house.

A most magnificent mid-Victorian Baroque gatescreen was taken from here and can now be seen gracing St John's Church of Ireland church in Tralee. A triple gateway of exquisite curvilinear ironwork is framed by four limestone pillars capped by immaculately chiselled honey-coloured sandstone lions, sejant rather than Crosbie rampant, and a pair of Vanbrugh obelisks borne on balls over fluted friezes with scallop shells.

TCD (Beaufort MSS); Lewis 1837; *IFR*; Bence-Jones 1988; Williams 1994; NIAH; Lawrence photograph (6380C); O'Connor 1999.

6. ARDTULLY CASTLE, Kenmare; pre-1841.

At the church, by a beautiful river-lined avenue, are the remains of a commodious gabled structure rendered indescribable by rampant vegetation. It lies at the access to an 1840 house subsequently replaced by a Scots Baronial pile for Sir Richard John Theodore Orpen, which also lies in ruins after its burning in the 'Troubles' of 1921.

Bence-Jones 1988; Williams 1994.

7. ASKIVE COTTAGE, Sneem; pre-1842.

Opposite the entrance is a modest gabled, rubble-built, one-bay affair to a Bland family property, tenanted in 1837 by a Dr Browne. The house was burnt in 1922.

Lewis 1837; Bary 1994.

8. AUGHANAGRAN, Ballylongford; pre-1841; *demolished.*

Neither the house nor the porter's lodge of the O'Connors survives.

BAHAGHS LODGE (see BAHOSS)

9. BAHOSS, Caherciveen; pre-1841; *demolished.*

The house, and perhaps its gate lodge, built in 1833 upon the marriage of Charles O'Connell to Kate, daughter of 'the Liberator'.

Lewis 1837; *IFR*; Bary 1994.

10. BALLARD, Tralee (2).

North entrance; pre-1841; *demolished.*

South entrance; *c.* 1855; architect probably William Atkins; *demolished.*

For Francis Crosbie, clerk of the peace, is this

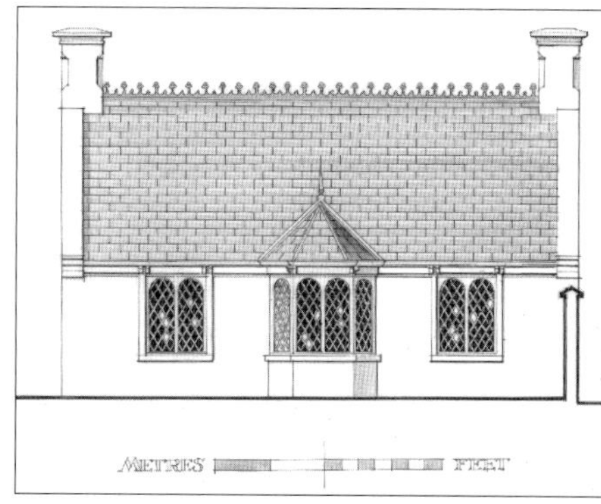

fine gatescreen of palmette-topped railings to concave quadrants terminating in four stone pillars chamfered to octagonal section, squinching to oversized square cappings. This detailing is identical to that at South Hill [*q.v.*] and Oak Park [*q.v.*], which points to the work of architect William Atkins. The lodge was a pretty single-storey standard structure, with corbelled kneelers to skew-tables rising to octagonal stone chimney-stacks on each gable. Bipartite latticed casement windows flanked a projecting semi-octagonal glazed hall, like a mini-conservatory, its semi-octahedral roof rising to a spiky hip-knob and ornamental cresting. The gable to the footpath connected to the entrance sweep by a wall containing an arched postilion opening.

Griffith 1853–63; Slater 1846; 1856; 1870; McMorran and O'Keeffe 2005.

11. BALLARD LODGE, Tralee; pre-1841; *demolished.*

A lodge for the Foley family had been taken down before 1938, when the house had become 'Glenview'.

12. BALLINRUDDERY, Listowel (3).

Alternatively known as 'Woodford', the sad remnants of a once-beautiful demesne of the Fitzgeralds, knights of Kerry, now minus its thatched mansion, rhododendron-lined avenue and all three porters' lodges.

Bary 1994.

13. BALLINTAGGART, Dingle (2).
The house, built in 1830 by Samuel Murray Hickson, has two contemporary gate lodges.

Secondary entrance; *c.* 1830.
The blocked-up stone shell of a single-storey lodge with a three-bay front of round-arched openings.

Main entrance; *c.* 1830.
A modest single-storey standard rendered cottage on a square plan, its pyramidal roof rising to a central chimney-stack. Occupied.

Bary 1994.

14. BALLYARD, Tralee; *c.* 1830.
A series of three grand octagonal ashlar pillars frame the carriage gates and, at right angles, forward of them a screen wall penetrated by two Tudor-style label-moulded openings, one a postern gate, the other a window to the lodge which monitored arrivals. Otherwise ruinous, it was probably built by Peter Thompson not long after he erected his house in 1828.

Bary 1994.

15. BALLYBEGGAN CASTLE, Tralee; pre-1841; *demolished.*
What appears from the first OS map to have been a pair of lodges, presumably built by James O'Connell after he bought the estate from the Husseys in 1822.

Bary 1994.

16. BALLYCARTY, Tralee; pre-1892; *demolished.*
Like the big house, no trace survives of the mid-Victorian gate lodge of the Nash family.

17. BALLYHEIGUE CASTLE, Ballyheigue (2).
Colonel James Crosbie incorporated earlier structures into his new romantic castle 'in the later English style of architecture', to a design of Richard and William Vitruvius Morrison around 1809, and thereafter embellished the rather bare estate with entrance lodges.

Village entrance; *c.* 1810; architects probably R. and W.V. Morrison.

A rather dull and formal composition, though in the context of this unprepossessing village relatively striking. Lancet-headed, Y-traceried Gothic windows suggest a date contemporary with the big house on a height beyond. Otherwise it contrasts with the Picturesque informality of the castle in being a symmetrical design of two tall, square, castellated towers containing minimal porter's accommodation of a single room each, linked by a crenellated carriage opening of a two-centred arch. The towers are relieved with mock arrowloop ornamentation. Alongside has been added a single-storey extension, intended to be in keeping but in random coursed stone facings contrasting with the regular coursed ashlar of the original. Maintained.

Country entrance; *c.* 1835.
An isolated single-storey standard rendered cottage below a hipped roof, its side walls extending to create a verandah across the face, carried on two intermediate post supports. Occupied.

Neale 1820–3; Lewis 1837; Bence-Jones 1988.

18. BALLYHORGAN SOUTH, Listowel; pre-1841.
The ruinous remains of a gate lodge built for Francis Gentleman or his son Robert (1787–1846). Hoop-topped railings and gates survive.

LGI (1904).

19. BALLYMACADAM, Castleisland; pre-1841; *demolished.*
Up to 1815 a property of the Crosbies, earls of Glandore, its gate lodge replaced by a modern house.

Taylor and Skinner 1778; 1783; Wilson 1803; *BPB* (1929).

20. BALLYNABLOUN, Portmagee; pre-1842; *demolished.*
A seat of the O'Connells, neither the house to which nor what was the most westerly lodge in the country survives. The latter, which was opposite its gates, had gone by 1896.

LGI (1904).

BALLYNAMAUNAGH (see MOUNT PROSPECT)

21. BALLYNOE, Causeway; pre-1841; *demolished.*
A gatekeeper's lodge built either by the Stroughton family or their later tenants, the Pierces.

Bary 1994.

22. BALLYSEEDY CASTLE, Tralee (2).
Now a hotel but previously a grand Georgian pile of the Blennerhassett family, it has a perfect introduction at the base of the avenue.

Main entrance; *c.* 1780.

A pair of single-storey lodges, the bow fronts of which reflect those on the big house. Each has a leading three-bay façade of pointed-arched windows, now blocked-up, projecting into a vast circular forecourt that incorporates a segment across the road. The main bodies of the lodges lurk behind screen walls, unmaintained, roofless and overgrown, but still containing windows with margined glazing bars which suggest later inserts of around 1840. In contrast to the whitewashed harled quadrants and lodge walls, the main carriage pillars are in ashlar, supporting incongruous modern lanterns, the secondary postilion pillars having birds atop rather than Blennerhassett dolphins. A once-impressive composition that begs restoration. There is a similar arrangement at Lucan House, Co. Dublin.

Secondary entrance; pre-1841.
An unpretentious single-storey hip-roofed structure, now derelict.

Bence-Jones 1988.

23. BARRY'S GLYNN, Killarney; pre-1841; *demolished.*
Of lodge, avenue and large curved entrance sweep nothing is left. Once a property of the Brennan family.

Bary 1994.

BAUNCLUNE or BUNECLOON (see THE REEKS)

BATH LODGE (see MASSEYVILLE)

24. BEAUFORT, Killarney; pre-1841; *demolished.*
Impressive square Georgian ashlar entrance pillars survive, with nice contrasting limewashed concave quadrant walls, probably built by the Hon. Deane Crosbie or the Revd Frederick Ferriter Mullins, who succeeded to the estate.

Taylor and Skinner 1778; 1783; Wilson 1803; Bary 1994.

25. BEDFORD, Listowel; pre-1841; *demolished.*
Of the main house and its gate lodge, built by Colthurst Bateman or his son of the same name, nothing survives.

LGI (1904).

26. BELLEVILLE, Killarney; pre-1841; *demolished.*
An estate in 1824 of Lt.-Col. George H. Maybury.

Pigot 1824.

27. BELMONT, Tralee; *c.* 1830.
In a state of advanced dereliction is this single-storey hip-roofed lodge with three limewashed rubble elevations, the fourth, forward of the gate pillars, rather more sophisticated, of coursed stone with a small label-moulded window. Of later date and sitting awkwardly alongside is one of two concave quadrants in crude vermiculated stones, containing a postern opening. The lodge is contemporary with the house, which was built in 1826 by Peter Thompson for his daughter Alicia on her marriage to Revd

Arthur Blennerhassett Rowan (1800–61), who lived on here as archdeacon of Ardfert until his death.

Bary 1994; McMorran and O'Keeffe 2005.

28. BREWSTERSFIELD, Killarney; pre-1841; *demolished.*

Neither lodge nor house survives on a property taking its name from the Brewster family, from whom it was inherited by the Herberts of Cahernane [*q.v.*].

Bary 1994.

29. BURNHAM, Dingle (2).

A large house built in 1790 for Thomas Mullins, 1st Baron Ventry of Burnham. He and his son seem subsequently to have neglected the property, for it was described in 1838 as being 'unrelieved by even one tree on the lawn which surrounds it, has a bleak and desolate appearance', despite a year earlier the occupant and the family's agent David P. Thompson's having commenced improvements to house and estate which may have included the earlier of the gate lodges.

East lodge; pre-1841; *demolished.*

The Mullins returned to live here in 1841, and Dayrolles Blakeney De Moleyns, for his father had assumed that ancient family surname, succeeded to the title and estates in 1868, adding a second gatekeeper's lodge.

West lodge; *c.* 1870; architect not known.

An attractive and solid single-storey standard structure with fleur-de-lis cresting to a hipped roof and the ridge of its projecting hallway, and ornamental perforated and scalloped fascia and bargeboards. Built in neat rubble construction with cut-stone quoins, dressings and chimney-stack; to the avenue elevation is a semi-octagonal bay window with transomed and mullioned latticed lights. Occupied and immaculate, the most westerly surviving gate lodge in the country.

Lewis 1837; Fraser 1838; *BPB* (1929); Bary 1994.

BUSHFIELD (see KILCOLEMAN ABBEY)

30. CAHERNANE, Killarney; pre-1841; *demolished.*

A lodge swept away by recent road-widening, built by the Herbert family to serve their old Queen Anne-style house, subsequently replaced by the present mansion in 1877.

Bary 1994; Williams 1994.

31. CARHOOBEG, Churchtown; pre-1841; *demolished.*

A property in 1852 of Edward McSweeney, its lodge a shell by the turn of the twentieth century.

Griffith 1853–63.

32. CASTLE COVE, Caherdaniel; pre-1896; *demolished.*

No trace remains of the mid-Victorian lodge to a property of the Jermyn family.

33. CASTLEISLAND RECTORY, Castleisland; pre-1841; *demolished.*

A rectory built on Kilbanavan glebe in 1818 for a total of £1,300, a goodly sum which may have included the gate lodge and explained by the then incumbent being the Revd William Crosbie, later to become the 4th and last Lord Bandon until his death in 1832.

Lewis 1837; *BPB* (1929).

34. CASTLELOUGH, Killarney; pre-1841; *demolished.*

The lodge, which lay opposite its gates, had gone by 1938. Probably built by the Lawlor family, who sold the property in 1850 to Thomas Cotter, first proprietor of the hotel which it became.

Bary 1994.

35. CHURCHTOWN, Churchtown; pre-1841/*c.* 1845.

The first OS map shows the previous entrance to have been in the form of a semicircular forecourt, the left-hand quadrant of which was terminated by a gate lodge by the road's edge. Built by the Blennerhassett family, it was replaced by the surviving delightful complex, which consists of a limewashed harled single-storey standard lodge with two-over-two sash windows on each side of a panelled door, below a steeply pitched hipped roof with high eaves to accommodate loft space, all contrasting with an elegant entrance sweep of four tall punched ashlar pillars with moulded cappings and unmatching pineapple finials. The decorative wrought-

iron carriage gates and their two postilion counterparts are hung on secondary iron posts topped with urn finials and charming oval sunflower paterae. Reflecting the lodge are whitewashed quadrant walls. Presumably an improvement for Revd Edward Fitzgerald Conyers (d. 1854), rector of Knockane [*q.v.*], who lived here after his marriage to Catherine, daughter of Sir Robert Blennerhassett, from 1822. Now Beaufort Golf Club.

BPB (1929); *IFR*.

36. CHUTE HALL, Tralee; pre-1841; *demolished.*

Both house and porter's lodge have gone, to be survived by a big and impressive gatescreen of about 1820, comprised of five out of six remaining limestone ashlar pillars with blocked corniced cappings framing a triple gateway of spear-topped carriage and postern gates with matching railings to extensive concave quadrants. Built for Francis Chute (d. 1849).

LGI (1904); McMorran and O'Keeffe 2005.

37. CLEENY, Killarney; *c.* 1845; *demolished.*

A property of Maurice J. Brennan in 1852, the valuation of that year identifying a lodge to his property, not obvious on the 1841 OS map nor on the ground; assumed demolished.

Griffith 1853–63.

38. CLOGHERS, Tralee; pre-1841/*c.* 1865.

An original lodge from the time here of the Yielding family may be incorporated into the present building, which is a single-storey four-bay structure, gabled with a like projecting hall. Harled, with two diagonally set chimney-stacks and a mix of perforated and foiled bargeboards and some carved soffit brackets; later single-bay addition to the right-hand side. Probably from the residency

of Edward Mulchinock, as is the gatescreen of cast-iron pillars with finials and pointed recessed panels that confirm a mid-Victorian date, as do the concave quadrants with similar panelling.

Slater 1870; Bary 1994.

39. CLONMORE, Tralee; *c.* 1870.
Built off a heavy plinth in blotchy random coursed sandstone is a standard single-storey lodge below a shallow hipped roof with similarly treated hall projection. Modernisation has seen the loss of its chimney-stack and the insertion of unfortunate replacement windows. Occupied. Probably built by the Huggard family.

40. CLOONALOUR, Tralee; *c.* 1905.

A long, low, single-storey structure below a shallow hipped roof with a stone chimney-stack having a corbelled capping; sash windows with shouldered rendered surrounds. To the front elevation is a projecting room of later date with a small Arts and Crafts-style casement window identical to those in the lodge to nearby Park-na-doon [*q.v.*]. Occupied. There is an impressive and extensive tripartite gateway with concave quadrant railings and solid ashlar pillars with moulded plinths and cappings. A lodge added at the turn of the twentieth century by Gerald Bailey which now gives onto a modern housing development.

COLTSMANN'S CASTLE (see FLESK CASTLE)

COOLCLOGHER (see SOUTH HILL)

41. COURTEENE HALL, Killarney; pre-1841; *demolished.*
The lodge may have dated from 1828, when work to the house is recorded to have been carried out by James Courtayne.

O'Donovan 1806–61.

CRAG (see ROCKVILLE)

42. CROTTA, or CROTTO, Abbeydorney; pre-1841; *demolished.*
Not a vestige is to be found of the gate lodge or the house that architect Sir Richard Morrison extended *c.* 1819 for the Carrique Ponsonby family.

IAA.

43. CULLENAGH, Churchtown; pre-1841; *demolished.*
A property in the early nineteenth century of Kean Mahony.

44. CURRAGHLEHA, Tralee; 1870.
A modest single-storey building with clipped eaves to a hipped roof having earthenware fleur-de-lis cresting, over a three-bay front elevation with door to the right-hand side in limewashed harled walls. Derelict. An entry for May 1870 in the Valuation Book notes 'Gate lodge in progress'. Built for Major William N. Leigh.

45. DANESFORT, Killarney; *c.* 1800.
The ivy-shrouded shell of a once-typical single-storey standard Georgian Gothic gate lodge with lancet openings, probably with a hipped roof but subsequently raised by a storey. Built for Vice-Admiral Samuel Butcher (1770–1849).

LGI (1904).

DEER PARK (see DOONEEN COTTAGE)

46. DERRYNANE, Caherdaniel; *c.* 1800.

The quintessential standard single-storey Georgian Gothic gate lodge, built by Maurice O'Connell, uncle of 'the Liberator'. Located opposite its entrance is this steeply hip-roofed structure with lancet, Y-traceried sash windows and a sheeted door in rendered walls. Now well restored and maintained as holiday accommodation.

At a lodgeless secondary gate is a charming rustic belfry tower.

IFR.

47. DERRYQUIN CASTLE, Sneem (2).
On the divine Kenmare River coastline, a house certainly existed here in 1814, was castellated by 1837 and had an early lodged gate on the main road.

Front entrance; pre-1842; *demolished.*
Built for Francis Christopher Bland I or his son, James Franklin Bland I (1799–1863), opposite the gates off a cruciform plan was a porter's lodge which had been removed by 1895. Surviving are later chunky tiered gabled cappings to chamfered gate pillars.

Rear entrance; *c.* 1870; architect probably J.F. Fuller.
Remote from pillars similar to those of the front gate is this pleasant mid-Victorian 1½-storey steeply gabled structure in rubble stone facings, dominated by a projecting semi-octagonal bay room. Built for Francis Christopher Bland II (1826–94), who had commissioned his relation James Franklin Fuller to further embellish the castle, which was demolished in 1969. Occupied.

Loot 1814; Lewis 1837; *LGI* (1904).

48. DICK'S GROVE, Dysert (2).
A once-handsome house and demesne of the Meredith family, now almost totally lost but for its stable block and two eccentric gate lodges.

Castleisland gate; *c.* 1800.

A remarkable survivor is this single-storey drum lodge built off a circular plan, with a conical slated roof rising steeply to a cylindrical brick chimney-stack. It would originally have had its eaves broken by gablets to four opposing sides, one now projecting to accommodate an entrance hallway. Clearly beloved of its owners but none the better for the choice of modern windows, modern slip sills, timber cladding and mock stone finish, though a flat-roofed extension does not detract. Probably built for Richard Meredith, who succeeded to the property on the death of his father in 1802.

Farranfore gate; pre-1841/*c.* 1875/*c.* 1910.
A delightful single-storey amorphous structure, perhaps incorporating that shown on the first OS map, basically hip-roofed but having evolved down the years in extensions cranked at differing levels to follow the

curved, sloped avenue access. To the rear is a projecting hall with quirky pyramidal roof, its windows with round arches in a series of gablets. Sadly, by 2001 it was abandoned, burnt and boarded up.

LGI (1904); Bary 1994.

49. DOONEEN COTTAGE, Killarney (2).
Forming part of the greater Kenmare estates, the house, which accommodated a succession of Lord Kenmare's tenants and his estate managers, was in the twentieth century named 'Deer Park' in the townland of that name.

South lodge; pre-1841; *demolished.*
A structure that had been removed by 1938.

Upper park lodge; 1909; architect J. Wornell.

An important Arts and Crafts bungalow in the Lutyens manner. A charming single-storey affair with attic space, a flat-roofed dormer to which penetrates a steeply hipped roof in earthenware tiles complete with valleys and bonnets. Three-bay, that to the left dominated by a roughcast gable over a canted bay window, alongside a recessed porch and tripartite squared casement window to the right-hand side. The chimney-stacks are unfortunately bland rendered replacements, but the whole is lovingly maintained and enhanced by delightful 'buttressed' topiary. White roughcast quadrant entrance walls lead to red-brick pillars with sawtooth-pattern copings and cappings. Secondary iron posts with pineapple finials and chinoiserie gates with palmette crestings.

In line with his predecessors, the 5th earl placed his faith in an English architect, in this case the relatively obscure John Wornell of 19 Ludgate Hill, London, a drawing of whose survives. The builders were J. Hearne and Son of Waterford. The lodge, now central to a farm in its own right, seems to be but one of two proposed to have been executed to Wornell's designs.

IB (11 June 1910).

52. Dromore Castle, Kenmare, Templenoe entrance.

50. DROMIN COTTAGE, Ballybunion; pre-1841; *demolished.*
Nothing remains of this property, in 1819 occupied by Francis Creagh.

Leet 1814.

51. DROMIN, Listowel; *c.* 1820.
A single-storey harled two-bay cottage, its door to the left-hand side, below a hipped roof. Semi-ruinous. Two ashlar pillars with peculiar vase finials contrasting. All built for James W. Raymond.

Leet 1814.

52. DROMORE CASTLE, Kenmare (2).
Overlooking this idyllic stretch of coastline sits the fairytale castle designed by Sir Thomas Deane and his son Kearns. Completed around 1838 for Revd Denis Mahony, who did not add gate lodges until just prior to his death in 1851.

Templenoe entrance; *c.* 1850;

architects Deane and Woodward.
By 1850 the talented but short-lived Benjamin Woodward had joined the Deane practice and designed a gatehouse to Annesgrove, Co. Cork [*q.v.*], and this almost identical composition. An impressive castellated Tudor Revival essay, stepping from the pointed-arched postilion opening in the screen wall, through a similarly arched carriage doorway with hood moulding and simple shield dripstones, to the two-storey crenellated gatehouse with its first-floor oriel window overlooking the entrance, terminating in the lofty square stair-turret with its arrowloop lights. All in rubble stone, having a variety of bipartite and tripartite dressed mullioned windows with label mouldings; to the side a typical Woodward battered chimney-stack. Totally derelict and bleak, with its northerly aspect and setting of mature trees, demanding salvation, like its Annesgrove counterpart, by such as the Irish Landmark Trust.

Blackwater entrance; *c.* 1850; architects probably Deane and Woodward.

Elevated opposite its gates is this house in the Picturesque English cottage manner, sufficiently commodious as to suggest that it had more than the role of housing a gatekeeper. A standard 1½-storey gabled structure with a plethora of ornamental fascias and bargeboards to gablets, gables and that of the projecting single-storey hallway; central battered stack, scalloped slate courses and small squared-pane windows and roughcast walls add to the effect. Occupied.

LGI (1904); Williams 1994.

53. DROMQUINNA, Kenmare; *c.* 1874; architect probably Thomas Drew.

Latterly a hotel, as a grand private house it seems to have evolved through three main building phases, the middle of which would have seen the addition of the gate lodge. It is a charming and quirky Picturesque cottage composition, single-storey off an L-plan, much gabled like the big house with decorative perforated foiled bargeboards, delicate hip-knobs and scalloped slate bands to a roof which catslides over miniature window projections. To the leading avenue gable is a bay window retaining some of its original latticed glazing, while alongside is a little entrance hall, gabled in its own right, almost as an afterthought. Rendered and occupied, it bears a striking affinity with the gate lodge to Tubber-na-Carrig, Co. Down. Some of the splendid mid-Victorian stone Gothic entrance pillars survive, with tasty concave iron sawtooth-topped quadrants on dwarf walls. The *Irish Builder* magazine in 1873 records 'Mansion at Drumquina, nr. Kenmare for Colonel Columb. Thomas Drew, archt.' Presumably this was General George Thomas Colomb (1819–74), like his architect later elevated.

IB (15 October 1873); Dean 1994.

54. DUAGH, Daugh; pre-1841; *demolished.*
Both house and lodge of the Fitzmaurice family were removed in the twentieth century.

55. DUNKERRON, Kenmare; *c.* 1830.
Dr Thomas Taylor, the noted natural historian, built himself the house and a gate lodge opposite his entrance in the early nineteenth century. This is an unusually substantial standard single-storey cottage with a distinctive hipped roof and oversailing eaves. It had bipartite cast-iron latticed casement windows, a pretty feature now sadly lost to recent modifications. The gabled breakfront hall with ornamental woodwork dates from the time of the property passing to the Herberts of

Cahernane [*q.v.*] in the early twentieth century. The walls recently roughcast.

Bary 1994.

56. DUNLOE CASTLE, Beaufort (2).
South lodge; pre-1841; *demolished.*
North lodge; pre-1894; *demolished.*
What was once a seat of the Mahony family is now the site of a hotel.

EDENBURN (see MAGH)

57. ENNISMORE, Finuge (2).
The house, since demolished, was an antique property of the Hewson family, its porters' lodges of differing periods.
Inner gate; pre-1841; *demolished.*
Outer gate; *c.* 1860.
A standard 1½-storey cottage with symmetrically placed loft gablets and a central single-storey gabled hall projection with a fanlit doorway. Its roof steeply pitched, with small slates over limewashed walls. Occupied. Built for George Hewson.

58. ERASMUS SMITH SCHOOL, Tarbert; pre-1841; *demolished.*
The school was established here by the Erasmus Smith Foundation in 1795, and the architect, James Pain, carried out alterations to the schoolhouse in 1833, when he referred to a 'Thatched Building remote from the house', which may have been the gatekeeper's lodge shown on the first OS map, sufficient in size to have also provided classroom accommodation.

59. FAHAGH COURT, Churchtown; pre-1841.
Opposite its gates is a much-altered and modernised lodge, standard single-storey originally, now enlarged with tall eaves and gabled dormers to attic space, the roof of which catslides over a central hall extension. Recent rendering, windows and synthetic slates. Occupied. Probably built by the Bernard family when the property passed from the Falveys.

Bary 1994.

60. FARMHILL, Killarney; pre-1841.
In its present two-storey gabled form with twentieth-century rendering ornament, it is difficult to imagine this building as having originated as a porter's lodge. Before 1894 it took on the additional role of post office, which it retains to the present. It perhaps originated when a Mr Bateman repaired the house in 1826.

Bary 1994.

61. FARRANAKILLA, Dingle; pre-1841; *demolished.*
A gate lodge surely contemporary with the building of the house in the early nineteenth century by barrister Peter Bodkin Hussey. It had gone by 1894.

62. FEALE VIEW, Listowel; pre-1841; *demolished.*
A modest holding in 1851 of James Connors.

Griffith 1853–63.

63. FENIT LODGE, Fenit; pre-1841; *demolished.*

Surviving the gate lodge is a grandiose pair of iron pillars, carriage and postilion gates from the late Victorian period. With all manner of decorative motifs—paterae, husk, anthemion, fleur-de-lis and trefoil—all framed by outer stone pillars and quadrants. All for John Charles Dennis Hurley, who inherited the estate in 1870.

LGI (1904).

64. FERMONT, Tarbert; pre-1841; *demolished.*
Like the house, alternatively called 'Pyrmount', its gate lodge opposite the gates had gone by 1921. Probably all for William Sandes (1773–1852), who came to the property in 1812.

LGI (1904).

65. FLESK CASTLE, Killarney; *c.* 1835.

In style, form and—sadly—condition, this is an appropriate and delightful prelude to the big house. Two-storey over a basement, opposite the old entrance avenue is this octagonal turret with castellated parapet and

label-moulded openings, that to the front door embracing a Tudor arch with pendant dripstone and quatrefoil-decorated spandrels. The whole is in convincing coursed stone-effect rendering. Now but a shell. Access between floors can only have been by ladder. If the forsaken, fantastic Gothic Revival castle in John Nash style was designed and built, as it is said, by its owner, John Coltsman, between 1809 and 1815, so too could the porter's lodge, but sometime later, before his death in 1857. A seat also known as 'Coltsmann's Castle' or 'Glenflesk Castle'.

LGI (1904); Bence-Jones 1988; Bary 1994.

66. FLESK PRIORY, Killarney; pre-1841; *demolished.*
John Stewart Coxon spent £1,200 on the house in 1828 and may then have built the gate lodge to complement it.

Bary 1994.

67. FOILDARRIG, Anascaul; pre-1841; *demolished.*
A hunting lodge of the earls of Kenmare, built in the 1830s and occupied for many years by their agent James Hickson, also to be found at Lansdowne Lodge [*q.v.*]. The gate lodge to a property that became known as 'Red Cliff' would have been contemporary.

Bary 1994.

68. FORT WILLIAM, Ardfert; pre-1841; *demolished.*
The first OS map of 1841 indicates a pair of lodges by the gate, now replaced by a modern bungalow to one side and a plain, single-storey, steeply gabled, four-bay structure to the other. The originals, like the big house, built for William Collis.

Bary 1994.

69. FROGMORE, Ballynahaglish; *c.* 1835.
A decent single-storey lodge below a shallow-hipped roof over nice exposed rubble stone walls, presenting a single-bay tripartite lattice-glazed window to the avenue and bipartite lights to the sides. Off a square plan, the roof rises to a central octagonal chimney-stack. Occupied. Four square punched limestone ashlar entrance pillars contrast pleasantly with whitewashed concave quadrant walls. Built by Revd Barry Denny.

Lewis 1837; Bary 1994.

70. GARRAHIES, Camp; *c.* 1810.
Not quite opposite the gates to what was a Fitzgerald estate is this modest single-storey lodge. Originally standard but extended by one bay to the right-hand side and with later two-over-two sash windows inserted in roughcast walls below a shallow-pitched roof with a clipped verge and corrugated iron finish.

71. GARRYANTANVALLY, Finuge; pre-1841; *demolished.*
Probably built by Alexander Elliott, both the house, also known as 'Tanavalla', and its lodge had gone by 1937.

72. GARRYARD, Listowel; pre-1937; *demolished.*
An estate in 1852 of Thomas Newman.

Griffith 1853–63.

GLENFESK CASTLE (see FLESK CASTLE)

73. GLENMORE, Ballynahaglish; *c.* 1845.

A pretty lodge raised off a square plan with a pyramidal roof, its eaves extending to form a verandah with post supports; two-bay façades with triangular-arched openings in rendered walls. Occupied. Small concave quadrant walls frame chunky octagonal entrance pillars with top-heavy cappings, all looking twenty years more recent than the lodge. A property now renamed 'Sea View', its gate lodge was first valued in 1880, when it was occupied by John O'Callaghan as gatekeeper to George Massey.

74. GORTROE or GURTROE, Killarney; *c.* 1845; *demolished.*
John Morrough Bernard, also recorded at Fahagh Court [*q.v.*], is noted here as occupant in 1852 on a property with a gate lodge, which does not appear on the 1841 OS map. The 1938 map shows it in outline, suggesting that it was by then ruinous.

Griffith 1853–63.

75. GRENAGH, Beaufort; *c.* 1820.
John O'Connell MP, a younger brother of Daniel 'the Liberator', came to live here in 1807, the year following his marriage, to repair, improve and extend the home. His improvements would have extended to the provision of gatekeeper's accommodation by the gate in the shape of this distinctive lodge. Standard single-storey and rubble-built, with an Irish crenellated parapet over a round-arched window to the park. Now a shell. Simple vertical iron strap gates are hung on basic rustic pillars, with dwarf concave quadrant walls lacking their railings. By 1850 O'Connell's spendthrift lifestyle had brought an end to his occupancy here.

Bary 1994.

76. THE GROVE, Anascaul; pre-1841; *demolished.*
In 1837 'the former residence of the Knights of Kerry, now of J. Hickson'. This was John Hickson, last sovereign of Dingle, who was resident here thirteen years earlier. Both the house and its lodge are lost without trace.

Pigot 1824; Lewis 1837.

77. GURTENARD, Listowel; pre-1841/*c.* 1875.

The surviving lodge is a replacement for a predecessor that would have been built in the time of John Church or his successor here, Stephen Edward Collis, residents in 1824 and 1837 respectively. Set well back from its entrance, it dates from when the property had become a seat of the earl of Listowel's agent—for that is what a plaque on the wall tells us, as well as the appellation 'Dandy Lodge'. Aptly named indeed is this mid-Victorian lodge with fine uncoursed rubble stone finish and brick dressings; raised off a T-plan, it rises to 1½ storeys to steeply pitched gables in Picturesque English cottage style. Sensitively restored with small-paned casement windows, perforated wave and foil bargeboards and red-brick banded chimney-stack. Occupied.

Pigot 1824; Lewis 1837; Bary 1994.

78. HAREMOUNT, Scartaglin; pre-1841; *demolished.*
A house, once of the Hare family, earls of Listowel, whose main seat was Convamore, Co. Cork [*q.v.*]. It lies ruinous and its gatekeeper's lodge opposite the gates has been replaced by a bungalow.

79. HILL GROVE, Caherciveen; pre-1842; *demolished.*
A property noted in 1814 and 1838 as being of Daniel O'Connell's agent, John Primrose; both house and lodge had gone by 1895.

Leet 1814; Fraser 1838.

80. HILL VILLE, Stradbally; pre-1894; *demolished.*
Another Kerry seat of the Hickson family, their house dating from 1833 but the lodge not added until after 1841.

O'Donovan 1806–61.

KENMARE (see KILLARNEY)

81. KENMARE CONVENT, Kenmare; *c.* 1863; architect possibly C.F. Hansom.

Contrasting with the extensive gabling and spired backdrop of church, convent and school is this little steeply hip-roofed building. Two-bay by one, single-storey with loft over, having a stone plinth, eaves course, toothed quoins and dressings to narrow Tudor-style windows, it has benefited from recent removal of rendering to reveal attractive coursed rubble walls, though emphasising a rather nasty later flat-roofed hall to its road front; chimneyless. Probably forming part of the commission of Charles Francis Hansom or his brother Joseph Aloysius, the latter sometime partner of E.W. Pugin and inventor of the cab.

Williams 1994.

82. KENT LODGE, Ballynahaglish, pre 1841; *demolished.*
The gate lodge may have been built by Major William Collis or, following his murder by intruders in 1821, his brother-in-law and successor here, George Collingwood. Surviving is a gatescreen with four pine-cone finials.

Bary 1994.

KILBANNIVANE GLEBE (see CASTLEISLAND RECTORY)

83. KILCOLEMAN ABBEY, Milltown; pre-1841; *demolished.*

Little remains of this once-fine demesne, the house and lodge having been demolished, the former an example of William Vitruvius Morrison's Elizabethan Revival style, an 1819 work-over of an older house for Sir William Godfrey, completed about 1837. The lodge may have been part of Morrison's commission. Surviving is a fine pair of ashlar entrance pillars with gabled cappings, apparently half of an original set, two having been purloined to grace the entrance to St John's New Cemetery, Tralee. The property was alternatively called 'Milltown' and 'Bushfield'.

McParland *et al.* 1989.

84. KILCREEN COTTAGE, Listowel; pre-1841; *demolished.*
A nineteenth-century seat of the Harnett family.

85. KILLARNEY BISHOP'S HOUSE AND CATHEDRAL, Killarney; *c.* 1850.

A standard single-storey, gabled, Picturesque English cottage-style lodge with perforated wavy bargeboards and pendant hip-knobs. In rendered walls is a Tudor-arched doorway in a projecting gabled hall. Suffering from modern window intrusions, it has been extended to the left-hand side, with another gabled hallway on the avenue elevation, an approach which leads to a complex that has A.W.N. Pugin's 'Irish masterpiece', St Mary's Cathedral, at its centre, the opening of which was presided over in 1856 by Bishop Cornelius Egan.

Atterbury 1995; Williams 1994.

86. KILLARNEY, Killarney (7).
The Browne family recovered the estates they had forfeited after the Battle of the Boyne, previously having lived at Ross Castle [*q.v.*], the 3rd Viscount Kenmare, Valentine Browne, building in 1726 a pleasant Queen Anne-style house. The first recorded gate lodges to the new demesne are early Victorian, built by another Valentine Browne, 2nd earl of Kenmare (1788–1853), who inherited in 1812. Either he or his executant architect must have possessed a library containing some of the pioneering architectural pattern-books of the day for the two designs replicated and surviving by their gates, the author of neither of which is known to have set foot in the country.

Deenagh Lodge; 1834; architect Thomas F. Hunt.

'The porter's lodge at this entrance is a very pretty thatched cottage, upon which, and upon the surrounding space, great pains have been bestowed.' Thus did Lacy in 1851 find this exquisite *cottage orné*, copied with very minor alterations from Design No. 2 in Hunt's *Half-a-dozen hints* (1825). Single-storey standard, with a steeply pitched hipped and decorative thatched roof which extends beyond the walls to form verandahs carried on rustic tree trunks, the eaves undulating in eyebrows over lattice-glazed, bracketed oriel windows on each side of the projecting gabled porch with its Tudor archways, highly ornate bargeboards, carved hip-knob and date-stone in the apex. Finished in simple roughcast and crowned by lofty octagonal chimney-pots, it is triumphantly and immaculately maintained in its new role as a tearoom for townsfolk and tourists.

86. Killarney, Killarney, Deenagh Lodge (T.F. Hunt design).

'Reen Cottage'; 1839; architect P.F. Robinson.

A highly decorative Picturesque English Tudor-style cottage, taken from Design No. 1 in Peter Frederick Robinson's *Designs for lodges and park entrances* (1833); 1½-storey on an informal plan, it shows minor alterations from the original in positions of fireplaces and their distinctive octagonal pots. The projecting porch differs also in displaying a delightful ogee-arched opening with date-stone over and, within, a surprise in an elaborate groin-vaulted ceiling. Steeply gabled with skew-tables and prominent kneelers, a gablet breaks the eaves with its fancy, carved wavy bargeboards. Here and in the two irregularly placed single-storey rectangular bay windows are label-moulded cast-iron latticed mullioned casements. In a rendered finish, it has latterly been extended into a commodious double pile. Quite why this charming and important lodge should lie abandoned and derelict is a puzzle, and its deterioration urgently awaits reversal. There is another version of this lodge at Parkanaur, Co. Tyrone.

Two gatekeepers' lodges on the Killorglin Road do not appear on the first OS map and may have been created as Famine relief.

Castlerosse gate; *c.* 1847; *demolished.*

Now the entrance to a golf club, with a modern structure by the gate.

Gortroe gate; *c.* 1847; *demolished.*

Victoria Lodge; *c.* 1845/*c.* 1861.

So called for, or since, Queen Victoria's visit to the estate in 1861, this perky little cottage probably owes its quirky appearance to its evolution from the simplest of single-storey standard hip-roofed cottages, to be later embellished for Her Majesty with a central projecting outsized gabled hallway with a Tudor-style arched doorway, foiled bargeboards and—its most distinctive feature—a chimney-stack rising majestically off the front wall and terminating in a pair of highly decorative earthenware barley-sugar pots, one of which is a dummy. Occupied. Nearby is a pair of big, square, cast-iron gate piers with palmette-topped gates.

Valentine Augustus Browne, the 4th earl of Kenmare (1825–1905), inherited the extensive estates on the death of his father in 1871 and took heed of Victorian travellers' comments on the 'indifferent', 'plain old building' and its 'bad situation'. He embarked on considerable improvements, which consisted of replacing the old house with a vast but ill-fated Tudor-style Arts and Crafts mansion on a new site, expending in all £59,000 in the process, and designs for additional porters' lodges, one of which was executed to the 'Western Domain', part of the commission of architect George Devey.

Lackabane gate; *c.* 1877; architect G. Devey.

IAA

A commodious and imaginative 1½-storey Arts and Crafts composition, gabled on an informal plan, well endowed with balustraded balconies, scalloped tile-hanging and liberal use of stone and brick, with ornamental carved woodwork to the jettied road gable. To the avenue is a two-storey canted projection, while the ridge intersection is marked by a lofty ornamental brick chimney-stack. Occupied and secreted by tall entrance gates and flanking walls.

Unexecuted design; *c.* 1877; architect G. Devey.

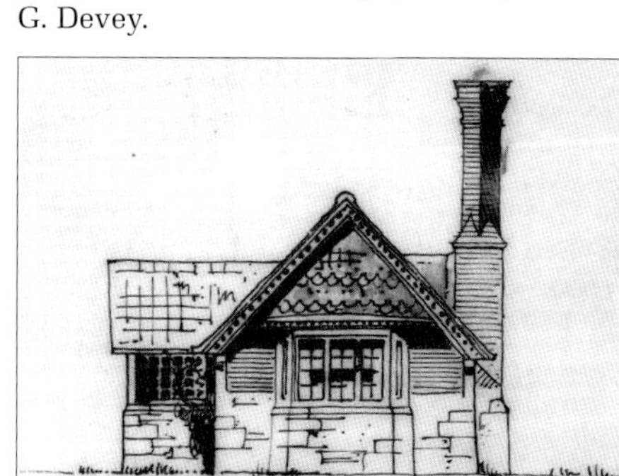

RIBA

Another Arts and Crafts composition depicting a more Spartan single-storey two-roomed layout, the pretty drawings for which survive to show an enchanting English cottage enhanced by a canted bay window with leaded lights and a decorative wooden porch in walls mixing diaper brickwork with

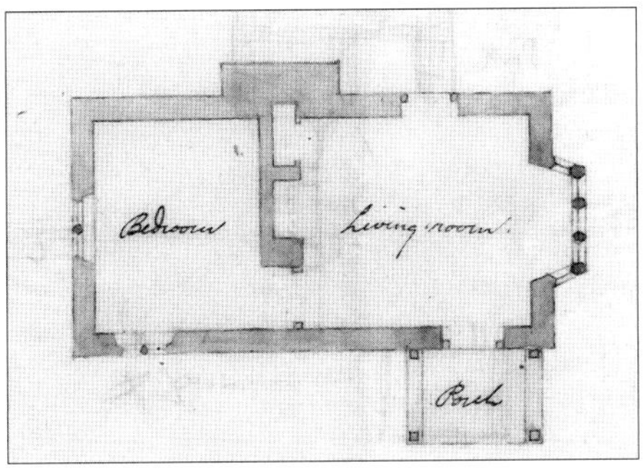

RIBA

battered stone. Above, more scalloped tile-hanging was intended to a gable with fancy carved bargeboards, the whole topped by a lofty brick chimney-stack. Perhaps an alternative design intended for the Lackabane gate.

Town gate; *c.* 1890; architect not known.

A solid single-storey Italianate lodge built off a cruciform plan, with harled walls having Classical mouldings to the deep coved eaves of the hipped roof, plinth and window surrounds, the latter spoiled by inappropriate modern intrusions. An impressive entrance screen known as 'the Golden Gates' consists of rusticated pillars with moulded cappings crowned by cast-iron gas lanterns—a tripartite gateway with good spear-topped gates and railings.

Today the magnificent estate survives substantially as a public park, graced by most of its fine lodges but lacking the great house, burnt down in 1913.

D.A. Beaufort 1788; Hoare 1807; Hunt 1825; Barrow 1836; Robinson 1833; Lacy 1853; *BPB* (1929); Bence-Jones 1988; Allibone 1991; Williams 1994; Dean 1994; Lawrence photograph (6946R); RIBA drawings collection (DEV 64:40–42); IAA photograph (37/0).

87. KILLARNEY LUNATIC ASYLUM, Killarney (2).
The site for this new provincial asylum was agreed in 1847 and the design by Sir Thomas Deane completed for admissions five years later. One of its gate lodges is contemporary with the complex built during the Famine, when it was criticised as being too elaborate.

Castleisland Road gate; 1873; architect probably Sir T.N. Deane.
An appropriate introduction to the great pile beyond is this 1½-storey steeply gabled Tudor Gothic gatehouse with irregular fenestration in a variety of arched openings dressed in cut stone contrasting with coursed random rubble facings, the attractive lancet doorway containing a sheeted door with

ornamental strap hinges. Moulded kneelers at the foot of layered skew-tables are repeated as features on the entrance pillars. The complementary chimney-stack has sadly been reduced to a nasty rendered stump and the lodge lies derelict and boarded up. Possibly to the design of Benjamin Woodward.

Tralee Road gate; 1887; architect J.F. Fuller.

An altogether less satisfactory composition, not helped by the imposition of modern windows and the probable loss of decorative bargeboards. A lumpy 1½-storey gabled structure built off a T-plan in coursed rubble with dressed openings and quoins. To one side a recessed porch with shouldered archway. Presumably dating from the time of additions to the main building to the designs of J.F. Fuller in 1887. In use. Now St Finian's Hospital.

Slater 1856; Williams 1994; O'Dwyer 1997b.

88. KILLARNEY UNION WORKHOUSE, Killarney; *c.* 1840; architect G. Wilkinson.
An institution commenced in 1840, almost inevitably to plans by the prolific George Wilkinson but not in his standard Tudor Gothic manner, here in a quite restrained Italianate style, as required by the local Poor Law guardians. In matching mode is this pair of single-storey lodges facing each other across the approach, lacking their original

uniting entrance screen. Remarkable for their generosity of size, each forming a double pile and matching the workhouse within in their shallow roof pitch with paired barge brackets and random rubble walls having contrasting ashlar quoins, door-cases and brick-dressed windows. Some large paired chimney-stacks survive. The right-hand block was extended *c.* 1902 to form a triple pile. In use. Although first admissions were not until 1845, the lodges appear on the first OS map of 1840.

PGI; *IB* (31 July 1902); O'Connor 1995; O'Dwyer 1997a.

89. KILLELTON, Ballylongford (2).
The fine old residence of the Hickie family lies ruinous and both its porters' lodges demolished, one dating from before 1841, the other, its replacement, deeper within the estate.

90. KILLORGLIN RECTORY, Killorglin (2).
Clearly an important living to warrant two lodges, or rather reflecting a wealthy incumbent such as Revd William De Moleyns, who was rector 1835–63, grandson of the 1st Baron Ventry of Burnham [*q.v.*]. Both have been demolished.

BPB (1929); Leslie 1940.

91. KILMEANY, Duagh (3).
Two surviving lodges post-date the arrival of the railway that cut through the property of Pierce K. Mahony, which also went under the names of 'Kilmorna' and 'The Rookery'.

Abbeyfeale gate; *c.* 1841/*c.* 1855.
A replacement lodge to a predecessor of the Gun family that was likewise located opposite the entrance. A single-storey standard 1½-storey building with steeply gabled roof and similarly treated central projection. Plain, with high clipped eaves and verges over rendered walls with modern windows. Occupied.

Listowel gate; *c.* 1855.
Identical to the above.

Bary 1994.

KILMORNA (see KILMEANY)

KILTEALY (see SEAVIEW)

92. KNOCKANE RECTORY, Churchtown; pre-1841; *demolished.*
The glebe house was built in 1828 with the aid of a loan of £461 from the Board of First Fruits and a gift of £276 probably from the family of the then incumbent, Revd Edward Fitzgerald Conyers, sums which may have gone some way towards providing a

contemporary gatekeeper's lodge. Revd Conyers nevertheless resided at Churchtown House [*q.v.*].

Lewis 1837; *IFR*.

93. KNOCKNAMAN TOWNLAND, Milltown; pre-1841; *demolished.*
A gate lodge to an anonymous house in the townland belonging to William Thompson in 1852; it had been removed by 1895.

Griffith 1853–63.

94. KNOCKNASEED, Rathmore; pre-1841; *demolished.*
A lodge built for the Duggan family, sited opposite what is today a very modest entrance.

Bary 1994.

LAKE HOTEL (see CASTLELOUGH)

95. LAKE VIEW, Killarney; *c.* 1870; architect possibly William Atkins.

The O'Connells lived on the estate, then known as 'Maulagh', at the beginning of the nineteenth century, leasing from the Herbert family. By 1869 James O'Connell (1786–1872) had been created a baronet and found his old house wanting, building the present Classical replacement and a gate lodge suitable to his new standing.

This is a pleasing three-bay symmetrical structure on a plinth, with rendered walls in gloss white finish, a hybrid composition combining Italianate features and Tudor label-moulded openings. The main body of the lodge is under a hipped roof with carved soffit brackets and gabled projections, one to the road, the other a hallway to the avenue front, both with paired slit windows and blank shields over. Occupied and pristine. The gates and railings have palmette finials, the pillars in ashlar, solid and chamfered with chunky corniced cappings, reminiscent of other such entrances about the county designed by William Atkins.

Bary 1994.

96. LANSDOWNE LODGE, Kenmare; pre-1895; *demolished.*
Of the fine old Georgian house, home to the marquis of Lansdowne's agents, or its gate lodge, built after 1841, nothing remains.

97. LASSINAGH, Ballynahaglish (2).
Early lodge; pre-1841; *demolished.*
Located to the north-west on the original avenue, the lodge may have become redundant when the later approach was formed.

Later lodge; *c.* 1845.

Presumably created for John Day Stokes is this once-fine single-storey Regency-style lodge. Originally presenting a short main front to the avenue with a single window set in a segmentally arched recess, it probably had balancing lower gabled projections from opposing side elevations, much as popularised by the Morrison architectural practice. What appears today is becoming indistinguishable from a modern bungalow with its unsympathetic choice of replacement windows. Contemporary with it is a very fine gatescreen with stone outer pillars and concave railed quadrants framing a tripartite gateway of four inner 'cage' posts, each with little crenellations, on which are hung gates with fleur-de-lis finials.

Bary 1994.

98. LEEBROOK, Tralee; *c.* 1810.

Built by Capt. Rowland Chute is this plain standard single-storey hip-roofed cottage with harled walls. Projecting towards the park is a later outsize hallway flanked by hideous flat-roofed additions. Of greater interest is a gatescreen of *c.* 1850, comprised of four square pillars containing carriage gates and concave ashlar quadrant walls, the right-hand one of which is pierced by a bipartite label-moulded Tudor-style opening with crenellations over, probably intended as the front windows of a replacement lodge, as actually realised at Ballyard [*q.v.*] and Belmont [*q.v.*] nearby.

99. LESLIE LODGE, Tarbert; pre-1841; *demolished.*
A seat sometime also called 'Shanaway', founded by the Leslie family, which passed to the Hallyburtons by marriage. The lodge may, however, have been built for the Parker family, tenants here between 1814 and 1846.

Leet 1814; Slater 1846.

100. LETTER or LITTOR, Ballylongford; *c.* 1800.
A small, gabled, single-storey structure with minuscule windows in limewashed walls, built by the Wren family. Derelict.

101. LISMORE, Tralee; *c.* 1860
A standard single-storey gabled lodge left undistinguished by modern 'improvement'—synthetic slates, plastic windows and cement-rendered walls. Recognisable are the original toothed quoins and door-case. There is a striking contemporary ornamental gatescreen with square iron gate posts having recessed panels and spiky knob finials, framed by concave railed quadrants with a repeating quatrefoil motif. Manufactured locally for Edward Day Stokes or his successor here, Stephen Huggard.

Griffith 1853–63; Bary 1994.

102. LISTOWEL HOSPITAL [NEW], Listowel; *c.* 1930; architect Vincent Kelly.

Built on the site of the Union Workhouse of 1845 is this hospital in the International style, and its striking gate lodge to match. It is a single-storey asymmetrical flat-roofed composition with a curved corner window, a canopy over extending to cap engaged columns, the fluting of which is carried into a porch recess. To the right-hand side is a porthole window, like the steel of the others replaced by plastic. There are similar lodges at the Cashel [*q.v.*] and Nenagh [*q.v.*] Hospitals, Co. Tipperary, also by Vincent Kelly. Contemporary rendered gate pillars, with modern lanterns atop, stop the original rubble convex quadrant walls of the old workhouse.

O'Dwyer 1997a.

103. LISTOWEL HOSPITAL [OLD], Listowel; pre-1839/pre-1900; *demolished.*
The old fever hospital was acquired as home to St Michael's College for boys, the new porter's lodge to which went the way of its predecessor.

LITTOR (see LETTER)

104. LOHERCANNON, Tralee; pre-1842; *demolished.*
An old seat originally of the Day family but subsequently let in the early nineteenth century to a succession of tenants.

105. LOUGH, Dingle; pre-1841; *demolished.*
The curved avenue led to a residence of the Hussey family.

106. MAGH, Ballymacelligot; pre-1841.
William Sealy in 1830 carried out improvements to his old family house at a cost of £2,000, which may have included the

building of the gate lodge. All that remains of this are two blocked-up openings and toothed quoins in a façade which also forms the right-hand entrance quadrant wall in a rusticated finish, terminating in punched limestone ashlar pillars. A property later renamed 'Edenburn' by Samuel Murray Hussey.

Bary 1994.

107. MASSEYVILLE, Ballynahaglish; pre-1841; *demolished.*
Presumably so called by a Massey, one of a series of marine residences along this stretch of coast. The porter's lodge was sited at an access that was common to the neighbouring properties of Bath Lodge and White Lodge.

MILLTOWN (see KILCOLEMAN ABBEY)

108. MOUNT EAGLE LODGE, Brosna; pre-1841; *demolished.*
Both the hunting lodge and its gatekeeper's cottage, built in 1830 by Capt. Charles G. Fairfield, have gone.

Bary 1994.

109. MOUNT HAWK, Tralee; *c.* 1850; *demolished.*
A fine early Victorian Classical villa built by George Day Stokes, which along with its lodge had been removed by 1990.

McMorran and O'Keeffe 2005.

110. MOUNT PROSPECT, Castleisland; pre-1893; *demolished.*
A house existed here in 1814 but the porter's lodge post-dated 1841, probably built by William E. Young.

Leet 1814; Bary 1994.

111. MOUNT PROSPECT, Killarney; pre-1841.
A property alternatively known by its townland name of Ballynamaunagh whereon a house was built in 1790 by John Murphy. Its gate lodge obviously received a mid-Victorian make-over, having been raised to provide loft accommodation and acquiring foil and wave bargeboards in the process. Originally a standard single-storey structure, it now lies derelict, lacking avenue and big house.

Bary 1994.

112. MOUNT RIVERS, Killorglin; pre-1841; *demolished.*
A seat of the Blennerhassett family, the porter's lodge to which was located opposite its entrance.

MOUNT ST JOSEPH'S PRESENTATION CONVENT (see RATHMORE)

113. MUCKROSS, Killarney (5).
The Herbert family has resided in this serene, much-visited spot since the late seventeenth century. Their first house on the site, built between 1720 and 1750, was by 1788 described as 'a very mean and ruinous structure', but in 1805 Carr found the second

113. Muckross, Killarney, Dromyrourk gate.

house 'a comfortable one'. In 1835 Robert Graham recorded 'the remains of Muckruss house', when the estate had become run-down. What he had found was the prelude to a grand rebuilding. Henry Arthur Herbert (1815–66), having inherited the property as a minor in 1823 on the premature death of his elder brother, on achieving his majority wasted little time in improving the place. In 1837 he married Mary Balfour of Whittinghame, near Edinburgh, where they encountered the young Scottish architect William Burn, who was to become the most prolific of the age, and he it was that they engaged to transform Muckross. The rebuilding programme saw the erection of a grand new Tudor Revival mansion, many estate workers' cottages and two replacement porters' lodges for those indicated on the 1842 OS map.

Dromyrourk gate; *c.* 1845; architect probably William Burn.
A delightful single-storey harled cottage on a simple square plan below a pyramidal roof, its outline enlivened by a variety of elevation tricks. The front two-bay façade is comprised of a gabled doorway alongside a canted bay window with small-paned sashes below a semi-umbrello roof. To one side elevation is a small gabled projection, while the opposing front displays an outsize staged chimney-stack. Perhaps lack of funds prevented the architect from providing a more appropriate Tudor Revival prelude to the big house.

Carrignafreaghan gate; *c.* 1845; architect probably William Burn.

Identical to the Dromyrourk lodge, situated opposite the boat-house entrance.

A second phase of building on the estate was prompted by the visit of Queen Victoria to Killarney in 1861, an event which, financially, the Herberts could have done without. Nevertheless, the Cork architect William Atkins was engaged to effect improvements appropriate for a royal welcome in the form of a noble *porte-cochère* addition to the house and a majestic lodged entrance to the demesne.

Knockreer gate; 1861; architect William Atkins.

An impressive Picturesque Tudor Revival 1½-storey gatehouse, its steeply pitched roofs exhibiting diamond-pattern slating and complicated ornate foiled bargeboards. Built in rubble stone with contrasting finely chiselled quoins and dressings to transomed and mullioned windows with latticed lights. To the leading gable is a single-storey canted bay window rising off a battered plinth, capped by a layered stone roof, and in the internal angle the arched doorway is under a monopitched canopy on decorative hewn stone piers. The complementary gatescreen with extensive ogee-walled and railed quadrants is punctuated by piers and hefty High Victorian buttressed and gabled carriage

pillars with the Herbert bearings and the motto PAWB YN EU ARFER ('Every man according to his taste'). The Gothic ironwork is rather more delicate, with shields and fleur-de-lis finials, by Perrott of Cork. There is a very similar gatescreen to the Sisters of Mercy Convent, Tralee [*q.v.*].

D.A. Beaufort 1788; Carr 1806; Heaney 1999; *LGI* (1904); Williams 1994; Lawrence photograph (5179C).

114. NURSERY COTTAGE, Tralee; *c.* 1860; *demolished.*
A property in 1852 of Patrick O'Sullivan, proprietor of the adjacent nursery.

Griffith 1853–63.

115. OAKPARK, Tralee (4).
Prior to the estate's transformation into Oakpark demesne it had alternatively been called 'Killeen' or 'Woodlawn', the lands having been given to Rowland Bateman after the Cromwellian wars. It would have been John Bateman (1792–1865) who built three gate lodges after 1841, only one of which survives, one within and another to the western approach having been demolished.

East entrance; 1866.
A modest single-storey standard building with a hipped roof, its walls roughcast and Virginia creeper-clad. Derelict.

In 1849 the estate was purchased by Maurice Fitzgerald Sandes (1805–79) of the Sallow Glen [*q.v.*] family. He commissioned the Cork architect William Atkins to design a quite unique new house in the Ruskinian Gothic style, with striking polychromatic brickwork and contrasting stone dressings. Commenced in 1857 in the year of Sandes's marriage, it was complemented by a suitably conspicuous gate lodge and entrance gates.

Main entrance; *c.* 1860; architect William Atkins.
Perhaps not quite complementary in that, curiously, there is a pink sandstone rather than brickwork contrasting with grey cut-stone quoins, voussoirs, corbelled eaves band, plinth, skew-tables, kneelers and

chimney-stacks. One may surmise that the imported English brick was sufficient only for the house. This is a corpulent single-storey standard lodge with, like the house, fine Venetian Gothic ogee-arched openings with foiled inserts. Hip-roofed with a gabled projection to the avenue, in the apex of which is a semi-quatrefoil feature with blank shield. The chamfered chimney-stacks reflect the entrance pillars, six of which punctuated the extensive gatescreen with railed concave quadrants. Two of the carriage pillars, their caps ornamented with acanthus leaves, have been relocated to accommodate modern traffic. There are similar chamfered pillars at Ballard [*q.v.*] and Coolclogher [*q.v.*].

LGI (1904); *LG* (1912); *IAR* (1998); Bary 1994.

OAK VILLA (see ANN'S VILLA)

116. THE PARK, Killarney; pre-1841; *demolished.*
A property of the Cronin family, which became the Castle Heights Hotel. The gate lodge lay vacant in 1852.

Griffith 1853–63.

117. PARKMORE, Currans; pre-1841; *demolished.*
A secondary seat of the Merediths of Dick's Grove [*q.v.*]. The gatescreen survives with 'candlestick' inner pillars and square outer.

118. PARK-NA-DOON, Tralee; *c.* 1905; architects Robert Walker and Son.

An Edwardian Arts and Crafts lodge, single-storey under a hipped roof which catslides above a rear hall and to the front over a break-front bay window with tiny squared panes. Roughcast, with banded window surrounds and big dominant corbelled chimney-stacks now rendered over what may be brick. Occupied. Moulded panelled gate pillars. Doubtless all part of the commission of the 'Handsome villa for W.H. McCowen J.B., cost £4,000; Robert Walker & Son of Cork', of which only its walls were left standing after a fire in 1917 that probably prompted William Henry McCowen to leave the country in 1920, having inherited hardware and shipowning businesses on the death of his father in 1901.

IB (20 May 1905 and 7 July 1917); McMorran and O'Keeffe 2005.

119. PLOVER HILL, Ballynahaglish; pre-1841; *demolished.*
Both the house, built in 1814 by Barry William Gunn, and its lodge have gone.

Bary 1994.

PYRMOUNT (see FERMOUNT)

120. RATHMORE, Rathmore; pre-1841; *demolished.*
Originally a property of the Cronin family of the Park [*q.v.*] but since the 1830s Mount St Joseph's Presentation Convent. The house survives along with an entrance screen of squat square limestone ashlar pillars and a rustic stile in one quadrant wall; the lost lodge was opposite it.

Bary 1994.

121. RATTOO, Ballyduff; pre-1841; *demolished.*
The porter's lodge, which had gone by 1921, was built by the Gunn family for an earlier house on the site.

RED CLIFF (see FOILDARRIG)

122. THE REEKS, Churchtown; pre-

1841/*c.* 1850; architect not known.
A property alternatively known as 'Bunecloon' or 'Whitefield', it has an immense entrance screen, becoming of The McGillicuddy. The lodge shown on the first OS map must be a predecessor of this surviving very smart Italianate composition. Single-storey and built off an L-plan below a shallow hipped roof with a bulky four-flue stack atop. All in a glossy white rendered finish, a break-front to the avenue elevation having three round-headed slit sash windows, to the road front a pair of the same and in the internal angle a flat-roofed hallway with Doric pi-

lasters. Occupied and immaculately tended. To a great pebbled forecourt are four octagonal ashlar inner pillars to a triple gateway, and another two distant containing extensive railed quadrants on dwarf walls. All built for Richard McGillicuddy (1790–1866), who inherited in 1827.

LGI (1904).

123. REENNAFURIRA, Sneem (2).

Rear entrance; *c.* 1860.

A long 1½-storey gabled lodge with gablets in a mild Picturesque manner, probably built by a Captain Hartley, who was leasing the property from the Fuller family. Occupied.

Front entrance; *c.* 1890.

A very plain late Victorian bungalow below a hipped roof, its left-hand bay a gabled projection alongside a recessed porch. Rendered, with twentieth-century windows.

Bary 1994.

124. ROCKBROOK, Farranfore; pre-1841; *demolished.*

A lodge doubtless contemporary with a house built by Francis Twiss in 1837.

Bary 1994.

125. ROCKVILLE, Castleisland; pre-1841; *demolished.*

Like the late Georgian gates are simple limestone ashlar pillars, contrasting with lovely Art Nouveau ironwork to the short flanking screens added by the Reidys, who succeeded the Miles family, builders of the lodge. A house later renamed 'Crag' after the townland.

126. ROSS CASTLE, Killarney; *c.* 1750; *demolished.*

Sometime in its chequered history the old O'Donoghue stronghold at the bridged crossing to Ross Island was guarded by a lodge, the evidence for which is a Thomas Walmsley painting of 1796. It may have dated from after the initial Browne family occupancy, when military barracks proper were built. These went out of use in 1825 and, judging by its absence from the 1841 OS map, it must have been demolished between these dates, when it returned to Browne ownership.

NGI

This lodge, or guardhouse, was a single-storey square structure with bipartite windows, a pyramidal roof and tall chimney-stack to one corner. Alongside was a pillared gateway.

Larner 2005.

127. ROSS COTTAGE, Killarney; *c.* 1830; *demolished.*

On Ross Island a delightful *cottage orné*, built by the earl of Kenmare, was described in 1845 as the residence of the head forester of the demesne. Sadly both it and its gate lodge, which lay in the shadow of Ross Castle [*q.v.*], have gone.

PGI.

128. ROSSDOHAN, Sneem; *c.* 1875; architect John Pollard Seddon.

Samuel Thomas Heard bought the island in 1873 and returned from India to create a subtropical garden as a setting for his peculiar new house, a creation of architect J.P. Seddon, a pioneer of the bungalow. It was burnt down in the 1920s and replaced, but its gate lodge, in like vein, survives.

At the crossing to the island is this unusual 1½-storey structure on an L-plan with hipped gables, one wing containing a single-storey canted bay viewing the approach. In the internal angle the previously open porch below a catslide roof is now enclosed. To seaward is a bulky two-stage chimney-stack, while the verges display corbel stones which once supported ornamental woodwork. All built in boulder-effect masonry containing inappropriate replacement windows. Occupied. Plain cylindrical rubble gate pillars.

Bence-Jones 1988; Darby 1983; Bary 1994.

129. ROUGHTY LODGE, Kenmare; pre-1842; *demolished.*

A property in the early nineteenth century of Captain Massey Herbert, set in beautiful country by the Roughty River.

Bary 1994.

130. ROYAL VICTORIA HOTEL, Killarney; pre-1841; *demolished.*

By all accounts—and there were many in the nineteenth century—a very fine establishment, its long-time proprietor being the admirable Mr Thomas Finn, appreciated amongst others on their travels by W.M. Thackeray. Capable of accommodating up to 60 visitors, it and its lodge may, from its name, have dated from 1837.

Thackeray 1897; Lacy 1853; Larner 2005.

131. RUSHEEN, Aghavallen; pre-1841; *demolished.*

Both the Crosbie family house and its lodge have gone, the latter by 1921.

132. SACKVILLE, Ardfert; pre-1842; *demolished.*

A house built in 1788 by Thomas Graves, dean of Ardfert and Aghadoe, the gatekeeper's lodge to which may have been contemporary or built by his successors, the Crosbies of Ardfert Abbey [*q.v.*]. Both lodge and home have gone, the former replaced by a twentieth-century bungalow.

Wilson 1803; Bary 1994.

ST CATHERINE'S COUNTY HOSPITAL (see TRALEE UNION WORKHOUSE)

ST FINAN'S HOSPITAL (see KILLARNEY LUNATIC ASYLUM)

ST JOHN'S CEMETERY (see TRALEE NEW CEMETERY)

ST MICHAEL'S COLLEGE (see LISTOWEL HOSPITAL [OLD])

133. SALLOW GLEN, Tarbert (3).

The mansion of the Sandes family has gone, to be survived by two of its porters' lodges.

North-west gate; *c.* 1810.

A 1½-storey three-bay cottage, with doorway to the left-hand side in limewashed harled walls and hipped gables over tiny loft windows. Built by William Sandes I (1736–1812) to what was described around 1803 as 'the new and handsome seat', it is occupied and seems to have outlived what was intended to be its successor across the road, opposite gateposts which are smaller versions of those to the other entrance.

South-east gate; *c.* 1855.

Presumably built by William Sandes II (1799–1867) is this Picturesque English cottage, originally two-bay with a steeply gabled roof, one bay as a breakfront. Mildly ornamental replacement wavy bargeboards and new plastic windows with chinoiserie glazing pattern, probably reflecting the originals. Otherwise extended sympathetically in the twentieth century to create holiday accommodation. Four stone gateposts with monolithic ball finials and nice decorative ironwork to a tripartite gateway.

Wilson 1803; *LGI* (1904).

134. SCART, Castlecove; pre-1842; *demolished.*
A charming Georgian villa of the Jermyn family, the gate lodge to which had gone by 1896.

135. SEAFIELD, Ballynahaglish; *c.* 1890.
A single-storey gabled cottage with wave and foil bargeboards and clipped eaves to its two-bay front window façade. Derelict and overgrown. Four good chamfered, punched ashlar pillars with tiered cappings and fine cast-iron gates to a disused avenue. Probably built by James Coffey after he had acquired a property previously called 'Eden Cottage' from St John Henry Donovan.

Bary 1994.

SEAVIEW (see GLENMORE)

136. SEAVIEW, Tralee; *c.* 1850.
A pleasant, unpretentious 1½-storey lodge, with tall eaves to a roof steeply hipped to accommodate loft rooms. Two-bay front elevation with doorway to the left-hand side in rendered walls painted in corporate colours to what is now 'Kiltealy House Hotel' but had been called 'Cahirconree'. Patrick Ryan was the occupant in 1852.

Griffith 1853–63.

SHANAWAY (see LESLIE LODGE)

137. SISTERS OF MERCY CONVENT, Tralee; 1894; architect not known.

A showy structure to a complex which developed from the 1860s in the convent chapel and orphanage to the school of *c.* 1891, with which the lodge shares many architectural details and the distinctive Tralee polychromatic mix of punched red limestone with white limestone quoins, plinth trim and window dressings. Single-storey on an L-plan and gabled, with mildly ornamental bargeboards having perforated toes and carved trussed apex features, the windows bipartite and tripartite openings with trefoil chamfered heads. In the internal angle is a flat-roofed entrance porch with shouldered arched support and a chamfered pier. Subsequently much altered and extended to the rear with commendable sensitivity.

The bold gatescreen pre-dates the lodge by around 30 years and identifies work within almost certainly by architect William Atkins, the pillars being nearly identical to his main entrance at Muckross [*q.v.*]. As there, the tripartite gateway has hefty buttressed pillars with gabled cappings having trefoil-sectioned ridges, each with Celtic cross motif. The screen extends with intermediate piers to convex quadrant dwarf walls and cast-iron railings with palmette finials.

NIAH.

138. SOUTH HILL, Killarney (2).
The first gate lodge that served the house built by John Leahy (1770–1846) in 1810 was close by at the end of a short avenue. By *c.* 1855 his barrister son of the same name (1810–74) had

transformed the house and located a replacement gatekeeper's lodge 100 yards further west, both to designs by William Atkins. To a property then renamed 'Coolclogher' after its townland Atkins produced this eccentric little building opposite its gates, perched on the banks of the River Flesk. Single-storey over a basement, it presents below a half-umbrello roof a canted front to the road having its own quirky breakfront gablet with skew-tables. Alongside is a gabled entrance hall at right angles with, as other openings, round-arched heads in glossy white walls with black highlights, all embraced by a moulded sill course and coved eaves band. Over are decorative cast-iron hip-knobs and large corbelled chimney-stack. Across the road are good chamfered ashlar gate pillars with four-faced segmentally pedimented cappings and 'Coolclogher' chiselled in below, supporting very fine cast-iron carriage gates with repeating Tudor Gothic tracery and helically twisted railed uprights.

LGI (1904); Williams 1994.

139. SPA LODGE, Ballynahaglish; pre-1841; *demolished.*
One of many marine residences on this stretch of Tralee Bay, all having ever-changing occupancy. A gate lodge that had gone by 1897.

TANAVALLA (see GARRYATANVALLY)

140. TARBERT, Tarbert; pre-1921; *demolished.*
A porter's lodge built after 1841 for Robert Leslie.

141. TIERACLEA, Tarbert; *c.* 1845; architect not known.

An exceptionally well-proportioned and understated entrance ensemble designed for Stephen Edward Collis (1794–1880). A fine gateway of four ashlar pillars with plain recessed panels and moulded cappings on which are hung cast-iron gates with fleur-de-lis finials and a highly ornate meeting rail, all framed by wide concave quadrant walls of continuous raised uncoursed hewn-faced panels. Across the road is the single-storey standard lodge under steeply pitched hipped roof with paired carved soffit brackets and banded ashlar chimney-stack. In harled walls are small-paned bipartite casement windows on each side of a double-leafed sheeted door with mouth-organ fanlight below a gabled canopy on carved wooden posts. The house was burnt in 1902, its lodge lying sadly derelict.

Bary 1994.

142. TORC COTTAGE, Killarney; *c.* 1815; architect not known.

NLI

Opposite the entrance is a pretty Regency single-storey porter's lodge, originally three-roomed and built off a T-plan, extending to the road in a canted front below a half-umbrello in an otherwise hipped roof from which rises a cluster of three octagonal chimney-pots at the junction of ridges. In stuccoed walls are delightful and intricate Y-traceried windows in Tudor Gothic arched openings. Extended sympathetically to the right-hand side; occupied. Across the road is a charming latticed cast-iron fence to a demesne which formed part of the neighbouring Muckross [*q.v.*] estate of the Herberts, variously used by them as retreat, dower house or when their principal seat was being rebuilt. Torc Cottage is now demolished.

Larner 2005; Lawrence photograph (2718R).

143. TRALEE CASTLE, Tralee (4).
Much of this fine demesne survives as a public park. It was originally the setting for a castle of the earls of Desmond, by whom it was forfeited and granted to the Denny family. Although the old castle was demolished in 1827, it was the intention of Sir Edward Denny, 4th baronet (1796–1889), who inherited in 1831, to build himself a new mansion here. This never materialised, but his preparations for it did in the form of tree-planting, the laying of gravel paths, the construction of an ornamental grotto and the furnishing of the place with gate lodges at three entrances to the park, only one of which remains.

Garryouth gate; *c.* 1840; *demolished.*

Castle Countess gate; *c.* 1840; *demolished.*

Denny Street gate; *c.* 1840; architect not known.

On the main approach from the town, looking to be of a later date is this fine Picturesque 1½-storey cottage with gable door, steeply pitched to accommodate attic rooms. Built off a T-plan, an entrance breakfront contains a hood-moulded Tudor-arched porch with a pretty slit window over, while ground-floor windows are label-moulded, transomed and mullioned and lattice-glazed in rendered walls. To the

avenue gable is a single-storey canted bay window with decorative bargeboards above, carved into a myriad of pendentives. A photograph of *c.* 1900 shows the lodge with ornamental octagonal chimney-stacks and nestling cosily into its park setting, from which it is now parted.

Inner gate; *c.* 1810.
Now unrecognisable through modernisation, but a 1960s photograph reveals a basic rustic hip-roofed single-storey cottage with a projecting gabled hall and diagonally set chimney-stack rising off the rear wall. It stood at the entrance to the old walled garden, subsequently occupied by Walsh Memorial Schools.

McMorran and O'Keeffe 2005; Diggin 1998.

144. TRALEE NEW CEMETERY, Tralee; *c.* 1875; *demolished.*

Surviving is a good pair of pillars and Gothic carriage gates, probably purloined from the Kilcoleman Abbey [*q.v.*] entrance. In quality ashlar, chamfered with steeply gabled cappings, one displays a plaque with the information: 'St. John's New Cemetery Opened 1860 by Rev. Anthony Denny Rector and Rev. John Mawe P.P.' Of the lodge there is no trace, but a sketch by Caroline Sloane shows a structure that appears High Victorian and later than 1860. It was 1½-storey with skew-tables and kneelers to gables, an irregular three-bay elevation comprised of lancet-headed openings, some below like relieving arches in stone walls, in a mix of single, bipartite and tripartite lights with latticed glazing. The effect is heightened by a bold plinth and large chunky chimney-stacks.

Diggin 1998.

145. TRALEE FEVER HOSPITAL, Tralee; pre-1841; *demolished.*
Described in 1837 as a substantial modern building, capable of accommodating 200 patients, it and its gate lodge have been replaced by Jeffer's Institute.

Lewis 1837.

146. TRALEE GAOL, Tralee; 1812; architect Sir Richard Morrison.

IAA

A symmetrical three-bay two-storey gatehouse, with hipped roof and central open pediment supported on console brackets penetrated by a round-arched window and below a gated carriage opening, like the flanking windows having prominent voussoirs. All windows set in rectangular recesses in conspicuously rusticated ashlar walls. A surprising survivor of a much greater complex, which has been largely removed.

McParland *et al.* 1989.

147. TRALEE MILITARY CEMETERY, Tralee; pre-1938; *demolished.*
The lodge was built after 1841 but has been replaced by a bungalow.

148. TRALEE UNION WORKHOUSE, Tralee; *c.* 1841; architect G. Wilkinson; *demolished.*
A lodge seems to have been in position before first admissions to the workhouse in 1844, a complex almost inevitably to plans of that most productive of architects George Wilkinson. Now St Catherine's Hospital.

O'Connor 1995; IAA.

149. TUBRID, Ardfert; pre-1841; *demolished.*
Neither the big house nor its porter's lodge survives. Originally a seat of the Crosbie family, which passed in the early nineteenth century through Townsend Gunn to the Hilliards.

150. TULLIG, Castleisland; pre-1841; *demolished.*
A property owned by the Saunders family, the gate lodge to which was derelict by 1893.

WHITE LODGE (see MASSEYVILLE)

WHITEFIELD (see THE REEKS)

WOODFORD (see BALLINRUDDERY)

151. WOODLANDS, Tarbert; *c.* 1800.
The pathetic remains of a little single-storey Georgian Gothic gatekeeper's lodge built in rubble stone, presenting a shallow canted front to the avenue, its road elevation blind but a two-window bay to the park. The house, which survives, is said to have been built by a Mr Craven, though it was occupied by Thomas O'Connor in 1814, when it was known as 'Aghana'.

Leet 1814; Bary 1994.

152. WOODLAWN, Killarney; pre-1841; *demolished.*
A gate lodge, removed by 1938, was built by Pierce Mahony (1750–1819) or his son of the same name (1792–1863). Their house is also no more.

LGI (1904).

WOODLAWN (see OAKPARK)

153. WOODMOUNT, Milltown; pre-1841; *demolished.*
Both the house and its gate lodge of the Eager family are lost without trace.

COUNTY LIMERICK

1. ABINGTON RECTORY, Cappamore (2).
Neither the original porter's lodge, which commanded the old eastern approach before 1840, nor its successor on the new southern avenue survives. A glebe house built in 1804 on twenty acres for Revd William Galwey (1762–1833) after he had moved from the adjacent Caherconlish parish [*q.v.*]. It was occupied by Revd William Francis Seymour (1823–99), the probable builder of that replacement, between 1872 and his death.

Lewis 1837; NIAH; Seymour and Leslie 2012.

2. ADARE MANOR, Adare (11).
Embraced by a meander of the River Maigue lies an idyllic and fascinating landscape with Irish ecclesiastical ruins and a variety of English domestic architecture, at the heart of which is the premier landed estate of the county in the seat of the Wyndham-Quins, earls of Dunraven. Here in 1788 the Revd Daniel Augustus Beaufort, again on leave from his flock, visited and noticed that 'The house is not grand and stands very low by the water' but failed to record on its formal north-western approach the splendid little eye-catcher which may have been the earliest of many gatekeepers' lodges to grace the demesne and adjacent deer-park.

The Gothic lodge; *c.* 1770; architect not known.

This is now a shell presiding over an early main avenue since isolated by later realignment. In a Batty Langley manner it presents a perfectly symmetrical three-bay principal front in cut stone, each ground-floor opening with an ogee head, the gable over relieved by a pair of *oeil-de-boeuf* windows which presumably lit an attic storey. Within are the remains of the fireplace in a semicircular recess to the living room. Now choked in ivy, it was probably built in the time here of Windham Quin (1717–89). The Knight of Glin remembers there having been a like structure at Tervoe [*q.v.*].

The succession to the estate in 1824 of Windham Henry Quin (1782–1850), 2nd earl of Dunraven, and his wife Caroline Wyndham signalled the demise of the old early Georgian house, about which the Revd Beaufort was so dismissive, and its gradual replacement by the grandiose rambling Tudor Gothic mansion we see today. Initially their architect was James Pain of Limerick, first mention of whom in connection with Adare is found in 1826. While documentary evidence is lacking, much of the ancillary work about the estate and village may be attributed to him.

Village gate; *c.* 1828; architect possibly James Pain.

It may well have been Pain, with his familiarity with the English Cottage Picturesque through his experience in the John Nash office, who was responsible for the series of delightful 1½-storey semi-detached cottages outside the gates, one of which served as porter's accommodation. Its steeply pitched thatched hipped roof is cut to reveal a tiny attic window, and catslides as a canopy supported by a pair of rustic tree trunks to form a porch to the front door, which is flanked by wide multi-paned casement windows in plain rendered walls. In complete contrast is the formal Classical gatescreen of great coursed random cut-stone ogee quadrant walls contained by four grand ashlar pillars crowned by ornamental urns, a design repeated as the principal entrance to the deer-park.

Abbey gate; pre-1840; *demolished.*
A lodge opposite its gates to the northern drive, which became isolated and redundant when that portion of county road was absorbed into the demesne in the mid-nineteenth century, to be superseded by the Limerick lodge further to the north-east.

Inner gate; *c.* 1830.
A plain single-storey lodge built off a T-plan below hipped roofs, in a rubble finish to walls with pilaster features as quoins. The avenue projection contains a nice tripartite window, flanked in the internal corners by nasty lean-to structures of differing dates; otherwise there are two-over-two sash windows.

West gate; 1830/*c.* 1860.
On the western approach is an unremarkable but pleasantly rustic two-storey gatehouse below a hipped roof which probably originated off a T-plan but subsequently extended with a back return. Bipartite casement windows with brick heads are framed by big corner rubble stone pilasters; '1830' is inscribed on a lintol to the gateway.

Work had commenced on the new mansion in 1832 and James Pain was involved in its construction until around 1850, during which time a programme of building estate cottages was also in progress, all dated about 1838 and to generous proportions. Four of these five almost identical buildings housed gatekeepers.

South-west outer gate; 1838; architect possibly James Pain.
At a now-abandoned entrance is this substantial two-storey gatehouse, a cube built in random uncoursed rubble, its steeply pitched skew-tables rising to solid chimney-stacks. Two-bay, with the doorway to the right-hand side in a cut-stone chamfered surround and pointed archway. Otherwise the windows have been enlarged with inappropriate modern casements, the eaves being broken by gablets to accommodate later raising of the second-floor pair; a conservatory spans the width of the lower storey; date-stone.

South-west inner gate; 1838; architect possibly James Pain.

Surviving unmodernised, with original fenestration in its first-floor window heads below eaves level, but oddly abandoned and derelict, allowing nature to take over. Date-stone.

Front deer-park gate; *c.* 1838; architect possibly James Pain.

Across the road from the demesne proper is by far the most self-conscious of this group of four gatehouses, with its conspicuous Tudor detailing in the bipartite windows, all with exaggerated chamfered surrounds and stone mullions, more pronounced kneelers to its skew-tables, large slates and chimney-stacks diagonally set on square bases. All delightfully shrouded in manicured Virginia creeper, which perhaps conceals a date-stone. The prestigious Classical entrance screen is the same as that to the main gates, with four lofty ashlar pillars having corniced cappings and urn finials, framing tall ogee quadrant walls of coursed random rubble off quarry-faced plinths.

Rear deer-park gate; 1840; architect possibly James Pain.

Like its three counterparts, this is a two-storey gatehouse in random uncoursed rubble off a square plan, with diagonally set chimney-stacks and large kneelers but plain window surrounds, those to the first floor as at the south-west outer lodge, raised with gablets to break the eaves with the inevitable increase in downpipes. Here, for variety, was a round-arched doorway, now a window with a ludicrous modern plastic window insert. Date-stone.

In 1850 the Adare estates were inherited by the 3rd earl of Dunraven, Edwin Richard Wyndham-Quin (1812–71), and, for whatever reason, there was a change of architect to complete the great house. The London practitioner Philip Charles Hardwick's commission extended to the provision of a delightful entrance lodge to grace a new gate created on the northern extremity of the demesne.

Lantern, or Limerick, lodge; *c.* 1860; architect P.C. Hardwick.

A striking and familiar landmark on the approach from Limerick is this fairytale composition, consisting of a two-storey octagonal structure in uncoursed limestone with a single central buttress and extremely narrow lead-latticed slit windows, those to the ground floor round-headed but to the upper storey trefoil-arched in steeply pitched gablets, which on alternate faces break the eaves to an octahedral roof. To the rear is a single-storey back return, and alongside a Tudor-arched carriage gateway with stepped gable connected by a little hip-roofed porch to the main structure.

Castleroberts gate; 1898; architect not known.

At the outermost boundary of the demesne is this conspicuous 1½-storey late Victorian Elizabethan Revival cottage. Built off an L-plan, the lower storey in quarry-faced masonry, with the attic floor decorated in black and white strapwork below hipped gables. One wing contains a tripartite mullioned and transomed casement light, the other a single-storey canted glazed bay window, whilst the roof catslides over the internal angle to form an entrance porch carried on ornamental carved posts. To the ridge is a cluster of three cut-stone octagonal

chimney-flues with exaggerated cappings. Presumably for Windham Thomas Wyndham-Quin (1841–1926), who had succeeded to Adare Manor in 1871 as the 4th earl of Dunraven.

Now a hotel.

Beaufort 1764–1808; Heaney 1999; *BPB* (1929); *Country Life* (15, 22 and 29 May 1969); Seoighe 1982; Williams 1994; Lee 2006.

3. AHABEG, Caherconlish; pre-1840; *demolished.*

A lodge probably built by either Richard Anderson Rose or his father Thomas Maunsell Rose (d. 1831), lost to road-widening.

LGI (1904).

4. AHNAGURRA, Ballylanders (2).

A property in 1837 of Thomas T. Adams, on which neither the house nor its two lodges survive.

Lewis 1837.

5. ALBERT VILLA, Limerick (2).

The seat in 1851 of William Finch, now lacking both its outer lodge and the pair within. Renamed 'Lanahrone' in the twentieth century.

Griffith 1853–63.

ALL SAINTS CHURCH OF IRELAND CHURCH (see STRADBALLY CHURCH OF IRELAND CHURCH)

6. ALTA VILLA, Rathkeale; *c.* 1810.

The once-grand mid-eighteenth-century Palladian-style house built by John Bateman, after whose death in 1792 a porter's lodge was added by his son of the same name. It is a simple single-storey hip-roofed cottage with limewashed harled walls, its main avenue front of two square windows, the entrance doorway to the road elevation. Unoccupied but maintained as a feature by the gates. Peter Griffin had acquired the estate by 1852, when his gatekeeper was Michael McMahon.

Griffith 1853–63; *LGI* (1912); Bence-Jones 1988.

7. ARDHU, Limerick; *c.* 1875; architect William Fogerty; *demolished.*

'Dwelling House and offices nr. Limerick for Thomas Revington. The building with its offices and gate lodge, are designed in the Italian villa style, and will cost c. £4,500. W. Fogerty, archt.' The entry in the *Dublin*

Builder magazine refers to a wealthy Limerick city merchant and his young, talented and short-lived local architect. The house survives at the centre of a hotel complex, its ill-fated lodge not in fact valued until 1878, built for Robert de Ros Rose, the subsequent owner.

DB (1 March 1865).

ARDVULLEN (see MILLMOUNT)

8. ASHBOURNE, Limerick; pre-1870; *demolished.*
A lodge, to an earlier house, built after 1840, a map 30 years later showing it to be of tiny square plan with a verandahed main front. Added by Richard Wilson, who is recorded here in 1850, his successor Revd John Delinege (1856) or Edward J. Synan (1870).

Griffith 1853–63; Slater 1856; 1870.

9. ASHFORT, Limerick; pre-1840; *demolished.*
A property in 1837 of Revd Joseph Jones.

Lewis 1837.

10. ASH HILL TOWERS, Kilmallock; pre-1840; *demolished.*

The death without issue of Chidley Coote in 1799 saw the end of that family's long association with the estate, it passing to that of his paternal grandmother, Jane Evans, in the person of his cousin and her grand-nephew Eyre Evans (1773–1856) of the Milltown Castle, Co. Cork [*q.v.*], family. He waited 30 years before refacing and extending the old Coote house into a symmetrical Romantic Castellated mansion under the direction of architect C.F. Anderson. Nothing at the gate is apparently from that phase of building, there being a twentieth-century bungalow on the gate lodge site while the gatescreen is clearly Georgian. This is comprised of extensive concave-walled quadrants framing V-jointed rusticated postilion openings on each side of graceful tall ashlar carriage pillars with moulded cornices and beautifully chiselled scroll-topped gate stops.

Lewis 1837; *BPB* (1929); Anderson *c.* 1847.

11. ASHROE, Moroe; *c.* 1820.

What appears to have been a single-storey standard, whitewashed, harled and hip-roofed lodge facing the road, subsequently opened up thereto and framed by concave wing walls, and similarly extended in dog-leg manner, that two-window-bay elevation parallel to the avenue behind a plain gatescreen; unoccupied but maintained. Probably built for John Evans, who is recorded here in 1814, and extended by his successor, Thomas P. Evans.

Leet 1814; Lewis 1837.

12. ASKEATON RECTORY, Askeaton; pre-1841; architect perhaps J. Pain; *demolished.*
A gatekeeper's lodge perhaps contemporary with 'The glebe-house, a large and handsome residence, built in 1827' and, if so, also designed by James Pain for Revd R. Murray.

Lewis 1837; IAA.

13. ATHLACCA RECTORY, Athlacca; *c.* 1825.

A single-storey hip-roofed rendered cottage, distinguished by its main single-bay front to the avenue of a window in a recess created by a pair of extending piers. Derelict. Probably of an age with the glebe house erected in 1822, which in 1837 'was a handsome residence situated on a glebe of 14 acres, the whole of which is tastefully laid out'.

Lewis 1837.

14. ATTYFLIN, Patrickswell (2).
An imposing seat of the Westropps, of whom John Westropp (1762–1839) built at least one of the porters' lodges, having succeeded to the place on the death of his father Ralph in 1806.

North gate; pre-1840; *demolished.*
The first OS map indicates a building with a cruciform plan.

South gate; *c.* 1830.
An unusually generous lodge for its age, of five bays below a steeply hipped roof, the windows six-over-six sashes below slightly segmental arches, the central three bays gathered in a breakfront below a catslide. Rendered, with its chimney-stack off centre; occupied.

LGI (1904).

15. BAGGOTSTOWN, Bruff; *c.* 1845.

Doubtless built by a John Bouchier, there being a succession of the family of that name resident here, one of whom (1811–85) succeeded to the estate on the death of another, his father, in 1845. This is a characterful little lodge, sadly neglected and overgrown. Single-storey standard below an oversailing shallow hipped roof, its main avenue front in a recess created by end piers, the transomed and mullioned cast-iron latticed windows flank a sheeted front door in limewashed harled walls, all below a single all-embracing Tudor label moulding.

LGI (1904).

16. BALLINACOURTY, Pallaskenry; pre-1840; *demolished.*
A property in the first half of the nineteenth century of the Davenport family, its porter's lodge having gone by 1923.

Leet 1814; Griffith 1853–63.

17. BALLINACOURTY LOWER, Pallaskenry; pre-1840; *demolished.*
A seat of the Evans family, its house and 44 acres in 1851 let to Thomas McFarland.

Griffith 1853–63.

18. BALLINACURRA, Limerick; pre-1840; *demolished.*
The estate in 1814 of Richard Wilson, which by 1851 had been acquired by Edmund Palmer. At the gates is a bungalow in gate lodge style, single-storey below a shallow hipped roof, wooden posts supporting a projecting porch.

Leet 1814; Griffith 1853–63.

19. BALLINCOLLOO, Bruff; pre-1840; *demolished.*
By 1927 the porter's lodge opposite the gates had gone, to a property in the early nineteenth century of the Bennett family, who by 1837 were letting it to Joseph L. Gubbins.

Leet 1814; Lewis 1837; Slater 1846.

20. BALLINGOOLA, Caherconlish; pre-1840.
Forward of the gates survives a plain single-

storey gabled structure with a corrugated-iron roof. A holding in 1814 and 1837 of the Revd Patrick Fitzgerald, vicar of Cahercorney.

Leet 1814; Lewis 1837.

21. BALLINORAN, Bruree; pre-1840; *demolished.*
A lodge, which had been removed by 1924, to a property in 1851 of the Revd James Ryan, parish priest of Bruree.

Griffith 1853–63.

22. BALLINVIRA, Adare; pre-1841; *demolished.*
A seat in 1814 of Thomas Fitzgerald, succeeded here by Gerald Browne Fitzgerald before 1837.

Leet 1814; Lewis 1837.

23. BALLYANRAHAN, Patrickswell; pre-1840; *demolished.*
A gatekeeper's lodge in 1840 sited next to a 'Thrashing Machine' on an estate of the Rose family.

Fitzgerald and McGregor 1827.

24. BALLYCAHANE COTTAGE, Crecora; pre-1840; *demolished.*
A property in 1814 of Daniel Cudmore, the lodge to which had gone by 1923.

Leet 1814.

25. BALLYCAHANE, Crecora; pre-1840; *demolished.*
By 1923 the lodge, to the seat in 1837 of Captain Scanlon, had been removed.

Lewis 1837.

26. BALLYCLOGH, Annacotty; pre-1840; *demolished.*
In 1837 a property of Paul Cudmore, who by 1870 had been succeeded here by Col. John C. Dixon, who may have been responsible for the surviving late Victorian gate sweep with its boldly vermiculated plinth.

Lewis 1837; Slater 1870.

27. BALLYCLOGH, Ballysheedy; *c.* 1800.

A single-storey late Georgian porter's lodge with a hipped roof, the slope to the avenue slightly curved to follow the short bowed façade, which has a single wide tripartite window, perhaps originally a 'Wyatt'. Walls limewashed and harled below a corbelled eaves band. Now lying derelict at the entrance to an old estate of the Furnell family. Presumably built for Michael Furnell (1758–1816), who inherited upon the death of his father in 1790.

IFR.

28. BALLYCULLEN, Askeaton; *c.* 1800.
A very dilapidated single-storey gabled cottage at the gate to a property until his death in 1807 of Carrol Patrick Naish.

LG (1875).

29. BALLYDONOHOE, Tarbert (2).
The seat of a junior branch of the Fitzgeralds of Glin Castle [*q.v.*], of whom Thomas (1800–60) inherited the place as a minor in 1806 on the death of his father, Capt. Gerald Fitzgerald, who had been dismissed from the army ten years before as a United Irishman.

West gate; *c.* 1820.
Not quite opposite the gates is a single-storey cottage with lofty eaves and hipped gables, its three-bay front having the doorway to the right-hand side.

East gate; *c.* 1845.
A single-storey standard lodge with carved soffit brackets to the oversailing eaves of a shallow hipped roof which now has a covering of incongruous concrete roll tiles, part of modernisation and extension. Occupied.

IFR.

30. BALLYHAUKISH, Hospital; *c.* 1845.

Both the house and its lodge were developed in the mid-nineteenth century, being valued in 1851 as a residence in chancery of George Carroll. A traditional, unassuming, single-storey standard gatekeeper's lodge, its rubble construction rendered in a stucco-effect finish below a hipped roof with off-centre chimney-stack. Derelict and boarded-up, outside its entrance.

Griffith 1853–63.

31. BALLYKEVAN LODGE, Ballingarry; pre-1841; *demolished.*
One of a number of seats in the vicinity of the Odell family, here in 1852 the residence of Crone Odell, whose gate porter was then Patrick Kennedy.

Griffith 1853–63.

32. BALLYKNOCKANE, Ballingarry; *c.* 1845.
A lodge built by William Scanlan sometime between the first Ordnance Survey of 1841 and the valuation of 1851. This is one of those lodges, peculiar to County Limerick, also to be found at Cappagh [*q.v.*], Glenville [*q.v.*] and Springfield Castle [*q.v.*], where the roof abuts a tall parapeted screen wall, here in coursed rubble construction, pierced by standard symmetrical three-bay fenestration to the avenue (the door since sealed). Single-storey, the roof is otherwise hipped to the rear. Derelict.

Griffith 1853–63.

33. BALLYLIN, Rathkeale; pre-1841; *demolished.*
A property in the first half of the nineteenth century of the Smith family, the lodge to which was a ruin by 1923.

34. BALLYMACREESE, Ballyneety; *c.* 1880.
A seat in the eighteenth century of the Greenes, it was acquired by the Shine family, who were in possession for the following century. The lodge, probably built by Jeremiah Shine, is a late nineteenth-century single-storey pebble-dashed bungalow, with wavy bargeboards to the main gables and that of the projecting hall.

LOI.

35. BALLYMURPHY, Crecora; pre-1840; *demolished.*
A house and lodge whose proprietor in 1837 was Eyre Powell Esq.

Lewis 1837.

36. BALLYNACARRIGA, Pallaskenry; *c.* 1850.
A single-storey five-bay lodge, gabled, as is the central breakfront with its perforated foil and wave bargeboards over a segmentally arched fanlit doorway. Rendered and much modernised. An estate in 1851 of Richard Dawson.

Griffith 1853–63.

37. BALLYNAGARDE, Ballyneety (3).
Here are the tragic and sparse remnants of a once-proud landed estate, its big house of

IAA

1774 lying a ruin and all of its pre-1840 lodges demolished. On the evidence of an old photograph, one of these was of considerable sophistication and may be that which appears from the first OS map to have been under construction in 1840 for John Corker (1784–1858) to designs of an unidentified architect. It was a superb design—a single-storey standard hip-roofed cottage wrapped up in a neo-Classical cloak of ashlar topped by an entablatured parapet. Six-over-six Georgian sash windows flanked a portico, its shallow pediment containing the Corker bearings, carried on two pairs of Doric columns with corresponding pilasters. Within is a segmental entrance screen with panelled doors leading to both of the principal rooms. A sturdy cut-stone chimney-stack crowned the ridge.

LGI (1904); Bence-Jones 1988; IAA photograph (31/41 Z2).

38. BALLYNAHINCH, Kilmallock; pre-1841; *demolished.*
A property in 1851 of Thomas Cleary.
Griffith 1853–63.

39. BALLYNANTY, Bruff; pre-1840; *demolished.*
Originally an ancient seat of the White family, which by the nineteenth century saw a succession of different families in occupation. In 1814 Charles Creed was resident and James Kelly by 1837.
Leet 1814; Lewis 1837.

BALLYNASH CASTLE (see MANTLE HILL)

40. BALLYNOE, Ballingarry (2).
The ancestral home of the Cox family, also known as Ballynoe Cox, for much of the nineteenth century was the seat of three successive generations of William Coxes. Their big house now lies derelict, both its north and west lodges demolished, one of which in 1852 had as gatekeeper John Dea.
Griffith 1853–63; *LGI* (1886).

41. BALLYNOLAN, Pallaskenry; *c.* 1850.
A plain whitewashed and harled gabled cottage with minimal skew-tables, its three-bay front with doorway to the right-hand side; occupied. An estate in 1826 of Revd Thomas Westropp, and eleven years later of H. Potter Esq.
Fitzgerald and McGregor 1827; Lewis 1837.

42. BALLYSHEEDY, Limerick; pre-1840; *demolished.*
A property of the Fitzgibbon family, the lodge to which, opposite the gates, had gone by 1924.

43. BALLYSHEEDY WEST, Limerick; pre-1840; *demolished.*
A seat in the nineteenth century of the Furnell family.

44. BALLYSTEEN, Askeaton; pre-1841; *demolished.*
A lodge perhaps contemporary with the big house built in 1809 by General John T. Westropp (d. 1825), who had inherited the place twenty years earlier.
LGI (1904).

45. BALLYSTEEN, Shanagolden; *c.* 1865.
A mid-Victorian faintly Picturesque single-storey lodge, with scalloped slates to a steeply gabled roof having complicated ornate carved bargeboards with sawtooth-pattern overlay. Harled front elevation having now two windows, extended to the right-hand side. Occupied. A holding in 1852 of James Murray.
Griffith 1853–63.

46. BALLYVORHEEN, Cappamore; pre-1840; *demolished.*
An estate in 1814 of General Edmund Burke, which had passed to T. Holland Esq. by 1837.
Leet 1814; Lewis 1837.

47. BALLYWILLIAM, Rathkeale (4).

47. Ballywilliam, Rathkeale, south lodge.

IAA

A once-important estate well served by lodge entrances, now either removed or approaching ruin. Much of the previous grandeur was seemingly due to the efforts of George Meares Maunsell (1785–1871), who inherited the property on his father's death in 1824 and clearly enlisted the assistance of leading architect Charles Frederick Anderson.

Deer-park lodge; pre-1841; *demolished.*

West lodge; pre-1841; *demolished.*

South lodge; *c.* 1835; architect C.F. Anderson.
An outstanding neo-Classical lodge, located conspicuously in its pathetic dilapidation across the road from its gates. Innovative but not unique, as there is a lodge identical in form and detail at Kilfrush [*q.v.*] in the county and so similar to those at Gurteen le Poer, Co. Waterford [*q.v.*], as to make attribution to Anderson safe. There are also like lodges at Woodfort, Co. Tipperary [*q.v.*], and Lauriston, Co. Cork [*q.v.*], which display the same features. Single-storey and built off a three-roomed cruciform plan with pedimented projections, that to the leading front having chunky baseless Doric columns '*ex antis*', each conspicuously contained in its own corner recess. What is particularly effective is the contrast in texture and colour between the harling of the main body of the structure and the tympana and the smooth chiselled surfaces of the limestone dressings. Framed by straight curtain walls that terminate in concave quadrants and stone pillars reflected in the entrance screen opposite. Where there were once six-over-six Georgian sash windows is now boarding, ineffective against the vandals, an important small piece of Ireland's architectural heritage awaiting a saviour.

North lodge; *c.* 1875.
Again opposite its entrance is this unusually commodious 2½-storey symmetrical three-bay gatehouse with tiny windows, as are those to the attic below hipped gables. Now partly roofless and approaching ruin, the harling parting to reveal its rubble construction and brick arches. Having all the appearance of a Georgian structure, the OS maps and the red-brick chimney-stack with sawtooth corbelling reveal it to be mid-Victorian, probably built for Daniel Meares Maunsell (1819–98) not long after his father's death.

IAA

LGI (1904); IAA photographs (S826/1 & 2).

48. BEECHLAWN, Limerick; *c.* 1850.
A lofty single-storey rendered hip-roofed lodge with a catslide over the hall projection and paired modillion brackets to soffits. Modern squared casement windows are contained in rectangular recesses with pediment motifs over having acroteria and, in the tympana, peculiar devices like bunches of bananas, a detail also to be seen on the earlier house within, perhaps to celebrate the success of a thriving grocery business in the city. This is a delightful Regency villa built by James Alexander, one of three Quaker brothers to have developed the area after the completion of Wellesley Bridge and prior to the emergence of the North Circular Road, the others creating Bellevue [*q.v.*] and Janeville [*q.v.*].
Griffith 1853–63; Bennis 1940.

49. BEECHMOUNT, Rathkeale (2).
About 1800 the *Post chaise companion* found here 'the elegant seat of the late Crosbie Morgell, Esq; with beautiful and extensive parks and gardens; the demesne containing above three hundred acres, well walled in; and on which nature seems to have been lavish of her favours, in the variety of swells with which it abounds, and by the vast number of plantations lately made thereon, with the most judicious taste', and so on to describe the elegant and roomy house which in 1805 was purchased by Thomas Lloyd, who may in so doing have acquired the gate lodges, the property by then already being 'well walled in'.

East entrance; *c.* 1800.

Elevated behind a shallow concave quadrant wall of a Classical pillared triple gateway is the roofless shell of a single-storey Georgian Gothic porter's lodge with hooded lancet openings to each face of its canted front, conspicuous for its cut-stone finish and bold eaves course.

West entrance; *c.* 1760/*c.* 1830.

A charming gatekeeper's lodge in the form of a 'keep', three storeys high off a square plan in very random uncoursed rubble, rising to a minimally battlemented parapet. An old photograph shows the early chinoiserie glazing pattern to the pointed openings in irregular fenestration, now replaced by inappropriate lead-effect plastic inserts. More sensitive alongside is a single-storey hip-roofed addition in like masonry and more pronounced lancet openings, probably added by the second Thomas Lloyd (*c.* 1771–1830) to be associated with the property. A lodge wrongly identified by Rosemary ffolliott as belonging to neighbouring Rathkeale Abbey.

Wilson 1803; *LGI* (1904); ffolliott 1971b.

50. BELLEFIELD, Limerick; pre-1840; *demolished.*
A property in 1814 of Christopher A. Marrett, which subsequently passed to Daniel Gabbett, who was here until his death in 1857.

Leet 1814; *LGI* (1904).

51. BELLEVUE, Limerick; 1861.

One of three neighbouring Regency villas, the others being Beechlawn [*q.v.*] and Janeville [*q.v.*], built by the Alexander brothers, local grocers and wine retailers, on what was to become the North Circular Road. The limestone entrance pillars and cast-iron gates are of *c.* 1830 and contemporary with the house, but the porter's lodge was added about 30 years later in a fussy but delightful Italianate style. Single-storey standard in a smooth rendered finish, its round-arched fanlit doorway is flanked by square windows below entablatures carried on scrolled console brackets with acanthus leaf aprons all set in rectangular recesses to ground level. Above is a moulded eaves band to the steeply pitched hipped roof, rising to new perforated scalloped ridge tiles and hip-knobs, part of a modern restoration, admirable but for the door and window replacements. Built for Isabella, widow of William Alexander.

Griffith 1853–63; Bennis 1940.

52. BELMONT, Castleconnell; *c.* 1845; *demolished.*
By the once-famous Shannon angling resort was this occasional residence of the O'Gradys, who let it out to the Massys until 1835 and then to the Stacpoole family, in whose time here the now-lost lodge was added.

53. BELVIEW, Athlacca; pre-1840; *demolished.*
A property in the early to mid-nineteenth century of the Yielding family, whose lodge had been removed by 1924.

Leet 1814; Lewis 1837.

54. BETTY VILLE, Crecora; *c.* 1820.
A seat until his death in 1835 of John Lee, in 1826 'a handsome thatched cottage, occupied by Capt. John Franklin', a tenant. Its gatekeeper's lodge lies derelict, a single-storey structure with short principal avenue front exhibiting a wealth of toothed dressings as quoins and window surround. A flat-arched postilion opening has a fluted band.

Leet 1814; Fitzgerald and McGregor 1827; *LGI* (1904).

BISHOPSBOURNE (see LOTA)

55. BOLANE, New Kildimo; pre-1841; *demolished.*
A small estate in 1837 of Arundel Hill, the lodge to which had gone by 1923.

Lewis 1837.

56. BOSKILL, Caherconlish; *c.* 1845/*c.* 1870.

A thoroughly rustic Picturesque composition, irregular on a T-plan, which probably evolved from a taller, steeply gabled structure to which was added a lower central extension and, to an original gable, a semi-octagonal projection below an equivalent roof with a single window overlooking the avenue. The whole is in whitewashed roughcast with mainly one-over-one sash windows, basic skew-tables and bands of large scalloped slates throughout. Occupied. The original building was presumably for Benjamin Frend (1779–1858), one in a long line of that name associated with the property, and the alterations for his son Benjamin Bunbury Frend (d. 1875).

LGI (1904).

57. BRACKEN BRAE, Limerick; pre-1902; *demolished.*
A lodge built after 1871 on the North Circular Road development, removed with the creation of the new entrance to a modern housing estate. A property in 1871 of Henry Dumarisq.

58. BRITTAS, Caherconlish; *c.* 1855.
A very unassuming single-storey three-bay structure with an irregular roughcast front elevation, having clipped eaves and verges to its gabled roof; equally basic gatescreen. Built for Thomas Keys.

59. BROOKLANDS, Limerick; pre-1924; *demolished.*
A porter's lodge built after 1840 to a holding in 1851 of Elizabeth Creagh.
Griffith 1853–63.

60. BROOKVILLE COTTAGE, Kilfinnane; pre-1841; *demolished.*
A property in 1837 of T. Massey MD, to which the lodge had been removed by 1928.
Lewis 1837.

61. BRUREE AUXILIARY WORKHOUSE, Bruree; pre-1840; *demolished.*
The gatekeeper's accommodation had been removed by 1924.

62. BRUREE COTTAGE, Bruree; pre-1840; *demolished.*
A property in 1852 of Michael Ryan.
Griffith 1853–63.

63. BRUREE, Bruree (4).
The seat of R. Fetherston Esq. in 1837, when there was a single lodge, apparently removed when the property was redeveloped around 1890 for Jonathan Robert Willington Shelton (1826–92) with the building of three further porters' lodges, all beyond the boundary of the demesne.

North entrance; *c.* 1890.

Opposite the gates is a substantial 1½-storey standard decorative house with a banded and corbelled chimney-stack to each gable, perforated earthenware cresting and a pair of carefully positioned dormer windows in a slated roof which catslides to create a front verandah with decorative carved fascia carried on four chamfered and bracketed wooden posts. Behind is a pair of bipartite two-over-two sash windows on each side of a panelled and sheeted front door with rectangular fanlight in smooth rendered walls. Framed by concave quadrant walls; carved wooden chamfered gateposts with trefoil, or shamrock, tops.

South entrance; *c.* 1890.
A plain two-storey, three-bay gabled gatehouse with segmentally headed windows, those to the lower storey bipartite on each side of a later gabled hall projection. Located across the road from its gates.

Railway entrance; *c.* 1890.
Distant from the demesne proper and separated from it by a road and railway line is this 1½-storey gabled composition in polychromatic brickwork with walled entrance quadrants to match. On each side of a single-storey gabled hall projection, below lofty clipped eaves, are pairs of one-over-one

segmentally arched sash windows dressed with cream brick, repeated as quoins and string-course in otherwise mellow orange brickwork; skew-tables rise to banded and corbelled chimney-stacks.
Lewis 1837; *LGI* (1904).

64. BRUREE LODGE, Bruree; pre-1840; *demolished.*
The residence in 1837 of J. Langton Esq.
Lewis 1837.

65. BUSHY PARK, Pallaskenry; pre-1841; *demolished.*
The first OS map shows what must have been an impressive entrance, with its pair of porters' lodges on each side of an extensive gateway, sadly gone by 1923. Also known as 'Bushy Island', it was home in 1814 and 1837 to Peter Low. By 1850 it had passed to John Peppard MD, whose gatekeeper was then James Sheehy.
Leet 1814; Lewis 1837; Griffith 1853–63.

66. CAHERASS COURT, Croom; pre-1840; *demolished.*
The big house and its lodge, on an estate purchased by Jeffrey Browning (d. 1845) from Lord Carbury in the early nineteenth century, have gone. On the site of the latter is a twentieth-century bungalow in 'gate lodge' style.
LGI (1904).

67. CAHERASS HOUSE AND FLOUR MILL, Croom (3).
A concern for much of the nineteenth century of the one family in the persons of David Roche (d. 1830) and his son of the same name (1791–1865), who was created a baronet in 1838.

North gate; pre-1840; *demolished.*

Inner gate; *c.* 1830.
A once-harled single-storey lodge, now a craft shop with its limestone rubble walls exposed, with brick dressings to its four-bay front elevation, its doorway now a window, all openings below segmental heads. Gabled with clipped verges and three brick chimney-stacks. A building that seems to have assumed the role of lodge, in having no avenue shown on the first OS map. There is a good ashlar gatescreen of convex-walled quadrants between four tall square pillars having cappings with concave curved friezes.

South gate; pre-1840; *demolished.*
In 1837 'a very powerful flour-mills, fitted up in superior style, with machinery of the most improved construction', and its prosperous mill-owner's house, all swept away by extensive road works, the demesne devastated.
Lewis 1837; *BPB* (1929).

68. CAHERCONLISH, Caherconlish; pre-1840; *demolished.*
A lodge possibly contemporary with 'a handsome modern residence, erected near the site of the old family mansion, by the proprietor, Major William Wilson ... surrounded by fine plantations and ornamental grounds', as recorded in 1837 by Samuel Lewis.
Lewis 1837.

69. CAHERCONLISH RECTORY, Caherconlish; pre-1840; *demolished.*
The *Post chaise companion* found 'a most excellent glebe-house and suitable offices, built in 1794, by the Rev. Mr William Galway (1762–1833) the incumbent, under the direction of his grace Lord Somerton, then archbishop of Cashel'. Its porter's lodge may have been contemporary, but what survives at the gate today is a later structure which serves neighbouring Castle Lodge [*q.v.*], both houses unusually having shared a common entrance and each listed in the 1852 valuation as occupied by the Revd Matthew Moore, incumbent from 1835 until 1867. The rectory now lies a ruin.
Wilson 1803; Griffith 1853–63; Seymour and Leslie 2012.

70. CAHERELLY CASTLE, Fedamore; pre-1840; *demolished.*
A property since the seventeenth century of the Furnell family, containing 'quarries of very excellent limestone', the castle on which in 1826 had 'lately been handsomely fitted up by Mr Hannan'. By 1851 it was occupied by Michael Furnell (1794–1867), who was also in possession of Caherelly Cottage [*q.v.*] in the same townland.
Fitzgerald and McGregor 1827; Lewis 1837; Griffith 1853–63.

71. CAHERELLY COTTAGE, Fedamore; pre-1928; *demolished.*
In 1837 'the residence of Mr Furnell, a neat building in the cottage style, with tastefully disposed grounds'. This was the same Michael Furnell as was letting out the neighbouring Caherelly Castle [*q.v.*]. The gate lodge was not added until after 1840.
Lewis 1837; Griffith 1853–63.

72. CAHERELLY EAST TOWNLAND, Fedamore; pre-1840; *demolished.*
An anonymous property occupied in 1851 by Revd John Fogarty, leasing from Thomas Wilkinson.
Griffith 1853–63.

73. CAHERLINE, Annacotty (2).
For long an estate of the same family, there being a William Gabbett as proprietor here from the seventeenth century until the death of the last in 1828, to be succeeded by his son, William Henry Gabbett, either of whom may have been responsible for the highly individual porters' lodges. Both are eccentric and naive, clearly from an inexpert hand, by the proprietor or his jobbing builder.

Main entrance; *c.* 1830.

An otherwise unremarkable single-storey roughcast, two-roomed, hip-roofed lodge were it not for its short avenue front, which is a flat parapeted wall against which the roof abuts. This contains a single window set in a rectangular recess over which is an arbitrary Tudor label moulding, too narrow to serve any function. Derelict.

Secondary entrance; *c.* 1800/*c.* 1830.
Just forward of the right-hand convex entrance quadrant and facing the road is a three-bay symmetrical standard façade, its windows now sealed, probably to what was originally a single-storey lodge. If so, it has subsequently been raised, blind, to become a substantial two-storey gatehouse. Overlooking the basic gatescreen is a large first-floor window set in an otherwise blind bow below a cantilevered gable. Whitewashed and roughcast, it lies in an advanced state of dereliction, a medium for varied saplings.

LGI (1904).

74. CAHERLINE, Caherconlish; pre-1840; *demolished.*
Another Gabbett family property, of the same name as their estate at Annacotty [*q.v.*], in 1837 'occupied by a farmer' and fourteen years later leased to Thomas Barry.

Lewis 1837; Griffith 1853–63.

75. CAHERMOYLE, Ardagh; pre-1841; *demolished.*
Here is the rare example of an Italianate house by Ireland's leading Gothic church architect, J.J. McCarthy, built in 1870 for Edwin William O'Brien. The now-lost and substantial gate lodge within the estate was associated with the previous house, home in 1837 to William Smith, the year of his death, upon which the property passed to the O'Briens through the marriage of his daughter and co-heir, Charlotte.

Lewis 1837; *BPB* (1929); Sheehy 1977.

76. CAHIR GUILLAMORE, Meanus (2).
No longer evident is 'the very beautiful and highly improved seat of Standish O'Grady' noted in 1816. The important late seventeenth-century house now lies in ruins and its entrance lodges demolished, both that in place by 1840 and its later replacement to the east.

Mason 1814–19, vol. 2.

77. CAMASS, Bruff; pre-1840; *demolished.*
Today a twentieth-century bungalow occupies the site of the porter's lodge to a seat from 1703 of the Bevan family.

IFR.

78. CAPPAGH, Rathkeale; *c.* 1830.

A modest, standard, single-storey limewashed, harled and gabled cottage with one-over-one sash windows on each side of a sheeted door. Small and unremarkable were it not for that feature peculiar to Limerick of one gable abutting a tall, flat-topped rubble stone screen wall, in this instance facing the road. This is an idiosyncrasy also to be found in the county in lodges at Ballyknockane, Caherline, Glenville and Springfield Castle. Built for Robert Peppard. Derelict.

Leet 1814; Lewis 1837.

CAPPAMORE GLEBE (see DOONE RECTORY)

79. CAPPAMORE PRESBYTERY, Cappamore; *c.* 1880.
A plain 1½-storey gabled affair with what was a symmetrical standard rendered front elevation; later single-storey back return. Occupied, its avenue now a public road.

80. CAPPANIHANE, Ballinleeny; pre-1840; *demolished.*
A seat of the Mason family until it was sold in 1854 as an incumbered estate.

Leet 1814; Lyons 1993.

81. CAPSWOOD, Pallaskenry; pre-1923; *demolished.*
On the evidence of the surviving gate pillars with their tapering recessed 'pylon' panels the lodge may have dated from around 1850, when General James Caulfield (1782–1852) was in residence.

Griffith 1853–63; *BPB* (1929).

82. CARTOWN, Pallaskenry; *c.* 1810.
Conspicuously located on a right-angled bend in the road, commanding the entrance, forward of its gates is this single-storey standard limewashed harled lodge with a hipped roof, behind which the chimney-stack unusually rises off the rear wall. The Gothic pointed-arched doorway gives away its Georgian origin, but the two-over-two sash

windows are from a later period and probably of an age with the mid-Victorian gatescreen, with its smooth-rendered convex quadrants and moulded recessed panelled pillars with outsize cappings. A seat in 1826 of a Mr Baldwin and 50 years later of John Mulqueen.

Fitzgerald and McGregor 1827; *LOI.*

83. CASTLEGARDE, Pallasgrean (3).
Waller O'Grady (*c.* 1794–1849), barrister and second son of seven of the 1st Viscount Guillamore of Rockbarton [*q.v.*], was in 1823 to marry Elizabeth, daughter of the 3rd Lord Massy of Hermitage [*q.v.*], in expectation of which he took this old Desmond castle and, with the probable assistance of architects George Richard Pain and his brother James, made it habitable as a romantic retreat. It was adapted and extended, and in the old bawn walls an impressive gatehouse was created as an inner 'defence' before the great forecourt.

Inner gate; *c.* 1823; architects probably G.R. and J. Pain.

Preceded by wide convex quadrant walls in a finely chiselled limestone, unlike the rest of the complex, the composition is dominated by the two-storey circular tower that is the porter's accommodation, lit by a variety of apparently whimsically placed windows with round-, flat- and pointed-arched heads below label mouldings, having squared and latticed sashes and casements, all sufficiently narrow to convey the medieval effect and provide the minimum of illumination. Above is a bold machicolated and crenellated parapet, a feature continued as ramparts to the adjoining carriage gateway, with its pointed archway hooded to the visitor and a pair of great wooden doors to bar entry. A square turret bears a tiny trefoil motif and is crowned by a sculpted eagle. To the rear the gateway is relieved by a pair of mock arrowloops, while the parapet is adorned by statues of Bacchus, Mars and an unidentified goddess, all standing on their individual corbels.

Rather less thought or expense seems to have been given to the outer gates.

West entrance; pre-1840; *demolished.*
A lodge located opposite its gates that survived until after 1927.

East entrance; *c.* 1845.
A single-storey roofless shell in harled rubble construction of irregular outline, a gable atop the right-hand window of its three-bay front. Seemingly undergoing alteration and restoration in 2001.

BPB (1929); de Breffny and ffolliott 1975.

84. CASTLE IEVERS, Athlacca; pre-1840.
A lodge made almost undatable by modernisation. Single-storey and hip-roofed, with a loft room lit by a roof window in a covering of synthetic 'slates' over a two-bay main front of replacement plastic windows in cement-rendered finish. Surviving is a good gatescreen of ogee-walled quadrants framing a railed triple gateway with four hexagonal cast-iron posts. An antique estate of the Ievers family.

85. CASTLE LODGE, Caherconlish; *c.* 1850.
A modest 1½-storey gabled cottage with high eaves to accommodate a central gabled entrance breakfront flanked by two-over-two sash windows.

This commands a common entrance to an avenue which forks to serve neighbouring Caherconlish Rectory [*q.v.*] and supersedes a pre-1840 lodge. In 1852 Revd Matthew Moore is recorded as occupying both houses.

Griffith 1853–63.

86. CASTLE OLIVER, Kilfinane (3).
Also known as 'Clondofoy' or 'Cloghanodfoy', it was in 1776 found to be 'a place almost entirely of Mr Oliver's creation, from a house surrounded with cabins and rubbish he has fixed it in a fine lawn, surrounded by good wood'. So did Arthur Young enthuse over the improvements of the Rt Hon. Silver Oliver (d. 1799), who on his death left it to his son, Richard Philip Oliver (d. 1843). The latter assumed the surname of Gascoigne but showed rather less affection for the place, and in 1826 Fitzgerald and McGregor found the estate to have fallen very short of Young's description; the proprietor having absented himself 'to reside in England many years since, the greater part of the timber is cut down, and the house and demesne much neglected'. His two sons having predeceased him in 1842, he must have set in motion the remarkable transformation of the property to the design of the Scottish-born architect G. Fowler Jones. His untimely death, however, meant that the works were overseen by his daughters and co-heirs Mary Isabella and Elizabeth (who were later to marry Trench cousins, one of whom was the 2nd Lord Ashtown) but with the assistance of an executant architect, Sir Thomas Deane of Cork. The resultant spectacular programme of rebuilding included a new mansion house and two striking porters' lodges.

Ballyorgan gate; 1846; architect George Fowler Jones.

IAA

The Builder

The most suitable prelude in material, detail and style of any lodge, best illustrated by quoting a contemporary description of the house in *The Builder* magazine (*above, middle*): 'The style mainly adopted is the Old Scotch Castle or Manor House style of Scotland, which prevailed during the Stuart period: it comprises occasionally the Jacobean, and features in common with the Elizabethan ... The stone is the old red sandstone found on the property.' In a now lichen-encrusted uncoursed random masonry is a two-storey 'keep' with slit windows, some trefoil-arched, and a corbelled parapet with stepped corner crenellations. From the foremost right-hand corner breaks a square stair-turret, which corbels out above the entrance doorway and rises above the ramparts to terminate in a pyramidal roof with an iron weather-vane. Above the front door is an Oliver-Gascoigne monogram plaque, while alongside is the segmentally pointed carriage archway with sheeted doorways and strap hinges, all below a stepped gable containing a plaque of O'Sullivan bearings, and supported on each side by battered piers with pyramidal cappings and ball finials. These piers are repeated as pillars to stop the widespread concave quadrant wing walls. A hopper head reveals the date of construction. Derelict.

Raheenroe gate; *c.* 1846; architect probably George Fowler Jones.

IAA

No less striking is this secondary entrance, the porter's accommodation of similar form to the main lodge but with a lean-to single-storey adjunct and a circular stair-turret rising from an octagonal base with a mock cross arrowloop and a plaque with the family's bearings. It also differs in being free-standing and unconnected with the gatescreen of convex-walled quadrants framing a triple gateway with pyramidal capped pillars. Even in its advanced dereliction this remains an evocative Romantic Castellated composition, with its splendid mountain backdrop.

South gate; pre-1841/*c.* 1860.

This would appear to be an early survivor from the late Georgian period—a simple but commodious single-storey standard lodge with a hipped roof, given a mid-Victorian face-lift. The front façade is now ashlar-clad, with rusticated quoins and openings with moulded surrounds and elaborate keystones, framing one-over-one sashes and a fanlit doorway. Occupied.

Young 1780; Fitzgerald and McGregor 1827; *The Builder* (23 November 1850); *BPB* (1929); Bence-Jones 1988; *IFR*; Williams 1994; Howley 1993; IAA.

87. CASTLE PARK, Limerick (2).

Both the lodge in place by 1840 and another built thereafter have been demolished. A peculiar castellated Palladian house, formerly 'Smithfield' after its builder Charles Smith, it later became the residence of Christopher Delmege (1785–1863).

LGI (1904); ffolliott 1971a.

88. CASTLETOWN, Pallaskenry (2).

Two lodges that were extant in 1841 have been removed to an estate long associated with the Waller family.

89. CASTLEVIEW, Castleconnell; *c.* 1840.

Originally a single-storey standard lodge built for Thomas Spooner White, it has latterly suffered much abuse, its round-headed doorway blocked up and with a modern monopitched roof. A property now called 'Shannon View'.

Griffith 1853–63.

90. CASTLE VIEW, Newcastle West (2).

In 1826 this was 'a very handsome house belonging to the Rev. T. Lock with a well-planted demesne'. The same Revd Thomas Locke, the local rector, was still in residence here twenty years later but by 1851 had been succeeded by the new incumbent, Revd Robert M. Rodwell, whose gatekeepers were then Thomas Sheahan and John Cotter. Towards the end of the century the house was still serving as Newcastle rectory, with a pair of lodges flanking the southern gate and one to the northern avenue, just as they were in 1841, all since removed.

Fitzgerald and McGregor 1827; Slater 1846; Griffith 1853–63.

91. CASTLE VILLE, Limerick; pre-1937; *demolished.*

In 1840 this was 'Newcastle Cottage' and lodgeless, but by 1870 it was grander and home to John Rickard Tinsley, wealthy merchant and ex-mayor of the city of Limerick.

Slater 1846; 1870.

92. CHERRY GROVE, Croom (2).

The 1840 OS map shows two gate lodges at the entrance, that which survives and what was undoubtedly its predecessor across the road, which doesn't.

This is a standard 1½-storey affair with harled walls, missing bargeboards and the remains of paired carved soffit brackets over its main front, the three bays of which are in a rectangular recess. Probably dating from around 1835 and thus built for the Harding family, who are recorded here in 1826 and twelve years later, although a James Barry is also mysteriously noted as resident in 1837 and 1846, one or the other presumably being a tenant. Prior to this it was home in 1814 to Edward Cripps.

Leet 1814; Fitzgerald and McGregor 1827; Lewis 1837; Fraser 1838; Slater 1846.

93. CLARE VIEW, Tarbert; *c.* 1835.

Here are the sad remnants of a typical Irish gate lodge from the reign of William IV. Single-storey standard, with an exaggerated oversailing shallow-hipped roof showing paired carved modillion brackets to the soffit, here continued singly about the verge of the porch gable, which magically cantilevers out, having been deprived of its columned support. Now completely stripped of its harled finish to reveal its fine rubble construction, and a semblance remaining to suggest bipartite casement windows, presumably once small-paned. Nicely limewashed harling survives in concave quadrant walls that once framed a tripartite gateway, now missing its carriage pillars to accommodate a cattle grid. All reflecting the deterioration of a once-proud property of the Revd Richard Fitzgerald (1801–85), descended from the knights of Glin and long-time resident here.

Lewis 1837; *LGI* (1904).

CLOGHANODFOY CASTLE **(see CASTLE OLIVER)**

94. CLONLONG, Limerick; pre-1840; *demolished.*

In 1851 the house, gate lodge, flax factory, offices and land of John Norris Russell (d. 1859), founder and proprietor of the establishment, a property he had inherited through his maternal grandfather John Norris.

Lewis 1837; Griffith 1853–63; *IFR*.

95. CLONMACKEN, Limerick; pre-1840; *demolished.*

Hugh Weir in his 1986 *Houses of Clare* records 'a single storey gate lodge and early twentieth-century wrought iron gates on cast iron pillars are set into a stone gateway'. The mid-eighteenth-century gentry house was the residence in 1814 and 1826 of Alderman Henry D'Esterre but by 1837 it lay unoccupied.

Leet 1814; Fitzgerald and McGregor 1827; Lewis 1837; Weir 1986.

96. CLONSHIRE LODGE, Adare (2).
Initially an estate of George Fosberry, who was recorded here in 1814 before moving on to his main seat of Curraghbridge [*q.v.*] nearby. His legacy to Clonshire is a delightful example of Irish Palladian cottage rustic.

Main entrance; *c.* 1790.

With just a modicum of thought given to its design is this single-storey structure below a hipped roof, the short three-bay main front comprised of a pair of round-headed niches on each side of a central window now containing an incongruous modern casement window horribly at odds with the layers of basic limewashing to the harled walls. Derelict and overgrown. This is not a unique form, for there are like lodges at Castle View, Glanmire, Co. Cork [*q.v.*], and Clonacody, Co. Tipperary [*q.v.*]—by chance or from the inspired hand of the same provincial architect?

After the Fosberrys' departure, the property became home to Col. John Dickson until the arrival around 1850 of Samuel D. Power, whose family added another lodge.

Secondary entrance; pre-1923; *demolished.*
A lodge erected after 1840.

Leet 1814; Fitzgerald and McGregor 1827.

97. CLORANE, Old Kildimo; pre-1923; *demolished.*
A property associated with the Fosberry family from the late seventeenth century but let to the Hunts in the early nineteenth century before the lodge was built by George Fosberry (1806–75), who had returned here by 1851.

Leet 1814; Griffith 1853–63; *LGI* (1904).

98. CONIGAR, Mungret; pre-1841; *demolished.*
Samuel Lewis advises in 1837 that 'the late country residence of the bishop, called Cunegar, situated in the centre of a fertile district, has been purchased, under the Church Temporalities Act, by Charles Wilson Esq., and is now in the occupation of a farmer; the entrance lodge has been converted into a barrack for the constabulary police force stationed here'. Neither barracks nor lodge survived until 1923.

Lewis 1837.

99. COOLE, Caherconlish; *c.* 1845; *demolished.*
In 1837 'also the residence [the other being Caherelly Castle, *q.v.*] of Mr Hannan, in well-planted grounds ornamented with shrubs and evergreens'. In 1840 the property was lodgeless but the 1851 valuation records one to the estate when occupied by Revd John Fogarty.

Lewis 1837; Griffith 1853–63.

100. COOLEEN, Athlacca; pre-1840; *demolished.*
A seat in the early nineteenth century and before of Joseph Mason, the lodge to which had gone by 1924.

Fitzgerald and McGregor 1827.

101. COOLRAINE, Limerick; pre-1840.
There survives a plain single-storey gabled cottage with a three-window main front in rendered walls, much modernised, elevated and occupied. A property in the mid-nineteenth century of John Vereker.

Slater 1846; Griffith 1853–63.

102. COOLRUS, Ballin; *c.* 1835.
A modest lodge occupied in 1851 by James Lynch, gatekeeper to the Harte family, of whom Sir Richard Harte was in 1807 knighted as mayor of Limerick by the duke of Richmond. A standard 1½-storey structure, rendered, with clipped verges to its steep gables and a flat-roofed central entrance breakfront. Occupied.

Fitzgerald and McGregor 1827; Griffith 1853–63.

103. COOLYHENAN, Ballysimon; *c.* 1830.
A plain single-storey standard cottage with an oversailing hipped roof, a traditional Irish gate lodge now lying derelict up a lengthy track. A seat in 1837 of Jeremiah Shine.

Lewis 1837.

104. COOPERHILL, Mungret; pre-1841; *demolished.*
Both the fine 1741 house and the gate lodge of the Cooper family are but memories of a once-proud estate.

105. CORBALLY COTTAGE, Limerick; *c.* 1920; *demolished.*
A property in the nineteenth century of the Fitt family on Mill Road. The short-lived porter's lodge does not appear in the valuation books until 1921 during the occupancy of Alma G. Fitt. By local tradition it was circular in plan and shared by neighbouring River View [*q.v.*].

106. CORBALLY, Limerick; pre-1840; *demolished.*

Assuming the gate lodge to have been of an age with the surviving gatescreen, it dates from the time here of Poole Gabbett, corn merchant of the Corbally Mills. The entrance is a triple gateway but with the carriage gates hung on a pair of archways that form postern openings, each in cut stone with recessed panel piers supporting an entablature with die. These are framed by wide ashlar shallow concave quadrants. An impressive design, possibly by James Pain or his erstwhile pupil C.F. Anderson, for there are similar trabeated entrances in the province at Lota Park and Lauriston, Co. Cork [*q.v.*], and Gurteen-le-Poer, Co. Waterford [*q.v.*]. Now totally neglected and redundant to a house which became the RC bishop's palace before the property became the site for St Munchin's College in 1962.

Lewis 1837; Slater 1846.

107. CORGRIG, Foynes; pre-1840; *demolished.*
The estate of the Griffin family in the early nineteenth century, its gate lodge opposite an entrance from which the avenue had been diverted to another access by 1923.

108. COURTBRACK, Limerick; pre-1840; *demolished.*
Garret Hugh Fitzgerald retired in 1817 from a captaincy in the army; he rose thereafter to become a pillar of Limerick society, being its mayor in 1838, and settled on nineteen acres here, on a property that included a powder magazine in 1850. He was noted for a remedy for potato blight, which was ignored; the Famine spelt ruin for him, and he was forced to sell Courtbrack in 1851 before dying, aged 61, at Geraldine Cottage.

Griffith 1853–63.

109. COURTBRACK VILLA, Limerick (2).
A property which saw a succession of different occupants down the nineteenth century, being enlarged and developed into 'Westbourne House', later to become a Convent of Mercy.

South entrance; *c.* 1845.
A 1½-storey gabled affair with a similarly treated breakfront, built sometime between 1840 and the 1851 valuation, when a Captain Rogers is recorded here.

North entrance; pre-1937; *demolished.*
A secondary lodge erected after 1840.

Griffith 1853–63.

COURTENAY CASTLE (see NEWCASTLE WEST)

110. CRAGBEG, Clarina; *c.* 1845.
An estate in the late eighteenth century of the Vokes family, who were succeeded by Richard Parsons before Major Thomas Pakenham Vandeleur (d. 1875) of the Kilrush, Co. Clare [*q.v.*], family came here, probably just after his first marriage in 1827. It was he that built this lodge, which lies next to ruined; 1½-storey standard and gabled, with a lower projecting gabled hall which shares the main eaves line over harled walls. In better condition is a good ashlar entrance screen with trabeated postern openings.

Taylor and Skinner 1778; 1783; Leet 1814; Fitzgerald and McGregor 1827; *LGI* (1904).

111. CRAIG COTTAGE, Limerick; *c.* 1865.
A much-abused and nondescript single-storey three-bay cottage with a shallow-pitched gabled roof; derelict. A property by 1902 called 'Cragfield', residence in 1865 of a Mrs Hunt, part of a speculative development on the North Circular Road by Ambrose Hall.

112. CROOM UNION WORKHOUSE, Croom; *c.* 1852; architect probably George Wilkinson; *demolished.*
An institution that opened for admissions in 1852.

O'Connor 1995; IAA.

113. CROOM CASTLE, Croom; pre-1840; *demolished.*
A standard 1½-storey gabled structure near an old castle of the Fitzgeralds that lay vacant for many years before John Corker of Ballynagarde [*q.v.*] fitted it up and furnished it in the castellated style around 1825.

Fitzgerald and McGregor 1827.

114. CROOM, Croom; *c.* 1845/*c.* 1880/*c.* 1920.
Big ogee-walled quadrants and pillars with peculiar vases atop make up a gatescreen leading to a gate lodge that seems to have evolved as a tiny gabled single-storey structure with perforated ornamental bargeboards from which projects a lower hall, a back return and, alongside, another single-storey gabled building with a tripartite window apparently of twentieth-century origin, the whole ensemble in a roughcast finish. Some work could conceivably date from 1880, when the renowned church architect J.J. McCarthy was carrying out ill-defined additions and alterations to the big house for Henry Lyons (1828–85), who had inherited it on the death of his father in 1853. Griffith does, however, notice a lodge here in 1851 that is not obvious on the 1840–1 OS map.

Griffith 1853–63; *IB* (1 April 1880); *LGI* (1904).

115. CROOM RECTORY, Croom; pre-1840; *demolished.*
'The glebe-house is a handsome edifice, erected on the new glebe, in 1813, by aid of gift of £100 and a loan of £800 from the late Board of First Fruits', according to Lewis in 1837, some of the expense possibly going towards the erection of the porter's lodge. The OS maps are unusually detailed in showing it with a canted front to the avenue and a central back return.

Lewis 1837.

116. CURRAH CHASE, Askeaton (7).
The grand and romantic estate once of the de Vere family, beautifully wooded and watered by them, and which incorporated the associated properties of 'Holly Park' and 'Farm Lodge'. The whole was accessed by an abundance of gates with attendant gate lodges, rich in quantity if not quality, judging by the few that survive on site or on record. One can only surmise that James Pain in 1827–8 and the English architect Amon Henry Wilds a year later may have offered designs for lodges when they were then engaged by Sir Aubrey de Vere Hunt (1788–1846) to work on the estate. By 1841 there would appear to have been five lodges already in place, although in 1837 Samuel Lewis seems only to have noticed those on the perimeter of the estate: 'there are three entrances to the park, of which the lodge at that from Adare is the most handsome'.

Stonehall gate; pre-1841; *demolished.*
In 1850 the gatekeeper was Thomas Farrell.

Kyleavarraga gate; *c.* 1820.
Next to Farm Lodge, and seemingly the lodge that Lewis considered to be on the Adare approach, is this commodious single-storey structure below a steeply hipped roof with gabled breakfronts, one accommodating the doorway and the other a single-bay window to the avenue. Limewashed and harled, it lies derelict on the southernmost boundary of the estate.

Lisnamuck gate; pre-1841; *demolished.*
A lodge which once commanded the south-western approach has now been replaced by a twentieth-century bungalow.

Deer-park gate; pre-1841; *demolished.*
A lodge that occupied a site opposite the gates, west of the house on an inner boundary of the estate.

Currah Chase north gate; 1840.
The modern date-stone may indicate the origin of this single-storey gabled cottage built in limestone rubble facing with brick dressings, almost lost in modernisation and additions in like materials. The serrated bargeboards indicate a late Victorian embellishment.

Kilcornan gate; *c.* 1850; *demolished.*

'Hollypark, the ancient residence of the Taylor family, now the property of Sir Aubrey de Vere', and to which he or his son added this extensive gatescreen, with its four grand punched ashlar pillars having roll-topped plinth tops and four-sided semicircular pedimented cappings with shields in their tympana. Partly railed with postern gates.

West gate; *c.* 1865; *demolished.*
Here is a very grand pair of tall ashlar Classical carriage pillars of around 1790, with splendid pine-cone finials on moulded corniced cappings and having scroll-topped gate stops, the whole framed by rubble stone quadrant walls. This seems to have been unattended until the building of a generously proportioned 1½-storey gabled gatehouse in Picturesque mid-Victorian mode with a back

IAA

return, its gables and gablets ornamented with basic wavy bargeboards and slender hip-knobs over rendered walls with brick-dressed two-over-two sash windows. To the avenue gable was a single-storey wooden porch similarly adorned.

In 1941 the big house was reduced to a shell by fire, the estate now in care as a forest park.

Fitzgerald and McGregor 1827; Heaney 1999; Lewis 1837; Fraser 1838; Griffith 1853–63; *LGI* (1912); Bence-Jones 1988; Colvin 2008; IAA photograph (31/58 Z30).

117. CURRAGHBRIDGE, Adare (2).
An estate of the Fosberry family, of whom George Fosberry built the earlier of the lodges, probably after inheriting the property on the death of his father Francis in 1810.

North gate; *c.* 1815.
A plain, harled single-storey cottage with skew-table gables.

South gate; pre-1923; *demolished.*
A porter's lodge built after 1840.

LGI (1904).

CURRAGOUR **(see SHANNON VIEW)**

118. DARRAGH, Ballyorgan; *c.* 1835.
'... [T]he seat of F. Bevan Esq., is pleasantly situated, and extensive improvements are in progress around it.' What Lewis witnessed in 1837 may have included this gate lodge for Frederick Massy Bevan, who had succeeded to Darragh on the death of his father in 1826. Faced in coursed stone with brick dressing, the gabled structure presents a principal short front with a small segmentally headed window in a like-arched recess and over a tiny light to a loft room. On the side elevation is a little shallow-pitched roofed porch. Derelict.

Lewis 1837; *LGI* (1904).

119. DERK, Pallasgrean; pre-1840/*c.* 1900.
Having replaced the earlier lodge on the site is this Elizabethan Revival lodge with ornamental strapwork to a gable which projects from an otherwise square-planned structure, its pyramidal roof rising to a central chimney-stack, built in what appears to be an early example of reconstituted stone. Occupied. A modest gatescreen contains a pair of postilion openings. For long a property of the Considine family.

120. DERRYKNOCKANE, Knocknapaul; *c.* 1835.
A standard single-storey porter's lodge

stripped of its protective harling to reveal a substantial fabric of coursed rubble and brick dressings. Now also lacking its shallow pyramidal roof, leaving its central cut-stone chimney-stack precarious. To the rear is a large, steeply pitched gabled extension, likewise reduced to a shell, perhaps with a view to rehabilitation. An estate in 1837 of George Gloster.

Lewis 1837.

121. DOONE RECTORY, Cappamore; pre-1840; *demolished.*
A lodge, removed before 1901, which may have been contemporary with the glebe house built in 1808 for Revd Richard Chadwick (1751–1815), incumbent from 1781 until 1811, or added during improvements to the property carried out for £1,143 in 1831.

O'Donovan 1806–61; *LGI* (1904) Seymour and Leslie 2012.

122. DOONEEN, Crecora; pre-1840.
A house 'Lately built by Villiers Peacock' in 1826, its lodge perhaps contemporary. It survives as a plain single-storey affair, gabled to the avenue, extended alongside as a double pile and so modernised as to make dating difficult.

Fitzgerald and McGregor 1827.

123. DREHIDTARSNA RECTORY, Adare; pre-1840; *demolished.*
A porter's lodge possibly of an age with the glebe house that was erected in 1828, the rector then being Revd Richard Maunsell.

Lewis 1837.

124. DREW'S COURT, Ballyagran; pre-1840; *demolished.*
A seat from the early eighteenth century of the Drew family, descended from that of Ballyduff, Co. Waterford [*q.v.*].

DROMARD (see MOUNT BROWNE)

125. DROMKEEN, Pallasgrean; pre-1840; *demolished.*
The pleasant mid-eighteenth-century house of a branch of the Hussey de Burgh family.

126. DROMKEEN HOUSE, Pallasgrean; *c.* 1830.
Opposite the gates is the derelict single-storey standard cottage with harled rubble walls below a hipped roof with conspicuous Regency paired carved soffit brackets. An estate of the Croker family in the nineteenth century.

LGI (1904).

127. DROMORE CASTLE, Pallaskenry (2).
Despite its gutting in the 1950s this remains one of the most spectacular ruins in the country. A neo-Irish castle commissioned in 1866, barely before his poor father was cold, by William Hale John Charles Pery, 3rd earl of Limerick (1840–96), from the English architect Edward William Godwin, who also proposed a highly appropriate design as an introductory gatehouse.

Unexecuted design; *c.* 1870; architect E.W. Godwin.

RIBA drawings collection

A delightful perspective sketch by the architect, offered to his client for the boundary of his demesne, in the form of a great defensive gatehouse in stone on a rectangular plan, rising four storeys with—but for the postilion access archway to one side—a symmetrical road front. Central to this is a cavernous segmentally arched carriage opening, over which is a plaque with the family bearings on a façade that is otherwise minimally fenestrated with the narrowest of arrowloop windows. Crowning all this is a vast machicolated parapet with Irish crenellations, behind the ramparts of which is a gabled attic storey. Godwin based this sketch closely on a survey drawing he prepared of Kilmacleurine Castle on a tour of Ireland in 1869.

Main entrance; *c.* 1870; architect possibly E.W. Godwin.

What transpired at the gate is somewhat less dramatic yet a creation sufficiently innovative to attribute to Godwin in the absence of documentary evidence. In immaculately tooled rough-faced random coursed masonry, with smooth stone as quoins and chamfered mullioned and transomed tall windows, which contain latticed leaded lights in Tudor manor style. Raised off an L-plan with two bold gables, one of which catslides over the internal angle to form a canopied porch; they are relieved by sculpted plaques, one a simple quatrefoil, the other intricately chiselled into the Pery arms: three lions passant on a shield surmounted by a hind's head rising from a coronet. Plain eaves and bargeboards are ornamented with carved brackets and dainty hip-knobs; on the main ridge a stone chimney-stack rises off a plinth with a wide moulded capping. Occupied and well maintained. The entrance sweep has spiky octagonal posts.

BPB (1929); *Country Life* (12 November 1964); Bence-Jones 1988; Soros 1999.

128. EDENMORE, Limerick; 1869; *demolished.*
Neither the house nor its lodge survive, having succumbed to the demand for denser housing. The lodge was built for the Very Revd Maurice C. Day, subsequent to his acquiring the property from John Copley Singleton.

129. EDWARDSTOWN, Ballyneety; pre-1840; *demolished.*
The property in 1851 of John Russell, the lodge to which has gone and his house now an ivy-covered ruin.

Griffith 1853–63.

130. ELM PARK, Clarina (3).
'It is a fine place, with an indifferent house but that will soon be remedied as a new one is in rapid progress of advancement.' Thus found Robert Graham on a visit on 8 August 1835, work being undertaken to designs by brothers George Richard and James Pain for Eyre Massy (1798–1872), who had succeeded as the 3rd Baron Clarina in 1810. He, significantly, had in 1828 married the teenaged Susan Elizabeth Barton, daughter of the immensely rich wine merchant Hugh Barton of Straffan, Co. Kildare. Her dowry enabled the creation of a Romantic fairytale castle and an appropriate new entrance in like style.

South gate; pre-1841; *demolished.*
What was originally the main approach to the old house was announced by a pair of lodges flanking the gates, probably built by the 1st baron, also Eyre Massy (1719–1804).

East gate; *c.* 1840; architects probably G.R. and J. Pain.
Central to an extensive entrance screen, of concave Irish crenellated quadrant walls terminating in circular turrets, is a great, forbidding castellated gatehouse, raised asymmetrically in fine punched ashlar to two storeys under an irregular battlemented parapet. The loftier breakfront tower contained the Tudor-arched carriage gateway

130. Elm Park, Clarina, east gate (IAA).

flanked by buttresses, over which was a bipartite window below a machicolation with mock cross arrowloop which breaks the parapet. On each side the porter's accommodation extends with a minimum of fenestration with its slit windows, while to the left-hand side is the lower postern entrance, its Tudor-arched doorway emphasised by quarry-faced toothed stone dressing. The effect, seen in a photograph of *c.* 1900, is much reduced by modern intervention, with the loss of its contextual planting, the conversion of the bipartite window to a single light, the reduction of the carriage opening to a front door and the removal of a pair of diagonally set chimney-stacks. Occupied. Although attributed by Jeremy Williams as the work of C.F. Anderson, it is likely that he was working in a supervisory capacity for the Pains.

North gate; 1864.
A secondary entrance, which gives access to the farmyard, is commanded by this substantial 1½-storey gabled lodge, built on an elevated site in mellow Flemish bond brickwork, with a single-storey gabled hall projecting from the left-hand side. Modern window intrusions.

Sadly, all that survives on the demesne are outbuildings and two lodges, Eyre and Susan Elizabeth's pride and joy having been burnt down in 1922 and subsequently demolished.

Heaney 1999; *IB* (1 January 1878); *BPB* (1929); Williams 1994; O'Donnell 2005; Lee 2006; IAA photograph (31/62Z1+N).

131. ENNISCOUSH, Rathkeale; *c.* 1835.
A single-storey standard lodge with limewashed harled walls below a gabled roof, the high eaves to which have conspicuous carved paired modillion brackets. Derelict. Built for John Hewson, older brother of James Hewson of Hollywood [*q.v.*], whose family was associated with the estate since the eighteenth century.

IFR.

132. FAHA, Patrickswell (2).
A house built in 1773 by John Tuthill, to which two lodged entrances were added.

Patrickswell gate; pre-1841; *demolished.*
The lodge was sited opposite the entrance to the southern avenue.

Clarina gate; *c.* 1835/*c.* 1870.
Behind wide and crude concave-walled entrance quadrants is a lodge originally built for George Tuthill and altered after his death in 1859, probably by the Russell family of Shelbourne [*q.v.*], who were in residence by 1870. A 1½-storey gabled cottage, initially built in rubble stone facings with smooth quoins and brick dressings, seemingly subsequently raised from a single storey with a rendered upper storey and reroofed with alternate scalloped slate coursing. Occupied.

Lewis 1837; Slater 1870.

133. FANNINGSTOWN CASTLE, Croom (3).
A nineteenth-century castle, home to the Jackson family until 1860, when it was sold as an incumbered estate. From *c.* 1895 James F. Bannatyne was in residence, adding three ill-fated porters' lodges, one being a replacement for that built before 1840.

Bence-Jones 1988; Lyons 1993.

FARM LODGE (see CURRAH CHASE)

134. FEDAMORE, Fedamore; *c.* 1845; *demolished.*
In 1840 'Fedamore Cottage' was lodgeless, but ten years later the property, then of John and Edward Synan, was valued with one, built either for them or for their predecessor in 1846, Revd J. Comyn.

Slater 1846; Griffith 1853–63.

135. FERNBANK, Limerick; 1926; *demolished.*

Sister Mary C. Merriman

The Cleeve family arrived in the city in the late nineteenth century and established a chain of creameries, enabling one of the brothers, Charles Frederick Cleeve (1851–1928) to build himself a smart residence and a porter's lodge on the Shelbourne Road, next door to their toffee factory.

This was a characterful little 1½-storey gabled lodge with an informal two-bay narrow main front, finished in roughcast with an abundance of brick highlighting in toothed quoins, dressings and a rectangular single-storey flat-roofed bay with squared casements extending alongside the front door. Over was a lofty central gablet window with carved bargeboards, as those to the main side gables. Removed in the 1960s to make way for a school extension for the Salesian Sisters, whose convent the house had become.

IFR; Spellissy 1998.

136. FINNITERSTOWN, Adare; *c.* 1840.
A hip-roofed single-storey standard lodge with clipped eaves and two-over-two sash windows in sepia-washed harled walls. Derelict. Built for Frederick Maunsell, whose gatekeeper in 1851 was John Slattery.

Slater 1846; Griffith 1853–63.

137. FORT, Charleville; pre-1840.
Probably originating as a single-storey standard lodge that was subsequently raised to accommodate loft space and extended by a bay to the right-hand side. Modernised with replacement windows. Occupied. A property in 1851 of David Hartigan.

Griffith 1853–63.

138. FORT LODGE, Charleville; pre-1840; *demolished.*
A holding in 1851 of Honoria Carroll, the lodge to which had gone by 1923.

Griffith 1853–63.

139. FORT ELIZABETH, Monaster; *c.* 1835.
A 1½-storey harled three-bay cottage with high eaves to its steeply pitched roof, with minimal skew-tables, which catslides to form a porch over the right-hand bay. Occupied. The residence in 1837 of Revd John Croker.
Lewis 1837.

140. FORT ETNA, Patrickswell (2).
While the 1791 Palladian-style house built by the Peacock family survives in good heart, it does so without any of its entrance lodges. Two of these were in place by 1841, one well to the south at the deer-park, the other by the village. The latter was, however, superseded by another when the arrival of the railway severed the old avenue.

Despite the Peacocks' losing interest in the property around 1835, when they leased the estate for many years to John Waller O'Grady of the Killballyowen family [*q.v.*], Thomas Peacock's widow was renting one of the lodges in 1851 from Alexander O'Grady Rose.
Lewis 1837; Griffith 1853; *LGI* (1904; 1912).

FORT UNION (see RINEROE)

141. FOYNES VICARAGE, Foynes; pre-1923; *demolished.*
The rector in 1876 was Revd Robert Gabbett (d. 1889).
LOI.

142. FRANKFORT, Ballingarry (2).
A seat in 1814 of Samuel Adams, which by 1837 was home to Richard Standish.

South entrance; pre-1841; *demolished.*

North entrance; *c.* 1810.
A tiny, derelict, single-storey gabled cottage, with a single window and door to its principal front.
Leet 1814; Lewis 1837.

143. FRIARSTOWN [1], Crecora (2).
Here in 1837 Lewis found 'The ancient residence of the Hunt family', one of their two houses of the same name in close proximity. The valuation of 1850 found Vere David Urquhart Hunt (1794–1854) in residence, with an estate boasting two gate lodges; only one of these is identifiable on the 1840–1 OS map but neither appears on that of 1924. Home in 1814 to William Hunt.
Leet 1814; Lewis 1837; Griffith 1853–63; *LGI* (1904).

144. FRIARSTOWN [2], Crecora; *c.* 1845.

In 1826 Fitzgerald and McGregor recorded that 'Vere Hunt has built a handsome house', presumably prior to his moving to the 'old' Friarstown House [*q.v.*] on the death of his father William. He was succeeded here by his second son, Henry Hunt (1820–66), the builder of the lodge. A well-tended single-storey standard lodge below an almost pyramidal roof rising to a central chimney-stack, its eaves extending over harled walls containing wide bipartite square-paned casement windows with prominent basic unchiselled label mouldings. Good contemporary cast-iron gates.
Fitzgerald and McGregor 1827; Griffith 1853–63; *LGI* (1904).

145. FRIARSTOWN, Fedamore; pre-1840; *demolished.*
A seat in 1852 of James H. Barry, the porter's lodge to which was situated opposite its gates.
Griffith 1853–63.

146. GALTEE VIEW, Galbally; pre-1928; *demolished.*
A lodge probably built when the main house was 'improved' in 1861 by Thomas Fitzgerald.

147. GERALDINE, Limerick; *c.* 1845.
Here are the remains of a tiny suburban single-storey standard stone-built structure with brick dressings, latterly much added-to. A property in 1837 and 1851 of Pierce Shannon, an iron merchant in the city.
Lewis 1837; Griffith 1853–63.

148. GLENBEVAN, Croom; pre-1840.
A gatekeeper's lodge that was opposite the gates to a seat in 1837 of Joseph Bevan, who probably developed the estate after the death in 1826 of his father, Henry Bevan of Camass [*q.v.*].
Lewis 1837; *IFR.*

149. GLENBROOK, Ballinleeny; pre-1840; *demolished.*
Despite being offered for sale as an incumbered estate in 1854, it remained in Mason family hands, the proprietor three years earlier having been Myles Mason. Their lodge had gone by 1923.
Griffith 1853–63; Lyons 1993.

150. GLENDUFF CASTLE, Broadford; *c.* 1810.

A sad, abandoned little Georgian Gothic porter's lodge in an unkempt wooded setting. Harled below a hipped roof, but unusual in having its three-bay symmetrical façade compressed into its leading short front, comprised of pointed-arched openings, the doorway tallest with a fanlight—all boarded up. An estate in 1814 of Jones Stevelly (*c.* 1763–1833), youngest son of a rich Cork merchant who also had a Dublin residence, Croydon in Clontarf.
Leet 1814.

151. GLENEFY, Galbally; *c.* 1845.

A solidly constructed single-storey two-roomed cottage below a hipped roof. Extraordinarily ill-lit, with a tiny window to the rear room and that to the avenue dependent upon minute sidelights to the front door, which are set in a recess to the short principal façade, faced in big random uncoursed cut stone blocks. Otherwise in rubble build, it lies derelict. A seat in 1851 of George Latham Bennett.
Griffith 1853–63.

152. GLENLARY COTTAGE, Kilfinnane; pre-1841; *demolished.*
A lodge originally located opposite its gates had been removed before 1928. A property in the mid-nineteenth century of James Keyes.
Griffith 1853–63.

153. GLENSTAL CASTLE, Murroe (3).
The great Norman Revival castle was commenced in 1837 by the Limerick lawyer and railway engineer Sir Matthew Barrington (1788–1861) to designs from the relatively obscure English architect William Bardwell, after rejecting many proposals from local practitioners. The mansion took until 1853 to complete and the equally innovative and singular lodges followed a lot later, added by Sir Croker Barrington (1817–90) after his succession in 1872; that at the eastern boundary was a replacement for an earlier, pre-1840 lodge.

Secondary entrance; *c.* 1875; architect not known.
A most irregular composition, dominated by a pyramidal-roofed, square, three-storey Italianate tower, raised in rubble stone with a shouldered-arched doorway, semicircular-headed upper windows and a corbelled eaves band. To this abuts a single-storey skew-tabled projection, alongside which is the main body of the lodge in punched ashlar, with the same eaves band and shouldered openings. Single-storey it extends to the avenue in a canted front from which projects further a little gabled porch with a moulded eaves band, which returns to form an open pediment containing a Barrington chevroned

shield over the shouldered entrance archway. Occupied and immaculately maintained, with modern lead-effect glazing and synthetic slated roof, it succeeds an earlier lodge on the site.

Main entrance; pre-1840/*c.* 1874; architect not known.

A delightful and original little single-storey gabled porter's lodge, which reflects the big house beyond in some of its Romanesque detailing. Faced in a mellow lichen-encrusted, coursed quarry-faced stone, apart from a small projection below a catslide roof to the rear, it is built basically off a simple rectangular plan, a short elevation to the avenue abundant in eccentric features. Each corner contains an angled window behind colonnettes with grotesque masks in their composite capitals. Above is a layered stone skew-table gable, rising from moulded kneelers to an acroterion crowned by a wrought-iron finial into which is worked the 'CB' monogram of Sir Croker. Below are the sculpted Barrington bearings and a tall shouldered-arched window, off-centre to accommodate the charming porch with its round-arched voussoirs arranged in sawtooth pattern, springing from a dog-tooth course. In its moulded skew-tabled gable is a quatrefoil motif over which is a pyramidal finial, a feature repeated on the carriage pillars, here crowning layered cappings. A replacement that must date from 1874, when its valuation rose by £2.

The castle now accommodates a boys' school, the property in the capable hands of the Benedictine Order.

BPB (1929); *Country Life* (3 October 1974); de Breffny and ffolliott 1975; Williams 1994.

154. GLEN VIEW, Ballyneety; *c.* 1875.

The lost house is survived by its gatekeeper's lodge, a single-storey standard hip-roofed structure faced in coursed punched ashlar with toothed quoins, dressings and soldier arches. To the front is a later glazed porch; occupied. Built in the time of John Russell, who is recorded here in 1851 and 1876. The neat entrance screen, with its concave railed quadrants and remaining cast-iron octagonal pillars, looks to date from *c.* 1845.

Griffith 1853–63; *LOI*.

155. GLENVILLE, Ardagh; *c.* 1840.

A single-storey lodge, much improved and extended but still retaining that distinctive feature peculiar to the county of the main elevation being in the form of a simple flat-topped screen wall, against which the structure abuts here in pleasant rubble stone pierced by two six-over-six sash windows with round-headed relieving arches. There are like lodges in County Limerick at Cappagh, Ballyknockane and Springfield Castle. Two of the pillars of a tripartite gateway are inscribed 'Glenville House' and crowned with pyramidal cappings, all contemporary. An estate that has been in the Massy family since 1763, the entrance and lodge dating from the time here of Captain John Massy (1773–1846), who inherited the property on the death of his father in 1830.

IFR.

156. GLENWILLIAM CASTLE, Ballingarry (2).

A house built in 1797 for Revd William Massy, which by repute was lost at the card-table by his grandson, William Hamon Massy, the property being 'in chancery' by 1852, along with its two gate lodges, before it was acquired by Edward Atkinson (1801–76) of Skea House, Co. Fermanagh, who carried out improvements and additions to the house and built the northerly lodge, apparently to designs of James Pain.

South entrance; pre-1841; *demolished.*

This is remembered as a two-storey gatehouse.

North entrance; pre-1841/*c.* 1860; architect probably James Pain.

What seems to be an early single-storey standard hip-roofed cottage has been given a Classical face-lift of ashlar with a blocked and corniced parapet that continues about the central breakfront, which contains an undersized front door with rusticated surround. To each side the one-over-one sash windows have architraves and keystones, the whole framed by toothed quoins.

LGI (1904); Bence-Jones 1988; *IFR*.

157. GLIN CASTLE, Glin (4).

The most attractive of marine estates on the shores of the River Shannon, home since the thirteenth century of the Fitzgeralds, knights of Glin, and the setting for folly buildings and an alluring group of castellated entrances as preludes to the crenellated mansion. Lt.-Col. John Fraunceis Fitzgerald (1791–1854), 25th knight of Glin, succeeded to the place on the death of his father in 1803 and set about fancifying the scene soon after his coming of age. Initially he concentrated on romanticising the plain old Georgian house and thereafter turned his attention to the demesne and its gates, where it is difficult to doubt that he enlisted the assistance of the Limerick-based architect James Pain, for the results bear the touch of the latter's erstwhile master, John Nash.

Glin gate; *c.* 1820; architect possibly James Pain.

Country Life

On the northern approach from the village is this delightful and informal composition dominated by the simplest of unadorned crenellations to archway and lodge. The three-centred arched carriage opening is flanked by a square turret to one side, relieved by mock arrowloops, and on the other by two-storey single-bay porter's accommodation with squared sash windows

157. Glin Castle, Glin, Tarbert gate.

Country Life

in Y-traceried pointed arches. To the side is a single-storey wing in like manner, the whole strikingly finished in whitewashed roughcast. Latterly the archway has been expertly adapted to permit modern traffic access by raising the arch with the incorporation of Gothic cross arrowloops, and the turret lifted correspondingly with quatrefoil windows for relief.

Inner gate; *c.* 1830.

A relatively unprepossessing single-storey structure below an oversailing shallow hipped roof, its squared casement windows set in rectangular recesses in masonry walls with crudely applied rendered quoins. To the left-hand side of the two-bay main front projects a later extension in matching style.

Tarbert gate; 1836; architect possibly James Pain.

On the southern avenue is this striking entrance (*above*) in the fashion of the Glin gate, with the same square-towered gatekeeper's house, pointed windows and crenellations, but here appearing in duplicate as a pair to flank the three-centred arched carriage gateway and framed by long, low, straight curtain walls containing lancet postern doorways and decorated with 'medieval' cross arrowloops, the whole terminating in circular turrets. Once perfectly symmetrical, it has recently had its right-hand curtain wall raised to better proportions and innovative pointed quatrefoil windows inserted to illuminate new accommodation behind. With its basic castellations it is faced in rubble sometime coated in whitewash.

Bathing gate; *c.* 1815; architect possibly James Pain.

Country Life

This delightful caprice lies just west of the house, across the public road from the shoreline. A lodge certainly, if not to house a gatekeeper then a place for lords and ladies to dally or prepare for bathing, each room having a separate access and both with fireplaces for drying out. It is another Castellated Gothic composition in whitewashed harling, comprised of a pointed-arched pedestrian doorway in a crenellated screen wall flanked on one side by a round ornamental turret with mock arrowslits and on the other by a circular two-storey tower with lancet windows and doors. In the interests of decorum, neither room has direct access to the other except externally, where levels have been playfully landscaped by the designer to contrive short flights of steps between, with the further device of a balustraded landing or rampart. A splendid eye-catcher, perhaps the work of James Pain, who was employed on the local parish church in 1815.

LGI (1904); *Country Life* (26 February and 4 March 1964); Malins and Glin 1976; Gaughan 1978; Howley 1993; Lee 2006.

158. GORTNASKAGH LODGE, Bruff; pre-1840; *demolished.*

A seat in 1851 of Michael Fitzgerald, whose lodge had been removed by 1927.

Griffith 1853–63.

159. GRANGE HILL, Holycross (3).

Of two pre-1840 lodges to an estate of Edward J. Corker there is no sign, one to an inner gate having gone by 1927. That to the public road looks to have been replaced by the existing structure, built around 1865, probably by Peter John de Salis, 5th count (1799–1870), rather than by his son, who only outlived him by six months, or by his grandson, the 7th count, who did not reach his majority until 1885. It was about this time that the house became 'Loughgur'. This is an unusual essay in duality, of ample proportions. Single-storey in a random punched ashlar, two matching hipped gables each contain a chamfered mullioned bipartite window with toothed dressed surrounds. These flank a central recessed porch, the eaves of which are carried on carved wooden brackets. Centrally positioned to the ridge above is a wide four-flue chimney-stack. Clearly architect-designed—identity not known. Occupied.

Although a property by 1826 of the de Salis family, it seems that they were mostly absentees.

Leet 1814; Fitzgerald and McGregor 1827.

160. THE GRANGE, Sixmilebridge (2).

The shell of the great three-storey Georgian mansion is a forlorn sight, once the proud seat of the O'Grady family. It was Thomas O'Grady (d. 1861) who inherited it, on the death of his father Standish in 1816, with an early, pre-1840 porter's lodge. This main entrance he upgraded with a new lodge and gates, and added another on the back avenue.

Main gate; *c.* 1850; architect James Pain; *demolished.*

David O'Keeffe

The architect responsible is identifiable by the grand gatescreen's being identical to those at Carrigoran [*q.v.*] and Kilkishen [*q.v.*], Co. Clare, Derry Castle, Co. Tipperary [q.v.], and Convamore, Co. Cork [*q.v.*]. The wide, straight, triple gateway is flanked and greatly extended by tall ashlar convex quadrant walls that frame four cut-stone pillars, with raised and fielded panels and round pedimented cappings, which contain hefty contemporary cast-iron carriage gates and postern gates beyond in matching railings. The gatekeeper's lodge was a precocious little Italianate affair, very much a reduced version of that at Convamore. Single-storey standard in ashlar and notable for open pediments to the main gables and that of the central hall projection, all conspicuous for their bold mutule brackets. Another Pain hallmark was evident in the pair of chimney-stacks rising off the back wall. A fine little building, ignominiously demolished in favour of a bland bungalow alongside.

Secondary gate; *c.* 1850; architect probably James Pain.

In contrast is this 1½-storey standard lodge in the English Picturesque Cottage style, steeply gabled with fretted foiled bargeboards, an ornamental feature which extends beyond as fascia boards and similarly embellishes the little single-storey hall projection, its doorway below a mouth-organ fanlight. In harled walls, the squared casement windows are highlighted by plain unmoulded labels over. To the road gable is a little semi-octagonal bay window with equivalent roof. Occupied and recently having been subjected to plastic window replacement. The round carriage pillars have 'bap' cappings.

LGI (1904).

161. GREENMOUNT, Patrickswell (2).
'The very handsome and improved demesne of John Green' in 1826, the newly built house and its two complementary porters' lodges have all gone.

Fitzgerald and McGregor 1827.

162. GRISTON, Ballylanders; pre-1841; *demolished.*
The 'fine old place which belonged to Charles Massy' in 1826 had been removed by 1928, by which time its gatekeeper's lodge had become 'Griston Cottage' in its own right.

Fitzgerald and McGregor 1827.

163. GROVE, Ballingarry; pre-1841; *demolished.*
Both the house and its lodge (the latter opposite its gates), in 1814 and 1826 of Colonel William Odell MP, had gone by 1923. Only the stables remain.

Leet 1814; Fitzgerald and McGregor 1827.

164. GROVE, Rathkeale; pre-1841; *demolished.*
A house marked as 'In ruins' on the first OS map; its lodge was gone by 1923.

HAMPTON LODGE (see SUNVILLE, Limerick)

165. HARDING GROVE, Bruree; *c.* 1840.
A standard single-storey rendered hip-roofed lodge with clipped eaves, lying deserted. A property in 1837 of Henry Harding.

Lewis 1837.

166. HEATHFIELD, Kilmeedy; *c.* 1825.

A perfectly preserved little single-storey gatekeeper's lodge, built off a square plan with a shallow pyramidal roof rising to a stone chimney-stack. The elevations are single-bay: a sheeted door to the avenue, and to the road a bipartite small-paned casement window, the mullion of which stops the internal partition dividing the two rooms. All in an exposed fabric of neat coursed rubble, probably originally a base for harling. Maintained. Built by Edward Lloyd (1793–1867). Alongside are low quadrant walls and plain carriage pillars with oriental lions atop, sejant rather than rampant of the Lloyd family crest, moved to here from Knockaderry [*q.v.*].

IFR; *The Irish Ancestor* **5** (2).

167. HERMITAGE, Castleconnell (4).
Lost along with two of its early lodges is this stylish house, built for a banker called Bruce in 1800. He had little time to enjoy this superb site overlooking the Shannon, for by 1814 it was home to Lady Massy, presumably Margaret, widow of the 3rd baron, who had died two years previously. Thereafter it remained in the possession of the Barons Massy until 1916, before being burnt down five years later.

Inner gate; pre-1840; *demolished.*
A lodge that commanded the access to a river walk and seems to have been shared by the properties of Castleview [*q.v.*], Woodlands [*q.v.*], Belmont [*q.v.*] and Shannon Lodge [*q.v.*].

Middle gate; pre-1840; *demolished.*

Ruan gate; *c.* 1810.

Opposite the entrance to the northern approach is this Georgian Gothic lodge, probably added on the advent of the Massys. Single-storey standard and gabled but not quite symmetrical, with three pointed-arched openings and the doorway fanlit, all now with plastic Y-tracery and panelled door. In pleasant random rubble facing, its moulded hoods, dripstones and keystones look to be later twentieth-century embellishments; the puny chimney-stack is off-centre on a synthetic slated roof. Across the road is a fine contemporary gateway of big limestone rubble concave quadrant walls framing a pair of tall, slender, ashlar carriage pillars with delicately chiselled cornices and beautiful swagged Coade stone urns.

Ballynacourty gate; *c.* 1860.

To mark the access to the southern avenue is a very impressive cast-iron mid-Victorian gatescreen of ogee railed quadrants and matching carriage gates with repeating flower motifs and gadrooned finials recurring on the four pillars, the outer with round-arched panels, the inner pierced with intricate intertwining foliage. Opposite, and of an age, is the single-storey standard hip-roofed lodge, Italianate with moulded semicircular-arched hoods and dripstones in rendered

walls. The double-leafed sheeted front door is framed by a gabled canopy supported by a pair of basic Doric columns. Modernised with concrete roof tiles and replacement windows. Built for Hugh Hamon Ingoldsby Massy, 5th baron (1827–74).

Leet 1814; *BPB* (1929); Bence-Jones 1988; Kelly 1990.

HERON COURT (see LOTA)

168. HIGHMOUNT, Milford; pre-1841; *demolished.*
A seat in the early nineteenth century of the Walker family.

HOLLY PARK (see CURRAH CHASE)

169. HOLLYWOOD, Adare (2).
Two outstanding lodges built opposite their entrances a century and a half apart to a seat in 1814 of James Raymond, which by 1837 was the residence of James Hewson (b. 1783), who added the early lodge, perhaps as an improvement to mark his marriage in 1824 to his cousin, Mary Hewson.

Old entrance; *c.* 1825.

A fine example of a Regency porter's lodge, its short show front a single bay of a segmentally arched bipartite window with unusually early margined glazing to its one-over-two sashes. Finished in limewashed harling below a hipped roof with clipped eaves, in its dilapidation it searches for its lost gates opposite, supplanted by its successor nearby.

New entrance; *c.* 1990.
An admirable modern interpretation of a late Georgian Classical gatekeeper's lodge. Built essentially off an L-plan in a crisp rendered finish, its single-storey standard three-bay front comprised of two wooden six-over-six sash windows, correctly hornless, flanking a minimal central breakfront below the oversailing eaves of a hipped roof. The entrance doorway has a pair of two-over-one sashed sidelights. It stands at the heart of a wide segmental forecourt defined by concave

railed quadrants terminating in tapered stone 'pylon' pillars with recessed panels that reflect the six opposite, which contain a tripartite gatescreen in the manner of J.B. Papworth.

Leet 1814; Papworth 1818; Lewis 1837; *IFR*.

170. INCHIROURKE, Askeaton; pre-1923; *demolished.*
A seat in the nineteenth century of the Hunt family, the lodge to which was built after 1841.

171. INDIA VILLA, Limerick; pre-1870; *demolished.*
A lodge probably added to the villa in the Corbally suburbs when the property passed from Francis Brew to William Phayre around 1850.

Slater 1846; Griffith 1853–63.

172. ISLAND, Castleconnell; pre-1840; *demolished.*
A gate lodge opposite the gates to an estate of the de Burgho family, presumably built either by the first baronet, Sir Richard de Burgho (d. 1790), or his son of the same name (d. 1839).

BPB (1861).

ISLANDMORE (see TOURINE or TOUREEN)

JANEVILLE (see SHANNON LAWN)

173. JOCKEY HALL, Crecora; pre-1840; *demolished.*
A property in 1826 of Major Tomkins, which eleven years later was 'now occupied by a farmer'.

Fitzgerald and McGregor 1827; Lewis 1837.

JONESBOROUGH VILLA (see PARK COTTAGE)

174. KENMARE CASTLE, Hospital; *c.* 1810.
An unprepossessing single-storey gabled structure built in stone rubble, not quite opposite the gates to a stylish single-storey villa erected by Joseph Gubbins, of the Kilfrush [*q.v.*] family, next to the old castle of the earls of Kenmare, probably around the time of his marriage in 1805.

Leet 1814; Lewis 1837; *LGI* (1904).

175. KILBALLYOWEN, Bruff (3).
The family of O'Grady had been established here since 1309, although the recently demolished house was in 1837 'a handsome modern building in a richly planted demesne', then of Gerald de Courcy O'Grady II, who had succeeded to the ancient estate on his father's death in 1812 and was probably its builder prior to his marriage a year later, when he may also have added at least two of the unassuming gatekeepers' lodges.

North entrance; *c.* 1820.
On the road's edge forward of its gates is this derelict single-storey standard structure in a stuccoed finish below a hipped roof with clipped eaves. Manned in 1851 by John Ward.

Middle entrance; pre-1840; *demolished.*
A lodge located opposite its gates, its porter in 1851 Hugh Connors.

South entrance; *c.* 1810.
A single-storey building in harled rubble construction on a square plan with a pyramidal roof, its single-bay elevations having tiny window openings. Approaching ruin, having spent its final days as a rugby clubhouse. The gatekeeper in 1851 was William Connors.

Lewis 1837; Griffith 1853–63; *IFR*.

176. KILBALLYOWEN TOWNLAND, Bruff; pre-1840; *demolished.*
An anonymous holding of 50 acres in 1851 of Thomas Fitzgerald, whose gatekeeper was then John Connolly. Sometime around 1850 the public road was realigned to sever the old avenue, marooning the lodge and hastening the demise of the whole property by 1900.

Griffith 1853–63.

177. KILFRUSH, Hospital (2).
Joseph Gubbins commissioned architect Charles Frederick Anderson to develop his estate around 1835, to include a large, unprepossessing Classical mansion and at least one porter's lodge of considerably greater presence.

South entrance; pre-1840; *demolished.*

North entrance; *c.* 1837; architect C.F. Anderson.

A very fine neo-Classical single-storey lodge built off a cruciform plan in immaculate punched random stone, each of its wings pedimented, that to its main front single-bay with a basic Doric column '*ex antis*' in a recess to each corner. This is the successful format also employed by Anderson at nearby Ballywilliam [*q.v.*], at Gurteen-le-Poer, Co. Waterford [*q.v.*], and probably at Lauriston, Co. Cork [*q.v.*], and Mooresfort, Co. Tipperary [*q.v.*]. Now lacking its original sash windows, it has also had an additional more steeply

pitched roof applied to the original. It otherwise survives well maintained behind a manicured hedge, monitoring its gatescreen across the road. This is a triple gateway with spear-topped leaves hung on four cylindrical pillars with square plinths and cornices, a design also to be seen at Sunville [*q.v.*] and in County Tipperary at Grenane [*q.v.*], Lismacue [*q.v.*] and Mooresfort [*q.v.*].

Lewis 1837; *LGI* (1904); Williams 1994.

178. KILKEEDY RECTORY, Clarina; *c.* 1860.
A plain 1½-storey gabled cottage with clipped verges and eaves, built in coursed limestone rubble with brick dressing to its three-bay front, the doorway to the left-hand side with the remains of a decorative porch. A glebe house built in 1792, long known as 'Vermont', it was home to the long-time rector Revd Richard Dickson.

Lewis 1837.

179. KILLACOLLA, Killacolla; pre-1840; *demolished.*
A property in 1851 of Patrick Carroll.

Griffith 1853–63.

180. KILMALLOCK UNION WORKHOUSE, Kilmallock; *c.* 1841; architect probably A. Deane; *demolished.*
Opened for first admissions in 1841, a workhouse built to designs of Alexander Deane.

O'Connor 1995.

181. KILMORE, Ballinleeny; pre-1840; *demolished.*
Surviving at the gate are four small stone pillars with ball finials to an estate in the early nineteenth century of Thomas Lynch that by 1837 had passed to the Tuthill family, who in 1852 were letting it to Col. William Jones, whose gatekeeper was then Edmond Morrisey.

Leet 1814; Lewis 1837; Griffith 1853–63.

182. KILMOYLAN, Cappamore; pre-1840; *demolished.*
A seat since the early eighteenth century (but for a break of 40 years) of a member of the White family with the Christian name of Newport.

IFR.

KILMOYLE (see WESTFIELD)

183. KILMURRY RECTORY, Annacotty; pre-1840; *demolished.*
A porter's lodge possibly contemporary with the glebe house of 1790.

Lewis 1837.

184. KILPEACON CHURCH OF IRELAND CHURCH, Crecora; *c.* 1820.
A tiny single-storey hip-roofed cottage, given a modern rendered face-lift. Perhaps built when the church was enlarged in 1820.

Lewis 1837.

185. KILPEACON, Crecora; pre-1923; *demolished.*
A seat developed after 1841, with a lodge probably built by Patrick J. Spillane, resident here in 1876.

LOI.

186. KILPEACON HOUSE, Crecora; *c.* 1855.

A fine villa built *c.* 1810 to replace an old castle on the site, surely to designs of Sir Richard Morrison but which remained lodgeless until the estate was purchased as an incumbered property by George Gavin in 1850. The dapper lodge dates from his time here, having subsequently had a back return added and its front door modernised to ill effect. Single-storey standard below a shallow hipped roof that oversails on paired soffit brackets, it is crisply rendered with a plain eaves band and architraved surrounds to casement windows on each side of the breakfront hallway. The cut-limestone chimney-stack is reflected in the carriage pillars, which have a James Pain feel with their moulded recessed panels and four-sided round-pedimented cappings. Scroll-topped stops to chunky decorative cast-iron carriage gates. In pleasant contrast are whitewashed stuccoed quadrant walls.

Lewis 1837; McParland *et al.* 1989; Lyons 1993.

187. KILPEACON RECTORY, Crecora; pre-1840; *demolished.*
A lodge that may have dated from the rebuilding of the glebe house in 1817.

Lewis 1837.

188. KILRUSH COTTAGE, Limerick; pre-1840; *demolished.*
A property in 1851 of Dennis O'Connor, the access to which was originally from the north, accompanied by a 'turret' by the gate. The house was subsequently approached from the newly constructed North Circular Road to the south.

Griffith 1853–63.

189. KILSCANNELL, Ardagh; pre-1923; *demolished.*
A lodge built after 1841, probably by William Gibbings, who is recorded here in 1870, having come to a property previously of Richard Condon.

Slater 1846; 1870.

190. KNOCKADERRY, Newcastle West; *c.* 1810; *demolished.*

IAA

An ancient seat of the D'Arcys and subsequently of the D'Arcy Evans family, whose quaint gatehouse remains only in the memory and in an old photograph. It was a two-storey, hip-roofed, three-bay symmetrical affair, apparently in limewashed finish and with a bold eaves band over the main front of wide round-arched ground-floor openings with similarly headed narrow windows over, on each side of a matching niche. A pair of lions have been moved from the gate piers to those of Heathfield [*q.v.*].

Lewis 1837; IAA photograph (27/33); English 1973.

191. KNOCKARD, Doon; *c.* 1862; *demolished.*
A plain 1½-storey lodge in harled rubble construction below a steeply gabled roof. Derelict. Presumably built by Richard Scott when he erected his new house in 1862.

192. KNOCKTORAN, Kilmallock; *c.* 1880.
Opposite its gates is a single-storey standard gate lodge on a square plan, with a chimney-stack to the end of each ridge of its synthetically slated hipped roof. One-over-one bipartite sash windows flank the central doorway in walls with stucco effect carried about basic projecting corner piers. Derelict. Probably built for the proprietor, James Napier Webb (1813–88).

LGI (1904).

193. KYLEGLASS, Limerick; 1862; architects perhaps J. Fogerty and Son.
A once-quaint single-storey standard rendered lodge, notable for an eaves band and carved modillion brackets to its oversailing hipped roof with off-centre chimney-stack. Big square window openings with exaggerated chamfered reveals, also to be found in the lodge to Summerville [*q.v.*], are hideously disfigured with replacement windows on each side of a nasty later lean-to hallway which obscures the original semicircular-arched doorway. A similarly chamfered slit window survives to the road

with its square-paned casement. The Valuation Book records the lodge to be 'in progress' in 1862 to a property of Revd Benjamin Jacob, chaplain to the Female Blind Asylum.

Slater 1846.

194. LACKA, Castleconnell; pre-1840; *demolished.*
A small estate in 1851 of William Homan, before whom John George McKay was the proprietor.

Slater 1846; Griffith 1853–63.

LANAHRONE (see ALBERT VILLA)

195. LANDSCAPE, Pallasgrean; *c.* 1845.
A lodge, like the main house very derelict, with the avenue a muddied grass track. Single-storey standard with a hipped roof and stone corbelled eaves over limewashed harled rubble construction, the casement windows bipartite with multi-rectangular cast-iron glazing pattern, much as at the lodge to Mount Catherine [*q.v.*], where Revd M. Lloyd Apjohn was in 1851 the lessor, but here resident. Matching unassuming gatescreen of similarly finished carriage pillars and modest gates with pretty scroll-topped meeting rails.

Griffith 1853–63.

196. LAUREL HILL CONVENT, Limerick; pre-1870; *demolished.*
Previously a lodgeless private house which was acquired in 1844 as a convent by Mother D'Houer, superioress of the Faithful Companions of Jesus, the mid-Victorian addition being short-lived.

Lenihan 1967; Spellissy 1998.

197. LAURELVILLE [1], Limerick; 1857; *demolished.*
A lodge built on a property of Joseph Robinson upon his letting it to Stephen O'Donnell.

198. LAURELVILLE [2], Limerick; pre-1840.
A villa in the Corbally suburb associated in the mid-nineteenth century with the Bindon family. Their lodge survives as a single-storey flat-roofed structure given a modern castellated parapet, its two-window-bay front forward of the entrance gates alongside.

Griffith 1853–63; Slater 1856.

199. LEMONFIELD, Crecora (2).
A residence in 1814 and 1837 of Henry Bevan, who probably built the original lodge, that within being added by his son, George Purdon Bevan.

Outer gate; pre-1840; *demolished.*
The porter's lodge was located opposite the entrance.

Inner gate; *c.* 1845.
A ruinous lodge that has suffered a direct hit from a fallen mature tree. Single-storey in a harled rubble finish, its short principal front having housed the doorway apparently in a flat parapeted wall against which the gabled roof abutted, another instance of that type of structure which is peculiar to the county and

is also to be found at Ballyknockane [*q.v.*], Cappagh [*q.v.*], Glenville [*q.v.*] and Springfield Castle [*q.v.*]. One of the gatekeepers in 1851 was Michael Purcell.

Leet 1814; Lewis 1837; Griffith 1853–63; *IFR.*

200. LICKADOON CASTLE, Limerick; pre-1840; *demolished.*
A lodge, which had been removed by 1924, to a seat of a branch of the Hunt family.

201. LIFFORD, Limerick; pre-1840; *demolished.*
A seat in 1814 of Revd John Hoare, who by 1851 had been succeeded by Francis John O'Neill. The lodge had gone by 1937 and by the end of that century was replaced by a nice little gate-lodge-style bungalow, single-storey on a square plan, in clay facing brick below a pyramidal roof.

Leet 1814; Griffith 1853–63.

202. LIMERICK ARTILLERY BARRACKS, Limerick; 1807.

Jim Shaw

Jim Shaw

Thirty years after its foundation, Samuel Lewis recorded 'The Artillery Barrack, in the Irish town, for 6 officers, 194 men, and 104 horses, with a hospital for 35 patients'. What was then a thoroughly well-kept military parade ground has now become a run-down home to small industrial units. So, too, the once-smart guardhouses that flanked the narrow entrance, each matching in fine punched limestone ashlar to its arcaded façades. Short principal fronts to front and back are topped by pediments, the tympana of which were rendered and contained oculi. Two-bay to the visitor and three-bay within, their fenestration has been subjected to much unfortunate alteration down the years, and a carriage archway that united the rear elevation is no more.

Lewis 1837; NIAH.

203. LIMERICK LUNATIC ASYLUM, Limerick (2).

Mulgrave Street gate; 1826; architects F. Johnston and W. Murray; *demolished.*

The second of nine such institutions to be completed throughout the country, mainly to a standard plan which included a forbidding screen wall to the street through which carriage access was gained via a pair of tall doors carried on rangy pillars flanked by short wing walls containing postilion doors. These were monitored by a pair of single-storey twin pedimented lodges, blind with toothed quoins to the visitor, facing each other across the entry with three-bay fronts. Removed last century to present a less intimidating aspect to what is now St Joseph's Hospital.

Roxborough Avenue gate; *c.* 1865.
An unassuming two-storey gabled gatehouse with a standard three-bay ground-floor elevation in stucco-effect walls, with a single-storey projecting hall having skew-tables and block kneelers. Above are two symmetrically placed windows.

Lewis 1837; Lenihan 1967; O'Dwyer 1997a.

204. LIMERICK UNION WORKHOUSE, Limerick; 1840; architects Thomas and Kearns Deane; *demolished.*
A simple single-storey two-room structure with a single window to rear and a front elevation which was flush with a bipartite gateway alongside, the whole screen terminating in convex quadrant walls. First admissions were received in 1841 to an institution that now forms the core of St Camillus' Hospital. The gate porter in 1850 was William Bourke.

Griffith 1853–63; O'Connor 1995; Williams 1994.

205. LIMERICK WATERWORKS, Limerick; 1858; *demolished.*
The North Strand reservoir was constructed in 1858 by Limerick Corporation.

206. LINFIELD, Pallasgrean (2).
Originally the seat of the Apjohn family, which by marriage became Lloyd property.

They assumed that additional surname but preferred to live at their residence of nearby Landscape [*q.v.*], in 1837 leasing Linfield to Darby O'Grady. By 1928 the house was in ruins and both lodges—the one to the main gate in place by 1840—having followed it into obscurity.

Leet 1814; Lewis 1837; Griffith 1853–63; *IFR*.

207. LISKENNETT, Croom; pre-1840; *demolished.*

A property in 1826 of Patrick McMahon, which eleven years later had passed to Roger Keating Sheehy (*c.* 1804–84). By 1851 it was occupied by Francis S. Walker, whose gate porter was then John McEniry.

Fitzgerald and McGregor 1827; Lewis 1837; Griffith 1853–63; *IFR*.

208. LISSURLAND, Strand; pre-1841; *demolished.*

A lodge located opposite the gateway to a seat in the nineteenth century of the O'Brien family.

209. LOMBARDSTOWN, Caherconlish; pre-1840; *demolished.*

A holding of Thomas O'Brien in 1851, leased from the Wolfe family. Its lodge across the road from the entrance had gone by 1928.

Griffith 1853–63.

210. LOTA, Limerick; *c.* 1860.

A development that formed part of the mid-Victorian suburb of North Circular Road, in 1865 the residence of Edward Collins. This is a bold little Italianate lodge of the period, raised on a tall plinth as a single-storey standard structure in smooth rendering below a hipped roof. Its windows with lugged moulded surrounds flank an incongruous gabled porch with narrow access to the fanlit panelled door, its walls in conspicuous channelled rustication carried about the semicircular archway as 'sunburst' voussoirs. Now undergoing imaginative modernisation and extension. Good chamfered ashlar entrance pillars. Subsequently renamed 'Bishopsbourne', the property now goes under the name of 'Heron Court'.

Slater 1870.

211. LOUGHANANNA, Mitchelstown (2).

North entrance; pre-1928; *demolished.*

South entrance; *c.* 1895.

Contemporary with the big house is this sturdy single-storey lodge, built off an L-plan in expressed stone rubble with toothed brick dressings below a hipped roof, its lean-to porch roof under the main eaves. Derelict. Entrance pillars with dainty stone vases. A mountain retreat at the foot of the Galtees, originally created by the earls of Kingston but completely redeveloped around 1895 by Abel Buckley.

LOUGH GUR (see GRANGE HILL)

212. MANTLE HILL, Askeaton; pre-1841; *demolished.*

At one time also known as 'Ballynash Castle', a seat in 1814 and 1837 of John Hunt.

Leet 1814; Lewis 1837.

213. MARTINSTOWN, Kilmallock; 2009; architect Michael Healy.

A remarkable reproduction of Robert Adam's design for the North Lodge to Kedleston Hall, Derbyshire (1761–2), here created for J.P. McManus. A towering neo-Classical semicircular-arched carriage gateway is faced with a pair of engaged Tuscan columns carrying an entablature and mutuled pediment. Supporting are twin parapeted lodges, each single-bay with correct six-over-six sash windows, the whole in a beautifully chiselled golden limestone ashlar transported from the Chipsham Quarry in Rutland. Framed by extensive concave railed quadrants to form a great segmental forecourt, which is mirrored in that across the public road with its triple gateway, the carriage pillars of which are crowned by exquisite Classical urns. Elevationally the

Above: North Lodge, Kedleston Hall, Derbyshire.

archway differs from the original in the columns being unfluted, a lack of triglyphs and the pediment being steeper, perhaps to comfortably display a coat of arms. An admirable addition to the landscape and a triumphant reawakening of the Irish tradition of gate-lodge-building.

Mowl and Earnshaw 1984.

214. MARYVILLE, Fedamore; pre-1840.
A single-storey gabled structure, much removed from its original manifestation by modernisation and extension. A property in the nineteenth century of the Finch family.

215. MASSY LODGE, Ballylanders; pre-1841; *demolished.*
A summer residence in the Galtee Mountains built *c.* 1800 for Hugh, the 3rd Baron Massy (1761–1812), whose main seat was Hermitage [*q.v.*] in the county. The architect C.F. Anderson claimed to have carried out work here in the early nineteenth century, referring to the place as 'Aldborough' after its townland.

BPB (1929); Bence-Jones 1988.

216. MILFORD, Limerick; pre-1840/*c.* 1900; architect not known.

A property which has seen a succession of owners, from the Revd Mr Widenham in the late eighteenth century, Lord Kiltarton in 1814, the Limerick banker George Maunsell in 1826, the Fitzgerald family in 1837 and 1851, through to the Massys of Hermitage [*q.v.*], who remained here for much of the remainder of the nineteenth century. The early gate lodge was replaced by the present striking example of Arts and Crafts architecture, built single-storey off an L-plan in a red brick, its windows wide, transomed and mullioned with tiny squared glazing, all set below segmental relieving arches. In the internal angle the porch is set below a catslide roof supported on carved wooden posts. While the half-timbered-effect apex to the avenue is simply gabled, that to the road is partly hipped and jettied on earthenware corbels and a breakfront. Reroofed with modern concrete tiles, it was built for Lt.-Col. Henry Thompson Russell (1875–1953).

Taylor and Skinner 1778; 1783; Leet 1814; Fitzgerald and McGregor 1827; Lewis 1837; Griffith 1853–63; *IFR.*

217. MILITARY CEMETERY, Limerick; 1856.
A single-storey standard lodge with a chimney-stack to each main gable; these have plain clipped verges in contrast to that of the entrance breakfront, which sports pretty perforated foiled bargeboards with trefoil toes. Built in limestone rubble facings, with toothed brick quoins and dressing to the panelled front door with mouth-organ fanlight and the plastic imitations of six-over-six sash windows. In the leading apex is the date inscribed in a stone shield, perhaps also indicating the date of the first burial. By 1937 the graveyard was 'disused'; the last interments appear to have been those of Welsh Fusiliers in the early twentieth century.

Spellissy 1998.

218. MILLFARM, Hospital; pre-1840; *demolished.*
A mill complex that by 1840 seems already to have fallen into ruin and in 1851 was not included in the valuation.

Griffith 1853–63.

219. MILLMOUNT, Kilmallock; pre-1841; *demolished.*
Another property of the Gabbett family, latterly renamed 'Ardvullen'. Surviving at the entrance are good tall ashlar pillars with tapering recesses in the Egyptian 'pylon' fashion, popular in the Regency period.

220. MILLTOWN, Pallaskenry; pre-1841; *demolished.*
A seat in the early nineteenth century of the Bevan family, and subsequently home to Revd Arthur Champagne in 1837.

Lewis 1837; *IFR.*

221. MONASTER, Monaster; *c.* 1810.

An intriguing example of a rustic Irish Palladian porter's lodge. As originally conceived, its leading short front containing the doorway was set in a large semicircular-arched recess flanked by a pair of similarly headed niches, all springing from common stone impost blocks in whitewashed harled walls. A credit to its builder, John C. Heffernan, who would be distressed to see some of the alterations since visited upon it, from the extending bargeboards which replaced the old clipped verges, thus fouling the niche heads, to a plastic window installed in the previous door opening, and an extension built flush with the show façade rather than set back in deference to it.

Leet 1814.

222. MOUNT BROWNE, Rathkeale; pre-1841; *demolished.*
A property now known as 'Dromard', a residence in 1814 and 1838 of John S. Browne.

Leet 1814; Fraser 1838.

223. MOUNT CATHERINE, Pallasgrean; *c.* 1825.
An estate that came to Peter Smithwick through his marriage to an Apjohn of Linfield [*q.v.*] in the mid-eighteenth century and remained in his family for much of the succeeding century. A single-storey steeply hip-roofed cottage with two-bay elevations, rendered with vermiculated quoin stones. The windows are small-paned, just as those to the lodge at Landscape [*q.v.*], another property with Apjohn connections. Occupied. Perhaps built by Michael Smithwick (d. 1857) around the time of his marriage in 1825.

IFR.

224. MOUNT COOTE, Kilmallock (3).
An estate from the seventeenth century of the Coote family, in 1837 'of Chidley Coote, Esq., a spacious and handsome modern mansion, finely situated in the centre of an ample and picturesque demesne, highly improved by the proprietor with ornamental plantations'. This Chidley Coote (1776–1843) since inheriting the property in 1792 had known but one entrance and gatekeeper's lodge.

West entrance; pre-1841/*c.* 1870; architect not known.

Charles Aldworth Coote (1811–97) had succeeded to Mount Coote on the death of his eldest brother in 1869 and would seem to have been responsible for the surviving lodge, either a thorough rework of its predecessor or a complete replacement. Single-storey and double-pile in an Italianate Baroque manner, with stuccoed walls beneath a gabled roof with exaggerated oversailing bargeboards carried on protruding ridge, purlin and eaves members with fancy carved ends. To the avenue extend two flat-roofed, sturdy-framed rectangular bay windows, while to the road projects a like-roofed glazed porch with leaded lights and dentilled eaves. Crowning a striking lodge is a bridged 'Vanbrugh' chimney-stack rising from the central gutter.

In 1925 this branch of the Cootes failed in the male line and the demesne was acquired by the Lillingston family, who created additional lodged approaches.

South entrance; *c.* 1925.
A commodious single-storey Arts and Crafts building, its hipped roof finished in tiny slates over a four-bay ashlar front to the avenue; good contemporary wooden gate. Occupied.

East entrance; *c.* 1925.
Another Arts and Crafts bungalow, much as that to the rear avenue.

Lewis 1837; *LGI* (1912); *LG* (1937); Bence-Jones 1988.

225. MOUNT COURTENAY, Abbeyfeale; *c.* 1850.
A single-storey rendered and gabled lodge with carved paired soffit brackets over its two-window-bay avenue front. Extended and occupied, built on a property in the mid-nineteenth century of William Courtenay, 10th earl of Devon (1777–1859), the latest in a succession of family absentees, and then occupied by Cornelius L. Curtin.

Griffith 1853–63; *BPB* (1929).

226. MOUNT MINNETT, Kilteely (2).
A property in 1814 of William Gabbett (d. 1824) and in 1837 of his son of the same name, one of whom added the early porter's lodge.

North gate; *c.* 1820.
Opposite the gates is a plain single-storey cottage with a two-window-bay front in limewashed rubble below a hipped roof. Derelict.

South gate; *c.* 1860.
Built by yet another William Gabbett is this two-storey gabled single-bay gatehouse with, alongside, an attached three-window-bay single-storey gabled structure. Derelict.

Leet 1814; Lewis 1837; *IFR*.

227. MOUNT RUSSELL, Kilfinnane; *c.* 1825.
Looking to have originated in the time here of Patrick Russell (1795–1828), who inherited on the death of his father in 1819, is this much-modernised and pebble-dashed single-storey standard three-bay lodge below a hipped roof. Occupied.

LGI (1904).

228. MOUNT ST LAWRENCE, Ballyneety; pre-1840; *demolished.*
A seat in 1851 of Joseph Hannon, the lodge to which had been removed by 1928.

Griffith 1853–63.

229. MOUNT ST VINCENT CONVENT, Limerick; *c.* 1852; architect probably J. Neville.
The Sisters of Mercy acquired a property called 'Mount Kenneth', and to designs of Dundalk architect John Neville developed the site with an orphanage, school, chapel, convent and a dozen widows' almshouses, the foundation stone being laid in 1851. By the road is what is now a bipartite gateway with three surviving chamfered cut-stone pillars with four-sided triangular foiled Gothic cappings. Monitoring the entrance is a relatively plain single-storey standard gate lodge, certainly having lost something in modern improvements, with its inappropriate recent casement windows and doorway in an otherwise limestone ashlar wall, with corbelled eaves to a steeply pitched roof with conspicuous plinthed, banded and corbelled cut-stone chimney-stacks to each limestone rubble gable; curiously flimsy perforated curved and foiled bargeboards.

Lenihan 1967; Williams 1994.

230. MOUNT SHANNON, Annacotty (3).
The sadly decimated house and demesne of the Fitzgibbons, of whom the 2nd earl of Clare, John (1792–1851), on inheriting it in 1802 created 'one of the finest mansions in the south of Ireland', according to Lewis in 1837. He had remodelled it in 1809 to designs of Lewis Wyatt, James Pain having carried out the supervision and perhaps having been responsible for many of the ancillary buildings. Despite unanimous appreciation of the place by tourists and topographers in the early nineteenth century, its demise was hastened by the 2nd earl's generosity in Famine relief, reflected today in the condition of its porters' lodges.

Garraunykee gate; pre-1840; *demolished.*

Mount Shannon gate; pre-1840; *demolished.*

Lisnagry gate; *c.* 1820; architect possibly James Pain.

Here are the tragic remains of a once-pretty *cottage orné* with a shallow hipped roof rising to a tall chimney-stack, its eaves over the three-bay avenue front supported on forked tree trunks at each corner recess, between which is a canted bay window, the rubble and brick walls now lacking their original harled finish. Surely by James Pain, fresh from the influence of his erstwhile mentors John Nash and the Reptons.

Heaney 1999; Lewis 1837.

231. MOUNT TRENCHARD, Foynes (2).
Previously called 'Cappa' until the close of the eighteenth century, when it was the seat of Stephen Edward Rice (d. 1831), whose union with Catherine Spring in 1785 had issue in the Spring-Rices; their son Thomas (1790–1866) was created 1st Baron Monteagle of Brandon in 1839, and in his time their late Georgian house had a main approach from the east.

East entrance; pre-1841; *demolished.*
Located opposite its gates, the lodge lay a shell in 1923.

Thomas Spring-Rice (1849–1926) succeeded to the property on the death of his grandfather and added a second lodge on the western avenue.

West entrance; *c.* 1875.
A 1½-storey structure built in random quarry-faced stone below a shallow-pitched roof with gables featuring decorative wooden 'trusses' to the apexes. Occupied and spoilt in alterations.

BPB (1929).

232. MOYLISH, Limerick; pre-1937; *demolished.*
A property in 1850 and 1870 of Lawrence Kelly, a prosperous butcher in the city, whose lodge was built after 1840.

233. MULKEAR, Annacotty; pre-1840/*c.* 1875; architects J. Fogerty and Son.

A residence between 1824 and 1838 of Revd Josiah Crampton after he moved from Shannon Lodge [*q.v.*], probably leasing from the Tuthill family, the early lodge to which was replaced when the house was transformed for Alexander Bannatyne, corn merchant and miller. He rather confusingly rechristened it with the name of an earlier neighbouring house—Woodsdown [*q.v.*]. This is a splendid little lodge in the Italianate style by local architects Joseph Fogerty and Son. Single-storey standard, built off a cruciform plan with a bold plinth in a crisp smooth-rendered finish below a roof hipped to each wing and individually to both end elevation breakfronts. Semicircular-arched windows with ornamental surrounds and corbelled sills are framed in rectangular recesses, while the hall projection has similarly headed sidelights and door opening. Occupied and immaculately maintained, but with unfortunate door screen and window replacements. The wide contemporary mid-Victorian railed quadrants are contained by formidable chamfered pillars having pyramidal cappings and deep friezes with brackets in the manner of J.S. Mulvany. Now St Vincent's Centre.

Pigot 1824; Fraser 1838; Lyons 1993; Williams 1994; IAA.

234. MUNGRET COLLEGE, Mungret; *c.* 1860; *demolished.*
What originated in 1826 as the Church of Ireland rectory became the site for a monastery before, in 1858, an ill-fated attempt to create an agricultural college.

Lewis 1837.

235. NANTINAN, Ballinagrave (2).
An estate of the Royse family since the mid-

eighteenth century, from which time the main entrance dates, though now lodgeless.

North gate; pre-1841; *demolished.*
Impressive, very tall ball-finialled pillars are nicely set off by high-walled concave quadrants, each of which contains a round-headed niche and lancet-arched postern opening with decorative ironwork. Presumably built for the Revd Thomas Henry Royse, rector of Nantinan. The lodge had been removed by 1923.

South gate; *c.* 1830.
The secondary approach retains its gate lodge, a derelict single-storey standard porter's cottage, harled below an oversailing hipped roof. Probably contemporary with the replacement villa built by Thomas Henry Foorde Russell Buckworth Royse, who inherited the property in 1809.

LG (1853).

236. NEWBOROUGH, Patrickswell; *c.* 1810.
Originally a standard single-storey harled hip-roofed cottage, subsequently converted to an L-plan with the addition of a wing projecting parallel to the boundary wall and tripartite gateway alongside. A property in 1814 of Revd J. Croker, and twelve years later of Christopher Adamson.

Leet 1814; Fitzgerald and McGregor 1827.

NEWCASTLE COTTAGE (see CASTLE VILLE)

237. NEW CASTLE, Limerick; pre-1840; *demolished.*
A seat in 1814 of Denis O'Brien and in 1837 of Mathew O'Brien, whose gatekeeper's lodge had gone by 1937.

Leet 1814; Lewis 1837.

238. NEWCASTLE WEST, Newcastle West; pre-1841; *demolished.*
An old castle of the Fitzgeralds, granted in 1591 to the Courtenay family, subsequently earls of Devon, who were conspicuous by their absence, the house built by them in the grounds mainly occupied by their agent, in 1824 and 1846 identified as Albert Furlong. At the gates to what was alternatively called 'Courtenay Castle' the first OS map indicates a lodge with a bow to its short avenue elevation.

Pigot 1824; Lewis 1837; Slater 1846; Bence-Jones 1988.

239. NEWCASTLE WEST UNION WORKHOUSE, Newcastle West; *c.* 1845.
A simple four-bay hip-roofed structure, much modernised, to a workhouse designed by Sir Thomas Deane, which opened for admissions in 1841. Now St Ita's Hospital.

O'Connor 1995.

240. NEWGARDEN, Castleconnell; pre-1840; *demolished.*
A seat in the late eighteenth century of the Purdons, which by 1814 had passed to the Ryves family but by the mid-nineteenth century appears to have fallen into disrepair.

Taylor and Skinner 1778; 1783; Leet 1814.

241. ODELL VILLE, Ballingarry (2).

241. Odell Ville, Ballingarry, south gate. IAA

A big, unassuming, astylar Georgian house, built around 1780 for John Fitzcharles Odell on an estate most notable for its delightful contemporary gate lodge at the early main entrance.

South gate; *c.* 1780.
In contrast with the big house is this quintessential Georgian Gothic single-storey standard lodge, with pointed arches to Y-traceried sash windows on each side of a sheeted doorway in limewashed harled walls below a steeply hipped roof with off-centre brick chimney-stack, all once beautifully set off by concave rubble quadrant walls but now disgracefully overgrown and allowed to go to ruin.

In 1860 Helena Mary, only child of John Odell, married Edmund Morony and the property passed to him; presumably this was when the main entrance was moved to the north and the old lodge isolated.

North gate; *c.* 1865.
A pleasant, solid little single-storey lodge of two bays by one in random ashlar facings below a soffit of paired carved brackets to a steeply pitched hipped roof; plastic windows.

LGI (1904); de Breffney and ffolliott 1975; IAA photographs (S/549/6 & 7).

242. ORELAND, Limerick; *c.* 1865.
A mildly Italianate standard single-storey lodge below a hipped roof with paired carved soffit brackets, mimicking those on the villa within. The avenue elevation is distinguished by recessed panels formed by plain pilasters framing square windows and a central elliptically arched porch recess. All in smooth rendering on a stone plinth. Unoccupied. Built for John McKern, forming part of the mid-Victorian suburban development of North Circular Road. Contemporary concave railed quadrants and matching carriage gates are contained by equally forthright chunky pillars with moulded recesses and 'Oreland' inscribed in the friezes under four-sided 'gabled' cappings.

NIAH.

243. PARK COTTAGE, Limerick; 1856.

A charming Georgian Gothic look-alike porter's lodge, single-storey standard and built off a square plan, its shallow pyramidal roof rising to a central chimney-stack. Y-traceried sash windows below lancet heads are displayed in conspicuous applied channel rustication with exaggerated 'voussoirs'. Sullied by later flat-roofed additions in a late Victorian glazed hall to the main front and extension to the right-hand side containing an original window salvaged from the previous side elevation. A property in 1856 of James Barry, letting to James Monsell; subsequently renamed 'Jonesborough Villa' and latterly 'Janemount'.

244. PARK, Limerick; pre-1937; *demolished.*
A lodge built after 1870 to mark the house becoming the residence of the Roman Catholic bishop of Limerick.

245. THE PEOPLE'S PARK, Limerick; 1875; architect not known; *demolished.*
The fine residential Pery Square developed by James Pain, with at its heart the Spring-Rice column of 1828, railed in and enclosed as a public park by 1874, has at its main access, in limestone ashlar, a grand triumphal Doric archway, tripartite with semicircular archivolted and keystoned arches, the postern openings flanking a grand carriage gateway, the mutuled entablature to which is inscribed with the information: 'Pery Square; In Memory of Richard Russell; The land being given by the Right Honble

245. The People's Park, Limerick.

NLI, Lawrence Collection

The Earl of Limerick; 1875'. The tragedy of all this is clear from a late Victorian photograph which shows the archway to have been attended by a sophisticated single-storey neo-Classical porter's lodge, apparently built off a cruciform plan with porticoed and pedimented fronts. Quite what warranted its removal is quite inconceivable.

Lawrence photograph (2697C); Spellissy 1998.

246. PLASSEY, Limerick (2).
Both lodges, one of which was in place by 1840, have been removed, to a property originally known as 'Ballykilty' but subsequently renamed by its famous later owner Robert Clive (1725–74). In the early nineteenth century it became home to local banker Thomas Maunsell before the house was transformed into a grand Italianate pile in 1863 for Richard Russell (1803–71), a rich mill-owner, who probably added the second lost lodge. Now at the centre of the National Institute for Higher Education.

LGI (1904); Bence-Jones 1988; Spellissy 1998.

247. PORTLAND, Limerick; *c.* 1845; *demolished.*
A house and lodge built between 1841 and 1851 in the North Circular Road suburb by William Murray.

Griffith 1853–63.

248. PORTNARD, Cappamore (2).
A property of Revd Rickard Lloyd (d. 1856) in 1826, when the house was approached via a single lodged gate.

North entrance; pre-1840.
A ruin with only one rubble wall surviving.

South entrance; 1880.

A very solid 1½-storey standard gabled lodge built in random coursed quarry-faced stone with brick toothed dressings, now rendered over. The double-leafed sheeted front door has a mouth-organ fanlight below a flimsy gabled canopy carried on hefty sculpted stone corbels, on each side of which are multi-paned casement windows. To one gable is a brick relieving arch with basic foiled and wavy bargeboards over. Built for Rickard E. Lloyd.

249. PROSPECT, Annacotty (2).
Both the pre-1840 lodge, serving the estate in the time of the Powell family, and that added around 1845 by Eyre Lloyd (1803–76) have been demolished.

Fitzgerald and McGregor 1827; *IFR*.

250. PROSPECT, Limerick; *c.* 1850.
A plain, single-storey hip-roofed lodge has its main Virginia creeper-clad three-window-bay façade turning its back to the road to face what is now a training college. Previously 'Prospect Hill', it was home in 1850 to William Saunders.

Griffith 1853–63.

251. PROSPECT LODGE, Kilmallock; pre-1841; *demolished.*
A property in 1851 of Michael Hayes.

Griffith 1853–63.

252. RAHEEN, Annacotty; pre-1840/*c.* 1870.

The original lodge may have dated from the time here of John Clarke, in residence in 1824. By 1851 it was home to John Gueran, and 25 years later to W.J.H. Moreland, presumably responsible for the present replacement. Although off a simple rectangular plan, it is quaint for its irregular outline, 1½-storey with hipped gables that have wavy bargeboards like the central gablet, the slit window to which lights the attic space. Three-bay with doorway to the left-hand side, it is constructed in squared coursed rubble, recently sensitively restored with convincing squared casement windows within shallow segmentally arched openings.

Pigot 1824; Griffith 1853–63; *LOI.*

253. RATHANNY, Hospital; *c.* 1820.
A traditional single-storey standard hip-roofed gatekeeper's cottage with sepia-washed harled walls. Derelict. A seat in 1814 of John Sheeran but by 1837, and after, a property of the Bennett family.

Leet 1814; Lewis 1837.

254. RATHBANE COTTAGE, Limerick (2).
A property in 1846 of Thomas P. Vokes RM, with two pre-1840 lodges, which five years later he was leasing to merchant Horatio Nelson Seymour, one of the lodges being occupied by John Rich. That which survives appears to be a replacement of *c.* 1860, 1½-storey standard and hip-roofed with a gablet above the front door. Modernised with synthetic slates, having segmentally headed openings in sand/cement-rendered walls. Occupied.

Slater 1846; 1870; Griffith 1853–63.

255. RATHFREDAGH, Newcastle West; *c.* 1865.

Opposite the gates is an unassuming, solidly built single-storey gabled lodge in random ashlar facings, its two-bay main front of small-paned tripartite windows in contrasting toothed punched cut-stone dressings, the quoins matching. To the ridge is a paired chimney-stack in finely chiselled stone, whilst the bargeboards have a simple sawtooth pattern applied, rising to dainty hip-knobs with pendants. A seat for much of the nineteenth century of the O'Grady family of Rockbarton [*q.v.*] and Cahir Guillamore [*q.v.*], now a Cheshire Home with its lodge abandoned behind a railed screen. Probably built when the new house was being erected in 1860 for the Hon. Richard O'Grady.

256. RATHKEALE ABBEY, Rathkeale; pre-1841.
An estate in the late eighteenth century of the Pigott family, who subsequently leased it to George Leake, followed around 1837 by J. Hewson Esq. The old porter's cottage lies in ruins, with but a single-bay rubble wall left standing.

Taylor and Skinner 1778; 1783; Wilson 1803; Lewis 1837.

257. RATHKEALE RECTORY, Rathkeale (2).
A glebe house built in 1819 on ten acres was clearly a prosperous living to warrant two gatekeepers' lodges, both in existence in 1841. By 1923 that to the main eastern approach had gone, while the other on the northern avenue was unhatched on the OS map of that year, suggesting its ruin.
Lewis 1837.

258. RICH HILL, Annacotty; pre-1840; *demolished.*
A seat in 1814 of John Howley and 23 years later of William Howley, having earlier been established by the Rich family.
Leet 1814; Lewis 1837.

259. RICHMOND, Limerick; pre-1840; *demolished.*
The residence in 1826 of Joseph Fisher (d. 1830).
Fitzgerald and McGregor 1827; Bennis 1940.

260. RICHMOND PARK, Patrickswell; pre-1840/*c.* 1845.
The plainest of single-storey hip-roofed structures with its short main front to the avenue, having replaced a predecessor at the other side of the access. Built as Richmond 'Villa' by Henry Westropp, it remained in 1851 the residence of a descendant of the same name.
Fitzgerald and McGregor 1827; Griffith 1853–63.

261. RIDDLESTOWN PARK, Rathkeale (2).
The very fine house built *c.* 1730 for the Blennerhassett family, to which one of its lodges barely survives.
East entrance; pre-1841; *demolished.*
West entrance; pre-1923.
Built to the secondary gate after 1841, it lies ruinous.
Bence-Jones 1988.

262. RINEROE, Adare; pre-1840/*c.* 1914.

A holding in 1814 of T. Potter that by 1837 had been renamed 'Fort Union', probably by the then occupant, John Christy. The early porter's lodge has been replaced by the remaining Arts and Crafts cottage. Built off a simple rectangular plan, it is enhanced by the irregular roofscape of its attic storey, the single window to the main front of which is contained in a gable, its upper floor further defined by a rendered finish above the brick two-bay ground floor, the entrance door having a sidelight below a lean-to canopy with carved bracket support. Modern small-paned plastic windows suggest quadripartite, tripartite and bipartite predecessors, those to the attic having bellcast hoods in the Voysey manner. Presumably dating from about 1914, when the valuation of the property was considerably raised owing to improvements carried out by Lord Dunraven.
Leet 1814; Lewis 1837.

263. RIVER BLEACH MILL, Castleconnell; *c.* 1800.
An antique single-storey hip-roofed lodge with harled walls is located forward of its entrance; a sophisticated tripartite 'Wyatt' window on the single-bay short main front surveys the gates in its derelict state. Once commanding the access to a thriving bleaching business in 1824 of James Fisher, which by 1851 had been converted to a woollen mill of Joseph Harrison.
Pigot 1824; Griffith 1853–63; Hogg 2000.

264. RIVERSDALE, Galbally; *c.* 1840.
A plain, square, single-storey lodge below a pyramidal roof, its two-window-bay rendered elevation to the avenue, now lies derelict to a seat in 1837 of Hugh Massy (1796–1881).
BPB (1929).

265. RIVERSFIELD, Kilmallock; pre-1841.
A large single-storey structure, square in plan below a pyramidal roof, with a two-window-bay front to the avenue. Possibly a replacement. Occupied. A property between 1824 and 1856 of Thomas Weldon, prior to which it was occupied in 1814 by a Captain Sargent.
Leet 1814; Pigot 1824; Slater 1856.

266. RIVER VIEW, Limerick; pre-1870/*c.* 1920; *demolished.*
A property in 1851 of ironmonger John Abell and nineteen years later of Mrs Elizabeth Sykes, to which a replacement porter's lodge, circular in plan, was built and reputedly shared with neighbouring Corbally Cottage [*q.v.*].
Griffith 1853–63; Slater 1846; 1870.

267. ROCKBARTON, Holycross (2).
Now lying ruinous is the once very fine mansion of Standish O'Grady (1766–1840), which he complemented with gatekeepers' lodges at his gates around the time of his raising to the peerage as 1st Viscount Guillamore in 1831.
Secondary gate; *c.* 1835.
Opposite the entrance to the stable yard is a long, single-storey standard cottage in random rubble facing below a hipped roof. Occupied and maintained, with modern plastic window replacements.
Principal gate; *c.* 1830; architect perhaps James Pain.
Before the intrusion of hideous modern windows this was a lodge of some distinction, now only apparent through the survival of a soffit to its hipped roof of paired carved modillion brackets with moulded coffer ornament between and a moulded cornice to the big central porch recess. The latter contains a tripartite doorway with sidelights, while in the flanking bays are wide window openings which may have contained tripartite sashes in harled walls. Just as James Pain was working for the O'Grady family at Castle Garde [*q.v.*] so too was he here.
BPB (1929); Glin *et al.* 1988.

268. ROCK LODGE, Castleconnell; pre-1840; *demolished.*
A property in 1826 of Messrs Grady, later to be associated with the Corbett and Gillie families, its lodge having been superseded by a twentieth-century bungalow.
Fitzgerald and McGregor 1827; Griffith 1853–63; Lenihan 1967.

269. ROCKHILL, Bruree; pre-1840; *demolished.*
An estate in the first half of the nineteenth century of the Cushin family.
Fitzgerald and McGregor 1827; Lewis 1837.

270. ROCKSPRING, Limerick; pre-1870; *demolished.*
A lodge built after 1840 to a property in 1851 of Joseph King Moore.
Griffith 1853–63.

271. ROSELAWN, Annacotty (2).
Both lodges, one existing in 1840, have been demolished. A seat in the mid-nineteenth century of the Matterson family.
Griffith 1853–63; Slater 1856.

272. ROSSAKIPPANE, Dromcolliher; pre-1841; *demolished.*
An estate in 1851 of Patrick Fitzgerald, the gate lodge to which had gone by 1924.
Griffith 1853–63.

273. ROXBOROUGH, Limerick (2).
Neither of the pre-1840 porters' lodges survive to a demesne of the Vereker family, ennobled in 1816 as the Viscounts Gort.

274. RUTLAND, Limerick; pre-1840; *demolished.*
A property recorded in 1826 and 1870 as home to the Russell family, much leased out between those dates.
Fitzgerald and McGregor 1827; Slater 1870.

275. RYVES CASTLE, Knocklong (2).
A long-time seat of the Ryves family, initially known as 'Castle Jane', which was served by a single lodged entrance. The place was let to tenants in the early nineteenth century before it was acquired *c.* 1855 from William H. Ryves by John Franks (1803–81), who employed architect William Atkins of Cork

to rebuild the house, renamed 'Ballyscaddan' after the townland, and to provide two almost identical new porters' lodges.

East gate; pre-1840/*c.* 1855; architect William Atkins.

Replacing a predecessor is this solid structure built off a square plan, with a standard single-storey three-bay front in squared random coursed stone below a shallow pyramidal roof rising to a tiny chimney-stack. A projecting skew-table-gabled porch has lancet side windows and door opening, flanked by cast-iron latticed-glazed narrow casement windows. Derelict. Nearby are contemporary cast-iron carriage gates on pillars with four-faced pedimented cappings, framed by coursed stone convex quadrant walls.

West gate; *c.* 1855; architect William Atkins.
Almost identical to the main lodge but for pronounced keystones and a bargeboarded porch, now sporting an unfortunate plastic appendage, a material which has spread to the window openings. Carved modillion brackets to the soffits. Occupied.

Taylor and Skinner 1778; 1783; Griffith 1853–63; *LGI* (1904); Bernelle 1992.

276. ST JOSEPH'S HOSPITAL, Limerick; *c.* 1900; *demolished.*
Built *c.* 1900 like a big Elizabethan Revival Arts and Crafts house, totally alien in style but as an infirmary adjunct to the main hospital, which was the Limerick Lunatic Asylum [*q.v.*], on the one side and the equally grey County Gaol on the other; it came with a short-lived lodged entrance, to Mulgrave Street.

NIAH.

277. ST MARY'S CATHEDRAL, Limerick; 1813; architect James Pain; *demolished.*
According to Lewis in 1837, the medieval cathedral was 'surrounded with graduated battlements', which relate to Irish crenellations also repeated on the boundary wall, and in 1813 James Pain was to replicate these on the parapet to his new gatehouse, built to mark the carriage access but which by 1879 was already considered surplus to requirements, had become derelict and was removed.

In wholly appropriate rubble stone facings, the symmetrical two-storey gatehouse presented a central Tudor gateway to Bow Lane, flanked by blind walls of buttresses carried up to define the three-bay upper storey, with its label-moulded mullioned Gothic-style windows with latticed glazing, flanking a large ecclesiastical quatrefoil feature. This was Pain's first work on coming to Ireland, a creation that was only to outlive him by two years.

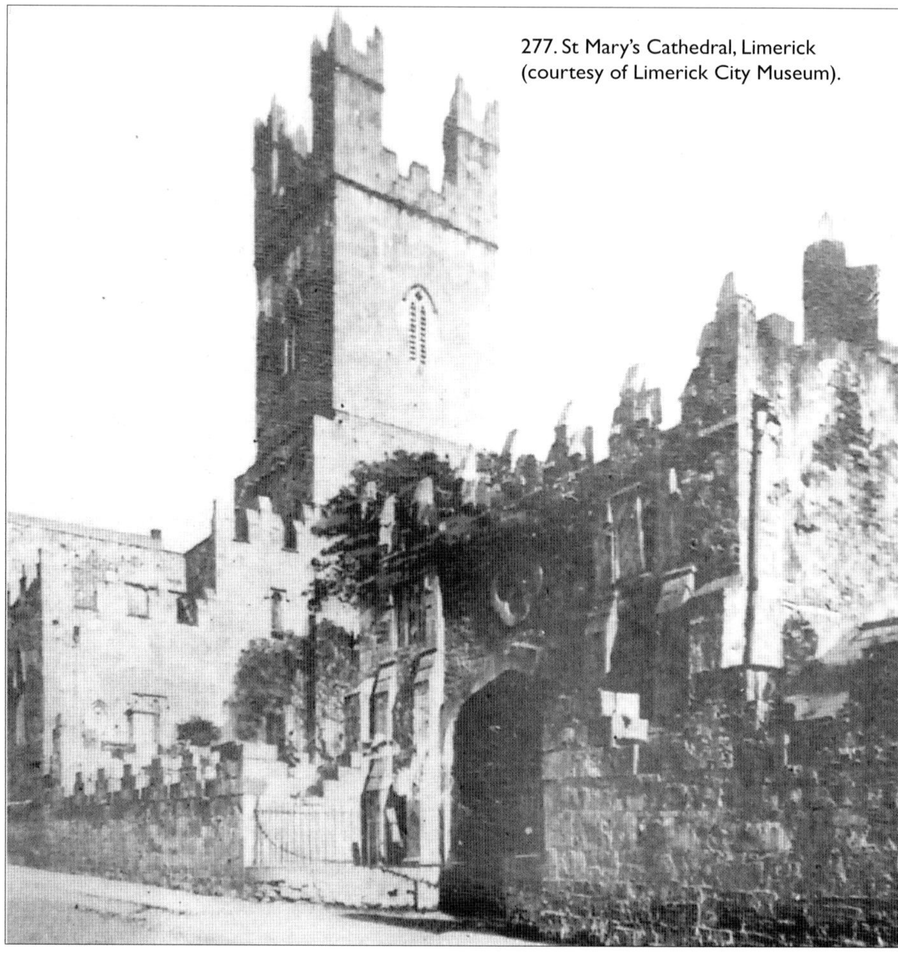

277. St Mary's Cathedral, Limerick (courtesy of Limerick City Museum).

Lewis 1837; Lenihan 1967; Lee 2006; Limerick Museum photograph (LM0000-5293).

278. SANDVILLE, Ballyneety; pre-1840; *demolished.*
A lodge, which had gone by 1928, to an estate of the Barry family previously called 'Fryarstown', probably built by John Barry (1779–1839).

LGI (1904).

279. SCART, Rathkeale; pre-1841; *demolished.*
A property recorded as the residence of a James Condon between 1814 and 1856, possibly the same as at Wellmount [*q.v.*] nearby.

Leet 1814; Slater 1856.

280. SCARTEEN, Knocklong; pre-1840/*c.* 1865.
Replacing a predecessor at the other side of the entrance is this singular three-bay single-

storey lodge, an exercise in duality with its pair of steep gables breaking forward, each with large windows below wide label mouldings in rendered walls, flanking the doorway under the linking eaves; roof otherwise hipped to the rear, with a grand chimney-stack looming from behind the ridge, now sadly in an advanced state of dilapidation. Nearby is a surviving pair of quarry-faced pillars. Built for Thaddeus Richard Ryan (b. 1837), who had succeeded to the estate on the death of his father John (1800–63).

LGI (1904).

281. SHAMROCKVILLE, Limerick; 1907; architect possibly G.R. Ryan.

A delightful and quirky little composition, faced in a maroon-coloured brick laid in contrasting white mortar to English garden wall bond. Single-storey and almost square in plan below a hipped roof which rises to a big corbelled brick chimney-stack, its three-bay front elevation highly articulated by the left-hand breakfront bay, with a multi-paned window under a catslide roof projecting sufficiently to permit a side-entry doorway from the central gabled porch with a canopy displaying minimal half-timbered work to its apex. Neglected. Contemporary quarry-faced stone pillars with 'cushion' friezes below the cappings, and nice carved wooden gates of the same period as the typical 'Stockbroker's Tudor' villa within. All developed on land of 'Tivoli Cottage' [*q.v.*] for George R. Ryan (*c.* 1863–1932), engineer and building contractor, who was possibly his own designer.

IAA.

282. SHANNON GROVE, Pallaskenry; pre-1841.
A very fine early eighteenth-century house of the Bury family, earls of Charleville, of Charleville Forest, Co. Offaly, from whom it passed into the ownership of Bolton Waller (1769–1854) around 1835. At the entrance was a large two-storey gatehouse, now lying in ruins.

Lewis 1837; *LGI* (1904); Bence-Jones 1988.

283. SHANNON LAWN, Glin; *c.* 1835.
A seat in 1837 of Daniel Harnett, from whose time here dates the porter's lodge, now a roofless shell. Originally single-storey standard over a basement with a hipped roof, the front door to which is located in a central canted recessed porch.

Lewis 1837.

284. SHANNON LAWN, Limerick; *c.* 1856.
One of the original three houses to form part of the North Circular Road suburb, when it was initially called 'Janeville'; its lodge was added by John Thomas McSheehy, agent and city treasurer, who altered the name of the place. Single-storey with a shallow hipped roof, the walls now finished in roughcast, the front elevation containing a central casement window flanked by segmentally arched recessed panels. Occupied.

Griffith 1853–63.

285. SHANNON LODGE, Castleconnell; pre-1840.
Much disguised by subsequent alterations down the years, this appears to have been a single-storey standard lodge, its three-bay front to the avenue gabled. Now partly raised a storey, with two chimney-stacks added and a flat-roofed bay extending from the park front. Good railed entrance sweep, with octagonal limestone carriage pillars having fancy cappings. A property, latterly renamed 'Stradbally', in 1814 of Revd Josiah Crampton, in 1824 of William White and in 1837 of John White.

Leet 1814; Pigot 1824; Lewis 1837.

286. SHANNON PARK, Limerick; pre-1840; *demolished.*
Alternatively known as 'Dromroe', in the early nineteenth century this was the residence of the O'Farrell family until it was sold by Michael Richard O'Farrell in 1858 as an incumbered estate, the accompanying lithograph in the advertisement illustrating a plain, hip-roofed, single-storey gatekeeper's lodge with an irregular three-window-bay façade to the avenue.

Leet 1814; Lyons 1993.

287. SHANNON VIEW, Limerick; pre-1840; *demolished.*
Home in 1824 to Frederick Holland, attorney, it was subsequently occupied by a succession of different owners, becoming 'Curragour' by 1870 and latterly 'The Priory' in the twentieth century.

Pigot 1824.

288. SHANNON VILLE, Limerick; pre-1902; *demolished.*
A lodge built after 1841, possibly by Matthew McNamara, resident here in 1851.

Griffith 1853–63.

289. SHELBOURNE, Limerick (2).
Originally built by William Petty Fitzmaurice, 2nd earl of Shelbourne and marquis of Lansdowne (1737–1805), it was subsequently occupied by the Gabbett family, of whom Robert Gabbett added the first lodged entrance between 1841 and 1850; the second, at the North Circular Road gate, was probably built for Thompson Russell (1801–80), a subsequent resident. Both lodges have been demolished, surplus to the requirements of the property's present use as a school.

Griffith 1853–63; *LOI*; *LGI* (1904); Spellissy 1998.

290. SMITHFIELD, Rathkeale; *c.* 1820.
By a lost avenue is this derelict single-storey harled cottage, its two-window main front below a steeply hipped roof. A seat in 1814 and 1826 of Richard Smith.

Leet 1814; Fitzgerald and McGregor 1827.

291. SOUTH HILL, Limerick; pre-1840; *demolished.*
An estate in 1837 of Samuel Evans which subsequently passed to Peter Tait, who restored the house after a fire in the 1860s to designs of William Fogerty of Limerick.

Lewis 1837; *DB* (1 March 1864).

292. SOUTHVILLE, Limerick; pre-1840; *demolished.*
The property in 1850 of John Spillane, tobacco and snuff manufacturer in the city.

Slater 1846; Griffith 1853–63.

293. SPRINGFIELD CASTLE, Dromcolliher (4).
An estate that passed by marriage from the Fitzmaurices to the Deane family, Lords Muskerry, in 1775. Two pre-1841 lodges opposite their gates on the southern approaches have been demolished, having been replaced at different avenues by the 3rd baron, Matthew Fitzmaurice Deane (1795–1868), who had succeeded to the property in 1824 on the death of his brother.

Rear entrance; *c.* 1845.
At the distant northern gate is a single-storey hip-roofed affair, notable for remarkable surrounds to the windows of its two-bay main front. These are later twentieth-century added frills in a New Zealand Maori manner which precisely reflects the extraordinary archway at the main gate.

Front entrance; *c.* 1845.

Over the access is a pair of concrete beams, one bearing the inscription *Forti Et Fideli Nihil Difficile*, the motto of the Deanes, supported by big tapering limestone ashlar pillars flanked by wing walls containing triangular-arched postern openings. Beyond that again are octagonal pillars, probably redeployed from an earlier gate, surmounted by lofty finials, all apparently a whimsy of Robert Matthew-Fitzmaurice Deane-Morgan, 5th Baron Muskerry (1874–1952), when he had to rearrange the big house after it had been destroyed by fire in 1921. Deep within, marooned by subsequent road realignment, is further architectural eccentricity in a most peculiar cottage, gabled on a cranked plan, partly single-storey and partly 1½-storey, its leading gable abutting a tall leading roughcast screen wall, rectangular just as in the gate lodges to Ballyknockane [*q.v.*], Cappagh [*q.v.*] and Glenville [*q.v.*].

BPB (1929); Bence-Jones 1988.

294. STAGDALE, Galbally; pre-1841; *demolished.*
A demesne of the Croft family, from whom it was acquired by the Massys of Glenwilliam Castle [*q.v.*], described in 1826 as 'The noble residence of Hugh Massey'; by 1837 it was the residence of William Massy.

Fitzgerald and McGregor 1827; Lewis 1837; Seoighe 1982.

295. STONEHALL, Askeaton; *c.* 1855.
Opposite the gates is a plain, single-storey standard harled cottage with mini-skew-tables to a steeply pitched roof. Derelict. A seat in 1851 of Edward Coplen-Langford.
Griffith 1853–63; *LGI* (1904).

STONETOWN (see STRAND)

296. STONEVILLE, Rathkeale; pre-1841; *demolished.*
The early eighteenth-century house of the Southwells was purchased in 1758 by William Massy. The lodge may have been added by James Fitzgerald Massy when a stable range was built in 1802. In 1923 it was known as 'Eagle Lodge' in its own right.
Bence-Jones 1988.

297. STORMONT, Castleconnell; pre-1840; *demolished.*
Previously called 'Island House' of the de Burgho family, it was occupied in 1824 by John C. Kelly, its lodge having been removed by 1938.
Pigot 1824.

298. STRADBALLY CHURCH OF IRELAND CHURCH, Castleconnell; pre-1840/*c.* 1920.

The church of All Saints was erected in 1809 and enlarged in 1830, its early porter's, or sexton's, lodge being replaced by the present edifice in the last century. It is 1½-storey, gabled and raised off an L-plan, with a catslide roof over the internal angle, forming an entrance porch with dumpy colonette for support. Tripartite and quadripartite windows have quarry-faced stone dressings in smooth-rendered walls. Occupied.
Lewis 1837.

STRADBALLY (see SHANNON LODGE)

299. STRAND, Limerick; *c.* 1820.
Alternatively known over time as 'Stonetown', this was another suburban property of the Gabbett family, of whom around the turn of the eighteenth century it was home to Daniel Gabbett. Behind huge stone boundary walls as a barrier against modern traffic is a remarkable survivor in this plain, lofty, single-storey-with-loft hip-roofed lodge with tall eaves and short main front to the approach. Occupied.
LGI (1904).

300. SUMMERVILLE, Bruff; *c.* 1835.
A standard single-storey gatekeeper's lodge built off a square plan, with a shallow pyramidal roof rising to a central chimney-stack. Square windows, transomed and mullioned with latticed chinoiserie glazing pattern, set in rectangular recesses to ground level. Derelict, with its rubble and brick fabric exposed in either restoration or destruction. A property in 1851 of the ubiquitous Revd Joseph Gabbett (1806–83), rector of Kilmallock, leasing from Alcock Otley. Ribboned ball finials to gate pillars.
Griffith 1853–63; *LGI* (1904).

301. SUMMERVILLE, Limerick; *c.* 1870; architects possibly J. Fogerty and Son.

An early house built by the Harvey family in the Courtbrack suburb and subsequently much tenanted, its distinctive little lodge probably added by James Bannatyne. Single-storey on an essentially square plan, with a hipped roof and central chimney-stack, from which project gabled breakfronts or wings which extended to a cruciform base. The front projection to the avenue has an entrance doorway and side windows in an otherwise blind elevation; the walls are smooth-rendered with deeply chamfered window reveals, also to be seen in the lodge to Kyleglass [*q.v.*], below boldly carved soffit brackets. Impressive wide railed gatescreen, partly straight and partly concave quadrants, framing chamfered stone pillars with four-faced semicircular pedimented cappings. A similarity in plan with the lodge to Mulkear [*q.v.*], also for the Bannatyne family, points towards work by J. Fogerty and Son.
Slater 1870; Bennis 1940.

302. SUMMERVILLE, Pallaskenry; pre-1841; *demolished.*
A property in 1848 of Michael O'Donnell, whose gate porter was Michael Grady.
Griffith 1853–63.

303. SUN VILLE, Kilfinnane; pre-1841; *demolished.*
Otherwise known as 'Sun Vale', this was an estate in 1814 of James Godsall which by 1837 was the residence of Edward Sayers. The site of the lodge is now occupied by a chalet bungalow.
Leet 1814; Lewis 1837.

304. SUNVILLE, Limerick; 1856; *demolished.*
A plain, two-storey, hip-roofed gatehouse in a roughcast finish, with modern replacement windows to its symmetrical front of three-bay ground floor and two-window upper storey below a soffit with paired carved soffit brackets. A property originally called 'Hampton Lodge', to which the lodge was added when Edward Cruise (1802–87) acquired it from John Vanderkist.
Spellissy 1998.

305. SUNVILLE, Pallasgrean; *c.* 1835; architect perhaps C.F. Anderson.

A pleasant 1½-storey English Picturesque cottage, with simple wavy bargeboards to its conspicuously steeply pitched gables. Some windows with label mouldings in roughcast walls, the long, tall-eaved road façade sparsely fenestrated. From the avenue gable projects a single-storey gabled hall, a lean-to extension on the opposing front. Tripartite gateway with cut-stone drum pillars having square cornices in the manner of architect C.F. Anderson at Kilfrush [*q.v.*]. Built for Thomas Kearney.
Lewis 1837; *PGI.*

306. TEMPLEMUNGRET, Mungret; pre-1924; *demolished.*
A property of the Kennedy family at the turn of the twentieth century, its lodge erected after 1840.

307. TERVOE, Mungret (2).
In 1835 the Scottish tourist Robert Graham wrote of the property of William Thomas Monsell (1754–1836): 'entering at one gate and going out the other and I was gratified in doing so. The house is old fashioned but respectable.' By the following year, that of his death, Monsell had greatly extended and improved the house, perhaps also upgrading the entrances, where lodges were in place by 1841, ten years later being occupied by porters Mary Rourke and Mrs Stokes. Today the property is destroyed, the mansion having been demolished in 1953, with an ivy-covered ruin at one gate and a twentieth-century bungalow at the other. The Knight of Glin recalls one of the lodges being similar to the Gothic lodge at Adare Manor [*q.v.*].
Heaney 1999; Griffith 1853–63; Potter 2009.

308. THORN VILLE, Limerick (2).
The Valuation Book records two porters' lodges having been added to the property by 1870 for Windham Gabbett (b. 1844). Neither survives.
LGI (1904).

309. TIVOLI COTTAGE, Limerick; 1910; architect not known.

An ostentatious little single-storey standard Italianate lodge below a pyramidal roof, with console brackets in pairs to the oversailing eaves and scrolled brackets to the banded chimney-stack, repeated below the sills to windows with moulded surrounds in rectangular recesses. Projecting centrally from rendered walls is a glazed hall with open-pedimented gable. Occupied and overlooking an innovative cast-iron tripartite gatescreen of four circular railed 'birdcage' posts with decorative tops and insets. All for Sir Vincent Nash. Overthrows to the postilion gates announce 'Villiers School', revealing the property's present use.

LOI.

310. TOOMALINE LOWER, Doon; pre-1840; *demolished.*

A seat for much of the nineteenth century of the Marshall family, the lodge to which had been removed by 1927.

311. TOOMALINE UPPER, Doon; *c.* 1840.

A plain single-storey standard lodge built in rubble stone, its hipped roof with clipped eaves. Derelict. A property of Patrick Kilbride in 1851, when the gatekeeper was Michael Russell and the house was let to Richard Bradshaw.

Griffith 1853–63.

312. TOURINE, Croom (3).

An estate for much of the early nineteenth century of James Dennis Lyons, who inherited nearby Croom House [*q.v.*] on the death of his father in 1837 and sold the place to Robert Maxwell, one of whose gate porters in 1851 was Patrick Keane. The property by about 1860 was in the possession of John Joseph Roche Kelly (1835–98), who promptly let it to Edward J. Smith, by which time the house had been renamed 'Islandmore'.

West gate; *c.* 1820.

A single-storey standard lodge, snugly wrapped in thick creeper to the eaves of its undulating hipped roof. Sometime extended into a double pile and its front door sealed up between a pair of bipartite mullioned windows with squared panes. Occupied and controlling a fine gatescreen of ashlar quadrant walls framing a wrought-iron triple gateway of spear-topped rails, its leaves hung on circular pillars like snooker-cue racks.

South-east gate; *c.* 1820.

A nice pair of whitewashed semi-detached cottages, each with a two-window front to the roadside below a hipped gable roof. Occupied.

North-east gate; *c.* 1820/*c.* 1865.

What was probably an early nineteenth-century lodge with clipped gables and whitewashed harled walls now forms a back return to a taller single-storey gabled affair with carved paired soffit and verge brackets over coursed limestone walls, with a two-window bay elevation to the avenue. Perhaps added when architect W.S. Cox was building farm offices for Smith in 1866.

Griffith 1853–63; *LGI* (1904); IAA.

313. TREANLEWIS, Kilmallock; pre-1840; *demolished.*

A property in 1851 of Timothy Roche, whose porter's lodge seems to have served as a temporary auxiliary workhouse, the first OS map showing it to have been of considerable area. It had gone by 1923.

Griffith 1853–63.

314. TULLYBRACKY RECTORY, Holycross; pre-1840.

Ruinous to waist height are the remains of an octagonal lodge, rubble-built with brick dressings. Now across the road from a later entrance, it having been marooned around 1835 by the 'New Line' of road. Perhaps contemporary with the glebe house, which was erected in 1813 and by 1837 'of Rev. John Fitzgerald, the grounds of which are laid out with much taste and densely planted'. He had been the rector since 1821 and alternatively could have included the lodge as part of his improvements.

Lewis 1837.

315. UREGARE, Bruff; pre-1840; *demolished.*

In 1804 a 'Seat of the late General Gabbett', by 1837 it was home to a Mrs Gubbins.

Wilson 1803; Lewis 1837.

VERMONT (see KILKEEDY RECTORY)

316. WATERVILLE, Ardagh; pre-1841; *demolished.*

Probably the same as 'Waterfield, a good old mansion, is the residence of J. Creagh'. Mentioned by Lewis in 1837, a John Creagh being recorded here 23 years earlier.

Leet 1814; Lewis 1837.

317. WELLESLEY FARM, Abbeyfeale; pre-1841; *demolished.*

A concern in 1851 of John Hartnett, which included a quarry, tuck mill and osiery in addition to two houses with offices and good acreage.

Griffith 1853–63.

318. WELLMOUNT, Rathkeale; *c.* 1845.

A plain, harled 1½-storey gabled cottage, strangely blind to the avenue, with its sole doorway and a window to the rear and a window to each peak. Derelict. A 79-acre holding in 1846 of James Condon, a name also to be found at Scart [*q.v.*] nearby.

Slater 1846; Griffith 1853–63.

WESTBOURNE (see COURTBRACK VILLA)

319. WESTFIELD, Limerick; *c.* 1850; *demolished.*

A house and lodge which formed part of the mid-Victorian Limerick city suburb of North Circular Road, the gatescreen of which survives with the earlier name of 'Kilmoyle' inscribed on chunky limestone pillars framed by short concave-walled quadrants. A residence in the mid-nineteenth century of Arthur Russell, provision merchant in the city.

Slater 1846.

320. WHITEHILL COTTAGE, O'Briensbridge; pre-1840; *demolished.*
An estate in 1846 and 1870 of James Crawley, the lodge to which had gone by 1938.
Slater 1846; 1870.

321. WOODFIELD, Dromcolliher; *c.* 1860.

A standard single-storey lodge with scalloped slate courses to its oversailing shallow hipped roof, from which extends a gabled entrance canopy with mildly ornate bargeboards carried on carved wooden bracket supports. To each side are one-over-one sash windows below label mouldings in rendered walls. Contemporary carriage pillars with friezes and corbelled cappings and rubble stone quadrant walls. A seat in 1852 of Henry Daly. By 2017 both gatescreen and lodge abandoned and overgrown.
Griffith 1853–63.

322. WOODLANDS, Castleconnell; pre-1840; *demolished.*
A property in 1824 of Lt. J.S. Rich, while Captain John Sampson Rich is recorded here as late as 1870. The lodge is remembered as 'single storey with a rounded front'.
Pigot 1824; Slater 1870.

323. WOODPARK, Castleconnell; pre-1840; *demolished.*
A house occupied in 1846 by Thomas Devit, the gate lodge to which had been removed by 1938.
Slater 1846.

324. WOODSDOWN, Annacotty; pre-1840; *demolished.*
An old estate of the Gough family, best known as the birthplace of Field Marshall Lord Gough. The place was sold off in 1875 by a descendant, William Gough Gubbins, and absorbed into the neighbouring Mulkear property [*q.v.*], which adopted both the 'Woodsdown' name and its gate lodge.
Spellissy 1998.

325. WORLDSEND, Castleconnell; *c.* 1810.

A lodge undergoing complete restoration in 2001 when stripped of its harled finish to reveal a rubble construction and that it originated unusually with a four-bay single-storey entrance front of pointed-arched openings below an oversailing hipped roof, doubtless beginning with Y-traceried sash windows to complete the Georgian Gothic picture. An idyllic seat in 1814 of Thomas Frend Maunsell (d. 1833).
Leet 1814; *IFR.*

COUNTY TIPPERARY

1. ABBEYVILLE, Clonmel; pre-1840; *demolished.*
An eight-acre holding on the banks of the River Suir, recorded as far apart as 1824 and 1870 to have been home to a Revd Richard Maunsell.
Pigot 1824; Slater 1870.

2. AGHNAMEADLE RECTORY, Toomyvara; *c.* 1840.

Cowering below the demesne wall is this charming single-storey hip-roofed lodge with scalloped slates over harled walls, a semi-octagonal projection from one side creating an L-plan. Like the so-called 'River Glebe' within, looking older than suggested by Lewis, who recorded that there was 'neither a glebe nor glebe house' in 1837. Alongside is a little railed entrance with hoops, top and bottom, matching carriage gates and iron posts. Both the rectory and its lodge must date from the incumbency (1833–46) of Revd Thomas Knox (1807–71).
Lewis 1837; Leslie and Crooks 2010.

3. AGLISH GLEBE, Aglish; pre-1903; *demolished.*
A lodge was added perhaps around 1859, during the incumbency (1839–69) of Revd Arthur Marshall Franklin Browne (d. 1869), when work was being carried out to the church, its glebe house, attached to the parish of Offane, having been built in 1816.
Lewis 1837; IAA; Knox 2008.

4. ANNAGHBEG, Drumineer; *c.* 1825.
An antique property of the Minnitt family, of whom Joshua Minnitt (1778–1830) erected the present house in 1824. Its porter's lodge opposite the entrance appears contemporary, despite its near-ruinous and overgrown state. Single-storey and hip-roofed with a two-window-bay main front of bipartite casements in harled walls, its entrance doorway at the left-hand end. Very rustic entrance screen.
LGI (1904); NIAH.

5. ANNAGH LODGE, Borrisokane (2).
Another seat of the widespread Minchin family, who had settled here by the early eighteenth century in the person of Charles Minchin, who left a son to carry on the line after being killed in a duel in 1736.

North entrance; pre-1840/*c.* 1900.
Now a singular-looking affair, resulting from an early twentieth-century build which reorientated the main entrance front to the road and may incorporate the previous principal three-bay avenue elevation of the earlier single-storey standard lodge, which has received channelled rusticated rendering and the eaves of the steeply pitched hipped roof raised with a deep limestone frieze. From the right-hand side of the new entrance front projects a gabled hall, and to the left-hand side a distinctly Egyptian-flavoured tapering window surround in a subtly battered roughcast wall; chunky casement windows and banded and corniced red-brick chimney-stack. A lodge perhaps originating from the time of the present house, which John Minchin inherited in 1825 but which was transformed by his grandnephew Falkiner John Minchin (1831–1916), who also added the secondary cottage.

South entrance; pre-1903; *demolished.*
Gatekeeper's accommodation built after 1840.
IFR.

6. ANNER HOUSE AND MILLS, Clonmel; pre-1840; *demolished.*
Here in 1837 were recorded the extensive flour mills and residence on 40 acres of Barclay Clibborn.
Lewis 1837.

7. ANNER PARK, Clonmel; pre-1840; *demolished.*
A porter's lodge built to command the entrance to the old castle of the Mandevilles before the latter was given a fairytale cloak *c.* 1848 by architect C.F. Anderson for the Revd Nicholas Herbert Mandeville, who altered its name from 'Ballinahy' in the process.
IFR; Williams 1994.

8. ANNERVILLE, Clonmel; pre-1840; *demolished.*
Erected to serve the predecessor to the present late Victorian house on the site, presumably by William Riall (1768–1843) of the Heywood [*q.v.*] family, who had acquired the estate *c.* 1820 from Pierce A. Butler.
Leet 1814; Pigot 1824; *LGI* (1904).

9. ANNE'SGIFT, Fethard (2).
A gracious big mid-Georgian house, a residence of John Jacob Gledstanes, from whom it passed by the marriages of his daughters Sarah and Anne to George Ponsonby and Col. Wray Palliser of neighbouring Derryluskan [*q.v.*], who before 1824 leased it to Major George Gough of adjacent Ardsallagh [*q.v.*]. Neither lodge built before 1840 survives that to the main entrance, gone by 1906.
Leet 1814; Pigot 1824; *LGI* (1904); *BPB* (1929).

10. ARBOUR HILL, Birr; pre-1839; *demolished.*
A property until 1771 of Maurice Keatinge, which by 1837 had passed to J. Antisell Esq. In 1903 the porter's lodge was serving as 'Riverstown Dispensary'.
Lewis 1837; *LGI* (1904).

11. ARCHERSTOWN, Thurles; pre-1840/*c.* 1870.
The seat of the Langley family since *c.* 1780, the original lodge to which was doubled in size by Henry Langley (1820–99) after he succeeded in 1858 to the property, which he also complemented with a contemporary gatescreen. The new single-storey standard hip roofed structure has end elevations faced in random uncoursed high-quality punched limestone ashlar, contrasting starkly with the bold quarry-faced avenue front containing two-over-two sash windows in chamfered reveals. The oversailing roof is distinguished by a finish of large scalloped slates and a punched limestone banded chimney-stack. Ogee railed entrance quadrants are stopped by urn-topped cast-iron carriage posts, which carry ornamental gates with an anthemion-finialled meeting rail.
LGI (1904).

12. ARDMAYLE, Cashel (2).
A house of the Prices is recorded here in 1783 but it remained lodgeless until the mid-nineteenth century.

North entrance; *c.* 1860.
Attending on an older entrance screen is a plain standard lodge with oversailing hipped roof built in the time of Richard Price.

South entrance; *c.* 1880.

A striking if far from pretty single-storey standard cottage with shallow clipped-eaves hipped roof over walls of random uncoursed rock-faced masonry extending to voussoirs above the one-over-one sash windows, which flank the projecting gabled hall containing a sheeted door; derelict. Built for Thomas E. Price.
Taylor and Skinner 1778; 1783; Slater 1856; Bassett 1889.

13. ARDSALLAGH, Fethard (2).
An estate in the late eighteenth century of the Chaloners, which passed about 1810 to George Gough (1775–1841), yet another soldier from that noted military family of Woodstown, Co. Limerick [*q.v.*], and to whom can be credited at least one of the lodges.

Cashel gate; pre-1840; *demolished.*
A lodge located opposite the entrance on the northern approach.

Fethard gate; *c.* 1830.

An elegant pair of rusticated stone entrance pillars, now lacking finials, dating from the late eighteenth century are presided over by this pleasing later porter's lodge. Single-storey and of that form popularised in Ireland by Richard Morrison, with a short main one-bay elevation to the avenue, in this case a tripartite casement window with fancy latticed glazing pattern below an oversailing shallow-pitched hipped roof with eaves high enough to accommodate a pair of balancing hip-roofed outshots to the side elevations—typically a closet and an entrance hall. All in a bland modern rendering, tiny original slates to the roof and vacant. There is a like lodge at nearby Racecourse Hall [*q.v.*] and similar glazing to the neighbouring Springhill [*q.v.*] lodge.

Wilson 1803; Leet 1814; *BPB* (1929).

14. ARRAGHSLEA, Bansha; *c.* 1825/*c.* 1870.

Apparently dating from 40 years earlier than its building here, a situation which may be explained by its having been the lodge that once attended the original main entrance to Spring House, taken down and re-erected here when that public road was absorbed into the estate. It subsequently served the house built *c.* 1850 by Francis Wise Low as a 'caretaker's house' within the Spring House [*q.v.*] property, when it was briefly called 'Kilshane' before its later independence.

Single-storey standard and built off a square plan, its oversailing shallow roof rises to a central chimney-stack. In limewashed walls six-over-six sash windows flank a semicircular porch recess in which the doorway is placed to one side. A pleasantly proportioned building, now complete with satellite dish and louvred window shutters, it presides over a semicircular entrance screen of concave rubble quadrants and bullet-shaped limestone carriage pillars, perhaps also salvaged from elsewhere but both inscribed 'Arraghslea'. The narrow carriage opening also leads to the sad shell of Joseph Welland's 1859 Church of Ireland church.

15. ASHGROVE, Borrisokane; pre-1840; *demolished.*
A delightfully situated estate overlooking Lough Derg, presumably founded by a Mr Ash, who is noted here in 1803, but which by 1837 had passed to Benjamin Talbot. The lodge had gone by 1903.

Wilson 1803; Lewis 1837.

16. ASHLEY PARK, Dromineer (2).
A seat until his death in 1817 of John Head, of that family of Derry Castle [*q.v.*], after which in 1824 it was purchased by George Guy Atkinson; one of these two built the early lodge.

North gate; pre-1840; *demolished.*
A lodge which had been removed by 1903 from an entrance supplanted as the main approach soon after.

South gate; *c.* 1910.

A conspicuous tripartite archway, its semicircular-arched carriage gateway flanked by a pair of similarly headed lower postern openings framed by tall piers constructed in quarry-faced limestone, a copy of the earlier entrances to nearby Kilteelagh [*q.v.*] and Johnston Park [*q.v.*]. In like facings is the uncommonly generous two-bay two-storey gatehouse, its rustic walls setting off smooth, chamfered, dressed, narrow Gothic lancet windows with replacement Y-traceried casements, affording little illumination. To the rear is a similarly uncoursed rubble yard wall with mock arrowloops and crenellations. A strange mix of styles created for Major Thomas B. Biggs-Atkinson, who after marrying an Atkinson daughter assumed her surname.

IFR.

17. ASH PARK, Templemore; *c.* 1830.

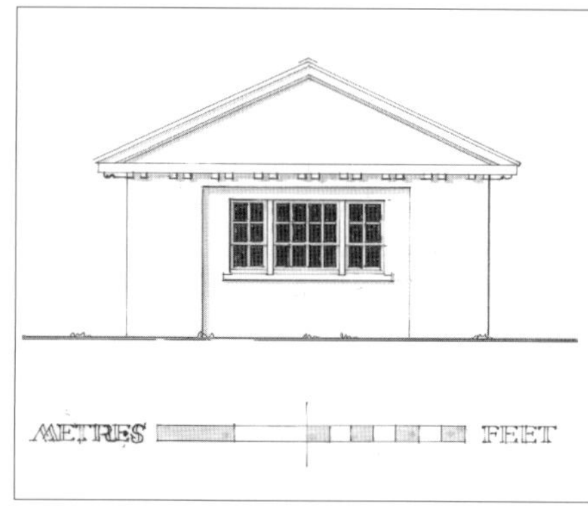

A once-impressive but now hopelessly derelict lodge, its principal front single-bay, with a wide window set in a rectangular recess below a full-width pediment carried on paired carved modillion brackets, which continue to the soffit of the eaves over the road elevation, with its three bays in like recesses. Built by James Butler. To the rear gate in 1840 was a 'Constabulary' station.

Leet 1814; Lewis 1837.

18. ATHASSEL, Golden; *c.* 1845.
An unpretentious single-storey standard cottage, with modern window and door replacements in roughcast walls below a shallow-pitched hipped roof rising to a cut-limestone chimney-stack; occupied. A property in 1846 of Richard Creaghe.

Slater 1846.

19. ATHLUMMON, Thurles; *c.* 1862; *demolished.*
A lodge built as part of improvements to the property by Vernon William Russell MD, after he purchased it in 1860 from Richard Alfred.

Slater 1870.

BALLAHOOLAGH (see PASTOR VILLE)

20. BALLINAMONA, Cashel; pre-1840; *demolished.*
A house and its porter's lodge probably built by a William Murphy, a name recorded as resident here as far apart as 1814 and 1889.

Leet 1814; Bassett 1889.

21. BALLINARD, Lattin; pre-1840; *demolished.*
An ancient seat of the Chadwick family.

BALLINGARRANE (see SUMMERVILLE)

22. BALLINGARRY, Ballingarry (S); pre-1840.
Once a standard single-storey gabled affair, now much improved, rendered and extended on the left-hand side to a five-bay front with a central gabled hall projection; occupied. A property in the Slieveardagh Hills in 1814 of Michael Carroll, which by 1851 had passed to Clement Carroll, whose gatekeeper then was Patrick Bryan.

Leet 1814; Griffith 1853–63.

23. BALLINLINA COTTAGE, Golden; pre-1840; *demolished.*
A small estate in 1853 of Charles Green, whose porter's lodge by 1906 was a shell.
Griffith 1853–63.

24. BALLINLONTY, Borrisoleigh; pre-1840; *demolished.*
The Fogarty family were resident here in the first half of the nineteenth century.

25. BALLYANNY, Nenagh; *c.* 1830.

A derelict traditional Irish single-storey standard gate lodge, with wide windows in limewashed walls of rubble construction below a clipped-eaves hipped roof with a tiny off-centre diagonally set brick chimney-stack, undoubtedly built by James Meagher, who is recorded as proprietor here in 1824 and 1837.
Pigot 1824; Lewis 1837.

26. BALLYBOE, Clonmel; *c.* 1850.
A farm of 352 acres in 1853 of James O'Donnell, to which survives a 1½-storey gabled lodge with Picturesque carved wavy bargeboards. Extended as single-storey in a single bay to the right-hand side and having a lean-to porch supported by a pair of metal posts; cement-rendered. Occupied.
Griffith 1853–63.

27. BALLYBRADA, Cahir (3).
On the western bank of the River Suir, a property for over a century of the Fennell family, the main entrance to which for much of that period was on the southern approach.

Ardfinnan gate; *c.* 1800.

A rustic single-storey lodge on a square plan, its hipped roof rising to a bulky chimney-stack, subsequently raised a stage in search of draw. Its irregular two-bay limewashed rubble avenue front contrasts with sophisticated surviving gate pillars in ashlar with moulded cornices and pedestalled ball finials. An attractive ensemble created for William Joshua Fennell.

Middle gate; *c.* 1880.
An incoherent three-window-bay cottage in roughcast and stone, with a hipped gable to the road containing a recessed canted bay window, alongside a gabled hall projection.

Cahir gate; *c.* 1880; architects Otway and Watt.

Despite its incongruity in the Tipperary landscape, here is a very fine Arts and Crafts composition by a short-lived architectural partnership of James Otway and Robert Watt, who also designed the house and stables for the new proprietor, Abraham Denny. It is 1½-storey, its attic accommodation contained in an earthenware tile-covered steeply hipped roof lit by tile-hung dormers and gablet, which to the fore projects to create a delightful three-sided verandah carried on cast-iron posts and decorative balustrade screening roughcast walls, one of which to the road displays a multi-paned canted bay window to the parlour. Elsewhere are other quirks, such as a coved soffit and ornamental lozenge glazing to a first-floor oriel which has a hipped gable with terracotta poppy hip-knob. In contrast, alongside is a pair of tall Classical carriage pillars with V-jointed rusticated masonry, swagged friezes, moulded cornices and elegant pedestalled ball finials, on which are hung decorative iron gates bearing the date '1905'—to a design by architect A.E. Murray, working for the then proprietor of the estate, Charles Edmond Denny.
IAA; NIAH.

28. BALLYCARRON, Golden; pre-1841; *demolished.*

An impressive Classical gatescreen comprised of four V-jointed rusticated limestone pillars framing a straight screen of whitened rendered walls, each containing a pedimented arched postern opening with toothed dressed jambs. Bence-Jones records a Gothic lodge facing it across the road, now sadly lost without trace. Perhaps all of around 1820 and built for Thomas Butler (1782–1863), who succeeded to the estate on the death of his father in 1801.
IFR; Bence-Jones 1988.

29. BALLYCOLLITON, Dromineer; 1865.

Opposite its gates is this remarkable 2017 restoration of a long-derelict lodge that always appeared older than when built. Single-storey below a hipped roof and standard but for asymmetrical fenestration, now enhanced by exposure of its limestone rubble fabric and red-brick dressings. Admirable replacement latticed casement windows and sheeted door with complementary lozenge vision panel. A true eye-catcher that would not now be recognised by its original builder, Charles I. Webb, without its previously crucial harling.
Valuation books.

30. BALLYDAVID, Littleton; pre-1840; *demolished.*
Just visible in a lithograph produced for the sale of the property in 1854 as an incumbered estate is a glimpse of a single-storey hip-roofed structure behind the boundary wall. The proprietor in 1814 was Marcus C. Russell and 40 years later John Russell.
Leet 1814; Lyons 1993.

31. BALLYDINE, Carrick-on-Suir; *c.* 1845.
Opposite what is now a non-existent avenue is an unassuming 1½-storey gabled standard gatekeeper's lodge to a seat for long of the Power family until being acquired by the 3rd earl of Clonmell in 1855. Subsequently renamed 'Ballynoran'.
Lyons 1993.

32. BALLYDUFF, Birr; pre-1839; *demolished.*
An estate in 1837 of B. Walker Esq., the lodge to which had gone by 1903.
Lewis 1837.

33. BALLYGRIFFIN, Golden; *c.* 1815.
A standard harled hip-roofed structure with a cut-stone projecting soffit, now lying sealed up. One of the properties in the late eighteenth century and early nineteenth century of the Meade family, earls of Clanwilliam, its lodge probably built by the 3rd earl, Richard (1795–1879), who inherited the estates in 1805.
BPB (1929).

34. BALLYKISTEEN, Tipperary (2).
The Irish seat of Sir John Thomas Stanley, 1st baron (1766–1850), which was occupied by his agent Thomas Bolton in 1837, when there was one gate lodge on the northern approach.

Front entrance; pre-1840; *demolished.*
The house was occupied after Stanley's death by Robert Hewston, who added the secondary lodge.

Rear entrance; *c.* 1855.
To the southern avenue is a standard single-storey porter's lodge in a good punched random ashlar, with faintly segmentally headed openings below a shallow pyramidal roof. The effect is spoiled by a hideous modern flat-roofed hall-cum-sunroom.

Binns 1837; Griffith 1853–63; *BPB* (1929).

35. BALLYMACKEOGH, Newport; pre-1840; *demolished.*
A property since the seventeenth century of the Ryan family.

36. BALLYNACOURTE, Tipperary (2).
On the slopes of Slievenamuck was the peculiar house of the Massy-Dawson family, who added gate lodges to the property at different periods.

East gate; pre-1840; *demolished.*
West gate; 1873.

A solid, steeply gabled, single-storey English Picturesque cottage raised off an L-plan, with a semi-octagonal bay window and equivalent roof to the leading gable and alongside in the internal angle a gabled hall, over the front door of which is a plain slate plaque with the date and monogram 'G.H.M.D.', despite the proprietor then being George Staunton King Massy-Dawson (1816–97). All rather sanitised by crisp modern rendering, the insertion of plastic windows and the probable loss of ornamental bargeboards.

BPB (1929).

37. BALLYNACREE, Emly; pre-1840; *demolished.*
A property in 1846 of Michael Manning, to which the porter's lodge had been removed by 1906.

Slater 1846.

38. BALLYNAVIN CASTLE, Cloghjordan; pre-1840; *demolished.*
A lodge, which had gone by 1906, to an antique house, residence in the nineteenth century of the Robinson family. Valued at a mere ten shillings in 1850, when it was occupied by Michael Gleeson, porter to Revd Robert Robinson.

Griffith 1853–63.

39. BALLYNERA, Thurles; pre-1840; *demolished.*
A property settled in 1730 on Thomas Pennefather, whose descendant in 1837 was Richard Pennefather, also recorded here fourteen years later, when his gatehouse was occupied by John Cassidy.

Lewis 1837; Griffith 1853–63; *LGI* (1904).

BALLYNORAN (see BALLYDINE)

BALLYOWEN (see NEWPARK)

40. BALLYPHILIP, Ballingarry; pre-1840; *demolished.*
A seat in the early nineteenth century of Ambrose Going, whose gate lodge was located opposite the entrance and in 1850 lay vacant.

Griffith 1853–63.

41. BALLYQUIVEEN, Silvermines; pre-1904; *demolished.*
A mid-nineteenth-century development by Henry Darby Head.

BALLYSORRELL DEMESNE (see CRAWFORD'S LODGE)

BALLYSTANLY or BALLYSTONELLY (see COUNTY KILDARE)

42. BALLYWALTER, Dundrum; *c.* 1845; *demolished.*
The seat in the early nineteenth century of the Wayland family, from whom it passed through marriage to the Coopers.

LGI (1904).

43. BANSHA CASTLE, Bansha; pre-1840; *demolished.*
In 1837 Lewis found 'the seat of E[dmund] O'Ryan, Esq., an elegant building in the castellated style', since when it has been stripped of the Romantic trappings of architect C.F. Anderson and of its gate lodge, which had gone by 1906.

Lewis 1837; Williams 1994.

44. BANSHA, Bansha; pre-1840; *demolished.*
The estate in 1837 of Robert Hare Clarke of the Graiguenoe Park [*q.v.*] family, which soon after was let to Revd B.H. Bannen.

Lewis 1837; Slater 1846; 1870; *LGI* (1904).

45. BARNA, Newport; pre-1840; *demolished.*
The Lee family purchased the property in 1688 and remained here for centuries. All that remains at the entrance is a pair of carriage pillars with undersized ball finials, or outsized pedestals, the lodge having gone by 1938.

LGI (1904).

46. BARNANE, Templemore (2).
The Carden family had been here since 1701 and their residence reflected almost 200 years of evolution before falling into ruin after their departure in the 1920s. Architect Thomas Newenham Deane benefited in his relationship with the family both at Templemore Abbey [*q.v.*] and here, where John Rutter Carden (1811–66), who had inherited the estate as a minor in 1822 and grew up to be known as 'Woodcock' through his being so often shot at by his tenants, engaged him to carry out works to the house and to add a couple of gate lodges in a dark forbidding limestone.

South lodge; *c.* 1863; architect Sir T.N. Deane.

Like the house in a Tudor Revival manner, this is a roomy 1½-storey structure on an L-plan, raised in uncoursed ashlar with bold skew-table gables, quite a puny chimney-stack, a mock cross arrowloop, a blank shield to the leading gable and label mouldings to windows. To the internal angle is a long entrance verandah with lean-to roof carried on spindly iron posts. Ogee entrance quadrants meet in a pair of complementary four-sided triangular-capped carriage pillars with recessed shafts.

North lodge; pre-1840/*c.* 1863; architect Sir T.N. Deane.

Replacing a predecessor on the main avenue is, in like detailing, a single-storey version of the south lodge, with a huge mock cross arrowloop motif dominating one gable as relief above a label-moulded window. Here the construction is of coursed punched ashlar of high quality, with a pair of more forthright banded and capped stone chimney-stacks. All now hugely extended and modernised with synthetic replacement slates, plastic windows and a ghastly 'take-away' plastic door in what was an attractive little hall projection, now sporting a hipped roof; to the main roof is a bungalow dormer. Now lacking any carriage pillars, but with more ogee entrance quadrants having muscular contemporary ironwork.

LGI (1904); Bence-Jones 1988.

47. BARNE PARK, Clonmel; pre-1840; *demolished.*
The grand mansion of the Moore family has been exposed for all to see through a road realignment that deprived it of privacy, its entrance gates and porter's lodge.

48. BARNLOUGH, Bansha; pre-1840; *demolished.*
A seat in the early nineteenth century of the Smithwick family to which the lodge was opposite the gates, shown on the first OS map as having an L-plan.

LOI; Bassett 1889.

49. BARONA, Caher; pre-1840; *demolished.*
Another estate of the Perry family of Woodrooff [*q.v.*], a Samuel Perry being resident here in 1837 and as late as 1870.

Lewis 1837; Slater 1870.

BARONNE COURT (see TINNAKILLY)

50. BEECHWOOD, Nenagh; pre-1840; *demolished.*
The splendid and elegant house of the Toler family, earls of Norbury, of Durrow Abbey, Co. Offaly, now deprived of the *gravitas* of its own lodged entrance.

51. BEHAMORE, Cloghjordan; pre-1840; *demolished.*
'Behamore Castle', so called in 1837, was then of Benjamin Hawkshaw and before him the residence in 1814 of Revd Thomas Hawkshaw, its lodge a ruin in 1903.

Leet 1814; Lewis 1837.

52. BELLE ISLE, Portumna (2).
A seat from the mid-eighteenth century of a branch of the Yelverton family, whose Dublin house was Fortfield.

Portumna gate; *c.* 1840.
Looking somewhat older is this single-storey hip-roofed porter's lodge, its main short front to the avenue displaying a single pair of casement windows in harled rubble walls. Now ruinous. Probably built by Barry John Yelverton, 3rd Viscount Avonmore (1790–1870).

Carrigahorrig gate; pre-1840; *demolished.*
The lodge to the main entrance is survived by a once-excellent gatescreen comprised of very extensive concave roughcast quadrant walls containing postern openings with quoined dressings, the copings carried over as lintels and emphasised by dies. In contrast are outer and carriage pillars in cut stone, corniced with friezes. Now much abused and in poor shape.

BPB (1929); Bence-Jones 1988.

53. BELLEVILLE, Templemore; pre-1840; *demolished.*
A residence in 1814 of George Bennett, which ten years later had been acquired by Charles Joseph Kelly Monck (1791–1849), who remained here until the death of his elder brother, when he unexpectedly succeeded to the viscountcy and the estate of Charleville, Co. Wicklow, but which he didn't live long to enjoy. Thereafter the property was absorbed by the Cardens into their Templemore Abbey demesne [*q.v.*].

Leet 1814; Pigot 1824; *BPB* (1929).

54. BELLEVUE PARK, Newinn; pre-1841; *demolished.*
The lodge to a demesne of the Roe family had been removed before 1906.

55. BELLPARK, Borrisokane; pre-1840; *demolished.*
A property in 1837 of T. Robinson Esq.

Lewis 1837.

BEN GURRAGH (see CAHER ABBEY UPPER)

56. BIRCH GROVE, Roscrea; *c.* 1830; architect possibly R. Elsam; *demolished.*
A late eighteenth-century house of the Birch family, of the local distillery, who engaged the maverick and nomadic English architect Richard Elsam to carry out eccentric additions to it. He may also have been the designer of the curious gatekeeper's lodge located opposite the gates; 1½-storey with a symmetrical three-bay ground-floor main front, above the pointed-arched central doorway of which was an attic window contained in a quirky gable of concave skew-tables giving a distinctly oriental feel—an attic storey which may well have been a later addition to a basic standard lodge.

Lewis 1837; IAA photograph (S/135/4).

57. BIRDHILL, Birdhill (2).
Neither the pre-1840 lodge at the southern gate nor that built later in the century on the northern approach survives. A property in the late eighteenth century of the Going family, of whom the proprietor in the early nineteenth century, barrister and police magistrate Richard Going, was murdered in 1821, as was his elder brother John eight years later.

Taylor and Skinner 1778; 1783; Leet 1814; *LGI* (1904).

58. BIRD HILL, Clonmel; pre-1840; *demolished.*
The pleasant park and villa in 1824 of Thomas Taylor.

Pigot 1824.

BIRR CASTLE (see COUNTY OFFALY)

59. BORRISLEIGH RECTORY, Littleton; pre-1840; *demolished.*
A '... very spacious and handsome glebe-house built by Rev. Mr Thomas Grady in 1791' on Littleton Glebe, the gate lodge to which opposite its gates may have been contemporary. Grady was still here in 1814, when the tourist A. Atkinson visited to find that the rector of Ballybeg's 'taste for improvement appears evidenced by those rich plantations which ornament his concern, and which were the first thing of that kind I had noticed on a glebe-house demesne in the course of my travels'.

Wilson 1803; Atkinson 1815.

60. BRITTAS CASTLE, Thurles (2).
A property in the mid-eighteenth century of Oliver Grace, which passed through the marriage of his daughter in 1859 to Henry

56. Birch Grove, Roscrea (IAA).

Langley. It is from the time of his son, Henry Grace Langley (1756–1821), here that the early lodge dates.

Inner gate; *c.* 1810.

Deep down the southern avenue is what was a Georgian Gothic porter's lodge, subsequently much extended and altered down the years. Originally three-bay symmetrical of three lancet openings in a gabled front, the bull's-eye attic window over has now been replaced and the front door blocked up, to be replaced on the side elevation by a gabled hall projection with Irish pilaster quoins and ornamental carved fascia boards; chimney-stack with corbelled band to capping. There is a good contemporary late Georgian gatescreen.

A double tragedy was to strike the property with the burning down of the old house *c.* 1820 and its spectacular replacement, designed by W.V. Morrison for Major Henry Langley (1784–1834), being abandoned when the unfortunate client was killed by falling masonry during construction. The place was in 1853 purchased by Colonel William Knox (1808–92), who added a new gatekeeper's lodge on the western approach.

Outer gate; *c.* 1855; architect perhaps S.U. Roberts.

A generously proportioned and conspicuous single-storey standard lodge, with projecting verges to a shallow-pitched roof of Italianate feel, punched limestone quoins contrasting with white-rendered walls, but otherwise Tudor Revival with label mouldings to a variety of openings, all with chamfered reveals and toothed dressings. To the end gables are paired elliptically arched windows with a dividing mullion; square-headed windows flank the central porch projection with ogee-arched side lights and a wide entrance opening with a straight arch, now partly bricked up to create an enclosed hallway, below a blank shield. To the end apexes are mock arrowloops and to the junction of the ridges a white-rendered chimney-stack on a blue limestone plinth. All redolent of the work of S.U. Roberts, it commands an earlier entrance of *c.* 1820 comprising plain ashlar pillars containing concave-walled quadrants with postilion openings, the lintels of which are continuations of the copings.

IFR; Bence-Jones 1988.

61. BROOKFIELD, Ballinderry; *c.* 1845.

A two-storey hip-roofed gatehouse with clipped eaves, its symmetrical main front of three-bay ground floor and two-bay second storey. A property in 1851 of John Parker.

Griffith 1853–63.

62. CABRAGH CASTLE, Thurles; pre-1840; *demolished.*

A lodge opposite the gates to a seat in the early nineteenth century of the Fogarty family.

63. CAHER ABBEY, Caher; *c.* 1835; architect possibly William Tinsley.

A good, solid, Classical villa built in 1830 by Richard Grubb (1780–1859) of the adjacent Abbey Mills, with which the equally no-nonsense porter's lodge is contemporary; single-storey standard with rendered walls containing openings in rectangular recesses below a hipped roof. Of considerably greater pretence is the extensive gatescreen, its two grand stone pillars, much as those to Melview, Clonmel [*q.v.*], attributable to William Tinsley, with recessed panels to tapering 'pylon' frontispieces, friezes with floral paterae and cappings with acroteria. Here they are flanked by railed convex outer quadrants and inner straight screens that terminate in pairs of cast-iron posts, which carry the carriage gates, as recommended by J.B. Papworth. The gatekeeper in 1850 was Denise Callaghan.

Papworth 1818; Griffith 1853–63; Grubb 1972; *IFR.*

64. CAHER ABBEY UPPER, Caher; pre-1840; *demolished.*

A seat in 1814 of Joshua Fennell; the family's gatekeeper in 1850 was John Morrissy.

Leet 1814; Griffith 1853–63.

65. CAHER COTTAGE, Caher; *c.* 1820.

A derelict standard structure with a clipped-eaves hipped roof above harled walls which contain one bipartite window with central sash box, all in contrast with the so-called 'Swiss Cottage', the exquisite *cottage orné*, in 1835 'chiefly used for picnic parties', built *c.* 1820, according to Fraser, for Emily, wife of Richard Butler (1775–1819), 1st earl of Glengall, probably to designs of John Nash.

Heaney 1999; Fraser 1838; *DEP*; Bence-Jones 1988.

66. CAHER PARK, Caher (2).

After vacating Caher Castle in the eighteenth century, successive Barons Cahir lived in their adjacent town house, and it was not until after the death of the 11th baron and 2nd earl of Glengall, Richard Butler (1794–1858), that his daughter Margaret, who that year had married Lt.-Col. Richard Charteris, engaged the Belfast architectural practice of Lanyon, Lynn and Lanyon to design a new mansion for the Kilcommon demesne, a commission which included two new entrance screens and a porter's lodge.

South gate; pre-1840; *demolished.*

'The grand entrance to this fine demesne is situated about a furlong from the town, and is formed by a capacious semicircular sweep, composed of rich granite, the gate piers on each extremity being of castellated construction. From the nice gate-lodge a fine gravelled walk of about a mile in length leads to the light iron bridge constructed by Turner of Dublin.' Although the early 'nice' lodge has gone, the grand entrance described by Thomas Lacy in 1862 remains, his 'castellated construction' probably referring to the conspicuous vermiculated face to V-jointed rusticated blocks that frame the smooth ashlar concave-walled quadrants containing lugged architraved postilion openings, which flank noble ashlar carriage pillars with dentilled cappings and supported by piers in like finish to the outer pillars.

Town gate; *c.* 1863; architects Lanyon, Lynn and Lanyon.

Another wide Classical gatescreen, crowned by a pair of beautiful 'House of Dun' urns with bas-relief figures on tall chamfered pillars with moulded friezes and cappings. Architect W.H. Lynn had no qualms about presenting his lodge alongside in a contrasting High Victorian Gothic with eccentric detailing. Single-storey, built off an L-plan, having a twin gable to the road and a curious arrowhead projection to the gate forecourt, which contains two segmental pointed-arched windows set in half-hipped gablets, its roof rising steeply with canted

slates to an ornamental wrought-iron hip-knob. The boldly bracketed eaves carry a secret gutter and lion gargoyle outlet to a hopper head. All in a subtle granite and limestone mix, with decorative relieving arch to the main flat-headed shouldered window below skew-tables with decorative chiselled hip-knobs as stops to a fleur-de-lis-crested ridge. All highly fanciful, from a period when Lynn was offering similar designs at Ballydrain, Co. Antrim, and in County Dublin at Ashurst and Mount Temple.

The equally eccentric house of 1861 was destroyed by fire exactly a century later.

DB (1 September 1861); Lacy 1863; *DEP*; Dean 1994; 2016; Williams 1994; IAA photographs (S/169/6-8).

67. CAHER RECTORY, Caher (2).
A plain, single-storey, hip-roofed structure on an L-plan, with modern square-paned windows. Built *c.* 1860 in the time (1858–71) of Revd John Morgan (1819–1909), seemingly to replace a predecessor on a different site, which was probably contemporary with the glebe house built in 1809 by aid of a gift of £100 and a loan of £750 from the Board of First Fruits during the incumbency (1803–22) of Revd John Wallace.

Lewis 1837; Knox 2008.

68. CAMUS PARK, Cashel; pre-1906; *demolished.*
A lodge built after 1840 to a property of the Cooper and Chadwick families, who intermarried.

LGI (1904).

69. CAPPA MURRAGH, Dundrum; pre-1840; *demolished.*
A seat in 1814 and 1837 of John Green.

Leet 1814; Lewis 1837.

70. CARRICK-ON-SUIR, Carrick-on-Suir; pre-1840; *demolished.*
A rare surviving example in the country of a Tudor manor house, built *c.* 1568 by the 10th earl of Ormonde onto their older castle. By the end of the eighteenth century it was in a state of neglect and tenanted, its lodge probably dating from the period of occupancy of John Wogan, sovereign of the town in 1824 and 1837.

Pigot 1824; Lewis 1837; Bence-Jones 1988.

71. CARRICK-ON-SUIR FEVER HOSPITAL, Carrick-on-Suir (2).
An institution of early foundation, when the lodged approach was from the north by the dispensary, superseded by that on an avenue from the west by the twentieth century.

72. CARRIGATAHA, Ardfinnan (2).
A seat in 1837 of William J. Fennell, both porters' lodges to which, built before 1840, one opposite its gates, had gone by 1906.

Lewis 1837.

73. CASHEL INFIRMARY, Cashel; pre-1900/*c.* 1940; architect Vincent Kelly.
Swept away was a short-lived porter's lodge built after 1840 to the older town infirmary, making way for this replacement in the International style, like the new hospital block. Single-storey, flat-roofed and smooth-rendered, its symmetrical three-bay front, to the rear of its gatescreen, continues without as a convex quadrant containing a tripartite window monitoring arrivals. Identical to the pair at Nenagh Hospital [*q.v.*] and that at Listowel Hospital [*q.v.*] by the same architect. Now known as Our Lady's Hospital.

O'Dwyer 1997a.

74. CASHEL PALACE, Cashel; *c.* 1784; architect possibly Oliver Grace.

At the gates to the dignified palace of the Church of Ireland archbishops of the diocese, built from 1729 to designs of Sir Edward Lovett Pearce, is this delightful Georgian Gothic cottage, not standard but on a generous asymmetrical C-plan. Single-storey, its avenue front contains a pair of Y-traceried lancet windows in a semicircular-headed recess alongside a pointed-arched doorway with a matching panelling pattern. To each side project canted wings under corresponding roofs and with like fenestration, all in roughcast walls with a stone spring-course. This may date from around 1784, when architect Oliver Grace was carrying out alterations to the palace and adding outbuildings for Revd Charles Agar (1760–1810), bishop of the diocese (1779–1801).

Country Life (31 August 1972); IAA.

CASHEL UNION WORKHOUSE (see ST PATRICK'S HOSPITAL)

75. CASTLE CAMBIE, Coolbaun; *c.* 1800.

Also known as 'Castletown', a property in 1783 of the Cambie family, with the most peculiar of gatekeepers' lodges by the gate. Perhaps originating as a single-gabled block with its three-bay short front to the visitor, it may sometime later have had the two flanking structures alongside added to form an entrance forecourt. Otherwise relatively plain, in roughcast with clipped verges and very derelict. Perhaps not unique, for the first OS map suggests something similar at nearby Finnoe [*q.v.*]. Located forward of an extensive and likewise crude gatescreen with inelegant ball finials to pillars.

Taylor and Skinner 1778; 1783.

76. CASTLE FFOGARTY, Thurles (2).
The ancient seat of the O'Fogarty family, from whom it descended through marriage to Thomas Lenigan about 1770. Both pre-1840 lodges have been removed.

LGI (1904).

77. CASTLE GRACE, Clogheen; *c.* 1840.

Backing onto the huge flour mills of Samuel Grubb and Sons is this sophisticated and ample porter's lodge. Single-storey standard with a chimney-stack to each gable, its whitewashed harled walls contain six-over-six sash windows flanking an unusually chaste door-case of Ionic pilasters, framing a raised and fielded eight-panel door below a semicircular 'spoke-and-cobweb' fanlight, all below an oversailing soffit. Built by Samuel Grubb (1787–1859), who had purchased the property in 1820.

Grubb 1972; *IFR*.

78. CASTLE OTWAY, Templederry; pre-1840/1857.

Originally 'Cloghonan Castle', a fine mid-eighteenth-century house to which was bizarrely attached a mock keep a century later, when a replacement gatehouse was erected, similarly incongruously having an inappropriate appendage. All this was instigated by Captain (later Vice-Admiral) Robert Jocelyn Otway (1808–84), who had inherited the place from his cousin in 1848. This is commodious two-storey porter's accommodation in stucco-effect rendering, with Tudor-style label mouldings to openings and quatrefoil feature on gable. From the avenue front projects a single-storey entrance hall, while to the rear is attached a cut-stone octagonal stair-tower with mock arrowloops.

LGI (1904); Lyons 1993.

79. CASTLE PARK, Golden; *c.* 1845; architect probably W. Tinsley.

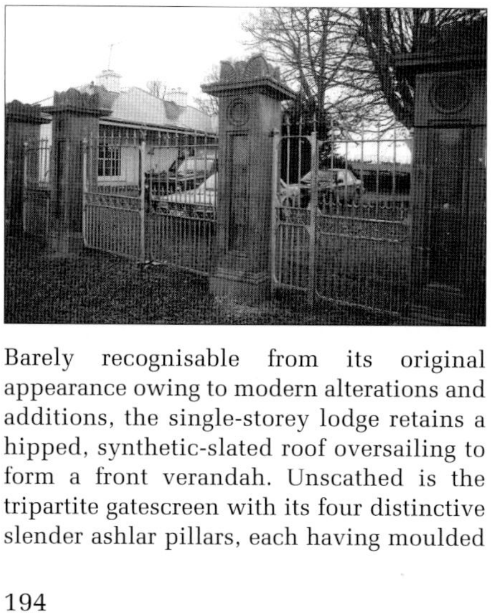

Barely recognisable from its original appearance owing to modern alterations and additions, the single-storey lodge retains a hipped, synthetic-slated roof oversailing to form a front verandah. Unscathed is the tripartite gatescreen with its four distinctive slender ashlar pillars, each having moulded plinths, recessed rectangular panels and roundels below extended cappings with bold fan-sculpted acroteria atop, much as those at Woodroofe [*q.v.*] and Grove [*q.v.*]. All doubtless by Clonmel architect William Tinsley, who is known to have built a new house at Golden for Richard Creagh in 1842 and extended it four years later, although Lewis mentions 'a spacious and well-built mansion' here in 1837.

Lewis 1837; Forbes 1953; IAA.

CASTLETOWN (see CASTLE CAMBIE)

80. CASTLETOWN-ARRA RECTORY, Portroe; *c.* 1830.

A charming and unusual little building, facing the road with steep, mildly skew-tabled gables, 1½-storey in whitewashed harling to walls with a subtle batter. The two-bay front is comprised of a bipartite window of six-over-six sashes and, alongside, a projecting single-storey gabled hallway with herringbone-boarded door below a pointed arch. Above two attic slit windows to one gable is a peculiar triangular blind silled recess. Probably built slightly later than the glebe house of 1820 during the incumbency (1823–36) of Revd Robert Gabbett (1774/5–1836).

Lewis 1837; Leslie and Crooks 2010.

81. CASTLE WALLER, Newport; pre-1840; *demolished.*
A Cromwellian settlement of the Wallers, which by 1837 had descended to Sir Edmund Waller (1797–1851), whose gate lodge had been removed by 1938.

BPB (1929).

82. CASTLE WILLINGTON, Nenagh; *c.* 1830.
A tiny, harled, standard, gabled single-storey cottage with square window openings and a corrugated-iron roof; derelict. A seat in 1824 of James Willington (1790–1862), who had succeeded to it three years before.

Pigot 1824; *LGI* (1904).

83. CIALMANTHA, Birdhill; *c.* 1840; architects probably J. and G.R. Pain.

'Lord Bloomfield is building a handsome lodge, in the Elizabethan style, which commands many fine views, and has laid out an extensive nursery, from which considerable plantations have been made on the surrounding mountains.' Thus Samuel Lewis in 1837 described the pretty hunting lodge under construction for Benjamin Bloomfield (1762–1846), the 1st earl, with its multi-gabled elevations and decorative bargeboards, doubtless to plans of brothers James and George Richard Pain, who were working for Bloomfield in 1835 at his other property of Laughton, Co. Offaly. Their commission would have included this once-complementary Picturesque English cottage lodge in like style, 1½-storey on an L-plan, raised in pleasant rubble stone facings with chamfered dressed mullioned windows, that to the leading avenue gable a single-storey semi-octagonal bay below a layered stone roof. The main roof is decorated with large scalloped slates and crowned by a pair of lofty octagonal stone chimney-stacks. Inexplicably dilapidated and overgrown.

Lewis 1837; *LGI* (1904).

84. CLASHAPHOOCA, Clogheen; *c.* 1820.
A standard single-storey gatekeeper's lodge with a shallow hipped roof and extending eaves. Harled brick walls contain openings set in rectangular recesses to ground level. All of an age with the big square house, whose early occupant was Edwin Taylor, agent to Lord Lismore of Shanbally Castle [*q.v.*].

85. CLASHLEIGH, Clogheen; *c.* 1810.
In 1837 one of the seats of Samuel Grubb, the miller, corn merchant and brewer also associated early in the nineteenth century with Clonmel and nearby Coolville [*q.v.*]. Opposite the gates is a run-of-the-mill two-storey three-bay gabled house, remarkable only for its slate-hung walls.

Grubb 1972.

86. CLIFTON, Ballingarry (N); pre-1840; *demolished.*
The Sheppards settled here in the mid-eighteenth century, altering its name from 'Killcullenmore' to that of their place of origin near Bristol.

LGI (1904).

87. CLONACODY, Fethard; *c.* 1790.
A large Georgian house of the Kellett family, whose lodge is a delightful rustic Palladian

87. Clonacody, Fethard.

cottage. Single-storey below a hipped roof with whitewashed harled walls, the short main front three-bay, with a pair of round-headed niches flanking what may have been the doorway, now reduced to a window with a wholly inappropriate plastic insert which fails to spoil the effect; occupied and extended to the rear. Probably by chance there are similar lodges at Castle View, Glanmire, Co. Cork [*q.v.*], and Clonshire, Co. Limerick [*q.v.*].

Lewis 1837; Bence-Jones 1988.

88. CLONMEL AUXILIARY LUNATIC ASYLUM, Clonmel; *c.* 1865; *demolished.*

What had been the Clonmel House of Industry was adapted as a workhouse in 1841 before becoming the male Lunatic Asylum with the division of sexes, when the District Lunatic Asylum [*q.v.*] became for women only. In 1865 the additions of gate lodge, physician's house and laundry were valued.

O'Connor 1995.

CLONMEL CEMETERY (see ST PATRICK'S CEMETERY)

89. CLONMEL COLLEGE, Clonmel; pre-1840; *demolished.*

The institution moved here *c.* 1830 and was built to appear more as a big country house at an expense approaching £5,000, which may have included the provision of its porter's lodge.

Lewis 1837.

90. CLONMEL DISTRICT LUNATIC ASYLUM, Clonmel; *c.* 1835; architect W. Murray; *demolished.*

A typical second-class asylum for the county of Tipperary to designs by William Murray, whose drawings for its gate lodge survive and show it to have had a standard plan to be found throughout the land. Signed and dated as early as 1832, they are of a standard single-storey format below a hipped roof, with a central pedimented breakfront containing a segmentally arched fanlit doorway, flanked by like-headed eight-over-eight sash windows. One corner has Murray's characteristic chamfer, while the octagonal hallway gave onto kitchen and bedroom, each 12ft 6in. by 14ft. Probably faced in ashlar, the chimney-stack familiarly banded.

Lewis 1837; O'Dwyer 1997a; NAOPW drawings (5HC/4/884-3).

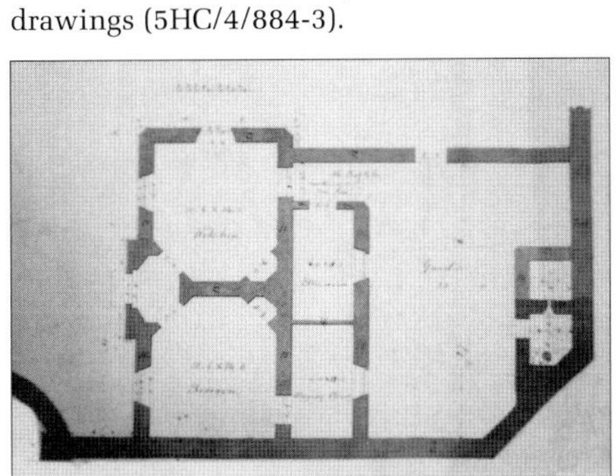

90. Clonmel District Lunatic Asylum, Clonmel, plan (National Archives).

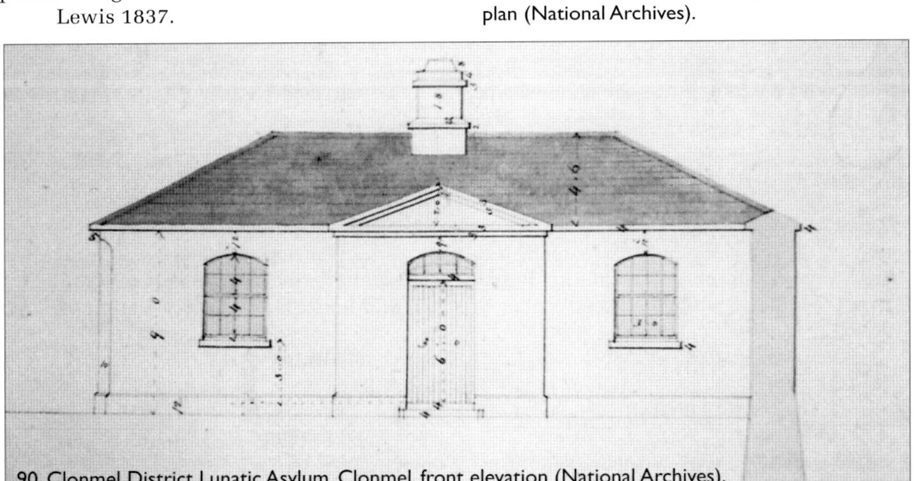

90. Clonmel District Lunatic Asylum, Clonmel, front elevation (National Archives).

91. CLONMEL FEVER HOSPITAL, Clonmel; pre-1840; *demolished.*

An institution in operation by 1812 with its adjacent dispensary, 'both handsome and commodious buildings on the north side of the town'.

Lewis 1837; O'Donnell 1999.

92. CLONSINGLE, Newport; pre-1904; *demolished.*

A lodge built after 1840, probably for Robert Saunders Young, proprietor in 1856 and 1870.

Slater 1856; 1870.

93. CONGOR, Borrisokane; pre-1840; *demolished.*

Another seat of the Falkiner family of neighbouring Mount Falcon [*q.v.*], home in 1837 to Frederick Falkiner (b. 1760), after whose death it was by 1851 leased to Nicholas Biddulph (1803–88).

Lewis 1837; Griffith 1853–63; *LGI* (1904).

94. COOLE, Clonmel; *c.* 1840.

A thoroughly modernised single-storey standard gabled lodge, with original features still recognisable in chamfered stone surrounds to windows and its Tudor-arched front door with trefoils to the spandrels, a feature repeated in the new perforated canted red crestings to the main ridge, those of window gablets and projecting hall. Roughcast and occupied. A property in 1851 of Thomas Morrisey, spirit dealer, of Irishtown, Clonmel.

Slater 1846; Griffith 1853–63.

95. COOLE, Newport; pre-1840; *demolished.*

A seat in 1851 of William Waller.

Griffith 1853–63.

96. COOLNAMUNNA, Cloghjordan; *c.* 1835.

A ruinous lodge, of which just discernible are the remains of a hipped roof to a single-storey structure of harled rubble. Home in 1852 to Patrick Mackey, gatekeeper of Edward Kennedy. In stark contrast, dating from around 1850, is the pristine and opulent cast-iron gatescreen (*see overleaf*), containing two plain ashlar pillars and railings with claw feet meeting carriage pillars of foliage topped by cappings with the Kennedy crest: an arm, in armour, embowed, in hand a scimitar. Gates to match, with a meeting rail crowned by a fine poppy finial. All from the works of Kennan and Sons of Dublin.

Griffith 1853–63.

96. Coolnamunna, Cloghjordan

97. COOLVILLE, Clogheen; *c.* 1800.
A charming development by Samuel Grubb (1750–1815), miller and corn merchant, which includes the elegant villa, ruined mill building and attractive entrance from the village. Behind tall ashlar carriage pillars with ball finials, studded sheet doors with

ornamental strap hinges and quadrant walls with postern door is this pretty single-storey harled standard cottage with steeply gabled thatched roof and sheeted front door, flanked by what were six-over-six sash windows, now replaced by look-alikes; to the road a later lean-to addition. Admirably maintained.

IFR; Grubb 1972.

CORBALLY ABBEY (see CORVILLE)

98. CORDANGAN MANOR, Tipperary; *c.* 1865.
An estate in the first half of the nineteenth century of the Cooke family which remained lodgeless until it was acquired by Horatio Hamilton Townshend (1830–97) of Woodside, Co. Cork [*q.v.*]. His lodge is a

single-storey gabled rendered structure with a three-bay avenue front of segmentally arched moulded surround openings to bipartite one-over-one sash windows and doorway to the right-hand side. Now enclosed by a later gabled glazed hallway. Further relieved by toothed quoins, carved perforated foiled bargeboards and a solid brick chimney-stack. To the rear is an elevation mirroring its front. Distant are modest carriage pillars with pyramidal cappings and ball finials.

IFR.

99. CORRABELLA, Ardfinnan; *c.* 1825.

Fronting the carriageway, alongside and forward of its gatescreen is a standard single-storey hip-roofed lodge with a semicircular fanlit doorway, but with signs of later improvements in its two-over-two sash windows in pebble-dashed walls and late Victorian cappings to the carriage pillars, the tympana of their four-faced pediments ornamented with a Gothic trefoil motif; railed concave quadrants. A property in 1851 of William Mulcahy.

Griffith 1853–63.

100. CORVILLE, Roscrea; pre-1840; *demolished.*
Samuel Lewis in 1837 found '... a handsome structure in the Grecian style, and is seen to great advantage terminating a long avenue from the entrance gate'. The seat of the Hon. Francis Aldborough Prittie (1779–1853) since *c.* 1810, before which it was the residence of a Mr Mansell.

Wilson 1803; Lewis 1837; *BPB* (1929).

101. CRANAGH CASTLE, Templetuohy; pre-1840; *demolished.*
A house of 1768 attached to a medieval round tower, long an estate of the Lloyd family, the lodge to which had been removed by 1905.

Bence-Jones 1988.

102. CRANNA, Birdhill; pre-1840; *demolished.*
A seat in the nineteenth century of the Going family.

103. CRAWFORD'S LODGE, Templetuohy; *c.* 1810.
A single-storey standard gabled porter's lodge with harled walls. Extended by a one-bay 1½-storey addition to the right-hand side; modern canopied porch. Also known as 'Ballysorrell Demesne', a property in 1814 of Thomas Crawford.

Leet 1814.

104. CREGG, Carrick-on-Suir; *c.* 1825.

To a typical late Georgian gentry villa is this singular single-storey gatekeeper's lodge, its bold eaves with paired carved brackets carried around the main short avenue gable to form a shallow pediment confused by later continuous-bracket bargeboard additions. Below this in a deep recess in rendered walls is a sexpartite casement window with latticed glazing pattern rising to innovative spokes in round arches. To the road elevation are two-bay recesses with bipartite lights. To the park is a later addition in like manner to form a double pile. All proudly maintained. Thomas Lalor died in 1812, to be succeeded by his only son, Thomas Edmund Lalor (d. 1847), who added the lodge.

Lewis 1837; *LGI* (1904); ffolliott 1971b.

105. CROGHAN, Birr (2).
The estate in 1824 of Francis Drought, the lodges to which have had mixed fortunes.

Principal entrance; *c.* 1820.
Immaculate but much 'improved' is this single-storey standard three-bay hipped-roof cottage, with a projecting hip-roofed hall flanked by round-headed windows with spoke-topped glazing. Extended into an L-plan.

Secondary entrance; pre-1839; *demolished.*
A lodge that was located opposite its gates.

Pigot 1824.

CROSSAGE (see PRIOR'S LODGE)

106. DANGANSALLAGH, Roscrea; *c.* 1790.
A standard lodge with tiny openings in limewashed rubble walls below a clipped-eaves hipped roof with huge slates; derelict. A property in the early nineteenth century of the Middleton family.

DARLING HILL (see KNOCKEEVAN)

107. DEBSBOROUGH, Nenagh; pre-1840; *demolished.*
For two centuries since 1702 these lands

were always in the hands of a John Bayly. In the twentieth century both the big house and its porter's lodge were replaced by something of their time.

LGI (1904).

108. DEERPARK, Cashel; pre-1840; *demolished.*
Previously a property of the Butlers but by 1837 had passed to John Hare, for whom architect C.F. Anderson supervised the building of a new house as recorded in his c.v.

Lewis 1837; IAA; Anderson *c.* 1847.

109. DEERPARK, Cloghjordan; pre-1840; *demolished.*
A property associated with Cangort Park, Co. Offaly, nearby, in 1837 of William Trench (1798–1849), leasing to A.J. Robinson.

Lewis 1837; *BPB* (1929).

110. DERRY CASTLE, Ballina (2).
Beautifully situated on the banks of Lough Derg, Arthur Young in 1777 found 'the seat of Michael Head, Esq. ... within fifteen years this gentleman has improved Derry so much, that those who had only seen it before, would find it almost a new creation. He has built a handsome stone house, on the slope of a hill rising from the Shannon, and backed by some fine woods.'

North gate; pre-1840; *demolished.*
Neither Head's fine old bow-fronted house nor its original main porter's lodge survives.

Around 1850 the estate was acquired by Francis Spaight (1790–1861), who made improvements to it which included an alternative approach to the house from the south and Limerick. A new gate lodge and entrance screen were added to designs by James Pain of that city, attributable on the strength of the gates being identical to those at Convamore, Co. Cork [*q.v.*], by him. There are also like gatescreens in County Clare at Carrigoran [*q.v.*] and Kilkishen [*q.v.*], and at Grange, Co. Limerick [*q.v.*]. Pain nevertheless seems to have been at pains to vary his lodge designs, for all differ, although a common trait is their chimney-stacks all rising off the rear walls.

South gate; *c.* 1850; architect James Pain.

A single-storey standard gabled lodge with tall eaves, in a smooth rendered finish with a moulded top plinth, and to the projecting hall a door having a moulded lugged architrave and in the apex over a limestone shield bearing the Spaight crest of 'three pheons of the field'. Otherwise modest, with modern door and windows. The impressive entrance screen is comprised of four tall

limestone pillars with raised and fielded panels and semicircular pedimented cappings. Between, three straight ornamental cast-iron sets of railings contain carriage and two postern gates, all so positioned as to form a conspicuous vista stop to the public approach.

Young 1780; *LGI* (1904); Bence-Jones 1988.

DERRYLAHAN PARK (see WALSHPARK)

111. DERRYLUSKAN, Fethard (2).
A big house of the Palliser family, of whom John Palliser (1760–1833) just before his death engaged the Clonmel architect William Tinsley to remodel it. At least one of the porters' lodges may be by him.

North entrance; pre-1840; *demolished.*
On the site is a twentieth-century bungalow that may just reflect its predecessor. Symmetrical, single-storey and three-bay, with a distyle Tuscan portico flanked by squared Georgian-style plastic windows in roughcast walls below a hipped roof. Other than the sheeted pediment, an acceptable replacement.

South entrance; *c.* 1830; architect possibly William Tinsley.

A singular single-storey standard lodge with hipped gables and limewashed rubble walls, the three-bay avenue front composed of cut-stone trimmed lancet openings, the left-hand

window and central doorway having had their functions subsequently reversed. To the park is a surprise in a grand Classical Venetian window—another detail from the Georgian era, but the robust section of Y-tracery to the Gothic window suggests a later date, perhaps from the time of Tinsley's commission. He was then working in that style on Rockwell House [*q.v.*]. Sadly the lodge lies neglected and overgrown, but not too far gone to preclude restoration.

LGI (1904); Forbes 1953.

DERRYO (see GREENHILLS)

112. DONEGAL, Ballycleraghan; pre-1840; *demolished.*
A property in 1851 of John O'Halloran, leasing from Arthur Riall of neighbouring Westgrove House. In 1840 a 'Police Barrack' had been established at the base of the south avenue, with the gate lodge on the eastern approach.

Griffith 1853–63.

113. DONNYBROOK, Ballymackey; *c.* 1845.
A single-storey standard plain gabled lodge with small windows in rendered walls. Occupied and extended into a double pile. Built by William Poe, a name associated with the property in 1814 and 1856.

Leet 1814; Slater 1856.

114. DONOHILL RECTORY, Cappaghwhite; *c.* 1880; *demolished.*
A short-lived gate lodge presumably contemporary with the rectory of 1880 built on the arrival that year of Revd Hawtrey Browne (1840–1908), incumbent until his death.

NIAH; Seymour and Leslie 2012.

115. DOVEA, Borrisoleigh (2).
A seat of John Trant (1819–87) from the death in 1838 of his father, Captain John Frederick Trant.

East gate; *c.* 1865.
A wide late Victorian gatescreen with banded quarry-faced features to pillars, behind which is a single-storey standard gatekeeper's lodge, roughcast with a steeply gabled roof and high eaves to accommodate the lower gabled hall projection. Finials but no fancy bargeboards survive; occupied.

West gate; *c.* 1850.
A plain, roughcast, two-storey, three-bay gabled house, identified in 1905 as a 'Constabulary Barrack', now a private house.

LGI (1904).

116. DROMARD, Templemore (2).
Two lodges probably built by Frederick Lidwill sometime between the death of his father in 1839 and his own demise in 1868.

East entrance; *c.* 1840.
In 2000 for sale as a site containing the remains of a single-storey gabled lodge with catslide breakfront, extended to the right-hand side. In harled rubble with chimney-stacks to each gable; very derelict and overgrown, with ivy and cottage roses extending over the roof.

West entrance; pre-1904.
A ruin with only one wall standing.

LGI (1904).

117. DROMINAGH, Ballinderry; *c.* 1870.
A property of Edward Biggs in 1851, acquired not long after by James Esmonde (1828–94), who added the porter's lodge. Approached via a humpback bridge is a standard cottage with a very steeply pitched hipped roof accommodating attic rooms lit by roof windows in a green slated finish and paired joists exposed in the soffit; sash windows in Virginia creeper-clad walls; occupied.

Griffith 1853–63; *BPB* (1929).

118. DRUMMONA, Dundrum; *c.* 1845.
Below the level of the road and opposite its gates is the ruin of a tiny single-storey standard hip-roofed lodge to a property in 1851 of Revd William R. Sandys.

Griffith 1853–63.

119. DUNDRUM, Dundrum; pre-1840; *demolished.*

The handsome mansion of the Maude family, Barons de Montalt and from 1793 Viscounts Hawarden, of whom Cornwallis Maude (1780–1856), the 3rd viscount, who inherited the 2,400-acre estate in 1807 from his brother, was probably responsible for the lost lodge and its impressive surviving gatescreen. Wide and straight, with highly ornamental cast-iron railings and matching gates topped by fleur-de-lis and anthemion motifs alternating, all contained by four solid, squat ashlar pillars with tapering 'pylon' recesses and four-sided shallow pedimented cappings crowned by modern lanterns. The gates are hung off secondary iron posts, as advised by J.B. Papworth (see Fig. 6, p.8) All from *c.* 1825.

BPB (1929).

120. DUNESKE, Caher (2).
Richard William Smith (1833–*c.* 1923) in 1873 commissioned architect Sir Thomas Drew to develop the property with a large mansion house and at least one porter's lodge.

South gate; *c.* 1880; architect possibly Sir Thomas Drew.
A two-storey hip-roofed gatehouse in mellow rubble facings with red-brick dressings and toothed quoins. The main front has a two-bay upper storey over a three-bay ground floor enhanced by a decorative half-timbered gabled porch; occupied.

North gate; *c.* 1875; architect probably Sir Thomas Drew.

A characterful little gatekeeper's cottage, single-storey on an L-plan, with part-gabled and part-hipped roof having coved eaves above smooth rendered walls, the openings having moulded surrounds and, in the internal angle, an integral porch with shouldered flat arches. Recently extended sympathetically and reoccupied. Straight triple gatescreen of an age with four dainty stone pillars with recessed panels.

IFR; Bence-Jones 1988.

121. ELM HILL, Nenagh; pre-1840; *demolished.*
A seat in the early nineteenth century of the Middleton family.

122. EMLY RECTORY, Emly; pre-1840; *demolished.*
To a glebe house possibly built to designs of Thomas Cooley in the incumbency (1782–1817) of Revd Anthony Armstrong was added a gate lodge, which had been removed by 1906.

Seymour and Leslie 2012.

123. E.T.M. VILLE, Clonmel; pre-1840; *demolished.*
An estate until his death in 1815 of Edmond Theobald Mandeville Butler, from 1796 the 6th Viscount Galmoyle, and until 1853 the residence of his wife Elizabeth. The lodge had gone by 1950.

IFR.

124. FAIRY HILL, Ballingarry (N); pre-1839; *demolished.*
The 'well planted' demesne of W.H. Cox Esq. in 1837.

Lewis 1837.

FANNYVILLE (see LISKEVEEN)

125. FETHARD ABBEY, Fethard; *c.* 1800.
A plain two-storey gabled roughcast gatehouse, three-bay with its door to the left-hand side; derelict. Home in 1851 of Patrick Kennedy, gatekeeper to proprietor William H. Latham.

Griffith 1853–63.

126. FETHARD RECTORY, Fethard; *c.* 1840.
To a glebe house designed by Richard Morrison is a later lodge; single-storey standard with an oversailing hipped roof and eaves with exposed rafter toes and scalloped fascia boards. A wide, sheeted, fanlit doorway is flanked by two-over-two casement windows in roughcast walls. Built during the long incumbency (1812–63) of Revd Henry Woodward (1775–1863).

Pigot 1824; Slater 1856; Seymour and Leslie 2012.

127. FINNOE, Borrisokane; pre-1840; *demolished.*
At the entrance to the seat until his death in 1843 of Thomas Maunsell Waller remains a series of fine V-jointed rusticated Georgian gate pillars but nothing of the gate lodge opposite. The 1840 OS map shows it to have been of the same outline as that at nearby Castle Cambie [*q.v.*]—a triple pile, the central third recessed.

LGI (1904).

128. FISHMOYNE, Borrisoleigh; *c.* 1790.
Here are the sad remains of a pair of Georgian Gothic lodges forming part of a straight gate sweep, windows and postilion openings having pointed arches in harled walls meeting at big carriage pillars. This was an impressive entrance to the seat of a junior branch of the Carden family of Templemore Abbey [*q.v.*], built either by John Carden (d. 1794) or his younger brother Richard Carden (d. 1812), who succeeded him to the estate.

LGI (1904) Bence-Jones 1988.

129. FORTESCUE, Templemore; *c.* 1880; architect not known.
A development for Richard Lloyd (1850–98), second son of J.J. Lloyd of Lloydsborough [*q.v.*] and Cranagh Castle [*q.v.*], consisting of

129. Fortescue, Templemore.

a 'Hansel and Gretel' villa of 1887 and a comparatively less fanciful but attractive gate lodge, 1½-storey standard, gabled and constructed with sandstone rubble facings, toothed red-brick dressings to openings and limestone quoins. From one gable extends a single-storey annexe, like the projecting hall and main gables having ornamental carved fascias and bargeboards rising to spiky hip-knobs complementing red pantiled roofs.

LGI (1904); NIAH.

130. FORT WILLIAM, Cloghjordan; *c.* 1800.

A pleasant single-storey hip-roofed cottage with limewashed harled walls and an informal three-bay main front with four-paned casement windows and doorway to the left-hand side. The roof has clipped eaves, tiny slates and a modern brick chimney-stack; derelict. In 1852 a Miss Crawford was the gatekeeper to a property of Thomas Dance, prior to which it was in 1814 and 1837 an estate of Anthony Parker.

Leet 1814; Lewis 1837; Griffith 1853–63.

131. FOX HALL, Newport; pre-1840; *demolished.*

The seat until his death in 1820 of Richard Anderson Rose and subsequently of his two sons, Richard Anderson and Wellington Anderson Rose. The property had come to the family through marriage with the Andersons. Their porter's lodge had gone by 1904.

LGI (1904).

132. GAILE, Holycross; *c.* 1820.

The gatescreen is comprised of simple square pillars flanked by ogee quadrant walls, their copings continuing as lintels to little postilion openings. Opposite at a road junction is what was a single-storey standard hip-roofed, limewashed and harled cottage, now with its door blocked up. An estate in the first quarter of the nineteenth century of Richard Phillips.

Pigot 1824; *LGI* (1904).

GALTEE CASTLE (see MOUNTAIN LODGE [1])

133. GARRANE, Toomyvara (2).

Front entrance; pre-1840; *demolished.*

Rear entrance; *c.* 1850.

A spacious standard lodge with harled rubble stone walls and very steeply pitched hipped roof. A property in 1850 of Bryan Kennedy, whose sole gatekeeper then seems to have been a Mrs Ryan in a lodge valued at six shillings, which may account for its demise.

Griffith 1853–63.

134. GARRANLEA, Newinn; pre-1850.

A gate lodge evident neither on maps nor on site but identified by the valuation of 1850 as occupied by John Quirk, gatekeeper to James Keating, proprietor of house, offices, corn and flour mills, leasing from Leonard Keating, who is recorded here in 1814.

Leet 1814; Griffith 1853–63.

135. GARRAUN, Fethard; pre-1840; *demolished.*

A lodge opposite the entrance to a holding in 1814 of John Butler had been removed by 1906.

Leet 1814.

136. GARRYKENNEDY, Portroe; pre-1840/*c.* 1860.

An old property of the Watson family, which was sold in 1857 as an incumbered estate to the neighbouring landowner of Landsdown [*q.v.*], William Parker, who replaced an older gate lodge with this pleasing cottage of rustic sophistication in its tree-trunk columns *in antis* between rubble piers of the gabled breakfront hall. Single-storey standard and hip-roofed, with rubble walls having toothed brick quoins and dressings to windows with modern 'lead effect' inserts. Over the front door are shallow foiled bargeboards with trefoil perforations. Probably originally rendered like its relation at Landsdown.

Lyons 1993.

137. GARRYVANUS, Thurles; pre-1840; *demolished.*

A lodge, removed by 1905, to a farmhouse which in 1851 lay vacant though the land was farmed by James Lenigan, its gate porter then being William Cummins.

Griffith 1853–63.

138. GLENAGYLE, Toomyvara (2).

North gate; *c.* 1870.

Lying abandoned is this attractive little building, single-storey standard, built in harled rubble with quarry-faced voussoirs to windows and the arrowhead doorway, all below a crude open pediment to its gabled breakfront. A hipped roof with carved soffit modillion brackets is conspicuous for its scalloped slate finish and paired square chimney-stack.

South gate; *c.* 1870.

Much as its counterpart though plainer, but sporting the same quarry-faced voussoirs. Similarly derelict, with a nasty flat-roofed addition to the hallway. A property in 1876 of Stephen M. Lanigan.

LOI.

139. GLENALBERT, Roscrea; pre-1840; *demolished.*

A seat in 1837 of Albert F. Maxwell, the gate lodge to which was a shell by 1954.

Lewis 1837.

GLENAM (see COUNTY WATERFORD)

140. GLENCONNOR, Clonmel; pre-1840/*c.* 1880.

Built around 1797 as a dower house to neighbouring Summerville [*q.v.*] by Solomon Watson and called 'Larchgrove', it subsequently lay vacant before being let to a succession of tenants. By 1876 it had been acquired by William Byrne, who carried out considerable improvements and additions to the house and built a replacement gate lodge. This is a commodious, square, single-storey standard structure with a steep hipped roof, from which projects an outsized hallway

with an open pediment supported on pilasters which are repeated on all corners, acting also to frame openings with straight arches, rounded corners and shouldered banded surrounds in smooth rendered walls.

LGI (1904); *LOI*; Bence-Jones 1988.

141. GOLDEN HILLS, Golden; pre-1840; *demolished.*

The seat in 1814 of Henry White, at the entrance to which was a round or 'inkpot' lodge that had gone by 1906.

Leet 1814.

142. GORTAGARRY, Toomyvarra; pre-1840; *demolished.*

A property in 1851 of Thomas Harden, the lodge to which had been removed by 1904.

Griffith 1853–63.

143. GRAIGUENOE PARK, Holycross; *c.* 1840; architect possibly C.F. Anderson.

A residence created in 1833–5 for Charles Clarke (1803–79) by architect C.F. Anderson, to which was being built in 1840 a porter's lodge that now presides over a lost demesne, avenue and big house. Single-storey and square, with an oversailing very shallow hipped roof rising to a minimal chimney-stack. Three-bay by three-bay, that elevation to the road having a blind recess flanked by very fine replacement six-over-six sash windows in coursed rubble walls dressed in toothed cream brick, perhaps revealed after removal of an original harled finish—to good effect. To the front door is a modern wooden *porte-cochère* as part of an admirable rehabilitation.

Lewis 1837; *LGI* (1904); IAA.

144. GRANGEMORE, Cashel; pre-1840; *demolished.*

A lodge, lost to road-widening, occupied in 1850 by Mrs Sexton, gatekeeper to William Smithwick.

Griffith 1853–63.

145. GRANTSTOWN HALL, Golden (2).

A mid-Victorian bargeboard Gothic villa built for brothers Major Charles William and

Henry William Massy (1816–95), both porters' lodges to which have been demolished but are survived at the main entrance by a Romantic castellated gatescreen of six round turrets, four of which contain, flanking the carriage opening, a pair of pointed-arched postilion gates with crow-stepped gables. Beyond are crenellated angled curtain walls, all in a pleasant tooled rubble stone.

LGI (1904); Bence-Jones 1988.

146. GREENFIELD, Cappaghwhite (2).

On the death in 1846 of Col. William Purefoy, Edward Bagwell (1819–83) inherited the estate, assuming the additional surname of Purefoy, and added two gate lodges at the entrances, neither of which is particularly distinguished.

North gate; *c.* 1850.

A plain, elongated, 1½-storey gabled three-bay affair in sand/cement rendering, with a single-storey flat-roofed hall extension.

South gate; *c.* 1850.

Once a standard single-storey lodge with oversailing hipped roof, now much enlarged into an L-plan. Good contemporary gate sweep of shallow concave railed quadrants and six low square pillars.

LGI (1904).

147. GREENHALL, Birdhill; *c.* 1845.

Opposite the gates is a derelict standard single-storey lodge with limewashed rubble walls and a stone eaves course to its clipped hipped roof. A property of the White family in the eighteenth and nineteenth centuries.

148. GREENHILLS, Moneygall; pre-1840; *demolished.*

A property purchased by William Minchin in 1703 but sold around 1854 as an incumbered estate by his clergyman great-great-grandson of the same name, before emigrating to New Zealand. He left behind a mansion described in 1801 as 'modern, elegant and spacious' but which now lies a ruin, its gate lodge opposite the gate gone. Before its demise the property was renamed 'Derryo'.

Coote 1801; *IFR.*

149. GREENMOUNT, Newcastle; pre-1840; *demolished.*

A property lately renamed 'Kenilworth', associated in the nineteenth century with the Prendergast and Mulcahy families.

150. GRENANE, Tipperary; *c.* 1840; architect perhaps C.F. Anderson; *demolished.*

For long an estate of the Mansergh family, of whom Richard Martin Southcote Mansergh

(1800–76), on the basis of the gate pillars being identical to those at Mooresfort [*q.v.*] and Kilfrush, Co. Limerick [*q.v.*], employed architect C.F. Anderson, whose commission may also have included plans for the gate lodge. The extensive gatescreen is comprised of a triple gateway with matching railings framed by six drum pillars with square bases and cappings. There are also like gates to Lismacue [*q.v.*].

LGI (1904).

151. GRENANSTOWN, Toomyvara; *c.* 1850.

A modest gate sweep and lodge, the latter single-storey with pebble-dashed front but otherwise harled; chimney-stack to each clipped gable but with carved continuous-bracket bargeboards to the projecting hall. Occupied. Built for Count Edward P. D'Alton.

152. GRENE PARK, Dundrum; *c.* 1800.

Opposite the entrance is an unusually large lodge for its age. Single-storey standard, with a not-quite-symmetrical three-bay main front of small bipartite casement windows on each side of the sheeted door in newly rendered walls. Derelict, with an original slated hipped roof. A seat in 1814 of Patrick Grene.

Leet 1814.

153. GREYFORT, Borrisokane; pre-1840; *demolished.*

An estate until his death of Major Bigoe Armstrong Stoney (1762–1827), thereafter being the property of Henry Owen Saunders (1805–80) but let to tenants, as he resided at Kilavalla in the same county. Little remains of note at the gates except a gadrooned capping to one gate pillar.

LGI (1904).

154. GROVE, Fethard (4).

Thomas Barton (1694–1780) purchased the estate in 1752, and his great-grandson William Barton (1790–1837) made many improvements to the property, which included work to the entrances, much to designs of the architect William Tinsley. The gate lodges have fared badly over time.

West gate; pre-1840; *demolished.*

South gate; *c.* 1835; architect possibly W. Tinsley; *demolished.*
Surviving is a good gatescreen similar to those at Castlepark [*q.v.*] and Woodroofe [*q.v.*]. It is a triple gateway contained by four cut-stone pillars with moulded recessed panels and distinctive cappings with acroteria. In contrast are roughcast wing walls.

East gate; pre-1906; *demolished.*
The latest of the lodges, erected after 1840.

Town gate; *c.* 1835; architect possibly W. Tinsley.

An innovative gatescreen comprising a triple gateway with four cast-iron secondary pillars with nice anthemions, framed by a pair of peculiar stone pillars with incised shafts and four-gabled cappings as bases to fluted column stumps. Beyond are shallow quadrant walls with recessed rectangular panels. Within is a much-modernised single-storey standard gabled lodge, with plastic windows below stylised entablatures set in rectangular recesses on each side of a gabled entrance breakfront with round-arched porch which used to contain a doorway. To opposing ends are windows in segmentally headed recesses; roof covered in synthetic slates and lacking its chimney-stack.

This may well be the lodge referred to by Mary Healy in the 1930s, where 'Mrs Morrissey gave birth to eleven children, there was no running water inside or out, and water had to be fetched from the creamery a quarter of a mile away'.

LGI (1904); Forbes 1953; Bence-Jones 1988; Somerville-Large 1995.

155. GURTEEN, Ballingarry (N); 1890.

A large single-storey lodge with plain rendered walls on a square plan recessed on each corner giving angled windows and an entrance porch, having chamfered posts supporting the eaves of a pyramidal roof covered in pantiles and rising to a three-flue cluster chimney-stack. For long the nineteenth-century seat of George Smyth, it remained lodgeless until 1890, when the property had become associated with Percy Bicknell through his marriage to Sarah Smyth. Now an agricultural college.

156. GURTEEN, Rathcabban; pre-1839; *demolished.*
Remaining are squat Georgian entrance pillars with friezes of fluting and rosettes below corniced cappings, whilst the lodge across the road has gone. A seat in 1837 of John Lalor.

Lewis 1837.

157. HARLEYPARK, Callan (2).
East gate; *c.* 1835.

Outside its gatescreen is a large standard lodge with wide windows of multi-square-paned cast-iron glazing. Roughcast, with tiny slates to the roof; deserted.

West gate; pre-1840; *demolished.*
A lodge that stood opposite the gates to a secondary avenue.

A seat of the Poe family, of whom James Purefoy Poe (1777–1851) would have built the main lodge.

LGI (1904).

158. HARVEST LODGE, Lorrha; pre-1840/*c.* 1860.
Opposite the entrance is a 1½-storey gabled porter's lodge in limewashed harling, with a symmetrical three-bay ground-floor front and two-bay above in a pair of gablets with ornamental foiled bargeboards. Probably an original structure of around 1830 and raised a storey about 30 years later, both stages for Thomas Johnston Stoney (1780–1869).

LGI (1904).

159. HELEN PARK, Killenaule; *c.* 1840.
An elegant late Georgian villa in 1814 of Oliver Latham, from whom it passed by marriage of his daughter to James Ryan, builder of the tiny single-storey standard hip-roofed cottage with wide eaves over harled walls; doorway now sealed up. Like its avenue, now disused.

Leet 1814; Pigot 1824; *LGI* (1904).

160. HERMITAGE, Nenagh; *c.* 1840.
A standard single-storey gatekeeper's lodge, with a gabled breakfront and a hipped roof with carved paired modillion brackets to the soffit; derelict. Built by the Jackson family.

161. HEYWOOD, Clonmel; pre-1840; *demolished.*
A lodge, removed by 1950, to a property in 1814 until his death in 1855 of Charles Riall, a branch of that family of Old Conna Hill, Co. Dublin.

Leet 1814; *LGI* (1904).

162. HIGH PARK, Cappaghwhite; pre-1840/*c.* 1870.
A lodge presumably built for Revd John Hunt (d. 1837) as a single-storey standard affair, either replaced or remodelled by his son Vere Hunt (b. 1814), perhaps by raising of the eaves to its oversailing hipped roof to accommodate a little gabled projecting hall with carved bargeboards and narrow side lights. On each side in rendered walls are simple mid-Victorian one-over-one sash windows. The brick chimney is contemporary with the gatescreen ironwork: railed quadrants and matching gates hung on cast-iron posts with 'morgenstern' finials.

LGI (1904).

163. HILTON, Cloghjordan; pre-1840; *demolished.*
A lodge built either by Richard Dancer or, after his death in 1818, by his second son, Thomas Dancer (1777–1857).

BPB (1929).

164. HILTON, Mullinahone (2).
A property in the early nineteenth century of the Pennefathers, whose early porter's lodge of before 1840 was located opposite their gates, to be replaced in the time here of John Blackmore by the surviving structure on the park side. Single-storey standard with a chimney-stack to each gabled end, built in harled stone, its wide window openings on either side of a slight entrance breakfront below a catslide; derelict. Probably built at the same time as the conspicuous round turret gate pillars with cut-stone crenellated cappings of *c.* 1870.

Griffith 1853–63.

165. HOLYCROSS CHURCH OF IRELAND CHURCH, Holycross; pre-1840; *demolished.*
The lodge may have been contemporary with the 'handsome modern edifice with a tower' of 1821, noted by Samuel Lewis in 1837, built during the incumbency (1817–33) of Revd William Edward Lloyd (1788/9–1854).

Lewis 1837; Seymour and Leslie 2012.

166. HONEYMOUNT, Monegall (2).
North entrance; *c.* 1790.

A delightful little Georgian 'inkpot' lodge, built in rubble stone to an internal diameter of 17ft, its symmetrical three-bay elevation with central doorway, cut-stone surrounds defining their lancet heads. Just apparent is a stone eaves course to what would have been a conical roof. Sadly now derelict, but not beyond being stabilised as a folly feature by the gates.

The Minchin family was here in the mid-eighteenth century, to be followed by John Evans in 1814 before the place was acquired by John Lloyd, recorded here by 1837, probably the same Captain Lloyd noted in the 1851 valuation, when the gatekeeper was James Doyle.

South entrance; *c.* 1850.
An altogether plain single-storey standard affair with one-over-one sash windows in rendered walls and clipped eaves to its hipped roof. Similarly abandoned.

Leet 1814; Lewis 1837; Griffith 1853–63; *LGI* (1904).

167. HYMENSTOWN, Newinn; *c.* 1800.
Remote from its entrance is a very derelict, sizeable, standard hip-roofed cottage, with small windows in harled walls and a little lean-to breakfront hall below eaves high enough to permit attic space above the right-hand side. A seat in the late eighteenth century of Nathaniel Robbins and in 1814 of George Robbins.

Leet 1814; *LGI* (1904).

168. INANE, Roscrea (2).
An estate in the late eighteenth century and early nineteenth century of the Curtis family, who would have established the early gatekeeper's lodge.

Front entrance; *c.* 1800/*c.* 1860.
What may originally have been a standard single-storey harled rubble-built Georgian Gothic lodge, with lancet windows on each side of a square-headed doorway. Probably raised to 1½ storeys with gabled attic rooms when decorative bargeboards were added and a square chimney-stack built alongside its diagonally set Tudor-style predecessor. Now disfigured by plastic window intrusions. The early modernisation may have been carried out by the new arrivals around 1820—the Jackson family, in the person of Peter Jackson, whose successor, Frederick Adolphus Jackson, was in residence by 1846 to add the triple gateway, with its four channelled gate pillars with moulded, round-headed panels, and the secondary lodge.

Rear entrance; pre-1904; *demolished.*
A short-lived building located at some distance from its gateway.

Taylor and Skinner 1778; 1783; Leet 1814; Pigot 1824; Slater 1846.

169. INCH, Borrisoleigh (3).
The seat from the early eighteenth century of the Ryan family, their splendid house of 1717 built by John Ryan.

Side entrance; pre-1840; *demolished.*
Bouladuff entrance; *c.* 1825.

On the southern approach is a delightful single-storey standard lodge, with wide windows in whitewashed harled walls below an oversailing shallow hipped roof with a brick chimney-stack; derelict and boarded up, and preceded by an extensive railed concourse of concave quadrants with an abundance of hooped tops and anthemion motifs repeated in the matching carriage gates and iron pillars. Presumably built by the eldest of John Ryan's great-grandsons, Daniel (d.s.p.(trans: died without issue) 1831), succeeded at his death by his younger brother George Ryan (1791–1875), who added a third lodge.

Borrisoleigh entrance; *c.* 1845.
Single-storey and four-bay, with steeply pitched gables, tiny lean-to porch projection and small windows in limewashed rubble walls. Derelict, but a backdrop for mock orange and cottage roses.

LGI (1904).

INDAVILLE (see OLD COURT)

170. ISLANDBAWN, Nenagh; pre-1840; *demolished.*
A property in 1824 of Minchin Lewis.

Pigot 1824.

171. JOHNSTOWN PARK, Dromineer; *c.* 1820.

The splendid house noticed in 1777 by Arthur Young as being built by Peter Holmes now lies a ruin. By 1824 the place was the residence of the Prendergast family, who probably created the striking entrance comprised of a triple round-arched gateway in ashlar with buttress dividers and complete with imposts, intrados and keystones. There are identical archways to Kilteelagh [*q.v.*] and the later Ashley Park [*q.v.*] copy, both nearby. Commanding the grand forecourt from without is the less-sophisticated traditional single-storey standard hip-roofed lodge, quite elongated, with square windows in limewashed harled walls.

Young 1780; Pigot 1824.

172. KILBEG, Cappaghwhite; *c.* 1840.
Apparently a rare instance of the vernacular four-bay single-storey linear cottage with steeply hipped roof, built as a gate lodge to a property in 1837 of S. Bradshaw Esq.

Lewis 1837.

173. KILBOY, Silvermines (2).
This important house, designed by William Leeson around 1780 for Henry Prittie (1743–1801), created 1st Baron Dunalley a year before his death, was a tragic loss to the arsonists of the 1920s but is survived by two fine entrances.

Nenagh gate; *c.* 1780; architect possibly William Leeson.

173. Kilboy, Silvermines, Silvermines gate.

At the northern entrance is an unusual and commodious 1½-storey gabled standard lodge faced in mellow stone rubble, arranged about a central pedimented frontispiece with a concave rococoed porch containing a round-headed fanlit doorway. This is flanked by rectangular-paned casement windows in recesses with three-centred arches below an eaves band. To the road front is a tripartite casement under a narrow attic window, both in rectangular recesses. Beautifully restored and maintained, its detailing is suggestive of canal architecture of the late eighteenth century which may indicate Leeson in relaxed mode. Low-lying, it has scant sight of its entrance. This is in the form of a triple ashlar Classical archway, or rather three independent round-headed archways, the outer postern ones linked by short railings to the larger central carriage opening, like the others with imposts, alternate raised voussoirs and keystone but having a peculiar corbelled shelf below a blocking course with die.

Silvermines gate; pre-1840/*c.* 1960.

At the main southern entrance is another grand gateway of *c.* 1780, again of three arches, here combined, the central carriage opening marked by a crowning pediment over a semicircular arch springing from a thick stone course with moulded intrados and keystone, otherwise in coursed rubble construction. To each side piers curve to lower postern arches, similarly dressed below flat copings. Within is a lodge of twentieth-century creation, either a complete rebuild or transformation into a lovely *cottage orné*. In mellow rubble stone construction, it has a three-bay avenue front with wide, shallow, segmentally arched entrance capped by a thatched hipped roof, within which the upper attic is lit by a big eyebrow lunette window central to the composition.

Both entrances have been admirably rescued from the dilapidation of the mid-1950s.

Lewis 1837; *BPB* (1929); Bence-Jones 1988.

174. KILBRAUGH, Ballingarry (S); *c.* 1870; *demolished.*

A lodge built probably during a period of development on the site by Robert Ashby around 1869, when the valuation rose considerably.

175. KILCARREN, Carrigahorrig; pre-1840/*c.* 1860.

A 1½-storey cottage with a brick chimney-stack to each main gable and tall eaves with carved soffit modillion brackets over cement-rendered walls. Probably a replacement for a previous lodge; occupied, with a later single-storey extension to the left-hand side. A property associated in 1814 and 1851 with Ralph Smith, though let in 1837 to Alexander Carew.

Leet 1814; Lewis 1837; Griffith 1853–63.

176. KILCOLEMAN, Nenagh; pre-1840; *demolished.*

An old estate of the Finch family, in 1837 'a handsome and well-planted demesne containing some very fine oak timber'.

Lewis 1837.

177. KILCOOLEY ABBEY, Urlingford (5).

On the Kilkenny border is the once-grand estate of the Barker family, named after a Cistercian abbey on the site, the mansion having been erected around 1790 along with a grand gateway for a new approach to designs by Michael Coffey for Sir William Barker. Four of its lodges were already in position before the building of a five-mile-long boundary wall as Famine relief for William Ponsonby-Barker (1795–1877), who had succeeded to the property on the death of his father in 1834. In 1850 two of his gatekeepers are named as Mary Hill and James Smee, while a third lodge lay vacant. None of those that survive are particularly notable.

North gate; pre-1840.

A three-bay gabled cottage, rendered nondescript by later extensions and 'improvement'.

North-west gate; *c.* 1820.

Known as 'George's Park' in its own right is what may also have functioned as a yard and farm manager's house, being a four-bay, two-storey hip-roofed structure complete with outbuildings and, to the road, distinguished by a rubble-built three-centred arched gateway surmounted by a little Gothic belfry to the parapet. Alongside is a plain postilion gateway in the wall, balanced by a plain gabled building to the right-hand side.

West lodge; *c.* 1820.

An unprepossessing gabled affair, forward of a good, extensive, straight Georgian gatescreen.

South lodge; pre-1905; *demolished.*

Inner lodge; pre-1840; *demolished.*

Griffith 1853–63; *IFR*; *IAR* (Winter 2003); IAA.

178. KILFEAKLE, Thomastown; *c.* 1780.

The shell of an antique lodge remains in rubble stone, with one blocked-up window projecting beyond, and once commanding, the forecourt of a rustic entrance screen. Built for either Roger Scully (1713–83) or his son James Scully (1737–1816), who succeeded the Bunbury family here around 1810.

LGI (1904).

179. KILGARVAN, Ballinderry; *c.* 1855.

Opposite the gates, seemingly disinterested, turning a single-storey gable with ornamental wavy bargeboards to the road is a lodge seemingly built for the proprietor in 1851, Solomon B. Cambie.

Griffith 1853–63.

180. KILLAGHY CASTLE, Mullinahone; pre-1840; *demolished.*
A sixteenth-century tower-house of the Tobin family, to which the Despards added a Tudor Gothic wing in the early nineteenth century. Their porter's lodge had gone by 1906.

Bence-Jones 1988.

181. KILLENAULE RECTORY, Killenaule; pre-1840; *demolished.*
A big glebe house of 1773, sometime called 'Upham', it and its lodge perhaps erected during the long incumbency (1773–*c.* 1822) of Revd Samuel Riall.

Wilson 1803; Seymour and Leslie 2012.

182. KILLENURE CASTLE, Dundrum (2).
The romantic sixteenth-century stronghold of the O'Dwyers, to which was added a plain late eighteenth-century house of the Cooper family, who built two porters' lodges.

East entrance; *c.* 1830.
A single-storey structure on an L-plan with a symmetrical three-bay avenue front below an oversailing, very shallow hipped roof which catslides over the hall projection. The occupant in 1850 was Ellen Cleary, porter to William Cooper (1772–1850), who had succeeded to the property on the death of his father Samuel in 1831. Plain triple gateway with square stone pillars.

West entrance; pre-1840; *demolished.*

Griffith 1853–63; *LGI* (1904); Bence-Jones 1988.

183. KILLOSKEHANE CASTLE, Borrisoleigh (2).

A medieval tower-house given a Georgian extension by the Willington family, whose early gatekeeper's lodge has gone. With the failure of the male line on the death of John James Willington (1815–62) the property was purchased by Colonel (later General) Albert Fytche (1826–92), who gave the place a fanciful make-over to plans of Sir Thomas Newenham Deane in 1867. The client from that date until 1871 was British chief commissioner of Burma, thus missing the building of his Irish seat. Deane's commission also included a design for the replacement gate lodge.

A highly ornate Tudor Picturesque single-storey gabled lodge, raised off a T-plan in rubble stone facings with label-moulded, mullioned, dressed stone bipartite and tripartite casement windows with latticed glazing. The rectangular bay window to the road has a Chinese-style roof below a gable decorated with wooden sheeting, and delightful trefoil carved bargeboards with incised decoration over that again. In the internal angle is contrived a hip-roofed entrance porch with carved wooden arched support. To the roof serrated cresting has replaced the cast-iron original, a ridge broken by a cut-stone chimney-stack part-chamfered as per the gate pillars. The latter form part of a tripartite gateway with ornate ironwork hung on beautifully chiselled pillars with poppy finials, shamrock motifs to friezes and heraldic shields as fanciful as the architecture.

IB (1 October 1867); *LGI* (1904); Bence-Jones 1988; Williams 1994.

183. Killoskehane Castle, Borrisoleigh.

184. KILLOUGH CASTLE, Holycross (3).
Another antique castle adapted in the Georgian and early Victorian periods, latterly by the Hon. Bowes Richard Daly (1814–88), fourth son of the first Baron Dunsandle, and brother of the second and third barons, who added two lodges to the extremities of the estate to supersede an earlier one within.

North gate; *c.* 1855.
Originally a standard 1½-storey lodge with roughcast walls and steeply pitched roof, extended by a bay to the right-hand side. A single-storey gabled hall projection contains the doorway in a semicircular-arched recess.

South gate; pre-1952; *demolished.*

Griffith 1853–63; *BPB* (1929).

185. KILMORE RECTORY, Silvermines; *c.* 1850.
A glebe house built in 1812, to which a gate lodge was added during the incumbency (1847–83) of Revd Andrew Armstrong Jones (1816/17–90). It lies in ruins.

Lewis 1837; Griffith 1853–63; Leslie and Crooks 2010.

186. KILMOYLER, Caher (2).
A big mid-Georgian house, home in 1783 to the Creagh family but which about 1810 passed from a Colonel Butler to Denis O'Meagher, who may have made his mark with the addition of at least one of the porters' lodges.

West gate; *c.* 1810.

Opposite the entrance but not quite on an axis with it is a charming Georgian Gothic cottage. Single-storey and square on plan below an almost pyramidal roof, its three-bay symmetrical front has three lancet openings, the central one sheltered by a later projecting gabled hall with a matching pointed window head, all in pastel-pinkwashed livery. Across the way is a later triple gateway of four tall ashlar pillars with unconventional cappings.

East gate; pre-1840; *demolished.*

Taylor and Skinner 1778; 1783; Wilson 1803; Leet 1814.

KILSHANE (see SPRING)

187. KILTEELAGH, Dromineer; *c.* 1865.

At the entrance to an estate also known as 'Shannonvale' is an imposing triple archway with round heads in uncoursed limestone, its impost blocks, voussoirs and keystones chiselled, rising to stepped copings and with dividing piers, just as at nearby Johnstown Park [*q.v.*] and Ashley Park [*q.v.*]. Like the latter, this may be a copy of the former, perhaps dating from the rebuilding of the house in 1865 to designs by James Rawson Carroll for Lt.-Col. Wills Crofts Gason, who had acquired the property just after his marriage three years earlier. Just as at Johnstown Park, across the concourse is a basic, and probably contemporary, single-storey standard gabled rendered lodge with thatched roof, as is the traditional hip-roofed cottage attached at right angles to it.

LGI (1904); IAA.

188. KILTINANE CASTLE, Fethard (3).

The castle of the Butlers, Lords Dunboyne, a gate lodge to which within the demesne was removed on the advent of the Cooke family, who added two lodged entrances to the boundary of the property in a distinctive Romantic vein, appropriate to the architecture within.

North gate; *c.* 1830.

A plain single-storey hip-roofed lodge in pleasant stone construction with brick-dressed openings. By the roadside is a triple

188. Kiltinane Castle, Fethard, south gate.

lancet-arched gateway flanked by tall, mellow rubble convex crenellated quadrants. The little postern gates (one sealed up) frame the great carriage gate with a plain parapet contained by a pair of unusual full-height 'arrowhead' turrets, castellated and relieved by mock arrowslits. Immaculately maintained as the main entrance.

South gate; 1842.

Another innovative entrance in the form of a castellated gatehouse, the porter's accommodation integral to each side of and above the Tudor-style carriage archway, which is flanked by two-storey breakfronts with crow-stepped gables containing sealed-up label-moulded windows over a lower storey which was always blind, with only pairs of ornamental cross arrowloops for relief in the uncoursed rubble walls. Above the carriage archway is another 'blind' window with label moulding-cum-string-course, between which and the crenellated parapet is an informative plaque stating 'Built by Robert Cooke Esq. A.D. 1842 Wm. And Ml. Cody Masons'. All effectively located at a T-junction, creating a vista on the Clonmel approach and framed by concave quadrant walls with crenellated copings terminated by little square 'flankers'. Unoccupied but maintained.

IFR; Bence-Jones 1988.

KINGSWELL (see SADLEIR'S WELLS)

189. KNOCKEVAN, Ballycleraghan (2).

William Pennefather acquired the property known as 'Darling Hill' around 1810 from the Carleton family, but it was his son Richard Pennefather, baron of the exchequer in Ireland, who engaged the young Clonmel architect William Tinsley to enlarge the house and provide at least one new gate lodge. While the house has gone, its lodges linger on.

Village gate; pre-1840/*c.* 1850.

Largely rebuilt and extended, there is still evidence of a once-pretty lodge in the Picturesque English cottage manner, 1½-storey on an L-plan. Its gables no longer have ornamental bargeboards but the main gable sports a tiny 'arrowhead' oriel window, while that attic storey is defined by the suggestion of jettying, its roof catsliding on one side to form a porch to the front door in the internal angle. The gable to the single-storey wing terminates in an 'arrowhead' bay window with, as elsewhere, lead-effect latticed glazing pattern, perhaps to remind of previous cast-iron casements. This must be a replacement, for the first OS map of 1840 indicates a lodge on the site prior to Tinsley's commission.

Country gate; pre-1840/1848; architect W. Tinsley.

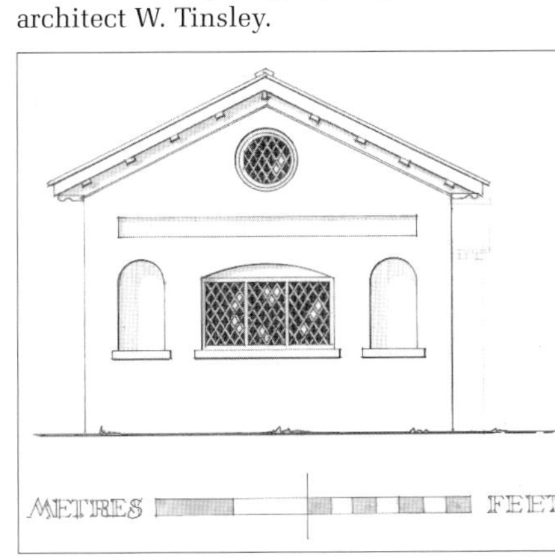

In contrast to its counterpart at the other entrance, this is Tinsley with his neo-Classical/Italianate hat on—an eccentric design of strange proportions but nonetheless attractive. Basically single-storey, with loft space accommodated by tall eaves with carved modillion brackets to the soffit of a shallow gabled roof. To the road is a three-bay front, a little gabled hall projection flanked by a pair of blind 'windows', or rectangular recesses, in stucco-effect rendered walls. From the opposing elevation to the park the interior is lit by two bipartite windows with cast-iron latticed casements. The avenue show-front gable is an odd amalgam of elements: the main wide, segmentally arched window is flanked by a pair of round-headed niches and topped by an embracing rectangular recessed panel over which is an oculus, and above that again the verge is highlighted by a continuation of the eaves brackets. There is a like elevation to the lodge at Merlin, Co. Waterford [*q.v.*]. On the opposing, rear elevation symmetry is dispensed with in a back door alongside another bipartite latticed window and a blind oculus in the apex. In 2000 a sad, dilapidated sight, with some faint hope of its restoration. The gatescreen in a similar state, a lonesome anthemion motif surviving at an overgrown avenue.

Wilson 1803; Leet 1814; *LGI* (1904); Forbes 1953.

190. KNOCKGRAFFON RECTORY, Newinn; pre-1840; *demolished.*

'... [O]n a glebe of forty acres joining the church-yard, procured by exchange by his grace Lord Somerton, Archbishop of Cashell, in 1784, has been built under his grace's direction, by the Rev. Nicolas Herbert, the present incumbent of the parish of Knockgraffon, a most commodious glebe-house and offices; which have a very pleasing effect, as seen from the road: towards building this house which cost 1300l. the sum of 250l. was bequeathed by the Rev. Hugh Bolton, formerly incumbent of this parish.' Thus recorded the *Post chaise companion* of *c.* 1804, with no mention of a gate lodge, but there is little doubt that it was erected in the time of Revd N. Herbert, for—remarkably—he was still resident in 1837, by which time the glebe lands had increased to 60 acres.

Wilson 1803; Lewis 1837.

191. KNOCKLOFTY, Clonmel (3).

One of the premier estates of County Tipperary, with its mansion of the Hely Hutchinson family, earls of Donoughmore, pleasantly located on the banks of the River Suir. Before 1880 there was but one lodged entrance to the grounds, created probably by John Hely Hutchinson (1757–1832), the 2nd earl, who succeeded to the title and estate on the death of his brother in 1825.

Main entrance; *c.* 1830.

At first sight a single-storey standard hip-roofed lodge in Regency style with an oversailing shallow-pitched hipped roof, but in fact revealed at the rear to be a two-storey gatehouse. Its avenue front of six-over-six sash windows and door, all set in segmentally arched recesses to ground level, was originally painted to contrast with the harled finish. Like a skinned rabbit, it has been stripped of this weather protection to reveal a limestone rubble fabric with red-brick dressings, exposed as never intended.

The magnificent limestone ashlar carriage pillars have likewise been vandalised, with the loss of their original innovative blockings and finials with scrolls supporting cockatrices nesting in coronets. Surviving to the fore are beautifully tooled roundels with the family armorials containing the motto *Fortiter Gerit Cruceum* ('He bears the cross patiently'), above which on each face is a grotesque mask, moustachioed with streaming sideburns, flared nostrils, pointed ears and a coronet. The triple limestone gateway is completed by a pair of modest flat-arched postilion gates, the whole only saved for posterity in its original state in an old photograph.

John Luke George Hely Hutchinson (1848–1900), who succeeded as 5th earl in 1866 on his father's death, set about improvements to the property, to include another couple of lodged gates in a typical late Victorian manner.

East entrance; *c.* 1880; architect not known.

A single-storey standard lodge with hipped roof over walls of bold roughcast, its openings emphasised by toothed red-brick dressings with keystones to three-centred arched windows, a material repeated in its slender chimney-stack. A triple gateway is divided by elaborate cast-iron pillars and flanked by matching concave railed quadrants terminating in ashlar pillars with more ironwork in decorative scrolled supports.

South entrance; *c.* 1880.

Opposite its gates in nice rubble stone with toothed brick dressings and two-over-two sash windows, the three-bay main front with door and grouped side light to the left-hand side sheltered by a gabled canopy with brackets and sheeted apex. Crowned by a steeply hipped roof with off-centre chimney-stack; three-bay side elevation.

BPB (1929); Bence-Jones 1988; IAA photograph (16/61Z1).

192. KYLE PARK, Borrisokane; pre-1840; *demolished.*

A property in the nineteenth century of the Stoney family, of whom George Stoney (1774–1810) or his successor Thomas George Stoney (1808–86) would have built the lodge.

LGI (1904).

193. LACKENACOOMBE, Cappaghwhite; pre-1840; *demolished.*

Another holding in 1850 of Samuel Cooper of nearby Killenure [*q.v.*].

Griffith 1853–63.

194. LAKEFIELD, Fethard; *c.* 1835; architect probably W. Tinsley.

The young architect William Tinsley's first major commission resulted in this impressive Italianate-style villa for William Pennefather (1819–72) of the New Park [*q.v.*] family. The house was complete by 1833 and its porter's lodge was in place by 1840. This is an unusually commodious single-storey standard structure on a square plan, with smooth rendered walls below a pyramidal roof. Three bays by two, its rectangular-paned casement windows each set in a rectangular recess with unusual paired corbel motifs to the head, a feature to be seen also on the lodge to Rocklow [*q.v.*]. To the side elevations are recessed panel pilasters off a bold plinth. The gatescreen has plain pillars and ogee railed quadrants.

LGI (1904); Forbes 1953; Bence-Jones 1988.

195. LANDSDOWN, Portroe; pre-1840/*c.* 1860.

A very fine Palladian-style slate-clad house of 1779 built for William Parker, whose successor and namesake in the mid-nineteenth century would appear to have replaced an earlier lodge with this single-storey standard hip-roofed cottage of generous proportions and a pleasant rural pedimented breakfront containing a pair of Doric columns *in antis*, flanked, in roughcast walls, by narrow rectangular-paned casement windows but with two-over-two bipartite sashes to the road elevation. It monitors a contemporary gatescreen of wide, concave, railed quadrants and matching carriage gates in decorative cast iron with tall stone pillars. William Parker acquired the adjacent estate of Garrykennedy [*q.v.*] in 1858 and gave it an almost identical lodge.

LOI; Bence-Jones 1988.

196. LANESPARK, Killenaule; pre-1840; *demolished.*
A seat of the Lane family, whose gate porter in 1850 was William Croak, whose lodge had been removed by 1905.

Griffith 1853–63.

197. LANGLEY LODGE, Drangan; *c.* 1830.
Now called 'Priesttown House'. Across the road from its entrance is a basic single-storey gabled building with a three-bay front, the door to the left-hand side. A property of the Langley family, of whom Lawrence Langley, who sold the place in 1853, probably built the lodge after succeeding on the passing of his father Oliver in 1825.

LGI (1904).

LARCHGROVE (see GLENCONNOR)

198. LESERRAGH, Ballinderry; pre-1903; *demolished.*
A property in 1851 of Richard Pierce, the lodge to which was built after 1840.

Griffith 1853–63.

199. LISBRYAN, Ballingarry (N); *c.* 1850.
Opposite the gates is a very derelict single-storey standard lodge with distinctly large window openings on each side of a double-leaf door below a rectangular fanlight, set in a slightly canted breakfront; subsiding hipped roof. The estate was acquired by Thomas Bunbury around 1835, becoming his residence for about 40 years, a handsome big Palladian house having been built around 1775 for the Faulkner family.

Lewis 1837; *LOI.*

200. LISDUFF, Moneygall; pre-1840/1886.
A fascinating and unusual late Georgian Gothic house, in 1814 of Samuel Smythe and by 1840 having an early porter's lodge, the site of which is now occupied by a replacement, built by the subsequent owner, Thomas Meara. This is an uncommonly commodious affair: a two-up/two-down structure with an attic, two-bay to the avenue and with pronounced quoins, presenting a single-bay gable to the visitor, the door now missing its porch, but above a loft window in stucco-effect rendered walls is the date in relief 'MDCCCLXXXVI', at which time it was home to gatekeeper Cornelius Hays. Despite the accommodation offered, abandoned and windowless.

Leet 1814.

201. LISHEEN CASTLE, Templetouhy; pre-1840; *demolished.*
A remarkable mock castle of the Lloyd family, a ruin since its burning in 1900, its gatekeeper's lodge certainly briefly outlasting it.

Williams 1994.

202. LISHEEN, Golden (2).
A seat of the Judkin-Fitzgeralds, baronets, both lodges to which have been demolished, the earlier of before 1840 and its replacement built prior to 1906.

203. LISKEVEEN, Littleton (2).
Here are the dilapidated remains of two fine lodges of a once-prosperous demesne created by Samuel M. Going.

Main entrance; *c.* 1860; architect not known.

This was once a very attractive and decorative building, a single-storey standard affair with moulded surrounds to windows and a doorway with ornate fanlight, in stucco-effect walls sheltered by a shallow-pitched hipped roof which oversailed sufficiently to form a surrounding verandah originally featuring fancy post supports. Doorless and with windows now staring, its dereliction is highlighted by a well-preserved and conspicuous gatescreen comprised of extensive ogee railed quadrants contained by stone outer pillars, its single carriage gateway in matching ironwork framed by a pair of cast-iron pillars of entwined foliage climbing to anthemions contained in hooped tops—all very much as at Sadleir's Wells [*q.v.*].

Secondary entrance; *c.* 1860.
A 1½-storey gabled lodge with high eaves to roughcast walls, with bipartite windows of one-over-one sashes on each side of the doorway with rectangular fanlight. Derelict.

Slater 1856; 1870.

204. LISMACUE, Bansha; *c.* 1840.
The castellated Tudor Gothic house was designed by William Robertson of Kilkenny for William Baker in 1813. Two years later the client was murdered, and the entrance at the base of the great lime tree avenue remained lodgeless until after Robertson's retirement from practice. The lodge built for Hugh Baker (1798–1868) has no architectural pretensions, although what remains of the gatescreen has drum pillars with square

plinths and capping slabs, just as are apparent at Grenane [*q.v.*] and Mooresfort [*q.v.*] in the county, at Kilfrush, Co. Limerick [*q.v.*], and at Cangort, Co. Offaly, where there is work attributable to C.F. Anderson. The lodge is a pleasant single-storey standard structure with whitewashed harled walls, with modern windows and doorway with rectangular fanlight below a hipped roof; occupied.

LGI (1904); Heron 1999.

205. LISMORTAGH, Killenaule; pre-1840; *demolished.*
A seat in 1814 of Matthew N. Sankey, but from about 1820 of the Millet family.

Leet 1814; Pigot 1824.

206. LISSENHALL, Nenagh; pre-1954; *demolished.*
A secondary property of the Otway family of Castle Otway [*q.v.*] until sold through the incumbered estate court in 1853 to the sitting tenant, William H. Carroll, who in the 1870s was carrying out building improvements that may have included provision of the gate lodge.

Lyons 1993.

LITTLETON GLEBE (see BORRISLEIGH RECTORY)

207. LLOYDSBOROUGH, Templemore (2).
A late Georgian house, the residence of a succession of John Lloyds. The lodge by the main gate and the 'schoolhouse' at the rear entrance, both in place by 1840, have been demolished.

208. LODGE, Puckaun; *c.* 1840.
A plain two-storey, three-bay gabled gatehouse, presumably built for Maurice Studdert (1802–67).

IFR.

209. LONGFIELD, Goold's Cross (2).
A house of *c.* 1770 built by Richard Long, the estate with its two gate lodges being purchased around 1850 by Charles Bianconi of horse-drawn transport fame.

South gate; pre-1840; *demolished.*

North gate; *c.* 1830.
A standard single-storey lodge with roughcast walls and a shallow hipped roof with high extending eaves; well maintained.

Bence-Jones 1988; Nolan 1985.

210. LONG ORCHARD, Templetouhy (2).
Originally an estate of the Doghertys, it passed on the death of John Lalor in 1828

through his eldest daughter's marriage to Edmond Power of Gurteen le Poer, Co. Waterford [*q.v.*], to their son Edmond James Power-Lalor (1817–73), who added at least one of the porters' lodges.

Town gate; pre-1905; *demolished.*

Country gate; *c.* 1855.

Opposite the entrance is this nondescript single-storey standard roughcast gabled lodge; occupied.

LGI (1904).

211. LORRHA RECTORY, Lorrha; pre-1903; *demolished.*

Although the handsome glebe house dates from 1816, its gatekeeper's lodge was not added until after 1840, probably sometime during the long incumbency (1832–74) of Revd Archdeacon Edmund Dalrymple Hesketh Knox (1801–84).

Lewis 1837; Leslie and Crooks 2010.

212. LOUGHKEEN RECTORY, Ballingarry (N); pre-1840; *demolished.*

A lodge probably contemporary with the building in 1829 of the exceptionally large and late glebe house, home to the long-serving rector Revd Francis Synge (1790–1870), incumbent from 1824 to 1858.

Lewis 1837; *IFR*; Leslie and Crooks 2010.

213. LOUGHLOHERY CASTLE, Caher; pre-1840; *demolished.*

A seat at the turn of the nineteenth century of the Dogherty family, which about 1810 was acquired by the Quinns. In 1850 Edward Hack was gatekeeper to William Quinn.

Wilson 1803; Leet 1814; Griffith 1853–63.

MANTLE HILL (see CASTLEPARK)

214. MARLFIELD, Clonmel (3).

The Bagwell family obtained the estate on the banks of the River Suir in 1781 from the bankrupt Stephen Moore, and four years later Col. John Bagwell had built a new mansion. His son William Bagwell died unmarried in 1825, leaving the property to his young nephew John Bagwell (1811–83), who upon coming of age commissioned the local architect William Tinsley to furnish plans for a grand entrance to the estate.

East entrance; 1833; architects Sir John Soane/William Tinsley.

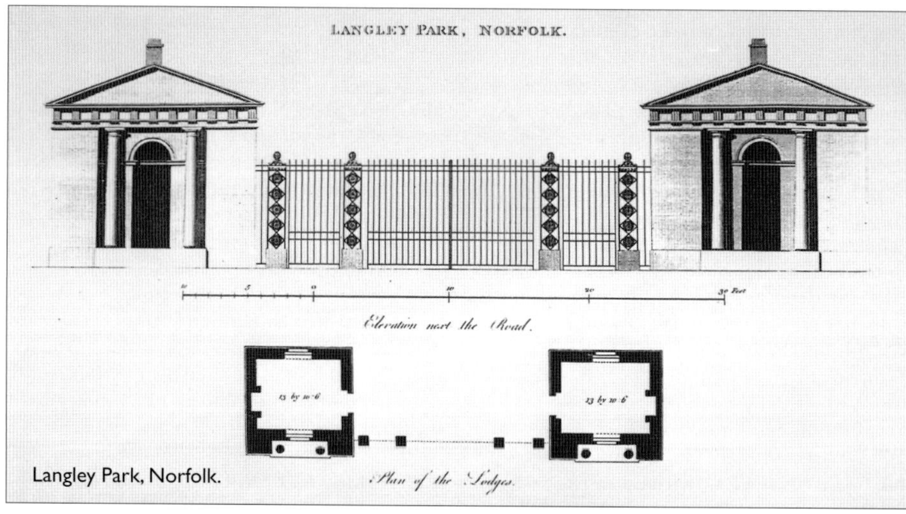

Langley Park, Norfolk.

The most sophisticated of Tinsley's work, explained by its being a replication of Sir John Soane's design for a pair of lodges to Langley Park, Norfolk, with which he was familiar through the publication of the plans in the English architect's *Plans, elevations and sections of buildings* (1789). Originally twin single-storey one-roomed cubes with hipped roofs and pedimented breakfronts to the road, each of which contains a pair of Doric columns *in antis* framing round-headed niches. These Tinsley has substituted for windows on Soane's design and has similarly replaced a triglyphed frieze for one of fluting relieved by paterae. To each pediment is an octagonal chimney-flue to the apex, while Tinsley has designed identical fronts to face each other across the entrance in the form of single windows below giant paterae in semicircular-arched recesses flanked on one side by a niche and on the other by a V-jointed pier to match the carriage pillars, which define a triple gateway and railings. Presented in a honey-coloured sandstone, each lodge has subsequently been extended with considerable sensitivity.

West entrance; *c.* 1835; architect possibly William Tinsley.

A generously proportioned 1½-storey gabled English Picturesque Cottage in roughcast finish, with transomed and mullioned multi-paned casement windows. To the right-hand side of the three-bay avenue front is a little

projecting single-storey gabled hall with a roof of scalloped slate courses and, like the main gables, having pretty perforated cusped bargeboards with quatrefoil toes and rising to a turned hip-knob which stops perforated canted earthenware cresting. The rectangular bay window gives a splendid view of the park from that gable end. The grand late Victorian chimney-stack in red brick with plinth and corbelled capping suggests much later alteration and extension of the lodge. Across the road is an arched entrance to the farmyard.

Side entrance; *c.* 1860.

Alongside a pointed-arched gateway with crenellated parapet in rubble stone is a 1½-storey gabled standard lodge with tall eaves to accommodate the shallow-pitched single-storey hall projection. A pleasant cottage in roughcast finish, with square-paned sash windows and plain bargeboards.

Soane 1789; Wilson 1803; *LGI* (1904); Forbes 1953; O'Donnell 1999.

IAA

214. Marlfield, Clonmel. East entrance.

215. MARLHILL, Newinn; pre-1840; *demolished.*

A lodge opposite the gates to an estate in 1814 of Edward O'Meagher.

Leet 1814.

216. MELDRUM, Cashel (2).

An old estate of the Letham family, around 1810 acquired by Richard Lloyd.

Front entrance; pre-1840; *demolished.*

Rear entrance; *c.* 1780.

Still in farm use is this antique cottage lodge in harled stone and mud construction, gabled with windows to each end and a front elevation blind but for a low, lean-to entrance breakfront. Within is a vernacular limewashed stepped chimney-breast and a loft room over.

Taylor and Skinner 1778; 1783; Leet 1814.

217. MELVIEW, Clonmel (2).
The residence of David Malcomson (1765–1844) of the local mills, probably built to plans by Clonmel-based architect William Tinsley, whose hand is apparent in the Cashel Street gatescreen.

Front entrance; *c.* 1825; architect probably W. Tinsley.

A triple-railed gateway conspicuous for its Egypto-Greek Revival stone pillars with tapering recessed panels, clearly influenced by a design from J.B. Papworth's *Rural residences* (1818) but crowned by a Tinsley trademark in their anthemion-sculpted acroteria. Commanding the entrance is the elevated single-storey hip-roofed lodge, its principal one-bay front addressing the visitor with a segmentally arched tripartite window in stuccoed walls framed by raised V-jointed stone quoins. There is a similar gatescreen at Caher Abbey [*q.v.*].

Rear entrance; pre-1840; *demolished.*

Now a convalescent home.

Papworth 1818.

MERLIN (see COUNTY WATERFORD)

218. MERTON, Cloghjordan (3).
A seat in the nineteenth century of the Hall family, none of its pre-1840 lodges have survived, one within having been removed by 1903.

219. MILLGROVE, Caher; pre-1840; *demolished.*
A property in 1824 of Thomas Jackson which by 1850 was the residence and corn mill of William Walpole, whose gatekeeper then was Pat O'Brien. The gatescreen displays the date '1854'.

Pigot 1824; Griffith 1853–63.

MINELLA (see COUNTY WATERFORD)

220. MOBARNAN, Cashel; *c.* 1810.
The ruin of what was a sizeable standard lodge built in stone with a pointed door head, which may have had similarly arched windows. Gabled, with a loft room. A Georgian Gothic cottage probably built by Samuel Jacob, the proprietor in 1814.

Leet 1814.

221. MODREENY, Cloghjordan (2).

221. Modreeny, Cloghjordan, Cloghjordan gate.

A good late Georgian house to which were added sophisticated wings by Sir Amyrald Dancer (1768–1843), who succeeded as 5th baronet at the age of eight and further embellished the demesne with two gate lodges.

Cloghjordan gate; *c.* 1835; architect perhaps Richard Morrison.
A handsome Classical lodge appropriately elevated on a platform, its ashlar pedimented frontispiece with a pair of Doric columns *in antis* approached up a flight of steps. From there the canted recessed porch has two panelled doors leading unsocially to separate day and night accommodation. Single-storey with a hipped roof, the otherwise rubble facings contain bipartite casement windows with margined glazing. There are like lodges at Ballindoolin, Co. Kildare, Thornton Lodge, Co. Dublin, and, significantly, an unexecuted design for the Baronscourt, Co. Tyrone, estate by the Morrison office. The complementary gatescreen is as fine, comprised of extensive railed ogee quadrants framed by V-jointed rusticated pillars and cast-iron carriage posts.

Modreeny gate; *c.* 1825/*c.* 1890.

A lodge much altered in late Victorian times from its original manifestation as a single-storey structure with canted front to the avenue. It was subsequently raised a storey by the 7th baronet, Sir Thomas Johnston Dancer, who succeeded to the place in 1872, its road elevation becoming the main front, with a central single-storey gabled hall projection added below a pair of attic gablets with two-over-two casements, all with basic scrolled bargeboards and little turned hip-knobs. The transformation was completed by red earthenware hip and ridge tiles, with a big banded and corbelled late nineteenth-century brick chimney-stack. Concave railed entrance quadrants are contained by square outer pillars and octagonal inner ones with simple recessed panels.

BPB (1929); Dean 1994.

222. MODREENY HOUSE, Cloghjordan; *c.* 1825.

A perfectly symmetrical and quintessential Irish porter's lodge, single-storey and originally with limewashed harled walls containing small two-over-two sash windows below a hipped roof with paired carved modillion brackets to the soffit; derelict. The ashlar carriage pillars with plain friezes are framed by straight railings on dwarf walls, harled as are the quadrant walls beyond.

Built either by Lt.-Gen. Michael Head or, after his death in 1827, by his only child, William Henry Head (1809–88), whose principal seat was Walshpark [*q.v.*], for the house lay vacant in 1852.

Griffith 1853–63; *LGI* (1904).

223. MODREENY RECTORY, Cloghjordan; pre-1840/*c.* 1880.
The original lodge may have been contemporary with the building of the glebe

house about 1813 during the incumbency (1801–*c.* 1831) of Revd Edwin Palmer (b. *c.* 1759), so what graces the entrance today is either a reworking or a replacement, recently expertly rehabilitated. Facing across the forecourt to the gatescreen is a single-storey standard gabled lodge in pleasant rubble stone facings with toothed brick dressings to transomed and mullioned casements, the upper panes latticed, and the doorway below a wooden bracketed canopy, the wavy bargeboards to which are carried beyond as ornamental fascias; to the ridge is red clay perforated scalloped cresting. All work probably dating from the amalgamation of the parish with that of Cloghjordan in 1874 during the short incumbency (1873–5) of Revd Martin Carysfort Proby.

Lewis 1837; Leslie and Crooks 2010.

224. MONAINCHA, Roscrea; *c.* 1830.

To complement 'An elegant villa in the Italian style' in 1837 was this single-storey two-roomed cottage, single-bay and bow-ended to the avenue, with an equivalent roof over white harled walls. Rather more ornate are the pillars to the triple gateway, with four-sided pedimented cappings, friezes with panels containing pairs of oval paterae, and raised and fielded panels to the shafts; spear-topped gates. All for the proprietor in 1837, George Birch.

Lewis 1837.

225. MONAQUIL, Silvermines; *c.* 1835.

A seat in the late eighteenth century of Philip Going, after whose death it passed by marriage to the Atkins family, who were probably responsible for adding the lodge. Standard single-storey with roughcast walls below a steeply hipped roof which extends over a back return to form an L-plan. A similarly roofed porch is carried on a pair of cast-iron columns; occupied.

Taylor and Skinner 1778; 1783; Lewis 1837.

226. MONROE, Nenagh; *c.* 1820.

A harled and ochre-washed single-storey cottage with a plain two-window-bay front below a hipped roof, now being improved and enlarged. Matching rustic triple gateway. In 1837 'the neat cottage residence of R[ichard] Power'.

Lewis 1837.

227. MONTEVIDEO, Roscrea; pre-1840; *demolished.*

A porter's lodge sited opposite the entrance to a property in 1846 of Thomas Parsons.

Slater 1846.

228. MOORESFORT, Lattin; *c.* 1835; architect probably C.F. Anderson.

A singular lodge design but not unique, as there are almost identical lodges at Ballywilliam [*q.v.*] and Kilfrush [*q.v.*], Co. Limerick, Gurteen-le-Poer, Co. Waterford [*q.v.*], and Lauriston, Co. Cork [*q.v.*], thus attributable to architect Charles Frederick Anderson. Conspicuously located on a right-angled corner of the public road and facing across the gatescreen forecourt, it is a single-storey standard gabled structure faced in limestone ashlar; its six-over-six sash windows flank a pedimented hall breakfront with Doric columns '*ex antis*' to its corner recesses and framing a panelled doorway with a round-arched fanlight, once spoked. Relieving recessed panels above the windows display paterae, and all nicely set off by low concave wing walls. The gatescreen has cylindrical carriage pillars with square bases and slabs to cappings, identical to those at Grenane [*q.v.*] and Lismacue [*q.v.*] and at Kilfrush, Co. Limerick. Lodge extended into a double pile to the rear and in use as holiday accommodation. Built for Maurice Crosbie Moore to a property subsequently purchased by a different branch of a family of that name in the 1850s.

Lewis 1837; *LGI* (1904); *IFR*.

229. MOUNTAIN LODGE [1], Ballyporeen (2).

A hunting lodge built *c.* 1785 by Robert King (1754–99), 2nd earl of Kingston, of nearby Mitchelstown Castle, Co. Cork [*q.v.*], and further developed by his son George King (1771–1839), the 3rd earl, who added a porter's lodge to the property.

Inner gate; pre-1840/*c.* 1875.

What survives forward of the entrance, derelict and overgrown, looks to be a replacement lodge. Single-storey and three-bay below a hipped roof with projecting central like-roofed hallway of side entry and faced in pleasant uncoursed rubble. There are two-over-two sash windows to the main structure and a later addition to the rear. Probably built for Nathaniel Buckley (1821–92), cotton millionaire of Manchester, who purchased the estate in 1873.

Outer gate; *c.* 1895; architects perhaps Darbyshire and Smith.

Abel Buckley, who inherited the place on his brother's death, transformed the house into a Gothic mansion and accordingly renamed it 'Galtee Castle', creating another lodged entrance further down the avenue, perhaps also a design by Manchester architects Darbyshire and Smith, albeit relatively modest. Three-bay in good random cut-stone facings, with dominant stacks to each gable and the monopitch canopy to the front door having scalloped-end wooden boarded sides; extended by a bay to the left-hand side. Both lodges survive the big house, which was dismantled around 1940.

IAR (2002).

230. MOUNTAIN LODGE [2], Ballyporeen; 1908; architect probably F.W. Higginbotham.

Around the time when Cornelius O'Callaghan (1775–1857), 1st Viscount Lismore, was creating his spectacular mansion of Shanbally Castle [*q.v.*] nearby to designs of John Nash, so too was he building himself his shooting-box of Galtee Lodge 'in a situation of much beauty in a glen of the Galtees and surrounded it with a plantation of about 150 acres', which remained without a porter's lodge until the turn of the twentieth century.

'Glengarra Lodge' is an immaculate single-storey Edwardian lodge with a pyramidal roof rising to a central chimney-stack, square on plan but for a verandahed entrance porch, with door and window of the three-bay avenue front behind carved post supports rising off dwarf walls. Otherwise constructed in random cut stone with conspicuous white pointed red-brick toothed quoins and dressings to two-over-two sash window openings. Built for sisters Lady Constance Butler and Lady Beatrice Pole Carew, who succeeded to the property on the death of their cousin, the 2nd Viscount Lismore, in 1898, probably to designs of

Frederick W. Higginbotham, who was then working at Shanbally.

Lewis 1837; *PGI*; Debrett 1920; *IAR* (2002).

231. MOUNT BRUIS, Tipperary; pre-1840; *demolished.*
A seat until around 1850 of the Dogherty family, its gate lodge removed before 1906.

232. MOUNT DUDLEY, Roscrea; pre-1840; *demolished.*
The estate in 1824 of Shelton Dudley.

Pigot 1824.

233. MOUNT FALCON, Borrisokane; pre-1840.
A house built in 1720 by Richard Falkiner, which became home to a succession of the family of that name down the years. Their lodge now lies a ruin.

LGI (1904).

234. MOUNT KENNEDY, Templederry; pre-1904; *demolished.*
A property of the Kennedy family, the lodge to which was added after 1840.

235. MOUNT PLEASANT, Nenagh; pre-1840.
Opposite the gates is the shell of a standard lodge of rubble stone construction. A seat in 1814 of John Short, which ten years later had passed to George Jackson.

Leet 1814; Pigot 1824.

236. MOUNT RICHARD, Carrick-on-Suir; *c.* 1825; architect probably J.B. Keane.

A distinguished entrance, the lodge to which belongs to that genre whose source was a design in John Soane's *Sketches in architecture* (1793) [see Fig. 5, p. 6], developed as a gate lodge throughout the country by Richard Morrison. This is a variant of it by his erstwhile assistant J.B. Keane, and there are identical examples by him at Rockgrove, Co. Cork [*q.v.*], and Stradone, Co. Cavan (demolished). A short single-bay elevation forms the principal front, a tripartite window with segmental head being set in a recess formed by two projecting piers, each with moulded panels and laurel wreath motifs over. The recess is exaggerated by the oversailing hipped roof with carved modillion brackets to the soffit, while the otherwise blind side elevations had gabled projections—an entrance hall and balancing closet. All done up in a stucco-effect finish. Unfortunately, the original main window is lost to a modern steel replacement and the closet projection to a flat-roofed extension. To the road is the noble gatescreen, comprised of four bulky ashlar pillars with tapering pylon-like faces, the inner pair with more laurel wreaths to hefty cappings, both supported by gadroon-topped piers. Between are concave railed quadrants to match the carriage gates, which are hung on cast-iron secondary pillars, just as recommended by J.B. Papworth, from whose *Rural residences* (1818) [see Fig. 6, p. 8] this design was taken. Sadly, a feature particular to Mount Richard is missing: two antlered bucks' heads that graced the top of the main pillars, indicating the crest of the family within—the Powers. Beyond is a relatively unassuming villa in Morrison mode. This would all seem to have been commissioned by Edmond Power (1775–1830), proprietor of the local coalmines.

Soane 1793; Papworth 1818; Lewis 1837; *LGI* (1904); Dean 1994.

237. MOUNT RIVERS, Newport (2).
A seat of the Phillips family.

North lodge; pre-1904; *demolished.*
A lodge built after 1840 opposite the gates.

South lodge; *c.* 1845.

On a sylvan site is this charming limewashed harled cottage below a pyramidal roof rising to the central chimney-stack. To the avenue is a three-window-bay elevation with door and window to the road front. Maintained derelict. Not obviously attributable to architect James Pain, who carried out additions to the house in 1850 for Richard E. Phillips.

Slater 1856; IAA.

238. MOUNT ST JOSEPH NUNNERY, Roscrea; pre-1840; *demolished.*
The lodge may have been of an age with the original late eighteenth-century convent building but was removed to make way for the brooding school extensions of *c.* 1860.

239. MOYALIFFE, Thurles (2).

The remaining lodge is a replacement for a predecessor closer to the road and probably built in the time here of Revd William Carew Armstrong (d. 1839). This would have formed part of improvements to the estate carried out by his grandson, Edward Marcus Armstrong (1829–99), also of Chaffpool, Co. Sligo. Dating from *c.* 1880, a once-presentable single-storey gabled lodge of irregular plan and outline, the main body of which presents a grand segmentally arched window to the old avenue, with the front door to the internal angle of one of the lower wings projecting from each side. Faced in a pleasant uncoursed rubble, enhanced by contrasting red brick as toothed dressings, arches and a central banded and corbelled chimney-stack, which breaks the ridge of serrated earthenware cresting. Derelict, it now presides forlornly over a muddy track. In 1851 the gatekeeper in the old lodge was Andrew Dwyer.

Griffith 1853–63; *LGI* (1904).

240. MOYNE RECTORY, Moyne; pre-1840; *demolished.*
A lovely glebe house dating from 1820, the gate lodge to which may have been contemporary. If so, probably dating from the incumbency (1815–*c.* 1824) of Revd John Torrens.

Lewis 1837; Seymour and Leslie 2012.

241. NEDDANS, Ardfinnan; *c.* 1810.

Prominently located outside its basic gatescreen, facing down the road is an almost characteristic late Georgian traditional Irish porter's lodge, but not quite symmetrical, like that to Grene Park [*q.v.*]—perhaps by the same jobbing builder. Single-storey standard with small square window openings in limewashed walls below an oversailing hipped roof with original slates and a centrally positioned chimney-stack. Endearing but derelict. Possibly built for Francis Mulcahy (1784–1862).

Griffith 1853–63; *LGI* (1904).

242. NENAGH CHURCH OF IRELAND CHURCH (OLD) AND GRAVEYARD, Nenagh; *c.* 1820.
An undistinguished two-storey, gabled, cement-rendered gatehouse with modern casement window openings, built against the early church tower, the remains of the previous parish church abandoned in 1860 for the new one in St Hannan Street. The gatekeeper prior to this in 1851 was Mary Bird during the incumbency of Revd James Hill Poe.

Griffith 1853–63; Bassett 1889.

243. NENAGH DISTRICT HOSPITAL, Nenagh; *c.* 1935; architect Vincent Kelly.

In the International style is this remarkable pair of flat-roofed single-storey lodges flanking the entrance to the hospital, built in the same manner—a highly appropriate introduction. Outside the gatescreen, their curved corners contain tripartite windows and extend within to symmetrical three-bay entrance fronts facing each other across the approach in a smooth rendered finish with clearly defined plinths. There are similar versions at Cashel District Hospital [*q.v.*] and that at Listowel, Co. Kerry [*q.v.*].

O'Dwyer 1997a.

244. NEWCASTLE, Newcastle; *c.* 1840.
A seat of the Mulcahy family lies in ruins, to be survived by its derelict gate lodge. Single-storey, big and hip-roofed, with two chimney-stacks, finished in traditional limewashed harling and presenting a short one-windowed bay to the avenue. Alongside is a modest entrance of uncoursed rubble concave quadrant walls and plain ashlar carriage pillars with spear-topped gates.

Griffith 1853–63; *LGI* (1904).

NEWGROVE (see ST KIERAN'S)

245. NEWHILL, Littleton; pre-1905; *demolished.*
A lodge built after 1840 opposite the gates to a seat in 1851 of John Thomas Going.

Griffith 1853–63.

246. NEWPARK, Cashel; *c.* 1835.
A good mid-eighteenth-century house built by Richard Pennefather on an estate to which a smart new lodged entrance was added by

his grandson, Captain Mathew Pennefather (1784–1858), after he inherited the property in 1831. A quite pretentious gatescreen is comprised of extensive concave railings on dwarf walls contained by four stone pillars with moulded plinths, recessed panels and projecting cornices over friezes with minimal fluting and pretty floral paterae; on the two outer pillars are weighty ball finials. Presiding over all this is a much-renovated single-storey standard lodge with oversailing shallow pyramidal roof of synthetic slates, its openings having Tudor label mouldings to modern plastic lead-effect windows but a nice panelled door below a spoked rectangular fanlight, all in crisp modern rendering on an original stone plinth. It extends considerably to the rear in sensitive additions. Captain Pennefather's gate porter in 1850 was James Ryan. A property renamed 'Ballyowen'.

Griffith 1853–63; *LGI* (1904).

247. NEWPORT, Newport; pre-1840; *demolished.*
A seat of the Waller family, the porter's lodge to which had been removed by 1904.

248. NEWTOWNANNER, Clonmel (2).
The lovely estate to which, in 1783, Sir Thomas Osborne (1757–1821) succeeded as 9th baronet on the death of his father, between 1798 and 1802 greatly enlarging the house to its present manifestation. The improvements he carried out to the grounds may have included the provision of the early gate lodge.

East entrance; pre-1840; *demolished.*
Nothing remains of the lodge, but the 1850 valuation refers to 'Two' gate lodges here, which suggests a pair.

As Sir Thomas had married late in life and his only son outlived him by only three years, the property was inherited by his infant daughter, so it was his young widow, Catherine Rebecca, who managed Newtownanner until her death in 1880. In that time she greatly embellished the park with picturesque features, forming ornamental lakes and canals and creating vistas to a temple and grotto, and was responsible for a grand new entrance to the place.

West entrance; *c.* 1845; architect possibly C.F. Anderson; *demolished.*
Only a late Victorian photograph survives as testimony to the splendour of this gateway and lodge, apparently constructed in limestone ashlar, which rose to an entablatured parapet to partially conceal the hipped roof of a single-storey structure which had a central canted or semi-octagonal hall projection and equivalent roof over. The windows were casements with ornamental cast-iron hexagonal glazing pattern, and to the junction of the ridges was a row of three octagonal chimney-flues. This was screened by a wide triple gateway in that trabeated form whereby the carriage pillars double as postilion archways, each flanked by piers with recessed panels carrying entablatures with dies. This was a format employed by Charles F. Anderson in his design for an entrance to nearby Gurteen-le-Poer, Co. Waterford [*q.v.*], and possibly also at Lauriston, Co. Cork [*q.v.*]. He also worked at the neighbouring estate of Anner Park [*q.v.*], so an attribution to him seems reasonable.

Griffith 1853–63; *BPB* (1929); *Country Life* (8 and 15 September 1988); IAA photograph (1/97 Z1+N).

248. Newtownanner, Clonmel, west entrance.

IAA

249. NOAN, Ballinure (3).
A typical big late Georgian gentry farmhouse, home for almost 200 years of the Taylor family, whose old lodge, built before 1840, lay off a now-discontinued loop of the public road. The direct male line failed and the estate was sold in 1853 as an incumbered estate to Stanley Black, after having been let for years to Francis Mulcahy of Neddans [*q.v.*]. Black was here from 1859 to 1876, during which period he added two new gate lodges.

Rear entrance; *c.* 1860.

A replacement for the Taylor lodge at the end of an extended avenue, it is a generous single-storey standard affair built in rubble stone with piers defining three-bay by two-bay elevations, the recesses thus formed harled, with distinctive tripartite sash windows of rectangular-glazed side panels framing a central latticed section. The hipped roof with all its rafters exposed is crowned by a hefty chimney-stack. Elevated and remote from its simple gate sweep of ball-finialled carriage pillars flanked by convex quadrants of railings with claw feet. Terminally derelict.

Front entrance; *c.* 1860.

An unassuming single-storey standard gabled porter's lodge, with bipartite cast-iron latticed casement windows in roughcast walls. Extended to a double pile.

Slater 1846; *LGI* (1904); Lyons 1993.

250. OAKLANDS, Clonmel; *c.* 1820/*c.* 1860.

A strange hodgepodge of a building that may originally have been quite sophisticated, judging by the Doric pilasters defining the bays of a single-storey standard gabled lodge with a very tall entablatured eaves band which indicates loft space. Latterly it has been prettified with Tudor Picturesque features, such as the additions of ornamental foiled bargeboards to the main gables and those of a latticed porch, and label mouldings above the bipartite one-over-one sash windows, all presented in a smooth render; derelict. Alongside are chaste V-jointed rusticated cut-stone pillars to a tripartite gateway with contemporary spear-topped late Georgian ironwork, perhaps of an age with the fine big house built by Simmons Sparrow of the Suir Island mills in Clonmel but subsequently occupied by a succession of owners, such as the Bagwells of Marlfield [*q.v.*] and the Phipps family in the mid-nineteenth century.

Bence-Jones 1988.

251. OAKVILLE, Clonmel; pre-1840; *demolished.*
A property in the mid-nineteenth century of the Hon. George Ponsonby Prittie (1808–71), clerk of the peace.

Slater 1846.

252. OLD COURT, Borrisokane; *c.* 1845.
A property in 1851 of the Brereton family, whose gatekeeper then seems to have been Jane Horgan, occupying a 1½-storey structure with a cut-stone eaves band taken across its gable ends. The main front is a two-window bay in rubble stone walls; cut-stone chimney-stack. In 2000 undergoing renovations.

Griffith 1853–63; *IFR.*

253. OLD COURT, Cashel; *c.* 1825.
Now known as 'Indville', at its entrance are the remains of a plain, steeply hip-roofed rendered lodge, with a tiny window and doorway to its main avenue front. Approaching ruin, and a sad introduction to the smart Regency villa within. Nearby are huge ashlar gate pillars with concave quadrant walls, at one time forming part of a clear boundary by the public road but now hemmed in by later housing. Sometime in the early nineteenth century the residence of Patrick Littleton.

ORMONDE CASTLE (see CARRICK-ON-SUIR CASTLE)

PARSONAGE (see KNOCKGRAFFON RECTORY)

PARSON'S GREEN (see TULLAGHORTON RECTORY)

254. PASTOR VILLE, Newcastle; *c.* 1825.

A sometime presbytery house to the parish of Newcastle, occupied by Revd Michael Meighan in 1814 and by Revd Edward Larkin in 1851, when his gatekeeper was Mary Mahony. Valued then at a paltry five shillings, it amazingly survives on a beautiful site by a babbling brook, overlooking a grassy track, the remains of an avenue abandoned after a new access was formed to the house, which late in the century became 'Boolahallagh' after its townland. It lies forlorn and isolated as a tiny single-storey standard structure with wide windows in rendered walls below a chimneyless shallow hipped roof.

Leet 1814; Griffith 1853–63.

255. PEGSBOROUGH, Tipperary; *c.* 1825.

A seat at the turn of the nineteenth century of Edward Stanley, 12th earl of Derby (1752–1834), and possibly named after one of the Margarets in that family. It was the residence in 1814 of Henry Smithwick but it was more likely his successor who built the lodge, Captain George Bradshaw being recorded here in 1824. It appears to the avenue as a standard single-storey three-bay structure with a shallow hipped roof, but its principal front addresses the road's edge as a single window in an elliptically arched recess in stucco-effect walls below oversailing eaves marked by paired carved soffit brackets. To the ridge is a large paired chimney-stack. Alongside the derelict lodge is a postilion opening beside a plain carriage gateway.

Leet 1914; Pigot 1824; *BPB* (1929).

256. PHILIPSTOWN, Cappaghwhite; *c.* 1845; *demolished.*
A lodge built sometime between the first OS of 1840 and its being recorded in the valuation of 1851 as occupied by Denis Ryan as porter to Hugh Brady Bradshaw.

Griffith 1853–63.

257. PORTLAND, Portumna; pre-1840/*c.* 1855.
The Stoneys were associated with this estate since the early 1700s. The existing lodge, probably a three-bay standard single-storey structure, was apparently raised a floor to 1½ storeys with a pair of gablets to the attic; gabled with harled walls and a single round-headed window to the road elevation. The work was carried out for Thomas Butler Stoney (1813–93), who succeeded to the property on the death of his father in 1830.
IFR.

258. POWERSTOWN, Clonmel (2).
A seat in 1814 of George Green, of whose influence precious little survives. A lodge to the west in Carriglen townland was a ruin in 1950, as is that to the front entrance, manifest only as a front elevation, blocked up with a lancet-headed doorway, which suggests a date of around 1800.
Leet 1814.

259. POYNTSTOWN, Ballingarry (S); pre-1840; *demolished.*
A property in the eighteenth century of the Cooke family which by 1850 was being let by Fennell Cooke to James Morris, whose gatekeeper was a Mrs Freny. The lodge had gone by 1905.
Taylor and Skinner 1778; 1783; Griffith 1853–63.

PRIESTTOWN (see LANGLEY LODGE)

260. PRIOR PARK, Dromineer; pre-1840; *demolished.*
A house commenced in 1779 for James Otway which by the nineteenth century had become the residence of George Waller (d. 1833), his son William Thomas Waller living on here until 1898. The lodge had been removed by 1903.
LGI (1904); Bence-Jones 1988.

261. PRIOR PARK TERRACE, Clonmel; *c.* 1830; *demolished.*
An early nineteenth-century development of seven houses in a fashionable area of the town given additional exclusivity by its attendant porter's lodge, which had nevertheless been removed by 1950.
O'Donnell 1999.

262. PRIOR'S LODGE, Thurles; pre-1840; *demolished.*
Samuel Lewis in 1837 recorded that 'Prior Lodge, the property and residence of Rev. Dr [John] Prior is situated on a small but tastefully disposed demesne'. The estate was renamed 'Crossage', its gate lodge gone by 1905.
Lewis 1837.

THE PRIORY (see TEMPLEMORE ABBEY)

263. PROSPECT, Dromineer; pre-1840; *demolished.*
A property in 1824 of John Falkiner and in 1837 of J.S. Handcock which continued in the nineteenth century to be home to a succession of occupants. By 1903 the lodge had gone.
Pigot 1824; Lewis 1837.

264. RACECOURSE HALL, Cashel; *c.* 1825.

An extensive semicircular forecourt to an impressive gatescreen of concave railed quadrants and a triple gateway contained by six late Georgian pillars, four of which display friezes with well-chiselled fluting framing floral paterae, a feature also to be seen at Newpark [*q.v.*]. Behind one quadrant is a symmetrical single-storey hip-roofed lodge, its single-bay leading front spoiled by an insensitive modern casement window in cement-rendered walls. To opposing side elevations are balancing little hipped roof projections tucked in below the oversailing main eaves. At Ardsallagh [*q.v.*] is an almost identical lodge. An estate in 1824 of Avary Jordan, whose gate porter in 1850 was James Kirby.
Pigot 1824; Griffith 1853–63.

RAHEEN (see COUNTY WATERFORD)

265. RAHEEN PARK, Thurles; *c.* 1830.

A pleasing single-storey standard lodge of long, low lines, its sheeted door and bipartite casement windows in limewashed harled walls framed by corner piers to give it a sense of permanence despite its dereliction; hipped roof with chimney-stack on the rear wall. It combines with a good contemporary gatescreen as a single gateway, four square stone pillars and concave railed quadrants with fancy finials to form an impressive semicircular concourse. A seat in the early nineteenth century of the Wilson family.

266. RAPLA, Nenagh; pre-1840; *demolished.*
Little remains of this estate of the Willingtons, the big house a ruin and its lodge replaced by a bungalow. On the death of Jonathan Willington in 1818 it was acquired by William Cooper Crawford, who by 1850 was letting it out.
Pigot 1824; Griffith 1853–63; *LGI* (1904); Bence-Jones 1988.

267. RATHCOOL CASTLE, Fethard; *c.* 1840.
A seat initially of a branch of the Blake family, from whom it had passed to the Blackmores by 1824. What seems to have originated as a standard single-storey gabled cottage shows signs of a make-over by Charles Blackmore *c.* 1860, when the front door was moved to a gabled hall extension on the road gable, the previous opening becoming a window and, in common with the others, given a fashionable mid-Victorian moulded surround in harled rubble walls. To the chimney-stack is a faintly chinoiserie capping, while within is a very Irish vernacular cottage fireplace and loft space to the left-hand side. Derelict and windowless beside a plain entrance.

268. RATHRONAN, Clonmel; 1826; architect William Tinsley; *demolished.*
A Scottish visitor in 1835 found 'Sir Hugh Gough's ... It is a nice place of moderate size, with a magnificent avenue of limes, a piece of made water, very pretty garden and a lawn studded with some magnificent trees (oak and chestnut very remarkable)'. What he did not record was the gate lodge designed by the young Clonmel architect William Tinsley, who had been commissioned nine years before by Hugh Gough (1779–1869), 1st viscount, and field marshal by 1862.
Heaney 1999; *BPB* (1929); Forbes 1953.

269. RATHURLES, Nenagh; pre-1840; *demolished.*
A house built *c.* 1790 by John Brereton (1729–1813), to which was added a porter's lodge either by him or by his elder son, Thomas Brereton (1785–1860), but it had gone by 1904.
IFR.

270. REDWOOD, Lorrha; pre-1903; *demolished.*
A lodge built after 1840 for John Colpoys Bloomfield (1788–1881).
LGI (1904).

271. REGAILE, Holycross; pre-1840; *demolished.*
A property associated in the mid-nineteenth century with the Armstrong family.

272. REHILL, Clogheen; *c.* 1845; *demolished.*
In 1850 Thomas Butler was gate porter to

James Mulcahy, whose family remained in residence until 1880 despite the property's having been sold to Robert Murdock in 1853 as an incumbered estate. The valuation book notes the gate lodge as 'down' by 1902.

Griffith 1853–63; Lyons 1993.

273. RICHMOND, Cashel; pre-1840; *demolished.*
A property in 1837 of R. Butler H. Lowe, which by 1850 had been acquired by Dr Michael Cormack, whose gatekeeper was then Owen Callaghan.

Lewis 1837; Griffith 1853–63.

274. RICHMOND, Nenagh; pre-1840; *demolished.*
Surviving at the entrance is a good gatescreen with V-jointed rusticated stone mid-Georgian pillars. A seat in 1814 of Richard Gason and ten years later of his son, Richard Wills Gason, whose gate lodge and some of their house, which evolved over the centuries, have been demolished.

Leet 1814; Pigot 1824; Bence-Jones 1988.

RIVER GLEBE (see ACHNAMEADLE RECTORY)

275. RIVERSDALE, Borrisokane; *c.* 1845; *demolished.*
A delightful little early Victorian Classical single-storey-over-basement villa built *c.* 1845 for Thomas S.D. Robinson on the family estate of Ballynavin Castle [*q.v.*]. The contemporary porter's lodge, valued at £1.0.0 in 1850, was then occupied by John Callahan and John Tuohy.

Griffith 1853–63.

276. RIVERSTON, Nenagh (2).
A property in the first half of the nineteenth century of John Bennett, which seems to have been lodgeless until the advent of James Jocelyn Poë in the 1860s, after he had married his predecessor's daughter and sole heiress.

Town gate; pre-1904; *demolished.*
Surviving are plain Georgian corniced pillars framed by quadrant walls with lancet-topped niches, all from the Bennett era.

River gate; *c.* 1900.
An undistinguished square, two-storey, roughcast hip-roofed house, perhaps built after Captain James Hill Poë inherited the estate in 1895. Again there is an earlier gatescreen of two plain late Georgian stone carriage pillars.

Slater 1856; 1870; *LGI* (1904).

277. ROAN, Killenaule; pre-1840; *demolished.*
The seat in the early nineteenth century of Dennis Duan and by 1846 of Robert Percell.

Leet 1814; Slater 1846.

278. ROCHESTOWN, Caher; pre-1840; *demolished.*
A splendid house built *c.* 1807 for Dunbar Barton, probably to designs of Richard Morrison. He had come by the property through marriage to Elizabeth Riall, daughter of the previous proprietor. It was burnt in 1922 and has gone the way of its lodge, survived by an entrance sweep with five squat square pillars, all with ball finials.

Clonmel Herald (2 January 1808); Glin *et al.* 1988.

279. ROCK ABBEY, Cashel; pre-1840.
The ruin of a single-storey porter's lodge, overgrown and extending as the left-hand convex quadrant of its gatescreen, which it viewed through a single opening. The seat in 1846 of Captain George Minchin.

Slater 1846.

280. ROCKFORD, Nenagh; *c.* 1850.
Opposite the gates is an immaculate 1½-storey standard gabled gatekeeper's lodge, in nice rubble facings with limestone quoins and brick dressings. Very much restored. A property in 1851 of John Wolfe (1787–1858) of that family of Forenaghts, Co. Kildare, who had acquired Rockford through marriage in 1823 to the daughter of its previous owner, William Kingsley.

Griffith 1853–63; *LGI* (1904).

281. ROCKFOREST, Roscrea; pre-1840.
A much improved lodge, its short principal gabled front adorned with a basic modern flat-roofed 'portico', the only original feature manifest being the quoin stones. Probably originating from the time here of William Henry Hutchinson, who had inherited it on his father's death in 1820. The property passed through the marriage of his daughter to the Minchins of Greenhills [*q.v.*], of whom Stephen Minchin had Bridget Carey as his gatekeeper in 1851.

Lewis 1837; Griffith 1853–63; *LGI* (1904); *IFR*; Bence-Jones 1988.

282. ROCKLOW, Fethard; *c.* 1835; architect possibly W. Tinsley.

A late eighteenth-century house that passed from the hands of the Low family to Benjamin Frend around 1810. The lodge added by him before 1840 is a spacious single-storey hip-roofed structure, its main front being blind but for the central hall breakfront, which has an open pediment with paired corbel support above what was the doorway in a rectangular recess—now converted to a window in recent alterations and extension. To the avenue façade two windows are similarly set in rectangular recesses with more paired corbel features over, much as on the lodge to Lakefield [*q.v.*] attributable to Clonmel architect William Tinsley. All in a smooth rendering with a bold plinth and a later Victorian banded and corbelled brick chimney-stack to the ridge. Insensitive modern casement windows spoil the effect. In contrast are stone Tudor Gothic-style gate pillars with steep four-faced triangular cappings.

Taylor and Skinner 1778; 1783; Wilson 1803; Leet 1814.

283. ROCKWELL, Newinn; pre-1841; architect perhaps W. Tinsley; *demolished.*
The young architect William Tinsley's first Gothic house for client William Roe, a major remodelling of an existing structure around 1833. The lost lodge may have formed part of that commission. Later that century the estate was acquired by the Order of the Holy Ghost and the respected college for boys was established.

Forbes 1953.

284. RODEEN, Borrisokane; pre-1840; *demolished.*
The lost lodge was located opposite its gates and in 1852 was manned by Michael Moran, gatekeeper to Joseph Falkiner (d. 1857), founder of the property.

Griffith 1853–63; *LGI* (1904).

285. ROESBOROUGH, Tipperary; pre-1840; *demolished.*
A house, now in ruins, built at the turn of the nineteenth century by James Roe, its porter's lodge possibly contemporary.

286. ROOSCA TOWNLAND, Caher; *c.* 1860.
A house which 'never had a name', in 1851 the residence of Peter Banfield, probably the builder of the standard nondescript gate lodge. Gabled and roughcast with squared casement lights. Probably added when the old house was extended about 1860.

Griffith 1853–63.

287. SADLEIR'S WELLS, Tipperary; *c.* 1835.

Richard Sadleir acquired the house called 'Kingswell' around 1810 and changed its name, his family remaining here until about 1850, in which time William Sadleir created the present impressive entrance. Although the lodge is relatively plain, probably through modernisation, with the bland cement-rendered walls and plastic windows, extended to an L-plan from a single-storey standard hip-roofed affair, its gatescreen is extensive, with decorative convex railed quadrants having claw feet to the bottom rails and matching triple gateway, the cast-iron carriage pillars with foliage intertwining and climbing to anthemion motifs in hoop-framed terminals. At the extremities of the sweep are stone pillars, both their shafts and the tympana of the four-faced segmental pedimented cappings in a vermiculated finish. These would seem to be of later date, perhaps of *c.* 1870, after John Massy (1810–94) had been here for about fifteen years and had returned the name of the place to 'Kingswell'.

Leet 1814; Lewis 1837; Slater 1856; *LGI* (1904).

288. ST DAVID'S, Dromineer; *c.* 1845.

Samuel Lewis in 1837 must have been captivated by this property, 'A fishing lodge of the Very Rev. Gilbert Holmes, Dean of Ardfert, beautifully situated on the banks of the Shannon', then known as 'Urra Lodge'. The dean was succeeded on his death in 1846 by his eldest son, William Bassett Holmes (1820–83), builder of the porter's lodge opposite the gates.

This is an appropriately Picturesque cottage, 1½-storey gabled and in white roughcast, three-bay symmetrical with a projecting porch, over the segmental pointed archway of which is a pretty lancet attic window. To each side are replaced bipartite round-headed lights, while the roof displays modest carved bargeboards and trefoil-, or shamrock-, perforated earthenware cresting. The brick chimney-stack rises from the rear.

Lewis 1837; *LGI* (1904).

289. ST JOHN THE BAPTIST CATHEDRAL, Cashel; *c.* 1845/1912; architect W.H. Hill.

Within the precincts is this striking building, probably the sexton's house, to designs of architect William Henry Hill, for which tenders were invited in 1912. Three-bay symmetrical and single-storey, with tripartite four-over-four sash windows in roughcast walls on each side of a two-bay hall projection, the gable of which is in half-timbered effect. Opposing end elevations are canted below equivalent roofs, on the ridge of which are two balancing chimney-stacks. This would seem to be the replacement for a predecessor not evident on the 1840 OS map but valued ten years later, its appropriately named gatekeeper Joseph Lodge. Alongside is a segmentally arched gateway crowned by a fine pair of urns.

Griffith 1853–63; *IB* (16 March 1912).

290. ST JOHNSTOWN CASTLE, Drangan (2).

An old tower-house at the turn of the nineteenth century of the Jacobs, which by 1824 was in the possession of Richard Millet, who built a new house in the vicinity and possibly added the lodged entrances.

West gate; *c.* 1830.

Opposite the entrance is a derelict single-storey roughcast lodge with a front elevation of two windows. Extension to the right-hand side with a two-over-two sash window.

East gate; pre-1906; *demolished.*

The 1906 OS map indicated the lodge, flanked by gate access to either side. Built after 1840 and short-lived.

Wilson 1803; Pigot 1824; Lewis 1837.

291. ST JOSEPH'S INDUSTRIAL SCHOOL, Clonmel; *c.* 1880; *demolished.*

An institution established in 1880, financed by Arthur J. Moore MP of Mooresfort [*q.v.*].

O'Donnell 1999.

ST KEVIN'S FORT (see LISKEVEEN)

292. ST KIERAN'S, Rathcabban (2).

A property also known as 'Newgrove' down the years, seat in 1837 of J.W. Bayly, who may have built the earlier lodge.

Inner entrance; *c.* 1840.

A tiny three-bay cottage, its doorway to the right-hand side and six-over-six sash windows in harled walls below a gabled roof. Abandoned.

Outer entrance; *c.* 1860.

Opposite the gates, what was originally a single-storey standard steeply pitched hip-roofed lodge with tiny slates, exposed rafter toes and two chimney-stacks. Extended by a bay to the left-hand side, with bipartite eight-squared casement windows in harled walls. Derelict. Presumably erected on the advent of Frederick Willington (1823–89) of the Castle Willington [*q.v.*] family.

Lewis 1837; *LGI* (1904).

293. ST PATRICK'S CEMETERY, Clonmel; 1886; architect probably W.G. Doolin.

According to O'Donnell, Walter G. Doolin was appointed to design the two mortuary chapels, a gate lodge and the general layout of paths. The building contractor was Fermoy builder James Newstead, who completed the contract in 1885.

A striking 1½-storey High Victorian Tudor Gothic lodge with step gables, rising from an L-plan in uncoursed sandstone with limestone quoins and dressings to a variety of mullioned and transomed chamfered casement windows, and a shouldered arched doorway to the entrance formed by the roof catsliding over the internal corner. The roof is enhanced by geometrically carved bargeboards and alternately perforated

earthenware crestings that terminate in threatening dragons. The whole is topped off by a cluster of conjoined stone octagonal chimney-flues. Impressively elevated to command a wide gatescreen with concave stone quadrants and carriage pillars with moulded plinths and layered pyramidal cappings finishing in tooled finials; contemporary cast-iron ornamental railings and gates.

Williams 1994; O'Donnell 1999.

294. ST PATRICK'S COLLEGE, Thurles; *c.* 1836.

Described in 1837 as '... established in 1836 for the liberal education of R.C. young gentlemen upon moderate terms ...', and nine years later as a 'sumptuous building with a centre and wings'. Its gate lodge is anything but sumptuous, today presenting a sorry sight, set back from the fine limestone ashlar carriage pillars, chamfered with moulded cornices and crowned by fearsome eagles. The lodge, single-storey below an oversailing hipped roof with banded chimney-stack, has an irregular three-bay façade in roughcast, its doorway to one side. Derelict and boarded-up.

Lewis 1837; Slater 1846.

295. ST PATRICK'S HOSPITAL, Cashel; pre-1952; *demolished.*

To what was the Union Workhouse of 1842, a later lodge on Deerpark Road has been replaced by a twentieth-century bungalow.

296. SALISBURY, Clonmel; pre-1840; *demolished.*

A tall, three-storey late Georgian house, in 1814 occupied by Stephen Moore, who by 1837 was leasing it to Thomas Sadlier and thereafter to others.

Leet 1814; Lewis 1837.

297. SHANBALLY CASTLE, Clogheen (3).

One of the greatest losses to Ireland's architectural heritage was this masterpiece by John Nash in his Picturesque Castellated style, created *c.* 1810 for Cornelius O'Callaghan (1775–1857), 1st Viscount Lismore. Of its three early porters' lodges there is little trace.

South-west entrance; pre-1841; *demolished.*
Surviving are the extensive dilapidated remains of a gatescreen of shallow concave quadrant walls terminating in outer pillars with pointed-arched niches.

When George Ponsonby O'Callaghan, the 2nd viscount, died without male heirs in 1898, the peerage became extinct and the estates were left to his cousins, Lady Constance Butler and Lady Beatrice Pole-Carew, daughters of the 3rd marquis of Ormonde. It was Lady Beatrice who clearly found inappropriate the entrances to the great mansion that she had inherited, and from 1906 she engaged the Dublin architect Frederick W. Higginbotham to prepare plans for two new lodges over which there may have been much agonising, for one was not completed until eight years later.

East entrance; 1914; architect F.W. Higginbotham.

A distinctive single-storey gabled lodge in an Arts and Crafts Tudor Revival style. Gabled and built off an L-plan in uncoursed limestone facings, its wide windows are multi-paned casements below basic label mouldings. In the internal angle is a hall-cum-porch with post support to the lean-to roof, while the roof line is dominated by three great corbelled chimney-stacks. In one gable is the date-stone '1914', since when it has suffered the indignity of the loss of its big house, entrance gates and general context, and its own abuse with the blocking up of one window and another replaced by a hideously obvious plastic substitute.

North-west entrance; *c.* 1914; architect perhaps F.W. Higginbotham.
A three-bay chalet structure with two dormer windows in a clay roll-tiled gabled roof, a material repeated on the single-storey lean-to porch; brick dressings to wide windows and quoins.

Altogether too depressing to dwell on.

Debrett 1920; *BPB* (1929); *IB* (14 July 1906; 25 June 1910; 27 May 1911); Bence-Jones 1988.

298. SHANBALLY, Toomyvara; pre-1840; *demolished.*
A lodge opposite the gates to a property in the late eighteenth century of John Gason, who died in 1818 'having had numerous issue'—none of whom occupied their father's house, for by 1837 it was leased to Peter Smithwick (1806–94), who remained here into old age.

Lewis 1837; *LGI* (1904).

299. SHANNONVILLE, Portroe; pre-1840; *demolished.*
A seat overlooking Lough Derg, in 1837 of Bamblett Kent.

Lewis 1837.

300. SKEHANAGH, Templemore; pre-1840/*c.* 1940.
An estate of the Lloyds on which neither the original house nor gate lodge survives, the former having been burnt down, to be replaced *c.* 1920 by the present house, and the existing lodge built about twenty years later. This is a convincing impression of a building of *c.* 1845, with its label mouldings and perforated continuous bracket bargeboards apparently applied to an original single-storey standard structure with steeply pitched gables, and a seemingly single-bay extension to one side and further added to at the rear to form a double pile. Sand/cement-rendered wall finish, plastic windows, synthetic roof 'slates' and brick-built chimney-stacks reveal its recent origin.

NIAH.

301. SLEVOIR or SLEVYRE, Terryglass; *c.* 1870.
The old seat known as 'Firmount' was the residence in 1777 and 1804 of the Firman family but by 1837 was occupied by R. Monsell Esq. Stunningly located overlooking Lough Derg, the place was transformed around 1870, when a grand Italianate house with giant belvedere tower was created for Lt.-Col. James Francis Hickie (1833–1913), probably to designs of John McCurdy. At the gate there is no indication of the ostentation within, marked in 2000 by a single-storey rubble-built gabled cottage, then little more than a shell undergoing renovation.

Taylor and Skinner 1778; Lewis 1837; *LGI* 1904.

302. SOLSBOROUGH, Nenagh (2).

Long the property of the Poë family, it was inherited on the death of his uncle in 1857 by Henry Harrington Poë (1824–98), who commenced improvements by adding another storey to the house and replacing the old, pre-1840 gatekeeper's lodge with more social accommodation opposite the entrance gates.

This is a generous lodge in size and finish, single-storey, gabled and built off an L-plan in random ashlar with Irish pilaster quoins to the leading gable, which displays a plaque in the apex of the Poë arms—three crescents and a boar's head—over a glazed canted bay window with recessed under-panels. The extensive wing is three-bay, with round-headed sash windows and the doorway all within an entrance verandah screened by carved wooden posts. Across the road is an equally ornate gatescreen with decorative cast-iron railings and tripartite gateway set off by sturdy stone pillars with moulded recessed panels and outsized cappings. One pillar is inscribed helpfully 'Denis Hanly Builder Nenagh 1863'. Hanly may well also have been the designer, for in an 1870 directory he also describes himself as an architect. If so, he also designed the identical gate lodge to Glasshouse, Co. Offaly.

Slater 1870; *LGI* (1904); NIAH.

303. SOMERSET, Lorrha; pre-1840; *demolished.*
A recently removed lodge to the seat of the O'Meara family, whose replacement house of 1875 survives within.

304. SOPWELL HALL, Ballingarry (N) (4).
These were the lands of the Sadleir family since the 1600s, but the present splendid Palladian villa was built by Francis Sadleir around 1745; after his death in 1797, the estates passed through the 1754 marriage of his daughter Mary to Frederick Trench (1724–97) of Woodlawn, Co. Galway. Of the two early porters' lodges, that to the north has gone but the other survives at the south-eastern approach.

Picturesque lodge; pre-1840/*c.* 1860.
Remote from the road is a lodge that may have originated as a simple single-storey standard cottage, perhaps built in the time of Francis Trench (1757–1829) but probably developed by his son, Frederick Mason Trench (1804–80), 2nd Baron Ashtown, into the present four-bay 1½-storey affair with roughcast walls, quoins and a dormer window. The antique gatescreen has an unusual postilion stile opening.

It was this Lord Ashtown who carried out considerable improvements to the property to plans of the Ballinsloe architect J.F. Kempster, whom he was employing on his Galway estates. He was certainly responsible for the new main entrance and lodge.

Classical lodge; *c.* 1860; architect probably J.F. Kempster.
A striking single-storey standard hipped-roof lodge of generous proportions, with an elegant pedimented frontispiece in cut limestone having a pair of chaste Greek Doric columns *in antis*. Very correct on its own but curiously flanked by a pair of narrow windows of one-over-one sashes with

304. Sopwell Hall, Ballingarry (N), classical lodge.

corbelled sills and Italianate moulded surrounds taken about the segmental arches, all in stucco-effect walls framed by limestone quoins. To the end elevations are twin windows similarly treated, and to the ridge a big central three-flue stack with plinth and extending corniced capping. Rubble stone quadrant walls and plain pillars contain spiky-topped railings and matching carriage gates hung on cast-iron pillars with the familiar anthemion motifs in hooped tops.

Tudor Revival lodge; *c.* 1860; architect possibly J.F. Kempster.

At the northern entrance is this charming 1½-storey standard gabled lodge in mellow rubble facings with dressed and label-moulded openings. Pretty multi-squared glazed casements with wooden mullions flank a front door with rectangular fanlight below high eaves to accommodate the attic floor; minimal skew-tables and kneeler blocks.

One of Lord Ashtown's gatekeepers in 1852 was Michael Cummins.

Griffith 1853–63; *LGI* (1904); *BPB* (1929); Bence-Jones 1988.

305. SOUTH LODGE, Windgap (2).
Only one lodge, and it demolished, is evident on the OS maps of 1840 and 1906. The valuation of 1853 identifies two, however, with Michael Ryan and Mrs Shelly as gatekeepers to Richard C. Jackson, who succeeded Richard Branagan, proprietor here in 1814. A date-stone inscribed 'I.B. 1737' on the stables reveals the antiquity of the property.

Leet 1814; Griffith 1853–63; NIAH.

306. SPRING, Tipperary (2).
The lands, previously of the McCarthys, were acquired around 1820 by John Low of Cork, who set about building the present Classical villa, probably to designs of fellow Corkman John Hargrave, a commission which may have included the early porter's lodge. This was located about 500 yards south of the house by a public road subsequently absorbed into the demesne around 1870, at which time it seems to have been demolished. On the other hand, there is good reason to believe that it may have been dismantled and re-erected at the new western entrance to the estate and is that of early nineteenth-century appearance now associated with Arraghslea [*q.v.*]. Its successor on the present Caher–Tipperary road seems to have originated as a police station around 1835 but was 'surrendered' in 1872 and acquired by Francis Wise Low, who had succeeded to the estate around 1850 after the death of his brother Simon.

This is understandably generous accommodation for a gatekeeper, the main body of it being a 1½-storey roughcast structure with English Picturesque Cottage appearance, probably completely transformed when converted, as appears from its two-over-two sash windows and geometric-styled ornamental bargeboards. Two-bay to the road with gablets over, the end gable contains a single-storey canted bay window commanding the gates. From the opposing gable extends a single-storey gabled addition, while to the rear a single-storey return with a pair of round-arched sash windows with spoke-topped glazing is probably all that is recognisable from the old barracks. A property also known as 'Kilshane' down the years.

Wilson 1803; *LGI* (1904); Bence-Jones 1988.

SPRINGFIELD (see COUNTY WATERFORD)

307. SPRINGFIELD, Newinn; pre-1906; *demolished.*
A lodge built after 1840 at the gates to a mid-eighteenth-century farmhouse, property in the nineteenth century of the Doocy family.

308. SPRINGHILL, Killenaule; 1880.

Opposite the gates to an elegant Classical villa of *c.* 1810, home in 1814 to Dr Samuel Hemphill, is this equally smart single-storey standard lodge with a high, oversailing, steeply pitched hipped roof, with gutterless eaves, rising to a heavily corniced chimney-stack. Tucked in below the eaves is a little gabled porch with wooden post support, flanked by paired casements with latticed glazing, very much as at Ardsallagh [*q.v.*], all in a rendered finish. Dated 1880 but looking earlier. Probably built for Charles H. Hemphill.

Leet 1814; Bassett 1889.

309. SPRINGVALE COTTAGE, Tipperary; pre-1906; *demolished.*
A Regency villa, home in the mid-nineteenth century to Patrick Joseph Bourke, who probably added the porter's lodge. Around 1900 it became an adjunct of the bigger house, which was renamed 'The Vale'.

Slater 1846; 1856; NIAH.

310. SRADUFF, Birr; *c.* 1840.
A standard single-storey hip-roofed lodge with clipped eaves and wide windows on each side of a doorway with keystone to lintel over in harled rubble walls. Shown lightly hatched on the first OS map, which suggests that it was then under construction. Now abandoned and windowless, but not as decayed as the shell of its big house on the hill beyond. Built for Thomas Antisell, proprietor in 1837 and 1852 on a farm of 318 acres.

Lewis 1837; Griffith 1853–63.

311. STREAM VALE, Clonmel; 1860; *demolished.*
A mid-Victorian villa now known as 'Northfield'; it and its contemporary porter's lodge were a development for John Leslie Worrall.

312. SUIR CASTLE, Golden; pre-1841; *demolished.*
Another property in 1783 of Hugh Massy (1700–88), 1st baron, of Hermitage, Co. Limerick [*q.v.*], and Killakee, Co. Dublin, although the present house is a typical single-storey-over-basement villa of the Regency period, presumably built for the 4th baron, Hugh Hammond Massy (1793–1836), then letting to Joseph Robbins. There survives a good cast-iron entrance comprised of a triple gateway with pretty carriage posts containing palmette motifs in inverted hearts, all terminating in outer limestone pillars. A lodge that also served as a police station in 1841.

Taylor and Skinner 1778; 1783; Leet 1814; *BPB* (1929).

313. SUIR COTTAGE, Holycross; pre-1840; *demolished.*
A seat in the early nineteenth century of the Armstrong family.

SUIRMOUNT (see GREENMOUNT)

314. SUMMERHILL, Clonmel; *c.* 1825.

A superb late Georgian gatescreen served as introduction to the residence in 1814 and 1824 of Revd George Miles. Comprised of four Classical stone pillars with fluted friezes and moulded corniced cappings, those to the carriage opening crowned by excellent pedestalled pine cones. Between, in strikingly contrasting whitened screen stucco-effect walls, are postern openings, all the gates original with spear tops. Elevated to the left-hand side is a contemporary porter's lodge—single-storey below a hipped roof with banded stone chimney-stack, its short leading front two-bay of modern casements set in segmentally arched recesses in roughcast walls. All immaculately tended.

Leet 1814; Pigot 1824.

315. SUMMERHILL, Moneygall; pre-1904; *demolished.*
A seat in the mid-nineteenth century of the Shortt family, the gate lodge to which, opposite its entrance, was erected after 1840.

316. SUMMERHILL, Nenagh; pre-1900; *demolished.*
A property in 1846 of Major Laurence Dundas until his death in 1866, and for five years thereafter of his widow. He may have been the builder of the porter's lodge after 1840, the house having been erected in 1836.

Slater 1846; *LGI* (1904); NIAH.

317. SUMMERVILLE, Clonmel (2).

317. Summerville, Clonmel, Gortmore gate (IAA).

Also known as 'Ballingarrane' after its townland, this was an estate in 1824 of William Harding Bradshaw, letting from the absentee Watson family, to which both lodges, built before 1846 opposite their gates, have gone.

Ballingarrane north gate; pre-1840; *demolished.*
A recent bungalow now views the entrance from across the road. Surviving are tall pillars with pine-cone finials guarding the gate to the farmyard.

Gortmore gate; *c.* 1810; *demolished.*
Opposite the main gate with its V-jointed rusticated carriage pillars with fluted friezes and vase finials was a single-storey standard steeply hip-roofed Georgian Gothic porter's lodge with lancet-headed openings, that of the central doorway emphasised by a little gable over. Valued in 1850 for as little as seventeen shillings, it was subsequently enlarged in like manner with the addition of single-bay wings set back to each end. Swept away by road-widening after 1977.

Pigot 1824; Griffith 1853–63; IAA photographs (S/339/9810).

SWISS COTTAGE (see CAHER COTTAGE)

318. SYNONE, Cashel; *c.* 1865; *demolished.*
A long, five-bay, symmetrical 1½-storey gabled lodge, built around the time of the big house's creation for the Johnston family—a large, gabled villa farmhouse.

Slater 1870.

319. TEMPLEMORE ABBEY, Templemore (4).
Long known as 'The Priory', the estate was associated with the same family since John Carden settled here around 1650 and lived to the age of 105. After the castle succumbed to fire in the mid-eighteenth century, his descendants built a succession of replacements. William Vitruvius Morrison enlarged a Gothic cottage in 1819 for Sir John Craven Carden, 1st baronet, a year before his client's death. His son, Sir Arthur, only lived until 1822 and was succeeded by his younger brother, Sir Henry Robert Carden (1789–1847), at the time of whose death there were three porters' lodges to the property, none of which survive. It was the 4th baronet, Sir John Craven Carden (1819–79), who put the finishing touches to the estate, completing the mansion in Tudor Gothic style and commissioning designs for three new gate lodges, some perhaps to plans by Sir Thomas Newenham Deane, who was working at nearby Killoskehane Castle [*q.v.*] and for the Cardens at Barnane [*q.v.*]. All are of unusually generous proportions.

Adamstown gate; pre-1840.
At the north-western boundary is this ruin of a gabled rubble-built gatekeeper's lodge, accommodation in 1850 for porter Jeremiah Wall.

Abbey Road gate; pre-1840/*c.* 1860.

A substantial two-storey gatehouse, multi-gabled with skew-tables and kneelers in Tudor Revival manner, built off an irregular and extensive plan in uncoursed limestone ashlar with label mouldings to openings, lost to hideous refenestration on the avenue front. An informal elevation to the park has a later glazed entrance porch flanked by a two-storey breakfront to one side and a single-storey semi-octagonal bay window with equivalent roof to the other. A replacement lodge, the variety of materials, size and complex outline of which suggest that it evolved, perhaps at some stage accommodating the Cardens while work to the big house was being carried out.

Church Street gate; pre-1840/1853.

At the old eastern approach, superseding an earlier porter's lodge, is another sizeable building. Of 1½ storeys, raised in pleasant rubble facings off a T-plan formed by a central projection, like the main gables with a simple clipped verge. Flat-arched ground-floor openings and lancet-headed attic windows all display modern inappropriate glazing patterns to the detriment of the original Gothic effect. To the main ridge, symmetrically placed, are two matching banks of triple diagonally set stone flues in Tudor style, each on a hefty base, while to an internal corner is a single-storey lean-to hallway, over which is a cut-stone shield with the date of construction. A structure that may also have housed the steward to the demesne. Extensive railed surround on dwarf limestone plinth.

Richmond Road gate; *c.* 1860; architect possibly Sir T.N. Deane.

A result of the final building phase of 1856–63 is this conspicuous main entrance with its extensive gatescreen of four tall cut-limestone pillars with their scroll-topped piers, moulded cornices and curved cappings containing a triple gateway, the decorative ironwork to which only survives to the postilion openings. Behind one concave-walled quadrant is the striking 1½-storey Tudor Gothic lodge built off a T-plan in fine uncoursed limestone ashlar terminating in moulded kneelers and skew-tables with tiny ball finials. The showpiece elevation to the avenue displays elliptically arched chamfered bipartite label-moulded windows, that to the ground floor flanked by mock arrowloops and framed by buttressed corners, while that to the attic has blank shields to each side and a roundel over. To the park front is a blind lower floor with a pair of oriel gablets on curved corbels. The big chimney-stack base is probably now missing ornamental pots.

Lewis in 1837 records that 'One of the entrances to the Park is a remnant of the castle of the Knights Templar', perhaps that described by Wakeman in 1883 as 'a fine pointed archway'. It appears to have perished along with the outstanding Tudor Gothic mansion, which was destroyed by fire in 1922 and later levelled.

Lewis 1837; Griffith 1853–63; Wakeman 1883; Bassett 1889; *BPB* (1929); Bence-Jones 1988; McParland *et al.* 1989.

320. TEMPLEMORE RECTORY, Templemore; *c.* 1830.

Compared to the glebe house designed by Thomas Cooley in 1783, described in the *Post chaise companion* as one of the best in Ireland, the gatehouse is comparatively modest. A two-storey symmetrical house with a main front of two-bay over three-bay ground floor with projecting single-storey hall, gabled like the main body; rendered, with one-over-one sashes in paired openings. Probably built during the incumbency (1789–*c.* 1833) of the long-serving Revd Dr Henry Meggs Graves (1735–*c.* 1833).

Wilson 1803; Seymour and Leslie 2012.

321. Thomastown Castle, Golden (IAA).

321. THOMASTOWN CASTLE, Golden (3).

Country Life

The Mathew family has been associated with these parts since the 1600s and their old house formed the core of the turreted Gothic extravaganza, with its massive kitchen and stable courts adjoining, and its light blue painted livery creating a fantastic sight in the landscape. All this was created around 1812 by Richard Morrison for Sir Francis James Mathew (d. 1833), the 2nd and last Lord Llandaff, who had inherited the property in 1806. Of the two porters' lodges in place by 1840 off the Cashel–Tipperary road there is no trace, but an inner gatehouse survives just short of the approach to the outbuildings.

Of a pattern that the Morrison office also provided for their clients at Glenarm Castle, Co. Antrim, and Borris, Co. Carlow, it is an impressive two-storey structure in the Tudor Gothic Castellated manner, constructed of stucco-faced brickwork and stone dressings about a Tudor carriage archway flanked on one front by buttresses and on the other by square turrets with crenellated and machicolated tops which rise to frame carved family bearings and a label-moulded tripartite window for accommodation over. Spanning above are machicolated castellated ramparts, the whole liberally provided with medieval mock cross arrowloops, the outline enlivened by a lofty octagonal stair-tower to one side and a single-storey postern structure to the other.

Dating from *c.* 1815, it lies in an advanced state of dilapidation, a prelude to the huge ivy-covered shell of the Mathew mansion beyond.

Country Life (2 October 1969); *IFR*; McParland *et al.* 1989; IAA photograph (16/90 Z1); Dean 1994.

THORNVALE (see COUNTY OFFALY)

322. THURLESBEG, Cashel; *c.* 1845.

A single-storey standard gabled cottage with a projecting gabled hall, harled with a nice ochre wash finish; derelict. A property in the mid-nineteenth century of the Phillips family.

323. THURLES PALACE (RC), Thurles; pre-1888; *demolished.*

A lodge built after 1840, perhaps in the time of Archbishop Revd Dr Slattery.

324. THURLES RECTORY, Thurles; pre-1840; *demolished.*

A lodge that may have been contemporary with the building of the glebe house in 1820 during the incumbency (1815–28) of Revd George Forster (1770–1832).

Pigot 1824; Lewis 1837; Seymour and Leslie 2012.

325. THURLES UNION WORKHOUSE, Thurles; *c.* 1850; architect possibly George Wilkinson.

A tall building, rendered, with stone chimney-stacks to each clipped-verge gable, three-bay and astylar after being deprived of all its original Tudor Gothic detailing. Post-dating George Wilkinson's workhouse of 1842. Now horribly exposed by a roundabout.

O'Connor 1995.

326. TIMONEY PARK, Roscrea; *c.* 1850; architect not known.

'... [T]he seat of J.D. Hutchinson, Esq., is situated on rising ground surrounded by hills finely wooded, and by plantations covering 100 acres; the grounds are embellished with timber of stately growth, and contain some of the largest spruce and Scottish fir trees in the country. Great improvements have been made on this estate by the proprietor, and much rocky mountainous waste land has been reclaimed.' Such was the hope, confidence and ambition pertaining in 1836 that it is poignant today to witness the sad remains of that once-proud property, with its big house in ruins. But as a beacon is its gatehouse, surviving in pristine condition, built by the improving John Dawson Hutchinson (1796–1881), who had inherited Timoney Park in 1831. Two-storey and exceptionally large in an English Picturesque Cottage idiom, with perforated foiled bargeboards having quatrefoil-carved toes, it rises off an L-plan in mellow rubble stone facings, with brick dressings to tall casement windows arranged in bipartite and tripartite form. To one gable is a breakfront while to the other is a catslide-roofed projection; the main roof similarly catslides over the internal angle to form a hall with pretty Tudor-arched doorway and, alongside, a recess with brick pier support terminating in a cut-stone capital. Much extended sensitively to the rear.

J.D. Hutchinson died without male heirs and the rot set in.

Lewis 1837; *LGI* (1904).

327. TINHALLA, Carrick-on-Suir; *c.* 1790.

On the border with County Waterford is a gatescreen, plain but for the decorative carved urns to the carriage pillars—cupped in acanthus-leafed pedestals with fluted bodies, flower-headed rims and flaming stoppers. Alongside on the roadside is the ivy-shrouded ruin of a hefty Georgian Gothic lodge with a hipped roof over stone walls, cut-stone eaves course and lancet openings in dressed stone. An antique seventeenth-century farmhouse, the property of Patrick Power (*c.* 1751–1827) in 1824.

Pigot 1824; *LGI* (1904).

328. TINNAKILLY, Riverstown; *c.* 1835.

Now known as 'Baronne Court', this was the seat in 1837 of Arthur and Robert Robinson, at the entrance to which is an extensive forecourt with a segmental railed screen with six octagonal stone pillars having fluted friezes containing a triple gateway. Within is

328. Tinnakilly, Riverstown.

a sizeable gatekeeper's lodge, single-storey on a cruciform plan below an oversailing hipped roof with paired moulded modillion brackets to its soffits. Single-window bays flank the central symmetrical three-bay entrance projection, the whole neatly smooth-rendered with twentieth-century decorative banding to the narrow casements and external corners; stopping the ridges is a wide chimney-stack with moulded capping. All immaculate and well tended.

Lewis 1837.

329. TINVANE, Carrick-on-Suir; *c.* 1820.
What was a single-storey hip-roofed lodge, almost unrecognisable through improvement and extension, although a window in a segmentally arched recess to ground level on the road elevation is clearly original. The entrance screen has simple punched limestone pillars with modest cornices, blockings and plinths, and posts and chains to quadrants. Now 'Cedarfield Country Home', it was a seat of the Briscoes of Ballinter, Co. Meath, of whom Henry Whitby Briscoe (1777–1834) was resident in 1814 and until his death.

Leet 1814; *LG* (1886); Bence-Jones 1988.

330. TRAVERSTOWN, Silvermines; *c.* 1810.
The important eighteenth-century mansion, probably designed by William Leeson for Robert Going, has gone, with its once-fine gate lodge soon to follow.

Built for Thomas Going (1767–1841), despite its reduced state it is still recognisable as having had a designed principal short front with round-headed niches on each side of an elliptically arched opening (now blocked-up), an elevation which seems to have once been behind a tetrastyle portico. Single-storey and two-roomed below a hipped roof with clipped eaves, modernisation has seen the insertion of loft accommodation and the whole wrapped in bland cement rendering; derelict. The niche theme is repeated on the outer piers containing angled screen walls.

LGI (1904).

331. TULLAGHORTON RECTORY, Clogheen; pre-1840; *demolished.*
The porter's lodge opposite the gates had been removed by 1907. The glebe house ceased to be such after 1836, when the office of vicar was suspended and the residence became known as 'Parson's Green', Revd Charles Tuckey having been the last incumbent between 1802 and 1836.

Knox 2008.

332. TULLAMAINE CASTLE, Fethard; pre-1840/*c.* 1880.
Architect William Tinsley's venture into the Tudor Castellated style is this battlemented mansion for John Maher (d. 1850), built between 1835 and 1838. The lodge would seem to be of later date, presumably for Henry Maynard Harding, who was resident in 1876, and to replace an earlier lodge on the site when James Scully was proprietor.

Single-storey standard with a chimney-stack to each gable and generously proportioned, with pretty canted glazed windows in roughcast walls flanking a later gabled glazed hall-cum-conservatory.

Leet 1814; Pigot 1824; *LOI*; *IFR*; Forbes 1953.

333. TULLAMORE PARK, Nenagh; *c.* 1840.
Almost a shell is this single-storey standard lodge with a hipped roof and gabled entrance breakfront, the walls in stone facings with brick soldier arches, wedged in behind a concave-walled and railed quadrant, one of two framing a triple gateway of chunky cast-iron gates and pillars. Presumably built for Edward Finch, who died in 1843, to be followed by three of his sons, who succeeded to the place in quick succession.

Lewis 1837; *LGI* (1904).

334. TURTULLA HOUSE AND FLOUR MILLS, Thurles; pre-1840; *demolished.*
An early house acquired by Nicholas Maher, whose son, Valentine Maher (1780–1844), remodelled and enlarged it in Tudor Revival style to designs of William Tinsley in 1837–8. The lodge had been demolished by 1952, when the demesne had become a golf club.

IFR; Forbes 1953.

URRA LODGE (see ST DAVID'S)

THE VALE (see SPRINGVALE COTTAGE)

335. VERDANTHILL, Roscrea; pre-1840; *demolished.*
A late Georgian villa, in 1814 a seat of John Townsend.

Leet 1814.

336. WALSHPARK, Riverstown (4).
The Walsh family connection with the estate concluded in the 1850s, at which time the old house could be approached past three lodged entrances, all in place by 1839. Two remain, the other replaced on the coming of William Henry Head (1809–88) of the Modreeny House [*q.v.*] family. He considerably improved the property, renaming it 'Derrylahan Park', replacing the Walsh home with a fashionable new pile in the High Victorian Ruskinian Gothic manner in 1862–5 to designs of Sir Thomas Newenham Deane and building two new gate lodges.

West gate; *c.* 1780.
The remains of a single-storey gabled Georgian Gothic lodge with limewashed harled rubble walls, the main short avenue front displaying what was once triple pointed-arched fenestration, the central doorway (since reduced to a flat head) flanked by a pair of little lancet windows (now blocked-up). What was once a building of considerable architectural significance is now reduced to a sheep shelter.

East gate; *c.* 1800.
Now sidetracked by a realigned road is the ruin of a standard single-storey gabled lodge with tiny windows in harled walls.

Inner gate; *c.* 1865; architect probably Sir T.N. Deane.
On the western approach is this substantial 1½-storey gabled lodge built off an L-plan, its roughcast walls containing single, bipartite and tripartite windows, all dressed in chamfered stone with arrowhead arches. In the internal corner is a single-storey gabled hall.

Main gate; pre-1839/*c.* 1865; architect probably Sir T.N. Deane.
A replacement on the northern avenue for the Walshes' principal lodge is this impressive entrance in beautifully chiselled limestone, uncoursed. More Tudor in feel than the Gothic of Deane's big house, it fronts the road as a pair of tall carriage pillars with roll-moulded corners and corbelled cappings linked by a wall containing the shouldered-arched postern opening to the 1½-storey lodge, with its leading skew-tabled and kneelered gable containing a bipartite loft window with chamfered reveals above a rectangular bay window, lacking a side light to view visitors. To the avenue is an irregular façade with door and window and overhead a gablet with lancet light, very much in the Benjamin Woodward manner. From the opposing wall rises a lofty chimney-stack;

336. Walshpark, Riverstown, west gate.

336. Walshpark, Riverstown, inner gate (Perrott).

336. Walshpark, Riverstown, Main gate lodge (Perrott).

the ridges bear ornate fleur-de-lis cresting. All well rehabilitated but no longer the appropriate prelude to the Head house beyond, it having been torched in 1921.

LGI (1904); Williams 1994; O'Dwyer 1997b.

337. WATERLOO LODGE, Ballinderry; *c.* 1855.
Probably originating as a 1½-storey gabled Picturesque cottage on an L-plan with an Italianate rusticated feature to the road elevation, it has since been imaginatively altered and extended to one side with an eccentric oval window in rendered walls. Occupied. A property that probably originated after 1815, it being the residence of Revd R.P. Vaughan in 1837 and fourteen years later of Edward Biggs.

Lewis 1837; Griffith 1853–63.

338. WATERLOO LODGE, Caher; pre-1840; *demolished.*
A seat in 1824 of William and C. Porter O'Brien.

Pigot 1824.

339. WELLINGTON, Nenagh; pre-1840; *demolished.*
An estate in 1837 of W. Smithwick Esq., which, like the two previous entries, probably originated after the Battle of Waterloo.

Lewis 1837.

340. WOODENSTOWN, Newinn; pre-1840.
A junior branch of the Carews of Castleboro, Co. Wexford, lived here, represented in 1824 by Alexander Carew and thirteen years later by Robert Carew. The lodge had been removed by 1906.

Pigot 1824; Lewis 1837.

341. WOODROOFE, Caher (4).
The seat of the Perry family since the seventeenth century, its fine mid-eighteenth-century house demolished, the estate devastated and not one of its lodges surviving as built.

Clonmel gate; pre-1840; *demolished.*
A pair of lodges marked this entrance, which may have announced it as being the principal approach.

Caher gate; *c.* 1830.
Having been developed into a modern house, the only clue as to its previous appearance is in the ground-floor windows set in arched recesses, suggesting a Regency origin.

Rear inner gate; pre-1840; *demolished.*

Rear outer gate; *c.* 1830; architect possibly William Tinsley.

The lodge remains much modernised and extended but with some evidence surviving of openings set in semicircular-arched recesses; sculpted plaques in the walls display the Perry crest—a hind's head with pear-tree branch in mouth—decorated with swags. Presumably an entrance created for William Perry (1793–1869), who succeeded his father to the property in 1829. His architect may well have been William Tinsley of nearby Clonmel, for the four gate

341. Woodroofe, Caher, rear outer gate.

pillars are almost identical to those at Castle Park [*q.v.*] and similar to The Grove [*q.v.*] examples. Tall and slender with moulded plinths and recessed panels, the friezes are embellished with laurel wreaths below oversailing cornices with distinctive anthemion acroteria as cappings.

LGI (1904); Bence-Jones 1988.

342. WOODVILLE, Moneygall (2).
Another estate in this vicinity of the Minchin family, neither of the pre-1840 gate lodges to which survive.

343. WOODVILLE, Templemore; pre-1840; *demolished.*
A late Georgian villa built for Daniel James Webb (1780–1850), perhaps to mark his marriage in 1812 for he is recorded here in 1814. The lodge opposite the gates may have been contemporary and of some import, for it is seen as cruciform on plan on the first OS map. Captain Webb's gatekeeper in the year of his death was Margaret Whittaker.

Leet 1814; Griffith 1853–63; *LGI* (1904).

COUNTY WATERFORD

Kilculliheen parish north of the River Suir has been transferred several times between counties Waterford and Kilkenny; properties therein are treated under the latter (see Dean 2016).

ABBEY CHURCH AND GRAVEYARD (see COUNTY KILKENNY)

1. AFFANE, Cappoquin (2).
A now-ruinous house with seventeenth-century origins which down the years has changed families twice, passing to Major Edmund Browning on his marriage to the sister and heiress of the previous owner, Valentine Greatrakes. It remained with the Brownings until the death without male heir of Samuel Browning (1743–83), when it passed, through the wedding in 1762 of his sister Elizabeth, to Pierce Power (d. 1815). His descendants remained here until 1945, after which the place went into decline. It may have been Pierce Power who improved the two estate entrances.

East gate; pre-1841.

Rather peculiarly located at a Y-junction across the public road from the access is a ruinous three-bay harled lodge, almost completely overgrown but zealously protected by an angry farmer. The entrance screen was quite handsome but is now much neglected, consisting of a noble pair of ashlar carriage pillars with plain friezes, finely chiselled moulded cappings and bases for missing finials. To each side screen walls contain round-headed postilion openings complete with sophisticated imposts and keystones. The pretty contemporary ironwork to the gates of *c.* 1790, now giving onto a field, may be contemporary with its seemingly unrelated porter's lodge.

West gate; *c.* 1800.
A derelict single-storey standard hip-roofed cottage with clipped eaves and small window openings, facing the road alongside a gatescreen comprised of round gate pillars with rectangular recesses. Flanking are concave quadrant walls, one with a postern gate, the other having a blind recess for balance.

LGI (1863); *IFR*; Bence-Jones 1988.

ANNMOUNT (see COUNTY KILKENNY)

ARDKEEN (see ELVA LODGE)

2. BALLINAMONA, Waterford (3).
The long-time seat of the Carews, descended from that family of Castleboro, Co. Wexford, whose house now appears as late Georgian with wings, much altered down the years and rebuilt after a fire in 1889. Following the death of Robert Thomas Carew I in 1834, his elder son Thomas (1775–1853) set about a phase of improvements on the estate, with the creation of an additional entrance and the provision of two porters' lodges to the same pattern.

Ballindud gate; *c.* 1839.

Opposite the entrance to the north of the demesne is a perfectly symmetrical single-storey hip-roofed lodge on a T-plan, its leading wing having a semi-octagonal front with corresponding roof oversailing to form a verandah and carried on new fluted concrete columns. Now much added to in sympathy, but with synthetic 'slated' roof and stucco-effect sand/cement rendering. Across the road is an older triple gateway with plain stone pillars displaying elegant pineapple finials. The gatekeeper in 1848 was Catherine Broderick. Coincidence it may be, but there is an almost identical lodge to Torc Cottage, Co. Kerry [*q.v.*].

Coolgower gate; *c.* 1842.

In 1841 a short-cut avenue was being constructed between the two county roads leading to the secondary gate. Distant, and similarly opposite, lies an almost identical lodge, lacking only a verandah, in its original form, not having been subjected to modern improvements. The gatescreen has pillars familiar in the county, possibly the work of George Richard Pain. The triple gateway is comprised of elongated octagonal limestone pillars with reeded panels to the shafts and gadrooned 'splashes' to their cappings,

features also to be found at Ballyglan [*q.v.*], Derriheen [*q.v.*], Whitechurch [*q.v.*] and Woodhouse [*q.v.*].

South gate; *c.* 1855.
A single-storey two-bay lodge with half-doors to the right-hand side and casement windows in stucco-effect walls below a hipped roof with oversailing eaves which exhibits fancy carved wavy fascia boards. Probably built for Robert Thomas Carew II (1809–86) on succeeding to the property on the death of his father.

Griffith 1853–63; Bence-Jones 1988; *IFR*; Craig and Garner 1977.

3. BALLINDUD, Waterford; *c.* 1860.
Next to their main property of Ballinamona [*q.v.*], this was the Carew's secondary residence—seat of the younger son. Their lodge is a standard, unprepossessing affair, with segmentally arched windows in rendered walls below a steeply hipped roof; derelict.

IFR.

4. BALLYCANVAN, Passage East; *c.* 1830.
The sad remains of a once-proud demesne of the Boltons of Mount Bolton [*q.v.*], who also built nearby Faithlegg [*q.v.*] before selling both to the Power family in 1819. Ballycanvan descended into housing a succession of tenants, amongst whom were Samuel Roberts in 1814 and Richard Morris in 1837. The mansion now lies a ruin, at the gate a plain single-storey gabled structure.

Leet 1814; Lewis 1837; Bence-Jones 1988.

5. BALLYCAR, Waterford; 1894.
Matching the contemporary house is this dull Italianate affair in a drab grey rendering. Single-storey on an L-plan below a hipped roof with a moulded corniced and banded chimney-stack on a plinth to reflect the main plinth, moulded sill course and eaves frieze. In the internal angle is a minuscule flat-

roofed hall with a one-over-one sash window as elsewhere.

Built for Herbert William Davis-Goff (1870–1923) while he waited to succeed his father as 2nd baronet to the neighbouring property of Glenville [*q.v.*], which he did in 1917. Lodges to both seats lie back to back. Rather more innovative are the gate pillars, with their conspicuous 'crazy-paved' panels, rebated corners and complex cappings; the decorative ironwork is of an age.

Thom's (1910); *BPB* (1929).

6. BALLYGALLY, Ballyduff; *c.* 1815; architect probably Sir Richard Morrison.

If there was any doubt that this elegant villa by the banks of the Blackwater was conceived in the office of Richard Morrison it should already have been scotched for the visitor at the entrance gates to the demesne, for they are of a formula purveyed by Morrison throughout the island early in his career and are to be found elsewhere in the county at Clashmore [*q.v.*] and Moorehill [*q.v.*]. It is a triple gateway, with the familiar 'drum' carriage pillars flanked by a pair of larger square postilion ones with simple recessed panels. Within is the derelict single-storey lodge, now lacking much of its original character through neglect. Most of Morrison's lodges featured a leading short elevation, here with a three-bay symmetrical front rather than his usual tripartite windows, recessed below a full-width gable, or pediment, probably having incorporated a pair of columns *in antis*, now missing. About its verge are extended brackets carried around from the eaves. The narrow casement windows have cast-iron latticed glazing, perhaps replacements when a wing was added at right angles to the rear *c.* 1830. All apparently a commission for George Giles, who is recorded as resident in 1814. By the mid-nineteenth century it had become home to Nelson Trafalgar Foley.

Leet 1814.

7. BALLYGLAN, Dunmore East; *c.* 1810.
A big house built about the time of his marriage in 1771 by Sir Joshua Paul of Paulville, Co. Carlow. It was his son, Sir Joshua Christmas Paul (1773–1842), who added the porter's lodge not long after inheriting Ballyglan on his father's death in 1799. It is a single-storey cottage with modern rendering and Irish pilaster quoins below a roof with hipped gables. It is set well back from its gatescreen, which is comprised of four octagonal pillars with reeded recessed panels and gadrooned 'splashes' to the cappings, all of a pattern to be found at the gates to Ballinamona [*q.v.*], Derriheen [*q.v.*], Whitechurch [*q.v.*] and nearby Woodstown [*q.v.*], either created by a local mason or to designs of George Richard Pain.

BPB (1929); Bence-Jones 1988.

8. BALLYMABIN COTTAGE, Dunmore East; pre-1841; *demolished.*
A lodge to a property in 1851 of James Murphy that had gone by 1925.

Griffith 1853–63.

9. BALLYMAKEE, Newcastle; *c.* 1810.
Opposite a relatively sophisticated gatescreen with ball-finialled carriage pillars is a modest single-storey gabled cottage lying derelict. A property in 1837 of Edmund Mulcahy, whose family are recorded here from the early seventeenth century.

Lewis 1837; *LGI* (1904).

10. BALLYNACOURTY, Dungarvan; pre-1841; *demolished.*
An early nineteenth-century house built by Robert Longan, who is recorded here as late as 1856.

Pigot 1824; Slater 1856.

11. BALLYNADIGUE, Lismore; *c.* 1950.
Until 1893 known as 'Bellevue', it remarkably remained lodgeless until the mid-twentieth century, when Col. Johnson J. O'Brien added this apparently late Victorian cottage, its true age only revealed by a surviving Crittal McKinney steel window. Single-storey with a two-window-bay avenue elevation in roughcast below a hipped roof with a pretty fretted fascia board right around, all crowned by a hefty corbelled, dentil-coursed, red-brick chimney-stack with stone capping. The inner triple gateway with a pair of slender cast-iron fluted, knob-topped carriage posts may be contemporary, but the framing ashlar corniced pillars date from the time of Paul Shewcraft in the early nineteenth century.

Griffith 1853–63.

12. BALLYNAKILL, Waterford (2).
An antique house, much altered down the centuries, seat in 1783 of Hannibal William Dobbyn, it was purchased five years later by Nicholas Power (1725–94) of Knockaderry [*q.v.*]. After his death the property was occupied alternately by that family and tenants, of whom Lt. Robinson Thomas RN was one in the mid-nineteenth century and whose gatekeeper in 1848 was William Honan. Both this pre-1839 outer lodge and another within, added later, have been demolished.

Taylor and Skinner 1778; 1783; Wilson 1803; Lewis 1837; Griffith 1853–63; Craig and Garner 1977; *IFR*.

13. BALLYNAPARKA, Villierstown; pre-1841; *demolished.*
The gate lodge, located opposite its gates, to a house in 1837 of Thomas Joseph Fitzgerald had been removed before 1927.

Lewis 1837.

14. BALLYNATRAY, Clashmore (6).
In its stunning and romantic setting by the River Blackwater, the distinguished Classical mansion owes its appearance to a major rebuilding in 1795 by Grice Smyth (*c.* 1762–1816) and its survival to an inspired restoration 200 years later, which almost certainly saved it from oblivion. As befits an estate of this size and importance, it was heralded down the years by an abundance of porters' lodges at its plentiful entrance gates, some of which would benefit from the attention recently lavished on the big house. Only two inner lodges to the demesne would date from Grice Smyth's time here.

North inner gate; pre-1841; *demolished.*

South inner gate; pre-1841.
A ruinous single-storey gabled structure, survived by a pair of slender, V-jointed, rusticated limestone ashlar carriage pillars, each flanked by semicircular-arched postilion openings to create a triple gateway of able craftsmanship but naive design.

The four outer lodges on the periphery of the estate bounded by the public road date from the occupancy of Richard Smyth (1796–1858), who succeeded to the property as eldest son on the death of his father.

Newport Bridge gate; *c.* 1845.
On the northern approach is this quintessential and unassuming gate lodge, single-storey standard with terracotta-coloured harled walls below a hipped roof. Now lying abandoned and boarded up.

Western gate; pre-1927; *demolished.*
Replaced by a twentieth-century bungalow.

Glendine Bridge gate; *c.* 1845.
Barely visible behind rampant vegetation is this once-fine pair of lodges, or rather lodge, for this 'day and night' accommodation is in the form of single-roomed Classical cubes separated by a narrow carriage gateway with a pair of cut-stone pillars. Each is a single-storey box of a single-window bay back and front, below a parapeted roof defined by moulded stone copings and string-course. Now sealed up, lacking their rendered finish to reveal rubble construction and crying out

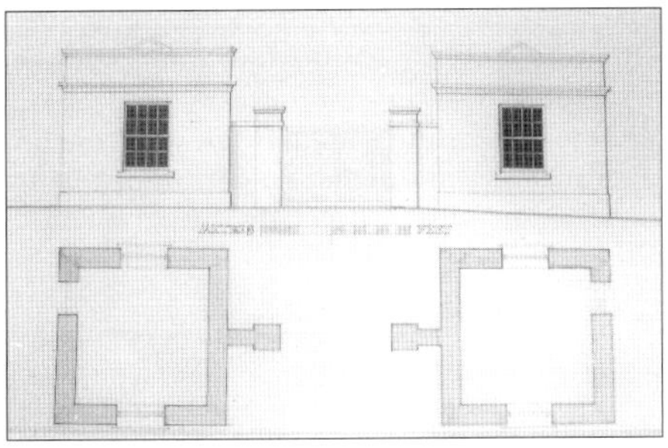

for restoration to their former glory.

Main gate; *c.* 1845.

Very definitely intended as the principal entrance is this triple gateway, which divides a true pair of porters' lodges, each two-roomed in its own right. Both matching single-storey standard, they face the visitor, their plain three-bay symmetrical fronts rather weighed down by ungainly parapets with recessed panels between dressed stone courses; conspicuously restored. Previously harled. This approach from the south was created via a causeway across a muddy river estuary.

Burke 1854–5; *LGI* (1904); Pike and Hodges 1911; Bence-Jones 1988.

15. BALLYSAGGARTMORE, Lismore (3).

Two of the most admired and illustrated entrances in the country, with their multiple lodges all the more remarkable for being the work of an otherwise unknown designer employed by Arthur Keily as a gardener—John Smith, no less, more credibly noted for his award-winning Oranges, Shaddocks, Noisette roses and White Muscat and Black Hamburgh grapes in the Youghal Literary and Scientific Institution Show. The young architect Henry Hill, in his *Diary of an itinerary in Ireland in 1831*, is guarded in his praise for what he found in the first known description of the gates, which were then nearing completion:

> 'Mr Kiely's [*sic*] grounds, about two miles from Lismore Bridge, worthy of the visitor's attention. An entrance gateway, great display of mountain stone in imitation of a castellated building, a particularly ugly arch of a Saracen character. However, there is considerable merit due to the gentleman who designed it (Mr Smith), who I could understand is but an amateur architect. In forming a new road to Mr Keily's house, advantage has been taken of a romantic spot to throw a bridge across. It promises to have a fine effect.'

15. Ballysaggartmore, Lismore, outer gate.

Three years later E. Hayden was more fulsome in his praise in a letter to the *Dublin Penny Journal* of 13 December 1834, in which his evocative sketches of both gateways were published:

> 'Sir—Permit me through the medium of the *Dublin Penny Journal* an opportunity of giving the public a brief description of the situation and scenery of Ballysaggartmore, the much improved residence of Arthur Keiley [*sic*], Esq., situate one mile west of Lismore, on the north side of the river Blackwater. The porter's lodge at the entrance to the avenue is composed of cut mountain granite or freestone, of a whitish colour, variegated with a brownish strata, which gives the whole a rich and pleasing appearance; it consists of a double rectangular building, in the castellated style, flanked by a round tower at either end, through which is a passage, and a carriage-way of twelve feet in the centre, over which is a perpendicular pointed arch enriched with crockets, and terminated with a finial; the buildings at either side of the gateway, although similar, form a variety in themselves; and the situation is so disposed as not to be seen until very near the approach: the gate is composed of wrought and cast iron; and is, I will venture to assert, the most perfect gothic structure, formed principally of wrought iron, in the Kingdom. It was executed by a native mechanic, and cost about one hundred and fifty pounds.
>
> Passing onward through the avenue, the road, which is perfectly level, leads through a beautifully romantic wood, neatly planted with all the varieties of fir, and other forest timber; and is naturally enriched by a limpid mountain stream, which, after passing over some very considerable rocks, and gliding down the glen, falls immediately into the Blackwater; over this stream, which in winter is often very rapid, stands the bridge, of which the prefixed engraving is a correct representation, consisting of three gothic arches, surmounted with richly embrazured battlements. A group of towers, embracing almost every shape and style of Gothic architecture, is erected at either end of the bridge; and the roadway leads under two very pretty obtuse Gothic arches. The greatest novelty in the whole is a round tower, erected on one of the arches. The stone used in the building has an agreeable reddish tint, and is all vermiculated, or, in other words, is a rusticated structure, which gives it somewhat the appearance of antiquity; this, and the gate-house, was designed and built under the inspection of Mr John Smyth.
>
> Almost adjoining the bridge is a pretty tunnel, through which a road is conducted from the town to the upper grounds; and the avenue, which leads onward to the house, has nothing more to boast of than a continuation of neatly disposed wood and shrubbery.—EH.'

Tradition has it that the money expended on the approach was to be but little compared with that projected to be spent by

Arthur Keily on his new mansion, intended to rival his brother John's Strancally Castle [*q.v.*]. This had been designed by George Richard Pain, who was clearly an inspiration for Arthur's Scottish gardener. Apparently the money ran out and his castle never materialised, for by 1854 Arthur Ussher (as he by then was, having taken the new name in 1843) was forced to sell the property through the incumbered estates court. In the sales documentation it was stated that the lodges cost £2,000 to build.

Outer gate; *c.* 1829; architect John Smith.
An extraordinary and beautifully executed identical pair of lodges brought together in a Picturesque composition, each at 45° to the ogee-arched carriage gateway. Tudor Castellated in the manner of John Nash, with all the required accoutrements of machicolated battlements, mock cross arrowloops, quatrefoil motifs, buttresses, label-moulded mullioned bipartite windows with latticed cast-iron glazing and octagonal turrets, and both lodges terminating in tall round towers. Each of these contains spiral stairs giving access to first-floor rooms. Unsociably, the porters could not reach these internally but, as Howley suggests, perhaps these were for the enjoyment of Mr Keily and family as belvedere tearooms. The exquisite iron gates repeatedly reflect the ogee arch over, a detail closely resembling that at Lacock Abbey, Wiltshire.

Inner gate; *c.* 1830; architect John Smith.
An altogether more muscular complex compared to the relative delicacy of the outer gate, here carried out in a design displaying the gardener's amazing eclecticism. Two miniature castles face one another across the span of a bridge of three pointed arches, differing and neither quite symmetrical, each with an eccentrically placed round tower dominating, with a selection of lower round and square crenellated turrets and boxes for the accommodation of estate workers. The rooms, some triangular, are divided by central carriage archways and poorly lit by narrow slit windows, as befits medieval fortresses.

After lying hidden from view in the undergrowth for a century, these extraordinary follies have been repaired and revealed for the enjoyment, once again, of the visitor.

Ballyduff gate; *c.* 1820.
Very much the poor relation and most unspectacular of estate lodges is this derelict single-storey standard lodge in harled rubble, below a shallow-pitched hipped roof that oversails to such an extent that there may well have once been post supports to form a pretty verandah on three sides. The diagonally set squared rubble carriage pillars have cappings with unusual Gothic arcaded indents and, along with the fleur-de-lis-finialled gate and railings, probably post-date the lodge by about 25 years.

Ballysaggartmore House has been demolished.

Dublin Penny Journal (13 December 1834); Heaney 1999; *Cork Constitution* (23 May 1837); O'Flanagan 1975; *Journal of the Cork Historical and Archaeological Society* **38** (1933), 30–7; de Breffny and ffolliott 1975; Bence-Jones 1988; Malins and Glin 1976; Howley 1993; Williams 1994; Craig and Garner 1977.

15. Ballysaggartmore, Lismore, inner gate.

16. BELLEVILLE PARK, Cappoquin; *c.* 1840; architect possibly Martin Day.

A striking single-storey standard, faintly Italianate lodge with shallow-pitched gables; its narrow windows, with cast-iron latticed lights and banded surrounds, flank a dominant hall projection with extending verges above a panelled front door having a segmental head and moulded architrave; rendered walls and a tall chimney-stack with plinth and corniced capping at the intersection of ridges. Diagonally set carriage pillars with round-headed recessed panels are flanked by postilion gates in straight screen walls terminating in convex quadrants. Possibly a design by Martin Day, to whom work in the big house, formerly called 'Bettyville', is attributable. Like Affane [*q.v.*] nearby, a seat until his death in 1842 of Samuel Poer or Power.

LGI (1904); Bence-Jones 1988.

BELMONT (see CAPPOQUIN)

17. BELMONT, Waterford; pre-1839; *demolished.*
A property in 1837 of John Roberts (b. 1773), who died that year, to be succeeded by a younger brother, Sir Samuel Roberts (1785–1848), whose gate porter in the year of his death was John Whelan.

Lewis 1837; Griffith 1853–63; *IFR.*

BELMOUNT (see COUNTY KILKENNY)

18. BELVEDERE LODGE, Waterford; pre-1839; *demolished.*
A dignified late Georgian villa overlooking the River Suir, a residence in 1846 of George Randall Penrose.

Slater 1846.

19. BISHOP'S PALACE, Waterford; *c.* 1850; *demolished.*
A distinguished mansion, now home to Waterford City Council, dating from the 1740s and attributable to architect Richard Castle. Its lost lodge was of much more recent foundation.

IAA.

20. BLENHEIM, Passage East; pre-1897; *demolished.*
A seat of the Ridgeway family, their house rather later than the eponymous battle and its lodge later still, built after 1841.

21. BLENHEIM LODGE, Passage East; *c.* 1830.
A plain single-storey gabled lodge that has suffered all manner of indignities in renovation and extension. It was home in 1848 to Mrs Mary Ronan, gatekeeper to proprietor Roger Sweetman, who had succeeded to the property in 1841 on the death of his father Pierce, merchant shipowner, who probably built the house on moving here in 1810 from his Waterford town house.

Griffith 1953–63; Whelan 1987.

BON SAUVEUR CONVENT (see CARRIGLEA)

22. BROOK LODGE, Passage East; pre-1841; *demolished.*
A Georgian house, originally of the Penrose family, which by 1837 had been acquired by

Simon Newport from George Penrose. It was subsequently inherited by Charles Newport Bolton through the marriage of his father, Revd Henry Bolton (1787–1854), in 1814 to Frances Newport.

Wilson 1803; Lewis 1837; *LGI* (1904).

23. CAMPHIRE, Villierstown; *c.* 1870.
Like nearby Cappagh [*q.v.*], an estate of Arthur Ussher (1683–1768), whose great-grandson, Christopher Musgrave Ussher (d. 1880), replaced the old homestead with a mid-nineteenth-century Italianate villa, and later added this sad, unprepossessing gatekeeper's lodge at an apologetic distance from its entrance. With a chimney-stack to each gable, the two-over-two sash windows are set in lugged surrounds in sand/cement-rendered walls with naive corner pilasters; adorned with a diminutive corrugated-iron gabled canopy on two wooden posts as an entrance porch. Derelict.

LGI (1904); Craig and Garner 1977.

24. CAPPAGH, Whitechurch (2).
An 1875 replacement house for Richard John Ussher (1841–1913), to succeed that of his great-grandfather, the same Arthur Ussher (1683–1768) as at Camphire [*q.v.*].

East lodge; *c.* 1845; architect perhaps John Robertson.

A prepossessing single-storey standard lodge with a paired octagonal stone chimney-stack to an oversailing hipped roof over an avenue front of three segmentally arched recesses containing a double-leaf panelled front door flanked by bipartite casement windows with an unusual and intricately margined wooden glazing pattern, all in smooth-rendered walls. In contrast is a fine pair of stone carriage pillars having bold plinths and projecting moulded cappings and shafts chiselled with raised and fielded panels, not unlike those to Headborough [*q.v.*], which tentatively points to the work of John Robertson; rubble stone concave quadrant walls and plain outer pillars. Built for Richard Keily Ussher (1778–1854), who succeeded to the estate as a minor of eleven on the death of his father in 1789.

West gate; *c.* 1870.
A 1½-storey gabled affair in nice random rubble, now almost unrecognisable following an imaginative transformation.

LGI (1904); Bence-Jones 1988.

25. CAPPOQUIN, Cappoquin (2).
Previously known as 'Belmont', this handsome Georgian house was built originally in 1779 by Abraham Hargrave for John Keane (1757–1829), probably to mark his first marriage in 1778. He was created a baronet in 1801, but all that can be attributed to him at the estate entrances is the main gate screen.

Principal gate; pre-1841.
A grand mid-Georgian entrance comprised of four sophisticated pillars crowned with flaming-urn finials and screen walls with segmentally arched postern openings. Within and thankfully remote is a hideously remodelled porter's lodge sporting a grotesque modern steeply monopitched roof. Of indeterminate age and promisingly derelict.

Secondary gate; *c.* 1890.
Opposite its gates is a modest single-storey gabled structure with a lower projecting gabled hall; pebble-dashed.

Taylor and Skinner 1778; 1783; *BPB* (1929); Craig and Garner 1977.

26. CARRIGANORE, Waterford; *c.* 1865; *demolished.*
A property in 1876 of Thomas H. Strangman, with a gate lodge built after 1839, probably when the house was extended in 1865.

LOI; NIAH.

27. CARRIGLEA, Dungarvan; *c.* 1830; architect not known.

A Tudor Revival house built about 1827 for John Odell (1801–47), attributable to the Pain brothers stylistically and by dint of the fact that Odell in 1827 had married a King daughter from the brothers' great pile that was Mitchelstown Castle [*q.v.*], Co. Cork. In the same pleasant honey-coloured sandstone and style as the house is the porter's lodge, a sturdy single-storey gabled structure raised off a T-plan, the downstroke to the avenue having a single-bay façade—the front door (now a window) with pointed-arched head in a peculiar frontispiece framed by a pair of buttresses to each corner, one of which doubles as one of four gate pillars (one missing) that formed a triple gateway. The windows are suitably label-moulded but with nasty modern inserts and there is an equally unsightly chimney-stack refurbishment. Sixteen days before John Odell's wedding, his sister Catherine had married Revd Percy Scott Smyth of Headborough [*q.v.*], which suggests an alternative attribution of the entrance to architect John Robertson.

Fraser 1838; *LG* (1886); de Breffny and ffolliott 1975.

CASTLE RICHARD (see GLENCAIRN ABBEY)

28. CHURCH OF IRELAND CEMETERY, Waterford; 1862; architect Abraham Denny.

IAA

A delightful Tudor Gothic composition, facing the road on John's Hill, which consists of a pair of steep gables joined by a low screen wall containing a postern door in a chamfered dressed opening to a pointed segmental arch. The left-hand gable in random uncoursed masonry has a pointed-arched carriage gateway, while that to the right is the one-bay end elevation of a 1½-storey lodge with skew-table and moulded kneelers, from which projects a single-storey semi-octagonal bay window with cut-stone roof. Over this is a pretty lancet attic window, retaining its original cast-iron latticed glazing bars. Dressings and quoins now enhance rendered walls which, as architect Abraham Denny's surviving drawing (dated 3 April 1862) shows, were originally in rubble facings, and the bay window is seen to have been an afterthought.

IAA drawing (ACC 93/138).

29. CHURCHTOWN, Carrick-on-Suir; pre-1841; *demolished.*
A late Georgian house, with a presumably contemporary gate lodge, in the early nineteenth century of John Power.

30. CLASHMORE, Clashmore; *c.* 1815.

A lost house of a branch of the Power family, survived by its charming farmyard and by a fine porter's lodge and entrance. The gatescreen shows the influence of a design by Sir Richard Morrison, with its squat, square outer stone pillars linked to smaller cylindrical carriage pillars by short rubble

walls, the whole framed by outer quadrants. Across the road, no longer having to monitor visits, is a standard single-storey lodge of considerable presence, not too much the worse for modernisation, with a large back return and a bland recent covering of sand/cement rendering. Distinguished by three round-headed openings, with new window inserts, flanking an elegant panelled door with spoked fanlight, all below an oversailing hipped roof. Occupied and nicely set off by a well-manicured low hedge. About 1840 Clashmore became a property of Francis Theophilus Henry Hastings, 12th earl of Huntingdon (1808–75), who in 1835 had married Elizabeth Anne, the only surviving daughter and heir of Richard Power, after whose death in 1857 the estate seems to have gone into decline.

Wilson 1803; Pigot 1824; *BPB* (1929).

31. CLASHMORE RECTORY, Clashmore; *c.* 1820.
A very derelict porter's lodge, probably of an age with the glebe house. Single-storey and rendered below a shallow hipped roof but without the regulation three-bay front, rather of a single squared sash window and the front door. Typically modest Establishment gatekeeper's accommodation.

NIAH.

CLASHNALOCHAN (see DUCKSPOOL)

32. CLONCOSKORAN, Dungarvan; *c.* 1810.
An antique seat of the Shanaghan family that passed through marriage to the Humbles, but by 1804 it lay in ruins. John Nugent Humble (1785–1834), created a baronet three years before his death, subsequently built it up again and probably added the unusually commodious gatehouse. Two-storey and square on plan below a hipped roof, the two-bay avenue front is comprised of window and doorway with round-headed arches in harled walls. It remains in use.

Taylor and Skinner 1778; 1783; Wilson 1803; *BPB* (1929); Craig and Garner 1977.

33. CLONEA CASTLE, Dungarvan (2).
Only one of the lodges identified by the 1851 valuation, when the gatekeepers were James Bucke and David Power, is now to be found. It is impressively positioned on the outside of a right-angled bend of the public road, passed on each side by an avenue—one to the house, the other the approach to the outbuildings. Single-storey and built off a T-plan below hipped roofs with carved modillion brackets to their soffits; rendered. The wing to the main avenue forms a recessed porch, the roof carried on three cast-iron posts. In 1804 Clonea lay in ruins but seems to have been restored after the death of Arthur MacGwire (1724–1810) by his son Walter, the eldest of eight brothers and the builder of the lodge *c.* 1830.

Wilson 1803; *LGI* (1904).

34. COOLNAMUCK COURT, Carrick-on-Suir (2).
A property with a tragic history, which in the early nineteenth century was the residence of Charles William Wall, with its two porters' lodges in place opposite their gates before 1841. The place was auctioned through the Incumbered Estates Commission on 25 May 1852 after its owner, James Wall, committed murder/suicide by driving himself and his family over a cliff in their coach and four. In 1857 it changed hands again, being bought by Revd John de la Poer Beresford (1814–66), who succeeded his brother two years later as 4th marquis of Waterford and inherited the Curraghmore estate [*q.v.*]. Coolnamuck Court and its two lodges were demolished in the later twentieth century, to be survived by a Gothic folly, a tower-house and one of its avenues, lined with old lime trees.

Leet 1814; Lewis 1837; *BPB* (1929); Lyons 1993.

CORBALLYMORE (see SUMMERVILLE)

35. COVE LODGE, Waterford; *c.* 1900; *demolished.*
Another late Victorian suburban villa development on the eastern approach to the city, in 1883 the residence of Alexander W. Heard, although its gatekeeper's lodge was probably added by his successor, William E. Jones, around the turn of the twentieth century.

36. CURRAGHMORE, Portlaw (12).
The premier estate of the county, 'unsurpassed in Ireland in size, romantic scenery and splendid woods' (Bence-Jones), and described by Girouard as 'very much a little world on its own, sealed off from outsiders by its woods and hills, and by the ten mile ring of its demesne walls'. The property of the de la Poer Beresfords, marquises of Waterford, in 1876 consisted of 39,883 acres containing the five mile by three mile demesne, but this only partly explains its being the most lodged in Ireland, for but few are located by the outer demesne wall; rather they are sited at gates to inner subdivisions, such as the deer-park, mostly out of sight. Surprisingly, with one exception, quantity is not matched by the quality that would befit such a grand setting. Of the five porters' lodges existing in 1841 four survive.

Portlaw entrance; *c.* 1820.

Forward of a triple gateway of four slender V-jointed rusticated stone pillars with big heavy cornices and ornate ironwork is this pleasant, modest, single-storey standard gate lodge, with steeply hipped roof and an original six-panelled doorway flanked by two-over-four sash windows in roughcast walls. John Barrow arrived at this gate in autumn 1835, where he was not so favourably received: 'here I also experienced a difficulty in gaining admission. In fact, I was rather uncivilly refused, and should have been sent away, had I not observed two decent-looking people on horseback coming out of the grounds, probably agents, who immediately procured me admission. Having passed the outer gate, all was civility within.' The lodge remains occupied.

Deer-park gate; pre-1841; *demolished.*
Having negotiated the Portlaw entrance *en route* to the big house, Barrow clearly did not experience any problem in passing the inner lodge by the deer-park boundary half a mile beyond on the eastern approach alongside the Clodiagh River.

Farmyard entrance; pre-1841/1849; architect William Tinsley.
A standard single-storey hip-roofed affair by the farm buildings and private cricket ground. Faced in ashlar with a moulded eaves band and four-over-four sash windows. Derelict and now gateless, it may be contemporary with the north-west inner lodge, with which it shares many characteristics. The architect identifies this and the model farm as his works in his memoirs, compiled after emigrating to America in 1851.

North-west inner gate; pre-1841/*c.* 1849; architect probably William Tinsley.
Situated within the demesne on the Carrick-on-Suir avenue is this standard single-storey hip-roofed lodge in ashlar finish with a moulded eaves band and four-over-four sash windows. Later red-clay ridge tiles are broken by a chimney-stack with concave corniced capping to match the four square stone entrance pillars. Derelict. Attributable to Tinsley on the grounds of its similarity to the farmyard lodge.

Clonagam lodge; pre-1841; *demolished.*
Presumably once located on a long-lost public road, since absorbed into the north of the demesne. Already ruinous by 1926.

Church lodge (1); *c.* 1825.

Next to the family chapel on the northern approach is this most peculiar little porter's lodge, derelict and suffering the indignity of having had a wide shed door punched in its leading front where the gatekeeper's threshold used to be. Single-storey and raised off an irregular five-sided plan with an equivalent roof configuration, its hip tiles rising to a complementary shaped brick chimney-stack. Below the oversailing eaves, harled walls contain tiny bipartite casement windows with cast-iron latticed glazing pattern. Adjacent is its successor from the turn of the twentieth century (see below).

Lissasmuttaun entrance; pre-1841; *demolished.*
On the western approach, this lodge was located in thick woodland on an inner boundary. Probably rendered redundant by the later lodge by Lowry's Bridge at the public road.

Sallyhene gate; pre-1841; *demolished.*

On the southern avenue and curiously remote from any apparent gate is this lodge, whose role seems to have been superseded by one of eight delightful Tudor Revival cottages arranged as four semi-detached pairs, each 1½-storey and gabled with a symmetrical three-bay front of uncoursed rubble comprised of tripartite latticed casements flanking a distinctive gabled carved wooden porch, its semicircular relieving archway carried on chamfered posts, a feature common to other cottages on the estate.

This development of estate cottages dates from the early 1870s, when architect Samuel Ussher Roberts is recorded as working on the house for John Henry de la Poer Beresford, 5th marquis of Waterford (1844–95), a phase of improvements which also extended to the building of the Tower Hill cottages and a new gate lodge at the western gateway.

Lowry's Bridge gate; *c.* 1873; architect probably S.U. Roberts.

Unlike the other cottages, this is arranged on an irregular L-plan to create a romantic and picturesque home. In Tudor Revival manner, faced in coursed rubble stone with dressed chamfered tripartite windows, the glazing pattern latticed and margined. To the leading gable is a blank shield below a tiny slit opening, while alongside projects the familiar pretty wooden gabled porch, with its semicircular relieving arch on bracketed supports leading to the similarly headed doorway. Above the sawtooth-slated bands of the roof is a cut-stone banded stack, just as those to the Sallyhene cottages. Nestling in an attractive complementary garden next to an entrance created south of its predecessor.

Whitestown Wood lodge; pre-1926.
A brick gabled structure built after 1841 but otherwise too ruinous to date accurately.

Henry de la Poer Beresford (1875–1911), after succeeding his father as the 6th marquis, pursued the policy of estate improvements, with the addition of two further porters' lodges at previously unmonitored gates.

Curraghballintea Wood lodge; *c.* 1900; architect not known.

A typically solid late Victorian 1½-storey standard gatekeeper's house. With simply carved foiled bargeboards to main gables and those of its two attic dormers, it has tall eaves to accommodate a central lean-to canopy carried on wooden posts, sheltering the front door. To each side, as elsewhere, are bipartite one-over-one original sash windows, all in pleasant rubble stone facings enhanced by red-brick toothed quoins and dressings. Guarding a considerably older gatescreen that has tall, slender stone carriage pillars with exaggerated cornices to cappings. Located distant from the public road on the north-western avenue.

Church lodge (2); *c.* 1900; architect not known.

Considerably more commodious than its surviving predecessor nearby (see above) is this well-proportioned late Victorian standard 1½-storey gatehouse, regrettably having its rubble finish coated in a drab grey rendering but still exhibiting its toothed red-brick quoins and dressings to square casement windows and original glazed sheeted door. The latter is sheltered by a conspicuous carved wooden gabled porch, clearly influenced by Roberts's design for the earlier cottages but more elaborate and accommodated by the high eaves of the gabled roof, with consciously symmetrically positioned flat-roofed dormer with square-paned bipartite casements and a pair of brick chimney-stacks.

Barrow 1836; Griffith 1853–63; *BPB* (1929); Forbes 1953; *Country Life* (7, 14 and 21 February 1963); ffolliott 1971b; IAA.

37. DERRIHEEN, Cappoquin; pre-1841; architect possibly G.R. Pain; *demolished.*

Previously called 'Little Bridge', home in 1783 and 1814 to the Greene family. If the surviving gatescreen is a guide, however, the lodge was built by the proprietor in 1837, C. Maunsell Esq. His architect may have been G.R. Pain, for the gate pillars with their reeded octagonal shafts and gadrooning to the domed cappings are almost identical to those at Ballinamona [*q.v.*], Ballyglan [*q.v.*], Whitechurch [*q.v.*] and Woodhouse [*q.v.*].

Taylor and Skinner 1783; Wilson 1803; Lewis 1837.

38. D'LOUGHTANE, Clashmore; *c.* 1830.
A large standard porter's lodge with a steeply pitched hipped roof, with an off-centre chimney-stack, over harled walls with cast-iron latticed casement windows on each side of an entrance of sheeted half-doors. Derelict. Nearby is a contemporary gatescreen of big rustic carriage pillars, flanked by screen walls containing on one side a round-headed postilion opening, balanced on the other side by a blind equivalent, both with buttressed piers; nice spear-topped gates. All presumably for Richard Power Ronayne, living here in 1837 after he had briefly lived at Newton [*q.v.*]. His family had married into the Powers of Knockaderry [*q.v.*].

Lewis 1837; *IFR*.

39. DONERAILE WALK, Tramore; *c.* 1830.
A quaint standard hip-roofed lodge with clipped eaves over rough-dashed walls, its openings set in recessed flat-headed recesses. Built for Hayes St Leger, 3rd Viscount Doneraile (1786–1854), of Doneraile Court, Co. Cork [*q.v.*].

BPB (1929).

40. DROMANA, Villierstown (5).
Another beautiful and romantic Waterford landed estate remarkable for being better known for one of its gate lodges than for the mansion perched above the River Blackwater. A property which passed to the Villiers family through their marriage to a Fitzgerald daughter in the late seventeenth century and which, thanks to their male line failing twice, descended in 1809 to young Henry Villiers-Stuart (1803–74), who, before he was created 1st Baron de Decies of Dromana in 1839, had already embarked upon extensive improvements to the place, which included the addition of at least four porters' lodges. His architect was Martin Day, already employed by the family before Henry's coming of age.

Cappoquin entrance; 1826/*c.* 1835; architect Martin Day.

IAA

The story goes that Henry Villiers-Stuart in 1826 returned from his honeymoon in Brighton with his Austrian wife, Theresia Pauline Ott, to be welcomed by a hastily built reminder of the Royal Pavilion in the shape of a temporary structure, generally accepted as having been reconstructed in the durable form we see today and for which drawings by Martin Day were prepared. Scottish visitor Robert Graham on 21 July 1835 found 'a remarkable bridge with a picturesque new church, having a pear-shaped cupola at the end of it. This bridge, I believe, makes the entry to this place.' What Graham mistook for a church was in fact a recently built precursor of what was, and remains, the only Hindu-Gothic structure in the country. Six years later the first Ordnance Survey map suggests that the present permanent building was in place, and in 1844 Flanagan found that 'Through this park is a noble avenue, and the entrance near Cappoquin is a costly fanciful structure: there is a wooden bridge over the Finnisk river'. Neither visitor notices a makeshift edifice. Regardless of its age, probably a rebuild of about 1830, it survives as unique and as one of the most extraordinary apparitions in the Irish countryside—a bizarre reminder of the Orient. It consists of a pair of identical one-roomed cubes as 'day and night' accommodation flanking the taller carriage gateway with its pointed Gothic archways front and back to give matching elevations, the rooms being lit by four elegant ogee-arched windows with intricate octagonal glazing pattern, all displayed in rectangular recesses. In golden sandstone ashlar, the rhythm continues within the vaulted archway, doorways facing each other with their moulded surrounds and ogee arches containing Y-traceried fanlights and, alongside, dummy doorways for balance. But the real delight is the fantastic roofscape, with its central copper onion dome and parapets of the most delicate of ironwork with quatrefoil motifs stopped by minaret-topped pilasters at all eight corners. The rickety bridge over the Finisk which now carries a public road rather than the old private avenue has been replaced by something more stable but with the loss of Martin Day's fancy Gothic balustrade, for which his drawings of various alternatives survive. Of his two 'Sketches' for the lodge, dated September 1849, one shows it as completed and the other as domeless but with an arcaded parapet and elaborately decorated cusped carriage arch. Quite why Day was preparing elevations as late as then

NLI

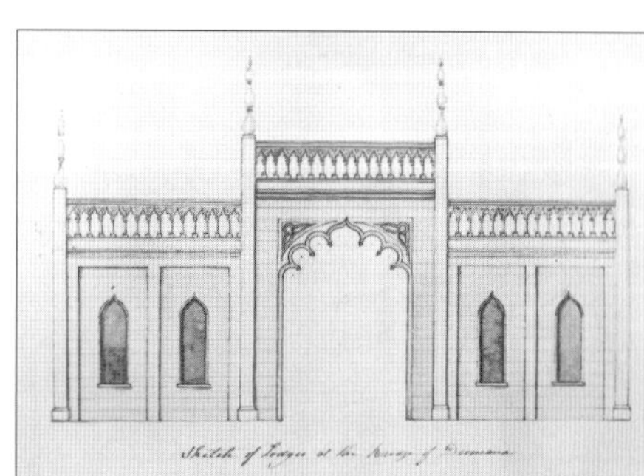

IAA

is not clear. It may be that they were proposals for additional enrichments to what existed. It would seem that the design was based upon Joseph Henry Good's 1832 North or William IV Gate to the Pavilion. Saved from ruin by a timely restoration by the Irish Georgian Society in 1968 but still under threat from vandals.

Triumphal archway; 1836; architect Martin Day; *unexecuted.*

IAA

A naive design which with a bit of refinement would have made the grandest impression at whatever gate it was intended for. The proposal was for a triple archway, the central of which is a round-headed double-height carriage opening, flanked by a pair of secondary, similarly arched lower gates, one a porch entry to a one-up/one-down 'Gate Keeper's House' integrated into one side, and the other a pedestrian passage access with unclassified space to each side and over. Above these gates are outsized roundels containing the date and the Villiers crest of demi-lions rampant. The bays are defined by lofty, detached, fluted Ionic columns, over which the entablature extends, the whole crowned by a stepped die displaying more family bearings.

Dungarvan gate; *c.* 1825.

Here are the sad remains of a pair of Classical lodges that formed part of a very fine gatescreen. Four tall pillars contained a carriage gateway and short railings of matching ironwork. Beyond, curtain walls contained postern openings, the whole terminating in two little single-bay porters' lodges, their windows in round-headed recesses framed by pilasters below pedimented gables. Now pillars and gates have gone, the left-hand lodge has been reduced to an overgrown rotting carcass and its erstwhile twin has been rather freakishly modernised and extended beyond all recognition.

South-east entrance; *c.* 1800.

A modest single-storey gabled cottage, now derelict.

Villierstown gate; *c.* 1855.

A commodious mid-Victorian 1½-storey gabled gatehouse built off a T-plan, having Tudor Picturesque detailing in a drab grey rendering relieved by bipartite squared sash windows below label mouldings. Ornamental bargeboards with quatrefoil perforations rise to carved hip-knobs, the ridge broken by a pair of octagonal stone flues with lancet recesses. Nearby is an impressive pair of lofty Classical carriage pillars in V-jointed rusticated stone, crowned by oversailing moulded corniced cappings. Probably earlier than the lodge, *c.* 1800, and now flanking a public road.

Heaney 1999; O'Flanagan 1975; Bence-Jones 1988; Guinness and Ryan 1971; Malins and Glin 1976; *IFR*; Craig and Garner 1977; Howley 1993; IAA photographs (23/46 R1,2,3,4+N).

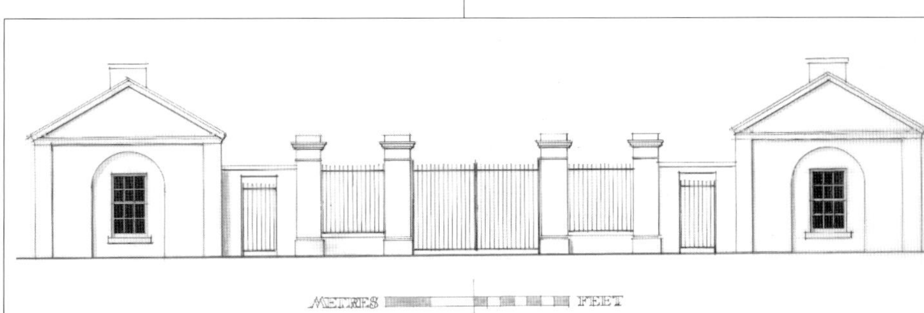

40. Dromana, Villierstown, Dungarvan gate.

41. DUCKSPOOL, Dungarvan; pre-1841; *demolished.*

An estate in the mid- to late eighteenth century of John Boate and his son Ussher, which by 1837 was the residence of John Matthew Galwey (*c.* 1790–1842) and subsequently of his son Edward, who lost the property and his money in the Famine. Latterly renamed 'Clashnalochan' and acquired by the Augustinian Fathers.

Taylor and Skinner 1778; 1783; Wilson 1803; Lewis 1837; *LGI* (1904); Bence-Jones 1988; *IFR.*

42. DUNGARVAN LUNATIC ASYLUM, Dungarvan; pre-1927; *demolished.*

An undistinguished modern replacement lodge for a mid-nineteenth-century predecessor sits on the site; 1½-storey, roughcast, with a crazy-paved plinth, squared casement and gables.

43. EASTLAND, Tramore; *c.* 1830.

A seat in 1837 of Pierce George Barron (1793–1864), whose porter's lodge is a single-storey hip-roofed two-bay cottage, its door and window set in segmentally headed recesses and both within a greater arched porch. Rendered and occupied. The main carriage pillars have stone cappings with gadrooned 'splashes', a feature prevalent in the county and suggestive of the work of architect George Richard Pain.

Lewis 1837; *IFR.*

44. ELVA LODGE, Waterford; *c.* 1864; architect J.S. Mulvany.

Architect John Skipton Mulvany benefited greatly from his association with the Quaker Malcomson family in County Waterford, being engaged on the houses of three brothers, Joseph at Mayfield [*q.v.*], Thomas at Minella [*q.v.*] and John here, all commissions that included the provision of gate lodges. Of unusually generous proportions, this is a typically forthright mid-Victorian design by Mulvany, in the neo-Classical style. Single-storey and built off a T-plan below a hipped roof, in a stucco finish with moulded opening surrounds, those to the gables having semicircular-arched heads. A plain eaves band extends through the projecting hall and beyond about the Tuscan tetrastyle portico, where it acquires triglyphs. Within the pronaos, framed by antae, the front door (now a window) is flanked by elegant round-headed niches. An impressive lodge at the entrance to Waterford Regional Hospital, by which it is shown scant respect, although as yet it does survive its big house, which for a time became 'Ardkeen'.

IADS (2000).

45. FAITHLEGG, Passage East (2).
A grand house built in 1783 by Cornelius Bolton but much altered and added to after being purchased in 1819 by Nicholas Mahon Power (1787–1873), whose improvements extended to the main entrance.

Principal gate; pre-1839/*c.* 1873.

A fine gatescreen from about 1845 comprised of simply recessed panel pillars and moulded cappings, the inner ones crowned by beautiful Power crests, antlered bucks' heads, and the outer topped by peculiar pumpkin-like devices; contemporary chunky iron railings and gates. Across the road is the porter's gatehouse, a conglomeration of building dates dominated by a two-storey gabled projection of one bay comprised of upper and lower paired round-headed Italianate windows with stone surrounds and squared casements in white rendered walls. Behind is a two-storey hip-roofed wing and a single-storey counterpart, which may be the remains of a standard original keeper's lodge, displaying a later segmentally arched window.

Inner gate; pre-1925; *demolished.*
A short-lived gate lodge within the estate, probably on the deer-park boundary, presumably built by Patrick Joseph Mahon Power, who succeeded to the property on his father's death.

After the departure of the Powers the place became a school, and latterly a hotel surrounded by a championship golf course.

LGI (1904); Bence-Jones 1988.

46. FLOWERHILL, Ballyduff; *c.* 1840.
A seat noticed by a succession of early nineteenth-century travellers as 'a new creation' (1835), 'a beautiful residence in the cottage style' (1837) and 'the sweetly-situated mansion of Barry Drew' (1844). Its pleasant lodge looks to be of slightly later date. Single-storey standard, its tall eaves and a skylight in its hipped oversailing roof betray attic accommodation. Raised on a prominent plinth, there is an inconsistency of stonework, starting in an uncoursed rubble finish and continued in regular square cut stone. Above the wide windows of square bipartite casements are relieving rectangular stone panels, while over the door is an oblong variant. The gatescreen is contemporary, with spear-topped railings and matching gates hung on iron posts with Georgian-style scrolled crowns. All seemingly for Barry Drew, of the family from nearby Macollop Castle [*q.v.*].

Heaney 1999; Lewis 1837; O'Flanagan 1975.

47. FORTWILLIAM, Lismore (2).
One of a group of gentlemen's seats by this beautiful stretch of the River Blackwater, this charming Tudor Revival villa was being built in 1835 to designs of J. and G.R. Pain for John Bowen Gumbleton, to replace his uncle's earlier house. Sadly, there is no trace of its lodges, that to the main gate being in place in 1841 and probably dating from the late eighteenth century, if its two surviving V-jointed rusticated stone pillars are any clue.

Heaney 1999; Burke 1854–5.

48. GARDENMORRIS, Kill (3).

A remarkable sight at this remote and antique seat of the O'Shee family is its sole surviving lodge at the main gate, a replacement for one of three built before 1841. Alongside and thrusting forward of the tripartite gateway, it is a striking 1½-storey structure, with its leading canted front below an equivalent half-umbrello roof sufficiently high-pitched to accommodate loft space lit by two curious arrowhead dormers emerging from a slated finish with scalloped and sawtooth courses and polychrome relief motifs. Crowning the ridge is a conjoined pair of diagonally set red-brick chimney-flues with jagged sawtooth specials, a detail repeated as eaves and sill courses and to the distinctly Romanesque windows with their segmental heads, that to the front bipartite and divided by a stone colonette, all set in rendered panels framed by brick pilasters. Stranger still is a little square appendage to one side with its own pyramidal roof, which should have served as the entrance hall were it not for the recessed corner porch below the rear hipped roof. All immaculately modernised but for the lead-effect plastic windows. Apparently dating from around 1880, as do the splendid contemporary wooden gates, with their Tudor Gothic arcading hung on earlier square ashlar pillars with swagged friezes and shafts chiselled with decorative bands. Atop there is an elegant pair of O'Shee swans *roussants.* Created for Nicholas Richard Power O'Shee (1821–1902) by an unidentified architect, perhaps the same inspired hand as had transformed the big house in French style a few years earlier.

IFR; Bence-Jones 1988.

49. GARRYDUFF, Clashmore; pre-1841; *demolished.*
A seat in 1814 and 1837 of Henry Garde, of whose fine property only the sad ruins of the house and its estate wall remain.

Leet 1814; Lewis 1837.

50. GLENABBEY, Clonmel; pre-1841; *demolished.*
A property in the mid-nineteenth century of Garret Richard Carey.

Griffith 1853–63.

51. GLENAHIRY LODGE, Newcastle; *c.* 1870; *demolished.*
In the late eighteenth century a hunting lodge of the Powers called 'Glasha', which by 1850 had been acquired by the earls of Stradbroke and around twenty years later by the Trench family, Barons Ashtown of County Galway, likely builders of the porter's lodge. In 1927 the house was 'in ruins'.

Taylor and Skinner 1778; 1783; Griffith 1853–63; *BPB* (1929).

52. GLENAM, Clonmel; pre-1927; *demolished.*
On the site of the lodge to this suburban house is a modern bungalow, perhaps incorporating its predecessor or replicating some of its characteristics, with an elevation to the avenue of three bays in an arcade of segmentally headed recesses and a moulded chimney capping. Otherwise all synthetic slates and plastic windows. A property in 1889 of Miss S. Grubb, although the lodge may date from around 1897, when Major Ralph Francis Xavier MacGeough Bond of the County Armagh family was in residence. A house since renamed 'Melbourne'.

Bassett 1889; *IFR.*

53. GLENBEG, Ballyduff; *c.* 1800/*c.* 1840.

A charming seventeenth-century seat of the Jackson family, afforded much recent care and attention, unlike its unfortunate porter's lodge, which lies derelict. Set back from its gatescreen and, like the big house, probably of more than one period, it is a basic 1½-storey cottage with clipped eaves and verges to vernacular limewashed harled walls. To the avenue is a simple two-window-bay front with, to the gable, an attic window with a Tudor label moulding, probably added later when the Picturesque conjoined brick pair of stacks was added. The tripartite gateway is comprised of bow-topped ironwork and spear-topped finials hung on four ashlar pillars with simple recessed panels, corniced cappings and nicely chiselled scroll-topped stops, all framed by extensive cruder harled rubble concave quadrants. All exhibiting work carried out in the time here of George Jackson and his son George Bennett Jackson.

Leet 1814; *LG* (1886).

54. GLENCAIRN ABBEY, Lismore (4).
A property previously known as 'Ballygarron' and until 1814 as 'Castle Richard', presumably after its owner, Richard Gumbleton. It was his son, Richard Edward Gumbleton, whose aspirations for the place were never quite realised and who renamed it in expectation of the house's transformation into the grand Tudor Gothic creation portrayed in Neale's views of 1820. He had engaged architect Richard Morrison but circumstances conspired against the completion of his plans; he died in 1819 when it was under construction, and those to whom he bequeathed the estate, his sister Louisa and her husband Henry Amyas Bushe, seem not to have had the will or the resources to complete the job. As a consequence, the property did not ever acquire lodges appropriate to it, the survivor of the two pre-1841 structures within the grounds being a nondescript standard gabled affair in a bland grey render of doubtful date. Bushe's granddaughter, Frances Maria, inherited Glencairn Abbey in 1879, married Ambrose William Power nine years later, and as late as the turn of the twentieth century commissioned two new porters' lodges.

Ballyduff gate; *c.* 1900.
A relatively plain 1½-storey building with rendered attic gables above a brick-faced ground floor, presiding over an earlier gatescreen.

Lismore Gate; 1902; architects W.H. Hill and Son.

A striking Edwardian gatekeeper's lodge, which also served as the local post office. It presents a perfectly symmetrical elevation to the road, its English garden wall bond red-brick lower floor displaying corner recesses, the eaves over which are supported by decorative cast-iron columns of a Composite Order, which flank a pair of semi-canted bay windows divided by a central buttress, the stone capping of which matches those to the gatescreen. Above is a flat-roofed bipartite dormer window and a central brick stack to a gabled roof, the apex of which is rendered and broken by the single-storey hall projection.

Neale 1820–3; *IB* (14 August 1902); *LGI* (1904); *LG* (1952); McParland *et al.* 1989.

55. GLENMORE [1], Ballyduff; *c.* 1845; *demolished.*
North of the Blackwater was a lodge not apparent on the first OS map but noted in the Griffith valuation of 1851 as a property of Arthur Ussher.

Griffith 1853–63.

56. GLENMORE [2], Ballyduff; pre-1926; *demolished.*
A property on the southern bank of the Blackwater, once of the Jackson family from nearby Glenbeg [*q.v.*], the lodge to which may have been built by Richard Cliffe, who is recorded here in 1851 and 1870.

Griffith 1853–63; Slater 1870.

57. GLENSHELANE, Cappoquin; *c.* 1845.
The pretty neighbouring hillside estate of the Keanes of Cappoquin House [*q.v.*], its lodge added by Sir Richard Keane (1780–1855) after inheriting from his father in 1829. Now almost completely overgrown, just detectable is a standard vernacular single-storey limewashed and harled cottage with oversailing hipped roof. Derelict and located outside its gates.

Griffith 1853–63; *BPB* (1929); Bence-Jones 1988.

58. GLENVILLE, Waterford (2).
A seat associated in the main with three individuals. In the early nineteenth century it was owned by John Greene (1801–70), who may have been responsible for the early, lost, porter's lodge to the east.

Ballynakill gate; pre-1839; *demolished.*
Greene's gatekeeper in 1848 was Edward Connell before the property was acquired by Michael Dobbyn Hassard, who is understood to have rebuilt the house in Italianate style. On his death it passed, through the marriage of his elder daughter Anna Maria in 1866, to William Goff Davis-Goff (1838–1917), who became a baronet in 1905, part of the celebrations of which may have been the formation of a later entrance closer to the city.

Cove gate; 1896.

Appropriate to its suburban setting is this Edwardian porter's lodge with traces of mock Elizabethan black-and-white work to one gable; single-storey in white rendering, raised off an L-plan, with a minuscule hall in the internal angle below a catslide roof. The two gables have very finely inscribed bargeboards and carved hip-knobs, although the effect is spoiled by modernisation, with an ugly picture window inserted in one and an outsized canted bay window added to the other. A contemporary tripartite gateway has stone pillars with multi-panelled faces and ogee cappings crowned by rusticated ball finials, all framed by railed ogee quadrants on dwarf walls. An entrance that outlives the big house, which was burnt and demolished in the 1950s.

Griffith 1853–63; *BPB* (1929); Bence-Jones 1988; *IFR*.

59. GORTMORE, Waterford; 1898; architect not known.

A delightfully ostentatious late lodge, repeating details more successfully than the same on the big house, all part of a small suburban development for Andrew Horn by a designer well versed in the Queen Anne Revival style. Single-storey below a pyramidal roof broken by a big cream brick battered chimney-stack and a gabled living room projection which exhibits a carved apex with spiky finial over the striking tripartite window, with its four-over-one sashes and central segmental mullion repeated in the pediment above. The projection is flanked by recesses, a single-bay porch to one side and a two-bay verandah to the other, both with decorative post support to segmentally headed eaves arches, features nicely set off by grey roughcast walls. Striking stone carriage pillars with pebble-dash-effect square shafts squinching to octagonal cappings.

NIAH.

60. GRACE DIEU, Waterford; *c.* 1860.
A property developed by James Anderson (1810–67) around the time of his marriage in 1842 to Margaret Carew on land belonging to his father-in-law of neighbouring Ballinamona [*q.v.*]. His modest house was drastically remodelled in the High Victorian Italianate style by his son, Thomas William Anderson, in 1891 to designs of A.E. Murray. Its gate lodge, impressively positioned opposite the entrance, does not seem to relate to either phase of building but rather belongs somewhere in between. Now lying ruinous, it was a standard single-storey hip-roofed affair with a gabled breakfront hall, ornamental bracketed eaves and round-headed openings with moulded surrounds, presumably once in stucco-effect walls—a relatively modest Italianate prelude to what lies beyond the gates.

IB (1 December 1891; 1 July 1894); *LGI* (1904); Bence-Jones 1988.

GRAIGUE LODGE **(see COUNTY KILKENNY)**

61. GRANTSTOWN SCHOOL, Waterford; *c.* 1810.

A commodious two-storey gatehouse below a hipped roof, of three bays with quoins. Doubtless built after 1808, when the school relocated here, under the guidance of principal Revd Mr J. Hughes, from Baron-Strand-street in Waterford, having outgrown its previous premises. The original private house on the site is recorded in 1783 as the seat of the Kearney family, to which the harled concave entrance quadrants survive, with the stumps of V-jointed rusticated stone carriage pillars, once with urns.

Taylor and Skinner 1783; Leet 1814; Lewis 1837; Craig and Garner 1977.

62. GREENMOUNT, Lismore; *c.* 1905; architect not known.

To the estate manager's villa as part of the great Lismore Castle [*q.v.*] property is this highly attractive little example of the mock Elizabethan style, being wholly clad in 'black-and-white' work. Gabled and partly 1½-storey to the rear with jettied oriel gablets, it extends to the avenue as single-storey with a full-width glazed front incorporating the entrance doorway, the casements all leaded below a gable projecting on a bracketed coving. Roughcast on a stone plinth, it lies abandoned and derelict, surely not beyond the resources of the Devonshire estates to maintain.

NIAH.

63. GURTEEN LE POER, Kilsheelan (3).

A charming antique demesne of the Power family on the south bank of the River Suir, its mansion being the third house on the property. Plans for this were drawn up in 1815 by architect Thomas Alfred Cobden but remained unfulfilled until 1863–6, when Samuel Ussher Roberts remodelled the earlier proposals in the same Tudor Castellated manner for Edmond James de Poher de la Poer, who had inherited the place on the death of his father in 1851. This apparent period of building inactivity did, however, realise the creation of three gatekeepers' lodges, which until then the estate lacked. Cobden having died in 1840, John William Power (1816–51), who succeeded his father to Gurteen House in 1830, commissioned Charles Frederick Anderson of Cork, who provided designs for two most imposing Greek Revival lodges to impress at new entrances created for them.

Clonmel gate; 1843; architect C.F. Anderson.

An estate map of 1824 prepared by S. Chaloner indicates a 'Grand Entrance' to the western extremity of the demesne, with an extensive forecourt but strangely avenueless. The 1841 OS map shows a new avenue formed, with the access 100 yards to the east and awaiting its attendant lodge. Single-storey with attic accommodation, this is a building of deceptively generous scale, faced in sandstone ashlar with pedimented gables to each end, the tympana of which contain loft windows, and that of the breakfront, which sports the Power crest—a buck's head.

63. Gurteen Le Poer, Kilsheelan, Clonmel gate.

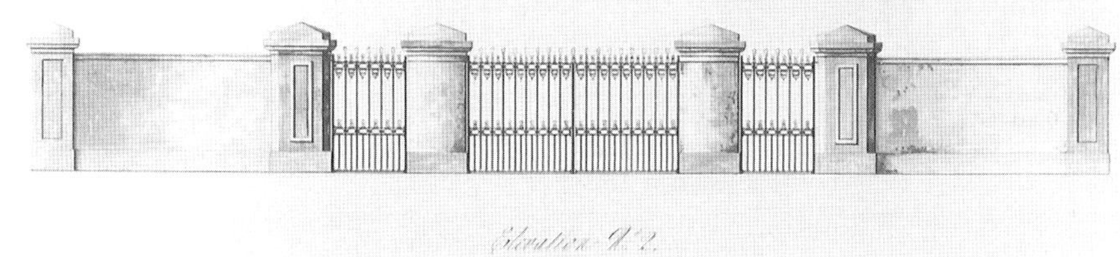

63. Gurteen Le Poer, Kilsheelan, Clonmel gate.

While the form lends itself to a conventional three-roomed layout, Anderson has contrived a most peculiar plan to suit his elevations and to accommodate a porch at both ends, each in the form of a pair of square pillars *in antis*—that facing the road, according to his drawing, not having a doorway. The three-bay avenue front has six-over-six sash windows in moulded and lugged surrounds, that to the breakfront, where one would expect the doorway, framed by a pair of Greek Doric columns in corner recesses, a favourite device of Anderson's, to be found at lodges to Lauriston, Co. Cork [*q.v.*], Mooresfort, Co. Tipperary [*q.v.*], and Ballywilliam [*q.v.*] and Kilfrush [*q.v.*], Co. Limerick, all attributable to him. Lest any doubt lingered as to the authorship of this entrance, the architect's watercolour drawings survive and his name is also inscribed in both entrance screens. Here the tripartite gateway is comprised of a pair of drum carriage pillars with square corniced cappings and, beyond, square panelled pillars contain concave quadrant walls.

Portlaw gate; 1843; architect C.F. Anderson; *demolished.*

Opposite a newly created gateway on the eastern approach to the house was another dignified Neo-Classical porter's lodge, tragically removed at the end of the last century for no apparent good reason. Similar in appearance to its western counterpart but lacking its porticos and a little more conventional in its internal layout. The frontispiece was identical, with its recessed corner columns, but here flanked by doorways, or at least one doorway, the other

63. Gurteen Le Poer, Kilsheelan, Portlaw gate.

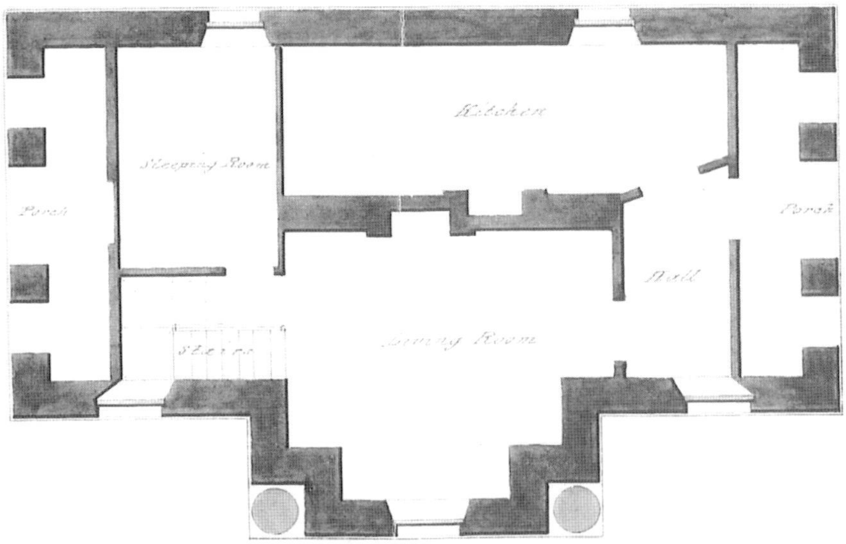

having been a dummy, complete with its own mock threshold step. The tympanum of the central pediment contained the family crest of 'a buck's head caboshed proper, attired or, between the antlers a crucifix or'. Forsaken across the way survives Anderson's splendid gateway, just as his drawing intended, examples of which are also to be found at Lota Park [*q.v.*] and Lauriston [*q.v.*], Co. Cork. A pair of trabeated postilion archways with panelled piers also perform the role of carriage pillars, the whole framed by concave quadrant walls and complemented with

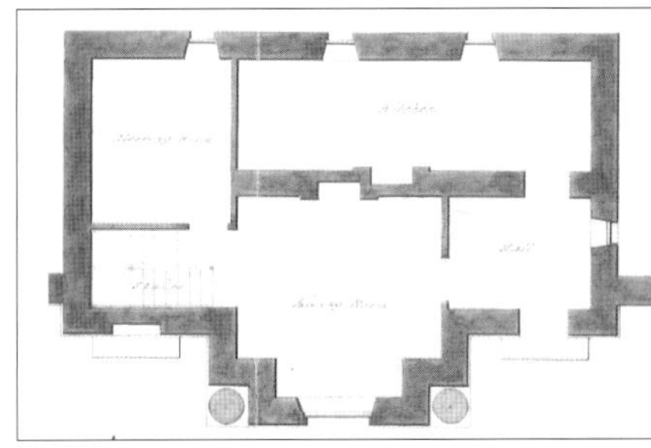

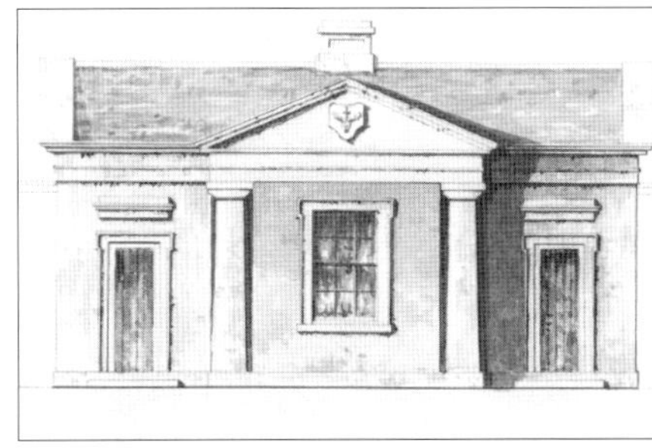

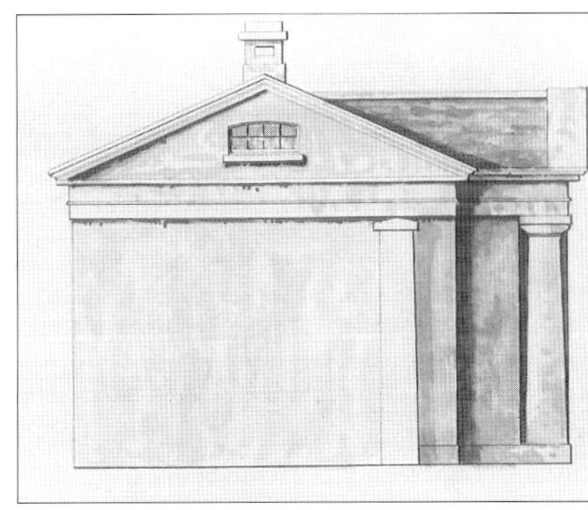

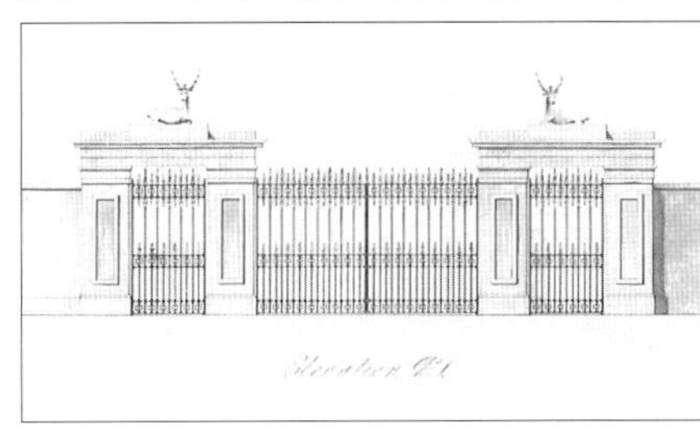

chunky ornamental iron gates. Missing atop the arches is a pair of Power bucks couchant.

Splendid as these Classical entrances are, they constitute inappropriate preludes to the medieval architecture of Roberts's later house. Did they form part of a more comprehensive and coordinated scheme by Anderson, alluded to by Frazer in 1838, which was thwarted by the Famine and then by the architect's mysterious and abrupt departure to America in 1849?

Middle gate; *c.* 1850; architect not known.

Situated at the access to the original southern avenue is this most singular of gatescreens, which is said to have been relocated from a site within the demesne and to have formed part of Cobden's commission around 1815. Separated by a wide gateless opening, in fine ashlar is an excellent pair of carved Tudor Gothic pillars, each in the form of a pointed label-moulded niche, with dripstones of crowned royalty, over which a machicolated and crenellated parapet runs between a pair of multi-gabled octagonal turrets. Across the public road, only loosely associated with its

63. Gurteen Le Poer, Kilsheelan, Portlaw gate.

entrance geographically and even less so stylistically, is the porter's lodge. A single-storey standard three-bay gabled affair with loft accommodation, conspicuous for being unusually elongated. Four beefy pilasters with recessed panels to corners and the central gabled frontispiece flank two pairs of engaged Doric columns *in antis*, which in turn frame bipartite casement windows in their own recesses. The panelled front door is below a round-headed fanlight, over which are incongruous carved Tudor Picturesque bargeboards. Equally disturbing are the newly synthetic-slated roof and the disastrous coating of grey roughcast applied to walls and columns.

Fraser 1838; *LGI* (1904); ffolliott 1971; Bence-Jones 1988; Williams 1994; IAA photographs (S/259/1&11); photographs and drawings in the collection of Count Anthony de la Poer; NIAH.

64. HAMMONDVILLE, Tramore; pre-1841; *demolished.*

A seat in 1814 of Samuel Hammond, which subsequently by 1846 was the residence of Lt.-Col. Robert Kettlewell. Latterly called 'Pickardstown', its lodge had gone by 1926.

Leet 1814; Slater 1846.

65. HARBOUR VIEW, Dunmore East; *c.* 1830.

Now at the gate to 'Pallas Stud' is a single-storey porter's lodge, smooth-rendered with a canted half-umbrello gable to the avenue. Two square outer pillars frame four octagonal stone posts to the tripartite gateway. An estate in the first half of the nineteenth century of William Morris and his son Shapland Carew Morris, whose gatekeeper in 1848 was Thomas Colbert.

Leet 1814; Griffith 1853–63; *LGI* (1904).

66. HEADBOROUGH, Villierstown (2).

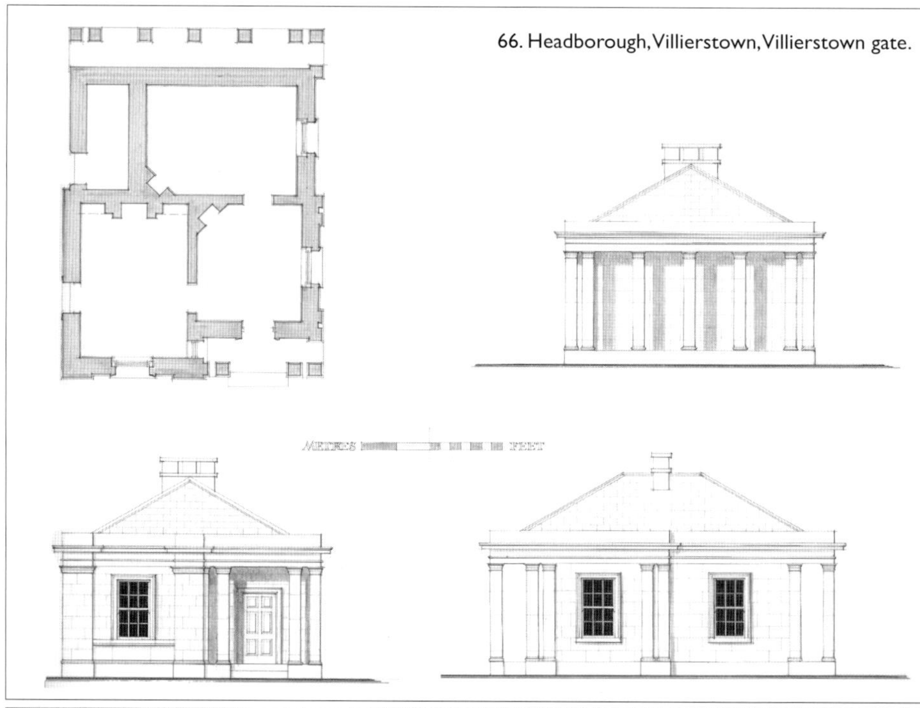

66. Headborough, Villierstown, Villierstown gate.

66. Headborough, Villierstown, Villierstown gate. IAA

An estate with a modest house and pleasant outbuildings but architecturally only notable for its distinguished principal entrance, added by Revd Percy Scott Smyth around the time of his wedding to Catherine Odell of Carriglea [*q.v.*] in 1827.

Villierstown gate; *c.* 1835; architect perhaps John Robertson.

An imaginative and informal neo-Classical lodge by an unidentified architect of some stature and masons of some skill; not quite unique, as there is a smaller variant of it at Tourtane [*q.v.*], where the Devonshire estate connection prompts reminders of the work of John Robertson for the 6th duke at Chatsworth House, Derbyshire, and detailing of his Park Lodge there of 1840–2, but there is no documentary evidence to support such an attribution. Despite its tragically being a roofless shell and deserted even by its gatescreen, which was moved down the road, it retains considerable presence thanks to its sophisticated detailing, finely tooled limestone ashlar and form. Single-storey, four-roomed and rectangular in plan, its erstwhile hipped roof was partly concealed by an entablatured parapet 'supported' by a series of square Doric columns and pilasters, creating panels which contained six-over-six sash windows in architraved surrounds. Three elevations are three-bay, that to the avenue having a panelled door approached by steps within a recessed porch screened by two pairs of columns. A most distinctive feature is an opisthodomus, a colonnaded screen to the rear façade which is blind and without any access from within, the three inner columns terminated by pairs of the same, to be admired from the public road. The tall, straight, spear-topped iron railings and matching carriage gates are contained by four noble pillars with raised and fielded panels below finely chiselled Smyth family bearings. It is difficult to understand what circumstances could possibly have justified the neglect of this important lodge and the parting with its gates.

Tallow gate; *c.* 1860.

Probably built for Percy Smyth (b. 1839), who succeeded his father as a minor in 1846, after his coming of age. Opposite the entrance is another dilapidated lodge in Classical mode. Single-storey, again with a parapeted roof over a two-bay main front, with broad windows in wide panels now coated in modern rendering, and abandoned—its windows boarded-up. A corrugated iron lean-to hallway to one end completes the scene.

LGI (1904); IAA photograph (23/54 Z6); Mowl and Earnshaw 1984; NIAH.

67. HERMITAGE, Dungarvan; pre-1841; *demolished.*

A property in the early nineteenth century of the Barron family, its lodge replaced by a bungalow.

68. HOLY GHOST HOSPITAL, Waterford; *c.* 1880; architect J.J. O'Callaghan.

In contrast with the architect's large, symmetrical institution is his asymmetrical gate lodge. High Victorian Gothic, with steeply pitched roof, built off a T-plan essentially in red sandstone rubble with limestone dressings in quoins, plinth, window surrounds, string-courses and alternate voussoirs in a pointed relieving

arch to one gable, a decorative plaque displaying a shield with the monogram 'HGH' in a bed of beautifully chiselled shamrocks. From the avenue gable overlooking the gate projects an arrowhead bay window with equivalent roof below main bargeboards perforated with more shamrocks. The roof, too, is relieved by polychrome work in a band of green canted slate, while the ridge is broken by a battered cut-stone chimney-stack of three conjoined octagonal flues. In the internal angle under a hipped catslide roof is the entrance hall and porch, the latter now glazed, as is required for its present role as a restaurant-cum-guesthouse, for which it has been admirably rescued from dereliction.

Williams 1994.

THE ISLAND (see LITTLE ISLAND CASTLE)

69. JANEVILLE, Tallow (2).

Both gate lodges, one opposite its entrance, dating from before 1841 when the Keilys were in residence, had gone by 1927.

Wilson 1803; Lewis 1837.

70. JOHN'S HILL, Waterford; pre-1840; *demolished.*

Of the original entrance survives a pointed-arched postern opening in one of the concave quadrant walls, with two large channelled rusticated carriage pillars, probably dating from the time here of barrister and MP Robert Paul, recorder of Waterford in the late eighteenth/early nineteenth century.

Taylor and Skinner 1778; 1783; Leet 1814.

71. KILBEG COTTAGE, Tallow; pre-1841; *demolished.*

A seat, in 1851 of John Parker, to which the lodge had gone by 1927.

Griffith 1853–63.

72. KILLOTERAN, Waterford; pre-1841/*c.* 1845.

If the first OS map is to be believed, this pretty little Regency-style porter's lodge had a predecessor on the site. Built in the time here of William Strangman, it is a simple single-storey rendered hip-roofed structure with an unusual two-bay main front to the avenue, door and window set in elliptically arched recesses. Spoiling the effect are an inappropriate modern plastic door and windows. There are contemporary modest octagonal carriage pillars with the familiar Waterford gadrooned 'splats' to the cappings.

Griffith 1853–63.

73. KILMACTHOMAS UNION WORKHOUSE, Kilmacthomas; *c.* 1853; architect probably G. Wilkinson.

A vast complex of buildings, with a capacity for 500 persons when it took its first admissions in 1853. The lodge is a modest, single-storey, single-roomed, stuccoed affair, gabled to the approach, having a brick chimney-stack banded and capped in granite; derelict. All inevitably by architect George Wilkinson.

O'Connor 1995.

74. KILMANAHAN CASTLE, Clonmel (2).

A large late Georgian house, castellated and given Tudor label moulding to its windows by Lt.-Col. Nuttall Greene (1769–1847), who succeeded to the property on the death of his father in 1813. Impressively located on a bluff overlooking the River Suir, it was approached by two main avenues, monitored to north and south by porters' lodges, both situated unusually remote from the public road.

South gate; pre-1841; *demolished.*

North gate; *c.* 1840; architect not known.

Now deprived of an associated boundary and its original role, this delightful Disney-like ensemble has become a Tudor Castellated eye-catcher. The four-centred arched carriage gateway is buttressed with shield motifs below a crenellated parapet, topped as are the flanking curtain walls, one of which terminates in an octagonal turret, the other containing a postern opening, a little square bartizan and a feature chimney-breast which rises as a stepped gable to the central stack. Behind this is the single-storey gatekeeper's lodge, likewise constructed in random rubble with a castellated parapet and similarly sporting its own octagonal turret and a bartizan. Occupied and lovingly maintained, its archway crenellations surviving as the loftiest of raised flower beds.

Sadly, the fortunes of the big house declined after the death of Col. Greene, who fathered nine daughters and five unmarried sons. The property was sold as an incumbered estate in 1852, eventually being acquired by the earls of Donoughmore, who had coveted it from Knocklofty [*q.v.*] on the opposite bank of the Suir. Their passion for the place must have waned, for Kilmanahan Castle was demolished in 1952.

Atkinson 1815; Heaney 1999; *IFR*; Lyons 1993.

74. Kilmanahan Castle, Clonmel, north gate.

75. KILMORE HILL, Tallow; *c.* 1880.
An elegant late Georgian villa, probably built by the young Revd William Perceval (1787–1880) and where he remained until his death. In that time the property was lodgeless, and it was his son, Richard Perceval (1819–98), who built the present structure. Single-storey and three-bay symmetrical with a hipped roof which catslides over the entrance breakfront, its ornamental canted cresting, perforated with trefoil motifs, is broken by two symmetrically placed chimney-stacks. Occupied, the walls in painted rendering. The good triple gateway of *c.* 1830 has two rather grand limestone ashlar carriage pillars.
Pigot 1825; Lewis 1837; *LGI* (1904).

76. KNOCK, Waterford; pre-1841; *demolished.*
The 1841 OS map shows the lodge unusually in the right-hand quadrant of a vast semicircular forecourt, forward of its gates. A 51-acre property in 1850 of Andrew Ryan.
Griffith 1853–63.

77. KNOCKADERRY, Kill; pre-1840; *demolished.*
A long-time seat of a branch of the Power family, which passed through the marriage in 1817 of heiress Anne Power to Maurice Ronayne of Tinhalla. By 1926 the lodge had deteriorated to a shell.
IFR.

78. KNOCKNAGEERAGH, Clashmore; pre-1841; *demolished.*
A lodge with a back return, to a residence in 1851 of John Power.
Griffith 1853–63.

79. LACKEN LODGE, Dungarvan; *c.* 1820.
In this remote hilly spot are the ruinous remains of a pretty porter's cottage, located well forward of its gates. In rubble construction is a standard three-bay front of a lancet-arched doorway flanked by little round-headed windows, all blocked up. Where the roof once was is rampant vegetation. Ornate cast-iron carriage posts support hoop-topped gates and railings. A property in the early nineteenth century of Dominic Tallon.
Lewis 1837.

80. LAKEVIEW, Dunmore East; pre-1841; *demolished.*
Another estate of the Morris family of nearby Harbourview [*q.v.*].

81. LANDSCAPE, Kilsheelan; *c.* 1900.
A single-storey, gabled, roughcast, three-bay symmetrical gate lodge, with chamfered piers framing the front door and windows in rectangular recesses, on a plinth. Occupied and not quite opposite an entrance, the main feature of which is an ancient tree in its centre. A seat of a branch of the Congreve family of Mount Congreve [*q.v.*].

82. LAURENTUM, Clashmore; pre-1927.
A not-quite-symmetrical standard gabled lodge built after 1841, lying in ruins and thus difficult to date. A property in 1851 of Richard Coghlan, who by 1870 had been succeeded by Laurence Dennehy.
Griffith 1853–63; Slater 1870.

83. LEOVILLE, Waterford; 1860; architect not known.

Very much a chip off the old block is this little lodge in Italianate style, like the contemporary make-over of its big house, which formed part of a mid-Victorian development for James Dobbyn. Single-storey and hip-roofed, with a carved serrated fascia board over rendered walls divided into panels by plain pilasters off a pronounced plinth. The main two-bay elevation to the footpath is comprised of paired round-arched one-over-one sash windows in moulded surrounds. To the avenue projects a later flat-roofed hallway with similar unembellished openings. Immaculately maintained. The first gatekeeper was Patrick Connolly.

84. LISMORE CASTLE, Lismore (3).
This magnificent edifice, precipitously perched overlooking the Blackwater valley, was founded in the time of King John on a previously important ecclesiastical site; it owes its present appearance to two families. In 1602 Richard Boyle (1566–1643), the future earl of Cork, purchased 42,000 acres in Cork and Waterford from Sir Walter Raleigh, and in the ensuing 30 years built the castle up to its basic existing form, to include the outer gatehouse, which remarkably survives much as conceived.

'The Riding House'; 1631.

'An avenue of pollarded elms leads up to it from the main road, and an enclosed way, with massive stone walls to either side, connects it with the gatehouse. With its two little towers, each surmounted by four gables, it is a singularly endearing piece of toy military architecture. It was started in June 1631, and finished about a year later; it cost, exclusive of the stone, which was quarried on the estate, about £50.' Thus did Girouard describe this attractive and durable guardhouse in 1964, its twin rubble-built three-storey towers flanking the round-arched carriage archway with a room bridging over, all with minimal leaded bipartite casement windows. Missing is the sculpted coat of arms of Lord Cork by Alexander Hills 'of Holborn tombmaker', created in 1634, which now adorns the inner gatehouse. Within is a staircase that links two levels of gardens.

The second great family to be associated with Lismore Castle, and remaining so to this day, is that of Cavendish, dukes of Devonshire, upon whom it devolved through marriage. It was the 'Bachelor Duke', the 6th, William Spencer Cavendish (1790–1858), who made such a favourable impression upon both the local populace and his Irish home. The latter received its present battlemented outline in two phases: after 1813, under the guidance of William Atkinson, and in the 1850s, when His Grace should have been more retiring, to designs of his friend Sir Joseph Paxton. According to a report by Curwen of 15 September 1813, the place was urgently in need of attention: 'the Duke of Devonshire purposes to rebuild the Castle of Lismore, and restore it to its ancient grandeur. A Castle, as at present, in ruins, comports with a town in a state of decay.'

Farmyard gate; *c.* 1850.
In a corner of the enclosed courtyard is a substantial single-storey standard gabled lodge in rubble construction, dominated by a central canted projection below an equivalent semi-octahedral roof; it has tiny, inadequate slit windows with cut-stone dressings and an extended lofty off-centre chimney-stack. At right angles is a rubble-built Tudor-arched entrance gateway with wooden boarded doors in cut-granite chamfered reveals, all below a crow-stepped parapet. This is attached to an obviously antique seventeenth-century stump of a round tower.

Castle farm gate; *c.* 1850; architect not known.

Conspicuous in an estate notable for its Tudor and Castellated buildings is this essay in the Italianate style, originally built off a cruciform plan, single-storey with shallow-pitched gables, their striking paired carved verge brackets carried beyond to the eaves. Rendered walls contain squared casement windows below bracketed entablatures. Similarly bracketed is the chimney capping to a row of three cut-stone stacks at the meeting of ridges. Sadly, the twentieth century saw the creation of flat-roofed additions to two internal corners flanking a front door with applied pediment over and two divorced round-headed side lights.

Not realised was a fabulous gateway intended for 'between Rawleigh's Mansion and the Broghill Tower'. The water-damaged drawing shows a grand Classical arch crowned by a Cavendish buck coveted on the

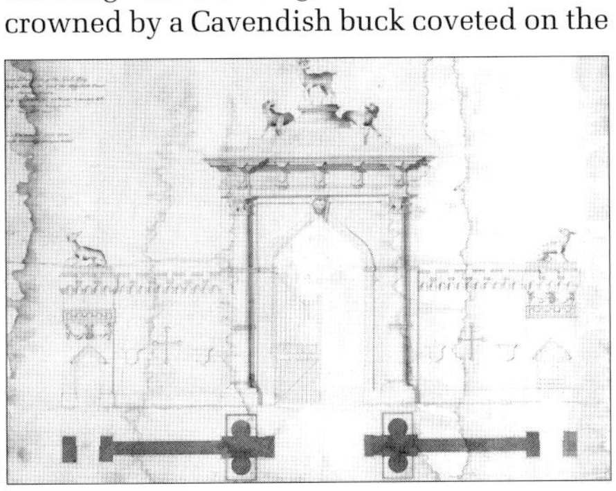

NLI

entablature and from the Gothic castellated curtain walls below by hungry hounds. A design of 23 May 1815 by one James Dwyer, commissioned by architect William Atkinson.

Curwen 1818; *BPB* (1929); *Country Life* (6 and 13 August 1964); Bence-Jones 1988; NIAH; NLI drawing (AD 2618).

85. LITTLE ISLAND CASTLE, Waterford; *c.* 1860.
Apparently a medieval castle in a romantic island setting, it in fact owes its rambling cut-stone appearance to a massive 1891 remodelling of an old sixteenth-century castle and later farmhouse by architect Romayne Walker for Gerald Purcell-Fitzgerald (1865–1946). In contrast, its lodge is a nondescript two-storey hip-roofed affair, much extended and probably raised a storey. Also known as 'Waterford Castle', it is now a hotel in a golf course accessed by ferry.

Lewis 1837; *IFR*.

MANOR OF ST JOHN (see ROANMORE [1])

86. MAYFIELD, Portlaw; *c.* 1855; architect J.S. Mulvany.

At the heart of what was the phenomenon of the Portlaw model village for mill-workers are the pathetic remains of a once-proud and industrious establishment of the vast cotton-weaving mills, the mill-owner's house and gate lodge, all lying in an advanced stage of decay. House and mills were founded by Edward May in the eighteenth century, but the place's brief glory days arrived with its acquisition in 1825 by the Quaker Malcomson family in the person of Joseph Malcomson (1798–1858). He developed the old house in two stages into the great, ungainly Italianate palazzo, initially to designs by Clonmel architect William Tinsley in 1849 and, after the latter's emigration to the USA two years later, in 1855 to plans of John Skipton Mulvany of Dublin. His commission included a new entrance and a porter's lodge, which is so positioned as to command access to both house and factory in perfect symmetry. Screen and lodge are effectively the heart of the radiating streets of the village. Framed by Classical granite outer pillars, shallow concave railed quadrants of ornamental ironwork by Richard Turner of Dublin, with fleur-de-lis finials, contain a tripartite gateway of two carriage gates hung on four cast-iron pillars with anthemion motifs flanking a straight railing with a central pedestrian gate on an axis with the path to the lodge, which leads past the mechanisms by which the gatekeeper could open and close the gates remotely—a system also to be found at Seaforde, Co. Down. In a rather subtler Italianate than that of the house, the single-storey shallow hip-roofed lodge addresses the village with a canted front under an equivalent oversailing roof, having a wide-open porch below a segmental arch in a pedimented and pilastered surround. Rendered walls contain four-over-four sash windows in moulded and lugged surrounds set off by toothed quoins. About the forecourt are rustic cast-iron railings, the same as at nearby Milfort [*q.v.*]. The Malcomson business went bankrupt in 1876. It is unbelievable that there can be such a lack of community pride as to have allowed this fine focal point to become the eyesore it is today.

Wilson 1803; Forbes 1953; Hunt 2000; *IADS* (2000); Craig and Garner 1977.

87. MAYPARK, Waterford; *c.* 1830.
A plain, roughcast, single-storey hip-roofed cottage with a similarly roofed projecting hall, bipartite sash windows and an off-centre chimney-stack; occupied. A seat in 1814 of Henry May, which by 1835 had become 'a comfortable house made out of an old castle and now called May Park, where Mr Mara [*sic*] lives, who is agent for Lord Waterford'. George Meara was still here in 1848, when his gatekeeper was Thomas Mack Murray.

Leet 1814; Heaney 1999; Griffith 1853–63.

MELBOURNE (see GLENAM)

88. MERLIN, Clonmel; *c.* 1825.
The once-quintessential Irish gate lodge, contemporary with its equally typical Irish Regency merchant's villa. Standard single-storey with exaggerated oversailing shallow hipped roof, but now having modern windows in roughcast, rather than harled, walls. To one end is a lean-to addition. Big square entrance pillars with simple blocked corniced cappings. A property for much of the nineteenth century of the Fayle family.

NIAH.

89. MILFORT, Portlaw (3).
A property of William Nicholson in 1814 and of A. Labertouche Esq. by 1837, when there was but one lodged entrance. Around 1845 Milfort was acquired by the Malcomson family of the nearby cotton mills and transformed architecturally. William Malcomson (1813–92), like his brothers at Mayfield [*q.v.*], Elva Lodge [*q.v.*], Minella [*q.v.*] and Woodlock [*q.v.*], probably

89. Milfort, Portlaw (NLI).

employed the services of John Skipton Mulvany to give the house an Italianate cloak and to create at least one of the two new entrances to the demesne. By the 1950s the house and its lodges had all been removed, although a photographic record of one of the latter reveals it to have been one of the architectural wonders of the county. In 1864 the *Dublin Builder* magazine informed its readers that 'An iron gate-lodge and entrance of original design and peculiar construction, is in course of erection for William Malcomson, near Portlaw, Co. Waterford. Mr William Turner, Hammersmith Works, Contractor.' This extraordinary structure was not solely of iron, for the 1927 OS map and a contemporary postcard view refer to it as 'Copper Lodge', doubtless referring to a conspicuous green roof finish. This was in the form of a great ogee dome that rose to the triple-flue chimney-stack, barely broken by tiny round-headed attic dormers with Gothic lights and extending its eaves sufficiently to create a verandah right around the ground-floor 'drum' accommodation. The eaves gutter was decorated with neo-Classical palmettes and carried on intricately fretted cast-iron arcading. Behind, the elevational treatment was Italianate, with moulded surrounds to round-headed windows and the segmentally arched porch opening. This remarkable exhibition of the capabilities of the Turner Ironworks of Ball's Bridge, Dublin, saw further outlet in the rustic fencing, the same as that to Mayfield, which divided the garden, and the contrasting exuberant and monumental gatescreen in the same material, with its grand carriage pillars of intertwining foliage rising to corniced cappings with wreath motifs as bases for elegant globe lanterns. The gates and screens beyond are again as at Mayfield and also at Woodlock [*q.v.*] and Tulira Castle, Co. Galway, though here with a more decorative foiled top. The secondary pillars were crowned by cast-iron urns, the whole terminating in fans. The reason for the lodge's removal and its fate are a mystery, but the gatescreen is to be seen in some of its former glory at Strancally Castle [*q.v.*].

DB (15 April 1864); *IADS* (2000); Lawrence photograph (4064C).

90. MILLBROOK, Clonmel; *c.* 1810.

A traditional two-bay single-storey lodge with oversailing hipped-roof eaves spoiled by a catslide hall addition over half of the main front. Extended more sympathetically to the left-hand side. Associated in the early nineteenth century with the Hughes family of the adjacent Suirville corn mills.

Slater 1846; Griffith 1853–63.

91. MINELLA, Clonmel (2).

In the 1840s this was 'Coleville House' of the Harvey family, but in 1864 the *Dublin Builder* magazine advised that 'Near Clonmel and adjacent to the River Suir, has been erected for Thomas Malcomsom a large mansion ... The stables and gate lodge are situated at a convenient distance and near the main road. Matthew Lynch, builder, Dublin, John S. Mulvany, archt.' Thomas Malcomson (d. 1872) was one of a number of brothers who commissioned the architect to plan residences in County Waterford, in this case in 1862, when a gate lodge design for his client was exhibited at the RHA—which of these two singular lodges was the subject is not clear.

Principal entrance; *c.* 1862; architect J.S. Mulvany.

If there was any doubt about Mulvany's involvement here it is allayed by details which display hallmarks of his work, from the bold corbelling of the entrance pillar cappings to his particular brand of straight arch to the windows with the corners rounded off. A gauche affair and as forthright as all his gate lodges, sitting on an elevated site, it is single-storey standard with a hipped roof to the main body of the structure and to its hall projection. Below the eaves is a deep frieze, plain but for disc motifs which crown pairs of deeply recessed pilaster panels on each side of the front door (now a window) with a moulded and lugged surround. All raised on a pronounced plinth in smooth rendering. There is a blind window to the road with sill corbelled, as elsewhere. Extended to the rear in like manner, but with the chimney-stack removed from the original structure, synthetic slates applied and plastic casements replacing the original sashes.

Secondary entrance; *c.* 1862; architect J.S. Mulvany.

Instantly identifiable as Mulvany's work, being a stuccoed version of his granite lodge at Mount Anville, Co. Dublin. Across the road from its gate, it is a single-storey design on a cruciform plan, the gables arranged as open pediments with striking mutules to verges continuing about the eaves as brackets. To the external angles the Classical pilasters frame openings that have the architect's favourite straight arches with rounded corners in plain lugged surrounds. From the leading gable extends a triangular bay window with its own equivalent roof, while at the intersection of the main ridges is a chimney-stack as a pair of conjoined square flues. There is a sensitive extension to the rear and a nice contemporary gatescreen to the road.

The house is now a hotel.

DB (15 May 1864); *IADS* (2000).

92. MOCOLLOP CASTLE, Ballyduff; pre-1841/1882.

On this once-proud demesne lie the ruins of the old Desmond castle and its successor, the residence of the Drew family, only survived by the fine outbuildings and its gate lodge, which is a late Victorian replacement for a predecessor. The earlier porter's lodge was surely built for a Francis Drew, for there were four of that name in succession, the last dying unmarried in 1839, to be succeeded here by his sister Olivia Maria Drew, who in 1841 married James Barry of Ballyclogh, Co. Cork [*q.v.*]. He died in 1881, but she recorded their union for posterity in a stone plaque on the gable of the replacement lodge that contains 'O' and 'M' intertwined with a 'B' as a monogram above the date '1882'. The gable is nicely framed by delicate fretted bargeboards continued as fascia boards to the eaves. Largely single-storey with a half-attic floor, the lodge is two-bay in a rendered finish, the ridge highlighted by a red earthenware canted cresting with trefoil perforations, broken by a red-brick corbelled chimney-stack. In 1883 Mrs Barry married her second husband, Lt.-Col. George Edward Hillier, but was widowed again only a year later.

LGI (1904); *IFR*; Craig and Garner 1977.

93. MOOREHILL, Tallow; *c.* 1825.

A triple gateway of a form normally associated with architect Richard Morrison, with its inner drum carriage pillars framed by larger outer square ashlar pillars with plain recessed panels and, beyond, contrasting rubble concave quadrant walls, much as at Ballygally [*q.v.*]. Within is the archetypal Irish gate lodge, single-storey below an oversailing hipped roof, nearly pyramidal owing to the almost square plan and rising to a central stone stack. There are wide sash windows with margined glazing, suggesting a later date, in limewashed harled walls on a stone plinth; lovingly maintained and sensitively extended to the rear. Modest and elegant wrought-iron entrance gates, by Heydens of Tallow, lead to the late eighteenth-century house built by the Hon. William Moore, the third son of the 1st Viscount Mount Cashell; after his death in 1810 he was succeeded by his son of the same name, also of Sapperton [*q.v.*], who built the lodge before his death in 1849.

BPB (1873); Bence-Jones 1988.

MOUNTAIN VIEW (see COUNTY KILKENNY)

94. MOUNT BOLTON, Fiddown; pre-1840; *demolished.*

A lodge presumably built by one of two short-lived John Boltons, either John senior (1783–1807) or his only son, John junior (1807–41).

LGI (1904).

95. MOUNT CONGREVE, Waterford (5).

Beautifully sited by the River Suir is the antique demesne of the Congreve family and their grand mansion, which unusually has a history of lodge-building spanning three centuries.

Middle gate; pre-1841/1950.

A Georgian lodge that was located to the right-hand side of what was then the main avenue to the big house. It was superseded as the principal approach with the formation of the Waterford entrance around 1845, but the building remained until it was replaced at the other side of the gate by one of three identical Georgian-style twentieth-century lodges as part of a remarkable revamp of the estate by Major John Congreve (1872–1957) and his son Ambrose, which also saw the birth of the famous azalea and rhododendron gardens. For all the world like something from 200 years earlier—George IV rather than George VI—is the single-storey standard porter's lodge in stucco effect on a square plan, with its pyramidal roof rising to a central chimney-stack partly hidden by a parapet. The three-bay avenue front is comprised of a recessed porch flanked by six-over-six sash windows, now replaced by casements. Contemporary with this is an extensive gatescreen of tall-walled concave quadrants contained by lofty pillars with recessed panels, moulded cappings and urns atop. The original carriage pillars may well be those to be found now at the Killoteran gate.

Portlaw gate; 1950.

Lodge and entrance are much as at the middle gate, although the gates are more elaborate, with the meeting rails enriched with the Congreve bearings and crowned by their crest of a falcon rising with wings extended.

Waterford gate; *c.* 1845; architect not known.

The new grand entrance was formed by John Congreve (1800–63), who succeeded to the estates as a minor on the death of his father in 1809. The impressive triple gateway is comprised of four square limestone ashlar

95. Mount Congreve, Waterford, Portlaw gate.

pillars with moulded cappings and spear-topped gates, all framed by convex-walled quadrants. The gatekeeper's accommodation is generous, contained behind a long five-bay avenue front, from the centre of which projects a room with a wide tripartite window with grey limestone surround in limewashed white walls. To each side are six-over-six sash windows and a double-leafed doorway, all below very shallow-pitched hipped roofs. All in pristine condition.

Killoteran gate; 1950.

Across the public road and severed by it from the demesne is this entrance which mysteriously leads nowhere; its twentieth-century astylar Georgian-style lodge, just as those at the Portlaw and middle gates, presides over its own gates, hung on what appear to be late eighteenth-century pillars of V-jointed rusticated cut stone with moulded plinths and railings. Perhaps they once graced the original main entrance but are now, like the lodge, out of sight and seemingly out of mind.

IFR.

96. MOUNT MELLERAY MONASTERY, Cappoquin; *c.* 1840.
'A great portion of this country belongs to Sir Richard Keane. He has lately bestowed 575 acres of it for one hundred years on an establishment of Trappists, who have rested in this country on the breaking up of the monastery of St Meillery in France. There are now sixty residents, and they have for the last two years been constructing great buildings on this ground.' Robert Graham, visiting on 21 July 1835, goes on to describe the impressive buildings, which probably did not then include the plain but commodious gatehouse, two-storey and three-bay, with bipartite one-over-one sashes and a fanlit doorway below a hipped roof crowned by two chimney-stacks. It commands an extensive gatescreen of wide concave-walled quadrants and ball-finialled stone pillars.

Heaney 1999.

97. MOUNT PLEASANT, Waterford; pre-1841.
The King family is noted here in 1814, and a Samuel King is recorded as resident in 1837 and 1876, his gatekeeper in 1851 being John Callaghan.

Mason 1814–19; Lewis 1837; Griffith 1853–63; *LOI.*

98. MOUNT RIVERS, Cappoquin (2).
The two ruined lodges tell of a disintegrating estate now lacking its big house, with only fine outbuildings remaining serviceable. A property that never seems to have had the security of a lengthy family relationship, in the early nineteenth century having had a succession of occupants: C.F. Musgrave (later of Tuourin Castle, *q.v.*) (1814), John Power (1824), Mr Peard (1835), Revd G. Gumbleton (1837) and Sir Charles Shaw (1851).

North lodge; *c.* 1810.
Single-storey, once stuccoed, with a window and doorway to the leading front below a hipped roof. Now a shell.

South lodge; *c.* 1820.
Square stone carriage pillars with scroll-topped stops flanked by sealed, segmentally arched postern openings and, alongside, the skeleton of a single-bay hip-roofed cottage, that window set in a segmentally headed recess to ground level.

Leet 1814; Pigot 1824; Heaney 1999; Lewis 1837; Griffith 1853–63.

NEW PARK (see COUNTY KILKENNY)

99. NEWTOWN, Tramore; *c.* 1830.
A standard single-storey lodge with harled walls below a hipped roof with a corbel course to its clipped eaves. Minuscule, derelict and cowering behind one of the tall, concave entrance quadrant walls, which frame plain carriage pillars; to one side is a postern opening below a segmental stone lintel with extended bearings. A seat in 1814 of Joseph Power (*c.* 1740–1826), who died childless; it passed briefly to his niece, Mary Power, and her husband, Richard Power Ronayne of D'Loughtane [*q.v.*], before becoming home to her nephew, Edward O'Neill Power (*c.* 1810–56), probably on his coming of age.

Mason 1814–19; Pigot 1824; Lewis 1837; *IFR.*

100. NEWTOWN LODGE, Waterford; pre-1839; *demolished.*
A property in 1824 of Meade Hobson, which by 1848 had become the residence of corn and tobacco merchant Joseph D. Lapham.

Pigot 1824; Griffith 1853–63.

NEWTOWN PARK (see SUIR VIEW)

NEWTOWN SCHOOL (see QUAKERS' SCHOOLHOUSE)

101. OLD COURT, Waterford; 1867; *demolished.*
The old palace of the bishops of Waterford, built in 1730 but given a Picturesque cloak after it passed to secular use. Before his succession to Rickett's Castle [*q.v.*] in 1877, this was probably work for John Thomas Medlycott (1823–96), who built the lodge in 1867, which was also the date of his first marriage. Now a hotel.

LGI (1904).

102. PAULSWORTH, Clashmore; pre-1841; *demolished.*
A lodge sited opposite the gates to an estate before his death in 1833 of William Gun Paul, barrister and younger son of Sir Joshua Paul of Ballyglan [*q.v.*]. Thereafter home to William Ryan, leasing from Paul's widow Marianna.

Griffith 1853–63; *BPB* (1929).

103. PEOPLE'S PARK, Waterford; *c.* 1880.

A municipal single-storey gabled lodge on a T-plan, with mildly decorative bargeboards, trefoil-perforated crestings, fleur-de-lis finials and a polychromatic red and cream brick chimney-stack that may reveal the original finish of the lodge, now smooth-rendered, with a variety of openings, flat and round-headed; from the avenue gable extends a rectangular bay window with its own hipped roof. The entrance screen is comprised of convex railed quadrants with chunky palmette-finialled ironwork to match a triple gateway contained by bold stone pillars with moulded recessed panels and exaggerated oversailing blocked cappings. Although a plaque records its construction date as 1900, it appears on a map of 1883!

PICKARDSTOWN (see HAMMONDVILLE)

PORTLAW (see WOODHOUSE)

PORTLAW WORKS (see MAYFIELD)

104. PRESENTATION CONVENT, Clonmel (2).
The Presentation nuns relocated their convent and college to this site in 1829 and built the great austere college block, to which at least one of the lodges was in place by 1850, with John Breen then as gatekeeper. Both lodges erected after 1841 are things of the past.

Griffith 1853–63; O'Donnell 1999.

105. PRESENTATION CONVENT, Waterford; pre-1950; *demolished.*
Sadly, it may never be known whether the commission for the Presentation Sisters by A.W.N. Pugin included the gate lodge. The great Gothicist architect is known to have paid visits in 1842 and 1845 to supervise the construction of his designs.

Atterbury 1995.

106. PROSPECT [1], Waterford; *c.* 1845; *demolished.*
The 1848 valuation records that the gatehouse of Thomas Sheppard of John's Hill [*q.v.*] lay unoccupied. A later valuation of 1880 records the building of a gate lodge for Samuel White in this townland of Ballytruckle, presumably a replacement.

Griffith 1853–63.

107. PROSPECT [2], Waterford; pre-1839; *demolished.*
A shopping complex now occupies the site on the Dunmore Road of a house and its porter's lodge, in 1814 of Charles Tandy.

Leet 1814.

108. QUAKERS' SCHOOLHOUSE, Waterford (2).
An establishment founded in 1798 about the house of 'Newtown' of the Wyse family.

Front entrance; *c.* 1800.
A single-storey standard lodge with eaves to its hipped roof high enough to accommodate attic space. White rendered walls had six-over-six sash windows on each side of a sheeted front door with a minuscule rectangular fanlight below a later bargeboarded canopy with ornamental quatrefoiled brackets; occupied. It commands a gatescreen of big square limestone ashlar pillars with plain cappings and postilion gate to one side.

Rear entrance; pre-1839; *demolished.*
A structure that was probably associated with the old walled garden, the access to which is sealed up.

Country Life (22 December 1966).

109. RAHEEN, Clonmel; *c.* 1825/1850; architect probably William Tinsley.
A very attractive villa, home in 1824 to attorney John Domville, perhaps its builder. Thereafter it was the residence of Thomas Greer, brewer and miller (*c.* 1769–1833), and then of his widow Elizabeth until *c.* 1870. At the entrance are late Georgian V-jointed rusticated gate pillars with moulded corniced cappings crowned by later lanterns. Tight alongside and probably contemporary with the pillars, but barely recognisable as such,

is a single-storey gate lodge with oversailing shallow-hipped roof, its short three-bay elevation to the avenue. Sometime later in the century, however, it was updated and transformed with a new face. The main front has been widened by the addition of 'cheeks', each with a round-headed niche and recessed panels above and below, which extend to embrace the original windows that flank the semicircular-headed doorway—all perfectly symmetrical and quirky and presented in a painted smooth rendering. To the sides these 'cheeks' create deep recesses or rustic arbours below the roof soffits. There is a 1½-storey version of this lodge at Knockeevan, Co. Tipperary [*q.v.*], by William Tinsley, which prompts attribution to him.

Pigot 1824; Griffith 1853–63; *IFR*; Forbes 1953.

RATHCULLIHEEN (see COUNTY KILKENNY)

110. RICHMOND, Cappoquin (2).
Although tracing its origins from 1704 and the earl of Cork of Lismore Castle [*q.v.*], the present big, square, late Georgian house dates from the time here of Michael Keane of the Cappoquin [*q.v.*] family. Both of its porters' lodges, however, would appear to have been built when the property was let to Major John Henry Alcock, recorded here in 1824 and 1856.

North gate; pre-1841.
Now obscured by modernisation and additions, the lodge may have been a standard single-storey hip-roofed cottage with rubble-built walls.

South gate; *c.* 1830.
A single-storey hip-roofed rendered structure, two-bay to the avenue, each of its bipartite one-over-one sash windows set in semicircular-arched recesses; occupied. The gate porter in 1851 was Mrs Grace Mansfield.

Leet 1814; Pigot 1824; Griffith 1853–63; Slater 1856.

111. ROANMORE [1], Waterford (2).
A seat of the Wyse family, before 1841 complete with its own gate lodge. Around 1843 Sir Thomas Wyse (1791–1862) significantly redeveloped the property, taking advantage of architect A.W.N. Pugin's involvement in designing the neighbouring Presentation Convent [*q.v.*] to engage him in planning a new house in his distinctive polychromatic Gothic manner, renaming the place 'Manor of St John', realigning the public road to enlarge his plot and building a replacement porter's lodge. One can only now speculate that the latter was also to Pugin's design, for it and its predecessor have both gone.

LGI (1904); Bence-Jones 1988; Atterbury 1995.

112. ROANMORE [2], Waterford; pre-1950; *demolished.*
Previously 'Pastimeknock House' and lodgeless, it took on its new name when that was discarded by the Wyse family at 'Manor of St John' (see Roanmore [1]). The lodge was built after 1841, when the property was home to the Condons.

Griffith 1853–63.

RIVER VIEW (see COUNTY KILKENNY)

113. ROCKETT'S CASTLE, Portlaw; *c.* 1861; *demolished.*
The seat for 50 years of Revd John Thomas Medlycott (1789–1877), which at the age of 72 he had completely transformed by architect Samuel Ussher Roberts at a cost of £4,500, which included a new Italianate house and perhaps the attendant porter's lodge, which one can only speculate was in like manner.

LGI (1904); IAA.

114. ROCKFIELD, Cappagh; *c.* 1835.
Also known as 'Rockville' in the past, a property for over a century of the Hely family, of whom Pierce Hely added the gate lodge. Plain and single-storey below a hipped roof, its two-bay façade to the avenue; much modernised, with rendered walls and new concrete interlocking roof tiles. Nearby are the entrance pillars, octagonal in section, much as found throughout the county but lacking any architectural detailing and impaired by crude oversailing cappings.

Pigot 1824; Lewis 1837; Pike and Hodges 1911.

ROCKSHIRE (see COUNTY KILKENNY)

115. ST ANGELA'S URSULINE CONVENT, Waterford; pre-1840; *demolished.*
'A school, also for the gratuitous instruction of poor females, has been established near the Ursuline convent on the road to Tramore.' Since Lewis recorded this in 1837 the site has been massively developed, but with the loss of its early lodge. The gatescreen with its extensive semicircular forecourt survives, with a cut-stone pedestrian opening to the left-hand side.

Lewis 1837; NIAH.

116. ST JOSEPH'S CONVENT, Cappoquin; *c.* 1903; architect probably S.F. Hynes.
Although exhibiting a three-bay elevation with its openings blocked up, it has been retained as an attractive feature by the gate. Quite quirky, the now-blind windows sport Tudor label mouldings on each side of a hood-moulded, segmentally pointed-arched doorway in rendered walls below a hipped gable. To the ridge are decorative tiles

stopped by hip-knobs. Doubtless part of the commission of Samuel Francis Hynes, from whose designs convent and schools were complete by 1903.

IAA.

117. ST JOSEPH'S CONVENT, Waterford; *c.* 1900.

An extensive hip-roofed affair, with cream brick in abundance in a sawtooth eaves band, string-course, quoins, dressings and segmentally pointed arches; five-bay to the avenue. Contemporary with the main institution on the hill.

ST JOSEPH'S CONVENT (see WOODHOUSE)

ST OTTERAN'S HOSPITAL (see WATERFORD LUNATIC ASYLUM)

118. SALTERBRIDGE, Cappoquin (3).

Although originating with the Hales family in the mid-eighteenth century and acquired by the Musgraves, it was the Chearnley family who were responsible for the estate's present manifestation, having inherited it about 1790. Richard Chearnley (1807–63) in 1849 engaged an as-yet-unknown architect to redevelop the place with a striking neo-Classical refacing of the house and the provision of new porters' lodges.

Glenribbeen Bridge gate; *c.* 1840.

On the western approach is this delightful five-bay cottage in pleasant rubble stone facing below a steeply pitched hipped roof with attic accommodation. Perhaps beginning as standard three-bay and subsequently extended in like manner to the left-hand side; multi-paned casement windows, some bipartite. Plain entrance pillars but more elaborate iron carriage gates with some Gothic detailing, also to be seen on the main gatescreen.

Fadduaga gate; pre-1841/*c.* 1849; architect perhaps John Robertson.

A conspicuous and unusually commodious four-roomed single-storey lodge rich in

Classical detailing, with, like the house, an abundance of Doric pilasters defining its bays. In limestone ashlar, with an embracing entablatured parapet partly concealing the hipped roof. Essentially three-bay, the central canted projection contains the entrance doorway flanked by wide eight-over-eight sash windows, which light the delightful octagonal hallway. Beyond, on each side are bipartite six-over-six sashes with chamfered stone mullions. Where the main and back return ridges meet is a dominant pair of stone chimney-flues, tall, hexagonal in section, reflecting the entrance projection but with a conflicting Tudor feel. The detailing is suggestive of the hand of John Robertson, who may also have been working for the local gentry at Headborough [*q.v.*] and Tourin [*q.v.*] close by. What is equally remarkable is that in 2000 this structure was a roofless shell and apparently in a state of terminal decline were it not for the Irish Landmark Trust, who triumphantly reincarnated it as a holiday let. Replacing an earlier lodge nearby, it is complemented by a wonderful and extensive tripartite gateway and railings in a stylistic mix of singular composite Classical pillars with engaged Doric columns and intricate Gothic ironwork with spiky arcaded top, pendants and intertwining roundel rail.

Cappoquin gate; pre-1927; *demolished.*

A mysterious short-lived lodge, built after 1841 almost opposite the Fadduaga gate, which commanded access to a sliver of land between the public road and that length of the River Blackwater known as Bishop's Fishery.

Taylor and Skinner 1778; 1783; Wilson 1803; Hoare 1807; *LGI* (1904); Bence-Jones 1988.

The Irish Landmark Trust

118. Salterbridge, Cappoquin, Fadduaga gate (after restoration).

119. SAPPERTON, Tallow; *c.* 1850.

The mid-eighteenth-century sister seat of the neighbouring Moore Hill [*q.v.*], both of the Moore family, a house that remained lodgeless for a century. Situated not quite opposite its entrance owing to a road junction, it is a plain single-storey, four-bay gabled structure, rendered and whitewashed, built for William Moore (b. 1816) after he succeeded to the estate on the death of his father in 1849.

BPB (1861).

120. SARAHVILLE, Kilmacthomas; pre-1840; *demolished.*

A property in 1814 and 1824 of James Barron, which by 1838 had been inherited by Morgan Barron and the lodge to which had gone by 1925.

Leet 1814; Pigot 1824; Fraser 1838.

121. SEAFIELD, Bunmahon (2).

A seat of the Anthony family, the lodges to which both seem to have been early twentieth-century cabins, both constructed of corrugated iron: one gabled and derelict, the other hip-roofed, reclad in weatherboarding and occupied.

122. SEAVIEW, Ringville; *c.* 1850.

In the mid-nineteenth century this was a marine property of Lord Stuart de Decies of Dromana [*q.v.*]. Its gatekeeper's lodge would have been an unremarkable single-storey standard cottage with high eaves and harled walls but for smooth banded verges and tiny brick diagonally set chimney-stacks to each gable and, over the front door, a cut-stone open pediment hood carried on wacky 'onion' corbels. Derelict and boarded-up.

SION HILL (see COUNTY KILKENNY)

SION LODGE (see COUNTY KILKENNY)

123. SPRINGFIELD, Clonmel; 1898; architect not known.

A good late Victorian single-storey Picturesque lodge, raised off an L-plan in English garden wall bond orange brick, with multi-paned bipartite casement windows below segmental arches. The steeply pitched roof has perforated earthenware scalloped

crestings between a squat corbelled brick chimney-stack and finely pierced bargeboards. Over the internal angle the roof catslides to form an entrance porch, its eaves carried on a pair of chamfered wooden posts at one end and at the other by an enormous stone corbel. To the road gable, above a pair of narrow windows is a peculiar cut-stone feature looking as though it should display an informative plaque. Concave entrance quadrants of railings on dwarf walls frame fine contemporary ashlar carriage pillars rising to composite cappings and elegant gadrooned urns. A property in 1898 of Frederick Quinn.

124. SPRINGFIELD, Portlaw; *c.* 1810.
Perhaps of an age with the attractive villa is its minute standard single-storey lodge with segmentally arched windows on each side of half-doors below an oversailing hipped roof. Unoccupied but maintained. A property of the Shaw family in the early nineteenth century.

125. STAR OF THE SEA CONVENT, Tramore; *c.* 1875.
A pleasant single-storey standard lodge with a hipped roof, its eaves lofty enough to accommodate the round-headed fanlight to the front door. Like the main convent, suffering from the insertion of inappropriate modern windows and doorway; extended. The short-walled gatescreen is dominated by six Classical pillars with moulded corniced cappings.

126. STRANCALLY CASTLE, Villierstown (5).
Beautifully situated overlooking the River Blackwater is the Romantic castle built for John Keily by James and George Richard Pain in the manner of their erstwhile master, John Nash. Unfortunately nothing of their work survives in its lodges. That to the north opposite the entrance from before 1841 is ruinous and overgrown. Nearby is the reassembled great iron gatescreen salvaged from its previous home at Milfort [*q.v.*], Portlaw. Two other pre-1841 lodges—one within the demesne and another close by to the farmyard across the public road—have

Kieran Heffernan

both been demolished. At the southern extremity of the property is a double cottage by an entrance gate of *c.* 1850, 1½-storey and sharing a big brick chimney-stack, built in random stone with a chamfered corner. Assuming the date to be correct, it may have been the last of Keily's ambitious building ventures, some of which, like the reconstruction of the village, remained unfulfilled, for he had to sell the estate to the Lloyd family by 1860.

Lewis 1837; Lyons 1993.

127. SUIRMOUNT, Clonmel (2).
A property in 1851 of Mrs Maria Fitzpatrick; both post-1841 lodges have gone.

Griffith 1853–63.

128. SUIR VIEW, Waterford; pre-1839; *demolished.*
A property, latterly renamed 'Newtown Park', which had a succession of ever-changing occupants in the nineteenth century, including a Captain Johnston in 1814 and Captain Edmund Richard in 1851.

Leet 1814; Griffith 1853–63.

129. SUIRVILLE, Waterford; *c.* 1820.
Apparently originating as a simple single-storey hip-roofed lodge, with an avenue front of three Gothic lancet windows with cast-iron latticed glazing pattern and an entrance doorway to one end. Subsequently extended towards the road, its new gable forming part of the perimeter wall, likewise roughcast, with a flat-arched postern gate. Alongside is a later pair of limestone ashlar carriage pillars and contemporary iron gates of *c.* 1870 with lion-mask features and foliated decoration. A villa in the late eighteenth century of Revd John Hewetson, in 1846 of George Hartforde and five years later of Captain Simon Newport.

Slater 1846; Griffith 1853–63; *LGI* (1904).

130. SUMMERLAND, Waterford; pre-1840; *demolished.*
A seat in the mid-nineteenth century of Samuel Strangman, the lodge to which had gone by 1950, when the property had been acquired as St Joseph's Novitiate.

Griffith 1853–63; Slater 1870.

131. SUMMERVILLE, Dunmore East; pre-1841/*c.* 1870.
A Victorian baronial house, built in 1870 by architects Otway and Watt for the Hon. Dudley Francis Fortescue (1820–1909) to replace the earlier house on the property, which he subsequently renamed 'Corballymore' after its townland. The architects may also have been responsible for the addition to the original gate lodge, thus forming an L-plan. This displays a most curious multi-latticed mesh feature to the gable, perhaps intended as roofspace ventilation. Previously a plain gabled cottage, with a canted bay to view the park rather than its gate.

BPB (1929); Williams 1994.

132. SWEET BRIAR, Tramore; *c.* 1850.
A suburban property in 1846 of George Roche, although its porter's lodge may date from the occupancy of James Budd, local grocer, timber and coal merchant. Initially a single-storey structure with oversailing hipped roof and a two-bay short front to the approach, it has since been considerably added to with a glazed hall and been modernised with replacement square Georgian-style look-alike windows in painted rendered walls.

Slater 1856; 1870; NIAH.

133. TEMPLEMICHAEL, Clashmore (2).
Around 1800 this was a 'modern country seat' of a Mr Freeman, subsequently home in 1837 to Captain Armstrong, now a scene of dereliction. Both lodges were across the public road by the old walled garden.

South gate; pre-1841.
A standard gabled cottage, ruinous and enveloped in ivy.

North gate; pre-1841; *demolished.*

Lewis 1837; Stalley 1991.

134. TIVOLI, Cappoquin; *c.* 1845; *demolished.*

In 1844 'the well-situate villa of Henry Dennehy' was observed by O'Flanagan, probably not long after its building, but strangely its porter's lodge escaped the notice of the Ordnance Survey, only an early nineteenth-century postcard recording its appearance for posterity. Conspicuous is the gabled roof of boldly oversailing eaves and verges with hefty hip-knobs and a central octagonal brick chimney-stack. The main rendered front to the road was comprised of four pointed-arched windows with multi-paned glazing. Nearby is a pair of carriage pillars in the form of pylons with recessed panels, the original boldly moulded plinths and cappings since crudely reconstructed and the previous exaggerated steeply angled four-faced pedimented top drastically simplified. Dennehy is listed in 1846 as a local attorney.

O'Flanagan 1975; Slater 1846.

135. TOURIN, Cappoquin (4).
Next to the ruin of the Roches' old castle is the stylish Italianate villa, probably dating from around 1860, built for Sir Richard Musgrave, 4th baronet (1820–74), after he succeeded to the estate in 1859. Only the two later gatekeepers' lodges survive.

Inner gate; pre-1841; *demolished.*
A lodge that commanded the north-eastern entrance by the river.

West gate; pre-1841; *demolished.*
An entrance distinguished by an extensive late Victorian wooden gatescreen.

North gate; *c.* 1870.

A 1½-storey substantial gabled lodge on an L-plan, with a single-storey canted bay window to the leading gable and a gabled porch projecting alongside from the internal angle. All rendered rather undistinguished by a drab grey finish, the insertion of ill-advised modern casement windows, enclosure of the porch and the probable loss of decorative bargeboards. In contrast is a wide and distinguished Classical gatescreen with limestone ashlar pillars, those to the main gate topped by elegant ball finials. A triple gateway with straight railings further extending in convex quadrants, the ironwork decorated with pretty scrolling.

Middle gate; *c.* 1850.
Outside the entrance is a 1½-storey gabled cottage in sandstone facings, the main front two-bay, with a pair of gablets over and a central chimney-stack above that again.

O'Flanagan 1975; *BPB* (1929); Bence-Jones 1988.

136. TOURNORE, Dungarvan; *c.* 1810.
A modest, single-storey, standard, harled gabled cottage; derelict. A seat in the early nineteenth century of the Boate family.

Leet 1814.

137. TOURTANE, Lismore; *c.* 1840; architect possibly John Robertson.
At the gates to the perfectly formal 1823 Classical villa is this superb little composition, with staid Classical elements imaginatively and expertly applied informally in the Picturesque spirit of the day. Not quite original, being based on its similarly asymmetrical big cousin at Headborough [*q.v.*], it is likewise formed in beautifully chiselled limestone ashlar with Doric details. Single-storey with a large back return below a shallow hipped roof, which oversails a two-bay principal front of wide sash windows with innovative latticed glazing pattern, and alongside a recessed porch approached up a flight of steps between a pair of square Doric columns *in*

137. Tourtane, Lismore.

antis that reflect an abundance of pilasters about the structure, framing openings. To the rear ridge is a row of three square chimney-flues united by a common capping. Almost unheard-of in a gate lodge, the architect has troubled to introduce interior design, with vaulted plaster ceilings to two rooms. Rightly treasured by its owners, as is the equally conspicuous, extensive and imaginative gatescreen, with low outer ogee quadrant walls flanking a triple carriage gateway with simple spear-topped ironwork by Heydens of Tallow, carried on four cut-limestone pillars, each on a square plinth, the shafts of which have chamfers that widen upwards to form an octagonal base for the corniced cappings. A tenant farm of the duke of Devonshire, occupied in 1837 by Thomas Foley, a connection which hints at the work of John Robertson, who was employed around the same time at Chatsworth House and Edensor village in Derbyshire.

Lewis 1837.

URSULINE CONVENT (see ST ANGELA'S)

138. VIEW MOUNT, Waterford; pre-1925; *demolished.*
A lodge built after 1841 to a property in 1870 of John Fanning.

Slater 1870.

WATERFORD CASTLE (see LITTLE ISLAND CASTLE)

139. WATERFORD LUNATIC ASYLUM, Waterford; *c.* 1835; architect W. Murray.
Now St Otteran's Hospital, it was originally founded in 1833 to designs by William Murray and opened in 1835 as a second-class asylum for 100 patients. The lodge by the entrance is clearly by Murray, exhibiting his recognisable detailing, such as the chamfered corner and segmental window heads to be found at other such institutions about the country, particularly that in Carlow town. Unlike the other examples, this rises to two storeys as a gatehouse, the resultant ungainliness suggesting the upper floor—in a drab grey rendering, unlike the punched limestone ashlar ground floor—to have been

a later addition. The central breakfront rises blind to a dainty shallow pediment, which projects from a hipped roof crowned by a bold cut-stone chimney-stack with plinth and banded capping, probably reassembled from below. The entrance doorway breakfront has been transformed into an unsightly glazed screen. Little remains of the original entrance gates.

IAA.

140. WATERPARK, Waterford; pre-1839; *demolished.*
A property in 1846 of Congreve Rogers.

Slater 1846.

141. WESTON, Waterford; *c.* 1860; architect perhaps S.U. Roberts.
A suburban seat overlooking the River Suir, in the mid-nineteenth century of land agent and county treasurer Edward Roberts, father of architect Samuel Ussher Roberts, who may have designed its tiny Italianate lodge, secreted behind the tall boundary wall and security gates. Single-storey, with its short canted front to the avenue containing the doorway with moulded architrave and four-

over-four side slit sash windows with roll-moulded surrounds in stucco-effect walls. Above is a semi-hexagonal roof with exposed carved rafter toes. Extending to the rear with a hipped end and six-over-six sashes.

Griffith 1853–63; Slater 1856; 1870.

142. WHITECHURCH, Whitechurch; *c.* 1825; architect possibly G.R. Pain.

The archetypal substantial well-appointed late Georgian Irish gentry house, with distinctive banded chimney-stacks identical to those at Woodstown [*q.v.*], a design attributed to George Richard Pain and replicated on the lodge here. This is a pleasant single-storey two-bay cottage of bipartite six-over-six sash windows to the avenue set in rubble walls, probably once limewashed and harled. The shallow hipped roof oversails to be carried on massive stone-slab soffits. The gatescreen is comprised of no less than six of those limestone pillars familiar in the county, to be found at Ballinamona [*q.v.*], Ballyglan [*q.v.*], Derriheen [*q.v.*], Woodhouse [*q.v.*] and neighbouring Rockfield [*q.v.*]. All by the same designer, their octagonal shafts chiselled with reeded panels and distinctive gadrooned 'splashes' to the cappings. The tripartite gateway with contemporary ironwork is framed by convex rubble quadrant walls. A seat in 1837 of Robert Power.

Lewis 1837.

143. WHITFIELD COURT, Kilmeaden; *c.* 1860; architect possibly J.S. Mulvany.

The handsome Italianate house of the Christmas family was built in two phases, the main body of *c.* 1841 for William Christmas, probably to designs of the wayward Daniel Robertson, to whom O'Dwyer also attributes its entrance gates on the strength of the architect's pillars at Dunleckney Manor, Co. Carlow. Their tiered monumentality could alternatively be ascribed to S.U. Roberts for

their affinity with those at nearby Woodlock [*q.v.*]. The triple gateway with latticed ironwork and family bearings is hung from great squat, square carriage pillars raised in two stages, the cappings in the form of blocking pieces with recessed panels containing lozenge motifs. The postern pillars, also in ashlar, are of rather more modest proportions, framed by straight screen walls of quarry-faced masonry. Assuming this work to be by Mulvany, it must be from twenty years later and contemporary with the addition of the twin belvedere towers to the house and the porter's lodge, in its contrasting, strikingly painted smooth-rendered walls. Single-storey on an L-plan below hipped roofs, the leading front contains a pair of round-headed slit windows bound by a common sill and double draped hood mouldings, not unlike that on the Woodlock lodge. Approached by steps is an open porch, entered beneath a single semicircular-arched hood moulding. The architect clearly gave little consideration to lighting the interior, for elsewhere are more one-over-one slit windows; occupied. It should also be mentioned that there are strong opinions on stylistic grounds that most of the work about Whitfield Court was to plans by local practitioner Abraham Denny, again without the support of documentary evidence.

LG (1863); *Country Life* (7 September 1967); *IAR* (1999); *IADS* (2000).

144. WOODBINE HILL, Ardmore; pre-1926; *demolished.*

On the old property in 1844 stood 'the handsome mansion of — Roch Esq., commanding a splendid prospect', but not so handsome that George Butler Roch (1794–1859) should not have replaced it two years later with the present house, perhaps also complementing it with the lost porter's lodge. Of an age is the surviving pair of sturdy octagonal carriage pillars with moulded cappings surmounted by relatively dainty gadrooned urns. Charmingly, alongside, probably remaining from the previous gatescreen, are two basic square pillars containing a delightful and quirky pedestrian turnstile spanned by a double iron overthrow archway.

O'Flanagan 1975; Burke 1854–5; *LGI* (1904).

145. WOODHOUSE, Stradbally; *c.* 1830.

An estate since 1725 of the Uniacke family, much improved in the early nineteenth century by Robert John Uniacke (d. 1851), who had inherited the property on the death of his father in 1802, building the present house and adding an appropriate entrance. Presenting itself as a single-storey structure to the road and avenue, it is revealed as a two-storey gatehouse to the rear under a shallow hipped roof. It projects beyond its gatescreen with rendered walls, its single window below a Classical 'entablature' hood on a pair of miniature consoles, set in a rectangular recess and further framed by limestone toothed quoins. Alongside is the wide gatescreen, comprised of a double gateway of decorative mid-nineteenth-century cast iron and a pair of chiselled limestone carriage pillars with reeded panels to shafts and gadrooned cappings, all as can be seen at the gates to Ballinamona [*q.v.*], Ballyglan [*q.v.*], Derriheen [*q.v.*] and Whitechurch [*q.v.*], except that here they are ovoid in section rather than octagonal. Perhaps indicating the involvement of architect George Richard Pain.

Mason 1814–19; *IFR.*

146. WOODLANDS, Passage East (2).

The lodges, in place before 1839, have been demolished, both perhaps having been contemporary with the building around 1830 of the refined villa of Michael Dobbyn, which was subsequently acquired by the Powers of neighbouring Faithlegg [*q.v.*] as their dower house. One of the lodges lay vacant in 1848.

Lewis 1837; Griffith 1853–63; Bence-Jones 1988.

147. WOODLOCK, Portlaw (2).

Another impressive County Waterford development for one of the prosperous Malcomson brothers, in this case George Pim Malcomson, and again architect John Skipton Mulvany benefited from his professional

147. Woodlock, Portlaw, east gate (NLI).

relationship with that family, designing in 1861 a large Italianate house which survives today as St Joseph's Convent. When the client, only four years later, sought plans for additions to the house, he turned to Samuel Ussher Roberts, and to him are attributable the surviving lodge and gates.

East gate; *c.* 1865; architect probably S.U. Roberts.

This is a particularly showy Italianate lodge and, although single-storey, is of large scale, accentuated by its high parapeted roof. Built in sandstone ashlar, now painted over, it is self-consciously symmetrical, its central room projecting to the avenue with a pair of round-arched windows below a double hood moulding with console bracket dripstones, flanked on each side by semicircular-arched porches, one of which contains the entrance doorway, the other curiously blind. A late Victorian photograph reveals that the main parapets have been lowered, with the loss of ornamental perforated panels and a loss of impact. As conspicuous is the impressive gatescreen, whose wide, rendered, convex quadrant walls frame a triple gateway with flamboyant cast ironwork almost identical to that which graced Milfort [*q.v.*], another Malcomson property nearby, and similarly from the Turner iron foundry in Dublin. These gates are hung on a pair of composite staged stone carriage pillars with tapering faces, wide cornices, pronounced plinths and secondary block cappings, a design to be found at Tulira Castle, Co. Galway, and presumably by Roberts, who may have been influenced by the entrance to Whitfield Court [*q.v.*], if not directly responsible.

West gate; *c.* 1861; *demolished.*

A tiny structure which may have been associated with that first phase of building.

Lawrence photograph (70R); *IADS* (2000).

148. WOODSTOWN, Dunmore East (2).

The pretty Regency villa built for Robert Shapland Carew (1787–1856), in 1834 created 1st Baron Carew, probably to designs of George Richard Pain. Dating from 1823, it was taken as an alternative marine residence to the family's main seat of Castleboro, Co. Wexford; its porters' lodges are of later dates.

Coastal gate; *c.* 1835; architect possibly G.R. Pain.

As is indicated by the 1841 OS map and confirmed by its generous accommodation, this charming creeper-clad structure was built as a 'School House'. In the English Picturesque manner, 1½-storey gabled, it is sited forward of its gates and monitors them through a single-storey canted bay window, which retains some of its original cast-iron latticed glazing. Three-bay to the road with attic gablets over, it remains occupied; conceivably also the work of Pain. Probably earlier is the sturdy pair of Classical V-jointed rusticated limestone carriage pillars with moulded plinths and cornices and scroll-topped stops.

Inland gate; *c.* 1845; architect possibly Daniel Robertson.

Opposite its entrance but well screened from it by vegetation is a gabled single-storey Tudor Revival gatekeeper's lodge on an L-plan, with a little gabled hall projecting from the internal angle. Ornamental gutters have serrated lips and fancy bracket supports, while to one gable is a cusped lozenge feature, the other having a Tudor-arched window below a shield displaying the monogram and boar passant crest of the Barron family, who purchased the estate in 1905. The architect may well have been Daniel Robertson, who was then working for Lord Carew at Castleboro, Pain having died in 1838. Unfortunately, the lodge has been covered in a bland, numbing masonry paint. In 1848 the porter was Miss Elizabeth Doyle.

Griffith 1853–63; *BPB* (1929); Bence-Jones 1988.

GLOSSARY

A GOTHIC *COTTAGE ORNÉ* LODGE

1. Pent
2. Cluster-column
3. Pinnacle
4. Crockets
5. Finial
6. Eyebrow eaves
7. Diocletian window
8. Lancet head
9. Y-tracery
10. Harling
11. Hexagonal
12. Ogee arch
13. Arrowloop or loophole (mock)
14. Trefoil window
15. Half-hipped gable
16. Broach
17. Diagonally set chimney-stack

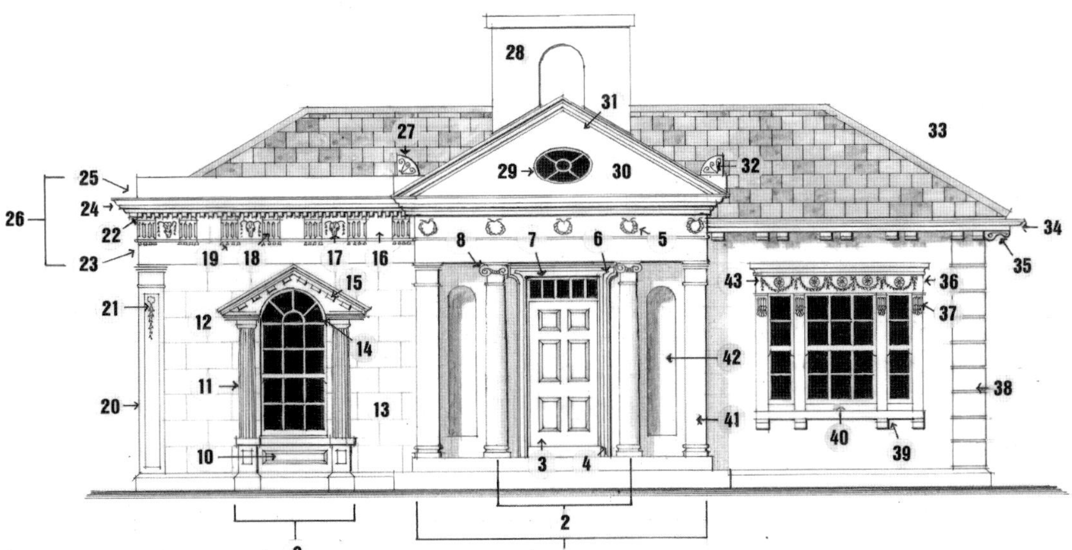

A NEO-CLASSICAL LODGE

1. Portico
2. Columns *in antis*
3. Panelled door
4. Architrave surround
5. Laurel wreath or garland
6. Lugged head
7. 'Mouth-organ' fanlight
8. Ionic capital
9. Aedicule
10. Under-panel
11. Doric column (fluted)
12. Open pediment
13. Ashlar (masonry) or stucco (applied)
14. Spoked head
15. Mutules
16. Metope
17. Bucrania (oxhead) or aegricane (ram's head)
18. Triglyph
19. Guttae
20. Pilaster
21. Margent
22. Dentil course
23. Frieze
24. Cornice
25. Blocking course
26. Entablature
27. Acroterion
28. 'Vanburgh' or bridged chimney-stack
29. *Oeil-de-boeuf* or ox-eye opening
30. Tympanum
31. Pediment
32. Anthemion motif
33. Hipped roof
34. Eaves
35. Modillion bracket
36. Flat entablature
37. Crossette
38. 'Irish pilaster' (quoins)
39. Bracketed sill
40. 'Wyatt' or tripartite window
41. Antae
42. Niche
43. Patera and festoon (or swag) ornament

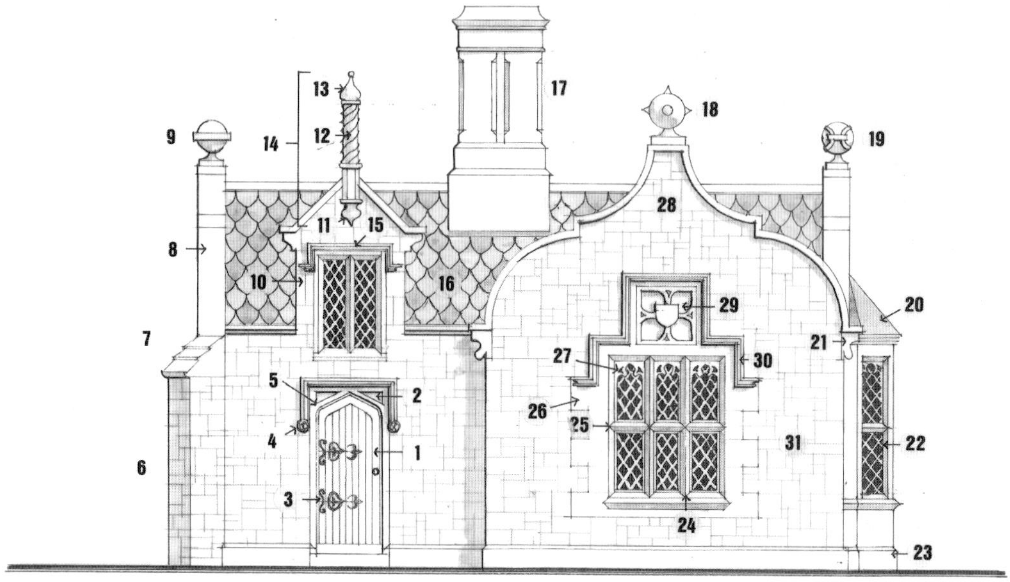

A 'TUDORBETHAN' LODGE

1. Sheeted door
2. Spandrel
3. Strap hinges
4. Dripstone
5. Tudor arch
6. Buttress
7. Weathering
8. Skew-table
9. Rusticated ball finial
10. Gablet
11. Pendant
12. 'Barley-twist' shaft
13. Finial
14. Hip-knob
15. Label moulding
16. Fish-scale slates
17. Coupled chimney-stack
18. 'Morgenstern' ball finial
19. Strapped ball finial
20. Half-umbrello roof
21. Kneeler
22. Latticed glazing
23. Plinth
24. Mullion
25. Transom
26. Dressing
27. Cuspidated head
28. Shaped or curvilinear gable
29. Foiled quarter with blank shield
30. Stepped label moulding
31. Squared, uncoursed masonry

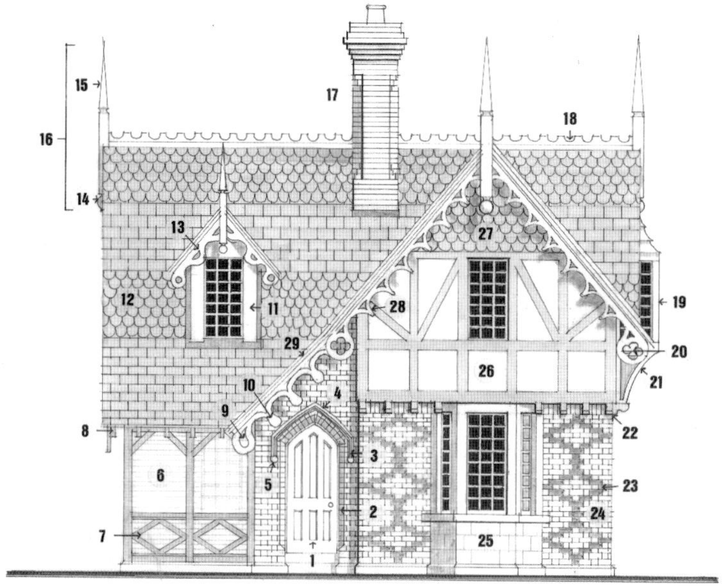

A PICTURESQUE ENGLISH COTTAGE LODGE

1. Panelled door
2. Chamfer
3. Hood moulding
4. Segmentally pointed arch
5. Dripstone
6. Verandah
7. Lozenge-pattern balustrade
8. Exposed rafter ends
9. Mouchette motif
10. Lobed bargeboard
11. Dormer window
12. Scalloped slates
13. Waved bargeboard
14. Pendant
15. Finial
16. Hip-knob
17. Modelled chimney-stack
18. Cresting (serrated)
19. Oriel window
20. Quatrefoil motif
21. Corbel
22. Jettying
23. Diaper work
24. Flemish bond brickwork
25. Canted bay window
26. Black-and-white work or half-timbering
27. Tile-hanging
28. Foiled bargeboard
29. Catslide roof

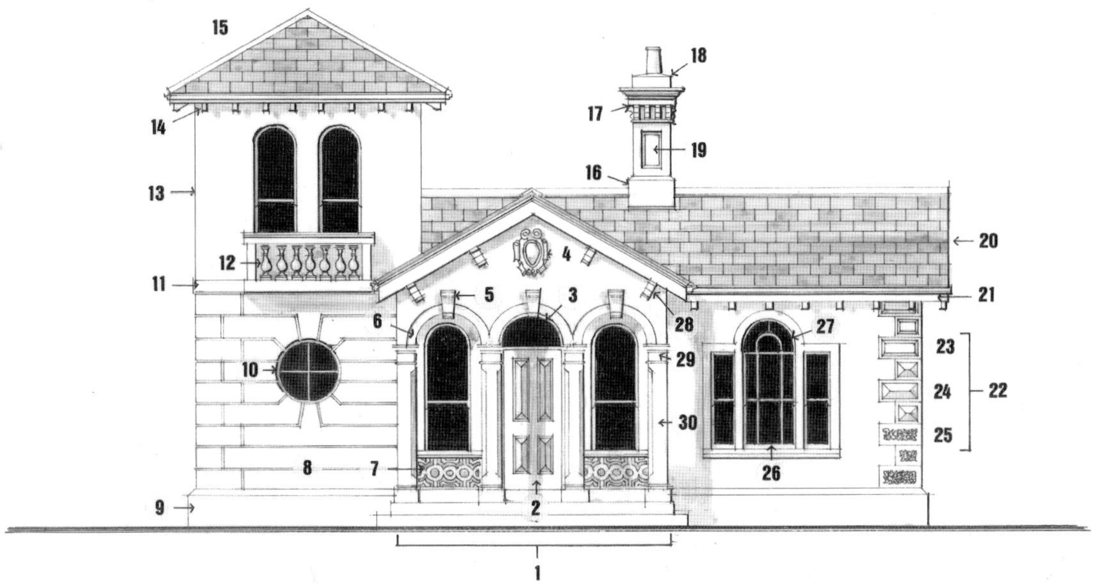

AN ITALIANATE LODGE

1. *Porte-cochère*
2. Raised and fielded panelled door
3. Fanlight
4. Cartouche
5. A cone (scrolled keystone)
6. Archivolt
7. Balustrade (fretted)
8. Channelled rustication
9. Plinth
10. Oculus
11. String-course
12. Balconette (balustrade)
13. Belvedere tower
14. Exposed rafter ends
15. Pyramidal roof
16. Plinth
17. Bracketed cornice
18. Blocked capping
19. Recessed panel
20. Gabled roof
21. Fascia
22. Quoins
23. Raised
24. Diamond-pointed
25. Vermiculated or reticulated
26. Venetian window
27. Margined glazing
28. Purlin ends
29. Impost
30. Pier

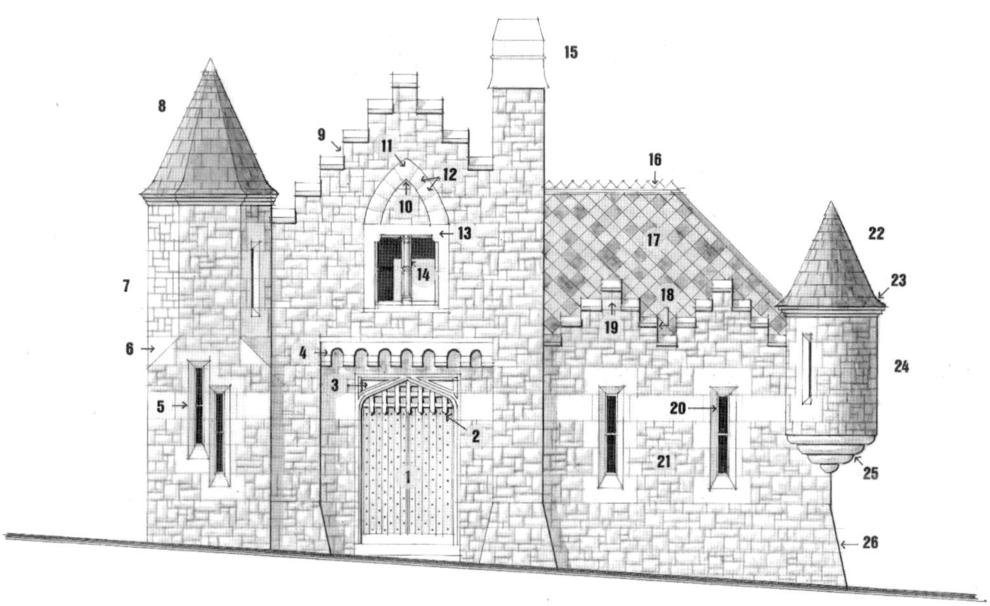

A CASTELLATED SCOTS BARONIAL LODGE

1. Studded doors
2. 'Portcullis'
3. Spandrel
4. 'Machicolation'
5. Batement window
6. Broach
7. Turret
8. Octahedral roof
9. Crow-stepped gable
10. Relieving arch
11. Keystone
12. Voussoirs
13. Shouldered arch
14. Colonette (banded)
15. Chimney capping
16. Cresting (sawtooth)
17. Lattice-pattern slating
18. Allure or ramparts
19. Crenellations (Irish)
20. Chamfered slit opening
21. Squared course masonry (quarry-faced)
22. Conical roof
23. Bellcast
24. Bartizan
25. Corbel
26. Batter

BIBLIOGRAPHY

Abbreviations

BPB	Burke's *Peerage and baronetage* (various editions; London, 1861, 1873, 1903, 1925, 1929).
DB	*The Dublin Builder.*
DEP	Burke's *Dormant and extinct peerages* (various editions; London, 1844, 1883).
IAA	Irish Architectural Archive.
IADS	*Irish Architectural and Decorative Studies: Journal of the Irish Georgian Society.*
IAR	*Irish Arts Review.*
IB	*The Irish Builder.*
IFR	Burke's *Irish family records* (London, 1976).
IGS	Irish Georgian Society.
JCHAS	*Journal of the Cork Historical and Archaeological Society.*
LG	Burke's *The landed gentry of Great Britain* (various editions; London, 1853, 1863, 1875, 1882, 1886, 1894, 1912, 1952).
LGI	Burke's *The landed gentry of Ireland* (various editions; London, 1886, 1904, 1912, 1958).
LOI	*Land owners in Ireland 1876* (reprint; Genealogical Publishing Co., Baltimore, 1988).
NAOPW	National Archives: Office of Public Works Collection.
NIAH	National Inventory of Architectural Heritage (available at http://www.buildingsofireland.ie/).
NLI	National Library of Ireland: Drawings Collection.
OS	Ordnance Survey.
PGI	*Parliamentary Gazetteer of Ireland 1844–1845* (3 vols) (Dublin, London and Edinburgh, 1846).
RIBA	Royal Institute of British Architects: Drawings Collection.
TCD	Trinity College Dublin.
Thom's	*Thom's Irish Almanac and Official Directory* (various editions; Dublin, 1844–1910).

A

Adam, R. 1990 *Classical architecture: a complete handbook.* Viking, London.

Allibone, J. 1991 *George Devey: architect 1820–1886.* The Lutterworth Press, Cambridge.

Anderson, C.F. *c.* 1847 *Architectural circular.* Privately published (Copy available in IAA.)

Atkinson, A. 1815 *The Irish tourist: in a series of picturesque views.* Courtney, Dublin.

Atterbury, P. (ed.) 1995 *A.W.N. Pugin: master of Gothic Revival.* Yale University Press, New Haven and London.

B

Barrow, J. 1836 *A tour round Ireland in the autumn of 1835.* J. Murray, London.

Bary, V. 1994 *Houses of Kerry.* Ballinakella Press, Whitegate.

Bassett, G.H. 1889 *The book of County Tipperary.* Sealy, Bryers and Walker, Dublin.

Beaufort, Revd D.A. 1764–1808 Unpublished travel journals. Trinity College Dublin Library.

Beaufort, L. 1781–1820 Unpublished travel journals. Trinity College Dublin Library.

Bence-Jones, M. 1988 *A guide to Irish country houses.* Constable, London.

Bennis, E.H. 1940 *Reminiscences of old Limerick.* McKern, Limerick.

Bernelle, A. (ed.) 1992 *Decantations: a tribute in honour of Maurice Craig.* The Lilliput Press, Dublin.

Binns, J. 1837 *Miseries and beauties of Ireland* (2 vols). Longman, Orme, Brown, London.

Bowen, E. 1984 *Bowen's Court.* Virago Press, London.

Brewer, J.N. 1825 *The beauties of Ireland.* Sherwood, Jones and Co., London.

Burke, J.B. 1854–5 *A visitation of the seats and arms of the noblemen and gentlemen of Great Britain and Ireland,* vols 3 and 4. Hurst and Blackett, London.

C

Carr, J. 1806 *The stranger in Ireland in 1805.* Richard Phillips, London.

Colvin, Sir H. 2008 *A biographical dictionary of British architects 1600–1840.* Yale University Press, New Haven and London.

Coote, Sir C. 1801 *A statistical survey of King's County.* The Dublin Society, Dublin.

Craig, M. 1982 *The architecture of Ireland: from the earliest times to 1880.* Batsford, London.

Craig, M. and Garner, W. 1977 *Report on buildings of historical/architectural interest in County Waterford.* An Foras Forbartha, Dublin.

Craig, M. and Glin, Knight of 1970 *Ireland observed.* Mercier Press, Cork.

Crookshank, A. and Glin, Knight of 2002 *Ireland's painters 1600–1940.* Yale University Press, New Haven and London.

Curl, J.S. 1993 *Encyclopaedia of architectural terms.* Donhead, London.

Curwen, J.C. 1818 *Observations on the state of Ireland* (2 vols). Baldwin, Cradock and Joy, London.

D

Darby, M. 1983 *John Pollard Seddon.* Victoria and Albert Museum, London.

Davis, T. 1973 *The architecture of John Nash.* Studio Books, London.

de Breffny, B. 1977 *Castles of Ireland.* Thames and Hudson, London.

de Breffny, B. and ffolliott, R. 1975 *The houses of Ireland.* Thames and Hudson, London.

De Latocnaye, J.L. de B. 1984 *A Frenchman's walk through Ireland, 1796–1797* [reprint]. Blackstaff Press, Belfast.

Dean, J.A.K. 1994 *The gate lodges of Ulster: a gazetteer.* Ulster Architectural Heritage Society, Belfast.

Dean, J.A.K. 2016 *The gate lodges of Leinster: a gazetteer.* Wordwell, Dublin.

Dearn, T.D.W. 1811 *Designs for lodges and entrances.* J. Taylor, London.

Debrett, J. 1920 *Debrett's Peerage and titles of courtesy.* Dean and Son, London.

Diggin, M. 1998 *Images of Ireland.* Gill and Macmillan, Dublin.

Doneraile Papers, National Library of Ireland.

Dooley, T. 2001 *The decline of the big house in Ireland.* Wolfhound Press, Dublin.

Dunne, S. (ed.) 1995 *The College: a photographic history of University College, Cork.* Cork University Press, Cork.

Dutton, H. 1808 *A statistical survey of the County of Clare.* Graisberry and Campbell, Dublin.

E

English, N.W. 1973 Some country houses near Athlone. *The Irish Ancestor* **5** (1), 17–23.

English, N.W. 1974 Some lost country houses near Athlone. *The Irish Ancestor* **6** (2), 79–84.

Everett, N. 2001 *Wild gardens: the lost demesnes of Bantry Bay.* Hafod Press, Bantry.

F

Fairbairn, J. 1986 *Fairbairn's crests of the families of Great Britain and Ireland*. New Orchard Editions, London.
ffolliott, R. 1958 *The Pooles of Mayfield*. Hodges Figgis, Dublin.
ffolliott, R. 1970 Entrance gates. *The Irish Ancestor* **2** (2), 128–30.
ffolliott, R. 1971a Some lesser known country houses in Munster and Leinster. *The Irish Ancestor* **3** (1), 49–50.
ffolliott, R. 1971b The charm of Irish gate lodges. *The Irish Ancestor* **3** (2), 102–4.
Fitzgerald, Revd P. and McGregor, J.J. 1827 *The history, topography and antiquities of the county and city of Limerick* (2 vols). George McKern, London.
Fletcher, Sir B. 1961 *A history of architecture on the comparative method* (17th edn). The Athlone Press, London.
Flynn, P.H. (ed.) 2013 *Franz S. Haselbeck's Ireland*. The Collins Press, Cork.
Forbes, J.D. 1953 *Victorian architect: the life and work of William Tinsley*. Indiana University Press, Chicago.
Fraser, J. 1838 *Guide through Ireland*. Wm Curry Jr and Co., Dublin.
Frost, J. 1893 *The history and topography of the county of Clare. Extracts from the journal of Thomas Dineley: Chapter 28*. Sealy, Bryers and Walker, Dublin.

G

Gandy, J. 1805a *Designs for cottages, cottage farms, &c*. John Harding, London.
Gandy, J. 1805b *The rural architect*. John Harding, London.
Gaughan, J.A. 1978 *The Knights of Glin*. Kingdom Books, Dublin.
General alphabetical index to the townlands and towns, parishes, and baronies of Ireland: based on the census of Ireland for the year 1851 (first published Dublin, 1861; Genealogical Publishing Co., Baltimore, 2000).
Glin, Knight of, Griffin, D. and Robinson, N.K. 1988 *Vanishing country houses of Ireland*. IAA and IGS, Dublin.
Goodwin, F. 1850 *Rural architecture* (3rd edn) (2 vols). Henry G. Bohn, London.
Griffith, R. 1853–63 *The primary valuation of rateable property in Ireland* (Munster). The Valuation Office, Dublin.
Grubb, G.W. 1972 *The Grubbs of Tipperary*. The Mercier Press, Cork.
Guinness, D. and Ryan, W. 1971 *Irish houses and castles*. Thames and Hudson, London.
Guy, F. 2017 *Cork city and county almanac for the years 1857–1876*. Forgotten Books, London.

H

Hajba, A.-M. 2002 *Houses of Cork. Volume I: North*. Ballinakella Press, Whitegate.
Hall, Mr and Mrs S.C. 1841–3 *Ireland, its scenery, character &c*. (3 vols). Jeremiah How and Parsons, London.
Heaney, H. (ed.) 1999 *A Scottish Whig in Ireland 1835–1838: the Irish journals of Robert Graham of Redgorton*. Four Courts Press, Dublin.
Heron, M. 1999 *The hidden houses of Ireland*. Gill and Macmillan, Dublin.
Hill, H. 1933 Diary of an itinerary in Ireland in 1831. *JCHAS* **38**, 30–7.
Hill, H. Unpublished notebooks. Cork City Museum.
Hoare, R.C. 1807 *Journal of a tour in Ireland 1806*. W. Miller, London.
Hogg, W.E. 2000 *The millers and the mills of Ireland of about 1850*. W.E. Hogg, Dublin.
Howley, J. 1993 *The follies and garden buildings of Ireland*. Yale University Press, New Haven and London.
Humphreys, J.A.W. 1979 The phenomenon of the grand entrance: an analysis of the development of Irish entrance gateways between 1660 and 1920. Unpublished thesis, University of East Anglia.
Hunt, T.F. 1825 *Half-a-dozen hints, or Picturesque architecture*. Longman, Hurst, Rees, Orme, Brown and Green, London.
Hunt, T. 2000 *Portlaw, County Waterford, 1825–76: portrait of an industrial village and its cotton industry*. Maynooth Studies in Irish Local History. Irish Academic Press, Dublin.

I

Inglis, H.D. 1835 *A journey throughout Ireland during the spring, summer and autumn of 1834* (2 vols). Whittaker and Co., London.

J

Jones, B. 1974 *Follies and grottoes*. Constable, London.

K

Kelly, A. 1990 *Mrs Coade's stone*. Self-Publishing Association, Upton-upon-Severn.
Killanin, Lord and Duignan, M.V. 1962 *Shell guide to Ireland*. Ebury Press, London.
Knox, Revd I. (ed.) 2008 *Clergy of Waterford, Lismore and Ferns*. Ulster Historical Foundation, Belfast.

L

Lacy, T. 1853 *Home sketches on both sides of the Channel*. London and Dublin.
Lacy, T. 1863 *Sights and scenes of our fatherland*. London and Dublin.
Larner, J. (ed.) 2005 *Killarney: history and heritage*. The Collins Press, Cork.
Lee, D. 2006 *James Pain, architect*. Civic Trust, Limerick.
Leet, A. 1814 *A directory to the market towns, villages, gentlemen's seats, &c*. Brett Smith, Dublin.
Lenihan, M. 1967 *Limerick: its history and antiquities* [reprint of 1866 original]. The Mercier Press, Cork.
Leslie, Revd J.B. 1940 *Ardfert and Aghadoe: clergy and parishes*. Church of Ireland Printing and Publishing Co., Dublin.
Leslie, Canon J.B. and Crooks, Canon D.W.T. 2010 *Clergy of Killaloe, Kilfenora, Clonfert and Kilmacduagh*. Ulster Historical Foundation, Belfast.
Lewis, S. 1837 *Topographical dictionary of Ireland* (3 vols). Samuel Lewis, London.
Loudon, J.C. 2000 *An encyclopaedia of cottage, farm and villa architecture* [reprint of 1846 edition]. Donhead, Shaftesbury.
Loudon, J.C. and Repton, H. 1840 *The landscape gardening and architecture of the late Humphry Repton*. Longman and Co., London.
Luckcombe, P. 1780 *A tour through Ireland in 1779*. Whitestone, Dublin.
Lugar, R. 1806 *Architectural sketches for cottages, rural dwellings, and villas*. J. Taylor, London.
Lyall, S. 1988 *Dream cottages*. Robert Hale, London.
Lyons, M.C. 1993 *Illustrated incumbered estates*. Ballinakilla Press, Whitegate.

M

McMorran, R. and O'Keeffe, M. 2005 *A pictorial history of Tralee*. The authors, Tralee.
McParland, E., Rowan, A. and Rowan, A.M. 1989 *The architecture of Richard Morrison and William Vitruvius Morrison*. IAA, Dublin.
McVeagh, J. 1996 *Irish travel writing*. Wolfhound Press, Dublin.
Malins, E. and Glin, Knight of 1976 *Lost demesnes 1660–1845*. Barrie and Jenkins, London.
Mason, W.S. 1814–19 *Statistical account or parochial survey of Ireland* (3 vols). John Cunningham, Dublin, Edinburgh and London.
Maxwell, C. 1949 *Country and town in Ireland under the Georges*. Dundalgan Press, Dundalk.
Mowl, T. 1984 The evolution of the park gate lodge as a building type. *Architectural History* **27**, 467–80.
Mowl, T. and Earnshaw, B. 1984 *Trumpet at a distant gate*. Waterstone, London.
Murphy, J.A. 1995 *The College: a history of Queen's/University College Cork, 1845–1995*. Cork University Press, Cork.

N

Neale, J.P. 1820–3 *Views of the seats of noblemen and gentlemen*, 1st series (6 vols). Sherwood, Neely and Jones, London.

Neale, J.P. 1824–9 *Views of the seats of noblemen and gentlemen*, 2nd series (6 vols). Sherwood, Gilbert and Piper, London.

Nolan, W. (ed.) 1985 *Tipperary: history and society*. Geography Publications, Dublin.

O

O'Connor, J. 1995 *The workhouses of Ireland: the fate of Ireland's poor*. Anvil Press, Dublin.

O'Connor, T. 1999 *Ardfert in times past*. T. O'Connor, Ardfert.

O'Donnell, E.E. 2005 *Father Brown's Limerick*. Currach Press, Dublin.

O'Donnell, S. 1999 *Clonmel 1840–1900: anatomy of an Irish town*. Geography Publications, Dublin.

O'Donoghue, B. 2007 *The Irish county surveyors 1834–1944*. Four Courts Press, Dublin.

O'Donovan, J. 1806–61 Unpublished Ordnance Survey memoirs and letters held by the Royal Irish Academy.

O'Dwyer, F. 1997a *Irish hospital architecture*. Department of Health and Children, Dublin.

O'Dwyer, F. 1997b *The architecture of Deane and Woodward*. Cork University Press, Cork.

O'Flanagan, J.R. 1975 *The River Blackwater in Munster: historical and picturesque guide*. Tower Books, Cork.

Ordnance Survey of Ireland 1991 *An illustrated record of Ordnance Survey in Ireland*. Ordnance Survey of Ireland, Dublin.

P

Pain, W. 1799 *The practical house carpenter*. J. Taylor, London.

Papworth, J.B. 1818 *Rural residences*. Ackerman, London.

Pigot, J. 1824 *Dictionary of Ireland*. Pigot and Co., London.

Pike, W.T. and Hodges, Revd R.J. 1911 *Cork and County Cork in the 20th century*. W.T. Pike, Brighton.

Plaw, J. 1795 *Ferme ornée*. I. and J. Taylor, London.

Plaw, J. 1800 *Sketches for country houses, villas and rural dwellings*. J. Taylor, London.

Potter, M. 2009 *William Monsell of Tervoe 1812–1894: Catholic unionist, Anglo-Irishman*. Irish Academic Press, Dublin.

Power, B. 2000 *White knights, dark earls: the rise and fall of an Anglo-Irish dynasty*. The Collins Press, Cork.

R

RIBA 1993 *Dictionary of British architects 1834–1900*. Royal Institute of British Architects, London.

Robinson, P.F. 1833 *Designs for lodges and park entrances*. Priestley and Weale, London.

S

Seoighe, M. 1982 *Portrait of Limerick*. Robert Hale, London.

Seymour, Ven. St J.D. and Leslie, Canon J.B. 2012 *Clergy of Cashel, Emly and Leighlin*. Ulster Historical Foundation, Belfast.

Shaffrey, P. and Shaffrey, M. 1985 *Irish countryside buildings: everyday architecture in the rural landscape*. The O'Brien Press, Dublin.

Sheehy, J. 1977 *J.J. McCarthy and the Gothic Revival in Ireland*. Ulster Architectural Heritage Society, Belfast.

Slater, I. 1846 *National Commercial Directory of Ireland*. Slater, Manchester.

Slater, I. 1856 *National Commercial Directory of Ireland*. Slater, Manchester.

Slater, I. 1870 *Royal National Commercial Directory of Ireland*. Slater, Manchester and London.

Smith, C. 1746 *The ancient and present state of the county and city of Waterford*. Smith, Dublin.

Smyth, C. 1893 *The ancient and present state of the county and city of Cork* [first published 1750] (3 vols). Cork Historical and Archaeological Society, Cork.

Soane, J. 1789 *Plans, elevations and sections of buildings: executed in the counties of Norfolk, Suffolk, Yorkshire, Staffordshire, Warwickshire, Hertfordshire, etc.* Taylor, London.

Soane, J. 1793 *Sketches in architecture: containing plans and elevations of cottages, villas and other useful buildings, with characteristic scenery*. Taylor, London.

Somerville-Large, P. 1995 *The Irish country house: a social history*. Sinclair-Stevenson, London.

Soros, S.W. (ed.) 1999 *E.W. Godwin: aesthetic movement architect and designer*. Yale University Press, New Haven and London.

Spellissy, S. 1998 *The history of Limerick City*. The Celtic Bookshop, Limerick.

Stalley, R. (ed.) 1991 *Daniel Grose: The antiquities of Ireland*. Irish Architectural Archive, Dublin.

Studdert, R.H. 1960 *The Studdert family*. At the Sign of the Three Candles, Dublin.

T

Taylor, G. and Skinner, A. 1778 *Maps of the roads of Ireland* (1st edn). W. Wilson, London and Dublin.

Taylor, G. and Skinner, A. 1783 *Maps of the roads of Ireland* (2nd edn). Reprint: Irish University Press, Shannon, 1969.

Temple, N. 1979 *John Nash and the Village Picturesque*. Alan Sutton, Gloucester.

Thackeray, W.M. 1879 *The Irish sketchbook*. Smith Elder and Co., London.

Townsend, B. 1997 *The lost distilleries of Ireland*. Neil Wilson Publishing, Glasgow.

Townsend, H. 1815 *A general and statistical survey of the county of Cork*. Graisberry and Campbell, Dublin.

W

Wakeman, W.F. 1883 *The tourist's picturesque guide to Ireland*. Dublin.

Weir, H.W.L. 1986 *Houses of Clare*. Ballinakella Press, Whitegate.

Whelan, K. (ed.) 1987 *Wexford: history and society*. Geography Publications, Dublin.

Williams, J. 1994 *A companion guide to architecture in Ireland 1837–1921*. Irish Academic Press, Dublin.

Wilson, W. 1803 *The post chaise companion, or, traveller's directory through Ireland* (3rd edn). J. and J.H. Fleming, Dublin.

Windele, J. 1849 *Historical and descriptive notices of the city of Cork and its vicinity*. Longman, London.

Y

Young, A. 1780 *Tour in Ireland, 1776–1779* (2 vols). T. Cadell and J. Dodsley, London.

APPENDIX

ORDNANCE SURVEY OF IRELAND: SIX-INCH COUNTY SERIES MAPS

County	1st edn	2nd edn	3rd edn
Clare	1842	1893–7	1913–18
Cork	1845	1901–6	1926–37
Kerry	1846	1892–8	
Limerick	1844	1901–4	1923–8
Tipperary	1843	1901–5	1938
Waterford	1843	1897–1905	1922–3

ARCHITECTS, BUILDERS (B), LANDSCAPE ARCHITECTS (L) AND MANUFACTURERS/CRAFTSMEN (M)

Letters and numbers in italics refer to counties and entries. Numbers set in bold type refer to the chapter on the history of the gate lodge in Munster, pp 1–19.

C = Cork
Ce = Clare
Ky = Kerry
Lk = Limerick
Ty = Tipperary
Wd = Waterford

PATRONS, PROPRIETORS AND PORTERS (P)

Letters and numbers in italics refer to counties and entries.

C = Cork
Ce = Clare
Ky = Kerry
Lk = Limerick
Ty = Tipperary
Wd = Waterford

C

E

F

M

O

U

V

W